Friends of the Family

Friends of the Family

The English Home and

Its Guardians, 1850-1940

George K. Behlmer

Stanford University Press

Stanford, California

1998

Stanford University Press
Stanford, California
© 1998 by the Board of Trustees of the
Leland Stanford Junior University
Printed in the United States of America
CIP data appear at the end of the book

For Jane

Acknowledgments

Had I known, early on, that making sense of the "Englishman's castle" would take twelve years, this book might not have gone forward. Long projects tend to incur large debts, and this is certainly true of *Friends of the Family*. Let me begin by thanking those institutions that helped to underwrite my research. The University of Washington provided crucial support through the Department of History's Keller Fund, the Graduate School Research Fund, and two sabbatical leaves. Additionally, grants from the Rockefeller Foundation, the American Philosophical Society, the National Endowment for the Humanities ("Travel to Collections"), and the National Institutes of Health (N.I.H. grant LM 03833 from the National Library of Medicine) made possible research trips to England.

Librarians and archivists on both sides of the Atlantic were unstinting with their time and technical expertise. In England, special thanks are due the staffs of the Bodleian Library, Bradford District Archives, British Library, Children's Society Archives, Coventry City Record Office, Cumbria County Record Office, Durham County Record Office, Gray's Inn Library, Greater London Record Office, Lambeth Palace Library, the Oral History Archives at the University of Essex, Public Record Office, Sheffield City Archives, Warwick County Record Office, and the Wellcome Institute. In the United States, I have received much help from the staffs of the Library of Congress, National Library of Medicine, Stanford's Jonsson Library of Government Documents, and Suzzallo Library at the University of Washington. Suzzallo's Inter-Library Borrowing Department stepped into the breach on the many occasions when travel beyond the Pacific Northwest proved unfeasible. Similarly, Suzzallo's Reference Department, and in particular Theresa Mudrock, Glenda Pearson, and Kristi Greenfield, managed—on shrinking budgets—to buy key research materials. Nancy Hines, in Classroom Support Services, gave sound advice on the photographs used in this book.

Several students and former students have assisted in various ways. Some scoured local newspapers for relevant police court cases. Thanks here go to Kathy Brown, Jeff Cowie, Will Prust, and Tony Reid. Lisa Nakamura shared her insights about Victorian neuropsychology, while Mark Scholz explained French conceptions of "home." Jon Crump, Matt Redinger, Byron Nakamura, and Mark Scholz helped greatly with word-processing.

Numerous colleagues read parts of this text as it took shape. My gratitude extends to Wayne Carp, Elisabeth Cawthon, Nadja Durbach, Bruce Hevly, Michael MacDonald, Randall McGowen, Maggie Miller, Mary O'Neil, Gail Savage, Ben Schmidt, Bob Shoemaker, David Smith, Martin Wiener, and Tony Wohl. I owe yet more to Jane Cater and Frank Prochaska, both of whom tackled the whole manuscript.

Over the years certain people have offered encouragement at times when the way ahead looked unpromising. Among these friends, I wish to single out Mel and Jeri-Beth Bowman in Seattle; and Leslie and George Hume in San Francisco. While living in London, I have been nourished by the hospitality and intellectual verve of Frank and Alice Prochaska. Peter McCartney and the late Alison McCartney likewise lent shelter and willing ears.

I recognize John Feneron and Peter Kahn at Stanford University Press for their welcome attention to detail. Dr. Norris Pope, Director of that Press, has long been supportive of my work.

Finally, I want to thank Jane Cater for her loving forbearance. Wise critic and steadfast mate, she, more than anyone, has sustained my spirit. To her I dedicate this book.

G.K.B.

Contents

Figures and Tables

Figures

Tables

Friends of the Family

Introduction

Of Castle, Home, and Sphere

"FAMILY" AND "HOME" are the most basic of imagined communities. These warm words, connoting as they do a realm beyond politics, encode a set of assumptions about how people should live. Benedict Anderson first used the phrase "imagined communities" to refer to nations. A nation, Anderson suggested, is necessarily an *imagined* political unit because, although its members will never know, meet, or even hear about most of their fellow-members, they nevertheless retain a mental image of their communion. Family members, unlike citizens, are presumed to be on intimate terms—save for the children of "broken" homes who cannot recognize absent parents, or those estranged mates who wish only to forget one another. Through our post-industrial mind's eye we still see nations as properly anchored in the bedrock of family life. Anderson argues that the modern nation is conceived as "a deep, horizontal comradeship."[1] At least in Western Europe and North America, the modern nation is also conceived as an aggregation of private family enclaves, an atomistic whole whose strength is directly tied to the health of its households.

The operative word here is "private." Justifiably or not, we persist in associating domestic privacy with the cultivation of solid citizenship. The much-lamented decline of "family values" is thus in large part a moral panic over the reproduction of character. At some point in the past, many social critics assert, there flourished a more traditional family, a well-armored "little commonwealth." Such a family, the critics insist, was equipped to mold conscientious citizens. And if this family flourished anywhere, it did so in that most famously domestic of cultures, Victorian England.

This book examines the Victorian cult of domesticity and how it shaped what we today would call "family policy." Through a series of linked essays, *Friends of the Family* aims to clarify what England's deification of the domestic meant in political terms between the high noon of Victorian culture in the 1850's and the coming of the Second World War. For it was during this ninety-year period that "the family" emerged as a subject of continuous political discussion. Such discussion tended to be fragmentary, addressing specific problems—domestic violence, juvenile criminality, and the fate of illegitimate children, among others—rather than focusing on "the family" writ large. England's middle classes not only set the agenda of family-focused debate but also supplied most of the leadership for a vast array of interventionist groups whose common goal it was to save the family, especially the working-class family, from itself. This much historians have long known. What remains less well understood is the extent to which working-class parents participated in a cultural "policing" process. The Victorian poor and their twentieth-century successors were never the inert lump of humanity that many well-to-do contemporaries, and some modern scholars, have supposed. Nor, for that matter, did the weight of schemes to regulate and elevate family conduct fall exclusively on the poor. Middle-class reformers, it will be shown, were not shy about dictating the terms of good parenthood to their own class. Thus, in the years between 1850 and 1940, England's self-appointed "friends of the family" are better understood as participants in a contested and, at times, even self-defeating mission of moral regeneration than as deployers of a social discipline designed to penetrate private life and subvert parental authority.

The policing of family life during this period was a liminal matter in two senses. First, the collision of private and public interests often occurred at the home's threshold (*limen*, in Latin). Literally, then, gaining access to a home—being invited across its threshold—might mark the crucial first step in a public campaign to re-moralize private life. Second and more broadly conceived, attempts to "save" the English home assumed a mutual infiltration of spheres. That is, since the quality of private family life was thought to determine the quality of public behavior, the boundary between public and private was necessarily porous. If, as a celebrated French historian has proclaimed, England was "the birthplace of privacy,"[2] the English home, epicenter of that privacy, nonetheless attracted a formidable guardian army. But there was rivalry within its ranks and confusion over its target. In 1948, the historian H. L. Beales assured a war-weary public that there had been a time, in the middle of the nineteenth century, when "[e]very Englishman's home was his castle." "There was a literature about the family," Beales allowed, "but it was a literature of praise, not of discussion."[3] Actually, there was a great deal of discussion, even hand-wringing, about the Victorian family. This reputed golden age of domesticity saw intense if inconclusive combat over the meaning of family and home.

To offer universal definitions for "family," "home," and "privacy" would be an exercise in cultural myopia since the diversity of forms masked by these deceptively simple terms is enormous. "Family" may be the most elusive. To take an obvious example, some cultures count as family all those individuals related through the female line of descent, while other cultures recognize only the male lineage. Within such societies a child may forge closer emotional bonds with an aunt or an uncle than with the biological parent who stands outside the line of descent. For the purpose of this book, however, "family" will be used in its Victorian sense to refer to a social unit that is, or is deemed ideally to be, patrilineal and nuclear. "Home," notes the anthropologist Mary Douglas, is always a localizable idea. In other words, a home must be situated in space, although not necessarily in a fixed space. A home can be a covered wagon, a boat, or a tent just as easily as a house built of brick and mortar. Home, conceived in these abstract terms, begins when space is brought under control and a regularity of furnishings is established.[4] To Douglas's notion of home English tradition added the element of comfort—comfort not as in luxury but as in a sense of well-being or contentment. A recent study has observed that the English language first used "comfort" to signify a level of domestic amenity in the eighteenth century. Applying crude functionalist logic, the author of this study asserts that if the English had sensed a need to represent the idea of comfort earlier, they would have invented a word for it.[5] True enough, "comfortable," used to suggest a state of "tranquil enjoyment and content," entered the language around 1770. Yet a roughly equivalent word, "homely," is far older. Used in its adjectival form to signify "the place where one receives kind treatment," this word dates from the late fourteenth century. Its adverbial forms meaning "intimately," "kindly," and "plainly" originated in the same period.[6]

As for "privacy," here again etymology cannot recover lived experience. Still, etymology is preferable to sweeping assertions based on "commonsense." The architects of a five-volume history of private life approached their subject daunted by its scope but curiously confident about conceptual boundaries. As Georges Duby explains:

We started from the obvious fact that at all times and in all places, a clear commonsensical distinction has been made between the public . . . and the private. In other words, a clearly defined realm is set aside for that part of existence for which every language has a word equivalent to "private," a zone of immunity to which we may fall back or retreat, a place where we may set aside arms and armor needed in the public place, relax, take our ease, and lie about unshielded by the ostentatious carapace worn for protection in the outside world. This is the realm where the family thrives, the realm of domesticity; it is also a realm of secrecy.[7]

Duby's Francocentric assumptions here are striking. To contemplate many a modern American home, bristling with weapons, is to realize that privacy and disarmament are hardly synonymous. More startling of course is Duby's assumption that the demarcation between public and private spheres has always been clear. We can only speculate about the origins of a need for privacy. It has been proposed, for example, that because we are temporarily defenseless while involved in the act of defecation, some sort of "protective isolation" surrounding excretory functions has been encouraged in all human cultures.[8] But socio-biological speculation aside, the sole certainty we have about the private realm is that its territory has

shifted over time. Indeed, as this book will show, the moral reso-
nances of "privacy" varied not merely over time but often simultaneously, depending upon the nature of perceived threats to family
order.

We must soon return to those troublesome categories, "private"
and "public." For now, though, two compressed genealogies will in-
troduce the most enduring metaphors of English domesticity. When
Ralph Waldo Emerson published *English Traits* in 1856, he had
spent a little over eight months among a people who plainly baffled
him. Then the core of the most powerful empire on earth, England
struck Emerson as a country full of strangely insular folk. The English seemed a staid and circumspect lot preoccupied above all with
domestic concerns. "Domesticity," declared America's great essayist,
"is the taproot which enables the[m] . . . to branch wide and high.
The motive and end of their trade and empire is to guard the independence and privacy of their homes." Unabashedly proud of their
wealth, the comfortable classes of mid-Victorian England allegedly
worshipped at the altar of real estate. "The house is a castle which
the king cannot enter," Emerson assured his readers. But the rich
were not alone in this worship. For "[w]hatever surly sweetness possession can give, is tasted in England to the dregs. Vested rights are
awful things, and absolute possession gives the smallest freeholder
identity of interest with the duke."[9] No doubt Emerson exaggerated.
We now know that home ownership was in fact unusual for the
mid-Victorian middle classes, and quite rare for those lower down
the economic ladder. The Registrar-General announced in his introduction to the Census of 1851 that, "The possession of an entire
house is . . . strongly desired by every Englishman; for it throws a
sharp, well-defined circle round his family and hearth—the shrine of
his sorrows, joys and meditations."[10] "Possession" here should be
construed loosely. Since perhaps nine out of ten urban middle-class
families rented their homes, preferring the economy and flexibility
of a fixed, short-term lease to the risks of owning what could easily
become a depreciating asset,[11] we must question Emerson's equation
of domestic pride with legal ownership. Yet in a broader sense he

was right. Home owners most Victorians may not have been, but proprietary they surely were.

That "A Man's House Is His Castle" was a declaration of domestic sovereignty understood at all levels of settled society, if often in different ways. By the mid-nineteenth century this adage had come to mean that an English subject should be safe from all outside harassment while at home. But perceptions of harassment varied widely, thereby opening up a fertile field for inter-class and interpersonal conflict. It was because their charitable visits could be seen as domestic meddling, for instance, that middle-class philanthropists who went door-to-door among the poor were warned to avoid any hint of intrusiveness (although, as we will see, the distinction between intrusion and perseverance was far from clear). To patrician ears, the cacophony of street musicians might constitute an assault on the castle.[12] For those who worried about the sanctity of plebeian homes, the occasional arrest of a man for being drunk in his own bed could smack of state tyranny.[13] Nor was the adage gender-exclusive. When young Walter squeezed through Mrs. MacStinger's front door in *Dombey and Son* (1846–1848), the landlady "immediately demanded whether an Englishwoman's house was her castle or not; and whether she was to be broke in upon by 'raff.'"[14] Many of the working-class wives who appear in the chapters to follow were no less territorial than the fierce Mrs. MacStinger.

When and how did this territoriality take shape? There is of course nothing peculiarly English about regarding home as sacred space. The biblical David, to cite an ancient example, flew into a rage when the head of Ishbosheth, son of Saul, was brought to him at Hebron. The two murderers, thinking they would do David a favor by slaying the offspring of his old enemy, had crept into Ishbosheth's house and killed him as he slept. For this act of domestic desecration the killers lost their feet and hands.[15] Still, it is safe to say that no Western society became so outspoken, so soon, about the inviolability of home as did England's. The articulation of this ideal dates from the late fifteenth century. Sir Edward Coke (1552–1634), the most distinguished lawyer and judge of his day, gave memorable form to an already familiar precept. In the third of his

Institutes (1628), Coke reasoned that "a man's house is his castle . . . for where shall a man be safe, if it be not in his house?" Similarly, in his report on Semayne's case (1605), Coke explained that "the house of every one is to him his Castle and Fortress, as well for defense against injury and violence, as for his repose."[16] Coke was echoing William Lambard and William Stanford, jurists from the previous generation who had used nearly identical language. Stanford, in turn, traced this convention back to a statute of 1478: *"la maison de homme est a lui son castel et son defence"* (a man's home is to him his castle and his defense).[17] The same sentiments materialize outside legal texts no later than 1581, when an Elizabethan schoolmaster, Richard Mulcaster, described a householder as "the appointer of his owne circumstance, . . . [whose] house is his castle."[18]

This proverbial conceit invites another question. Why did contemporaries choose to associate the home with a relic of the medieval past? After all, by the late sixteenth century Elizabeth's England was an internally secure state, one far less dependent on massive stone strongholds than earlier regimes had been. As of 1577 William Harrison could report that "there are very few or no castles at all maintained within England, saving only upon the coasts and marches of the country."[19] The answer that Lena Orlin offers is astute. The decline of the castle as a useful architectural form, she suggests, "released it to the realms of proverb, of metaphor, and even of legal pronouncement." That is, if every man's house could be his castle, then every house could become a self-sufficient bastion of individual privacy.[20] The equation of privacy with property seems to have been fundamental. Among the distinguishing features of early-modern England, certainly as compared to France, was the English reverence for private property. During the seventeenth and eighteenth centuries this reverence expressed itself in legal prohibitions against the billeting of troops in civilian dwellings and arbitrary taxation without representation, as well as in a ferocious criminal code and punitive sanctions against all debtors *except* those who mortgaged their land.[21]

But the most intriguing aspect of this "property fetish," this English obsession with the acquisition, retention, use, and inheritance of

things, may be its antiquity.[22] Seeking the origins of something so
vague as a reverence for property is risky business. All the same, a
few brave souls, chief among them Alan Macfarlane, have plunged
headlong into the thicket of causality. Macfarlane's provocative *Origins of English Individualism* (1978) argued that England had ceased
to be a "peasant" society as far back as the thirteenth century. Defining a peasant society as one that does not recognize the absolute
ownership of land vested in a specific individual, he went on to con-
jecture that well before the bubonic plague strained social bonds in
the 1350's, most ordinary English people were "rampant individual-
ists"—highly mobile both geographically and socially, market-
oriented and acquisitive, and emotionally tied to small kinship
units.[23] One might fault Macfarlane's readiness to generalize from
the parish records of two villages in Essex and Cumbria. It is considerably more difficult to dismiss his model, however.[24] Returning to
Coke's 1605 version of the house-as-castle trope, we see that he ex-
plicitly links the defense of one's home with the right to "repose."
Presumably, then, well before this date English public opinion had
accepted that a crucial attribute of ownership was the freedom to enjoy one's possessions, especially one's home, in private.

Over time, both "door" and "threshold" became synecdoches for
"castle." An often-quoted speech of William Pitt the elder against
the Excise Bill of 1763 provides an excellent illustration of proverbial embellishment—and, more to the point, allows us to track changes in the domestic-fortress image. These are the stirring words that
reference books put in Pitt's mouth: "The poorest man may in his
cottage bid defiance to all the forces of the Crown. It may be frail;
its roof may shake; the wind may blow through it; the storms may
enter, the rain may enter—but the King of England cannot enter."[25]

What Pitt actually said on the floor of the House of Commons in
late March 1763 we will likely never know. Modern reference
books appear to rely on the same authority for these epic words,
Brougham's *Historical Sketches of Statesmen Who Flourished in the
Time of George III* (1839). Two generations after the fact, Brougham
observed wistfully how the surviving shards of Pitt's speeches "bear
so very small a proportion to the prodigious fame which his elo-

quence has left behind." It is probable that the extended cottage metaphor, which Brougham reckoned the finest in all of Pitt's fabled oratory,[26] was the product of early-Victorian reconstruction. Closer in time to the speech was an anecdotal life of Pitt published in 1792, fourteen years after his death. Its summary of the Excise speech suggests more matter-of-fact language:

Mr. Pitt took no other part in the proceedings of this [parliamentary] session, until a bill was brought in, laying a duty upon Cyder and Perry [fermented pear juice], and subjecting the makers of these liquors to the laws of Excise. He opposed this bill very strongly; upon the dangerous precedent of admitting the officers of excise into private houses. Every man's house was his castle he said. If this tax endured, he said, it will necessarily lead to introducing the laws of excise into the domestic concerns of every private family, and to every species of the produce of the land. The laws of excise are odious and grievous to the dealer, but intolerable to the private person.[27]

If indeed Pitt harped more on tax collectors than sacred cottages, it would be useful to ask why Brougham's early-Victorian rendition assumed the shape it did.

The tax system of Hanoverian England offers a clue. Pitt's dim view of revenue men makes better sense when we realize that in the middle of the eighteenth century England's Excise Office was by far the largest single employer of state servants. Unlike the hated taxes imposed directly on consumers of various goods in *ancien régime* France, the excise was an indirect commodity tax levied at the point of either production or distribution. The excise was an "invisible" tax for consumers of salt, soap, candles, beer, and several other products, and thus dampened the social tensions that could flare when (as in France) consumers regularly locked horns with autocratic agents of the state.[28] But precisely because mid-eighteenth-century England *was* accustomed to a low-profile system of tax collection, the prospect of officials nosing about the homes of cidermakers seemed all the more worrisome. The Excise Office, when it sought revenue from a seasonal product such as hops, recruited large numbers of temporary tax-gatherers. In 1765, two years after Pitt's unsuccessful bid to halt the imposition of an excise duty on cider, no fewer than 962 officers were hired to help collect the new duties.[29] To the cider-making households around which these officers could now legally snoop, Pitt's rhetoric would have seemed far from fanciful.

When he warned about excise men interfering with the "domestic concerns of every private family," Pitt was, moreover, playing on deeply felt notions of citizen rights. By 1763 he had become the father figure of an English nationalism that was both Francophobic and suspicious of the landed oligarchs who dominated high politics. He was, in the words of a contemporary pamphlet, the man who had "so eminently distinguished himself in the great Cause of Liberty; who . . . has so often exerted his great abilities in opposing the unjust Encroachments of Foreign Enemies, and that Torrent of Bribery and Corruption, which had spread itself in our Country. . . ."[30] The military threat from France during the eighteenth century did much to shape a British—as distinct from an older and more narrowly English—national self-consciousness.[31] And it is clear that Pitt exploited popular discontent to enhance his own reputation. The "Great Commoner" nevertheless recognized that even in a political order where just one in six of the adult male population could vote,[32] there existed an unwritten yet widely shared moral consensus about the limits of officialdom. At a minimum, the so-called rights of "free-born Englishmen" included trial by jury, freedom from arbitrary arrest, a limited liberty of thought, speech, and conscience, and, not least important, immunity of the home from sudden entrance and search.[33]

The most spectacular violation of these notional rights was the impressment of civilians into the Royal Navy. By the middle of the eighteenth century the navy needed a shipboard force of at least 40,000 men in time of war.[34] Since volunteers could never satisfy its combat needs, the fleet resorted to the organized kidnapping of males between the ages of eighteen and fifty-five who "used the sea." It has been estimated that during the Seven Years War (1756–1763), over 90,000 such men were impressed—many at sea from homeward-bound merchant ships, but also from the ports and from in-

land towns with navigable rivers.[35] The Admiralty, whose orders unleashed press gangs at sea and ashore, defended this practice as a
royal prerogative and a practical necessity. The foes of impressment
retorted that nothing was so dangerous as an emergency measure
whose warrant could never be questioned.[36] Although impressment
has been blamed for everything from depressing the birthrate in
some areas (by scaring off "virile" males) to encouraging "liaisons"
between Englishwomen and foreign men (who were immune to sei-
zure),[37] the most remarkable fact about this unsavory practice was
that it did not ignite far *more* protest. The likely explanation rests,
again, with England's domestic sensibility. Press gangs might ran-
sack taverns in search of mariners; very rarely indeed did they dare
disrupt private homes. For few prizes would have been worth the
political cost of trespass.

But it was political and social strife across the Channel, as much
as any internal dispute, that caused a generation of English writers
to adjust their domestic metaphors. The French Revolution proved
profoundly shocking to the English on several scores. As Lynn
Hunt has shown, the distinctions between public and private life
grew very confused during the Revolution: at the peak of the Terror, "private meant factional, and privacy was equated with the secrecy that facilitated plotting."[38] The treatment of the French queen
gave English outrage a human focus. Marie-Antoinette's beheading
in early 1793 seemed a nightmare deed. Yet even back in October
of 1789, the mob's invasion of her private chambers in the palace at
Versailles had been enough to leave Mary Wollstonecraft, no royal
sympathizer, grasping for images of defilement: "The altar of humanity had been profaned—The dignity of freedom had been tar-
nished—The sanctuary of repose, the asylum of care and fatigue, the
chaste temple of a woman . . . , the apartment where she consigns
her senses to the bosom of sleep, folded in its arms forgetful of the
world, was violated with murderous fury." For Wollstonecraft, the
penetration of the queen's bedroom and her person appeared indis-
tinguishable.[39]

Earlier still, in the Revolution's first great *journée*, France's most
visible castle had been overwhelmed. Moated, crenelated, and

crowned by eight grim towers, its walls seventy feet high and five
feet thick, the late medieval Bastille (originally built as a defense
against the English) loomed above a working-class district of eastern
Paris. "Home" to just seven prisoners on July 14, 1789, the Bastille
had been captured when its inner drawbridge was lowered. There
immediately followed the most publicized demolition job in modern history. Between mid-July and late November the hulking fortress vanished stone by stone, a theatrical display that symbolically
deconstructed the absolutist state while creating a major tourist at-
traction.[40] Not surprisingly, for several decades thereafter English
paeans to the home would prefer the cottage, seemingly built on a
firmer footing of domestic content, to the now-tainted image of castle.[41]

   A second, and overlapping, genealogy of domesticity surrounds
the phrase "Home, Sweet Home." Whereas the castle (or cottage)
metaphor condensed English assumptions about household autonomy, "Home, Sweet Home" spoke to what historians have termed
the "affective" ideal of family life. The recognized source of this
phrase is a now-obscure operetta, *Clari; or the Maid of Milan*, that
premiered at London's Covent Garden Theatre on May 8, 1823.
The title figure is an innocent girl lured from her rural home by a
duke's false promise of marriage. Although showered with rich gifts
at his palace, Clari learns that the duke will never become her husband. Left alone in a magnificent room, Clari realizes: "'Mid pleasures and Palaces though we may roam,/Be it ever so humble,
there's no place like home!/A charm from the skies seems to hallow
us there,/Which, seek through the world, is ne'er met with elsewhere./Home! Home, sweet sweet Home!/There's no place like
Home! There's no place like Home!" As if anyone could now doubt
her homesickness, Clari pleads in the second verse to see her "lowly
thatch'd Cottage again." The Covent Garden audience was enthralled. A psalm had been written. Never mind that this psalm has
since been described as "a vacuum of a tune which nostalgia rushes
to fill."[42]

   Both the music and the words for "Home, Sweet Home" have
stirred controversy. Whether Sir Henry Rowley Bishop (1786–

Early sheet music for "Home, Sweet Home." Within a generation of its premiere in the 1823 operetta *Clari*, this song would become an English aural icon. Courtesy: British Library.

1855) created the melody or "adapted" it from a "Sicilian Air" remains uncertain. We do know that this composer, once hailed as "the English Mozart" and the first professional musician to be knighted, died destitute after setting notably low standards of paternal rectitude.[43] Money problems also dogged John Howard Payne (1791–1852), the American actor, playwright, and minor poet whose libretto would become a sacred text of Victorian culture. Legend has it that Payne, the first American actor to appear on a European stage, wrote "Home, Sweet Home" while starving in Paris. Actually, the early 1820's saw him solvent and occupying a top-floor apartment in the Palais Royal, a few flights above posh shops and restaurants: literally "'mid pleasures and palaces." Payne sold the rights to several melodramatic works, including *Clari*, for £250—a substantial sum at that time, although a pittance compared to the profit that the copyright would soon generate. His name did not appear on the early sheet music for "Home, Sweet Home."[44] Yet within a year of their operatic debut, Payne's words were cropping up in ballad collections across the British Isles. By the 1870's they had become a "second National Anthem," played on barrel-organs in city streets, embroidered and framed on working-class walls. Payne's mawkishness also inspired a series of satirical "variations" from a fellow American.[45]

Even if, as Payne may have claimed, the famous first verse came to him "as spontaneously as a sigh,"[46] he was ornamenting a very old theme. "The Backwoodsman," an American poem published five years before *Clari*, declared that: "Whate'er may happen, wheresoe'er we roam,/However homely, still there's naught like home."[47] These sentiments, in turn, match those of a "poetical broadside" that seems to have been published in London around 1792: "And to whatever place disconsolate folks roam,/At last they'll be forc'd to say this of their home,/Our friends are as true, and our wives are as comely/And, d— it, home's home, be it ever so homely."[48] In the previous generation we find Samuel Johnson reminding his readers that, "To be happy at home is the ultimate result of all ambition, the end to which every enterprise and labour tends, and of which every desire prompts the prosecution."[49] Dr.

Johnson's exact contemporary, the physician and poet Nathaniel Cotton, waxed no less lyrical about this "paradise below": "And they are fools who roam;/The world hath nothing to bestow,/From our own selves our bliss must flow,/And that dear hut our home."[50]

Dear hut or sweet home, this quintessentially English image in fact stretches back at least as far as the mid-seventeenth century. Earlier, in 1567, Richard Taverner (1505?–1575), a propagandist for both Crown and Reformation under Henry VIII, and later, under Elizabeth, high sheriff of Oxfordshire, became the first writer to convert the Latin proverbs of Erasmus into English. Taverner was no pedant. He aimed to provide not a faithful translation of the *Adagiorum Chiliades* ("Thousands of Adages") of 1508 but rather a folksy approximation of Erasmus's commentary on classical wisdom.[51] Interestingly, Taverner took few liberties with one proverb of special interest to us: *Patriae fumus igni alieno luculentior* (The smoke of home, brighter than others' fire). Erasmus explains that this phrase, found in Lucian's second-century A.D. *Praise of the Homeland* but with echoes in the *Odyssey*, refers to the longing for one's birthplace or "native land."[52] Richard Taverner's comment is rough-hewn, but identical in spirit: "The smoke of a mannes owne countrey, is much clearer than the fyer in a strange countrey. The countrey wherin we be borne, pleaseth naturallie everie man best, and he longeth continuallie to see it. . . ."[53] Erasmus and Taverner agree that the ancients were alluding to what we today might call patriotism.

Yet seventy years later the same Latin phrase triggered a very different association. In 1639, John Clarke published his *Paroemiologia*, a collection of "golden proverbs" gleaned, he tells us, from "vulgar mouthes" as well as great authors. Under the section headed *Domi Vivere* (Living at Home) appear several nuggets of wisdom, among them Erasmus's proverb, now rendered as: "Home is home be it ever so homely."[54] What could account for this pivotal shift in meaning? Several explanations may be offered, but none seems more plausible than the simplest—the affective antecedents of "Home, Sweet Home" had begun to cohere.

An identifiably English style of defining domestic space was older still. In her comparative study of New World possession rituals, Patricia Seed notes striking differences among the European colonizers. Frenchmen tried to reproduce the grandeur of royal processions wherever they could—processions that typically ended in formal speeches to the indigenous peoples. Spaniards also made speeches, but mostly as prologues to battle. The Portuguese, venturing farther into the South Atlantic than Europeans had ever done before, were understandably preoccupied with charting the heavens prior to subduing the heathens they met thereunder. Dutchmen, sailing in the wake of the Portuguese, charted not the heavens but harbors and coastlines, often in astounding detail. The English, however, laid down physical boundaries first. They fenced, hedged, and gardened the land they claimed. But above all they built houses.[55] For fixed dwellings established a legal right to the property upon which they sat, and property claims, as we have already seen, constituted a defining feature of English individualism. Small wonder that the English "back home" should have depicted their dwellings, and the family life that took place inside them, with such reverence. As for the English colonizers who "roamed" overseas, many could not afford to return. Yet they could, and did, seek to replicate "home" abroad.

One can overstate the case. Both in the early seventeenth century, when this adulation of the domestic was taking shape, and in the early twentieth, by which point it had become reflexive, there were dissenters. Around 1640, Joseph Beaumont, a shy Cambridge scholar, warned that "sweet Privacie" was "No Thing with Doors & Walls." "Home," the spiritually minded Beaumont wrote, "is every where to Thee/Who canst thine owne dwelling be."[56] Dispensing with rhyme, Bernard Shaw growled two and a half centuries later that, "Home life as we understand it is no more natural to us than a cage is natural to a cockatoo."[57]

Nor did the English have a monopoly on house-pride. The Dutch, for example, were not only the great map-makers of early-modern Europe but also among its most famous homebodies. Dutch wives reportedly waged an unceasing war on dirt. According to Sir William Temple, England's ambassador to The Hague, these women made a virtue of necessity. The damp Dutch air, Temple reasoned, threatened metal with rust and wood with mold, obliging wives "by continual pains of rubbing and scouring, to seek a Prevention, or Cure: This makes the brightness and cleanness that seems affected in their Houses, and is call'd natural to them, by people who think no further."[58] Then again, perhaps there was more to this cleaning frenzy than the demands of low-country climate. The seventeenth-century Dutch, after decades of rebellion against Catholic Spain, created the United Provinces of the Netherlands—Northern Europe's first republic, and an aggressively Calvinist one at that. The Dutch craved visible proof of their election. A booming maritime trade offered one such sign. Immaculate towns and homes offered another. As Simon Schama has put it, "To be clean, militantly, was an affirmation of separateness. What was cleansed was the dirt of the world that had obscured the special meaning of Dutch history and the providential selection of its people."[59] That the early-modern Dutch saw themselves as an indoor folk is clear. Their interior decoration, as well as the way that Dutch painting memorializes this decoration, is redolent of domestic intimacy, of an inward-turning family life. Yet it would be straining the point to insist that an atmosphere of intimacy was original to Dutch homes, or that the "idea of comfort" was "transplanted" from Holland to England.[60]

Suffice it to say that a recognizably modern form of domestic intimacy emerged earliest in Europe among the English and Dutch. Similarly, we need not linger over disputes concerning the rise of a modern, "affective" family. It seems plain enough that mothers and fathers often made deep emotional investments in their children, and in each other, long before the eighteenth century. To argue, as some scholars have, that parental indifference to the young was either an inevitable result of, or a key contributor to, high infant mortality rates is to ignore much compelling evidence to the contrary. For example, in his study of madness in Stuart England, Michael MacDonald found that among the mentally disturbed patients of an astrological physician were mothers who had experienced "searing grief" at the death of their children.[61] Also compressible is a scholarly quarrel over the persistence of "patriarchal" family forms.

If, as seems likely, the Reformation served to sanctify the rule of husbands over wives, and granting that Locke's political ideas by no means shattered the secular justification for patriarchalism, it nevertheless appears from scattered documents that in their home lives early-modern English husbands and wives often interacted more as emotional partners than as masters and minions.[62] At the same time, the polarities sometimes inferred from patriarchal thought—public versus private, political sphere versus domestic sphere—are central to an analysis of modern family regulation. The ambiguities masked by these labels defy neat resolution. They should, however, be acknowledged.

Over the past two decades historians have written at length about the separation of a public sphere of civil engagement from a private sphere of family life. Stimulated by the theoretical work of the German philosopher and sociologist Jürgen Habermas, as well as by feminist explorations of the "cult of true womanhood,"[63] such scholarship has enriched our appreciation of how gender tensions suffuse the exercise of political power. But there are also hazards attached to thinking in dichotomies. For distorted visions of the past tend to arise when a preoccupation with gendered "spheres" crowds out of consideration issues of "class" and "race."[64]

One such distortion involves the fate of the "true woman" at home. Writing thirty years ago about middle-class wives in mid-Victorian America, Barbara Welter painted an enduring portrait of the materialistic male "builder of bridges and railroads" turning the nation into "one vast counting house." Welter's predator of the public sphere rarely worried about the social consequences of his greed, however, since "he had left behind a hostage, not only to fortune, but to all the values which he held so dear and treated so lightly." Public man's "hostage" was, predictably, the bourgeois wife, into whose "frail white hand" he had thrust a "fearful obligation": namely, "to uphold the pillars of the [domestic] temple."[65] Although this historical caricature has since been refined and qualified, Welter's notion of a gendered division of labor that served to immure middle-class wives has continued to shape the thinking of American scholarship.[66] A more nuanced argument about the relationship between the formation of a middle class and the forging of a separate, private sphere for women has emerged in studies of English domesticity. Most importantly, in their landmark *Family Fortunes*, as well as in shorter essays, Leonore Davidoff and Catherine Hall have provided a detailed picture of how economic, religious, and political forces interacted to produce a provincial middle-class culture during the first phase of industrialization. They are quick to acknowledge that, despite the potent imagery of "separate spheres," the juxtaposition of "public" and "private" realms is misleading. This dichotomy masks the essential fact that middle-class privacy was built on the sweat of working men's and women's labor—whether in the public economy, as factory hands, or in the private home, as servants.[67] Davidoff and Hall are likewise sensitive to the conflicting demands of evangelicalism. They offer the important reminder that "serious Christianity" demanded quiet time for individual introspection even as it insisted that women busy themselves with the supervision of all household affairs. The authors of *Family Fortunes* nevertheless stand by their thesis that after 1750 a section of the English "middle ranks," seeking to formulate a domestic ideology that would distinguish their class from a morally lax aristocracy, began to adopt a "more domesticated, orderly life style" that not only extolled the pleasures of hearth and home but also defined a woman's rightful realm in newly restrictive ways.[68]

It is a backhanded tribute to the sweep of Davidoff and Hall's book that it has drawn such trenchant criticism. The most direct challenges have come from younger historians. Amanda Vickery and Dror Wahrman note that *Family Fortunes* mistakenly claims for the emerging middle class a cluster of domestic values that had in fact long been honored in English society. Furthermore, although the language of domesticity implied privacy, it was not necessarily synonymous with female seclusion and confinement.[69] The latter point is vital for the account of family regulation that follows. It was, after all, from the private sphere that mid-Victorian missionaries sallied forth to save working-class homes from godlessness, drink, and disease. Upon close examination, the boundaries between private and public spheres appear highly permeable. Pat Thane, analyzing the late nineteenth century, and Linda Colley, analyzing the late eighteenth, warn that the prescriptive literature which consigned the "passive" female to the sheltered realm of home must be read with caution. This literature may actually have *advanced* the case for female participation in conventionally male spaces. For the doctrine of separate spheres was implicitly contractual. "Women refrained, at least in theory, from invading the public sphere, the realm of action," Colley contends, "on the understanding that their moral influence would be respected and recognized." If, however, politics was inseparable from morality (as many Victorians maintained), then women, the putative guardians of morality, should enjoy some right of access to political affairs.[70] But the blurring of distinctions between public and private went beyond gender roles, or so *Friends of the Family* will suggest. This book will show, for example, how such "public" reforms as the creation of special courts for dealing with marital strife and juvenile crime were predicated on the assumption that these sensitive problems are best resolved in an atmosphere of "private" informality.

Much more could be said about the emergence of a private sphere in English society. Scholars of the early-modern period have identified a new sense of "psychological interiority" in everything from changing forms of confession, lying, and hospitality, to the spatial reorganization of country houses.[71] More must be said about the origins of working-class domesticity in England, a subject that just recently has begun to attract serious attention.[72] The study being introduced now cannot shed much light on these issues because it examines a later period in English social history, an era when the wisdom of "separate spheres" seemed beyond dispute (though dispute there always was) and the gospel of household privacy found preachers at nearly every level of the class structure. Instead, this book examines the reformist zeal unleashed when well-off citizens confronted the gulf between domestic ideal and reality.

Henry Mayhew witnessed this disparity more often than most. Journalist, fact-monger, and student of London street life, Mayhew (1812–1887) cocked an eyebrow when he heard hymns to home. It was, he allowed, natural that domestic pleasures should obsess a country rained on for an average of 178 days per year, but for those whose

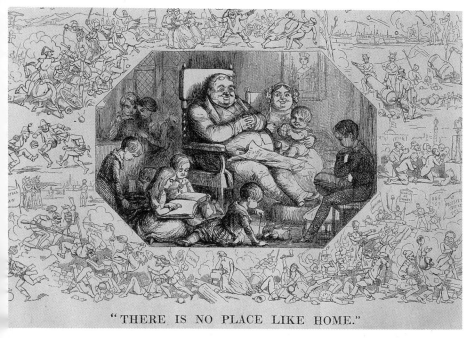

"THERE IS NO PLACE LIKE HOME."

This cartoon from *Punch* (early 1849) makes explicit the presumed link between domestic contentment and a stable social order. Here home-loving Britain appears immune to the Continental (and Irish) turmoil of 1848. In an equivalent gush of self-congratulation, a contemporary ballad entitled "My Own Dearest Home" was designed "to be sung to the Marseillaise."

shelter consisted of railway arches and stinking one-room cellars, the exaltation of "sweet home" could only magnify their misery. On one level, London's street people obviously grasped the ideal of domestic harmony: those who exhibited dogs, cats, rats, and pigeons in one cage—creatures "supposed to be one another's enemies and victims, living in quiet together"—called their displays "Happy Families." Yet the physical circumstances of their own lives had transformed urban street people into a distinct "tribe," Mayhew observed. They were the walking antithesis of settled privacy, and their freedom from the gravity of hearth and home was believed to excite secret envy.[73]

Victorian society was in fact riddled with troubling domestic contradictions. Journalists keen to document "moral improvement" among the masses eagerly noted the family pieties of the poor. During the early 1860's, for example, Hugh Shimmin reported how the denizens of a Liverpool slum court had begun to "gush forth in expressions which showed what a dear, very dear thing *home* is, be it ever so humble." Yet slum fathers were widely thought capable of molesting their daughters, while slum mothers stood accused of every other sin against "parental feeling."[74] Nor could the governing classes console themselves with the thought that they, at least, stood firm against threats to domestic purity. The furor over child prostitution that erupted in 1885 drew much of its force from revelations that "gentlemen" were the prime buyers of young flesh.[75]

Then, as now, politicians harped on the presumed links between strong families and strong nations. During a speech on "Conservative Principles" delivered in the spring of 1872, Disraeli reprised a standard Tory theme:

England is a domestic country. Here the home is revered and the hearth is sacred. The nation is represented by a family—the Royal Family; and if that family is educated with a sense of responsibility and a sentiment of public duty, it is difficult to exaggerate the salutary influence they may exercise over a nation. It is not merely an influence upon manners; it is not merely that they are a model for refinement and for good taste—they affect the heart as well as the intelligence of the people. . . .[76]

What few Victorians could have known was that the queen herself, paragon of domesticity, compared a woman giving birth to "a cow or a dog"; loathed the "terrible frog-like activity" of newborns; despised "baby worship"; and deemed the subject of breast-feeding "horridly disgusting."[77] But Victoria's subjects did know that all was far from well in many homes. On the one hand, domestic life in other European societies, particularly those of Spain and Italy, seemed "indifferent." Spouses there supposedly never experienced "the long cosy winter-evenings, wherein man and wife are thrown absolutely alone together, and forced to make the best of each other because they have nothing else to fall back upon." On the other hand, such intimacy could be suffocating. "Instead of love, and confidence, and serenity," an anonymous critic complained about English family life in 1876, "we have ill-tempers and selfishness, backbitings and quarreling, and any one abroad preferred to every one at home. . . . For the most part there is far more of tyranny, jealousy, and rebellion, than of those sweeter sentiments generally assumed."[78]

It would of course be foolish to argue that England's comfortable classes intervened in the private sphere solely to narrow a gap between domestic theory and practice. The self-appointed guardians of the English home had innumerable motives for their activism, by no means all of them high-minded. But just as it would be naive to suppose that these reformers ignored their own class interests when they visited a poor home or launched a new philanthropic venture, so it would be equally naive to assume that they were strangers to compassion. As fuel for social engagement, "compassion" may be no less potent, and certainly is no less complex, than "fear."[79] One survey of middle-class households in the 1890's revealed that they typically spent more on charity than on anything else in their budgets except food. Intriguingly, another survey of working-class families at the same time established that half of them gave weekly to charity. Whether this "kindness of the poor to the poor" was, as an Edwardian cleric believed, the barrier "which stands between our present civilization and revolution," there can be no doubt that common people contributed mightily to family welfare in an age before the building of a welfare "state." Much working-class charity has left no trace in organizational records; it would barely have figured in the calculation that, around 1911, annual giving to registered charities exceeded national spending on poor relief.[80] To see such massive benevolence as proof of a class conspiracy in action demands a tortured notion of cultural hegemony.

Further complicating the subject of family regulation is what has been labeled the "asocial egoism" of liberal theory.[81] Classical liberalism, at least as it was understood in England, cherished the rule of law, personal autonomy, individual equality, and the protection of privacy. In his *Thoughts and Details on Scarcity* (1795), Edmund Burke, normally seen as the father of modern English conservatism, offered an early distillation of this creed. Which duties the state ought to take upon itself for the common good and which it ought to leave to individual initiative, Burke recognized, was "one of the finest problems in legislation." Yet one truth seemed unalterable: that as legislators "descend from the state to a province, from a province to a parish, and from a parish to a private home, they go on accelerated in their fall."[82] Two generations later, Mill's *Principles of Political Economy* (1848) all but institutionalized this equation of freedom and privacy within liberalism. Thus, when reformers proposed to "save," "civilize," or simply "encourage" poor parents, these schemes often had to contend with stiff ideological resistance. Liberalism's doubts about social police are captured in Auden's epigram: "Private Faces in Public Places / Are Wiser and Nicer / Than Public Faces in Private Places." Less whimsical was the Victorian factory inspector who declared that he would sooner see a higher rate of infant mortality in textile towns than "intrude one iota farther on the sanctity of the domestic hearth and the decent seclusion of private life."[83]

But the resistance with which guardians of English home life had to contend ranged far beyond the confines of political theory. As this book will show, every attempt to discipline family conduct—or, in the Victorian vernacular, to fortify family "character"—required some sort of negotiation over the proper frontier between public and private needs. Strangers could not easily impose their moral values on a home. Whether they were charitable visitors knocking at the door, school attendance officials huddling in a public chamber, or psychotherapists waiting in their child guidance clinics, these strangers learned that their counsel would count for little unless the recipients saw some value in it. Parents and older children were often shrewd judges of the "help" on offer.

Family policy, whether devised by elected representatives, civil servants, or pressure groups within the voluntary sector, did not materialize in a demographic vacuum. Some basic characteristics of the English population should therefore be established. In the middle of the nineteenth century, England and Wales (treated here as a unit) had a population of 17.9 million. Toward the end of our period, on the eve of World War Two, this total had climbed to around 41.5 million. Thus, England's—or, for that matter, the United Kingdom's—population never matched that of Russia, Germany, or France, its main European rivals. More significant for our purposes was England's rapid urbanization. At the start of the nineteenth century only a quarter of its people lived in towns; by 1851 half did so; and by the end of the century more than three-quarters of the English population was urban. Cities larger than 100,000 absorbed most of the population growth. Greater London, with nearly 2.7 million residents in 1851, was the world's largest city. At the close of the nineteenth century, London, now a vast conurbation of six million, accounted for roughly 15 percent of the English population. By late twentieth-century Western standards, anyhow, households were very crowded. As late as 1911, when the first complete figures become available, 75 percent of the English people still lived in one- or two-room dwellings.[84] Social reformers were right to worry about overcrowding in the slums of East London or, worse still, of central Liverpool. Yet we probably should not assume, as one historian recently has done, that in these densely packed urban districts "the social control of nosey neighbours" was any more irksome than it had been in those early-modern English and American villages bluntly described elsewhere as "gossip-ridden, mean-spirited, endlessly litigious and generally rather nasty."[85]

England entered the second half of the nineteenth century scarred, but also hugely enriched, by industrialization. Contrary to the predictions of Marx and Engels, industrial capitalism did not destroy the nuclear family. Factory labor, for example, could not have torn apart many mid-Victorian mothers and children because comparatively few working-class mothers held factory jobs. In the cotton industry, England's largest employer of women outside the home, no more than a quarter of the female employees were married women; and among this minority, many were childless or had not yet embarked on procreation.[86] Nor, so far as we can tell, did industrialization rupture kinship ties. On the contrary, as studies of mid-Victorian Lancashire suggest, close kinship networks were probably stronger in urban than in rural areas of England. Michael Anderson contends that family ties were easier to maintain in relatively stable urban areas, where relatives often lived nearby, than in declining rural communities prey to migration and emigration.[87] So, functionally speaking, "family" and "household" were not always coterminous. A household, moreover, frequently sheltered individuals beyond the nuclear family core—servants, apprentices, and lodgers, not to mention distant kin. In 1851, just 36 percent of households contained a married couple, at least one child, and no one else.[88]

Legal notions of "family" added to this complexity. "The natural family," as the Census of 1871 declared, "is founded by marriage, and consists, in its complete state, of husband, wife, and children."[89] This nuclear family norm was enshrined in the common law, which required a man to support his wife and minor children, but no other kin. Meanwhile, England's statutory code of maintenance, embodied in the Poor Law of 1601 and not abandoned until 1948, recognized the claims of an extended family. For the Poor Law imposed an obligation not only on fathers and mothers to support children, and adults to support their elderly parents, but also on grandparents to support grandchildren.[90]

How, one wonders, if "family" was so variously understood, defined, and lived, can modern commentators be so categorical in their pronouncements on the "decline" of the nuclear family or the erosion of "traditional family values"? On what basis do they presume that a golden age of family autonomy once existed, an age when parents, left alone to nurture and educate their young, could raise virtuous citizens? If, on the other hand, this mythically autonomous family was in fact a psychic dungeon, a harsh "prison of expectations,"[91] why mourn its decline?

Although grounded in modern English evidence, this book offers a counter-narrative to popular lamentations about the fate of American and French families. Christopher Lasch brought out his *Haven in a Heartless World: The Family Besieged* in 1979. This elegant tirade against the "therapeutic state" argues that the "helping professions"—social work, child psychology, criminology, even home economics—have insinuated themselves into the home so thoroughly that the American family now retains almost no authority of its own.[92] Less elegant but no less influential, Jacques Donzelot's *The Policing of Families* (1977) likewise blames the enfeeblement of parenthood on a vague but sinister "tutelary complex." Donzelot describes the latter as "a whole series of bridges and connections between Public Assistance, juvenile law, medicine, and psychiatry" that, over the past century and a half, have made the French family "a sphere of direct intervention, a missionary field." Donzelot is at least forthcoming about what he calls his "team." Its captain is Michel Foucault and its turf is that wide realm of disciplinary practice "between the empty gesture of the voluntary and the inscrutable efficiency of the involuntary" called "policing."[93] Lasch is not a team player. Nor would he accept the curious proposition that voluntary gestures are "empty." Still, Lasch and Donzelot agree about the pernicious impact of "experts" on the modern family. Over time, they believe, a stampede of medical, legal, and educational specialists has thrown parents into bewilderment and home life into disarray. Neither critic seems aware that experts seldom speak as one, or that parents may resist specialist interference.

Perched far to the political right of Lasch and Donzelot is another pair of well-publicized social critics. Although Ferdinand Mount dwells on the English family and Gertrude Himmelfarb on Victorian morality, their ideological agenda are equally broad. Mount's journalistic *The Subversive Family* (1982) sketches a neo-libertarian view of the domestic scene. His nuclear family is every bit the haven that Lasch imagines, but with two key differences. Mount's "true defender of liberty and privacy" is specifically the working-class family, and its "permanent revolution" against the agents of state meddling is seen as largely successful. Because "intellectuals" have allegedly tried to suppress the story of how plain folk struggle against officialdom, however, Mount finds himself scolding "high culture" as well as invasive bureaucrats. The populist tone here should not surprise, coming as it does from a one-time policy adviser to Mrs. Thatcher.[94] What does call for comment, however, is Mount's radical juxtaposition of public and private. Rarely have the supportive inner realm of family and the threatening outside Other been so starkly delineated.

Gertrude Himmelfarb, a champion of intellectual history, would never pass as a populist. Yet very much like Mount she views the family as a repository of virtue. In her recent *The De-moralization of Society* (1995), Himmelfarb casts a fond eye back at some "conventional Victorian values" that were, she insists, honored in homes poor and prosperous: respectability, hard work, self-help, obedience, cleanliness, orderliness. Himmelfarb is right to argue, along with numerous historians before her, that such values cut across class lines. She may be thanked for reminding us that the Victorians saw self-help and charity as "opposite sides of the same coin." But to suggest, as she does in her book and elsewhere, that today's Anglo-American world should look to the Victorians for guidance in coping with illegitimacy, drug abuse, and welfare reform is more than merely simplistic.[95] Himmelfarb's distinction between the Victorian and the post-industrial era seems invidious. Her contrast between the self-responsible Victorian and the self-absorbed modern citizen minimizes the enormous energy that English reformers devoted to trying to *make* people more responsible, and not principally by shaming them.[96] It is precisely this moralizing thrust that *Friends of the Family* aims to examine.

This book will conclude with further reflections on "family values" and their political deployment. Before then, some of the most hotly contested campaigns to police the English home will be discussed in six topical chapters. Part I, "The Counsel of Strangers," investigates what happened when public advice encountered private domestic life. Part II, "The Adjudication of the Private," analyzes some of the ways in which courts accommodated demands that England's legal system address intimate family problems. This study will provide sufficient case detail to show how interventionist plans arise from the discrepancies between actual and imagined family life. Most of us have two families, as John Gillis points out: one that we live *with* and one that we live *by*.[97] Because the family we live with, in real time, often compares so unfavorably to the timeless ideal we imagine, a permanent sense of anxiety tends to envelop the former. Instead of removing idealized family life from its pedestal, we choose to dwell on the defects of ordinary homes. This has certainly been true for modern English society.

PART I

The Counsel of Strangers

ONE

Home Ministries

I T W O U L D B E difficult to overstate the importance that nine-teenth-century English society attached to preserving harmony in the home. As we have seen, the belief that domestic life should provide a "shelter . . . from all terror, doubt, and division" long predated the sanctification of the family commonly associated with the mid-Victorian writings of John Ruskin and Coventry Patmore.[1] A full generation before Victoria became queen, even the legal reformer Jeremy Bentham, a man supposedly immune to flights of sentimental fancy, had described the family as that "retreat wherein repose ought to be found" and the tenderest "emotions of the soul" nurtured.[2] The related strains of rapid industrialization and chaotic urban growth not only heightened concern about the stability of the family but also helped to popularize the home-as-haven ideal. In some respects this deification of the domestic represented wishful thinking. For as evidence began to show that many of the urban poor were actually living in the worst kind of squalor, England's middle classes appeared to hope that by articulating a vision of private virtue they might hasten its acceptance.

Preventive action would have to buttress noble thoughts, however. Parliament published two important reports on urban conditions in 1840 and 1844, both of which suggested that family life in the "populous districts" had become a nursery of vice. In an implicit attack on the housekeeping habits of working-class wives, these inquiries lamented that instead of "finding their comforts by [the] fireside," husbands were fleeing from the noise and filth of their own homes into pubs and spirit shops, there imbibing habits "in the highest degree anti-social." Equally troubling was the news that parental neglect had "neutralized" much of the progress achieved in church-supported schools.[3] At a time when labor militancy in the shape of Chartism already threatened the propertied classes, the prospect of a still less tractable generation of workers maturing in slum homes seemed especially grim. Thus, improved "tactics" for coping with the "dangerous classes" were required. "We cannot replant seignorial influence in England, or reinstate aristocracy on its olden throne," warned a reform-minded barrister in 1849. Yet the "higher orders" still had it within their grasp, through "chastening and Christianizing," to render the urban poor "discreet and temperate."[4]

No more potent moralizing strategy stood ready for use than a specialized form of parish charity. This was district visiting, an activity that sought to bring the word of God, along with advice about personal conduct and domestic management, into the homes of the poor. The men and, more commonly, women who undertook visiting are easily misunderstood today. On one hand, their mission has been attacked in crude Marxist terms as part of a "shrewd and quite ruthless combination of coercion, paternalism and cajolery" whose hegemonic force kept laboring folk quiet and conformist.[5] That most district visitors arrived at the doors of the poor with firm, class-based notions of right and wrong is incontestable. They also brought with them an evangelical faith, however, and the tenets of this faith, mediating between the public and the private, could operate at cross-purposes with their class interests. On the other hand, the Victorian "Lady Bountiful" carrying Bibles, soap, and throat lozenges into slum courts can be a vaguely comic figure, a cliché that suggests dilettantism.[6] In actuality this brand of benevolence often demanded major commitments of time and emotional energy. More broadly, as this chapter will argue, the perseverance with which district visitors sought to moralize the poor by modifying their domestic environment inspired other home ministries whose common concerns are now often overlooked. Those who became district nurses and health visitors, for example, would seem to personify the trend toward professional autonomy in work for women, while those middle-class ladies who conducted mothers' meetings would appear to trace a very different trajectory toward the maintenance of a conventional, family-centered separate sphere for the "gentle sex." These mid-Victorian inventions nevertheless all derived from district visiting their confidence in the efficacy of personal remonstration— as well as their worry about the alienating potential of unsolicited advice.

District Visiting

Although rural clergy traditionally sat with the sick, not until the last quarter of the eighteenth century did "friendly visiting" become a systematic part of local church work. The Methodists were pioneers here. John Wesley himself had been a sick visitor in the 1740's and Wesley's example inspired others among his fellowship to organize regular prayer meetings with cottagers. By concentrating their attentions on rural households, the Methodists were filling a spiritual void left by Anglican priests who in many areas had withdrawn physically as well as spiritually from their flocks. Another Methodist, John Gardner, brought this mission to London in 1785, where he established the Strangers' Friend Society, a charity whose scheme for helping the urban poor served as a model for what, a generation later, came to be known as district visiting. Other dissenting faiths soon entered the field of house-to-house philanthropy. By the early years of the nineteenth century even some Anglicans— evangelicals within the Established Church who had heard a "call to seriousness"—were joining the hunt for souls.[7]

The diversity among these visiting societies was striking. Members of the urban gentry dominated some organizations, the poor themselves ran others, but middle-class control was most typical. Many societies whose work we know today only through documentary shards limited their attentions to a few benighted streets, while others scoured whole cities. Within five years of its founding in 1828, for example, London's General Society for Promoting District Visiting had 10,455 families under observation thanks to the diligence of 573 visitors.[8] The GSPDV, like most large societies, was prepared to deal with a broad range of social problems, whereas smaller charities often chose to help only the aged poor, the blind, widows, or dock workers. Some societies existed to provide needy people with food, fuel, or clothing, yet the operating rules of others forbade the granting of "temporal relief" in any form. The great majority of district visitors were unpaid volunteers, although some of the larger societies, such as the London City Mission (founded in 1835), the Leeds Town Mission (1837), and the Manchester and Salford Town Mission (1837), used salaried agents. Several of the charities devoted to "domiciliary" work were strictly nondenominational and under lay control. If this array of home-centered philanthropy seems slightly bewildering today, it must have appeared far more so to the Victorian poor themselves, whose dwellings could become contested terrain for rival agencies. Gathered together, the visiting ranks were vast. In 1889, according to its first official count, the Church of England announced that 47,112 district visitors were active in just 80 percent of its English and Welsh parishes, a number that would grow to 74,009 by 1910.[9] Since dissenting Protestant, nondenominational, Catholic, and Jewish charities supervised at least this many agents, the combined visiting force could not have been far short of 200,000 (in a population of 36 million) on the eve of the First World War.

Although the visiting impulse likewise defies neat classification, four motivations predominated. The first followed from the evangelical concept of salvation. For some nineteenth-century Protestants, self-examination could not cease with the conversion experience because the danger of spiritual backsliding seemed all too real. Hence faith needed to be re-forged in the fire of adversity, as the diary of Mary Cryer, a mid-Victorian Methodist visitor, made plain:

I find the cross in canvassing from door to door for Missions, and perhaps not succeeding in one case in twenty; I find it still more in begging for a poor starving fellow-creature, and now and then meeting with a chilling repulse; . . . but, most of all, I find it in going door to door on the visiting plan, trying to persuade sinners to attend God's house, and flee from the wrath to come. . . . But O, when I have to make my own way, and meet the cold looks and even the rude rebuff of those who will not be subdued by kindness and courtesy, then nature does shrink. . . . Yet I dare not give it up: it is God's work. . . . I often think I ought not to be reckoned among the soldiers, till I burn with a nobler, warmer, bolder spirit, for the fulfillment of His love's redeeming plan.[10]

If some visitors took after Mrs. Pardiggle, Dickens's relentlessly "business-like and systematic" dispenser of religious tracts,[11] probably more approached this work with Mary Cryer's aching awareness of human frailty.

Such testing of one's spiritual armor could coexist with a second motivation for visiting, namely a zeal for restricting charity to the "deserving" poor. Both the axioms of political economy and the imperatives of salvation, after all, seemed rooted in higher law, and evangelical economics in the first half of the nineteenth century, as Boyd Hilton has shown, tended to assume that only checks on population and production could make the nation happier. Haphazard giving was therefore an unnatural and ultimately debilitating practice.[12] Yet at the same time, periodic crop failures and trade slumps produced human suffering too widespread to ignore. Thus, district visiting served to reconcile the competing claims of Malthusian theory and humanitarian conscience.[13]

Female visitors, who substantially out-numbered males in most societies, may often have been attracted to this work for a third reason: the opportunity it offered for developing a valued expertise outside the restrictive sphere of their own middle-class homes. A "rude rebuff," in Mary Cryer's words, was not always what came of knocking on a slum door. Even in very rough neighborhoods the conscientious lady visitor might hope to win a few "friends"—that is, poor people who appeared to welcome her advances. Anne Jemima Clough, a visitor in Liverpool and later the first Principal of Newnham College, Cambridge, cherished the familiarity she achieved with some of her clients. "The children know me, and speak my name," Clough revealed. "This was delicious to me, and worth more than a thousand praises."[14] By no means all female visitors shared Clough's concern about how the poor perceived her, but it would be perverse to imply that most such women went "slum-

ming" for the same reason they went shopping—to seek unchaper-
oned adventure in a cityscape of strangers and secrets. No doubt for
London ladies both shopping the chic West End and haunting the
grim East End served to accentuate their privileged status. After all,
decorous consumption in Oxford Street as well as charitable visiting
in Whitechapel Road proclaimed leisure, and thus wealth. Buying
hats and comforting the sick or dying were nevertheless very different forms of human engagement. Nor does the *flâneur*, that self-
conscious yet unseen spectator of urban life so closely associated
with the "modernist" sensibility of Baudelaire, bear much resemblance to the committed lady visitor. For although painfully aware
of moving between social worlds, she was highly visible and knew
nothing of the stroll without destination (*flânerie*).[15] It has been suggested that some women may have used door-to-door philanthropy
as a form of sexual sublimation, a way to "soak . . . up surplus energies."[16] Sexually fulfilled or not, female visitors surely derived a sense
of public accomplishment from their work at a time when most
roads to political power remained blocked.[17]

A fourth reason for undertaking house-to-house charity was to
reunite "the severed sympathies of the nation's classes."[18] From the
start, certain of its advocates had valued district visiting above all as
a kind of social cement. The famous example of Thomas Chalmers
in Glasgow did much to publicize this aspect of the work. Chalmers, a magnificent Scots Presbyterian minister, widely known theo-
logian, and, oxymoronic as it may sound now, popular mathemati-
cian, attacked the poverty and Christian indifference of his large St.
John's parish by carving it up into twenty-five smaller units. Each
unit, or "proportion," consisted of approximately fifty families
along with a church elder and a deacon, the former taking responsibility for the families' spiritual welfare and the latter for their physical needs. Chalmers's deacons were expected to become intimately
acquainted with the families under their supervision, and to show
them the path to economic independence. As Chalmers optimisti-
cally described the human chemistry involved in this configuration:
"There is a substantial, though unnoticed, charm in the visit of a superior. There is a felt compliment in his attentions, which raises an

emotion in the breast, the very opposite of that disdainful sentiment towards the higher orders of society, that is now of such alarming prevalence amongst our operative population."[19] Whether or not the poor of St. John's parish had been "charmed" into deference,[20] Chalmers's experiment seemed well worth replicating elsewhere.

In London, the General Society for Promoting District Visiting was the first large body to be organized along these lines. The rationale for the GSPDV's founding made explicit the hopes and fears that animated much visiting:

In the year 1828, the attention of a few individuals having been directed to the condition of the poorer classes in the metropolis, they were deeply concerned at the contemplation of the mass of wretchedness, profligacy, and ignorance which . . . appeared almost to defy every means of counteraction or improvement. The density of the population, combined with the difficulty and apparent hopelessness of individual exertion, had deterred many from making any efforts whatever to remedy this appalling evil; and thus the effect of the separation which for the most part exists between the dwellings of the rich and poor in London, was necessarily increased, and the salutary intercourse amongst the different classes of society which so frequently takes place in the country was thereby prevented. . . .

Societies already existed for visiting the sick, clothing the naked, and relieving the destitute. The doors of hospitals, infirmaries, asylums, and dispensaries were open to receive the victims of suffering, to whom much effectual assistance was administered. None, however, of these Societies were of an *aggressive* character: they relieved distress when it was brought before their notice . . . ; they endeavoured to deal with the effect, but they left the cause untouched and unassailed.

To supply this deficiency, . . . *a regular system of domiciliary visitation* was thought to be necessary, by which *every poor family might be visited at their own habitations, from house to house and from room to room*, and their temporal and spiritual condition diligently yet tenderly examined into, and appropriate treatment applied.[21]

"Social control" was therefore an acknowledged aim of district visiting, if by this vague phrase we mean an upper-class strategy for shaping the conduct of the poor. Because, as Mary Poovey has put it, efforts to homogenize high- and lowborn were conceived "within a problematic of visuality," the "ocular penetration" of working-class neighborhoods necessarily became a key feature of such philanthropy. But charitable visiting was far from a monolithic enterprise. Visitors themselves, we must remember, often disagreed about the proper method for "sow[ing] the seeds of a kindlier relationship . . . between the wealthy and the destitute."[22]

What may appear to late twentieth-century eyes as unseemly persistence was largely the product of an evangelical obsession with conversion. The periodical literature and instruction manuals aimed at visitors drove home the point that deathbed conversions were spiritual victories, however wretched a person's last hours on earth. As an "encouragement to perseverance," the *District Visitor's Record* told of the lifelong "infidel" stricken with cancer of the face. It was mere minutes before this sinner's agonizing end that he finally expressed a wish to hear more about "the all-atoning sacrifice of Christ." Readers learned that a "degraded" slum mother racked by consumption had found similar comfort because a lady visitor coaxed her to cough up the words "I am forgiven" just before her death.[23] Visitors were admonished to recall that the Lord sometimes worked in mysterious ways. Thus, if an oyster-diver could find a Gospel tract underwater wedged in a mollusk's shell, was it so strange that a London City Missionary should use a dying child to save the souls of her tramp parents?[24] No "race" was beyond rescue. For if James Crabbe's ministry to the Gypsies outside Southampton had already begun to transform these heathen wanderers into settled Christians, surely even more could be accomplished among the urban poor?[25]

Visitors waged a war on ungodly conduct as well as unbelief. Sabbath-breaking, cruelty to animals, drunkenness, and gambling were among the "sinful desires of fallen creatures" most frequently encountered during their rounds. Because the visitors' struggle against drink and betting often ended in failure, their rare successes demanded full publicity. When David Greer began patrolling his assigned neighborhood in West London, for example, card-playing was so popular that men allegedly used a corpse in its coffin as a gaming table, removing the two halfpence coins from its eyes to sweeten the first wager. Through Greer's exertions public gambling soon grew less common (or at least more furtive) in his district.[26] Couples "living tally"—as husband and wife, but unwed—received no sympathy from visitors. Lawfully joined couples who had taken advantage of the new (1837) option of civil registration rather than exchanging their wedding vows in church could expect to be lectured along with the more spectacularly reprobate.[27]

District visitors in the early- and mid-Victorian eras remained on guard against "artful" folks who "feign[ed] wretchedness," since the bodies of the poor were supposedly inured to hardships that would cause the comfortable classes real suffering. To avoid the "demoralizing" influence of scattershot charity it was often best that a married lady—someone who understood the principles of household management—should dispense relief. She could supply such essentials as oatmeal, soap, and tea to genuinely needy slum families, or else collect subscriptions to a provident fund that would pay interest in the form of coal or clothing at regular intervals.[28] During the last third of the nineteenth century, however, a less judgmental tone entered the visiting literature. By 1869, the same year that the Charity Organisation Society was founded to combat indiscriminate almsgiving, the London City Mission began to recognize that the wholesale demolition of tenement blocks had produced such terrible overcrowding that the poor naturally displayed a "reckless indifference to their temporal interest." The Christian Socialist–inspired West London Mission, formed in 1889, was probably the visiting charity most vocal in its condemnation of economic orthodoxy. Rejecting the "pessimistic fatalism" of Malthus, the "extreme Individualistic-Liberalism of the Manchester School," and the "biological laws of Darwin," the Rev. Hugh Price Hughes and his supporters attacked chronic underemployment rather than the purported fecklessness of the poor. Still, even the iconoclastic West London Mission placed great faith in the power of a visitor's "gentleness and sympathy" to comfort the dispossessed.[29]

All successful visiting schemes had to strike a balance between Christian zeal and off-putting intrusiveness. The most "womanly women," one clergyman asserted, naturally "shrink from forcing themselves upon . . . others just because they are poorer." Yet in some situations it was precisely the unexpected appearance of a lady striding across the threshold that could avert catastrophe, as a Manchester drunkard "saved" on the verge of suicide reportedly thought.[30] Properly undertaken, domestic visiting was "self-denying and humble" work, a "lowly and personal" service whose divine prototype was Jesus washing the feet of his disciples. But the spiritual basis for visiting could not be allowed to overwhelm its temporal demands. Vice, after all, "shrink[s] from detection," and it was therefore also the duty of respectable Christians to keep what Lord Shaftesbury termed "a moral and political, if not a physical, epidemic" from spreading among the urban masses.[31] There was ostensibly one role in which the visitor could ferret out disaffection while showing true sympathy to poor households—the role of "friend." Such a friend would listen attentively to everything that was said in a humble home; keep all confidences (although the secrets of the poor could be shared with clergymen); "avoid anything like dictation" when offering advice; resist the temptation to "gratify any vulgar curiosity"; refrain from "inquisitiveness" ("You are not an inspector"); shun politics; and "be always *respectful in manner*." Extremely few doors would remain closed to those who heeded these hints, visiting manuals declared.[32]

How often district visitors did in fact encounter working-class opposition, and on what grounds, is difficult to judge, not least because the visited have left extremely few accounts of their experience in this regard. Prisoners of drink, by the visitors' own admission, were frequently hostile to all overtures.[33] Yet even if outright hostility was rare, we should be cautious about accepting the generally optimistic assessments found in visiting literature. That the poor appeared to welcome missionary advances may say more about working-class survival strategies than about the ease with which visitors "surround[ed] themselves with an impregnable barrier of attachment." It is reasonable to assume that the receipt of visiting charity was often a negotiated process in which the poor, skilled in what Erving Goffman calls "impression management," were willing to perform rituals of deference as the price for material aid.[34] This is

A poor family (notably fatherless) shrinks from the advance of a "Lady Bountiful" and her well-dressed escort. This late-Victorian image recognizes only the invasive side of door-to-door philanthropy. Courtesy: Hulton-Getty Picture Collection.

not to say that unconditional friendship was impossible between visitors and the visited, but it was, probably, an unusual development. Ellen Chase, an American who became intimate with the poor of one Southeast London neighborhood during the 1880's and 1890's, managed to avoid an "embarrassing sense of intrusion" partly because of her sympathetic manner but partly also because, as a rent collector, she had the advantage of a clear contractual relationship with her clients.[35] As late as the Edwardian period district visitors were reminded that a key to winning a poor woman's confidence lay in relieving the monotony of her life: "A chat about your holiday in Scotland or Rome or Clacton-on-Sea, a description of the last play you saw, ball you went to, book you read . . . may carry you a great way into the affection of some tired housewife resting after Monday's washing." Perhaps such exotica did amuse some working-class women, although the sheer number of well-meaning visitors who could descend on her must have seemed as much an invasion as an entertainment.[36]

If many-sided, a visitor's mission nevertheless hinged on the guidance given to poor wives and mothers. It should come as no surprise that the first commandment of such guidance was to make homes as welcoming for husbands as possible, since notions of patriarchal authority pervaded the middle-class culture which supplied most visitors. Indeed, according to one handbook on pastoral practice, it was "too much a matter of . . . propriety to need urging" that the consent of husbands had to be obtained before a lady might take up parochial charity.[37] Once she had discharged her own home duties and won her husband's permission, the lady visitor could enlighten poor women about how to "manage" men. Because "a hungry man is an angry man," in the words of one visitors' guidebook, wives should do everything possible to have supper ready when their husbands returned from work. After supper, a man should be able to relax in his favorite chair by a well-laid fire. Only then would a sensible wife reveal her "budget of bothers." Even spring cleaning should be spread over months ("homeopathic doses") rather than days lest husbands lose their tempers. And if "beautiful order" failed to appease a man, his sullenness should be borne patiently.[38] Hovering over all these injunctions was the specter of male violence. Middle-class moralists realized that wife-beating was prevalent among the poor, although these critics often misunderstood the social meaning of such behavior.[39] In any case, district visitors carried the message that each household was a "little Empire" whose sovereign was the father. Fathers of course had some imperial responsibilities, chief among them bringing home an unopened wage packet. But mothers were charged with keeping peace in the realm.[40]

Children should not be allowed to breach the father's peace, and again it was primarily mother's duty to train her offspring "into habits of perfect and implicit obedience." Fervently evangelical visitors worried about what they regarded as the innate evil in a child's nature. To brand a child's conscience in such a way that the thought of eternity "thunders in [its] ears" was admittedly a job for both parents. Practically speaking, though, mothers shouldered most of this righteous burden.[41]

Less religiously driven visitors also expected that mothers would satisfy their children's basic material needs. Good nutrition, regular school attendance, and the protection of growing bodies particularly concerned middle-class "friends," and when maternal performance in these areas appeared unsatisfactory harassment could follow. One early nineteenth-century visitor confessed that only after a lengthy campaign had she shamed a woman into seeing a surgeon about her daughter's broken collar bone. The bone fused, and in time both mother and daughter reportedly came to appreciate this "timely interference."[42] Two generations later the tenor of visiting literature had turned still more interventionist, a trend that reflected worry about the residential segregation of the urban poor in general and growing disillusionment with slum-clearance schemes in particular. Slum mothers, it seemed, were in dire need of expert help: "Ignorance reigns in the kitchen, and perplexity in the parlour," warned a female physician. The so-called medicalization of motherhood, typically linked to social welfare reforms in the first third of the twentieth century, had its roots in the Victorian world of district visiting.[43]

Most of what we know about this ministry to working-class homes is based on evidence concerning London—a consequence of the fact that visiting tracts were typically published in, and dealt with, the metropolis. By shifting our attention briefly to another urban center and by analyzing organizational records rather than prescriptive literature, certain discontinuities between theory and practice emerge more clearly. Located almost two hundred miles north of London, the Yorkshire wool-manufacturing center of Bradford was both physically and culturally distant from the capital. In the summer of 1849, Mayor Titus Salt, a wealthy mill owner, pioneer of the alpaca trade, and soon-to-be builder of Saltaire, England's most elaborate model factory town, called a meeting of prominent men "to devise means for promoting the social and moral interests" of local citizens. Six months later the Bradford Town Mission emerged as the chosen vehicle for reaching those who lived in ignorance of Christian duty. Patterned after visiting work that had been operating in nearby Leeds since 1837, the Town Mission was "unsectarian," aiming "not to proselytize, but to evangelize" Bradford's poor.[44] Another aim received less publicity. The Managing Committee early on perceived a need for "Special Meetings or Lectures to counteract infidel or Socialist opinion amongst the working classes."[45] Disseminating gospel truths and preserving the economic and political order impressed Bradford's elite as complementary goals.

After a year of door-to-door investigation, four salaried missionaries had unearthed an "astonishing" amount of "home-heathenism." One agent kept a careful record of the 1,036 men and women he spoke with during that first year. He was shocked to find that only 41 percent of these adults had ever attended church, and just 27 percent did so regularly. By these measures of religiosity Bradford's laboring poor appeared to be considerably less devout than the population of England as a whole, assuming that the famous religious census of 1851 was at all reliable.[46] The bad news did not end here. Many children who attended Sunday schools read with great difficulty, and a "majority" of the girls found in brothels had attended these schools. Finally, the amount of "Sabbath desecration" was "almost incredible," probably because so many beer shops remained open on the Lord's Day.[47]

Fortunately for the city fathers, all of Bradford's Protestant sects supported the new Town Mission and a Ladies' Association threw itself into fund-raising. Equally encouraging was the "civil," sometimes even "cordial," reception of missionaries. The wool-combers seemed especially pleased to hear Bible stories. Some stubborn mill hands refused to separate politics from religion, but the missionary who dealt with most of them had, he thought, mounted an unanswerable defense of the status quo:

Some working men ... look upon us as sent out by, what they term, 'middle class men,' and are very free with their remarks about manufacturers, especially those who attend a place of worship, being oppressors. They sometimes tell us that we ought to visit the men who are 'robbing the hireling of his wages,' and reprove *them* for their sins. In reply to such charges, we readily admit that some masters may, doubtless, be designated 'oppressors,' but respecting professing Christians it is by no means universally correct. Moreover, if, in certain cases, men are tyrants, it is not in consequence of their being manufacturers. . . . I sometimes take advantage of such conversations and refer to the tyranny manifested by some working-men towards their wives and children, to show what overbearing, cruel masters they would make if they became employers.

As "proof" that these discussions had not been in vain, the missionary noted that a few of the former cynics now faithfully attended Sunday afternoon prayer services at the Mechanics' Institute.[48]

For the next ninety-three years Bradford Town Mission reports would assure readers that home-visiting was steadily eroding a mountain of sin. Deathbed conversions represented "brand[s] plucked out of the fire." Visitors left hundreds of thousands of evangelical tracts in the poorest dwellings. Railroad laborers, prostitutes, and the "pathologically" drunk earned painstaking attention, according to the annual reports.[49] Yet Mission records also show how unforeseen circumstances could alter the course of charitable effort. Money, above all else, proved a constant concern. Through congregational gifts, annual subscriptions, and odd donations, the Mission managed to raise £384 in 1850–51. During the following six decades its annual income rose only modestly while its philanthropic ambitions soared. One important result of financial uncertainty was a high turnover of missionaries, who often fell victim to cost-cutting schemes before they could earn the trust of families in their districts. Young single women, willing to work for less than married males, increasingly came to dominate the missionary corps, and this at a time when the decline of males in district visiting was being declared a national problem.[50]

Another unintended change in the Mission's work also stemmed from economic need. The mill owners and wool merchants who initially dominated the Managing Committee were staunch foes of indiscriminate alms, and the Mission's first agents accordingly denied nearly all requests for material relief. But in 1854 a sudden drop in demand for woolen goods temporarily brought hard times to Bradford. Widespread unemployment combined with an unusually harsh Yorkshire winter forced missionaries to distribute flannel clothing as well as godly tracts.[51] Thereafter they grew increasingly active in arranging such temporal aid as coal deliveries, ambulance transport, and lending libraries.[52] What gradually took place in Bradford was not a discernible transition from charity to social work, for the missionaries themselves remained oblivious to the emerging disciplines of social science. Nor did the material relief they came to provide somehow "establish and reinforce a division within [the laboring] mass which rendered it more manageable."[53] Rather, the visiting organization launched in Bradford, as in many other towns throughout England, found itself more a captive of circumstances than the warden of private lives.

Complaints about the conduct of district visitors intensified during the generation that preceded World War One. Some religious leaders griped about lady visitors who no longer appeared sufficiently "accountable" to their parish clergymen. Other critics attacked what appeared to be some visitors' "socialistic" embrace of feeding and clothing schemes for poor homes.[54] More consequential was the decision of activist ministers such as Canon Samuel Barnett to establish urban settlements. Barnett's Toynbee Hall, like most of these settlements, sheltered young, university-trained men who were expected to work with "passionate patience" in the surrounding slums as non-resident visitors rarely could do.[55] Late-Victorian visiting literature was sometimes its own worst enemy, portraying door-to-door charity as the preserve of snobs. Canon Barnett's wife, the bulldozing Henrietta, could imagine no legitimate excuse for a poor woman to pawn her family's clothing: "Does it not strike you as somewhat nasty and indelicate to allow our garments to mix with the ugly company of dirt and disease which they must often meet at the pawnshops?" she asked her genteel readers. Another veteran visitor found it amusing that the lower classes living nearby seemed to regard domestic advice "as gospel" so long as it appeared in print.[56] Middle-class defenders of the poor lashed out at such condescension. True, probably few district visitors understood what another well-born critic, George Orwell, would later describe as the "complicated meanness" of poverty.[57] They nevertheless constituted the advance guard of an army converging on the Englishman's castle.

District Nursing

District visiting inspired two, more specialized, forms of home-centered philanthropy that emerged in the 1860's. District nursing and health visiting were both exclusively female enterprises, devoted themselves to the physical well-being of working-class households, and, in time, shed the religious mantle that distinguished most of the older domiciliary work. Aiming to combine women's presumed superiority as family managers with the prescriptions of medical science, district nursing and health visiting sent new missionaries to knock on the doors of the poor. Once inside they discovered not only habits that begged to be broken but also unanticipated strength and resourcefulness.

Although the origins of district nursing are often traced to Liverpool, earlier steps toward what Frank Prochaska terms "missionary medicine" were taken in London.[58] In 1857, Ellen Ranyard, an ardent supporter of the British and Foreign Bible Society, hit upon the idea of using a charismatic, working-class woman to save the degraded poor. Mrs. Ranyard had recently moved with her husband and four children from Battersea to Bloomsbury, where, she was shocked to find, some of England's most "unvisitable" slums stood within a short walk of the British Museum. Most notorious was nearby St. Giles, a vast rookery whose shattered buildings and stench of human waste had appalled Engels a decade before.[59] Though dwellings in St. Giles remained "closed against all respectable approach," the Bible-selling success of "Marian B.," a poor but pious local woman, encouraged Mrs. Ranyard to recruit others like her.[60] Clean, tidy, humble, cheerful, and possessed of a keen evangelical spirit, Ranyard's "Biblewomen" were meant to provide the "missing link" between London's "sunken sixth" and their social superiors. But selling the Good Book on installment was not the Biblewomen's only charge. For Mrs. Ranyard believed that the poor needed a "gracious healing remedy for their actual miseries." Thus, while avoiding the "curse" of indiscriminate charity, Biblewomen could earn enormous goodwill by asking a simple question of destitute mothers: "Shall I make you more comfortable?" Washing her bed linen, scrubbing her floors, or preparing a few meals for her children may have constituted the sort of religious nurse-charring that Florence Nightingale so deplored, but in Ellen Ranyard's view the cure of body and soul were inseparable.[61]

The London Bible and Domestic Female Mission, or as it was better known, the Ranyard Bible Mission, grew remarkably fast. By late 1860, 137 full-time Biblewomen were penetrating "dens of iniquity" throughout the metropolis.[62] Paid twelve and a half shillings per week and plainly not afraid of dirt and vulgarity, these agents fired the imagination of a young Octavia Hill, soon to become England's most famous advocate of casework charity.[63] Stories of family restoration figured prominently in the Mission's literature. How long formerly drunken, violent, and filth-encrusted parents stayed "changed" as a result of the Biblewomen's intervention is impossible to know. Nor can we verify one of the Mission's key claims—that because its agents came as "sisters" into slum homes, poor mothers were willing to reveal their most private concerns. There are hints that such intervention may have brought a degree of emotional consolation. Mrs. Ranyard noted that at "Marian B.'s" first tea party the assembled wives agreed on one point: "they all had bad husbands."[64] Perhaps these and other poor women found some solace in the evangelical reverence for suffering? What seems certain is that the nursing component of Mrs. Ranyard's scheme proved very popular among a segment of the community used to paying neighborhood women for help with illness or, in grave cases, resorting to workhouse infirmaries.[65]

Responding to this enthusiasm, the Mission in 1868 sent forth "Bible-nurses" to provide "hospital work outside all hospitals." These women became London's first district nurses. Drawn, like the Biblewomen, from the churchgoing poor and required to live among the people they served, Ranyard's Bible-nurses presented a stark contrast to the largely middle-class women later associated with the Metropolitan and National Nursing Association.[66] Bible-nurses initially received just three months of hospital training—substantially less than most other district nurses—and probably spent more time with terminal patients due to the Ranyard women's interest in deathbed conversion. It is worth recalling, though, that Bible-nurses launched their medical mission at a time when the national ratio of doctors to population was 1:1,547, and far worse in some inner-city neighborhoods.[67] The Bible-nurses tended to provide simple but often very useful help. In 1893, for example, a Wandsworth mother went to work secure in the knowledge that a Ranyard nurse would spend several hours each day poulticing the abscesses on her young son's body.[68] The contributions of these women unquestionably helped to bridge a gap in the care of London's sick poor.[69]

Mid-Victorian Liverpool, although much smaller than London, had proportionally more citizens in desperate need of medical attention. Then the most overcrowded city in Britain, Liverpool was a public health nightmare. Fortunately, this teeming port also enjoyed a distinguished charitable tradition. It was one of the city's leading philanthropists, William Rathbone, who in 1859 hired a skilled nurse to ease the suffering in poor homes just as she had recently soothed his dying wife.[70] To what extent he later leaned on Florence Nightingale for advice in creating a district nursing scheme for Liverpool remains unclear. But it was definitely Rathbone money that underwrote the widely imitated system whereby a training school at the Liverpool Royal Infirmary produced nurses for neighborhood as well as for hospital and private work. A central organization, entirely dependent on charitable support, financed this professional training and paid the nurses' salaries, while a phalanx of amateur "Lady Superintendents" reviewed the case records, doled out supplies, and raised funds for the nurses' room and board.[71]

After 1868, the year that William Rathbone entered Parliament as a Liberal MP for Liverpool, philanthropic discussion of a similar scheme for London intensified. A private analysis of London's nursing needs published in 1875 found a worrisome dearth of females of "superior social station" to tend the sick poor.[72] With Florence Lees acting as chief analyst, this conclusion was foregone. Perhaps the most highly trained nurse of her time, Miss Lees (later Mrs. Dacre Craven) reputedly could also scrub a table and de-louse a slum home as well as the toughest charwoman. Such demanding work properly belonged to ladies, she insisted, not to "missing links" who preached as they nursed.[73]

The awkwardly named Metropolitan and National Nursing Association for Providing Trained Nurses for the Sick Poor became Florence Lees's personal weapon in her fight to carve out a professional niche for educated gentlewomen. By seeing to it that her nurses were decently paid, received a month's annual holiday, and had time to read and attend lectures, Lees tried to insure that they would not be "losing caste among their own kith and kin."[74] The Metropolitan and National Association won over many doctors with its policy that district nurses act only under a physician's direction. With a "well-trained, cultivated, and intelligent lady-nurse" to help him, predicted one medical journal, a doctor might now "trust his patient to remain at a distance, feeling sure that the state of the pulse, temperature of the body, and every changing phase of disease, would be accurately communicated to him by letter or telegram, and so enable him to regulate his visits . . . according to necessity."[75] Not all doctors were this accepting, of course. The idea that gentlewomen would willingly perform such "dirty work" as tending to bedsores baffled The Lancet in 1879. Thirty years later, a medical curmudgeon complained that, "The prescribing chemist, the herbalist, the bone-setter, and the quack medicine vendor are still with us, and there is, in addition, the district nurse to be reckoned with."[76]

By the start of the twentieth century district nursing had nonetheless become a national fact of life. The spread of this work from town to country owed much to the Queen Victoria's Jubilee Institute, a body established in 1889 with donations collected throughout the Empire as a tribute to the sovereign. "Queen's Nurses" met the most rigorous training standards of their day. Whether they or any other district nurses could accomplish all that Lees and Nightingale asked of them is another matter. In theory, this new health professional would "nurse the room"—dusting, washing, disinfecting, unsealing windows—as well as the patient. She would act as a "clinical clerk" for the doctor, yet be ready to improvise treatment if he were delayed. She would quickly distinguish between diseases that required prolonged attendance, such as puerperal fever, from

"A Queen's Nurse in Cornwall." This photograph from the *Queen's Nurses Magazine* (Jan. 1911) emphasizes the adaptability of such home-visitors. Courtesy: British Library.

those such as scarlatina, which demanded quarantine of a household. She would do her utmost to cheer up cheerless homes without almsgiving. This saint would become, her champions predicted, "the great civilizer of the poor," a purveyor of hygienic wisdom more influential than the doctor.[77]

The working-class reception of district nurses no doubt varied greatly from one community to the next. As Ellen Ross has noted, the nursing costumes these women wore, along with the practical aid they rendered to the needy, marked them as civic institutions. In London during the 1870's laboring men offered their subway seats to uniformed nurses.[78] Exhortations to treat patients as friends did not fall on deaf ears. Mrs. Crowie, a district nurse assigned to a London slum neighborhood in the mid-1880's, refused to let a former patient slide back into poverty. With this widow facing ruin from the impending repossession of her hire-purchase sewing machine, Nurse Crowie wrote directly to England's richest woman, the Baroness Burdett-Coutts, for help. It arrived. In a small Yorkshire town, another nurse accustomed to witnessing all manner of pain nevertheless broke down in tears at the "pitiful" sight of a mechanic watching his wife bleed to death from her slit trachea.[79] Perseverance was another endearing trait. The six district nurses active in late-Victorian Birmingham averaged 15.2 visits per patient, a frequency that may in fact have been comparatively low. Poor persons suffering from respiratory ailments such as bronchitis, pleurisy, and pneumonia were apt to receive especially close attention.[80] Despite the sensitivity of district nurses to being regarded as "parish charwomen," they continued in some areas to perform traditionally domiciliary services, most notably laying out the dead.[81] It is possible that at times working-class households may have viewed a nurse's "pokin' round" as the "harmless peculiarity" of a lady. But she was an unusual lady, prepared to brew beef tea or chop kindling if necessary. In cases where the presence of one outsider meant that fewer censorious neighbors needed to be on hand (as, for example, during childbirth), the lady nurse may actually have helped to preserve a vestige of privacy.[82]

Among the first generation of district nurses easily the most recognizable name is that of Margaret E. Loane. Between 1904 and 1911 Miss Loane, then a Superintendent of Queen's Nurses, published prolifically on the subject of working-class home life. This author of three health manuals, several short articles, and six full-length books has left nothing in the way of autobiography. Indeed, we know merely that she was born in Portsmouth, the daughter of a captain in the Royal Navy; that she was trained at Charing Cross Hospital; and that her district nursing experience covered both ur-

ban and rural assignments. Loane's writings leave much to be desired as cultural sociology. Her portraits of the poor are just that,
static impressions which cannot easily account for social change.
Nor can we be sure that the figures in her portraits are accurately
drawn, for Miss Loane entered humble homes as an authority figure
whose conversations with clients were rarely if ever un-self-con-
scious. Then too, Loane's informants may well have been unrepre-
sentative members of the working-class community, for as she herself confessed, "those who have regarded me with a friendly eye
have generally been eccentric persons not much in favour among
their neighbours."[83] Yet for all that she was an excellent listener, and
the impressions she recorded surely mirrored those of many other
veteran district nurses.

Margaret Loane fretted about the public reception of those under
her supervision. On one hand, she was protective of the district
nurse's social status. Thus she urged affiliates of the Queen's Institute to find "suitable" housing for their nurses, preferably in the
homes of professional men "well enough off to keep a capable servant." On the other hand, Loane was determined that local associations should get their nursing money's worth. Women assigned to
villages where patient caseloads were light, therefore, should make
"free-will offerings" of their time, perhaps giving lessons in fancy
needlework or spending extra hours chatting with bedridden patients.[84] But starting off on the right foot with poor families mattered above all. The first meeting was crucial, Loane believed: In
"knockerless, bell-less regions . . . a never-to-be departed-from eti-
quette demands that only the hand should be used; and it is desirable
that the neighbours should be able to testify that the first two or
three taps, at any rate, have been soft and low." Before going to a
poor home for the first time a district nurse should have learned the
family name. For "[t]o call [a woman] 'out of her name' is unpar-
donable, not to call her by it early and often is scarcely less wound-
ing to her feelings."[85] During this sensitive first contact, moreover, a
nurse's new friends should be encouraged to catalog their complaints, even when "culpable ignorance" or "sheer laziness" were the
root problems.[86]

The district nurse could not afford to act as a mere bearer of medical gifts, however. According to Loane, the working classes levied a toll on most philanthropic work:

It is impossible to deny that the poor demand a price for admission to their homes. Years ago, whenever I found a chronic sufferer, I tried to get people of leisure to interest themselves in the case, and I was pained and surprised to find how soon their visits ceased. At first—somewhat uncharitably—I attributed this to my friends' lack of 'grace to persevere,' but it gradually dawned upon me that the defection arose from their inability to meet the unhesitating and increasing demands that were made upon their purse by the relatives of the invalid. . . . [Genteel visitors] must pay their footing, must 'bring their welcome with them'; and the worst part of it was that there was no fixed scale of charges.[87]

Once she had been accepted into a household, and through repeated visits at different hours had gained a sense of family dynamics, the nurse, Loane was convinced, had a moral as well as a professional duty to make "other people's business" her own.[88] In practice this might mean advising wives on how to deal with violent husbands or alerting the National Society for the Prevention of Cruelty to Children about suspected cases of child abuse.[89] Margaret Loane could be grotesquely elitist in her assessment of working-class capabilities, particularly those of mothers. The "lack of discipline" that poor women allegedly displayed in their home-decorating habits struck her as juvenile. "[E]ven the most worthy among them," Loane sniffed, bought furnishings they could ill afford to use: to keep fireplace fenders from rusting, they blocked up their chimneys; and to save looking-glass frames from tarnishing, they sealed their windows.[90] Poor women were also like children insofar as they "find it almost impossible to believe that anything that has made a strong impression on the memory has not made an equally deep one on doctor, nurse, or district visitor, and attribute any oversight to wilful neglect." Hence the need for all such persons to record promises in their notebooks.[91]

Given this presumption of incapacity on the part of poor women, it followed that district nurses must to some extent operate as "inspectors" inside working-class dwellings. Careful to "avoid all fuss-ing and pettiness," the nurse-inspector should nonetheless use the "powers of minute observation that nature and training have given her." So equipped, she might go far toward improving both the health and the happiness of humble homes.[92] As one historian has recently observed, Margaret Loane's advice on domestic inspection typified how female professionals were urged to hone the skills of linguistic manipulation—skills which would have been suspect in men.[93]

Miss Loane's publications pay scant attention to the forces that militated against the exercise of such surveillance. The most signifi-cant of these was time. Especially in rural areas, the district nurse tended to devote as much of her day to moving between patients as caring for them; "going and returning" was a defining feature of country work, and a source of considerable frustration for many hospital-trained Queen's Nurses. One veteran district nurse assigned to a small country town in the 1890's estimated that she spent ten to fifteen minutes at each home, a bit more if patients were helpless or lonely. The introduction of the bicycle often encouraged nursing associations to enlarge a woman's district rather than permitting her to sit longer with the sick.[94] The minutes of two associations from rural Cambridgeshire suggest that financial and moral considerations may have shaped a nurse's routine more than the regulatory strate-gies outlined in Loane's work. With a combined population of 2,431 in 1911, the villages of Trumpington and Grantchester found themselves rationing the services of their only Queen's Nurse. Kept afloat by local subscriptions, this nursing association took a dim view of delivering high-cost home care such as oxygen therapy for acute pneumonia.[95] In the slightly larger orchard center of Soham, a powerful "Ladies Working Committee" decreed that its agent would not act as a midwife to unmarried mothers.[96]

During the interwar years the fixation with recruiting "ladies" faded within many district nursing associations, while the nurse her-self grew more multi-talented. After Parliament mandated the medi-cal inspection of schoolchildren in 1907, a new theater of work, that of part-time school nurse, opened up in several areas outside

London. In rural Somerset, for example, district nurses soon showed themselves to be far more skilled than doctors at convincing village parents that their school-age children needed to wear glasses or have bothersome adenoids removed.[97] Francis Fremantle, the County Medical Officer for Hertfordshire, hoped that this was just the start of a process by which the district nurse would become the linchpin of the nation's local health care system. Interestingly, Fremantle argued that a concentration of functions in the person of the district nurse would reduce public meddling with private lives. For if she were to take charge of all domiciliary work involving midwifery, tuberculosis care, sick schoolchildren, and health visiting, then just one official would need to "invade" the home.[98] The realization of Fremantle's wish never occurred. District nurses nonetheless continued for well over a generation to carry out what Charles Booth once termed England's most "directly useful" form of charity. Grants from local authorities to nursing associations gradually transformed this home ministry into something other than a pure expression of the voluntary impulse. Yet the intersection of professional training with "triumphant personality" would long continue to mark the district nurse.[99]

Health Visiting

Health visiting, like district nursing, became a secular mission, one dedicated to bringing the sanitary gospel into working-class homes. As with district nursing, however, health visiting in its earliest form owed much to an evangelical social conscience. The Ladies' National Association for the Diffusion of Sanitary Knowledge (LSA) was a London-based group of civic-minded gentlewomen organized in 1857. Embracing the conventional separate spheres dichotomy, these ladies sought to improve public health insofar as their "natural" talents allowed:

It is for man's comprehensive mind to devise schemes for draining and cleansing our towns, for improving dwellings, and for placing the necessaries of life within the reach of all; and it is for his strong hand to execute these schemes. . . . It is for woman, in her functions of mother, housewife, and teacher, to effect those urgently needed changes in infant management, domestic economy, education, and the general habits of her own sex, without which humanity could never attain to its destined state of bodily perfection, though all injurious external circumstances were changed.[100]

Leading male philanthropists such as Lord Shaftesbury and Charles Kingsley assured the LSA's founding members that they had embarked on work that was at once "chivalrous" and strategic, since Britain's colonial empire could ill afford continuing high levels of infant mortality in the ruling nation. The medical establishment agreed, and predicted, in a rush of optimism, that the "unobtrusive approach of educated women" would win welcome in the homes of their "less polished" sisters.[101] To advance this cause, socially prominent London women educated themselves by listening to doctors lecture on basic physiology at University College, or to female experts demystify the somewhat "dark and Haymarketty side of human life" at elegant drawing-room lectures.[102] LSA members also busied themselves distributing health tracts among the lower classes. Or to be precise, these genteel activists gave tracts to such front-line troops as district visitors and Biblewomen, who then read (or sold) them to poor mothers.[103]

In 1861, Mrs. Fison, an admirer of the Ranyard Biblewomen, persuaded the all-male Manchester and Salford Sanitary Association to create a "Ladies Auxiliary." The eleven working-class women selected to act as sanitary "missing links" became England's first paid health visitors.[104] The medical community in Manchester already favored the enforcement of a "rigid system of health police,"[105] and thus few among that city's governing elite would have lost sleep over the propriety of this new domestic patrol. As F. B. Smith has put it, early health visiting revolved around women who "exercised a certain charitable terror," ordering the cleansing of slum homes and returning to see that their orders had been obeyed.[106]

The Ladies' Sanitary Association nevertheless remained firmly under the control of privileged London women who saw to it that the branch societies organized in other towns followed their lead. The tracts they rained on poor households contained much health advice that was either accusatory or downright unrealistic. *How to Manage a Baby*, for instance, combined both of these unfortunate elements. Slum mothers learned that, "Almost every baby comes into the world quite strong and healthy enough to live long . . . ; it is we who cut life short, just as truly as we cut off tape with our scissors." A healthy infant was by definition an infant supplied with a basic wardrobe: "At least four frocks, six shirts, two flannel petticoats, two pilches [diaper covers], and twelve napkins [diapers]. . . ."[107] The tight-lacing of growing girls was tantamount to "Torture, or Murder."[108] Because "health is wealth," wise fathers should choose to live in "an airy part of town," even if this location meant higher rent and a longer walk to work.[109] Good mothers who detected "horrid smells" wafting over from a neighbor's house should never hesitate to send "a very nice civil sort of note" to the local Inspector of Nuisances, for an Englishman's home was not his castle when the castle stank.[110] These and dozens of other LSA pamphlets made it painfully clear that because family happiness demanded a healthy home, questions of water supply, drainage, ventilation, and diet were eminently moral matters.[111]

By 1882, LSA members had already given away or sold close to 1.5 million sanitary tracts and had lectured to many thousands of "the more intelligent and respectable" women at mothers' meetings throughout the country. It is doubtful that these zealous apostles of health made much headway among the desperately poor, for LSA literature laments the difficulty of teaching cleanliness to the "slattern."[112] Yet we should not discount the contributions that lady superintendents and their working-class visitors made to improving health in common homes. LSA representatives who had taken on the problem of infant mortality as "an almost life study" must have succeeded in convincing some mothers to stop feeding their babies indigestible food. On the supply side of the domestic equation, LSA involvement in "bread reform" helped coax at least a few millers to produce whole-grain loaves. The carbolic acid compounds that health visitors sold at discount prices to the poor were certainly effective as disinfectants and insecticides—even if, as medical journals charged, the wide availability of this poison offered despondent in-

dividuals an easy way to commit suicide.[113] It seems likely that the
sort of disinfecting fervor later shown in Dorothy Scannell's East
London home originated with the carbolic acid samples that health
visitors began passing around Poplar a generation before.[114]

Despite lingering male opposition to the idea that women could
perform "purely medical duties" (or should be admitted to the Sanitary Inspectors' Association),[115] both rural and urban authorities began at the end of the century to put health visitors on the public
payroll. In 1891, Florence Nightingale urged the leading citizens of
north Buckinghamshire to establish a training program for "Health
Missionaries," women who would receive instruction in sanitary
science yet retain the "sweet voice" essential to winning over cottagers. One year later the Buckinghamshire County Council appointed
three such women as full-time health visitors.[116] Soon thereafter the
Worchestershire County Council and the municipal corporations of
Manchester and Birmingham sent their own salaried visitors into
domestic battle. During the Edwardian years, England's corps of
health visitors grew dramatically, particularly after the 1907 Notifi-
cation of Births Act encouraged local authorities to use these wom-
en as infant welfare specialists. Counting both salaried agents and
volunteers, the Webbs reckoned that there were more English
health visitors—perhaps 1,800—than Poor Law relieving officers by
1910. In other words, this body was large enough to make an epidemiological difference. For the nation's infant mortality rate
plunged by 33 percent between 1900 and 1913, and what Arthur
Newsholme termed "education in hygiene" appeared to be at least
partially responsible for this public health coup.[117]

As it grew more professionalized, health visiting came to be seen
as fit work for educated women, thereby squeezing out the sort of
agent who had once contributed so much to the sanitary campaign
in Manchester. The increasing social distance between visitor and
visited probably aroused less working-class resentment than some
studies have implied, however. Granted, public health experts such
as George Newman, soon-to-be Chief Medical Officer to the Board
of Education, would not have cautioned visitors to exercise "insight
and tact . . . in their somewhat delicate duties" unless such a re-

minder was needed. Midwifery instructor Emilia Kanthack's haughty advice on how to engage poor mothers assumed that tact derived from "instinctive sympathy": "You will understand them right enough if you take an amazing interest in them as human beings, and you must be *very fond* of them *as a class*, even including the rather horrid, dirty individuals. Always think of the dreadful pity of it all!"[118] Visitors who carried out health research during their rounds may have struck mothers as impudent.[119]

But balanced against such evidence of cultural insensitivity are hints that "sanitary ladies" in many areas conducted their work with a zeal that earned respect rather than resentment from working-class communities. Looking back on his childhood in a Salford slum, Robert Roberts recalled with appreciation the health visitors who "worked bravely among us," distributing lime and whitewash brushes to "sweeten and purify" tenement homes.[120] Only twice during their first three thousand forays into working-class dwellings did Darlington's health visitors "meet with anything but a welcome." On the contrary, poor mothers in this Northern manufacturing town tended to express annoyance when the first home-visit was delayed, for such attention was "expected as a privilege and a right."[121] The attention of a lady health visitor, after all, could pay several kinds of dividends. In early twentieth-century Manchester she helped arrange seaside rests for sick children, whereas in Liverpool she assisted the Tired Mother's Holiday Committee.[122] The working-class mother may have been more impressed by a health visitor's ability to find work for an unemployed husband than by any sanitary lecture. Perhaps the appearance of a visitor at the door was welcomed primarily as a chance for the mother to air complaints about family and friends. Health visitors made recommendations on everything from patent foods to birth control methods, and at least some of their advice fell on receptive ears. Despite the fact that, unlike an inspector of nuisances, the health visitor had no legal authority to enter a private home, her mission might entail the prolonged disruption of household routine. Her supervision of persons suffering from pulmonary tuberculosis, for example, required that she persuade consumptives to sleep alone, use spittoons, burn all rags in-

Maternity and Child Welfare magazine (Dec. 1919) depicts the lady health visitor as a "friend" of the working-class mother—unlike the officious stranger who has been banished. Courtesy: British Library.

fected with discharge, and spend as much time as possible in the open air.[123] If the poor often balked at carrying out such directives, the evidence of such resistance is thin.[124]

Some advocates of health visiting, like certain champions of district nursing, proposed that female visitors be invested with broader powers so as to reduce the "over-inspection" of poor homes. Most prominent in this regard was Dr. A. Bostock Hill, the County Medical Officer for Warwickshire. Hill made sure that in addition to their educational work his visitors performed midwifery chores, assumed the care of tuberculosis patients, and reported housing defects to the medical authorities.[125] That the Warwickshire scheme was not widely copied speaks above all to the fractured leadership of England's public health movement. Many voices could be heard denouncing "maternal ignorance and fecklessness" during these years, but nothing remotely like a unified assault on working-class sanitary practices ever materialized.[126] Persuading the poor to do something as basic as open their windows did at times involve more than a trace of deception. But we should be wary of confusing means with ends. By 1937, the equivalent of 2,600 full-time health visitors were carrying out the hygienic commands of local government.[127] Although their work was intrusive, it was never intrusion based on a coordinated effort to replace parental authority with the tutelary force of social medicine. To speak of the health visitor's "Stalinist array of powers"[128] is to imagine the English home as a kind of *gulag*. This it assuredly was not.

From Mothers' Meetings to the Mothers' Union

While medical science was helping to legitimate the work of health visitors and district nurses, another home-centered campaign was attempting to moralize working-class family life through maternal fellowship. At the height of their popularity during the late-Victorian era, "mothers' meetings" drew a regular audience that numbered in the hundreds of thousands. Most mothers from the laboring classes would have been invited to attend such a gathering. Many pious women from the middle classes would have been expected to run one.[129] A commonly expressed goal of mothers' meetings was "to blend and unite classes that have been and still are too far separate." According to Elizabeth Twining, an early advocate, this sort of parish charity promised both to "elevate the poor . . . out of their low estate" and to "bring down thoughts of pride" among their social superiors. Other proponents saw a more concrete agenda: "the homes of the poor had to be made better."[130] Thus mothers' meetings can be classified as a form of family regulation whose agents did not need to knock on doors. Equally, however, they may be regarded as one of a number of domestic crusades whose objects of conversion—working-class wives—often accepted the resources offered as part of their own family survival strategies.

The first mothers' meetings were established in mid-Victorian London. In 1852, an agent of the London City Mission brought together several ladies eager to give Biblical instruction and twenty poor mothers willing to receive it. From scripture reading and prayer the format of these meetings expanded to include needlework and quiet conversation.[131] Mary Bayly, who organized a similar group in the potteries area of Kensington one year later, seized on the idea of supplying fabric at wholesale prices. Provided with good quality cotton prints, calicoes, and flannels, the women could make clothes for their families as they listened sympathetically to one another's domestic trials.[132] Mrs. Bayly also proved highly skilled at blending religious prescription with practical hints on home management. A meeting devoted to improved observance of the Sabbath, for example, might include tips on how to prepare much of the all-important Sunday dinner well in advance. Bayly's meetings were, moreover, wisely scheduled. As one mother observed, mid-evening found most of her children already in bed and her husband agreeable to a short absence because "we goes on with our work here."[133]

By the 1860's mothers' meetings had become familiar features of charity in London and were taking root in both urban and rural communities far from the capital. Visiting a remote village during the winter of 1865, one of Mrs. Ranyard's superintendents was delighted to find a majority of the local women gathered in a cottage kitchen listening to the "same blessed message" as slum mothers elsewhere.[134] Soon thereafter the Bradford Town Mission began using fortnightly mothers' meetings to promote churchgoing among "careless" wives.[135] In mid-Victorian Newcastle such gatherings frequently took place in Anglican parish halls, centers of sober entertainment in an age before radio or cinema.[136]

The rapid spread of mothers' meetings cannot be explained merely in terms of their entertainment value, however. To be sure, some patrons saw to it that faithful attendees were rewarded with holidays. The Congregationalist West London Mission offered the members of two mothers' meetings an "Annual Excursion." In the summer of 1890 this consisted of a train trip to rural Surrey complete with a luncheon at Lady Henry Somerset's home, an afternoon of wandering through country fields, group photographs, and, perhaps most luxurious, free child care.[137] For the members of remote rural meetings, an excursion to the big city would have seemed just as festive.[138] Still, the savings programs, blanket clubs, and bulk food-buying operations associated with many mothers' meetings probably constituted more powerful attractions for the majority of working-class women. When the national trade slump hit Manchester with particular severity during the late 1870's, for example, those meetings which offered provident plans saw dramatic growth in their memberships.[139] At least some poor women probably also found useful the medical and nutritional advice dispensed at mothers' meetings. The Ladies' Sanitary Association was keen to use these gatherings as occasions for preaching the gospel of soap and water.[140] Henrietta Barnett noted that her East End mothers took more "intelligent interest" in discussions of health than in the "goody-goody books" read at many meetings. Although working-class women often remained skeptical about assurance that oatmeal made a better breakfast than bread and butter, or lentil soup a wiser midday meal than chips and tea, they listened attentively to those who advanced these views. The counsel of district nurses appears to have carried special weight at mothers' meetings.[141]

Both the manipulative language occasionally found in promotional literature on the one hand and contemporary criticism of mothers' meetings on the other should be read with caution. Certainly one of the forces helping to popularize mothers' meetings was the difficulty that district visitors faced in winning a poor woman's undivided attention. The obstacles to "getting at the mothers" must at times have seemed insurmountable:

You go into a cottage, you long to have a quiet word with the careworn wife, whose husband is breaking her heart by intemperance, whose son is a rough, rude Sabbath-breaker. You find her at the washing-tub, with a crying babe in its cot, two or three dirty noisy children sprawling on the floor; you cannot ... speak to her with loving sympathy of her heart's grief; you make a kind remark or two, and then you have but to turn and leave the cottage, with an all but hopeless, yet longing desire that you could lift up that poor family, out of its depths, but, alas! where is your lever?

A lever, it seemed, was available in the "sacred exclusiveness" of maternal association.[142] The Rev. A. W. Snape, Rector of St. George-the-Martyr, Southwark, knew what he wanted when organizing the first mothers' meetings in his parish: "I wished to get the women out of their homes." Snape's words could be construed as evidence of a divide-and-conquer strategy to discipline the working-class family. But the frustrations of district visiting suggest a less conspiratorial logic. Too often haunted by a "sickening sense of ... failure," some evangelical visitors had concluded that gospel truths as well as the tenets of household economy were best imparted in the calm that could be found only *outside* the poor home.[143] It was a notable if unacknowledged irony that the same middle class responsible for articulating the ideal of home-as-sanctuary should devise this haven from the haven.

Mothers' meetings had their Victorian critics. In part this criticism was a response to the snooty tone that disfigured some of the charitable literature. A zealous supporter of the West London Mission would have been cheered to read that the packet of groceries offered as the prize for a sewing competition had stirred "unusual excitement" within the Craven Hall mothers' meeting. Other readers, such as Helen Bosanquet of the Charity Organisation Society, dismissed such activities as the pointless pursuit of "miserable little doles."[144] The clergyman who typified a mothers' meeting leader as "Mistress Agatha Comfort," a spinster grande dame "arrayed in mop-cap, with plentiful garniture of broad ribbon," was sketching a gentle caricature. But to stalwarts of socialist feminism such as those who established the Women's Co-operative Guild, "Mistress Agatha" embodied all that they resented about ladies who pontificated on domestic subjects beyond their ken.[145] Revealingly, though, the Webbs point out that the Guild began in 1883 "as a sort of Co-operative 'mothers' meeting' with co-operative literature being read to assembled wives bowed over their needles."[146]

Even if we accept the view that a gradual decline in needlework skills among working-class women led to the degeneration of some mothers' meetings into "mere parish gossip shop[s],"[147] it remains true that these institutions served as mainstays of maternal fellowship well into the twentieth century. During the First World War they provided emotional support for thousands of new widows, while during the interwar years many meetings broadened their range of discussion to include local government and international relations.[148] At the peak of their influence, in the last quarter of the nineteenth century, they did much more. Late-Victorian mothers' meetings articulated for a generation of poor women the hope that a mother's influence—"the power of littles"—might civilize even the roughest man.[149] The forbearance praised at mothers' meetings may sometimes have served to prolong the abuse that certain wives endured at the hands of their husbands. But for other poor women the reassurance that motherhood was a sacred calling rather than a curse proved welcome enough to insulate them from the taunts of neighbors who regarded as suspect any intercourse with posh folk.[150]

The evidence available suggests that Charles Booth was right in his assessment of mothers' meetings. Booth believed that although they did little to deepen the religiosity of working-class homes, neither were they typically used as vehicles for charitable fraud. What these gatherings *did* do was to answer "a real want" in the lives of "tired and worried women."[151] They also gave rise to other forms of local fellowship. Fathers' meetings were less common than their maternal equivalents, yet they, too, drew loyal audiences in some urban neighborhoods. Similarly structured around prayer and scripture reading, fathers' meetings offered laboring men a chance to vent their frustrations over nagging wives and unruly sons without seeking shelter in a pub. For social purity campaigners such as Ellice Hopkins, it seemed useless to preach self-restraint among young women so long as their fathers and brothers remained captives of impulse and strangers to holy writ.[152] Of more lasting significance, though, was the fact that mothers' meetings provided the foundation for modern England's most formidable religious society, the Mothers' Union.

Established in 1876, the Mothers' Union soon emerged as the quintessential expression of Anglican social conservatism. Mary Sumner, wife of the future Bishop of Guildford and a veteran of district visiting and village mothers' meetings, launched the Union to cleanse the "poisoned streams of sin and evil" which she saw undermining the nation. As Mrs. Sumner later assured a Mothers' Union audience, she had believed from the start that the only chance for reformation lay in "attacking the homes, where character is formed, and getting hold of the parents—above all, of the mothers—and persuading them to do their duty to the children."[153] Most mothers' meetings, according to Sumner, did not involve a full class spectrum. Thus, if "lady mothers" and "cottage mothers" were to find mutual understanding it would need to be in a more formal maternal association of rich and poor. Sumner's vision took shape as an international body which by 1913 would claim 414,000 members.[154]

The woman whose energetic leadership did much to popularize the idea of a cross-class alliance of mothers was herself the product of sheltered wealth. When she was four, Mary Heywood's father gave up his banking interests in Manchester and bought Hope End, the beloved childhood home of poet Elizabeth Barrett Browning. Foreign governesses taught the children French, German, and Italian, and their parents introduced them to the world beyond Hope End through annual carriage tours of the Continent. About the realities of working-class life young Mary knew virtually nothing, however. Even as a mature woman, while she was imploring poor mothers to train their children "in habits of obedience, self-control, and purity," she had servants to put on her stockings and cooks to protect her from plebeian fare. (She regarded herring as fit only for cats.)[155] Not surprisingly, therefore, the two-tiered organization that Mrs. Sumner introduced in the sprawling Diocese of Winchester accentuated class divisions.

Mothers from common walks of life enrolled as "ordinary Members" and paid no subscription fee. They received the much discussed "Members' Card" on which were printed Mrs. Sumner's guidelines for child rearing as well as the Mothers' Union prayer. The cards cost a penny each "but are better given if possible," observed a Union leader from Oxford, "in order that they may be withdrawn should the Member become careless." The quarterly *Mothers' Union Journal* featured educational and inspirational matter deemed suitable for "the poorer classes."[156] Ladies, by contrast, could become "Associates" of the Mothers' Union provided that they were communicants in the Church of England and paid an annual subscription of at least one shilling. For these women "there existed a separate quarterly, *Mothers in Council*, whose editor from 1891 to 1900 was the popular novelist Charlotte Yonge. Associates also received separate cards. When asked why rich and poor women should get different counsel, Union leaders were blunt: "Because their temptations are different." Thus, for example, the admonition that, "You are strongly advised never to send your children to the public-house," applied only to working-class mothers ("the words have no reality for an educated mother"). The injunction concerning sexual purity—"Do not allow your girls to go about the streets at night"—likewise dealt with a "class danger" and therefore belonged only on a Member's card.[157] Union advocates countered the charge that they were holding working-class women to a stricter moral standard by resort to a curious Biblical analogy. Just as it was easier for a poor man to enter the Kingdom of God than a rich man, they reasoned, so the poor woman should find the fulfillment of her "high [maternal] office" less taxing than a rich woman because the latter was burdened with servants ("hirelings") who distanced her from her children.[158]

Its sharply stratified structure mirrored the Union's hierarchical conception of society, a conception it shared with other Anglican family organizations and, more broadly, with the late-Victorian Conservative Party. Mary Sumner described her mission as seeking to "reinstate the home into its true position as the primal training place for children."[159] Her preoccupation with training in habits of discipline, obedience, and deference to established authority also characterized both the Girls' Friendly Society and the Church of

MOTHERS' UNION JOURNAL.

Mothers' Union.

PATRON.

Ther Majesty
Queen Alexandra.

PRESIDENT.

THE DOWAGER COUNTESS
OF CHICHESTER.

VICE-PRESIDENTS.

LADY HORATIA ERSKINE.
MRS. RANDALL DAVIDSON.
THE HON. MRS. MAC-
LAGAN.
THE HON. MRS. E. S.
TALBOT.

SECRETARY.

MRS. MAUDE,
The Church House,
Westminster.

TRAIN UP A CHILD IN

THE WAY HE SHOULD GO

Mothers' Union.

OBJECTS.

(1) To uphold the sanctity
of marriage.

(2) To awaken in mothers
of all classes a sense of
their great responsibility
as mothers in the training
of their boys and girls (the
future fathers and mothers
of the Empire), and

(3) To organise in every place
a band of mothers who will
unite in prayer, and seek
by their own example to
lead their families in purity
and holiness of life.

Motto: "Train up a child in
the way he should go, and
when he is old he will not
depart from it."

No. 90. [Circulation about 140,000.]   APRIL, 1910.   Price One Penny Quarterly. Post free, 1½d.

The contrast between genteel "Associates" and humble "Members" of the Mothers' Union was mirrored in the different quarterlies serving each constituency. The *Mothers' Union Journal* aimed to promote reverence for home, family, and empire among poor women. Courtesy: British Library.

England Waifs and Strays Society,[160] groups with which the Mothers' Union worked closely. Organizational ties to the GFS were especially strong. Dedicated to guarding young women during their vulnerable journey from girlhood to motherhood, the GFS sought to immunize a female labor elite against the notion that class conflict was inevitable. GFS leaders, like their Mothers' Union counterparts, saw the family as the wellspring of reconciliation. For in their idealized view happy families were necessarily places where the sharing of burdens defused anger and envy.[161] If more families could be taught to translate the GFS motto ("Bear ye one another's burdens") into reality, then the demand for "socialist" state action would disappear. It was of course the mother whose constant example of self-sacrifice could most forcefully imbue child minds with this presumed truth.[162] It was also mostly the mother's job—patriarchal theory notwithstanding—to see that discipline remained a defining feature of working-class home life. She was the true domestic sentinel, and her firm yet loving orders could halt the manufacture of "hooligans" on the one hand and "contemptibly softened individuals" on the other.[163]

The self-sacrifice that Mary Sumner had in mind did not end with poor mothers. Since "[r]eforms come from the head in the body politic, and circulate through the masses," Union leaders also took aim at "worldly" mothers too busy with shooting parties, yachting, and travel abroad to treat their children as anything more than "favorite lapdogs." Women of leisure, no less than their laboring sisters, had to be taught that motherhood was a vocation.[164] Maternal fecklessness, after all, knew no class:

Ask Lady Bountiful [or] the Hon. Mrs. Goodworks . . . simply this question: "Are your own daughters being trained and prepared in the duties and knowledge of the sacred wisdom of motherhood?" When they marry will they be, but for the nurses they are able to employ, one whit less ignorant or less foolish than the mothers you are so eager to train up in the class below your own?[165]

A well-to-do woman fully apprised of her maternal responsibilities would have her hands full seeing that servants did not threaten or bribe the children; that nursery rhymes did not overemphasize the grotesque; that champagne did not flow at dances where young and old mixed; or that boarding schools were not overly secular.[166]

But above all such mothers were urged to be on guard against what Mrs. Sumner and her fellow Union leaders perceived as an alarming rise of rebelliousness among daughters of privileged families. Anglican moralists such as Charlotte Yonge routinely denounced displays of impulsive behavior among girls.[167] In *fin-de-siècle* England, however, the spirit of "indefiniteness" contaminating music, painting, and poetry had apparently infected social relations as well, prompting young ladies to cast off time-honored restraints in the name of liberty. This so-called "revolt of the daughters," a revolt against the cloistered security of their upper-middle-class mothers, had already begun to disrupt family peace in some homes. Thus Mrs. Sumner urged her Associates to curb all forms of "fast" or "bold" behavior in their girls lest rampant self-indulgence launch a soaring divorce rate or, just as worrisome, an armada of spinsters.[168] According to the Mothers' Union, it further complicated the life of a well-born *materfamilias* that there was so much loose talk about "hysteria" at the turn of the century. Too often, it seemed, young women "seized with a mysterious disability to perform ordinary [household] duties" were being treated as psychically fragile—a diagnosis that wise mothers should treat with deep suspicion.[169]

When Union representatives lectured poor women about the duties of motherhood, therefore, they did so as parents whose conduct was likewise under scrutiny. Certainly, some of the advice that working-class mothers received from Associates must have seemed directed at beings from another planet. It was obviously one thing to insist on mothers' remaining "calm, gentle, patient, even-tempered, and very loving with your bab[ies]," and quite another for harried and half-starved slum mothers to honor this commandment.[170] Yet the river of advice that swept down from on high also carried eminently practical suggestions. The *Mothers' Union Journal*, for instance, offered labor-saving hints on everything from scrubbing wooden floors to forcing landlords to clear clogged drains. Nor is it unreasonable to assume that some women living in straitened circumstances might have taken solace in the Mothers' Union dictum that the key to a child's happiness lay not in the "gratification of every selfish desire" but rather in "care and thought and planning small pleasures."[171]

What cannot be denied is that the Mothers' Union continued to attract a great many poor women long after its founders had passed from the scene. By 1906 the organization had no fewer than 334 lady lecturers throughout England and Wales prepared to discuss all "important subjects connected with home-life."[172] Poor women who listened to these middle-class lecturers, or attended the more frequent local meetings of the Union, heard topical treatments of Tory themes. Thus, the sad collapse of the Italian runner Dorando on the last lap of the Olympic marathon in 1908 was offered as an object lesson in the importance of endurance training for life's race. Similarly, those who gave up their places on the *Titanic*'s lifeboats in 1912 became shining examples of selflessness.[173] It is difficult to know precisely what drew working-class women to the Mothers' Union because very little first-hand testimony from these women survives. Plainly, though, the Union could not have grown to embrace 600,000 members in 14,000 branches around Britain and overseas by 1938 unless sizable numbers of laboring women had found congenial its defense of home, monarchy, and empire, or its denunciation of dirt, drink, and divorce.[174] Once women won the franchise, this body wielded what Elizabeth Macadam called "powerful if semi-conscious parliamentary pressure owing to its enormous voting strength." For more than a generation after Mary Sumner's death (at the age of 92) in 1921, the Mothers' Union remained a staunch advocate of conservative family values. And in many cases it must have been preaching to the choir.[175]

The so-called "Golden Age" of parochial work within the Church of England spanned the late-Victorian and Edwardian years and coincided exactly with the rise to national prominence of the Mothers' Union.[176] But as we have seen, the Union was itself an outgrowth of earlier and by no means exclusively Anglican experiments in civilizing working-class homes through the medium of the mother. Although an evangelical drive to save benighted households lost much of its force during the first half of the twentieth century, its corollary, the visiting impulse, played a vital part in what José Harris has termed the "nationalization of culture."[177] That more modern visitors have gained professional standing as "social workers" should not blind us to the continuity between Victorian and post-Victorian home ministries. Nor should the coercive side of such effort receive undue notice. Across the Channel, philanthropy in Second Empire France (1852–1870) has been depicted as striving "to instill in [the poor mother] the elements of a tactics of devotion," thereby positioning her "to stamp out the spirit of independence in the working man."[178] The same accusation hurled at Victorian philanthropy would be misguided both because it ignores the fact that working-class women accepted charity selectively and because the mother was not the only target of reforming ardor. As John Stuart Mill understood, the family could never provide a "school of sympathy" while fathers rode roughshod over fragile emotions.[179] To save homes from the destructive influence of disease, ignorance, and brutality, new methods for winning the cooperation of both parents were essential.

TWO

The Policing of Parents

D URING THE last third of the nineteenth century, the phrase "parental responsibility" acquired a resonance that spoke of deepening national self-doubt. Most surveys of Victorian England offer a familiar list of developments that together undermined the "Age of Equipoise"[1] and ushered in a new era of anxiety for the governing classes. The "leap in the dark" toward greater political democracy taken with the Reform Act of 1867, the emergence of Germany as a military and economic powerhouse following its crushing defeat of France in 1871, the downward movement of prices and profits that began in 1873, and the challenge to religious authority posed by Darwinian biology all contributed to a palpable sense of unease among sections of the privileged population. Meanwhile, three seemingly unrelated social reforms, launched within a twenty-year period, intensified the examination of working-class family life. Between 1867 and 1871, Parliament gave teeth to the principle that all children should be vaccinated against smallpox. The Education Act of 1870 set in motion a campaign to create minimum standards for learning. Lastly, the mid-1880's saw philanthropists establish agencies whose controversial goal was the protection of children within their own homes. What these three reforms had in common was the policing of parental behavior. And what in turn linked them to the more widely recognized causes of national anxiety was the notion of "character."

The role of "character" in Victorian political argument cannot be reduced to ideological shorthand, a mere code word for the effort to impose middle-class notions of respectability on an uncivilized working class. Significantly, New Liberals as well as Conservatives often justified their starkly different conceptions of good government in terms of character development. The term "character" condensed widely shared assumptions about the personal qualities needed to cope with an increasingly complex and competitive world.[2] Both the individual citizen's quest for material security and Britain's fate in the struggle among nations for economic dominance seemed to depend on the same attributes—physical vigor, perseverance, and adaptability. Thus the security of the Empire hinged on the fate of the family, for it was above all family life that forged character. Or, as Samuel Smiles phrased it so succinctly, "Law itself is but the reflex of homes."[3] In 1901, C. F. G. Masterman, a prominent New Liberal, pronounced dead the "old astonishing creed that if each man assiduously minds his own business and pursues his own individual advancement and the welfare of his family, somehow ... the progress of the whole body politic will be assured."[4] Actually, political opinion at the turn of the century was deeply split on the question of how far family welfare should remain the responsibility of parents. Some of Masterman's contemporaries held with equal vehemence that any usurpation of parental functions would destroy that domestic intimacy in which the "moral obligations of life" were best learned. Charles Henry Pearson, a history don and colonial administrator, reasoned that,

In proportion as the family bonds are weakened, as the tie uniting husband and wife is more and more capricious, as the relations of the children to the parent become more and more temporary, will the religion of household life gradually disappear. ... Family life will be[come] a gracious and decorative incident in the system of such a society; but the family, as a constituent part of the State, as the matrix in which character is moulded, will lose its importance as the clan and the city have done.[5]

How might the family be preserved as the cradle of character without relieving parents of the "anxiety"[6] that allegedly helped to insure proper childrearing? The three social reforms mentioned above all addressed this question. Each devised new methods of family surveillance, and in this sense may be seen as elaborating the disciplinary impulse that animated the "home ministries" analyzed in the previous chapter. Yet just as the earlier domestic initiatives elude classification as expressions of a social control impulse, so the newer reforms examined here either failed in their totalizing ambitions to "civilize" the working-class family or else achieved partial success largely because the poor were prepared to police themselves.

Compulsory Vaccination

However intrusive the practice of district visiting, or of its lineal descendant, social casework,[7] the exponents of door-to-door philanthropy clung to the belief that their scrutiny of working-class home life was rooted in "friendship." No such justification could be advanced for the public health inspectors, truancy officers, and child protection agents who comprised an uncoordinated family police during the last decades of the nineteenth century. Their rationale for meddling with private lives was instead based on arguments about children's rights and the needs of the nation. Parents, these new disciplinary campaigns agreed, should not be free to inflict irreparable harm on their young. For blighted childhood eventually left its scars on the community as well as on individual bodies and minds. Conceived in these utilitarian terms, the policing of parental conduct appeared easily defensible to many among the comfortable classes. Yet striking a balance between public safety and family privacy proved immensely difficult in practice. The sanctity of the Englishman's Castle became a battle cry for those opposed to tampering with parent-child relations. It was far from clear, moreover, what preserving the home as the cradle of character might require in terms of social legislation.

The juxtaposition of parental prerogative and community need was nowhere more stark than in the realm of public health. The behavior of the nation's sanitary experts—its medical officers of health and inspectors of nuisances—seemed controversial enough. Medical officers of health (MOH) had served various urban governments, notably those of Liverpool and the City of London, since 1847, but it was not until 1856 that they formed their own professional society, and not until 1872 that all local authorities were obliged to appoint them. By the end of the century, 1,771 of these dedicated men served England and Wales, all of them qualified doctors and a few holders of the demanding Diploma in Public Health.[8] After mid-century some municipalities also began appointing inspectors of nuisances. It became the mission of these sanitary bloodhounds to sniff out (sometimes literally) a vast range of health hazards, from blocked privies to fever dens. In his famous *Essays on State Medicine* (1856), Henry Rumsey rued the fact that inspectors of nuisances "could only relieve the Medical Officer of a small portion of those inquisitorial and preventive duties which he is the most competent person to perform." Whereas Rumsey longed for a network of "Sanitary Courts" to prosecute the enemies of hygiene, not a few of his contemporaries worried that they were witnessing the creation of a despotic "health police." The house-to-house visitation undertaken by both inspectors of nuisances and medical officers of health struck some among the comfortable classes as thoroughly un-English—as activity suited perhaps to the autocratic regimes of central and eastern Europe but certainly not to the bastion of *laissez-faire* individualism.[9]

Rather than tread softly around the charge of domestic espionage, those who waged war on dirt made plain their impatience with the "ignorance and stupidity" of local authorities no less than with the slum dwellers who could or would not keep their rooms clean. To rhapsodize about "Home, Sweet Home" was absurd, one sanitarian pointed out, when home stank of sewer gas.[10] During the mid-1880's Whitechapel should have had at least twenty-six inspectors of nuisances to patrol about 5,000 tenement dwellings. There were, in fact, just two men available. What was true for London's East End applied to England as a whole: the nation needed many more sanitary officers, backed by stricter ordinances aimed against everything from overcrowding to spitting.[11] Small wonder, then, that such public health activism met resistance. It was the inspector of nuisances who usually had to confront citizens about health hazards in or near their homes, and it was therefore this junior partner of the sanitary team who caught the most flak. Men who wrote orders for the removal of health hazards from private premises might get scratched or punched for their diligence; those whose reports led to legal proceedings occasionally fared worse.[12] Verbal hostility from doctors in private practice was directed at the MOH, who sometimes found himself accused of trying to steal patients.[13]

But general criticism of the trend toward interventionist public health policy paled beside the focused fury of the antivaccination campaign. The issue of compulsory vaccination proved so divisive because the human stakes seemed so high. Smallpox, the viral sickness that vaccination sought to tame, was, as one London MOH observed, "the most loathsome of all diseases, and the most dreaded."[14] After an incubation period of ten to twelve days, the onset of classic smallpox symptoms is swift: a high temperature accompanied by intense muscular pain, often coupled with chills, severe nausea, and vomiting. Two to four days after these unpleasant preliminaries the characteristic smallpox blisters begin to appear on a victim's skin. There are several different clinical strains of smallpox. In the worst strain, variola major, the blisters can cover the body in a lunar landscape of densely packed, oozing craters. Should a victim survive an attack of variola major—which typically kills between 20 and 40 percent of an unprotected population—he or she may be blinded or crippled for life, and will frequently show deep facial scarring.[15] Smallpox is not infectious during the incubation phase, but once its lesions appear the disease can easily spread through direct skin contact or contaminated clothing. Smallpox, in other words, becomes most dangerous under crowded conditions. Although there is no known cure for the virus, it has only one host in nature, humans. A program of universal vaccination can therefore eliminate this scourge.[16]

Hagiographical accounts of Edward Jenner and his West Country experiments hold that as early as 1800 it should have been apparent to all thinking physicians that a small quantity of lymph taken from the blister of a calf infected with "cowpox" would, when injected into the arm of a healthy person, render the recipient far less likely to die from future smallpox attacks. Jenner's work was hailed as one

of the marvels of Enlightenment rationality, a brilliant example of
science triumphing over superstition.[17] By mid-century, smallpox
vaccination had become what the Epidemiological Society termed
the only true "antidote" to an infectious disease. Hence the pioneers
of public health in England, most notably John Simon, have been
praised for devoting enormous time and energy to building a comprehensive national vaccination system.[18] From this Whiggish view
of the rise of preventive medicine it follows that those who fought
state-sanctioned vaccination were at best blocking the path to progress. At worst, these resisters were deluded "fanatics" or else members of a vague but sinister "socio-political Establishment" dedicated
to keeping the poor so mired in disease and destitution that they
would meekly continue providing cannon fodder for the military
and wage slaves for the factories.[19]

There were, certainly, vested economic interests opposed to the
use of Jenner's vaccine. During the first third of the nineteenth century, for example, some doctors whose livelihoods depended on the
increasingly suspect method of arm-to-arm inoculation with live
smallpox virus denounced the new procedure. As for the antivaccination lobby that grew so clamorous during the latter half of the
century, its leadership boasted some memorable eccentrics located
on the fringes of Victorian science. John Gibbs, whose 1856 letter
to the Board of Health launched the campaign against compulsory
vaccination as an "atrocious cruelty," extolled the therapeutic power
of water. J. J. Garth Wilkinson, a prolific writer and speaker against
"blood assassination," was the leading homeopath of his day, as well
as a keen student of Mesmerism and the Swedenborgian faith. William Tebb, mainstay of the London Society for the Abolition of
Compulsory Vaccination, became obsessed with the hazards of
premature burial.[20] Deeply suspicious about the aims of allopathic
medicine, these and other prominent "antis" were charged in their
own day with "omissional infanticide," and since then have been re-
viled for their "absurd obstinacy." Fortunately, more searching studies of the Victorian antivaccination movement have helped rescue its
participants from what E. P. Thompson memorably termed the
"enormous condescension of posterity."[21] Yet the issue of parental

resistance remains murky. Were the mothers and fathers who became conscientious objectors to state-mandated vaccination of their
children acting out a script written for them by a coterie of cranks?
Or were parental objections grounded in deeply felt concerns about
the autonomy of their homes?

It is admittedly hard to distinguish between what parents, especially poor parents, were said to be thinking and what they actually
thought about compulsory vaccination. "Anti" leaders made much
of the point that compulsory vaccination was naked "class" legislation. From this premise agitators raced to the conclusion that conscientious objection therefore represented an expression of the
popular will, the action, according to P. A. Taylor, the antivaccinationist MP for Leicester, of ordinary people "defending their hearths
and their homes and their innocents." What Taylor failed to add
was that the best-publicized defenses of hearth and home involved
middle-class objectors.[22] Equally suspect was the claim that popular
hostility to cowpox vaccination derived from a widespread objection to the poisoning of a child with infected animal matter.
Granted, even before Parliament approved the first vaccination laws
in 1840 and 1841, no less a man of the people than William Cob-
bett had rejected the idea that caring parents could allow "the diseased blood . . . of a beast to be put into the veins" of their young.[23]
No doubt some poor parents subscribed to a version of the old hu-
moral physiology, and so shunned vaccination as an "unnatural"
mixing of vital essences. Others, perhaps, shared Garth Wilkinson's
related concern that "vaccination mingles in a communism of the
blood the taints of the community."[24] But the scattered evidence
available points to another possibility.

From the early nineteenth century if not before, working-class
parents in England had combined amateur inoculation with far
older folk remedies for smallpox. In Norwich in 1818, for example,
the poor turned to local women who "roasted" their patients back
to health—a treatment that first required the sick individual to sit
beside a roaring fire while drinking brandy, and later to spend at
least a week in bed virtually mummified by flannel. Placing an unprotected child next to, or in bed with, someone stricken with the

disease was apparently a standard practice in many working-class communities. Should such exposure fail to induce the desired infection (and consequent immunization), other steps might be required. When Roger Langdon, born in 1825, refused to catch smallpox from another boy, he was presented to "Old Nanny Holland," the village "nurse," who inoculated him with a stocking-needle.[25] Although these procedures seem crude today, they shared two reassuring features. First, either parents or neighbors performed them. Second, the preventive theory underlying all such procedures was comprehensible to the scientifically illiterate. When the state took up the challenge of eradicating smallpox, by contrast, its agents were strangers from another social world. Worse, they were strangers tainted by association with the Poor Laws and purveying a technique whose immunological action seemed mysterious even to the most sophisticated medical minds. Thus, compulsory vaccination surely struck some poor parents as a frontal assault on their domestic sovereignty.

Viewing the unvaccinated poor as England's great reservoir of contagion, the champions of public health gave short shrift to such concerns. Indeed, legislation passed during the mid-Victorian years revealed the sanitarians' goal of building an embryonic "national health service" around the power of state-directed vaccination.[26] The first small steps toward this goal came in 1840 and 1841, when Parliament allowed Poor Law guardians to offer free vaccination at the hands of medically trained "public vaccinators." With the rival practice of inoculation now declared illegal, sanitarians hoped that the masses would realize that the skilled lancet of a public vaccinator represented their only real defense against the ravages of smallpox. Lord Lyttelton's Act of 1853 aimed to hasten this understanding by making vaccination compulsory for all children within three months of birth. Although an unprecedented 408,824 English children under one year of age received public vaccinations during 1854, it soon grew clear that many poor parents were evading the new obligation. This should not have been surprising. Public vaccination, after all, posed health risks. Tellingly, *The Lancet* admitted that few doctors wished to see their own children injected at a public vaccination station, where physicians were paid, per "operation," out of the poor rates. Middle- and upper-class parents instead had their young vaccinated at home by private practitioners.[27]

The "operation" itself was simple. The circumstances under which it could be performed, however, might reasonably alarm a concerned parent. Through its National Vaccine Establishment, the government supplied public vaccinators with enough calf lymph to launch the prophylactic process. Unfortunately, lymph supplies were themselves less than pure. Children injected with government lymph developed "cowpox" as planned, and the blisters (or "vesicles") that appeared on their arms then became the source for further lymph transfer. Doctors were warned against trying to collect too much clear liquid from any one blister. But a public vaccinator short on time, as during a smallpox epidemic, might in his haste squeeze a child's arm and thereby force out a minute amount of blood along with lymph. If the donor happened to be infected with erysipelas (an acute inflammation of the skin and subcutaneous tissue) or congenital syphilis, these and certain other diseases could be transmitted to all children receiving the contaminated lymph, although mid-Victorian public health activists were loathe to concede this possibility.[28] Quite apart from concerns over the purity of lymph, Henry Rumsey conceded, poor parents were "justified in apprehending greater peril to the lives of their children" from exposure to crowds at the public vaccination station. Because the protective effect of vaccination could not yet be demonstrated with statistical precision, there was weight in the argument that England should pause on the road to compulsion.[29]

The standard-bearers of state medicine reasoned differently. Since smallpox vaccination had long been compulsory in Denmark, Sweden, and most of the German states, it struck sanitarians as outrageous that evasion of the law should leave London, the greatest city of Europe, vulnerable to the sort of epidemic that arrived in 1858–60.[30] London MOH, along with the Medical Department of the Privy Council, therefore urged a still more interventionist regime—one based, like the examination of suspected prostitutes authorized

"The District Vaccinator—A Sketch at the East-End." This line drawing from *The Graphic* (Apr. 1871) captures the unsavory atmosphere of a public vaccination station in East London. Such representations lent weight to claims that compulsory smallpox vaccination was an assault on "parental prerogative."

by the Contagious Diseases Acts, on the belief that public safety must take precedence over personal freedom. Accordingly, Parliament in 1867 empowered Poor Law guardians to appoint "vaccination officers." These were non-medical men assigned to ferret out parents who had "defaulted" on their responsibility. Section 31 of the 1867 Act, furthermore, gave local magistrates the right to levy repeated fines or, in lieu of fines, multiple jail terms against parents who refused to vaccinate their children. In the words of a prominent "anti," this extraordinary sanction guaranteed "the doom of Vaccination" since it "drove resistance to extremity, and set up an irreducible insurrection." While antivaccinationists were starting to decry the "relentless application"[31] of section 31 in some localities, sanitarians closed the disciplinary circle: new legislation, approved in 1871, made the appointment of vaccination officers mandatory.

Naturally enough the history of Victorian vaccination politics has concentrated on developments in the three decades that followed passage of the 1871 Act. Best known among these developments were, first, the "frustration of state medicine" whereby a tight-fisted Treasury denied the Medical Department of the Local Government Board sufficient resources to keep close watch over public vaccination services; and second, the shifting fortunes of an antivaccination lobby fractured along class and regional lines.[32] Neither focus can tell us much about the concerns of ordinary parents. The most informative court cases of conscientious objection involved not antivaccinators but rather parents who belonged to faith-healing sects such as the "Peculiar People." Accounts of distraught mothers and fathers whose recently vaccinated offspring died with bodies gone "entirely purple" or "filled with corruption" are no more helpful, compiled as they were by middle-class "antis."[33] Although the witnesses who appeared before the Select Committee of 1871 were also advocates of one kind or another, some of their testimony is suggestive. The friends of compulsion could not decide whether parents who had declared themselves conscientious objectors were, on the whole, "tolerably instructed" or among the "less educated."[34] But friends and foes alike agreed that some poor parents were determined to elude the public vaccinator. Their resistance might be passive, through failing to register the births of their children, or active, by moving often, sending a child to live outside the registration district, or even by emigrating. One former Board of Health clerk assured the Select Committee that two women in his London neighborhood had submitted their children to public vaccination and immediately afterwards "wiped or sucked out the poison."[35]

Those most committed to enlarging the scope of state medicine were ready to believe the worst about resisting parents. James Furness Marson, for thirty-five years the resident surgeon of London's Smallpox Hospital at Highgate, declared it "very suspicious" that fathers were "nearly always" the objectors. Asked to elaborate, he sketched a bleak picture of working-class paternity: "The father would like the family as small as possible that he had to work for; I am afraid that that is at the bottom of it."[36] Marson's class calumny apart, he was wrong to suppose that poor mothers more often smiled on public vaccination. Soon after Marson's pronouncement, Mrs. Brewer and Mrs. Wood, both poor, told the magistrate at London's Hammersmith Police Court that they failed to vaccinate their youngest children out of "dread" that they would later fall ill, as their older siblings had all done. Mary Ann Page, the wife of a laborer, went before the Reigate bench because she had refused to let the public vaccinator take lymph from her child's arm. All three women were fined token sums.[37] Since vaccination officers who took legal action against defaulting parents generally obtained a summons against the father, it may well have been true that men outnumbered women in court. Whatever their sex, those prosecuted for sabotaging the Vaccination Acts should not be allowed to air their "sophisms" in public, or so believed the *British Medical Journal*. Its editor, Ernest Hart, had led the British Medical Association's successful campaign to permit repeated fining of objectors, and he now set his editorial sights on magistrates who allowed these persons to convey "an impression of injustice and oppression."[38]

Public health zealots such as Hart were keen to minimize the signs of civil disobedience precisely because the wisdom of compulsion was still being challenged. As proof of the necessity for universal vaccination, sanitarians pointed to the dramatically different smallpox mortality rates among protected Prussian and unprotected French soldiers during the Franco-Prussian War. Yet the virulent pandemic of 1870–72 killed over 44,000 people in England and Wales. That is, the worst smallpox outbreak in a generation had started two years *after* the 1867 Act sent vaccination police into the field.[39] The sanitarians enjoyed support, but not unanimous support, from those whose mission was the civilizing of working-class family life. Many district visitors and model dwellings supervisors in London preached compliance with the Vaccination Acts, whereas the Ladies' Sanitary Association was strongly opposed to this "infringement of the liberty of the subject."[40] Probably most disturbing, however, were the mixed signals coming from magistrates' courts. Public health activists cheered judges who fined conscientious objectors the statutory maximum of twenty shillings, plus court costs, for each infraction of the law. But such cases could generate as much public indignation as support. When it was reported that Aaron Emery had been fined for conscientious objection even after producing a coroner's certificate to prove that another of his children had died from the effects of vaccination, probably few readers of *The Times* felt a warm glow of satisfaction. Antivaccinators milked the case of Charles Washington Nye, a watchmaker from Chatham who, like Emery, had already lost one child to the "deadly lancet." Nye had endured five separate jail terms, "working on the treadmill amongst the lowest criminals," rather than permit any of his surviving offspring to be vaccinated. Elsewhere, magistrates imposed steeply reduced fines against parents whose objection stemmed from personal loss.[41] John Cornforth, a Birmingham brassfounder, alleged that since two of his children had already died as a direct result of smallpox vaccination, refusing to condone the "murder" of his two youngest represented a "holy and just cause." Declining to pay his twenty-shilling fine, Cornforth appeared prison-bound when, in a remarkable display of contempt for the principle of compulsion, two "benevolent" policemen collected the money from spectators inside the courtroom.[42]

Throughout the 1870's and 80's, sanitarians advanced a distinctly schizophrenic view of antivaccination sentiment. On the one hand, they boasted that the antivaccination cause had "signally failed" to enlist public sympathy, noting that there had been "a fairly steady advance in obedience to the law" since compulsion took full effect in early 1872. By 1881 there were twenty children certified as vaccinated for every one who remained unmarked, yet the smallpox mortality rate was ten times higher among the "relatively few" unprotected children.[43] On the other hand, sanitarians vilified what seemed to be a growing band of misguided but influential persons bent on wrecking the machinery of compulsion. It was troubling enough when medical men lent credence to the antivaccination cause. Isolated instances of MOH certifying vaccination as the cause of a child's death, physicians lamenting the class bias of compulsion, or public vaccinators who themselves ducked the law were of course embarrassments.[44] It was more serious, though, when local Boards of Guardians began to obstruct justice. What occurred in the West Yorkshire town of Keighley boded ill for the future of state medicine. There, beginning in 1873, the Guardians had refused to prosecute objecting parents, even after an outbreak of smallpox. The intransigence of the Keighley Guardians cheered Northern "antis" and at the same time forced the Local Government Board to threaten a writ of *mandamus* against these renegades. Eventually, eight of the Keighley Guardians were jailed, but only after a "dense mob" had first registered its displeasure by ripping the clothes off several policemen who had been escorting the prisoners to York Castle. Guardians less confrontational than Keighley's mailed hostile resolutions to the Local Government Board, thereby "prejudicing many ill-informed persons against these wholesome laws."[45]

The medical press was right that leaders of the antivaccination cause seized every chance to inflame public opinion. No doubt some conscientious objectors would have been less eager to court "martyrdom" had they not been sure that their fines would be paid or their confiscated furniture purchased at auction with "anti" funds earmarked for such purposes. The raucous celebrations—complete with brass bands, banners, and, occasionally, rotten fruit to throw at the town hall—for "martyrs" returning from jail were carefully staged affairs. So were the funeral processions organized to honor infant victims of the lancet. And the stream of propaganda that tied together vivisection, grave-robbing, and compulsory vaccination, all the spawn of "Medical Despotism," was anything but spontaneous.[46]

Still, middle-class "antis" did not simply impose the idea of resistance on a clueless citizenry. The enforcement of the Vaccination Acts involved minute tyrannies, and these small wrongs, amplified by word of mouth and through local newspapers, created an audience receptive to the sort of anti-medical rhetoric so disturbing to the sanitarians.[47] When Job Eagleston, a poor man, appeared before the Bullingdon Petty Sessions in 1880, he was angry about more than the state's command that he vaccinate his young daughter. Eagleston assured the magistrates that he would have "none of the vile dirty stuff [vaccine] put into the veins of my children." In the next breath he lashed out against the local vaccination officer, whom Eagleston held responsible for spreading such lies about his wife's mental condition that she had been committed to a nearby asylum.[48] How many other parents were driven to defiance by what they viewed as ham-handed enforcement we cannot know. Ellen Chase, a volunteer rent collector in Southeast London, was amazed at the petty behavior of local health officials when smallpox appeared on Green Street. The parish doctor and the area's MOH shared the blame for allowing Mrs. Donnelly, a hawker of worsted mats, to make her door-to-door rounds while carrying an infected baby. These officials felt "so sore over the discredit thrown upon their respective departments," however, that they vanished after hauling away the child to a fever hospital: no one left instructions for disinfecting the baby's home or thought to burn Mrs. Donnelly's wares.[49] The 1871 Select Committee on Vaccination had recognized that where public health authorities planned to "disregard the wish of the parent, it is most important to secure the support of public opinion." This the sanitarians ultimately failed to do.

To parents who already entertained doubts about vaccination, the highly publicized example of Leicester could only have deepened their misgivings. This fast-growing Midlands town had suffered high mortality during the smallpox pandemic of 1871–72 despite being "well vaccinated." Thereafter, two developments transformed Leicester into the epicenter of resistance to compulsion. Under the leadership of J. T. Biggs, a waterworks engineer, local activists began to make antivaccination a central issue in all elections. Such political pressure gradually reshaped Leicester's Board of Guardians, who, after 1886, refused to prosecute any more "delinquent" parents.[50] Just as important, the town's unique approach to smallpox containment gave further encouragement to would-be resisters. Largely because of Dr. William Johnston, the assistant MOH, Leicester mounted an aggressive "sanitary defence" against the virus: doctors were obliged to report all cases of the disease within twelve hours of discovery; afflicted persons were immediately isolated in the town's Fever and Smallpox Hospital; the homes of those hospitalized were thoroughly disinfected; and persons known to have had close contact with the sufferers were kept under surveillance. Vaccination played no part in what became known as the "Leicester method." Operating instead on the assumption that smallpox, like all "zymotic" (infectious) diseases, was caused by "municipal and personal filth," Dr. Johnston and his assistants replaced some 4,000 of the old-style middens with more hygienic earthen or water closets.[51] English newspapers were impressed when more than 20,000 antivaccinators converged on Leicester for a well-choreographed protest in the early spring of 1885. A better gauge of parental feeling, however, was the fact that whereas in 1867 over 94 percent of Leicester's babies were vaccinated, by 1897 just 1.3 percent underwent this procedure.[52]

Leading "antis" greeted the Local Government Board's decision in 1889 to reopen the question of compulsion as a first step toward ending "a tyranny that will invade every home." William Tebb, for one, claimed that his society's propaganda effort had orchestrated the "revolt" of parents so effectively that by 1886, 90 percent of England's electorate opposed enforcement of the Vaccination Acts.[53] Tebb was vastly overrating his group's influence. Yet antivaccination sentiment did intensify during the 1880's and 90's for several reasons. Even among the privileged classes, skilled private vaccination could go wrong. In early 1891, for instance, the widow and two adult daughters of a leading London physician were revaccinated by Edward Cox Seaton, an acknowledged authority on smallpox and soon-to-be MOH for Surrey. Within three days of vaccination, Jeannette Marshall watched her arm swell alarmingly and turn septic, a frightening reaction that called for daily dressings of the wound.[54] How much more vulnerable were working-class children who had been subjected to a public vaccinator's hurried hand? Dr. Charles Creighton's article on vaccination in the ninth edition of the *Encyclopedia Britannica* weakened the scientific case for compulsion, pointing out that vaccination did not protect completely, and that even under ideal conditions the operation on very young children posed risks. Although medical men might dispute Creighton's analysis of post-vaccinial erysipelas data, they could not deny that their support for compulsion was becoming a professional liability.

"What is the use of forcing measures of safety upon an ungrateful public," wondered *The Hospital*, "when [a doctor's] advocacy of such measures results to himself in nothing but a monetary loss and personal odium?"[55] Finally, the smallpox virus itself seems to have mutated during the last decades of the nineteenth century. After the fierce pandemic of 1870–72, the disease grew both rarer and less lethal. Mild smallpox symptoms in the late-Victorian years were often confused with those of chickenpox. Thus, the incentive for parents to vaccinate their children was diminishing while the likelihood of misdiagnosis—and the resulting professional embarrassment—was increasing.[56]

The Royal Commission on Vaccination ultimately opened the door for those who claimed to uphold "Parental Liberty." This ponderous inquiry, which spanned seven years and weighed the testimony of 187 witnesses, came down squarely on the side of vaccination as the best available defense against smallpox. Nevertheless, even the pro-vaccination "Majority Report" agreed that compulsion in the name of public health had aroused "acute and widespread" opposition. If "agitators" had "intensified" public doubts about vaccination, cases of perceived injustice to individual parents nevertheless lay at the heart of public hostility. The remedy therefore seemed obvious: some allowance should be made for those parents with genuine fear about the vaccination of their young.[57]

Translating the Commissioners' guidelines into law proved no easy matter, but Lord Salisbury's Tory Government saw to it that the Vaccination Act of 1898 preserved the principle of conscientious objection. Henceforth parents who could satisfy a court that their opposition was sincere might legally shield their children from the public vaccinator. To disciples of sanitary science the 1898 Act seemed an abomination. Because children were, in part, "the property of the State," reasoned one irate doctor, legislation that viewed them as mere "chattels of their parents" was retrograde. Far from being rewarded for their selfishness, fathers who thwarted the progress of public health should be disenfranchised.[58]

The Vaccination Act of 1898 did not, as its medical foes had predicted, give immediate comfort to "monomaniacal faddists." Indeed, a key procedural change may actually have encouraged some parents to offer their children's arms. The new law abolished public vaccination stations, long attacked as breeding grounds of infection. Now, if parents requested a home visit, public vaccinators had to perform a "domiciliary" operation within two weeks. More than any other provision of the 1898 Act, home visits sent the cost of public vaccination soaring.[59] Simultaneously, though, arbitrary judicial readings of Clause 2 (the Act's "conscience" clause) stymied some objecting parents and reignited antivaccinationist feeling. Within the same court different magistrates might apply different standards to determine whether a parent "conscientiously believed" that vaccination would be "prejudicial to the health of the child." The Home Office ruled in 1906 that magistrates could not refuse a certificate of exemption merely because a parent's fears seemed irrational or ignorant.[60] In 1907 Parliament passed amending legislation that reduced conscientious objection to a straightforward declaration.

Yet even then one roadblock remained. In theory, mothers as well as fathers could declare themselves conscientious objectors. Much to the fury of English feminists, however, only fathers, as the legal guardians of their children, were actually allowed to register objections to vaccination in some localities. As late as 1921, a Ministry of Health official asserted that:

Mothers are potential anti-vaccinators; and, except among the upper classes of society, they are almost without exception opposed to vaccination. All they know is that when a baby is vaccinated, it suffers some minor pain and generally cries during the operation, that it becomes fretful and peevish for three or four days, that the mother's rest is disturbed at night by a wakeful child, and that unless attention is given to it, the vaccinated arm may become 'bad.' They hear of all sorts of calamities vulgarly and erroneously attributed to vaccination and to its results. As to the protective value of vaccination against such a terrible disease as smallpox they neither know or care.[61]

Remarkably, even after passage of the 1925 Guardianship of Infants Act—legislation designed to enhance gender equality—several judges and vaccination officers continued to uphold the fathers-only prejudice.[62]

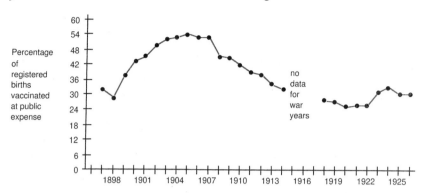

Figure 1. Public Vaccination Against Smallpox in England, 1897–1926. (Source: *Report of the Committee on Vaccination*, P.P., 1928, XII: 77–78.)

Despite this noxious residue of patriarchy, the resort to conscientious objection grew commonplace after 1907 (Figure 1). Medical experts in the 1920's admitted that the potency of government-supplied calf lymph varied; that some public vaccinators were clumsy with a lancet; and that "post-vaccinal nervous disease" constituted a real, if very rare, hazard.[63] Since an alert antivaccination lobby continued to pounce on such confessions, it is not surprising that by 1925 less than a third of all infants under the age of one were being vaccinated annually at public expense (while less than 14 percent of the same population were being vaccinated privately each year).[64] The successful resistance of English parents to compulsory vaccination is all the more striking when we consider that in early twentieth-century India, British doctors pursued resisting fathers into the jails.[65] At home, anyhow, "parental rights" had become a war cry.

School Attendance

Compulsory school attendance, like smallpox vaccination, posed a direct challenge to parental authority. Unlike the antivaccinationists, however, those who harbored doubts about elementary education in England never organized a coherent political opposition. This was true because very few among the politically influential classes dared deny—publicly, at least—that poor children required more efficient instruction. The decision to build a national, nonsectarian system of primary education in 1870 generated controversy above all on religious grounds.[66] A generation later, the foes of compulsory schooling would rail less against its secular bias than against the "burden of officialism" that had, it seemed, fallen on parent and child alike. "[I]n vaccination," complained one critic, "even if you cannot escape the infliction, you can at any rate suck the place and spit [the vaccine] out, but in education no one can ever spit out . . . the effects of being herded too young and too long with the riff-raff of the population . . . in one room in a stuffy Council School, five and a half hours a day, for nine years."[67] What shaped such alarmist rhetoric were two, often related, concerns. First, certain Edwardian conservatives insisted on viewing the administration of compulsory schooling as a specimen of "that universal confiscation of liberty sometimes called Social Reform and sometimes Socialism." The "Socialist bureaucrat," according to this critique, had gradually robbed "ordinary" parents of any sense of responsibility for the education of their young. Second, some self-appointed advocates of the poor held that the legal machinery behind compulsion pressed with "terrible severity" on working-class mothers and fathers. Central to both concerns was the school attendance officer, or "prowler," who on the eve of the Great War allegedly still inspired "intense fear" in the hearts and minds of poor parents.[68] The evolution of a school attendance police therefore invites closer consideration.

Irregular attendance had of course frustrated teachers long before Foster's Education Act of 1870 opened the era of universal schooling.[69] Given his experience in Glasgow, Thomas Chalmers assured readers in 1821 that urban parents "of all characters" would gratefully accept Sunday school instruction for their offspring. Where attendance at first proved disappointing, Sunday school teachers could, "by following up every case of absence with a week-day inquiry at the parents," insure future regularity.[70] Chalmers's confidence proved premature. For at least a century prior to 1870 some working-class parents had expressed a demand for elementary education by faithfully sending their children to Sunday, "ragged," or "adventure" ("dame") schools. Yet many other poor parents did not prize book learning, or else could not afford to part with the full-time earnings of their offspring.[71] It is possible (but statistically unverifiable) that the introduction in 1862 of the Education Department's Revised Code of Regulations, collectively dubbed "payment by results," may have driven some working-class pupils out of the schools then run by various voluntary bodies. The immediate aims of "payment by results" were to reduce government expenditure on basic education and to promote instruction in the "Three R's." Both aims were pursued by basing the size of government grants to elementary schools on the number of students in each institution who annually passed exams appropriate to their age-linked "standard." It is debatable whether the rote learning that "payment by results" encouraged was as hated among the poor as historians have generally supposed.[72] There can be no question, however, that the Revised Code placed a premium on regular school attendance. For although attendance was not made compulsory in 1862, the new regulations dictated that any child who went to school fewer than two hundred times a year (counting morning and afternoon appearances separately) would be ineligible to take the proficiency exam.

If we accept G. M. Young's claim that the Education Act of 1870 was, "for most English people, the first sensible impact of the administrative State on their private lives,"[73] we must remember that this landmark legislation neither established compulsory school attendance nor provided free elementary instruction. At the time that "Mundella's Act" of 1880 finally *did* demand universal attendance at an elementary school between the ages of five and ten, nearly 30 percent of the population in England and Wales lived in rural areas as yet untouched by any kind of compulsion. By 1900, an estimated 87.8 percent of English and Welsh children under twelve years of age were listed on elementary school registers, and on an average day 72.1 percent of them sat in a classroom.[74] Yet loopholes in the law—especially the partial exemptions for "half-time" children who worked in the fields or in the textile mills of Lancashire and Yorkshire—continued to rile those determined to make elementary education truly universal.[75] When analyzing the social impact of school attendance schemes, therefore, it is important to recall that school boards and their hired agents faced a legal code shot through with ambiguities. Under these circumstances it is hardly surprising that, in some communities, the "school board man" earned a reputation for overzealousness.

Who bore the brunt of educational policing? Although the statute of 1870 sought to bring England's most neglected children, the offspring of the "residuum," within the grasp of elementary education, it is probable that the hands of the first school attendance officers fell mostly on the "respectable" poor. Their children, after all, had likely attended some sort of school before 1870, and so would have been comparatively easy to trace. During the 1870's, newly formed urban school boards were often busy conducting censuses of their districts. The attendance rolls derived from these surveys would frequently have missed the children of parents who were constantly on the move in search of cheaper rooms, or whose "criminal and immoral" activities made them shy of the law.[76] In London, with its vast concentration of unskilled labor, the objects of school board scrutiny had good reason to hold grudges. It seemed hard enough when attendance officers tried to pluck children out of the small-scale ("sweated") workshops characteristic of casual labor in the metropolis, but worse still when, to make room for new schools, the authorities chose to level the tenements that so many poor families called home. The London School Board, moreover, appeared tight-fisted when it came to remitting school fees. In the mid-1880's just 4 percent of London elementary school pupils were granted free places—slightly under the national remittance rate of 4.43 percent but far below that of such Northern cities as Sheffield and Birmingham.[77]

Within the families of the "respectable" London poor, compulsory school attendance weighed most heavily on mothers. Girls were apt to be kept home more often than boys because mothers expected help with such traditionally female chores as washing and minding younger children. Both school attendance officers and teachers reinforced this double standard by condoning absences from a girl that would have smacked of "truancy" in a boy. As Anna Davin has argued, the readiness of London School Board officials to tolerate two or even more absences per week from girls "needed at home" sabotaged the formal equality of educational provision.[78] Yet the help extracted from school-age daughters rarely offset the added burdens being placed on mothers in wage-dependent households. For at the turn of the century, working-class mothers were losing their children's time and earning capacity to the demands of school, even as social legislation was imposing new childcare expectations upon them. The "terms of mothering" were being rewritten.[79] Naturally enough, then, some London mothers welcomed the end of their daughters' elementary education with ill-concealed glee. When the chairman of a metropolitan school board asked Mrs. Popert, a "jovial, well-nourished lady," to let thirteen-year-old Jane remain in the classroom for another season, this mother's answer was to wave Jane's birth certificate in his face: "[It] was, indeed, a moment of triumph, in which Mrs. Popert gloated with a perfectly indecent pleasure."[80]

A good deal is known about the enforcement of school attendance in London, and the evidence available suggests that this duty was far from pleasant. During the spring of 1872, an activist London School Board appointed its first forty-seven "visitors," twenty-five of whom were women, along with a superintendent of visitors for each of the Board's ten divisions. The predominance of women in district visiting work probably convinced Board members that female agents would be "more likely to influence the mothers, and less likely to excite resistance." Significantly, even a "first class" woman was judged willing to accept a pound per week, whereas the working-class men hired as visitors started with annual salaries of £80.[81] With each visitor initially responsible for 5,000 children and obliged to confront hostile parents "in their dens," London's female attendance officers soon began to resign. They were not replaced with women. Those visitors, male and female alike, who endured preferred to believe that whereas elementary school teachers were training the young, attendance officers were assigned "the more difficult task of enlightening the parents and bringing into their lives a higher moral tone." Spreading enlightenment could entail risk, of course. John Reeves, for sixteen years a visitor assigned to the rough Boundary Street district that lay between Bethnal Green and Shoreditch in London's East End, found that "parents would stand at the street door [of their poor dwellings] and threaten and abuse me in the most dreadful language, and nearly all the people in the street would come out and see what was the matter and sympathise in their view." Another visitor had a dead cat dropped on him from an overhead window.[82]

The "school board man" arrived at working-class doors offering more than moral guidance. He also distributed plenty of "Form A" notices, which enumerated for parents their new obligations under the education statutes. At the homes of children who had been absent repeatedly, or who had failed to give their teachers the required school fees each Monday morning, he presented the notorious "Form B," which "invited" parents to meetings of the local board "to show cause why you should not be summoned before a magistrate and fined." These "B meetings," as they came to be known, laid bare the inequalities of class and gender that typified compulsion. Seated at a table were the bourgeois gentlemen who represented the School Board, and standing behind them, now and then interjecting case details, were the male visitors. Ushered before this fraternity, one at a time, were the proletarian parents—"a stream of tired looking mothers with an occasional father"—whose children had run afoul of the rules.[83] By the Edwardian era, according to one observer, the sittings of a London school attendance sub-committee had acquired the status of a public confessional: "The parents come . . . to plead guilty of a civic failure and to make their defence. They wish to make out that they have done their best, but that circumstances have been too much for them."[84] As the example of Mrs. Popert should remind us, however, not all poor mothers were meek victims at these "Inquisitions." "[M]ore than one energetic dame" arrived ready to scold her social superiors for harassment.[85]

Obliged to learn the domestic habits of their districts, and often living in them, London's school attendance officers soon became recognized experts in the family lives of the poor. As early as 1875,

The "B meeting" of a local school board attendance committee. This image from George R. Sims's *How the Poor Live* (1883) views the war on truancy as an effort to discipline working-class parents as well as children.

the Clerk of the London School Board forwarded to the House of Commons a list of wife-desertion cases that visitors had unearthed in the course of their home inquiries.[86] Among the 110 witnesses who testified before the Royal Commission on the Housing of the Working Classes in 1884 and 1885, sixteen were London visitors. Some of them seemed better informed about local health "nuisances" than the sanitary officers themselves.[87] Charles Booth's monumental survey of poverty in London was based largely on the neighborhood data that school attendance officers had compiled. By 1886, when Booth and his assistants began to analyze the East End households of Tower Hamlets, visitors were still underpaid, overworked, and, most importantly, possessed no legal right of entry into a home. The visitors' impressions, in other words, were not always reliable. Yet without them, Booth's map of some 13,600 streets could not have been drawn.[88]

Predictably, the visitors' domestic expertise meant different things to different actors in the policing drama. The memoirs of

London School Board members praise the visitors' "careful and sympathetic work," eulogizing the "patience which no mendacity can baffle." To those charged with enforcing social discipline, it was cause for celebration that when "fishing for little children," visitors cast nets so fine that "few escape in the end."[89] To middle-class citizens categorically opposed to the regulation of private life, these benign fishermen instead became "beasts" who "live by spying and lying." And to many of those on the receiving end of the stick, the school attendance officer was, simply, the "punishment man."[90]

The ultimate "punishment" associated with attendance officers was not actually theirs to inflict. Only judges in courts of summary jurisdiction—police court magistrates—could order a fine or, in default of payment, a brief jail term for those who had violated the elementary education statutes. What critics of compulsion chose to ignore was that in some localities these magistrates hindered rather than helped the process of enforcement. Champions of compulsion believed that metropolitan magistrates at best resented the new duties thrust upon them and at worst wished to sabotage the visitors' work. The refusal of some magistrates to schedule enough time for the hearing of School Board cases had, complained a Marylebone headmaster, sent poor parents the message "that seven attendances in the week [out of a possible ten] are quite sufficient." R. B. Williams, the Superintendent of East Lambeth Division's twenty-two visitors, understood why a magistrate might reasonably dismiss charges which obliged parents to travel five or six miles to court. Williams could not comprehend, though, why police court justices failed to see that "it would be a true kindness in the end, both to the people and to their children . . . to fine at once, sharply, and to require immediate payment of the penalty, instead of granting further time for payment, which, in many cases, means . . . a large moral discount from the first effect produced by the summons."[91] Some London magistrates were more than merely obtuse, it seemed. When a parent who had been summoned repeatedly for his child's truancy received a fine of just sixpence, without costs, ridicule was heaped on the law. Alfred Plowden at the South Western Police Court clearly had no use for School Board cases. Upon learning from the father of an often-absent boy that he kept his son at home because the curriculum caused him to walk in his sleep, Plowden thumbed through the boy's textbook and pronounced it "quite enough to make anybody dream." The School Board's representative thereupon withdrew his summons.[92]

David Rubinstein has suggested that London magistrates refused to cooperate with the School Board and its visitors above all because these conservative, upper-middle-class jurists deplored the democratic implications of universal elementary education. "Help for the honest poor was acceptable," Rubinstein speculates, "but the hierarchical nature of existing English institutions should not be altered."[93] Although class-based motives surely helped shape the delivery of summary justice,[94] it would be wrong to depict magisterial opposition as essentially tactical. All of them barristers trained in the adversarial determination of truth, London's stipendiary magistrates were naturally perplexed, and often irked, when asked to divine a parent's intentions. Alfred Plowden spoke for many of his peers on the metropolitan bench when he confessed: "School Board cases are the only cases where I feel I have to *guess* at the truth, where I have nothing to take hold of or to reassure me that I have arrived at the right conclusion."[95] Since school attendance officers did at times misinterpret parental actions, London's magistrates were understandably loathe to punish an innocent person or make a "shuttlecock" out of a child.[96]

Beyond the metropolis the conduct of magistrates in school attendance cases stirred less controversy, partly, no doubt, because few provincial education authorities were as litigious as the London School Board.[97] In many rural areas the farmers who tended to dominate local school boards were also those who stood to lose cheap labor through rigorous enforcement of attendance bylaws. Still, even in some agricultural backwaters, such as Flora Thompson's Oxfordshire hamlet of Lark Rise, the "dreaded" school board visitor might appear at a cottage door to confront the mother of an absentee child.[98] School attendance officers in provincial towns also had their critics. In turn-of-the-century Manchester, the socialist editor Robert Blatchford damned them for behaving with "relentless cruelty" toward the poor, and cited cases of parents summonsed to the police court without first being allowed to defend themselves at a school board hearing.[99] We should note, though, that many attendance officers were less obsessed with refining methods of domestic surveillance than were other members of their communities. For example, it was a lady district visitor in Manchester who urged local attendance officers to check children's teeth for confirmation of age.[100] The *School Attendance Officers' Gazette* recognized that "degrading poverty," not parental stealth, was the real obstacle to universal education. Progress toward this goal had been achieved: in the course of one generation the average school-life of a working-class child had nearly doubled, from 3.76 years in 1870 to 7.05 years in 1897. Mere numbers alone failed to convey the attendance officers' worth, however, or so their professional association argued. Because these agents performed extensive volunteer service—from finding homes for orphans to keeping watch over fever dens—their value could not be judged solely on the basis of attendance percentages.[101]

If anything, the politics of school attendance grew more confused during the early years of the twentieth century. There had long been those who argued that compulsion was counterproductive. As the Cross Commission learned in the mid-1880's, some working-class parents saw the fixing of a school-leaving standard as a government-approved *maximum* for elementary instruction, and so withdrew their children from class at the earliest opportunity.[102] But during the Edwardian era, thanks in part to a deepening national concern with physical "efficiency" brought on by revelations of widespread weakness among volunteers for the Boer War,[103] the quest for "perfect attendance" lost some of its urgency. The practice of sending children younger than five to school began to draw sharp criticism. Since these boys and girls (who in 1902 constituted 10.9 percent of the English and Welsh elementary school population) ran the greatest risk of contracting an infectious disease in crowded classrooms, it made no sense for visitors "to exert any undue pressure [on] parents as regards the attendance of their younger infants."[104] Older children, too, were best left at home when their presence in the classroom posed health hazards. Once school medical officers were appointed in response to the 1907 Education (Administrative Provisions) Act, working-class parents more often found themselves prosecuted for sending their lice-ridden offspring to school. The "delicate" child, moreover, demanded special care. It was for this reason that some local education authorities on the eve of the Great War began to use trained nurses as attendance officers.[105] Thus, despite the shrill rhetoric of those who viewed attendance work as an assault on the "liberty of the subject," or the occasional charge that school board visitors surpassed even policemen in unpopularity among the poor, the job of enforcing England's elementary education codes was becoming more complex, demanding less "brawn" and more "brain" power, as an interwar probation expert later phrased it.[106]

Whether a more bureaucratically enmeshed school board visitor was also a more powerful agent of family discipline is questionable. In certain provincial towns, generally improving attendance figures cannot be attributed to the visitors' surveillance alone. Education authorities in late-Victorian Bootle, for example, gave considerable credit to such classroom bribes as sweets, toys, and clothing at Christmas; interesting "object lessons" on sparsely attended Friday afternoons; and the more common awarding of medals and certificates for outstanding attendance.[107] In Coventry, visitors did not launch a house-to-house survey ("visitation") of school-age children until 1908—three years *after* that city's "efficient" elementary schools had achieved a laudable attendance rate of 91.79 percent. Visitors in Edwardian Coventry seem to have had more trouble dealing with a punctilious school attendance subcommittee than with parents resisting compulsion. The former spent a good deal of time fretting about how well its officers "represent[ed] the dignity of the [Education] Authority in the eyes of the public."[108]

For sheer energy devoted to improving school attendance, few towns could match Sheffield. This iron and steel manufacturing center in south Yorkshire embraced the cause of compulsion early on. Its most prominent MP in the 1870's, A. J. Mundella, was a powerful advocate of universal elementary education, and a man who insisted that nothing short of Prussia's 97 percent school attendance rate should be acceptable.[109] Starting in 1875, the Sheffield School Board obtained quarterly returns of all local births, "with the view of tracing such children when they arrive at the age at which they should be compelled to attend School." By 1887, Sheffield had sixteen plainclothes officers patrolling city streets for school-age children and paying surprise visits to the homes of truants. At least one visitor used such "impure" language while remonstrating with the father of a problem boy that this parent attacked him. Although awarding officers cash prizes for improvements in school attendance figures proved unworkable, the opening of an industrial school for truants at Hollow Meadows in 1879 had the gratifying effect of removing habitual absences from the regular school rolls (and therefore also from the calculation of attendance percentages).[110] Yet these efforts failed to achieve the desired results: from 1889 to 1912, Sheffield's elementary school attendance rate never reached 90 percent, fluctuating instead between 78 and 89 percent.[111]

In 1905, eager to experiment with the much-discussed "Leicester system," Sheffield School Board authorities ordered its visitors in four districts to streamline the process by which teachers reported absences. Now supplied with the names of missing children by 10:30 on the morning of their absences, attendance officers could tackle the offending homes far sooner than was previously possible. Unfortunately for the School Board, this intensified pursuit of absentees left no time for other vital tasks such as tracking children who had moved into or out of the district. The experiment was abandoned.[112] Even in a town as staunchly committed to compulsory education as Sheffield, therefore, the enforcement of school attendance remained far less imposing than contemporary critics of the "education tyranny" would have us believe.

Indeed, perceptions of "tyranny" in the regulation of working-class family life were remarkably protean. Late-Victorian Leicester, as we have seen, was the epicenter of resistance to compulsory vaccination. Yet this same town devised the most intrusive system of policing school attendance in England. Leicester's citizens evidently found compulsion in the name of literacy far preferable to compulsion in the name of public health, perhaps because several years spent in a board school classroom seemed less lethal than a single carelessly handled lancet.[113] What remains obscure is the extent to which the poor themselves differentiated among various forms of domestic surveillance. For illumination we can turn to the reception of England's child-protection police.

The Prevention of Cruelty to Children

Where working-class neighborhoods sometimes saw the school attendance officer as the "punishment man," the National Society for the Prevention of Cruelty to Children's blue-uniformed inspector was the "cruelty man." Although both agents could be classified as ambassadors of what David Garland has termed the "penal-welfare complex,"[114] they obeyed different masters. Whereas school boards were public bodies elected to supervise primary education at the local level, the NSPCC was a voluntary organization that sought to centralize all efforts toward protecting children in their own homes. School boards carried out—with varying degrees of enthusiasm and efficiency—the letter of parliamentary law. The NSPCC, by contrast, was the first among England's myriad children's charities to take the lead in reforming legal codes while simultaneously trying to kill "the moral cowardice of the people on whom alone it can rely to put the law in place."[115] These interconnected roles as national pressure group and local watchdog of parental conduct gave the NSPCC a philanthropic cachet that fueled spectacular growth. From its founding as the London SPCC in 1884, when one inspector helped unearth just ninety-five cases of mistreatment, the Society rapidly built a bureaucracy that on the eve of World War One claimed to have 1,666 "centres of work," 258 full-time inspectors, and an annual caseload of 54,772 affecting 159,162 children.[116] The £903 of general income that sustained the infant Society during 1884 came from a small circle of metropolitan well-wishers, several of them subscribers to the venerable Royal Society for the Prevention of Cruelty to Animals (RSPCA). By 1908 the National Society's annual income would stand at £71,195, a treasury amassed from half a million subscribers scattered throughout the British Isles.[117]

The NSPCC's organizational roots in Liverpool and New York City, along with its subsequent rise to fame as an engine of moral reform, are by now well known.[118] Two cautions are nevertheless required. First, it would be wrong to imply that public anger over brutality to the young surfaced only after the founding of child-protection agencies. As Linda Pollock has demonstrated through sampling reports of cruelty to children in *The Times*, cases of gross mistreatment drew courtroom tears and magisterial wrath as far back as the 1780's.[119] During the early-Victorian period, John Stuart Mill, although a staunch believer in the "practical principle of non-interference," lamented the fact that parental power was "constantly abused" and urged legal intervention in defense of the defenseless. Mill's famous dictum that, "The domestic life of domestic tyrants is one of the things which it is the most imperative on the law to interfere with" referred in fact to those who terrorized the "lower animals." But his logic held true for all beings incapable of judging their best interests.[120] In both urban and rural settings, community anger over a parent's brutal behavior could transform neighbors into avenging mobs, as occurred at Preston, Lancashire, in the early 1850's and near Tonbridge, Kent, in 1871.[121] What distinguished the late-Victorian anticruelty campaign from such earlier expressions of concern was the creation of a systematic supervision of parents justified in the name of "children's rights."[122]

A second caution centers on the aims and tactics of English anticruelty work. The transatlantic scope of humane activism in the nineteenth century is important to acknowledge, not least because the emergence of animal and child protection schemes in England and America were closely linked. At the same time, however, American efforts to save the young from parental harm were conducted quite differently from those across the water. In her study of the Massachusetts SPCC (founded in 1877), Linda Gordon emphasizes the anti-immigrant thrust of its mission, noting that during the late nineteenth century about 70 percent of the MSPCC's Boston "clients" were foreign-born. The first U.S. reformers viewed cruelty to children as "a vice of inferior classes and cultures which needed correction and 'raising up' to an 'American' standard." No equivalent impulse colored English child protection efforts.[123] To be sure, the existence of Liverpool's large and notoriously rough Irish population helped persuade that town's civic elite that a new approach to civilizing the slum-dweller was worth trying. But in 1883 the founders of the Liverpool SPCC were far more worried about supplying the docks with docile unskilled labor than about Anglicizing the exiles of Erin.

A still more basic contrast between English and American child protection campaigns involved legal proceedings. The New York SPCC (founded in 1874), America's only large child protection agency to publish prosecution statistics annually, did not hesitate to haul abusive or neglectful parents into court. Approximately one-third of all the NYSPCC's cases investigated between 1887 and 1900 ended in criminal trials; between 1900 and 1913 its resort to prosecution reached nearly 43 percent. Thus "Teresa," a fictional ballet dancer in *fin-de-siècle* Manhattan, felt "overwhelming terror" when a fractured hip forced her into hospital and away from her baby daughter.[124] Appreciably different tactics prevailed in England. There, during the London (after 1889, National) Society's first five years, 16.2 percent of all cases were sent to a criminal court. This prosecution percentage then fell steadily, reaching 9.8 percent in 1898–99 and 5.6 percent in 1908-9.[125] "'Prevention' is the watch-word, 'Prosecution' the thing to be as far as possible avoided, and Family ties to be left intact"—so the Earl of Ranfurly, a longtime supporter, summed up the NSPCC's mission in 1910. Nor was the goal of family preservation a pious lie. Between mid-1889 and mid-1903, the NSPCC investigated reports of mistreatment involving 754,732 children, yet removed just 1,200 of these boys and girls (0.16 percent) from parental custody. English childsavers therefore meant it when they declared that, "The aim of the Society is to remove the evil from the home, and not the children."[126]

Despite such clear evidence to the contrary, some experts in English social history have erroneously implied that the NSPCC was keen to pluck children out of harmful homes.[127] This mistake is understandable if one considers only the ferociously self-righteous language of Benjamin Waugh, the Society's Director and zealot-in-chief from 1884 to his retirement in 1905. As the shrewd editor of his Society's monthly magazine, the *Child's Guardian*, as well as of its annual reports, Waugh missed few opportunities to proclaim the justice of what was actually a very controversial form of family intervention. Thus, the *Fifth Annual Report*, published while the Society's precedent-setting "Children's Charter" was clawing its way through Parliament, devoted several pages to the case of a woman whose maternal savagery had landed her in prison. During her trial it was established that she had, at various times, held a red-hot poker against her young son's back, bitten a chunk of flesh out of his arm, and whipped him on the face with a wire "scourge." Later, from jail, she wrote Waugh seeking news of her two children: "Let my faults be what they may in your eyes, I am not void of a mother's feelings." The Director's reply was less than conciliatory:

I am instructed to inform you that your two children are very well, even that pitiable, little half-dead and mutilated boy, against whom you committed the unspeakable cruelties for which you are now in prison. As to your having them both again, that is impossible. The one you tortured so . . . fiendishly you have made over to our Society, and he is in a Home till he is sixteen years of age. . . . As to the other child, he will be given to you, as we have already told you, on your release, should you demand him.

It is astonishing that you can so hypocritically talk of your 'suffering' by being deprived of your children—you whose crimes against one of them curdle one's blood to merely think of. . . . It is past belief that even you could call on God to be your judge in this matter. . . .[128]

Waugh, himself a Congregational minister, could afford to be harsh because the crime in question was diabolical. When no excuse for brutality seemed possible, Waugh and his Society agreed with the thesis that, "The rights and responsibilities of . . . worthless parents can only be spoken of in contemptuous irony, or pleaded as the excuse for a selfish and inhuman policy of non-interference."[129]

But such cases of wanton cruelty grew steadily more uncommon in the Society's experience, although naturally their shock value remained high. As NSPCC statistics demonstrate, the proportion of cases investigated that could be classified as "cruelty of violence" fell from 45.5 percent in 1889–90 to just 7.3 percent in 1913–14

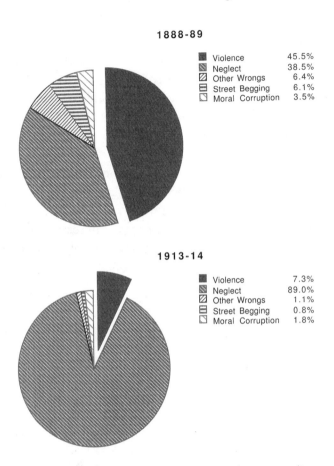

1888-89

■	Violence	45.5%
▨	Neglect	38.5%
▨	Other Wrongs	6.4%
▤	Street Begging	6.1%
◨	Moral Corruption	3.5%

1913-14

■	Violence	7.3%
▨	Neglect	89.0%
▨	Other Wrongs	1.1%
▤	Street Begging	0.8%
◨	Moral Corruption	1.8%

Figure 2. Classification of NSPCC Cases, 1888–89 and 1913–14. (Source: NSPCC *50th Annual Report*, Table 3.)

(Figure 2).[130] Most NSPCC supporters viewed the corresponding growth of cases classified as "neglect and starvation" as proof that the Society's vigilance had produced a true reformation in childrearing behavior. Such optimism may well have been unwarranted. Harry Hendrick has suggested that NSPCC leaders, like most middle-class moral reformers, were quick to admonish working-class parents for failing to provide their young with adequate food, shelter, clothing, or supervision. It was easier to charge poor parents with a "lack of self-consciousness" than to expose, much less explain, the sort of "unnatural" behavior that led parents to attack their own offspring.[131]

English childsavers gave relatively little attention to the aetiology of physical abuse. NSPCC leaders did not, for example, seek to answer a question that disturbed district nurse Margaret Loane: why was there sometimes a "single sufferer" in an otherwise well-treated family?[132] The Society's only thesis about the psychodynamics of family violence was that cruelty tended to reproduce itself. Even in "bad" parents there dwelled "indestructible [nurturing] instincts, though they are buried deep, stiff, cold, and silent." It followed from this premise that "in order [for] a child [to] suffer calamity, the parent must have previously suffered one, and in some senses a more serious one than the child's." Thus, "what was needed to be restored" to parents "was not saintly, but animal nature"; it was to "instincts, which men share with the beasts of the field, that we must look to remove and prevent the calamities to [children's] lives."[133] The childsavers' argument from instinct drew on widely shared assumptions about the survival value of parental love. If, as Benjamin Kidd put it in 1894, parental love was an evolutionary mechanism refined "through all those countless aeons of time," then to dwell on the counter-instinctual behavior of some fathers and mothers would have embroiled childsavers in disputes about the existence of an atavistic human type.[134] Given its doctrine that no parent was beyond reformation, NSPCC leaders spent a great deal of time and effort contending that cruelty was not related to poverty or drunkenness. The case data suggested otherwise, however. So, unable to deny that the bulk of its work *was* conducted in poor neighborhoods, or that alcohol *did* figure prominently in its cases, the Society hedged its bets by claiming that "a hateful court and slum respectability"—that is, a habit of mind rather than an income level—was the true enemy. To judge English childsavers by their own standards, therefore, we must decide how effectively they overcame the "horror of interfering"[135] that supposedly typified working-class culture.

As we have already seen, in cases of gross parental violence poor neighbors were not as reluctant to meddle as middle-class accounts would suggest. Nonetheless, the three child protection laws that

NSPCC supporters pushed through Parliament over a fifteen-year period shifted the operational meaning of abuse and neglect. The 1889 Act for the Prevention of Cruelty to Children was the most important of these. Although it placed new restrictions on certain forms of child labor, the 1889 Act's truly radical provisions were those which broadly defined ill-treatment as anything "likely to cause . . . unnecessary suffering, or injury to [a child's] health," along with clauses that specified jail terms of up to two years and fines as high as £100 for adults convicted of such offenses. The Act also let magistrates authorize "any person . . . bona fide acting in the interest of any child" to enter a private home, accompanied by a police officer, and remove from it all children listed on a warrant. The custody of boys and girls whose parents had been convicted of cruelty could now be transferred to a relative or other "fit person"— which meant, in practice, industrial schools or charities. That the 1889 Act represented "an essentially criminal rather than a social welfare approach" to childsaving is true. That it gave little thought to "children as victims" is demonstrably false, as the parliamentary debates over its passage reveal.[136]

Building on the "Children's Charter" were the NSPCC's amending Acts of 1894 and 1904. The former stiffened sanctions against abusive and neglectful adults, required a doctor to be called when needed for a sick child, and empowered policemen to remove suspected victims from their homes without a court order; the latter made it simpler to enforce maintenance orders against irresponsible parents, dispensed with the need for injured children to appear in court, and gave greater flexibility in prosecuting adults charged with sexually assaulting the young. Taken together, these three laws mirrored Benjamin Waugh's faith that by establishing "a new standard of right and wrong and community obligation," it *was* in fact possible to make parents moral by act of Parliament.[137]

The NSPCC generally wielded these expanding legal powers with restraint. Acutely aware that their status as arbiters of justice within the home was fraught with difficulty, NSPCC leaders erred on the side of caution in their prosecutions. To impress magistrates (and discourage lawsuits), the Society always used experienced counsel in court cases. Indeed, on one occasion it went so far as to provide counsel for *both* sides in a High Court case (*Queen v. Jane Tyrell*) involving a thirteen-year-old girl who had been convicted of soliciting for a carnal act. When an inspector's evidence appeared to contain a confession of guilt from an accused parent, the Legal Department at headquarters struck such material from the record before going to trial. Similarly, the Society opposed the idea that parents should be compelled to testify against one another in child cruelty proceedings.[138] On very rare occasions—usually where a parent refused to permit a medical procedure deemed vital by the Society—officials made highhanded use of the law. Such was the case in 1912, when NSPCC leaders won temporary custody of eight-year-old Alice Carter so that her speech-destroying cleft palate could be surgically repaired.[139] And it is true that magistrates who ruled against the child-savers sometimes earned criticism as "hasty," "fussy," or even "bigoted." But with an early twentieth-century conviction rate of 97 percent in the cases it brought to trial, the NSPCC was hardly impetuous.[140]

Did its courtroom caution spill over into the streets? Here the evidence is mixed. At the least we can say that inspectors were better positioned to exercise "unceasing surveillance" over working-class homes than most urban police forces.[141] As early as March 1889, the Chief Commissioner of Metropolitan Police issued orders directing constables to submit all reports of child mistreatment directly to the London SPCC. By 1907 Nottingham remained one of England's few large towns whose police took unilateral action in such matters. Likewise, many school boards routinely notified the nearest NSPCC branch when their visitors or attendance committees ran across a suspicious case.[142] The West London Mission was by no means alone among parochial charities in urging its helpers to keep "a sharp look-out" for signs of cruelty, and report these to "Mr. Waugh." To avoid "collision with the people," health visitors for the Manchester Ladies' Health Society quietly reported particulars of abuse or neglect to the childsavers, who in return agreed not to call lady visitors as witnesses during subsequent court proceedings. If, as *The Lancet* insisted, child protection had become a "gigantic" enterprise by the late 1890's, it was one with literally thousands of eyes.[143]

Yet the eyes that mattered most belonged to the poor. Both national and local statistics confirm this fact. Of the 23,124 cases reported to the Society in 1896–97, 58 percent came from the "general public," 24 percent from salaried officials such as policemen, school board visitors, and Poor Law relieving officers, and 18 percent from inspectors. By 1910, "cruelty men" were discovering just 8.8 percent of the Society's cases.[144] The apparent willingness of working-class people to "nark" on cruel neighbors can be explained only in part by the Society's strict policy of confidentiality. Cultural taboos against putting "oneself forward," together with fears that, once alerted, the "N-spectre" might find fault with the informer as well as with the cruel neighbor, drove some concerned but skittish folk to make anonymous reports. Anonymous tips accounted for a tenth of the cases reported during a test period in 1901, and a seventh of the cases analyzed in 1908. It is noteworthy that more than 80 percent of the anonymous leads received during both years were judged to be "well-founded."[145] The great majority of these faceless informants were not, then, motivated principally by a desire to vex next-door enemies.

The receptivity of working-class districts to the childsavers' work does not easily lend itself to explanation in terms of a social control model, however "complex," nor as a species of "patriarchy," however redefined.[146] Harry Ferguson sensibly warns that in studying English child protection practice we must be attentive to "intra-familial oppressions of age and gender."[147] Thus, when the all-male inspectorate invaded poor homes to shield the weak from the strong, cruelty men were, it would seem, adjusting a power relationship whose ideal type remained that of the kind but dominant father. This is an elegant representation of anticruelty work, and in certain cases may have been accurate. In many others, though, the lines of intra-family power were not so simply drawn. A Preston mother of six who in 1913 told her husband that she wished to fetch the "cruelty man" was driven from her home.[148] Yet one wonders how many other working-class wives did without warning what this Preston woman only threatened. For not every poor wife bowed to her husband's will: matriarchy in some poor homes could be a formidable fact. Growing up in the central Birmingham slum of Hockley, Kathleen Dayus had a 224-pound mother who was as fierce as she was large. "Our dad never hit us," Dayus recalled of her Edwardian childhood. "He would tell us off and show us the strap but he left the correcting to Mum, and she did enough for both. So we young ones tried very hard to behave ourselves when Dad was out and he was more times out than in. He always said he couldn't stand her 'tantrums'. . . ."[149] Margaret Loane may have been exaggerating when she observed of prewar family dynamics, "I doubt if the bare idea of fathers being equal to mothers in authority ever enters the mind of any cottage child under the age of sixteen."[150] Her hyperbole nonetheless underscores the point that NSPCC agents often dealt with households in which wives were as assertive and territorial as their husbands.

It is easy enough to understand why some middle-class commentators took the view that NSPCC "espionage" was justified. Well-to-do social critics decried the "want of self-control" among poor parents, a fecklessness that expressed itself in part as a sadly inconsistent approach to training their young. These children were allegedly "spoiled" up to the point where their "impudence" triggered harsh reprisals.[151] Hence if NSPCC intervention in the family lives of the masses could arrest the "decay of parental responsibility," or help blot out what G. R. Sims called the "Black Stain" of cruelty to children, then it would be honorable harassment.[152] Less easy to grasp, however, is the fact that in some working-class neighborhoods cruelty men were more than merely tolerated. "Thanks to you, sir, we are doing all right now," wrote an Oxford couple to the local NSPCC inspector after he had remonstrated with them to improve as parents. Another inspector was "reduced . . . to helpless laughter" when a mother against whom he had intervened announced to the street, "He's been as kind to me as a father!"[153]

Common folk did not accept "an informal, but very real, protectorship of children under observation"[154] because NSPCC cruelty men were paragons of tact. True, the Society's inspectors, nearly all

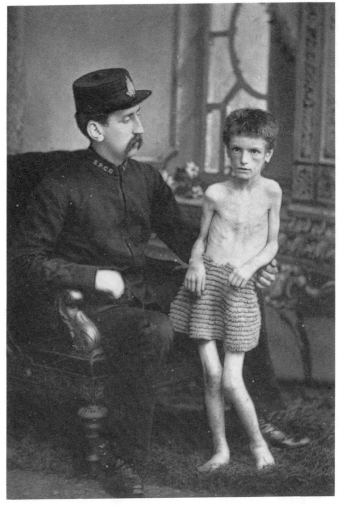

Entitled "Famine," this turn-of-the-century pose features a "cruelty man" from the NSPCC supporting a victim of parental neglect. In practice, separating criminal neglect from the ravages of poverty often proved difficult. Courtesy: NSPCC Archives.

of whom had working-class roots, tended to be mature, sober, and respectful of authority, with more than half of them joining the Society after serving as policemen or soldiers. Once tapped to be a "children's servant," moreover, the inspector-trainee was subjected to a rigorous course in law and community relations. They learned

the proper procedure for everything from weighing and photo-
graphing a starved child to constructing an economic profile for
each family investigated. Unlike inspectors of the RSPCA, NSPCC
agents, after they had completed a six-month probationary period,
were fully equipped to compile the long and detailed case invento-
ries upon which all subsequent action was based. Throughout their
apprenticeship these men had the strategic importance of courtesy
drummed into their heads—even as they were taught "to see through
a brick wall."[155]

Despite their careful training, some cruelty men nevertheless behaved in ways that seemed far from courteous. A middle-class London father became irate when his thirteen-year-old daughter was
subjected to coarse questioning during an indecent exposure case.
The NSPCC inspector who appeared in court asked the girl what
she had seen and, when she hesitated, rephrased his question: "Well,
was 'it' hanging out or what?" For a child reared in "sublime ignorance" of carnal concerns, such interrogation, according to her father, threatened greater "moral injury" than the original crime.[156]
More often the traumatized party was poor. The East London
childhood of Mrs. Benjamin before and during World War One was
full of material deprivation. But the extra pressure of a cruelty man's
visits drove her parents to take evasive action: all the children were
coached to answer "yes" when an inspector asked whether they had
eaten breakfast.[157] At roughly the same time, Stephen Reynolds and
his fishermen co-authors depicted the "National Cruelty 'spector" as
a censorious oaf who barges into one poor home without a warrant,
demands to see the mother's marriage certificate, and then proceeds
to check both the children's bedclothing and their hair for signs of
lice. Cruelty men of this ilk could aptly be described as "tearing"
their way through working-class districts.[158]

Such highhanded conduct was probably exceptional. Yet NSPCC
agents did sometimes exceed the bounds of propriety in their family
surveillance work and, just as surely, laboring folk continued to call
down the cruelty man on abusive or neglectful neighbors. The resolution of this seeming paradox lies in the segmented nature of working-class culture. Writing about proletarian life on the south bank of

the Thames, Alexander Paterson commented that, "Parental discipline is, in fact, a sure sign of prosperity and respectability." Likewise in Oxford at the turn of the century, working-class parents whose relative financial well-being set them apart from the residuum were precisely those who took advantage of the expanding facilities for juvenile supervision offered through both public and private child welfare organizations. Thus the domestic ideal of firm but steady parental guidance, rather than indifference punctuated by outbursts of rage, was gaining favor among self-consciously "superior" laboring people.[159] Robert Roberts's parents owned a small general shop in the slums of Edwardian Salford. The family was poor, although better off than most of its customers. Mrs. Roberts articulated her sense of respectability in several ways, among them an intolerance of parental savagery. "Whenever my mother heard of a heinous case," her son recalled, "she quietly 'put the Cruelty man on.'" So too in York, working-class informants often described the behavior of abusive parents as "shameful." One witness explained to Inspector Walter Jackson that she had decided to move, "as I cannot live next-door to . . . a brute."[160] The prevention of cruelty to children in prewar England obviously entailed the scrutiny of poor parents, but such scrutiny was, to a significant extent, invited.

The Battle over "Parental Responsibility"

Late-Victorian efforts aimed at shaping the conduct of working-class parents therefore varied widely in their success, if "success" is defined as the willingness of poor mothers and fathers to accept new forms of family surveillance. It was not until the Edwardian era, however, that the intrusiveness of home-centered social reform became the subject of national debate. What finally thrust this issue into the public eye? We know that public assistance to the needy did not turn suddenly inquisitorial at the start of the twentieth century. Pat Thane has shown that Poor Law administrators began to restrict the distribution of outdoor relief as far back as the 1870's, when paid officials called "cross-visitors" were first hired to insure that paupers told no lies about their domestic circumstances.[161] Although feminists were prominent among the Edwardian critics of household overinspection, we cannot reasonably cite feminism as the main force behind these critiques. It is worth remembering that well-born women known for sympathizing with the plight of poor mothers could never have compiled their portraits of family struggle without insinuating themselves into private lives. Florence Bell may have embraced an "implicit feminism," but this sensibility did not keep her from investigating nearly every ritual in the working-class homes of Middlesborough. Indeed, we find Lady Bell descending on humble households during funeral preparations ("in those moments of forlorn reaction worse to endure than the first deadening sorrow") and berating poor mothers for their "unwillingness to learn" about proper infant feeding.[162] The Edwardian protest against officialdom in the poor home was, rather, a focused expression of a broader unease with the growth of a modern regulatory state. The stock phrases associated with this protest are revealing. Both the "decay of home life" and the "erosion of parental responsibility" signaled a cultural concern with deterioration, and in fact represented another face of *fin-de-siècle* fears about the national character.

There were many among the comfortable classes who deplored the material hardships facing the Edwardian poor yet who balked at the idea that "inspection" was the key to social progress. The plight of the working-class home epitomized this thinking. As late as 1860 it was possible for the *Quarterly Review* to wax lyrical about the country-dweller's "little whitewashed and woodbined cottage," and to assert that the tidiness of these quaint roadside structures was not "the fruit of patronage, or espionage, or forcing, but the natural result of the public eye bearing upon humble life."[163] By 1902, according to a retired army officer, the growth of tenancies-at-will in rural districts was destroying country life through the "detachment of labour from local association." The essence of the problem was homelessness. For when they wandered from one farmer's cottage to another, agricultural laborers lost "[t]he special virtues of home, neighborliness, kindliness, [and] the loyalty to kith and kin that lies at the bottom of all social life."[164] Residential impermanence also worried England's urban élite, along with the shoddy construction of the "castles" that many laboring families inhabited.[165] But what was the price of saving homes, or for that matter lives, from flimsy disregard? If the price was an inspector "perched on every milestone" along life's route, as Herbert Preston Thomas put it in 1909, then perhaps it should not be paid. Thomas, himself a Civil Service veteran of nearly fifty years, saw the signs of regulation wherever he turned:

As soon as the child is ushered into the world by the legally qualified doctor, the Inspector of Registration arrives in order to see that its advent has been duly chronicled. Then follows the Inspector of Vaccination to ascertain that Dr. Jenner's rite has been properly performed. Then comes the question of education, and the Inspector of School Attendance appears on the scene. . . . When a modest cottage is built the Inspectors swarm. The Inspector under the local bye-laws objects to devices for economy in structure; the Inspector of Highways makes all sorts of stipulation as to roads; the Inspector of Nuisances is for ever girding at the dustbin. . . . If, oppressed by too much inspection, the wretched man takes refuge under the shadow of Bacchus, he may have to encounter an Inspector of Police, an Inspector of Inebriates, or an Inspector of Lunatic Asylums. Even after death he may not be free from inspection, for is there not the Inspector of Burial Grounds?[166]

A similar quandary faced those concerned about the supposed erosion of "parental responsibility." On the one hand, there seemed little doubt that the domestic life of the poor was in disarray. A tangle of modern woes, from high rents and the lure of the pub to married women working outside the home, had allegedly combined to make the snug worker's nest a "poetical dream." On the other hand, the eagerness of religious and philanthropic bodies to act *in loco parentis* with respect to the moral training of children had, it seemed, undermined poor mothers and fathers. "[T]hus," complained the police court missionary Thomas Holmes, "in order to teach the children religious principles we have our Sunday Schools, to teach them temperance our Bands of Hope; mercy, our Guilds of Mercy; in fact societies for teaching them all the cardinal virtues, with the Ten Commandments thrown in, but with very little attention to the fifth."[167] The preemption of parental duty posed eugenic as well as

Overinspection of "The Englishman's Home" (*Maternity and Child Welfare*, Dec. 1919). Early twentieth-century debate over the regulation of family life had a lighter side. Courtesy: British Library.

ethical dilemmas. For advances in public health and sanitation now kept alive many persons who in earlier times would have succumbed to various forms of "selective agency," and thereby enabled constitutionally weak individuals to "propagate their disabilities." This threat to the vigor of the English race made it all the more vital that well-meaning philanthropists not crush the sense of social obligation in parents-to-be.[168]

Edwardian alarms over the subversion of working-class parenthood offered different diagnoses of the problem. Whereas some critics stressed the misguided aims of voluntary effort, others emphasized the "bullying" and "espionage" that followed such "radical" social legislation as the provision of school meals, the creation of a school medical service, or the introduction of unemployment insurance. Nor could critics concur on the nature or strength of parental instinct.[169] Still, there was broad agreement that the creation of a public "overparent" to "direct" working-class mothers and fathers was a dangerous step.[170] Despite—or perhaps because of—the Liberals' welfare legislation of 1906–11, rhetorical attachment to the idea of the home inviolable gathered strength in the immediate prewar years. A language of defensive domesticity played particularly well in the capital, where the London County Council had begun to show what one historian calls an "appetite for managing other people's lives."[171] Major Guy du Maurier's melodrama, *An Englishman's Home*, opened in 1909 and enthralled London audiences. As literature it was beyond bad. Its artless blending of concerns over foreign invasion, racial deterioration, and the destruction of domestic harmony nevertheless generated such "wild excitement" that a recruiting office for the Territorial Army was opened in the theater.[172]

Yet reverence for the notion of domestic sanctuary extended well below the comfortable classes. Labor historians and political scientists have noted that the Edwardian poor were by no means enthusiastic about all forms of "progressive," "New Liberal," or "Fabian-inspired" social legislation. On the contrary, those reforms which sought to impose upper-class standards of behavior on the laboring majority (for example, the infant care provisions of the 1908 Children Act) were greeted with "critical hostility," while non-punitive reforms that aimed to improve the material world of the poor (such as laws to prevent food adulteration) were welcomed.[173] As we have seen, working-class mothers had long been accustomed to directives from "experts" concerning their children. Evasion was one common response to prying eyes, particularly those belonging to health professionals such as coroners and vaccination officers.[174] Grudging compliance was another. But what must be appreciated is that "house pride" among poor wives and mothers, or, in more formal terms, a general acceptance of the "male-breadwinner family model,"[175] also conditioned responses to interference from statutory authorities and voluntary visitors alike.

It is not surprising that economically advantaged sections of the urban proletariat should have embraced a domestic ideology based on the home as a refuge. Eric Hobsbawm and Gareth Stedman Jones have documented a gradual but decisive shift in the focus of working-class culture that dates from the 1870's. For fully employed artisans at least, this shift from a work-centered to a home-centered culture was encouraged by a substantial fall in the cost of living, a reduction in weekly hours of work, the creation of a half-holiday on Saturday afternoons, and, in some towns, by a growing spatial separation between home and workplace.[176] Thus, the artisan élite of Kentish London took great pride in their cottage-style houses, wherein "privatised and family-centered values" set their occupants apart from the transient poor.[177]

There is good reason to believe, however, that less privileged workers came to share many of these same values, if not the luxury of urban cottages with gardens, gates, and fences to tend or mend. In Edwardian North Lambeth, where weekly household incomes ranged from eighteen to thirty shillings, a "kind of dull aloofness" characterized the back streets and a "keep themselves-to-themselves" ethos prevailed among local wives.[178] One of Elizabeth Flint's clearest memories about her poor East London home was her Mum's clean-stove mania: "I do not recall the stove being anything but shiny and gleaming. . . . [A]ny slut could win praises from my mother if she happened to have polished up her range." Similarly, because cleanliness could deflect gossip, but more importantly because the conquest of dirt gave them a sense of control in an otherwise dark and disorderly cityscape, Northern wives often made the polishing of fire-irons and linoleum a sacred chore.[179] Writing in 1907, Margaret Loane had "no doubt" that the "conception and actuality of family life have vastly improved among the decent poor during the last fifty years." As proof of this trend she cited the growing habit among common folk of honoring familiy anniversaries. Children's birthdays had long been marked, but now the mother's (though less often the father's) birthday was usually celebrated, as were silver weddings. The importance of family bonds also manifested itself in a heightened awareness of kinship. "[A]sk the first little [working-class] girl of ten whom you meet," Miss Loane challenged her readers,

. . . and you will find that she can give you a complete list of her uncles and aunts (distinguishing the mother's brothers and sisters very clearly from the father's), and that she can tell you the names and ages of all her first cousins, and most probably knows the names of some of her mother's cousins and of her own elder cousins' children, besides those of several persons who, she is quite sure, 'are *something* to mother 'n father.' Even thirty years ago this would not have been; absent relatives were soon lost sight of, and a generation was long enough to obscure the relationships of those living in different parts of the same parish.[180]

The interwar years, according to one literary reading, marked the point at which "Englishness" became associated with domestic pleasure, while a "fetishisation of home" has been documented even in very disreputable urban neighborhoods during the 1920's and 1930's.[181] But the foundations of this "fetish" are plainly prewar. Although some of the Edwardian fuss over the family was a product of middle-class orchestration (as, for example, the revival of "Mothering Sunday" in 1913),[182] its echoes in working-class culture should not be forced into the Procrustean mold of *embourgeoisement*. The Edwardian poor were not simply aping the values of their social superiors when the former observed such rites of domesticity as that weekly eucharist, the midday Sunday dinner, held in that sanctum, the front parlor. Nor was the Edwardian rebellion against what the young Rebecca West, an ardent feminist and socialist, called the "rat-poison of housework" a working-class cause.[183] The poor but respectable mother took her enhanced status very seriously. And it was therefore those social police who most directly threatened her domestic regime that earned the rudest rebuffs.

The supervision of working-class motherhood by Edwardian champions of infant and child welfare is often decried as a classic case of middle-class cultural harassment. At best, according to this critique, the poor mother received a great deal of condescending advice about child management. At worst, a hoard of health visitors, physicians, and educators busied themselves with the "minutest detail of domestic and personal hygiene" in the name of the young, and by so doing created the phenomenon of the guilty or, in Edwardian parlance, "worried" mother.[184] Public health crusaders were undeniably quick to criticize traditional childrearing practices. They might brand working-class grandmothers "infanticidal experts," or exaggerate the dangers of drunken women "overlying" their babies in bed. Dr. Lewis Hawkes, a London general practitioner, assured the 1904 Inter-Departmental Committee on Physical Deterioration that he had grown "thoroughly sick and disgusted at the want of common sense of the mothers." "After I had been working about eighteen months in the Metropolitan Dispensary," Hawkes confessed, "my one idea was to take every child as soon as it was born and put it away in a Government home of some kind."[185]

Dr. Hawkes's words were those of a eugenic militant. It is certainly true that a declining birthrate among the "productive" classes drove some social critics to propose desperate remedies, from taxing bachelors to sterilizing "degenerates."[186] But the interactions between poor mothers and apostles of hygiene were by no means as confrontational as one might assume from eugenic battle plans. We have already seen that the attention of a female health visitor sometimes brought benefits that could offset the grating traces of Lady Bountiful benevolence. More broadly, as Deborah Dwork has argued, "maternalism"—the celebration of motherhood as a woman's highest calling—was not simply a middle-class ruse designed to fetter poor women and minimize the cost of infant welfare programs.[187] Many working-class women in the prewar years seem to have been discerning consumers of maternal services, a discernment encouraged by the structure of Edwardian charity. For in 1911 no fewer than eighty "health-promoting" societies were at work on a national basis. Largely uncoordinated and often overlapping,[188] these voluntary bodies were seldom in a position to dictate childrearing terms to matriarchs of humble homes.

At least some mothers were themselves concerned about the

threat of domestic disruption posed by certain child welfare measures. The provision of subsidized midday meals in public elementary schools is a case in point. Scholars digging for the roots of the
British welfare state have made much of the 1906 Education (Provision of Meals) Act, although the number of local authorities conducting school feeding programs grew very slowly. What mattered,
the conventional wisdom holds, was the precedent that the 1906
Act set for future state aid to defenseless portions of the population.[189] Contemporaries also were alert to the larger implications of
school feeding. Its supporters, drawn from a broad political spectrum, argued that when children were too hungry to learn, the state
must intervene to reinforce rather than supplant parental responsibility. Its critics, by no means limited to Charity Organisation Society sympathizers, replied that the underlying principle of "collective
parenthood" was fatal to family integrity.[190] As for the poor themselves, the suffragist and social worker Anna Martin observed that
mothers whose children took advantage of school dinners remained
"sincerely apprehensive [about] the demoralisation of the[ir] men if
the responsibility of the children's food is lifted from the shoulders
of the fathers." Martin was a shrewd analyst of working-class mores,
shrewd enough to realize that what verbal power poor women possessed often served to conceal their true feelings from strangers, especially well-born strangers. The Southeast London mothers she
met nevertheless revealed enough to show that they had a "dread of
being superseded and dethroned": "Each of them knows perfectly
well that the strength of her position in the home lies in the physical
dependence of husband and children upon her, and she is suspicious
of anything that would tend to undermine this."[191]

The child-focused bureaucracies that in some districts grew up
around elementary schools did theoretically threaten to subvert maternal (and paternal) power. If hungry scholars had to be fed, it followed that boys and girls with myopia, hearing loss, or body lice required medical attention. Thus, although the 1907 Education (Administrative Provisions) Act did not create the post of school medical officer, this legislation did require local authorities to conduct
medical inspections of all pupils at specified intervals. The Board of

Education went on to recommend that parents should be invited to attend the first inspection of their child, a protocol designed to "avoid misunderstanding" and "disarm prejudice."[192] Unfortunately, "misunderstanding" was bound to occur when the physical defects revealed through school medical inspection were then left for the parents to treat. The cost of addressing a serious medical problem was beyond most working-class budgets, unless families sought charitable help from a voluntary hospital or swallowed what amounted to parish relief from a Poor Law medical officer. The 1908 Children Act strengthened the hand of local authorities in prosecuting parents for failing to provide their young with adequate food, clothing, shelter, or medical attention. Finally, the Local Education Authorities (Medical Treatment) Act of 1909 obliged school officials to charge the cost of any medical treatment to the parents of the child, save in those cases where it was plain that they could not pay. In combination, this legislation was England's most concerted effort yet to stimulate a sense of parental "obligation" among the masses.[193]

The mostly middle-class foes of family "overinspection" protested the willingness of magistrates to convict poor parents for neglecting their new statutory duties, and assailed the school "care committees" that had emerged to oversee pupils' welfare. On both grounds the protesters were overwrought. Some magistrates, it is true, aggressively upheld the principle of parental accountability for a child's health. The police court at Eccles, in Lancashire, for example, threatened the father of a near-sighted girl with a stiff £1 fine if he did not buy her spectacles that very day. But at least as often the magistracy frustrated public health activists either by levying token fines or by dismissing charges altogether, particularly in "cleansing" (head lice) cases.[194] Children's care committees, created to wage "warfare against [parental] ignorance and carelessness," allegedly functioned to "administer" the child and, in the process, transform school bureaucracies into "veritable harrying machines."[195] It was the London County Council that in 1907 set out to recruit members for supervisory bodies attached to each of the capital's one thousand elementary schools. Drawn from such established charities as the

Children's Country Holiday Fund, the Invalid Children's Aid Association, and the Metropolitan Association for Befriending Young Servants, these volunteers were asked to oversee the feeding and medical inspection of pupils. Discharging such duties could be onerous. A dedicated care committee member, after all, was expected not only to stay in touch with teachers and keep track of which children had received free school meals, but also to visit recipients' homes, check that prescribed medical care had been obtained, and, after 1910, cooperate with the local Juvenile Labour Exchange to steer school-leavers away from "blind alley" occupations.[196] Had all care committee volunteers been as energetic as the hyperactive Margaret Frere, who helped devise the London County Council system, or as observant as the model members described in *The School Child and Juvenile Worker*,[197] England's large towns would have gained a formidable new regiment of family police. In fact, however, as late as 1925, only nineteen local authorities outside London were using care committees as integral parts of their educational programs. And within London, the supply of qualified volunteers always fell far short of the 6,000 to 9,000 individuals deemed necessary to operate the new service efficiently.[198]

A disciplinary system is not necessarily benign because it is inefficient. Thus it would be wrong to dismiss as groundless early twentieth-century linkages between an expanding application of the *in loco parentis* argument and the reputed "disintegration" of the English working-class family. Nor should we trivialize contemporary laments over the associated "decline of liberty." When E. S. P. Haynes attacked the "collectivist contempt for human personality" that he perceived at the heart of efforts to revitalize poor parents, he had a broad legal context in mind. Haynes reckoned that the "bureaucratic inquisition" of mothers and fathers was already pernicious, but when coupled with laws which effectively denied divorce to the poor, such harassment was bound to seem downright vindictive.[199] The Mothers' Defence League, founded by the freelance journalist Ada Jones Chesterton in 1919, gave organizational form to middle-class protests against meddling with the "deepest domestic concerns of the poor." Jones Chesterton was the sister-in-law of the author and literary critic G. K. Chesterton, who became President of the League, as well as a friend of Hilaire Belloc, whose diatribe against character-warping welfare reforms, *The Servile State*, provided the League's intellectual ballast.[200] Although it never gained wide popular support, the Mothers' Defence League apparently raised eyebrows among medical officers of health after it launched a door-to-door campaign to remind poor women that they could legally bar health visitors and tuberculosis nurses from their homes. The Chesterton circle had no use for maternity and child welfare workers who believed there was such a thing as "welcome intrusion." Yet at least one physician noted the irony that through their domiciliary rounds League members were "only adding another to the many well-intentioned visits with which harassed mothers had to contend."[201]

Granting, then, that the "overinspection" of working-class parenthood was a problem well worth addressing in early twentieth-century England, it nonetheless distorts the historical record to speak of such intrusion as a disciplinary "program." The now-famous diagram that first Margaret Bondfield, and soon thereafter Douglas Pepler, used to illustrate "The Invasion of the Home" actually underscores the fragmented nature of this process (see p. 128).[202] The counsel of strangers no doubt confused, even intimidated, some poor parents, but many of these strangers were just as confused about the limits of their jurisdiction. Thus, to argue that there was in operation a "neo-hygienist strategy"[203] designed to mend both body and character is not only to overstate the coherence of upper-class aims but also to understate the degree of stratification among the poor.

Robert Roberts provides a vivid portrait of the "English proletarian caste system" that existed in Salford at the start of this century. *The Classic Slum* may be tainted as historical evidence, given its author's determination to show the urban poor as massively inert: "ignorant, unorganized, [and] schooled in humility."[204] Roberts's emphasis on the fractured form of working-class culture nevertheless remains a useful caution to those who view laboring women and men as easily manipulated. We can go further. Along with the growth

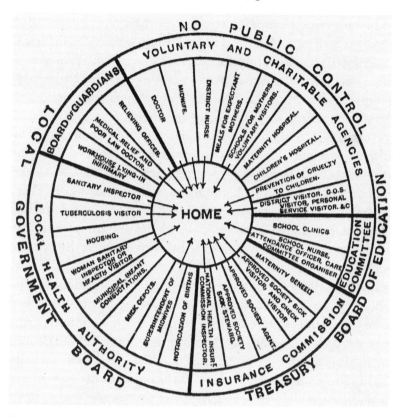

"The Invasion of the Home." From Appendix "A" of Douglas Pepler's *Justice and the Child* (1915).

of government-funded social services went an increased need for centralized administration; "bureaucracy bred rationalization," as one historian has summed up a complex and uneven development. The domesticity of the respectable poor often expressed itself as ambivalence toward the benefits of this embryonic welfare state. For they knew that "keep[ing] y'self to y'self"[205] in a home-centered world demanded vigilance against all who would encroach on their private lives.

THREE

Mental Science and the
Happy Family

I F THE NOTION of "policing" is broadened to include the prescriptions of psychology and psychiatry, then poor parents were
not alone in feeling the press of social regulation. English mothers
and fathers, we have been told, were never as cowed by the counsel
of scientific experts as their American counterparts. Geoffrey Gorer,
once acclaimed for his portraits of national character, surmised that
in the ethnic melting pot of America, partners were apt to bring different childrearing traditions to a marriage, and with them the potential for "endless clashes" over bringing up baby. To avoid domestic mayhem, Gorer explained, parents in the United States demanded expert advice. Demand created supply. Thus, mothers in
particular grew reliant on childcare professionals for both guidance
and understanding. But "[w]hatever system she may be following,
she can never have the easy, almost unconscious, self-assurance of
the mother of more patterned societies, who is following ways she
knows unquestioningly to be right." The American mother, Gorer
concluded, "is always more or less anxious, anxious lest she make
mistakes or forget part of the prescribed routine, anxious lest the
baby should not respond properly, often anxious lest she should after all have chosen the wrong [childrearing] method."[1]

In 1946, two years before this pronouncement, Benjamin Spock
published his now celebrated *Common Sense Book of Baby and Child
Care.* By the mid-1970's his manual would have gone through more
than two hundred printings and twenty million copies, making it
second only to the Bible in worldwide sales. Although Dr. Spock's

opening "Letter" to prospective parents urged them to "trust your own instincts" and therefore *seemed* to be a plea for family autonomy in an arena dominated by experts, *Baby and Child Care* has been attacked as a swindle, a therapeutic scam that feeds the "extravagant anxiety" of American parenthood precisely because it cloaks itself in "sweet positivity." That is, since Spock viewed children as naturally inquisitive, expressive, and honest, any behavioral problems that surface must by definition be the result of parental mismanagement.[2] The cult of Dr. Spock, according to Christopher Lasch, is the most obvious example of how proliferating medical and psychiatric advice "undermines parental confidence at the same time that it encourages a vastly inflated idea of the importance of child-rearing techniques."[3]

England, to be sure, produced no guru of Spock's stature, nor did an English equivalent of *Baby and Child Care* monopolize the field of childcare advice. Yet middle-class parents in this "more patterned" society also endured a barrage of expert opinion.[4] In 1938 Margaret Cole complained about "the books on baby-care which read as though they were designed to send a woman in her first pregnancy nearly out of her senses with worry." Such counsel was "paralleled by sermons on the care of the child's mind, compiled too often by persons who have had a hurried mixed meal of all the modern varieties of psychology, which set forth in detail all the ways in which a child's mind can be irretrievably ruined . . . by unwise conduct on the part of its parents."[5] The growing involvement of mental science in family matters was not a phenomenon confined to the interwar years. On the contrary, at least as far back as the 1880's medical generalists, together with specialists in the emerging disciplines of physiology, neurology, psychology, and psychiatry, were assuming ever greater importance as arbiters of household conduct. Mental science, like philanthropy, was shouldering some of the family welfare responsibilities once performed by organized religion. To the extent that they still valued theological guidance, the comfortable classes of late-Victorian England continued to heed their pastors. But just as laypersons (mostly laywomen, acting as district visitors) were coming to perform domiciliary tasks traditionally reserved for clerics, so students of the psyche were gradually gaining some recognition for their family services. Leonard Guthrie, a physician and authority on the nervous disorders of childhood, observed in 1907 that the English public had "learnt that morality is largely a question of health and temperament and environment." Hence "medical men [were] frequently called upon to advise in cases which formerly were dealt with by disciplinarians."[6]

It is clear that in England, as in America, mental health workers insinuated themselves deeply into debates about family governance. It is far from clear, however, that this process was part of a conscious professional strategy, or even that the practitioners involved were chiefly responsible for the domestic application of their research. As Janet Oppenheim has so convincingly shown, Victorian "alienists"—those who specialized in treating the insane—seldom could afford to pursue a therapeutic course that defied the wishes of their social and economic superiors.[7] This was true for England in large part because psychology and its kindred disciplines remained scientifically marginal longer there than in many Western industrial societies. Occupying as they did a comparatively low rung on the professional ladder, English experts in the science of mind found it difficult to win over a skeptical middle class. The advice these experts dispensed did make some privileged mothers and fathers more self-conscious about "parentcraft," but it would be fanciful to suppose that such advice constituted a unified "knowledge" whose aim was the subversion of parental power.

Physiological Psychology and Good Parenthood

The Victorian science of mind was shot through with uncertainty about basic mental operations. It would be tidy, and quite wrong, to suppose that nineteenth-century medicine dealt exclusively with physical illness and injury while English psychology contented itself with the diagnosis of mental defect. In fact, from the 1840's, if not earlier, medical philosophy and formal psychology were converging on a common interest in the mind-body relationship; at the same time that medicine was "moving toward holism by concerning itself with 'moral' causes, symptoms, and remedies, Victorian psychology was annexing physiology."[8] Thus, for example, such apparently distinct fields as neurology and psychiatry actually overlapped a good deal. What they shared was a preoccupation with neuroses. Although today the words *neurosis* and *neurotic* popularly suggest behavioral quirks best addressed in a therapist's office, in the middle of the nineteenth century they belonged to a huge medical category that included all diseases thought to involve the nervous system, but occurring without such visible structural changes as inflammation or lesions. Mid-Victorian neuroses encompassed most mental illnesses then known, from mania to melancholia. But neuroses also embraced poliomyletis, diabetes, and epilepsy—diseases whose physical origins, then unknown, have since been at least partially identified. So too, hysteria, hypochondriasis, and convulsions, all poorly understood, were classified as "functional nervous disorders." In 1882, the first edition of Sir Richard Quain's *Dictionary of Medicine* even listed tetanus among the neuroses.[9]

Thus, the wholesale application of the adjective *nervous* to mysterious forms of illness was a convenient way for Victorian doctors to cover holes in their medical knowledge. Yet at the same time an affliction of the nerves was one that might reveal its secret to the probing of experimental physiology. For early nineteenth-century science had taken long strides toward demystifying the human nervous system. Perhaps most importantly, Charles Bell (1774–1842), a Scots surgeon-turned-physiologist, had undermined the prevailing assumption that nerves were unitary fibers, proving instead that they consisted of bundles of filaments designed to perform different tasks. Bell's discovery (made independently in France by François Magendie) that there were separate spinal cord roots for sensory and motor functions gave weight to the notion that the properties of nerves might shape what is perceived in the mind.[10] If mind itself were an aggregation of nervous impulses, then by mapping the mind physiologists could learn much about the physical basis for thought as well as action. Although early-Victorian phrenology, with its focus on the relationship between personality and skull shape, hardly qualified as empirical science in the tradition of Bell and Magendie, it also helped promote the idea that the brain was the seat of consciousness.[11] Herbert Spencer's vague theory of cerebral localization owed much to the phrenologists. Since Spencer found "untenable" the proposition that the cerebrum was "a chaotic mass of fibres," he held that there must exist some "'physiological division of labour'" involving the "concentration of special kinds of activity in special places."[12] It fell to British neurologists, particularly John Hughlings-Jackson and David Ferrier, to prove experimentally that Spencer was right—that sensory-motor functions were indeed localized in the cerebral cortex.

By the 1870's physiological reasoning conditioned much psychological thought in England. William Carpenter's widely read *Principles of Mental Physiology* (1874) likened the brain to an open electrical circuit. Once "an Instinctive tendency, an Emotion, an Idea, or a Volition" reached an intensity sufficient to close this circuit, enough "nerve-force" would be "liberated," probably through chemical change in the ganglionic centers, to produce action.[13] Psychologists less knowledgeable about physiology than Carpenter were starting to conceive of such complex mental processes as attention and memory in terms of the "excitement," "agitation," or "vibration" of nerve cells. Certainly some English and American psychologists objected that to define mental activity as a chain of neural motions was to evade the question of how consciousness impinges on behavior. The self, in other words, remained more than the sum of its nervous parts.[14] Nevertheless, a generation after Ludwig von Helmholtz had precisely determined the rate at which impulses were transmitted through nerve fibers, it was difficult for psychologists *not* to be preoccupied with the behavior of "excitable living tissue." In fact, since nerve conductivity could now be measured, and, further, since the brain was coming to be seen as the "great central station" of the nervous system, it seemed only prudent for psychologists to begin analyzing mental health in terms of brain efficiency.[15]

"How the mind of man can be strengthened, widened, and made a more efficient instrument through the application of modern . . . physiological knowledge" therefore became a question of "intense interest" for some sections of the educated public.[16] A few scientific entrepreneurs did much to focus attention on nervous energy and the behavioral consequences of enervation. Henry Maudsley, whose early career as a medical officer in Northern lunatic asylums gave way to a prestigious and very lucrative private psychiatric practice in London, was confident that physiology, a discipline only recently "emerging from the fog" of metaphysics, would make possible a "positive science of mind." This science would show for the human nervous system what Lord Kelvin's second law of thermodynamics, propounded at mid-century, already demonstrated for the physical world: that there was a decreasing amount of usable energy in the universe. Among persons who had inherited a "tendency to disease" and consequently had "little vitality to spare," Maudsley warned, any added psychic demands threatened to release the "enemy that was lurking [with]in."[17] Still more self-promoting than Maudsley was James Crichton-Browne, another alienist whose professional ambition could not be contained within madhouse walls. Unlike Maudsley, Crichton-Browne was well versed in practical physiology, not only turning the West Riding Lunatic Asylum into a neurological laboratory but also launching his own postmortem study of brain tissue in patients afflicted with general paralysis.[18] Partly because he owned these experimental credentials, Crichton-Browne spoke with authority on the dangers of nervous exhaustion.

But it was James Sully (1843–1923), a psychologist with little training in physiology and none at all in medicine, who popularized the view that conscientious parenthood requires a basic familiarity with the laws of mental science. Sully's forte was synthesis rather than original research. His early publications, from the critique of German philosophy contained in *Pessimism* (1877) to the article on "Evolution" written for the ninth edition of the *Encyclopedia Britannica*, did not earn enough scholarly notice to propel him into academia.[19] By 1881 Sully was running out of professional options. Having recently failed in three competitions for university chairs, suddenly without a family allowance after his father went bankrupt, and now himself a parent for the second time, Sully decided to try his hand at the "hack-work" of writing textbooks. Since a popular summary of his field seemed to be needed, he set to work on what became *Outlines of Psychology* (1884). Due largely to his time spent studying the physiological research of Wilhelm Wundt in Germany during the early 1870's, Sully had already decided that a conceptual middle-ground was essential, a science of mind "as free from the almost puerile ... dogmatism of the materialists as from the prepossessions of the transcendental psychologists."[20] Not surprisingly, therefore, *Outlines of Psychology* was notable above all for its view of education as the "cultivation of sympathy" rather than brute memorization. Although Sully did not offer enough neurological analysis of fatigue to satisfy some experimentalists,[21] his first attempt at psychological synthesis nevertheless had the good fortune to appear just as a wave of public concern with educational "overpressure" was cresting.

Victorian doctors and psychologists had long warned that children in particular were prone to nervous exhaustion. Young bodies already taxed by the normal demands of growth had to be shielded from any activity that produced lasting fatigue. Since the nervous energy available to a child was thought to be finite, and because all developing organs needed a share of this precious fuel, good parents would monitor the stimuli reaching their sons and daughters. Alexander Bain, Professor of Logic and Mental Philosophy at Aberdeen, emphasized this balancing act in 1879:

To increase the plastic property of the mind, you must nourish the brain. You naturally expect that this result will ensue when the body generally is nourished: and so it will, if there be no exorbitant demands on the part of other organs, giving them such a preference as to leave very little for the organ of the mind. If the muscles of the digestion are unduly drawn upon, the brain will not respond to the drafts made upon it. Obversely, if the brain is constituted by nature, or excited by stimulation, so as to absorb the lion's share of the nutriment, the opposite results will appear; the mental functions will be exalted, and the other interests more or less impoverished.[22]

Often fully occupied with the demands of family survival, poor parents could ill afford to worry about translating the ideal of *mens sana in copore sano* into reality for their young.[23] Flora Thompson observed about the hardscrabble life in her childhood hamlet of

Lark Rise that its residents took no notice of the new psychiatric concerns. "Though food was rough and teeth were neglected," she recalled, "indigestion was unknown, while nervous troubles . . . had yet to be invented."[24] But among the comfortable classes of urban England, the risks of ignoring physiological wisdom seemed clearer than ever by the last quarter of the century. Doctors routinely scanned middle-class children for what contemporary medicine took to be the warning signs of nervous disorder: insomnia, nightmares, somnambulism, headaches, stammering, and daydreaming. Chronic headaches or, for that matter, such subtle associated symptoms as heaviness under the eyelids, twitching fingers, tooth-grinding, and drooping wrists (the "nervous hand") could be cause for grave parental concern.[25] Fragile because incomplete, a child's nervous system was both more "plastic" than an adult's, allowing the former to learn more easily, and subject to permanent harm from the "sudden derangement of nerve molecules" that could accompany minor frights. The stakes for parents, nurses, and teachers were high. According to William Preyer's influential *The Mind of the Child* (1882), all those charged with educating the young should understand that even a toddler with its weak will required "exercises" in obedience. Yet attempts to rein in an obstinate child could play havoc with its personality development, as well as its nervous system. Sully agreed that the power of discrimination was central to the proper growth of both character and mind, and consequently urged educators to rely on the "stimulus of change and novelty" as a pleasant means to this end. Parents and teachers often made "great," possibly "irreparable" mistakes when they punished what appeared to be childish willfulness. Far more often than not this presumed willfulness was merely a manifestation "of the *want* of Volitional control over the automatic activity of the Brain."[26]

What Denise Riley has described as the "ethical" thrust of physiological psychology[27] comes clearly into focus when we consider how mental science was harnessed to the cause of character formation. Middle-class parents in the late-Victorian period were obviously not the first to fret about moral development in their offspring. It is noteworthy that an advertisement for "spiritual science" appearing on *The Times*'s front page in 1853 gave top billing to just this concern:

PHRENOLOGY and SPIRITUAL SCIENCE

—A SEANCE every Wednesday, at 3 p.m. Consultations daily on the formation of character in children, deformities and imperfections of the brain, on all cerebral and nervous affections. Wonderful discernment of the cure of diseases.

—Phrenological College, 67, opposite the British Museum.[28]

Some mid-Victorian readers of skulls and auras joined the most influential psychologists and physiologists of the day—Bain, Spencer, Carpenter, and Maudsley—in suggesting that habit could leave a behavioral trace in the nervous system. Employing a watered-down Lamarckian notion of biological change, these experts helped popularize the view that by properly flexing the muscles of the will, a child might be able to build moral "force" and, under certain circumstances, pass on this acquired trait to its progeny. Alexander Bain's *On the Study of Character* (1861) drew the parallel between a generous reserve of "spontaneous energy" and a greater capacity for "Endurance, Patience, Courage, and Self-Reliance."[29]

Building on this work, Sully and other late-Victorian psychologists made much of character's contingent quality. That is, in addition to an individual's innate constitution, "every difference in external surroundings, family life, school discipline, profession, &c., serves to modify the character by developing certain special traits." By the end of the century, English mental science had reconceived character formation as an aspect of the physiology of habit, although some authorities, such as Dr. Alfred T. Schofield, urged that the study of character ("ethology") be accepted as a scientific subspecialty unto itself.[30]

With the moral as well as physical health of England's next generation hanging in the balance, it was natural that allegations of educational overpressure would disturb polite society in the mid-1880's. That worry and fatigue occupied the psychic center stage in a culture obsessed with the struggle for survival and fear of economic ruin is plain from such major novels as *Mary Barton, Bleak*

House, and *Hard Times*. The sheer speed of life in the world's first industrial nation—what Hughes termed "these racing railroad times" in *Tom Brown's School Days*—struck one social critic as the main reason why coronary disease had increased between 1851 and 1870.[31] By the late-Victorian years some medical guides were giving special attention to the diseases of overwork. The category "occupational neuroses" (adapted from the German *Beschaftigungsneurosen*) was now being used to denote the muscular spasm ("cramp") associated with excessive repetition in tasks as diverse as writing, sewing, and pianoforte-playing. Overwork in adults could produce full-blown dementia when accompanied by "deficiency of rest, by too absorbing singleness of thought on one topic, by too furious an enthusiasm," or when labor "enforces persistent urgency."[32] Where these pressures were brought to bear on schoolchildren, "disastrous consequences must result," Spencer cautioned in 1860. "Brain forcing" was a hallmark of much formal education, according to opponents of trial-by-examination, but it was at the elementary school level that the congestion of young minds seemed most dangerous. In 1879, the Russian psychologist I. A. Sikorskii became the first to study mental fatigue over the course of the school day. Shortly thereafter the German doctor Treichler voiced his concern about chronic headache and brain exhaustion in the Prussian state schools, an elementary system with many English admirers.[33]

If scholastic overpressure was an international concern, it found special resonance in England due to the confluence of two forces. Those opposed to the prevailing system of "payment by results" were keen to attack an educational bureaucracy that pushed often ill-nourished children through cramming sessions in the classroom and then piled on two or three more hours of home study each evening. By no means all these critics gave first thought to the working-class child hunched "with flushed and throbbing brow over book and slate" far into the night. Some were more worried about the professional status of elementary school teachers. Still others, sitting on the Anglican voluntarist right wing of the Tory party, had no use for state-sponsored education of any kind.[34] When such lay criticism received validation from the medical establishment, however, the resulting din summoned James Crichton-Browne into the fray as a supposedly impartial judge.

Crichton-Browne, having left his position as Director of the West Riding Asylum to become the Lord Chancellor's Medical Visitor in Lunacy at the end of 1875, now tackled a problem about which *The Lancet* and the *British Medical Journal* had already made up their minds. Cramming for standard examinations, along with home lessons for children under ten, seemed capable of inducing epilepsy, chorea, and other nervous afflictions, even though hard evidence for these suspicions was as yet lacking.[35] Much to the disappointment of some doctors, Crichton-Browne's round of visits to fourteen London elementary schools in March 1884 produced nothing of statistical value. On the contrary, his decision to inspect Board schools clustered together in slum-ridden Walworth killed any claim to representativeness that his subsequent report might have made. Just as troubling was Crichton-Browne's lame methodology. His finding that 46.1 percent of London's elementary schoolchildren suffered from "habitual headaches," for example, rested on a series of offhand pupil interviews. As for home study, "The fact that a large proportion of young children in London are now poring over books, racking their brains, straining their eyes, and rounding their backs, in the evening hours when they ought to be in bed, . . . is, I venture to think, a palpable evidence that overpressure exists."[36]

Grossly partisan, Crichton-Browne's Report to the Board of Education offered an easy target for the champions of compulsory education. Moreover, a parliamentary analysis of twenty-two overpressure cases, published in early 1885, proved that nearly all the stricken students had fallen ill or died from causes unrelated to their schoolwork.[37] Yet to a middle-class public increasingly prone to think of the young body as a fragile vessel, Crichton-Browne's concluding recommendation that teachers be taught physiology only reinforced the idea that good intentions alone were not enough to secure health and happiness in children. As Dr. Francis Warner put it in a series of lectures delivered to the Froebel Society, neither teacher nor parent could trust "simply to what is called intuitive knowledge." Instead, Warner argued, boys and girls should be sys-

OVER-PRESSURE.

School-Board Fogey. "I'M SORRY TO HEAR YOUR LITTLE BOY IS SO ILL, MRS. BROWN,—
AND HE WAS GETTING ON SO WELL AT THE SCHOOL! I MET THE DOCTOR, AND HE TOLD ME
IT IS 'PERITONITIS'!"

Mrs. B. (gloomily). "OH NO, SIR. TOMMY'S VERY ILL, SIR, SURE-LY; BUT I DON'T THINK
IT'S 'PELLY—PELLYTUM'——NO, IT AIN'T THAT, SIR; 'CAUSE, THOUGH HE WAS SO FORWARD,
HE COULDN'T SPELL WORDS O' MORE THAN TWO SYLLABLES, SIR!!"

England in the mid-1880's saw sharp disagreement over charges that compulsory
elementary education was damaging young brains. *Punch* (Oct. 25, 1884) was
skeptical about this "overpressure" panic.

tematically examined for physical defects, especially around the head, because by the "law of coincident development" a defective physiognomy provided the best clue to a defective brain.[38] Shortly after issuing this challenge, Warner launched a three-year study of 50,000 schoolchildren. Underwritten by an improbable troika of the British Medical Association, the Charity Organisation Society, and the British Association for the Advancement of Science, his survey represented England's last major exercise in craniometry and its first large-scale attempt to identify what Warner termed the "worst made" pupils.[39]

Mental science agreed, of course, that the scrutiny of young bodies and minds should not be limited to the schoolroom. Beginning in 1884, London parents could have their sons' and daughters' physical "powers" measured for threepence per child at Francis Galton's Anthropometric Laboratory in South Kensington. A graver duty was the watch that parents, teachers, neighbors, and doctors had to keep over depressed children, for the late 1880's and early 1890's saw what appeared to be a rise in the incidence of suicide among the young. The Registrar-General's statistics would later show that the persons most apt to take their own lives were actually men in their fifties or sixties. Nonetheless, a stew of social concern combining scholastic strain, corporal punishment, and the pressure of parental expectations fed a greater willingness to heed experts in the emerging field of child-study.[40]

Child-study or "paidology," as an American psychologist first termed it in 1893, has often been viewed as a discourse whose admonitory weight fell mainly on mothers. The "sacralization" of child life that Viviana Zelizer and Carolyn Steedman chart in Anglo-American society between 1870 and 1930[41] surely did heap new responsibilities on already full maternal plates. When Spencer scolded parents for "over-legislation in the nursery," by which he meant a slavish adherence to childrearing fashion ("French caprice" being the most "monstrous") rather than to the physiological needs of individual children, he obviously had mothers in mind. A generation later Wilhelm Preyer implored mothers to heed the "complicated" science of "psychogenesis," the study of mental development. There was, after all, a fine but crucial balance to be struck between concentrating the young brain and allowing it to lose power through "dissipation."[42] Mothers stood morally responsible for nurturing what, before the dissemination of Freudian theory, were already being called "unconscious faculties." "Probably the only reason" why a child's distinctive "faculties" did not blossom into practical talent was because its mother had not discovered and cultivated them during infancy. At the same time, experts cautioned, such cultivation must not lapse into neurotic anxiety lest the child grow emotionally brittle.[43]

The impossible demands implicit—sometimes explicit—in these warnings did not exhaust the prescriptions of child-study. Quite apart from the abundant late-Victorian advice literature on parenthood that ignored science as a sanctioning authority,[44] there was emerging a redefined notion of the paternal realm. Most of the works usually credited with legitimizing child-study as an academic field were in fact products of fathers observing their own offspring. Taine's "Note on the Acquisition of Language"(1876), Darwin's "A Biographical Sketch of an Infant"(1877), and Preyer's *Die Seele des Kindes* (1882) all used the authors' young sons as experimental subjects in home laboratories. However halting these steps toward domestic science may seem today (Darwin, for example, decided that "a tendency to throw objects is inherited by boys"), they inspired imitation, particularly in England.[45] More than anyone else it was James Sully who popularized child-study as a mix of amusement and sober necessity for middle-class parents of both sexes. Sully's first essay on this theme, "Babies and Science," was an awkward parody of childrearing stereotypes in the bourgeois home. Here, "science," engendered as "she," vindicates mothers and nannies by "redeeming the whole class of babies from the charge of being perfectly useless encumbrances." The interpenetration of biology and physiology, Sully wrote, was gradually converting "male scoffers" into "psychological papa[s]." Wielding the idea of cultural recapitulation, Sully explained why several of his married male acquaintances had so eagerly embraced child-study:

It is a doctrine of biology that the development of the individual roughly epitomises that of the race; that is to say, the study of infant life may be well fitted to suggest by what steps of intellectual and moral progress our race has passed into its present state. The attentive eye may thus find in seemingly meaningless little infantile ways hints of remote habits and customs of the human race.

Science having thus declared the infant to be a valuable phenomenon for observation, there has of late grown up among the class of scientific fathers the habit of noting and recording the various proceedings of the infant. Men who previously never thought of meddling with the affairs of the nursery have been impelled to make periodic visits thither in the hope of eliciting important psychological facts.[46]

Sully's initial discussion of child-study aimed to entertain. Soon, though, he began portraying this fashion as serious business. For the systematic observation of young children promised not only to shed light on human evolution but also to help breed an improved English race. The mid-1880's saw Sully speculating that the "babblings of infancy" might hold the key to understanding the relationship between speech and thought. This proposition would have seemed no more far-fetched than the idea, advanced seven years later, that the similar grip strength of apes and human infants revealed a common ancestry: baby behavior, if properly analyzed, could fill in the "gap between embryology and anthropology."[47] Even if such mysteries did not vanish under the glare of scientific parenthood, Sully reasoned, middle-class fathers and mothers should stay vigilant for signs of precocity in their offspring. True genius, as Galton had shown, tended to manifest itself early in life, and keep on blooming. But the merely clever child was "like a tree that bears fruit too soon." It therefore behooved parents to regulate precocity, for in the absence of regulation their clever young might suffer brain exhaustion and lapse into a prolonged period of "mediocrity."[48] No English psychologist of the period could match I. A. Sikorskii, Professor of Psychic and Nervous Diseases at the University of Kiev, for sheer alarmism over mental development in babies. According to Sikorskii, since an infant's "still tender, semi-liquid brain" could be damaged by tears and crying, it followed that the baby must be spared "all disagreeable impressions."[49] Home-grown experts on physiological psychology nevertheless issued stern warnings of their own on everything from a young child's diet (often lacking in brain-building fat) to its theological training (often far too complex).[50]

James Sully, who in 1892 finally found academic security when he became Grote Professor of Psychology and Philosophy at University College, London, contributed mightily to this avalanche of advice. Having suffered a nervous breakdown during his late twenties, Sully was personally committed to helping parents recognize the signs of mental fatigue in their offspring. No wonder that he preferred to err on the side of caution: better to risk worrying parents about their childrearing skills than allow the young to become psychic invalids. Thus Sully did not hesitate to advise on the "art-impulse" of children, or on their appetite for chasing animals, asking questions, and telling stories.[51] This commitment to applied science also expressed itself in his founding of Britain's first laboratory devoted exclusively to psychology. Seeking to extend Galton's anthropometric research, Sully obtained testing equipment from Germany, moral support from scientific and political luminaries, and space from University College. Teachers especially were encouraged to bring their "difficult" pupils to the laboratory for assessment. As his course syllabi showed, Sully viewed "Paedagogy" as a "regulative" field, an enterprise that had "the practical function of *guiding* action." On the strength of both word and deed, therefore, Sully deserves credit as one of the nation's pioneers in child guidance work.[52]

Although Sully conceded that nature typically trumped nurture in child development, he held out hope that, through assiduous study, parents could gain enough scientific insight to approach "perfection" in the moral training of their young. The most conscientious mothers and fathers would supplement parental instinct with the lessons of psychology.[53] Becoming "qualified" in child-study demanded much, however. Mothers, whose "acknowledged superiority in knowledge of child-nature" derived from their "higher gift of sympathetic insight," were essential participants. But because the average middle-class mother was supposedly too caught up in "baby

worship" to conduct a "cool and impartial process of scientific observation," Sully urged that the "coarser-fibred" father take charge of
the "experimental" tasks of recording an infant's gestures, sounds,
and mental progress.[54] Clearly, if such study of the child seemed
new, its recommended division of labor within the home remained
profoundly traditional. Some social scientists, especially in North
America, bridled at the suggestion that anyone other than neurologists and psychologists might make child-study genuinely experimental.[55] In England, though, James Sully's prominence within the
field of what later would be called child psychology went far toward
insuring that this emerging specialty would welcome middle-class
amateurs.[56]

Naturally, Sully's prose was far from the only force behind organized child-study. In 1894, several English and Scottish teachers,
much impressed with the ideas of the American psychologist G.
Stanley Hall, established the British Child Study Association. Its organ, *The Paidologist*, soon offered parents as well as educators insight
into child nature based on "systematic observation." By 1899 the
BCSA could claim over six hundred members, of whom Sully exercised the greatest influence on day-to-day business.[57] More medical in
focus was the Childhood Society, founded in 1896. Sir Douglas
Galton, an expert in hospital construction and kinsman of the great
eugenicist, served as the Childhood Society's first president, aptly
personifying that group's dual concern with the hygienic and ge-
netic welfare of the next generation. Eventually, in 1907, these two
organizations merged to form the Child Study Society. The ubiquitous James Crichton-Browne would later become its head.[58]

Discussions of observational child psychology in Edwardian England have emphasized its fissiparous path. So long as we limit our
analysis to credentialed specialists, it makes sense to chart the early-
twentieth-century splintering of this general field into such subspe-
cialties as pediatrics, anthropometrics, and psychoanalysis. It is true
as well, from the professional perspective, that the locus of child
psychology gradually shifted from home to school, a reorientation
premised on the growing belief that classrooms offered the most
promising site for reclaiming "nervous" and "defective" children.[59]

But largely hidden from history has been the work of well-read amateurs whose aim was just the opposite: to keep parents at the center of primary education. It was principally through their exertions that physiological psychology continued to paint middle-class parenthood as a "profession" rather than a mere condition.

The Parents' National Education Union

The extent to which child-study actually changed parental conduct is difficult to judge. Granted, by the start of the new century few steeped in the literature of applied psychology would have found amusing the mythical Victorian mother who instructed her nanny to find out what the children were doing and tell them to stop. Even if we accept the assertion that child-study prompted "thousands" of parents to keep detailed diaries of their children's behavior, a project that "greatly enhanced the self-confidence" of middle-class mothers and fathers,[60] we cannot easily deduce parental behavior from pedagogical chic. We can, however, show that the childrearing admonitions of Sully, Preyer, and Hall were folded into new schemes for early childhood education. Although these schemes varied widely in their curricular preferences, they shared the goal of promoting unforced, "natural" learning. Since the pace at which children acquired knowledge was to be dictated by individual tastes and curiosities, the learning environments within which children might thrive demanded an unprecedented degree of self-consciousness on the part of their parents. It was the Parents' National Education Union, organized in 1887 by a formidable headmistress named Charlotte Mason, which best argued the case that only through "strenuous incessant effort" could mothers and fathers hope to produce fully formed human beings.[61] As one critic complained, the recently established PNEU seemed to have as its "remorseless purpose" the articulation of a "revised code for parents." At least to some contemporaries, Miss Mason and her small but dedicated band of home education reformers appeared to be more menacing than most zealots afloat on a "tide of meddling" because the PNEU dissected private family affairs with the "probe of the surgeon."[62]

Charlotte Mason and those who gravitated to her made plain their intellectual debt to such foreign reformers as Pestalozzi and Froebel. Johann Heinrich Pestalozzi (1746–1827) had won only modest recognition as a philosopher but lasting fame as the oracle of a pedagogy that encouraged children to discover all they could through their own senses. When this Swiss educator urged "teach by THINGS," he meant that instructional methods and materials should be based on a hierarchy of sense experiences, and that through "object lessons" the young might naturally progress from observation to verbalization. Although "Father Pestalozzi" had set out to transform the education of poor children, failing health and falling income drove him to establish experimental schools, first at Burgdorf and later at Yverdon, near Lake Geneva, that attracted mostly well-off pupils and many adult observers.[63] The latter included several key figures in debates over British elementary education—Robert Owen, Andrew Bell, Lord Brougham, Maria Edgeworth—as well as some less prominent reformers who tried to replicate the Yverdon experiment. The few Pestalozzian schools established in southern England endured less than a generation.[64] But the notion that parents and teachers were guides, needed above all to encourage the young child's exploration of its surroundings, lived on, institutionalized in the curriculum of several teacher training colleges. Although Pestalozzi's tendency to divide up mental faculties with "the precision of a phrenologist" struck PNEU members as artificial, they nonetheless admired the way he had applied observational psychology to the learning process.[65]

The pedagogy of Friedrich Froebel (1782–1852) made a deeper dent in English educational practice. After visiting Pestalozzi's school at Yverdon in 1807, Froebel, then a young German tutor, threw himself into the task of redesigning learning environments. *The Education of Man* (1826), his first book, depicted humans as biological organisms for which education should provide mainly nourishment and freedom. Froebel's idea of the "mother-made-conscious" assumed that maternal instinct was necessary yet insufficient to "quicken" the "natural powers" of the young organism: a sense of purpose, added to instinct, would produce the best teacher.[66] It was

of course as the champion of enlightened infant teaching that Froebel's name became widely known. His advocacy of "child gardens"
in which the young would devote themselves to the touching and
handling of "expression work" gave rise to the founding of kindergartens throughout Western Europe and North America.

The first kindergarten teachers in England were liberal-minded
German emigrants whose numbers rose when reactionary governments gained control of many German states after the failed revolu-
tions of 1848. Soon, however, the cause won powerful advocates in
Charles Dickens and businessmen from the Montefiore and Rothschild clans, as well as the Home and Colonial Infant School Society, which in 1857 began training both governesses and elementary
teachers along Froebelian lines. Although the Froebel Society,
founded in 1874, would remain a middle-class body, kindergartens
organized as charities for the inner-city poor started to appear in the
1860's. Well before the Board of Education formally adopted "kindergarten" as an activity for pupils aged seven years and under in
1892, schools in several areas began to feature Froebelian "play" in
their classrooms. That groups of sixty or more children, trapped behind rigid desks, were now performing in unison exercises with
wooden blocks, beads, or sticks hardly thrilled kindergarten purists.
For teachers increasingly sensitive to charges of classroom overpressure, on the other hand, such "play" may have served to blunt accu-
sations of Board school tyranny.[67]

Flawed execution of kindergarten techniques aside, the Froebelian critique of mother-love helped amplify demands for a profes-
sionalization of parenthood. At its most insistent, this critique jux-
taposed the knowledge that came from close study of the kindergarten system with the "incompetent" middle-class mother whose ignorance of Froebelian precepts threatened personality development in
the young, and, by extension, the vigor of the race. The "Indulgent
Mother," the "Nervous Mother," the "Adoring Mother," even the
"Self-sacrificing Mother" (who tended to absolve her children of responsibility): maternal incompetence assumed many forms.[68] All
posed a threat to family, nation, and Empire. Less condemnatory,
and more common, was the view that Froebel's writing contained

the keys to proper parental "regulation" of home life. As Emily Shirreff, President of the Froebel Society, put it in 1884, "the due discharge of parental duty" hinged on the study of education.[69] The task of extracting "the Divine" from one's child was daunting, while the resources of the Froebel Society—whose 561 subscribers contributed a modest £182 in 1899—were not.[70] Still, kindergartens for privileged youngsters had become, as the Mothers' Union grumbled, a "fashion" in *fin-de-siècle* England. The headmaster and the school inspector could applaud this trend. For given Froebel's emphasis on the imitative power of little children, it followed that "hasty, careless, unobservant, slovenly, [or] hot-tempered" parents would reproduce these traits in small mimics. T. G. Rooper, an Inspector of Schools since 1877 and an early mainstay of the PNEU, was among those who saw Froebelian "philosophy" as a crucial corrective to parental "common sense."[71]

But Rooper did not control the Parents' National Education Union. Charlotte Mason did, and in her view neither Froebel nor Pestalozzi had given full consideration to "Psychology illuminated by Physiology." Mason's interest lay in harnessing mental science to the refinement of character. As she explained in an early editorial of her *Parents' Review*:

It is the study of that border-land betwixt mind and matter, the brain, which yields the richest results to the educator. For the brain is the seat of habit: the culture of habit is, to a certain extent, physical culture: the discipline of habits is at least a third part of the great whole which we call education, and here we feel that the physical science of to-day has placed us far in advance of the great philosopher[s] of fifty years ago. . . . Character is the result not merely of the great ideas which are given to us, but of the habits which we labour to form *upon those ideas*.[72]

In Miss Mason's hands the PNEU soon emerged as the nation's oracle of a physiology of character whose testing ground was the middle-class home.

It was in fact the perceived defects of home education that brought Charlotte Mason to public notice. Mason was born in 1842, the only child in a Liverpool merchant family. A sheltered

Charlotte Mason in 1864, at the age of twenty-two. Over the next half-century the reclusive Miss Mason would teach a moral physiology whose influence spread well beyond her Parents' National Education Union. Courtesy: Essex Cholmondeley, *The Story of Charlotte Mason* (J. M. Dent & Sons, 1960).

childhood filled with books ended suddenly at age sixteen when her mother died, followed soon thereafter by her father's financial ruin and death. Nearly destitute and lacking even distant relatives, Charlotte lived with friends until, at eighteen, she became a student at the Home and Colonial Training College for teachers in Anglican infant schools. Friendships formed there led to positions first as mistress at a Church-sponsored school in Sussex, and later as lecturer in education and human physiology at Bishop Otter College, Chichester, another of the few institutions where young, middle-class women could then receive anything like coherent preparation for elementary teaching careers. From Chichester, Mason moved north to Bradford in 1877, where she managed to split her time between teaching the young and tramping the countryside collecting material for her first book, a geography of the English shires. Five more years in Bradford found Mason adding volunteer work as a district visitor to her teaching and writing. But above all what preoccupied her during the early eighties was the belief that well-to-do parents needed training in the science of child management. The product of this conviction was a course of lectures delivered to Bradford ladies on "Home Education" in 1885. One year later these lectures were published together under the same title.[73]

Home Education offered a staunch defense of the separate-spheres argument. Mason held that in an age when a desire for professional recognition was spreading among educated women, the job of motherhood remained preeminent: "there is no promotion, no dignity, to compare with it." Indeed, maternal duties, particularly in connection with children under eight, demanded every bit as much "diligence, regularity, and punctuality [as] men bestow on their professional labours."[74] Yet at the same time Mason made it clear that within her natural sphere, the middle-class mother was free neither to treat her young as personal property nor to seek refuge in ossified "systems" and "methods" of education. Although she agreed with Pestalozzi that it was vital to demand of mothers "a *thinking* love," when thinking became mired in pedagogical shibboleths it acquired a woodenness apt to do more harm than good.

Mason knew her audience. The ladies she addressed were not about to sack their nannies and governesses. At the very least, however, the privileged mother should give her children her "freshest, brightest hours," while remaining ever alert lest "coarseness" in the hired help offend sensitive eyes and ears. Most importantly, mothers and fathers alike were morally obliged to obey "natural law," a behavioral code grounded as much in neurology as in the Bible. "[I]n nine cases our of ten," Mason maintained, "sensible good parents

trust too much to their common sense and their good intentions."[75]
Such an assertion came easily to one whose original aim had been to
publicize the educational implications of William Carpenter's *Mental Physiology*. Mason argued that study of the child brain was "not a
matter for the physiologist alone, but for every mother and father of
a family." Through such study parents could glimpse the scientific
truth underlying educators' demands for clean air, regular outdoor
exercise, and a controlled mix of mental stimulation and rest. Moreover, just as chronic mumbling in the child could produce hopeless
elocution in the adult, so moral habits could "make their mark on
. . . physical tissue" and thereby fix character. Like the physiological
psychologists she read so avidly, Charlotte Mason would not deny
the influence of heredity. But she (and they) could contend that,
"Habit may supplant Nature"—provided, again, that parents kept
constant watch over their young.[76]

Miss Mason set out during the autumn of 1887 to promote precisely this degree of domestic vigilance by organizing a "Parents'
Education Union" in Bradford. Mason's reform priorities were very
different from those of another, somewhat younger woman also
committed to educational change in late-Victorian Bradford, Margaret McMillan. McMillan's fame as the pioneer of nursery school instruction for slum children is well deserved, although the congruence between her socialism and her educational activism long remained vague.[77] Her involvement in Independent Labour Party politics and subsequent agitation for publicly financed school medical
clinics contrasts sharply with Mason's Tory-Anglican sympathies
and focus on childrearing in privileged households. Still, through
conviction as well as circumstance Charlotte Mason had much in
common with the better-remembered Margaret McMillan. Meager
family incomes forced both to carve out careers for themselves.
Both remained single and childless yet became champions of enriched childhood. Mason shared McMillan's belief that joy in learning required not only an aesthetically pleasing curriculum but also
small bodies strong enough to savor beauty.[78] Finally, both women
held that, as McMillan put it, "something more than parental love
and 'parental responsibility' are wanted" in educating the young.

For McMillan, this "something more" was the nursery school, a haven of health and harmony amidst the mean streets of urban England.[79] For Mason, the essential addition to home education was physiological understanding on the part of parents.

The organizational expression of Miss Mason's goals began as a local Bradford "parliament of parents" that met in one-day sessions to discuss the trials of child management. Formal papers were read so that "some half-dozen physiological and psychological truths" could be applied to such questions as, "How would you deal with a greedy or a sullen child, or a child with a too active brain?" Admission to these early Parents' Education Union meetings was designed to be "easy, but not too easy": nomination by two existing Union members was required, as was payment of an annual five-shilling fee to cover printing costs. A separate "artisan section" of the Union was established. The few members of this auxiliary group gathered in schoolrooms or at mothers' meetings, paid no fees, and heard lectures on childrearing geared to people "whose lot is cast within narrower lines."[80] Unlike many earlier advocates of home education, the PEU did not concern itself with offering an alternative to the brutal atmosphere of some boys' boarding schools. Nor did Mason's group share the National Home Reading Union's fixation with fighting impure literature, although both bodies certainly sought to raise the "intellectual tone" of households and to resist those "centrifugal forces of society" that threatened to pull apart the family unit.[81]

Whether to enlarge the Union's field of action became the key question of 1889. To answer it, Mason polled several leaders in education, science, and the Anglican establishment. The advice she received from two of these in particular convinced her that the Union should be moved to London and reorganized on a national footing. James Sully offered warm support. Just as encouraging to Miss Mason was the keen interest shown by Anne Jemima Clough, the first Principal of Newnham College, Cambridge. Before embarking on the campaign for women's higher education, Clough had spent ten years running a school for local children at Ambleside, a picturesque town in the heart of the Lake District. Mason admired Clough's work at Ambleside. It was Clough's former school, in fact, to which Mason went when she left Bradford and near which she built the Union's training college for governesses, the House of Education, in 1892.[82] Encouragement from such experts fostered optimism among a still small band of believers. By 1890 the *Parents' Review*, a monthly packed with distillations of physiological, psychological, and pedagogical theory, was being sold at six pence per copy. Nothing less than a transformation of the idea of home appeared possible. That "feeling we express in saying, 'The Englishman's house is his castle'" now seemed "a mere relic of . . . our barbarian days." The PNEU would lead English parents to realize that happy homes could only be the product of shared scientific research and personal experience.[83]

The size of the PNEU never matched its ambition. By the late 1890's its membership had passed two thousand, while the *Parents' Review* was serving a monthly subscribership of 2,300. Thereafter the Union grew very slowly, and then generally in towns where Church of England clergy actively participated. The PNEU's list of officers and Council members featured an impressive blend of aristocrats, Anglican bishops, Oxbridge college masters, and physicians (Sir James Crichton-Browne and Dr. Alfred Schofield being most prominent among the medical men). Although the ladies who tended to direct its branch activities no doubt drew other genteel women into the PNEU fold, these local leaders could also be liabilities. Lady Isabel Margesson, for example, treated London's Belgravia Branch as a fiefdom. When the Council refused to accept her demand that the PNEU define its pedagogical kinship with Pestalozzi, Froebel, and Spencer, one of the Union's most active centers was torn apart.[84] Too earnest to be fashionable, Miss Mason nevertheless remained firmly in control of the body she had formed.

It would be wrong, however, to measure the PNEU's influence solely in terms of size. Its House of Education at Ambleside soon became a magnet for gentlewomen seeking formal training as governesses. The physiology, foreign languages, and handicrafts offered there turned out the only professional governesses in England, and its graduates could expect starting annual salaries as high as £100.[85]

Scholars have given due consideration to the "widening sphere" of female work that marked the late-Victorian era. Employment as a nurse, clerk, typist, or teacher, Deborah Gorham explains, offered middle-class women "more money, status, and security than the older occupations of governess, companion, or needleworker."[86] It is worth adding that, in PNEU hands, the liminal role of governess was itself widening into a more rigorous—and valued—vocation. Lord Baden-Powell would later recall that a governess "imported from Miss Charlotte Mason's training college at Ambleside" had opened his eyes to the possibility of inculcating powers of "observation and deduction" in young males. "From this acorn" the Boy Scout movement grew.[87]

Still better known was the Union's correspondence school. Launched in 1892, it sought to provide "standardisation and rigor" for children of the "professional class," especially girls, who received much of their education at home. Along with an annual five-guinea fee, interested parents sent to PNEU headquarters profiles of each child's health, mental "powers," and general "tastes." In return, these parents obtained a learning schedule tailored to the individual student. "Brisk work and ample leisure" were the watchwords of this early version of the virtual classroom. To insure that overpressure did not damage young nerves, children under six were excluded from the "Home School," and all work not completed in the specified time was left undone. Otherwise the curriculum was demanding, with all students asked to tackle thirteen subjects through what Miss Mason termed the process of "narration." This involved reading a long passage from a book on the syllabus, "talk about it a little, avoid explanation, and then let [the student] narrate what has been read." At the end of each term PNEU headquarters mailed out, and later marked the answers to, exam questions for each of the books read.[88] Such a procedure, Mason declared, served to delight the imagination while it sharpened intellect and built character.

It was the PNEU's physiological analysis of character that best reflected, and reinforced, prevailing middle-class notions of personality development. District nurse Margaret Loane, in an assessment that rings truer of the Edwardian "haves" than of the "have nots," wrote that, "In nothing is the fatalism of the uneducated poor more strongly shown than in the way in which they accept their children's qualities and defects as innate and unalterable, and refuse to allow proper weight to circumstances and training." By contrast, Loane believed, "Middle-class parents are apt to run to the opposite extreme, and think that their children can all be shaped according to the exact type of character that they happen to admire."[89] Certainly Mason and her PNEU agreed that "character" was contingent, and dismissed out of hand the suggestion that character formation did not begin before age seven.[90] If, as the Union accepted axiomatically, "character is organised habit," then the molding of young personalities must start soon after birth. No less an authority than Michael Foster, doyen of experimental physiology at Cambridge, had reduced the link between volition and neurological growth to graphic simplicity. "The will," Foster wrote, "blundering at first in the maze of nervous network, gradually establishes easy paths. When once this is effected the slightest impulse seems to start the nerve current along the whole of the associated groups and produce[s] habitual action. The nerve current follows this route not now because it is guided by intelligence, but because this route offers the least resistance from habitual use."[91]

From volition as the product of neurological grooves etched by action, it was a short jump to the conclusion that parents must never rule arbitrarily. Mixed parental signals, after all, might confuse the developing "moral inhibitory centres" in young cerebrums. At the same time, mothers and fathers could not expect to see self-control emerge in beings who were themselves denied substantial autonomy.[92] Alfred Taylor Schofield, a London doctor who specialized in treating nervous disorders and, during the mid-1890's, served as Chairman of the PNEU Council, went further. Once generated, Schofield claimed, "will-power" resides in the child's unconscious mind. A rich supply of willpower would guard the child not only against apathy, cynicism, and greed, but also against the ubiquitous threat of nervous breakdown.[93] John Stuart Mill's infamous mental collapse was partly the result of overpressure, admitted a philosophy don to the PNEU's Reading Branch in 1907. But Mill's malaise was partly also the result of a "latent unconscious aspect of his self" that could no longer endure repression. Had his education honored emotional as well as intellectual needs, had his father allowed some room for the "animal tranquillity" that Miss Mason's curriculum preserved, perhaps Mill's breakdown could have been averted.[94]

Through its *Parents' Review* the PNEU issued a barrage of advice on proper child management. The broad range of issues addressed—from sullen temper to slouching gait, from the apparently "dull" child (who might need no more than a pair of spectacles) to the "backward" child (who could lapse into imbecility without great parental patience)—reflected the Union's eagerness to spare parents "a sense of distressing vagueness as to their complete duty."[95] Over time, advice on coping with special childhood defects receded as greater stress was given to the general problem of parental responsibility. Miss Mason had long depicted the young as a national treasure. What distinguished the Union's Edwardian from its late-Victorian voice, however, was the new emphasis on parentcraft as a patriotic skill. The Edwardian obsession with "national efficiency" found expression in PNEU literature as contempt for those privileged mothers and fathers who "muddle along through the battle of life" without a pedagogical compass.[96] Imperial strength flowed from knowledge, Mason declared in 1912. Parents were obliged to consume a "judicious intellectual diet" of physiology and social psychology. But they were also responsible for insuring that their offspring knew great books at an early age. Provided that a child in its seventh year had been taught to prize fine literature, Mason assured the *Times Educational Supplement*, it should be able to "relate"—if not actually read—*Pilgrim's Progress*, chapter by chapter. Indeed, she declared that a truly "Liberal Education" must grow out of reading in a home atmosphere of "sympathetic interest." The so-called silent reading technique associated with the name of Maria Montessori puzzled Miss Mason because in her view some degree of parent-child interaction was essential if books were to delight young minds.[97]

It was predictable that the sudden enthusiasm for Montessori's learning strategy would irk many PNEU members. Mason and her allies had always opposed blind adherence to any educational system. But when, after 1911, news began to spread about Montessori's miraculous success in applying "free development" principles to the preschool slum children of Rome, PNEU loyalists grew defensive. The Union's pedagogy was, they believed, every bit as well grounded in physiological psychology as Montessori's Casa dei Bambini, even though Miss Mason could not match La Dottoressa's scientific degrees. That young children needed both muscle and sense training hardly qualified as news to the PNEU faithful. And it was galling to be told that they and the English Froebelians could continue their useful work until enough trained teachers returned from Italy to inaugurate "expert education."[98]

What particularly troubled critics of Dr. Montessori was her conception of "freedom" and "imagination." After visiting schools in Rome and Milan, two agents of the *Journal of Education* griped that more floor space and lighter furniture were all that distinguished a Montessori classroom from a good English kindergarten. The "apostle of freedom['s]" so-called "didactic materials" appeared to induce boredom rather than creative inspiration. Another foe cast larger stones at the "cult" whose command to parents seemed to be, "'Enquire what the child demands and let him have it.'"[99] Although Montessori received a triumphant welcome when she first visited England in 1919, her reputation as the prophet of progressive education was never secure. There were, in addition to the traditionalist objections just mentioned, educational radicals who mocked Montessori's claim to have banished formal discipline. The novelist Ethel Mannin, for example, assailed the treatment of children who did not pay attention: isolating them within the classroom, Mannin wrote, smacked of "blackmail."[100] Charlotte Mason's adage had been, "The Child is a person." But now, at La Dottoressa's direction, this precept was apparently being contorted to mean that any display of childish imagination based on "credulity" rather than "intelligence" should cease.[101] English eugenicists might applaud such dicta.[102] Mason could not. For her, imagination, like faith, was the evidence of things not seen, and to deny the "kingdom of make-believe" while affirming the "arid realm of fact" was to impoverish the soul. Writing at the close of 1915, Miss Mason observed that, if nothing else, the horrors of total war were rousing Britain out of the "curious stolidity" that had characterized Edwardian culture. Now that a deluge was sweeping the land, it would be a further crime against civilization to reconstruct English education by ignoring a child's spiritual hunger.[103]

The PNEU's appeal, then, rested on precisely this blend of religious and political conservatism, applied physiology, and a character-building pedagogy that viewed the parent-teacher as one who encouraged, but did not intrude upon, self-discovery in the child. In different ways, declared the *Parents' Review*, both Wilhelmine Germany and Bolshevik Russia served to show the fatal consequences of a "one-sided education."[104] The immediate postwar years saw public elementary schools as well as privileged parents adopting PNEU syllabi. By mid-1920, 112 primary schools in twenty-three counties, along with seventy secondary schools, had rewritten their curricula to conform with Union practice. This list grew modestly during the twenties, and by 1930 included at least one industrial school.[105]

When Charlotte Mason died in January 1923, an estimated 40,000 English children had already been privately educated in compliance with PNEU standards. How many more were eventually exposed in state schools to lessons shaped by her belief in the child's "natural powers of appreciation" we cannot know.[106] But student numbers matter less than the cast of mind to which Miss Mason's group gave organizational form: an assumption that parents must themselves be trained before they are competent to participate in the education of their young. We should not equate England's PNEU with France's similarly named "Parents' School," founded in 1929, mainly because the latter was far more concerned with a falling birthrate. Certainly both bodies coalesced around what Jacques Donzelot calls "a project of pedagogical activation of family life," the "scene of a kind of permanent consultation between parents and educators."[107] Yet in England at least, such consultation was not a matter of educators browbeating parents into accepting new learning techniques certified by mental science. Parents, as the case of the PNEU suggests, were sometimes also the educators. Moreover, these activist amateurs kept alive a commitment to treating the child as an organism in need of physical as well as emotional nurture. It may be convenient to describe the focus of interwar child welfare work as shifting "from bodies to minds," but the rise to prominence of the "New Psychology" did not crowd out long-established concerns with habit, will, and character.[108]

Guidance for the "Maladjusted" Family

Between the end of the First World War and the start of the Second, we have been told, a "space" was created in English mental science for psychodynamic ideas. This process supposedly involved the replacement of a concern over neurological health with a concern over motivation, particularly in children. New definitions of parental adequacy accompanied this change, as did new forms of family intervention.[109] More chilling is the proposition that interwar England witnessed a medicalization of the mind. What allegedly occurred was a process by which the late-Victorian tuberculosis clinic—a new technology for "seeing" illness that "radiated" treatment modalities throughout the community—inspired an all-pervasive program for regulating private lives. In David Armstrong's Foucauldian terms:

The mind, as it was observed in the inter-war years, was . . . a fabrication of the disciplinary mechanisms of the Dispensary. The medical gaze shifted from body to mind: a focus on relationships and on interaction; a conceptualization of pathology as existing in the social body, constantly appearing, disappearing, reappearing; a need to know of its various manifestations and the development of technics for its observation; a gaze turned on the 'normal' population, as much as on the diseased, in an attempt to identify the incipient signs of instability; a medicine focused, not on the mind of the mad, but on the mind of the precariously sane.[110]

In actuality, interwar England's embrace of psychological medicine was tentative. To the extent that psychoanalytic ideas penetrated the therapeutic mainstream, moreover, they did so not at the level of medical discourse but rather through a dilemma of war. It was their success in treating "shellshocked" soldiers that gave advocates of the "New Psychology" a foothold in psychiatry.

Before the coming of the trenches and the mechanized slaughter they unleashed, English psychiatric practice had been the preserve of asylum doctors who believed that mental illness was often the result of hereditary weakness. In addition to providing asylum care for the certifiably mad, these alienists also laid claims to expertise in the disputed borderland between mental health and insanity. Like their rivals in neurology, late-Victorian psychiatrists wielded the catchy new diagnostic category of "neurasthenia" to reify what was in fact a wildly disparate cluster of symptoms previously ascribed to "shattered nerves" or "nervous collapse."[111] The psychic devastation of total war exposed not only the uselessness of neurasthenia as a diagnostic tool but also the hereditarian assumptions of traditional psychiatry. After all, some of the young men who filled what were called NYDN (Not Yet Diagnosed, Nervous) hospitals owned the best social and moral credentials. Had those who refused to go "over the top" into the teeth of machine-gun fire been limited to flagrant cowards, the British general staff might have continued its initial policy of shooting such men as deserters.[112] But in a war of attrition where the prospects for victory hinged on manpower and troop morale, the estimated 200,000 soldiers discharged from active service due to shellshock suggested that medical care, not execution, was in order. But how were mental health specialists at home (much less Army medical officers in field hospitals) to treat casualties whose "wounds" ranged from the loss of sight, speech, and hearing, to amnesia, chronic insomnia, and the paralysis of limbs?[113]

The old, somatic understanding of mental illness did not die easily where shellshock was concerned. Neurologists such as Sir Frederick Mott tried to salvage a physiological explanation by insisting that the concussion of artillery rounds tore small amounts of cerebral tissue or else ruptured nerves in the spinal pathway. When critics objected that shellshock symptoms also appeared in soldiers who had not been directly exposed to artillery fire, one materialist rejoinder was that the "wind of the bullet" caused trauma similar to the effects of shellblast.[114] Such arguments could not be defeated on purely theoretical grounds. Clinical practice cast grave doubt on them, however.

As Hugh Crichton-Miller told general practitioners in 1920, the wartime treatment of shellshock passed through three stages. At first, army doctors prescribed rest, sometimes supplemented by massage or electrical stimulation. The frequent failure of such therapy led physicians in specialist mental wards to use "suggestion"—"the process by which ideas are introduced into the mind of a subject without being submitted to his critical judgment"—in treating psychosomatic injuries. Although suggestion therapy often brought dramatic short-term improvement, too often men rehabilitated in this way broke down again upon return to the front lines. "[I]t was then," Crichton-Miller explained, "that the analytical method came seriously into vogue."[115] The "analytical method" of which he wrote was psychoanalysis. Just as neurologists had been studying "deep" nervous structures, realizing that peripheral motor function was itself dependent on evolutionarily "ancient mechanisms," so medical psychologists were starting to appreciate that the peculiar symptoms found among some neurotics were not random but instead signs of repressed moral conflict. Crichton-Miller and his psychiatric circle were grateful to Freud for the notions of repression, regression, and neurotic "complexes." At the same time, though, they rejected what they deemed Freud's misguided tendency "to see the origin of neurosis in a very hypothetical sexuality of infancy." These British clinicians had a clear peacetime agenda. They were eager to test their war-honed therapeutic skills on a civilian population, to transfer the lessons learned in treating shellshocked soldiers to helping civilians cope with "bad tempers, sexual obsessions, and morbid fears." Character flaws might now be addressed as psychoneuroses. But winning public acceptance for the New Psychology would require that they dissociate themselves from the "perversions" of Freud.[116]

Although the postwar New Psychology accommodated many shades of therapeutic opinion, its umbrella stretched only so far. Not found thereunder were several well-publicized schools of mental science. Most obviously excluded were the Freudian faithful. It may be true that some of these, such as Ernest Jones, Freud's chief

English advocate, made handsome livings; that at least one Freudian advice manual, J. C. Flugel's *Psycho-Analytic Study of the Family* (1921), flourished for a generation; and that shards of Freudian vocabulary—"inferiority complex," "sadism," "masochism," "id," "ego," and "libido"—were "bandied across the tea-cups or the Mah-Jong table" during the 1920's.[117] But if England's new psychologists were eager to classify "instinct," few wished to go as far as Flugel in declaring that parental love and adult sexual satisfaction were inversely proportional. Nor did many wish to identify themselves with orthodox Freudian psychoanalysis, a regimen that as late as 1926 was being accused of driving some patients to permanent insanity or suicide.[118] At the same time, those who considered all forms of the "talking cure" inherently dangerous were no more welcome in the New Psychology.[119]

Lastly, there was little room for mechanical, "behaviorist" models of personality development. Experimentally rooted in Pavlov's discovery of conditioned reflexes, behaviorism as expressed in Anglo-American psychology hammered home the importance of regularity in childcare practice. Starting with Luther Holt's late-Victorian schedules for feeding and toilet training, the behaviorist torch passed to Frederick Truby King, a New Zealand doctor whose version of mothercraft depicted breast-feeding as an exact science.[120] For devotion to the creed of stimulus and response, however, no contemporary could touch John Watson. Professor of Psychology at Johns Hopkins until his affair with a student drove him out of academia and into advertising, Watson's books on *Behaviorism* (1925) and *Psychological Care of Infant and Child* (1928) proclaimed the duty of experimentalists to "predict" and "control" human conduct through manipulation of the young. Watson scorned parents who hugged and kissed their babies. Employing an all-too-apt Pavlovian analogy, he observed that one did not train a watchdog by cuddling it on one's lap. Even the home irritated Watson: emotionally cluttered, it made a terrible laboratory.[121]

England's New Psychology likewise harped on the failures of parenthood and bemoaned the emotional disarray of many homes. But in stark contrast to the behaviorists, spokesmen such as Hugh

Crichton-Miller announced that "parents are not potters to mould clay, but gardners to protect bulbs." His *The New Psychology and the Parent* (1922) identified several childrearing habits that put the young at psychic risk. Relying on emotional bribery to curb masturbation, for example, was "desperately dangerous," while parents might do "immense harm" to toddlers by dealing harshly with their fears of animals or the dark.[122] Nevertheless, the New Psychology's greatest gift to the parent was "knowledge, not so much of the child, as of himself." Armed with a basic understanding of psychoanalytic principles, caring mothers and fathers might purge their mental lives of "unconscious bias" and so become "infinitely better" parents.[123] Crichton-Miller's book struck some contemporaries as highly germane to a nation whose falling birthrate rendered wise parenthood vital. Of more lasting significance, however, it marked a refocusing of guidance for parents. Along with another beacon of psychodynamic advice, Susan Isaacs's *The Nursery Years* (1929), *The New Psychology* turned from problems of child management to problems of meaning.[124] Middle-class parents in interwar England would henceforth hear and read much about childhood neuroses, and about the "maladjusted" families that created them.

Hugh Crichton-Miller's book was more than a therapeutic daydream. It served, in fact, to publicize the guidance being offered at his Tavistock Clinic, a psychiatric center opened in a gloomy Bloomsbury house on September 20, 1920. "H.C.M.," as his colleagues knew him, was a Scot whose medical training had taken place in Edinburgh and Northern Italy, and whose early expertise had been the mental health of the aged. During the war he became a recognized authority on shellshock treatment, first in Egypt and later in London, taking away from this work the conviction that psychoneuroses required "strict interactionist" therapy.[125] Not surprisingly, therefore, from its birth the Tavistock Square Clinic for Functional Nervous Disorders—the "Tavi," to its friends—operated as a mediating body. Here the insights of Freud, Jung, and Adler could and did mingle with those of a somatically based general medicine. Yet to laud the Clinic's therapeutic "flexibility"[126] was also to make a virtue of necessity. For in the beginning few members of its all-volunteer staff were psychiatrists in the traditional sense of that word: none, including Crichton-Miller, had trained for long years in mental hospitals, although several had treated battlefield neuroses. Thus, at a time when the idea of a psychiatric clinic operating independently of a hospital still verged on the heretical, the Tavistock was wise to promote itself as holding "no doctrine."[127]

Already suspect for its maverick staff, the Clinic similarly defied psychiatric convention by assuming that people with relatively minor behavioral and emotional flaws needed professional help. To attract patients, Crichton-Miller aimed to make the Tavistock as unimposing as possible:

The principle on which H.C.M. wanted the Clinic to develop was one of freedom from administrative and institutional bureaucracy, a place where a patient could come with a sense of privacy and confidence; a place where each person was seen punctually by appointment and always by the same doctor, in which there were no forms to fill in and no awkward details to be given in cold blood, so different from the dreaded long hours of waiting in the hospital out-patient departments, never knowing which doctor you might see. It is true that many patients and many referring doctors were at first nonplussed by this great difference from any then-existing medical institution. Only bare rooms with tables and chairs and an occasional couch; no apparatus, no dispensary, no medicine to take away, no white coats or syringes. . . .

Happily, patient surprise soon gave way to appreciation, or so the Tavistock's first historians claimed.[128] Neighborhood psychiatry had arrived.

Should we view the Tavistock's "personal touch"[129] style of guidance as proof that the "medical gaze" of psychotherapy was scanning new ground, that mental science, not content with inventing neuroses, was now busy constructing the neurotic culture? Perhaps in a literal sense, yes. Crichton-Miller and his backers believed that English mental hygiene would profit from an enlarged conception of the patient. To attract what he called the "educated poor"—students and clerks, overworked housewives and misunderstood children—the Clinic offered consulting hours that stretched from 9 A.M. to 10 P.M.; saw to it that patients were charged no more than five shillings (usually half that) for each hour-long consultation; and provided such outlets for "self-expression" as children's classes in painting and fencing and mothers' support groups.[130] In terms of their cultural critique, the Clinic's founders maintained that modern urban civilization was hostile to good mental health. Air pollution, for example, could cause "direct poisoning of the brain mechanism" or, more often, behavioral problems, through damaged thyroid glands. The unnatural pace and pressure of city life likewise warped the already precarious fit between the self and its social environment. The resulting personality maladjustments produced "inefficient" citizens. Hence a "holistic" course of therapy for many adults was a wise investment. For children, whose social worlds were more narrowly confined to family and school, such therapy stood a still better chance of success. Provided that parents told "the whole truth about [a] child's relationship with his other family members," the prospects for readjustment were excellent.[131]

This quest for full parental disclosure conjures up Armstrong's (and Foucault's) image of the new knowledge sought by the "medical gaze": "Whereas under the old regime the body of the patient had to be made legible to the physician's interrogation, under the new regime the body produced its own truth which required, not legibility, but encouragement. The patient had to speak, to confess, to reveal; illness was transformed from what was visible to what was heard."[132] Before accepting that the Tavistock Clinic did indeed represent a more refined and thus more insidious assault on family autonomy, however, we must consider carefully what was being asked of interwar parents. By the 1920's, of course, working-class mothers and fathers had been fending off would-be inquisitors for at least two generations: district visitors, district nurses, health visitors, school attendance officers, and other self-styled friends of the family had long been urging the poor "to speak, to confess, to reveal" with very mixed success. The extension of these tactics to middle-class parents after the Great War *was* novel, but the scale on which such intervention occurred was modest. In its first year of work, the Tavistock treated 248 patients, thirty-three of whom (13.3 percent) were children. By 1928–29, in its ninth year of work, the Clinic saw 481 new patients, 203 (42.2 percent) of them children. More telling, "a very high proportion of cases were seen once or only a few times."[133] Often, then, there would not have been time enough to extract "confessions" from parents. How eagerly parents sought help from the Tavistock we cannot know. We do know, though, that throughout the same nine-year period medical consultants and general practitioners combined to refer nearly three times as many patients to the Clinic as "parents, friends, and employers." Although the Tavistock saw itself as a social "clearing-house" for neurotic problems, physicians remained the housemasters.

Finally, the reasons for which children were brought to the Clinic are suggestive. Among the 326 new patients seen in the Children's Department between October 1, 1927, and March 31, 1929, such serious diagnoses as "hysteria" and "paranoid states" paled in number beside those of "bedwetting," "stammering," "nail-biting," "lying," and "delinquency."[134] Until 1932, when a cohort of younger therapists forced him to step down as Director of the Clinic, Crichton-Miller was fond of reminding parents about their obligation to raise not merely "good" but "happy" citizens. Yet the statistical trends just mentioned imply that parents most often brought their young to the Tavistock seeking help with disruptive household behavior, not because they were fretting about their children's inner peace.[135]

Both Hugh Crichton-Miller and his successor at the "Tavi," J. R. Rees, regarded psychotherapy as the "art of adjustment," an art whose success depended in part on the patient's "willingness to be reborn."[136] This fusion of theology and psychiatry—Crichton-Miller once assured a group of medical students that the only route to compassion for patients lay through "the Cross and the Manger"— did much to make the Tavistock's message more palatable to polite society. Blessed with friends in high places, its "holistic" approach to treating psychoneurotic problems proved very influential in two respects. First, the Clinic sponsored lectures on everything from endocrinology and sweet-stealing in children to the psychological side of nursing. These lectures provided intellectual ballast for a generation of psychiatric social workers and probation officers.[137] Second, the Tavistock's efforts to "adjust" the relationship between the child and its home constituted interwar England's first experiment in what would soon become known as "child guidance." Deborah Thom is right that in contrast to most English child guidance centers, the Tavistock clinic did not give much credence to social casework.[138] On the other hand, the Clinic's concern with juvenile delinquency was plain from the day it opened its doors in 1920. Among the few persons guaranteed to receive priority diagnoses were young persons under seventeen. Intelligence testing and speech analysis soon joined personality assessment and a full medical exam as standard features of any case brought to the Tavistock's Children's Department, opened in 1926. In 1931, one of that Department's leaders, Dr. C. L. C. Burns, left to take over the new Child Guidance Centre in Birmingham. Soon thereafter the Tavistock joined forces with psychoanalysts Edward Glover and Dennis Carroll in founding the Institute for the Scientific Treatment of Delinquency.[139]

By 1935, the standard handbook on probation could declare that, "Delinquency is not a disorder or entity in itself, but a fact of general maladjustment." According to such logic, juvenile crime represented a defect in mental hygiene and so demanded a "very thorough differentiation between individuals" rather than retribution apportioned by offense.[140] Interwar child psychology had done much to encourage this view. Both the Tavistock Clinic and Margaret Lowenfield's Institute of Child Psychology, established in 1928, catered to children "who found themselves at odds with society." The illustrative case history was their most impressive proof of how "unconscious motive" underlay many, perhaps most, delinquent acts. In the summer of 1929, for example, Crichton-Miller lectured probation officers about a ten-year-old boy who had been arrested for habitually traveling beyond the zone specified on his season railway pass. Only after careful investigation of the boy's background did psychotherapists learn that bright red hair was to blame for all his antisocial deeds. Children who called him "ginger" could be punched; adult teasing called for a different revenge. Thus, to spite a "non-intuitive" father who jokingly warmed his hands over the boys "fiery" hair, as well as a railway ticket collector who had branded him "copper nob," this child set out to "get his own back" through defiance of grown-up rules. Merely to punish the boy would be futile, Crichton-Miller concluded, since to do so would only confirm his sense of grievance against the adult world.[141]

An English children's court system had been created in 1908 precisely because penal reformers were keen to convert juvenile justice from a process of allocating blame to one of understanding deeds. This campaign receives close attention in a later chapter. For now, it is enough to point out that if juvenile courts created the potential for a new "psychological jurisdiction," bringing into collaboration the judge and the psychiatrist,[142] this jurisdiction in practice more often perplexed than encouraged the champions of mental science. William Healy's Chicago Juvenile Psychopathic Institute, opened in 1909, was America's first child guidance clinic and a monument to the idea that all young offenders should be scientifically examined to determine the origin of their "defects." Although Chicago's juvenile court had been in operation since 1899, as late as 1915 Healy was complaining about the "astonishing lack of any attempt to get down to the bed-level of causation" where juvenile crime was concerned. For Healy, whose multiple-factor analyses of delinquency anticipated those of Cyril Burt by a decade, this "bed-level" lay with the "impulsions" of early childhood. Significantly, in 1925 Healy was *still* lamenting the tendency of American juvenile courts to "generalize" about youthful conduct rather than going "as straight as we can to the individual's own inner mental life."[143] Given what appeared to Healy and company as the foot-dragging of American juvenile courts over the psychological assessment of their clients, it is not surprising that child guidance in the United States gradually turned away from the prevention of delinquency toward the clinic-based treatment of children with only mild behavior and emotional problems.[144]

England's child guidance movement also began by emphasizing "Preventive Psychotherapy." The notion that young offenders—along with habitual inebriates—needed the "gift of guidance" was hardly new. The police court missionary, a late-Victorian prototype of the probation officer, had aimed to steer the sinner back to the path of righteousness, and in so doing had deployed a redemptive psychology that likewise looked to motivation.[145] But it was the confluence of such long-standing philanthropic impulses with the New Psychology that gave rise to specialized child guidance work in interwar England. Certainly the ties between child guidance and other mental health campaigns were close. For instance, efforts to assist the "troubled" child and its parents overlapped with concerns about "defective" children. Mental deficiency, as defined by law in 1927, was "a condition of arrested or incomplete development of mind existing before the age of eighteen years, whether arising from inherent causes or induced by disease or injury." Conceived in these terms, mental deficiency appeared basically incurable. Prior to the 1920's, therefore, most voluntary effort in this realm consisted of selecting the worst cases for asylum care, while visiting less retarded children at home.[146] When it became known that certain grades of mental deficiency were "susceptible of adjustment in trained hands," however, bodies such as the National Council for Mental Hygiene (formed in 1922) began to study the "medico-psychological" health of children "in relation to education and parental responsibility." This cross-fertilization of child guidance and mental hygiene initiatives was clear in terms of personnel: both Hugh Crichton-Miller and Cyril Burt were members of the NCMH Executive Committee in 1930, while R. D. Gillespie, an Honorary Secretary of that group, had co-authored one of the period's leading textbooks on psychiatry. With the outbreak of war in 1939, London's Child Guidance Clinic joined the NCMH and the Central Association for Mental Welfare to create a Mental Health Emergency Committee.[147]

It nevertheless distorts the practice of interwar child guidance to regard these linkages as emblematic of a constantly probed "psychological family," much less a "perpetual medical gaze."[148] Cyril Burt recalled in 1953 that since no more than 15 percent of all cases referred to English child guidance clinics involved some pathological condition requiring a psychiatrist's diagnosis, these clinics had naturally been the domain of psychologists. The latter, after all, were best positioned to deal with "complex form[s] of maladjustment be-

tween the child's personality and ... environmental conditions."
But Burt was wrong. During World War One or soon thereafter,
this future panjandrum of mental testing may have run an *ad hoc*
child guidance clinic while serving as Psychologist to the Education
Department of the London County Council. And he did sketch a
plan for a psychologist-dominated clinic in Appendix II of his 1925
classic, *The Young Delinquent*. Unfortunately, Burt, who considered
psychiatrists to be "the least intelligent medicals," conveniently ignored the fact that nearly all the American-style child guidance clinics opened between 1927 and 1939 were supervised by doctors.[149]
Nor did these medical directors themselves form a united professional front. For throughout the interwar years mutual misgivings
persisted between clinic- and hospital-based child psychiatrists.[150]

Professional rivalry aside, what emerged in England during the
late twenties and thirties was something less than a child guidance
"Panopticon," the all-seeing disciplinary eye so often invoked by
Foucault and his followers.[151] If we treat the Children's Department
of the Tavistock Clinic as a separate sort of therapeutic center, then
England's first purpose-built child guidance clinic opened in Bell
Lane, Whitechapel, in 1927. The East London Child Guidance
Clinic derived its initial financing from the Jewish Health Organisation of Great Britain. For several years the latter had worried about
an apparent increase in "psychological maladjustment in home and
school" among the young of East London's Jewish immigrant community, not least because this population offered an easy target for
xenophobes obsessed with alien criminality. The East London
Clinic applied American "teamwork" principles, whereby therapeutic responsibilities were divided among psychiatrists, psychologists,
and psychiatric social workers. America's Commonwealth Fund had
in fact helped to train Dr. Emanuel Miller, the psychiatrist who supervised this clinic, as well as Sybil Clement Brown, its social
worker.[152] American largesse also made possible the formation of a
London-based Child Guidance Council in 1927, and the opening of
its training center and clinic at Islington in 1929. The Commonwealth Fund, an expression of "scientific philanthropy" whose
power flowed from Harkness oil money, had been impressed with

the receptivity to American child guidance methods on the part of English magistrates, education officers, and mental hygiene volunteers. It therefore agreed to bankroll not only much of the early clinical work in England but also a postgraduate mental health course at the London School of Economics.[153]

The London Child Guidance Clinic under Dr. William Moodie became independent in mid-1930, while retaining representation on the Council. Thereafter, clinics opened in several large towns, although Northern and Eastern counties saw few of them. By the end of 1938, local education authorities had replaced American philanthropy as the main support for these new therapeutic centers. England's thirty clinics reported 4,688 new cases in 1938. More than four times as many clinics offered some form of diagnostic service for children, but lacked the multi-disciplinary teams deemed necessary to earn the Council's "Group I" rating.[154]

What these institutions actually did must be distinguished from what ambitious clinicians wished them to become. In the United States, eight years after the first child guidance clinics opened, one could find a Yale psychologist urging "exhaustive" clinical inquiry into children's "development potentialities." Yet an analysis of case records from Philadelphia suggests that the therapeutic advice tendered to mothers and fathers reinforced rather than undermined parental authority.[155] Although no comparable cache of English case records has so far come to light, the clinical statistics contained in annual reports are revealing. Where Arthur Greenwood, Labour's Minister of Health in 1930, extolled child guidance work for addressing "the wider problems of character building, happiness, efficiency, life's aspirations, work and play, and social relationships of every kind," the day-to-day reality was more mundane. In that same year the London Child Guidance Clinic accepted 367 new cases. A "great majority" of these involved "conduct disturbing to others, rather than personality difficulties distressing to the child himself." The statistically typical child seen at William Moodie's clinic during the early thirties was between nine and twelve years old, possessed average intelligence, and had been referred by school officials or parents. Boys only slightly outnumbered girls on the Clinic's patient list, suggesting that delinquent acts, which boys were far more apt to commit, did not bulk large as reasons for referral. No child could be accepted for "full service" therapy, or even for single-session diagnosis, without the express consent of a parent or guardian. The degree of parental cooperation was reportedly "very gratifying." Indeed, the Clinic's social workers, who carried out family visits as part of full service treatment, often credited parents with making possible the complete "adjustment" of their children by seeing to it that "the atmosphere of the home became stabilised."[156]

Child guidance clinics presumably had an ulterior motive to depict parents as partners in the therapeutic process: evidence to the contrary might have cast these clinics in the role of family invader. Still, there is reason to think that many interwar parents welcomed clinical attention. Just as the Victorian poor often saw charity as a resource to be milked, so English mothers and fathers in the 1930's approached child guidance services as consumers.[157] The advice they received from clinic personnel may on occasion have been quite useful. Despite the aura of omniscience often attributed to them, child guidance clinics in fact defined their expertise rather narrowly. Most confessed that they could not help either "obvious cases of mental deficiency" or those of "purely physical illness," although hospital-based clinics, such as R. D. Gillespie's center at Guy's, had to see some of these children.[158] In theory, clinics accepted patients whose ages ranged from infancy to seventeen, but in practice few pre-schoolers and even fewer youths over fifteen were treated. Thus, clinics generally dealt with sane, more or less healthy, school-age boys and girls. Within this population, the team approach to treating scholastic "backwardness"—defined as a failure to keep pace with one's chronological peers in the classroom—yielded consistently high rates of "adjustment." This was true in part because defective vision and hearing, or poor reading and speaking skills, were comparatively simple to detect.[159] At a clinic, in other words, parents might reasonably have expected to get practical help with their children's scholastic problems.

Other, less easily classifiable forms of help could be obtained there as well. The Director of Plymouth's child guidance clinic noted in 1935 that when parents were angry at teachers, the former "come to a clinic as if to an ally."[160] Dr. Hunter predictably went on to warn against clinic personnel choosing sides in such cases, but the fact that some parents tried to enlist clinicians in their battles hints at the complex local politics in which the work of these bodies was enmeshed. It may well have been true also that overwrought mothers and fathers sought out a clinician because he or she listened well, and, unlike neighbors, could be trusted not to broadcast family secrets. The psychiatric professionals involved in this work sometimes cited case histories of obsessional parents who, in the name of enlightened values, were replicating their neuroses. Hence the vegetarian mother who thought she was teaching her child humanitarianism when she persuaded him not to kill slugs in the garden was actually projecting fears of her own aggression onto an unwitting boy.[161] In their dealings with parents and children, however, psychiatrists and psychologists alike shunned technical language, offering instead "an ordinary commonsense conversation." This folksy side of child guidance was no doubt partly tactical. One tried to put one's patients at ease, after all. But at least some clinicians may also have eschewed psychodynamic labels because they did not trust them. Dr. William Moodie, interwar England's most ardent advocate of child guidance, confessed to colleagues in 1938 that no one really understood why some nervous children became bed-wetters and others did not; mental science could often help with "enuresis," but could not say what it was. Even the definition of a "behavioral problem" bordered on tautology.[162]

According to the champions of child guidance, clinical diagnosis grew more accurate after the mid-thirties. This may have been true, but probably not for the reasons then offered. Child guidance had allegedly become a "more efficient therapeutic weapon" because clinicians were learning not to conceive of "'problem children' as a separate class, endowed by nature with an unstable mind and foredoomed to give trouble to themselves and others throughout their lives."[163] That such enlightenment emerged unproblematically from "scientific data" evades the issue of timing, however. More proximate factors were at play. English unemployment figures had begun to recede from their peaks of early 1933, for example, and in their wake the ethical implications of world depression were coming into focus. By the mid-thirties it was apparent to many that longstanding assumptions about the link between weak character and economic failure were no longer tenable. With the category of "unemploy-able" now suspect, the parallel classification of "problem child" would also have demanded rethinking.

Similarly, clinics may well have provided more "efficient" ther-apy for maladjusted children because one type of refractory patient, the persistent lawbreaker, was visiting clinics less often than in the past. The 1933 Children and Young Persons Act should have *in-creased* the number of disturbed youth sent to clinics since this stat-ute imposed new obligations on local authorities to investigate the social environments of children judged to be "in need of care and protection." Yet the much-publicized juvenile crime wave that swept over England during the early thirties so concerned shop owners, magistrates, and police that their enthusiasm for "progres-sive" treatment of delinquency wilted.[164] There were a few commu-nities, notably Exeter, where juvenile courts increased the flow of delinquents to clinics after 1934.[165] The experience of Birmingham was more typical, however. With C. L. C. Burns directing that city's Child Guidance Clinic and Geraldine Cadbury, a beacon of progressive penality, sitting on its juvenile bench, Birmingham ap-peared custom-made for the therapeutic treatment of young offend-ers. Nevertheless, in 1937 its juvenile court sent just sixteen chil-dren to Burns's clinic.[166]

The English child guidance movement by no means collapsed with the coming of World War Two. On the contrary, the uproot-ing of children from their homes during mass urban evacuations not only magnified neurotic symptoms (particularly enuresis) but also brought these to the notice of host families. The Government there-fore had to open special hostels for "unbilletable" boys and girls. The 1944 Education Act later compelled local education authorities to offer some form of child guidance service in their areas.[167] The campaign against juvenile maladjustment stimulated action on re-lated fronts as well. John Bowlby's controversial theory of "mater-

nal deprivation," often seen as an *ad hominem* attack on female autonomy, was actually the culmination of research launched in 1936
while working at the London Child Guidance Clinic.[168] Moreover, if
children required "psychological understanding," then husbands and
wives could not long be denied equivalent help. Marriage guidance
as a therapeutic specialty sprang in fact from the same psychodynamic thesis: that "[p]ersonal happiness can only be achieved . . . if
an individual is an integrated personality."[169]

That well-adjusted youth rarely came from homes where parents
were at odds constituted a basic tenet of child guidance propaganda.
Dr. C. W. Kimmins, Chief Inspector of Schools for the London
County Council, assured readers in 1926 that "eminent psychiatrists . . . have not known of a single case of nervous breakdown
where the patient was reared in the happy surroundings of a good
home." Eight years later, "experts" from the Institute of Medical
Psychology (as the Tavistock Clinic had become known) and the
London Child Guidance Clinic pleaded with the public for "more
scientific handling of . . . matrimonial discord" as a defense against
"the kindred social problems of divorce and child delinquency."[170]
Some police court magistrates were deeply involved in marital
peacemaking, but, as the next chapter will discuss, this social service
was effectively reserved for the poor. For middle-class spouses there
existed no equivalent source of advice. The pronouncements of
moral reform groups such as the Mothers' Union and the White
Cross League stressed "self-control" where procreation was concerned, advice "so vague as to be useless" in the struggle against dysgenic parenthood.[171] Thus, what the founders of marriage guidance
in England aimed to do, as Jane Lewis has suggested, was to preempt
radical attacks on monogamy by stressing the importance of sexual
fulfillment within marriage. Marriage guidance represented a balancing act between the "growing demand for greater individual liberty"
and concern over the social costs of "family failure."[172]

Although volunteers connected with Liverpool's Personal Service
Society opened a marital counseling bureau in 1936, the nucleus of
a national marriage guidance movement came together two years
later in London. The immediate spur to action was the 1937 Mat-

rimonial Causes Act, legislation that broadened the grounds for divorce. A. P. Herbert's Act had dramatically increased the number of
spouses seeking to dissolve broken unions. This perceived threat to
family stability drove a small group of clergymen, doctors, and social workers to form a committee whose twin concerns would be
the wise preparation for marriage and the "treatment of disharmo-
nies" within it. Members of the resulting National Marriage Guidance Council recommended sexual abstinence before marriage but
the pursuit of sexual pleasure, including the informed use of contra-
ception, once vows had been exchanged.[173] It was this stance that had
forced activists such as Herbert Gray, a Presbyterian minister, and
E. F. Griffith, a physician, to break away from the more cautious
British Social Hygiene Council. Progress was slow. Marriage guidance remained largely a matter of organizing lectures for doctors and
probation officers until the first counseling center opened in London in 1943. Several more years would elapse before trained "marriage counselors" became recognized members of the social service
community.[174]

If determined to do so, one could argue that marriage guidance
formed part of a grand, panoptic ambition to medicalize mental life.
David Mace, a Methodist clergyman who became Secretary of the
National Marriage Guidance Council in 1942, declared that, "Marital disharmony may rightly be regarded as a disease." Conversely,
Mace held, "There is a condition of positive marital health which
brings immunity." Finding, and maintaining, marital health was no
simple task. Certainly the idea that spouses could be "left to sort out
their 'private affairs' by themselves is quite fallacious."[175] We should
realize, however, that David Mace's rhetoric was far from representative of the movement he briefly led. One year after publishing his
book on *Marriage Counselling* (1948), Mace left England to become
Professor of Human Relations at Drew University in New Jersey, a
career move that underscored his atypical attentiveness to the language of therapeutic fashion. But behind closed doors, therapists had
few incentives to confound their patients, old or young. Marriage
guidance, like child guidance, was caught in a web of social, economic, and cultural constraints whose restrictive force was more

than sufficient to frustrate the designs of a colonizing mental science. To speak of the "psychologizing" of the English family is therefore to recognize only the most grandiose designs of a very few clinicians. Such a term moreover obscures the solace that some interwar parents and children apparently did derive from the counsel of strangers.

PART II

The Adjudication of the Private

FOUR

Summary Justice and Working-Class Marriage

A S W E H A V E S E E N, the policing of family life engaged many actors during England's era of international preeminence. These actors occupied both government and voluntary spheres, although with the important exception of public health and education officials, the most zealous waged their campaigns for home "improvement" independently of the state. We turn now to the realm of the judicial, where state agents took the lead in regulating domestic conduct. That courts encountered serious difficulty in adjudicating family matters is not surprising. The fact that judges and their community officers should have shown so disunited a front in pursuing this work, on the other hand, demands attention.

England's criminal justice system has been depicted as evolving from a preindustrial form in which wide judicial discretion served to legitimate the social order, to a new form where the need to impose industrial discipline on an increasingly urbanized work force produced less harsh but more systematic punishments. According to this vision, the wheels of Victorian justice ground both more gently and more intrusively than they had a century before, since along with the abolition of many capital crimes and the diminishing resort to incarceration went an intensified examination of private lives.[1] As Jennifer Davis has made clear, however, historians of crime often underestimate the degree of continuity between eighteenth- and nineteenth-century law enforcement, particularly at the local level. Significantly, both eighteenth-century justices of the peace and nineteenth-century police court magistrates enjoyed great latitude in their dealings with the poor people who appeared before them.[2] Nowhere is the highly personal and unsystematic nature of modern summary justice better displayed than in the police court's adjudication of disputes between husbands and wives. Long before divorce became a practical option for most working-class couples, the English police court provided a stage upon which the full range of matrimonial drama was played out.[3] These dramas sometimes assumed a coercive character, with legal energy directed toward sustaining inequalities of class and gender. But the application of bourgeois ideals concerning marriage, family, and the law was hardly a straightforward matter. Instead, the realities of working-class culture and the flexibility of summary procedure itself often combined to make this theater of justice highly improvisational.

The Peculiar Origins of Matrimonial Jurisdiction

Magistrates' courts, sometimes called "petty sessions" but more often known as "police courts," originally had no authority to meddle with marriage. Their rise to prominence as England's "great clearing house of crime"[4] was gradual and in large part accidental. What transformed them into their modern shape was the vast extension of summary jurisdiction that occurred between the late seventeenth and the late nineteenth century—a shifting of ever larger shares of the criminal caseload from jury trials to the magistrates themselves. Historians have only recently begun to explore in depth the power that early modern justices of the peace, acting individually or in pairs, wielded over a broad range of "victimless offenses." Persons summarily convicted of vagrancy, idleness, begging, drunkenness, and uttering profane oaths might have been fined, whipped, or committed to hard labor in a house of correction. So too, eighteenth-century justices in some places acquired or simply assumed the right to punish those caught holding poacher's tools, damaging hedges, or liberating turnips.[5] But not until the nineteenth century, when concern for national safety gave way to worry about the efficiency of local government, were large classes of "indictable" offenses heaped on magistrates' plates. The Criminal Justice Act of

1855, to note one important example, allowed magistrates to try cases of theft and embezzlement of objects worth less than five shillings. The right to deal summarily with juvenile felonies also arrived during the mid-Victorian years.[6] Thereafter, a thick pile of parliamentary statutes designated magistrates' courts as the proper venue for everything from landlord-tenant disputes to drunken driving charges. By the early twentieth century it was in local magistrates' courts that the overwhelming majority of criminal prosecutions began and ended, for only a small fraction of the cases brought before these bodies were sent up for trial to the higher courts of Assize and Quarter Sessions. A "quiet, almost unnoticed and typically English revolution" had taken place, a revolution in which "the jury ha[d] left the jury box and taken its place upon the bench." And just as "typically English" is the fact that those who presided over most magistrates' courts remained untrained amateurs until 1949.[7]

The amateur tradition among magistrates did not hold everywhere, however. First in eighteenth-century London and later on in several more cities, salaried barristers known as stipendiary magistrates were appointed to mete out criminal justice.[8] The power they exercised was remarkable in a culture so suspicious of unsupervised authority. The stipendiary magistrates could single-handedly decide how a person charged with any crime might be dealt with, and given the rapidly lengthening reach of summary jurisdiction during the nineteenth century, their pronouncements were likely to be final. It is not difficult to understand why England's urban élites found the stipendiary useful as a mediator between the state and "the most depraved and abandoned classes of our population" in places where the physical separation of rich and poor had grown most pronounced. Beyond serving as an "immediate and visible representative of law and government" for "many thousands in our big towns," he supposedly acted as the "consulting lawyer of the poor."[9] As the *Saturday Review* explained, "Everybody who finds himself in a little difficulty, and cannot at the moment think of anybody else to consult, takes the liberty of popping in upon the police magistrate and asking his advice in a friendly way. He sits like the Kadi in the gate, and every passer-by may have a word with him." Victorian

London's twenty-three stipendiary magistrates performed this double duty for the comparatively modest sum of £1,200 per year—a case of the "great underpaid" preserving calm among the "great unwashed."[10]

The perceived effectiveness of police court magistrates, salaried or amateur, was yet more impressive in view of the courtroom conditions they faced. Late-Victorian and Edwardian accounts of the police court ambiance tend to stress either the "picturesque" or the "degrading" elements of this judicial theater, depending on the observer's tolerance for crowds, noise, and strong odors.[11] Sixteen years after his first visit to London's Lambeth Police Court in 1894, missionary Thomas Holmes's memory of that "horrible wonderland" had not lost its edge: "I breathe again the sickening whiff of stale debauch, . . . the chloride of lime is again in my throat, and my nostrils tingle with it."[12] Commenting on Westminster Police Court at roughly the same time, another critic thought it absurd that antivaccinators should be prosecuted amidst sanitary conditions so "hot and poisonous" as to fell the court's own officers. As late as 1905 *The Lancet* complained that throughout London "the medical man, the man of law, the expert witness, and other respectably inclined persons are compelled to 'hob-nob'" with the verminous poor in these tribunals. Although Margaret Nevinson worked as a rent-collector in the slum-ridden East End, she was not prepared for what greeted her at Thames Police Court. Having come to obtain an eviction order, Miss Nevinson was alarmed to find herself jammed tight in a lobby where she was one of the few women without marks of violence. No one else seemed subdued by these signs of brutality, however. "Along the walls were large placards requesting silence, but the noise was deafening, and although at intervals an officer of the Court sprang out from the inner sanctum and bayed at the people like some furious mastiff: 'Be quiet, be quiet,' he only checked for a second or so the hubbub of voices."[13]

In London, the police courts were required by law to remain open from 10 A.M. to 5 P.M., Monday through Saturday, with holiday closings only for Christmas and Good Friday. If stipendiaries and lay magistrates elsewhere had less relentless schedules, all police

APPLYING FOR PROCESS AND ADVICE.

According to the account in George Sims's *Living London* (1902), when the doors of a metropolitan police court opened each morning, "the crowd elbows and jostles its way inside with the impatient eagerness of a gallery audience entering a Shoreditch music-hall." First to be seen were those seeking either a summons or counsel from the magistrate.

court justices faced the additional pressure of courtrooms often packed with observers. Once the initial "applications" phase of the court's business had concluded—a period lasting anywhere from twenty minutes to two hours during which "his worship" dispensed both summonses and advice—the general case phase of business began. At this point the courtroom's space for visitors would usually fill with friends and enemies of the accused, as well as the merely curious.[14] Although the contributions of the pub and the music hall to English working-class culture have been well documented, the phenomenon of police court proceedings as popular entertainment has so far gone unnoticed. Anecdotal evidence suggests that unemployed male laborers along with women in the course of their daily shopping often sought refuge at the back of the courtroom. In cold or wet weather all seats allotted to the public were quickly snapped up, forcing the rest of those drawn by the lure of local melodrama to stand for hours at a time.[15] When exasperated magistrates tried to trim the size of public viewing areas or to keep the curious outside longer than was customary, loud anger might be the reaction.[16] Nor could a magistrate expect to scold his audience into staying away. After Mr. De Gray branded the ragged habitués of his courtroom "scum of the earth," appearances, but not numbers, temporarily changed in the visitors' section: some of his regulars tried to disguise themselves by wearing their neighbors' best clothes.[17] Small wonder that the veteran stipendiary Alfred Plowden compared his task to "playing Hamlet in a barn," or that the imaginary magistrate in Galsworthy's *The Silver Box* speaks in a "paternal and ferocious voice."[18]

Reporters also tested magisterial patience. Both daily and weekly newspapers pursuing mass readerships saw the police court as a treasure trove of lurid and comic "bits." As early as 1844, metropolitan reporters howled to the Home Office when a reconfiguration of Clerkenwell Police Court left them seated too far from the dock to catch all the delectable evidence.[19] At London's Bow Street Court, one judge complained, a case involving charges against "superior" persons could draw as many as thirty or forty reporters from all over the Kingdom. If there arose anything vaguely sensational in such proceedings, "the whole dialog is furnished [in print], and every question and answer set out, together with the demeanour of the audience."[20] More irksome, though, was the readiness of reporters to pounce on the "semblance of the slightest injustice" in a magistrate's words. Especially in London, where the constituencies of over a hundred MPs lay wholly or partly within the Metropolitan Police district, a judge's remarks might ignite a parliamentary fire.[21] The fascination of the press with police court proceedings did sometimes have laudable consequences, of course, as when reported cases of dire poverty stimulated offers of financial aid, employment, or even a new home. But for the most part, overworked magistrates found it exasperating that reporters lay in wait to parade "[t]he quip, the jest, the thoughtless word . . . before a wondering world." The only judges in England to sit without wigs and gowns, police court magistrates must at times have felt more like casualties than ambassadors of justice.[22]

Police courts nonetheless remained bulwarks of the propertied classes for at least a century, beginning around 1850. What made these tribunals so important as sites for the recapitulation of élite values was their popularity with the English working classes. At the same time, it would be reductionist nonsense to speak of the nation's police court network as a "carceral archipelago" in the Foucauldian sense of a decentered penality so pervasive as to resist identification.[23] The poor, "rough" as well as "respectable," understood that magistrates possessed coercive legal power: there was no ambiguity on this point. If anything, as we shall see, working-class petitioners tended to overestimate a magistrate's discretionary power. The more serious interpretive danger here is the temptation to assume cause from effect. That the nineteenth and twentieth centuries watched humble folk make daily use of police courts to punish members of their own class for theft and assault is incontestable. That this was true does not, however, constitute proof that the disciplinary goal of a ruling élite had been achieved, or that the poor had learned to internalize the rule of law as defined by the rich. Rather, it makes more sense to argue that the poor sought legal relief from police courts as a supplement to, not merely a substitute for, the informal rituals that enforced their own indigenous notions of right and wrong.[24] Well before the close of the Victorian era, working-class applicants had grown accustomed to seeking support from "the beak"[25] principally because "the beak" was deemed to be capable of distinguishing between the just and the narrowly legal.

In part, the popularity of summary justice was attributable to its philanthropic associations. Whether they served rural or urban districts, nearly all nineteenth-century police courts maintained a "poor-box." An emergency relief fund to which local donors contributed on an irregular basis, the poor-box could be opened to support everything from mass outdoor relief during periods of high unemployment to the purchase of Christmas gifts for selected children. It was not uncommon for magistrates to give from their own pockets when the poor-box was empty, though few would have gone as far as Pinero's Mr. Posket and recruited all their servants through the "unhappy medium" of the police court.[26] Beginning in the mid-1870's, a rising tide of sentiment against "indiscriminate charity" seems to have pressured London magistrates away from granting outdoor relief. Still, even on the home turf of the Charity Organisation Society certain courts continued thereafter to orchestrate large-scale appeals during times of economic distress.[27] The gradual restriction of poor-box aid to individuals who appeared in court probably did not mean a falling off in the volume of charity, since press coverage of cases was reaching a steadily wider audience. Cecil Chapman remarked in 1932 that newspaper accounts of "pitiable" defendants were apt to generate a "storm" of charity which the magistrate was then obliged to calm. Once readers learned about the woman who could not afford a dog license for her only friend, £600 in money and clothes poured in upon the startled magistrate.[28]

If poor-box philanthropy served to humanize the police court, the willingness of magistrates at times to break ranks with other agencies of social discipline must likewise have served to invest police court justice with an aura of equity. Stipendiaries in London were often prepared to dismiss charges brought by Poor Law authorities, school attendance officers, and NSPCC inspectors when such complaints appeared to be directed against parents who were doing their best under trying circumstances.[29] Both in London and other large cities, however, police court magistrates most commonly locked horns with the police. Believing that trial by jury was "held in almost superstitious esteem," and concerned lest popular opinion come to view magistrates as "creature[s] of the police," some judges took care to prevent constables from acting as both witnesses and prosecutors in court.[30] At the level of law enforcement, magistrates tended to vacillate over tactics for the suppression of street prostitution and gambling—vacillation that frustrated city police departments.[31] Periodically this tension surfaced in public. When, for example, Liverpool police summonsed a publican for allowing her two young daughters to frolic in the bar just before closing time, they earned a mocking rebuke. Dismissing the summons, "His Worship even hazarded the remark that 'publicans as well as other people might occasionally allow their children to dance!'"[32] James Timewell was so outraged with what he took to be a case of police brutality in London that he wrote and published his own exposé. The most encouraging outcome of the complaint he lodged before Southwark Police Court was the attentiveness of the magistrate, who not only advised Timewell on how to go about prosecuting the policemen involved but also made room for the case on seventeen separate occasions.[33] Canon Barnett, dean of the settlement house movement, was right that police courts occupied "the very centre of observation and information" in an urban district, and that accounts of their cases "are read . . . when nothing else is read except football news."[34] Under these circumstances the fact of magisterial independence from other official bureaucracies must have been widely appreciated.

Summary justice thus accommodated a variety of class-based strategies. Magistrates in the late nineteenth and early twentieth centuries were typically products of the upper middle class—anything but "born" experts on proletarian life. Yet because they constituted the base of England's judicial pyramid, they tended to couch their claims to social recognition in terms of an acquired knowledge about the habits of the poor. As for the poor themselves, those who brought complaints to police courts hardly expected to find one of their own upon the bench. But they often did hope to find there a judge whose daily experience had made him receptive to their problems.

The most suggestive study of English police courts holds that they began to decline as a working-class resource toward the end of the nineteenth century. We are told that there was a "tendency . . . for the working class to desert the courts, as centres for advice and problem-resolution emerged elsewhere."[35] Quite the opposite was in fact true. Throughout the first four decades of the twentieth century, courts of summary jurisdiction became more than ever "the visible representative of 'justice'" that common people heard about in speeches and sermons.[36] By 1934, just over a thousand of these tribunals were dealing with 98 percent of persons found guilty of larceny, 80 percent of those punished for fraud, 68 percent of all judged guilty of violence against the person, and 58 percent of the sexual offenders.[37] More revealingly, the great bulk of working-class complaints about family matters also went before the police courts. They were, for example, the only places where an unmarried mother might obtain child support from a putative father: by the mid-thirties roughly 7,000 "bastardy" cases were being heard each year.[38] But most significant of all in terms of the police court's role as a "centre for advice and problem-resolution" were disputes pitting wives against husbands. Prior to the First World War, more than nine out of ten matrimonial complaints received summary treatment.[39] During the interwar years between 12,000 and 17,000 formal petitions for judicial separation were heard annually in police courts. How many other individuals obtained advice on marital matters is impossible to know, though scattered evidence drawn from the memoirs of magistrates and police court missionaries, along with newspaper accounts of cases, suggests that for every person who actually saw a marital complaint through to trial, perhaps three more sought relief of some kind without invoking the formal machinery of justice. Between the late nineteenth and the mid-twentieth centuries, therefore, hundreds of thousands of working-class people pinned their hopes for physical and emotional rescue on the understanding of police court magistrates and their assistants.[40]

It was the monumental cost of obtaining a divorce that drove the poor, especially poor wives, into the arms of summary justice. The Matrimonial Causes Act of 1857[41] represented a watershed in English social legislation since it made divorce a civil action rather than the concern of church law. This "secularization of divorce" was far from democratic, however. By stipulating that all suits had to be brought before a single, specialized Divorce Court in London, the 1857 Act built an economic fence that only the most determined working-class suitor could scale. An uncontested divorce case cost about the equivalent of thirty weeks' pay for the average male wage-earner in the Edwardian period (and about ninety-three weeks' pay for a contested case). These relative expenses would not have been much, if at all, lower a generation earlier.[42] That working-class spouses accounted for 17 percent of the divorce petitions filed in

England as early as 1871 is astonishing in an era when organized legal aid was unavailable.[43] Still, poor petitioners constituted a small segment of a tiny population. For the vast majority of ordinary people, English law long after 1857 continued to require that marriage remain, in Gladstone's words, "not a mere indulgence of taste and provision for enjoyment, but a powerful instrument of discipline and self-subjugation."[44]

There were, nevertheless, limits to the "self-subjugation" that the rich might demand from the poor. During the mid-Victorian years motherhood outside marriage became increasingly onerous due to the combination of a harsh Poor Law policy governing support of illegitimate children, a declining proportion of women in well-paid manufacturing work, and a wave of pressure for moral probity.[45] Desperate circumstances could drive single mothers to desperate acts, as the infanticide panic of the 1860's made graphically clear. By softening the Poor Law's bastardy provisions in 1872 and intensifying philanthropic aid to "fallen" women, the comfortable classes believed that they could prevent a continuing "slaughter of the innocents."[46] No sooner did the perceived nightmare of mass infanticide start to recede, however, than a new horror, again associated with poor women, began to discomfit polite society. The working-class wife, it appeared, all too often became a victim *because* of her marriage vows. Lurid newspaper accounts of wife-beating and feminist anger at the refusal of an all-male legislature to attack such outrages helped force this issue into prominence.[47] Confusion among magistrates as to the best punishment for wife-beating lent greater urgency to the problem. As Parliament discovered in 1875, magistrates often chose to deal summarily with assaults on women under section 48 of the 1861 Offences Against the Person Act. Thus, an "aggravated" assault—one causing serious bodily harm—carried a statutory maximum of just six months' imprisonment with hard labor, whereas if a magistrate elected to send the same case for jury trial at Assizes or Quarter Sessions, conviction in the higher court might mean up to five years' penal servitude.[48] A legally astute magistrate such as the Recorder of Portsmouth could offer guidelines by which to assess the gravity of a husband's offense: blows delivered with the arm or the fist "may often be excused, [but] . . . the foot never." Yet magistrates elsewhere, as in Liverpool, seemed to countenance the worst forms of male violence in their "kicking districts."[49]

Judicial wisdom generally favored the reintroduction of flogging to deter brutal husbands. Fortunately for poor women, Frances Power Cobbe did not. A feminist best known for her unyielding hostility to vivisection, Cobbe reasoned that a husband who had been flogged for assaulting his wife would more likely seek revenge than reconciliation. Her case was compelling. It was also well publicized after the *Contemporary Review* published her famous "Wife-Torture" essay in the spring of 1878. The only meaningful protection that a magistrate might offer a battered working-class woman, Cobbe insisted, was a judicial separation whereby she and her children could legally live apart from her husband.[50] Within days of its publication, "Wife-Torture" caused a quiet convulsion in the criminal law. For, roused by the essay, Lord Penzance managed to wedge Cobbe's judicial separation scheme into a bill on divorce procedure then wending its way through the Upper House. Their Lordships found little to trouble them in this new clause, nor would members of the House of Commons when their own deliberations began soon thereafter. What Parliament apparently did not grasp is that in providing such relief for poor women, the Matrimonial Causes Act of 1878 was lodging potentially broad matrimonial jurisdiction in the lowest criminal courts.[51] Although distinguished jurists would for a generation lament this backdoor enhancement of summary justice, the police courts themselves grew steadily more important as arbiters of working-class marriage.

The 1878 Act hardly revolutionized the status of poor women. It empowered magistrates to grant an order of non-cohabitation to a wife whose husband had been convicted of aggravated assault upon her. Additionally, magistrates might require a husband to make weekly contributions toward his wife's "maintenance," and allow her custody of all children up to the age of ten. Much to the dismay of late-Victorian feminists, however, the Act restricted these benefits to cases in which the magistrate was "satisfied that the future safety of the wife is in peril." In far too many police courts the "future safety" standard gave magistrates an excuse to avoid interfering with patriarchal prerogative, "even when marital authority has been enforced by the breaking of arms or jaw, by throttling to well-nigh strangulation, by cutting with knives, by biting, kicking, and striking with clenched fist, [and] by dragging upstairs and downstairs by the hair."[52] In 1880, the magistrates at Croydon denied Mrs. Long's plea for a separation order, despite the fact that her husband's abuse had driven her from home fifteen times during recent years. It was their "invariable rule" to refuse such orders, as they had no wish to split up a home.[53] At Macclesfield, one year later, magistrates seemed more disturbed by the application of rough justice against a wife-beater than by the beating itself. One autumn night in the Cheshire village of Alderly, the sounds of violence coming from the house of a man named Bredbury were enough to draw a crowd. Fearing that a murder might result, neighbors broke down Bredbury's door, fixed a halter around his neck, and with it led him "amid the jeering and scoffing of the crowd" toward a pond to be "ducked." A man who happened to be holding the halter when the village constable arrived was brought to court on a charge of drunk and disorderly conduct. Though the defendant escaped with a caution, his judges seized the occasion to condemn what they termed a "disgraceful" remnant of the "old bull-baiting days."[54]

The human impact of the 1878 Act is difficult to gauge. It may be true that in some cases the hope of gaining protection encouraged otherwise reticent women to air their marital woes in court, and that by doing so they merely provoked their tormentors.[55] In other cases, magistrates were grateful for any extra leverage in dealing with domestic violence. However uneven implementation of the Act may have been, its existence allowed Parliament to address the problem of domestic violence among the masses—and, one could add, to avoid confronting wife-beating as a more pervasive evil—by gradually restaking the boundaries of summary justice. Three further adjustments of the criminal law were important in this piecemeal process of social reform. First, the 1886 Married Women (Maintenance in Case of Desertion) Act[56] authorized magistrates to order a husband to pay maintenance directly to the wife he had deserted, instead of requiring her to prod the parish into collecting from him. Second, the 1895 Summary Jurisdiction (Married Women) Act[57] declared that magistrates might now grant separation orders not only to a wife whose husband had been convicted of an aggravated assault against her, but also to a wife who left her husband owing to his "persistent cruelty" or "willful neglect to provide reasonable maintenance" for her and their children. Interestingly, the 1895 Act was the product of pressure from the magistrates of Essex rather than from outraged feminists: legal "anomalies" evident in the 1878 legislation had impelled those responsible for applying the law to press for its improvement.[58] The Act of 1895 fell short of constituting the "poor woman's charter of freedom," largely because it stipulated that a wife treated with "persistent cruelty" had to leave her home *before* she could apply for a separation order. Even so, it did liberalize her custody rights.[59] Lastly, section 5 of the 1902 Licensing Act[60] permitted magistrates to grant separation orders where either husband or wife was deemed to be an habitual drunkard. Here was discretionary power far exceeding that of a Divorce Court judge.[61]

Elizabeth Wolstenholme Elmy echoed the thinking of many English feminists when she argued that no amount of tinkering with the criminal law could effectively shield poor women until the magistracy had shed its "sex-bias."[62] A police court's power to regulate working-class marriage had nonetheless grown formidable by the start of the twentieth century. And common people were now flooding these courts to demand what they reckoned were their "rights" as well as to plead for protection.[63] Did poor petitioners get what they came for? To assess how police courts understood and applied their new domestic jurisdiction, a closer examination of the court in action is needed. Such an examination will make concrete the limitations of summary justice as a mechanism for policing the private lives of ordinary people.[64]

Regulating Marriage in Southwest London

There was no such thing as a "typical" English police court. The stark difference in legal training between stipendiaries on the one hand and lay magistrates on the other is the most obvious factor rendering broad comparisons risky. Other, less salient, differences may have contributed just as much to variations in the way that police courts dealt with marital complaints. These included the legal acumen of the court clerk, upon whom magistrates relied for technical guidance (and, sometimes, dialect translation);[65] the size of a court's average daily caseload; the availability of a capable "missionary" or probation officer to investigate complaints; and the nature of relations between individual courts and local regulatory bodies such as school boards, Poor Law unions, and the police. But if a search for typicality is hazardous, it does not necessarily follow that close scrutiny of one court's marital work need be misleading, so long as the aim of analysis is to suggest a range of possible relations between court and community.

The community analyzed here was in fact an assortment of urban and suburban neighborhoods known collectively as Southwest London. When it opened in 1841 in Love Lane, the tribunal serving this area was called Wandsworth Police Court. Later, in 1889, the court moved to Putney Bridge Road, and once more, in 1893, to Lavender Hill, close by the metal maze of railway tracks radiating from Clapham Junction depot. By the end of the nineteenth century this institution, rechristened the South-Western Police Court, served not only the highly urbanized Battersea, Clapham, and South Lambeth districts, but also sprawling Wandsworth, chiefly middle-class Barnes and Putney, and a deep wedge of suburbia extending south well past Wimbledon.[66] From the perspective of high culture, London south of the Thames appeared nearly featureless. Sir Walter Besant summed up genteel prejudice in 1899 when he explained that:

In South London there are two millions of people. It is therefore one of the great cities of the world. It stands upon an area about twelve miles long and five or six miles broad—but its limits cannot be laid down even ap-

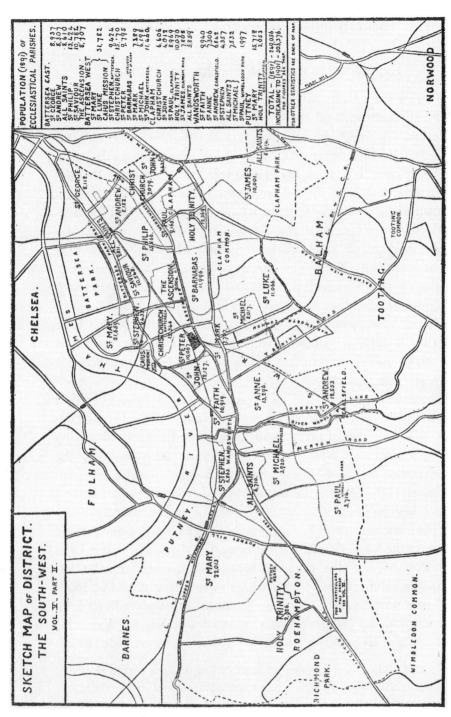

The catchment area for the South-Western Police Court. From Charles Booth's *Life and Labour of the People in London, Third Series: Religious Influences* (1902).

proximately. It is a city without a municipality, without a centre, without a civic history; it has no newspapers, magazines, or journals; it has no university; it has no colleges, apart from medicine; it has no intellectual, artistic, scientific, musical, literary centre—unless the Crystal Palace can be considered a centre; its residents have no local patriotism or enthusiasm . . . ; it has no theatres, except of a very popular or humble kind; it has no clubs, it has no public buildings, it has no West End.[67]

Since Southwest London, which contained perhaps a third of this population, could not even claim the Crystal Palace, it presumably ranked lower still on Sir Walter's scale of cultural attainment. From an industrial perspective the view was quite different. Among many engines of employment, the eighteen square miles under South-Western Police Court scrutiny included the great gas-production and railway complexes in Battersea, along with the Watney distillery, the starch-works of Orlando Jones, and the Price candle factory in Wandsworth.[68] Rapid industrial expansion in the latter half of the nineteenth century tempted speculative builders to throw up street after street of workers' dwellings—relentless rows of brick warmed if at all with plaster bay windows.[69] By the early 1930's, both the industrial boom and the fast-growing population that accompanied it had slackened considerably in Southwest London. Demographic data compiled at this time nevertheless show the area's main boroughs as comparatively well-off. Both Wandsworth, the largest and most populous Metropolitan borough, and Battersea enjoyed lower-than-average London rates for infant mortality, overcrowding, and unemployment. Both boroughs, moreover, possessed large parks and commons.[70] Thus, if the South-Western Police Court district was far from fashionable, neither was it unusually grim.

As a site for studying summary justice in microcosm, Southwest London holds two practical advantages. The first is its weekly newspaper, the *South Western Star*, which, beginning in 1889, offers a continuous record of local life.[71] The *Star* kept a close watch on police court business, prodding (one suspects) its reporters to note not only case particulars but also the comportment of all parties.[72] A second advantage is that the South-Western district became judicial headquarters for the controversial Claud Mullins, who in the 1930's emerged as England's leading advocate of "domestic courts." If we compare Mullins the reformer with Mullins the working magistrate, some of the legal strategies for intervening in working-class marriage gain greater clarity.

Half a century before Claud Mullins entered a police court, magistrates in Southwest London were learning that their new matrimonial jurisdiction was fraught with frustration. As a result, judicial patience and sympathy did not always prevail on the bench. According to one veteran of police court routine, even when magistrates could not grant marital relief, applicants tended to leave a courtroom "strengthened in some degree to bear [their] heavy burden[s]" because they had received "kindly" attention.[73] The unhappy husband who appeared before Mr. Garratt in 1901 received no such boost to his morale. The man had reluctantly summonsed his wife for assault. Instead of extracting from this "fierce and vigorous looking dame" a pledge to keep the peace, however, Mr. Garratt taunted the husband, asking, "Why don't you just run away?" "I'll walk away, Sir," the decrepit man replied as his wife glared at him "vengefully": "I should have to, I can't run."[74] Although nothing more than frayed nerves could explain the magistrate's insensitivity here, it appears likely that Garratt's sarcasm was strategic, intended to reinforce the norm of male assertiveness. At least one of Garratt's colleagues so prized the ideal of patriarchal dignity that he urged the husband of a "shrew" to leave his wife.[75] Occasionally, therefore, magistrates found that the regulation of working-class marriage involved having to choose between competing notions of right conduct.

More often it was the working-class wife who bore the brunt of judicial disdain. One Monday morning in 1904, a "frightened and respectful old lady" came before Mr. Francis. After curtsying, she blurted out that her husband had repeatedly threatened to shoot her. As Francis launched a volley of questions aimed at establishing the time and place of the alleged threats, the woman grew steadily more perplexed. She had endured her husband's foul temper for thirty-two years. Why, then, was the magistrate so concerned about recent details? In the end Francis did grant the old lady a summons for assault, though not before ridiculing her fears.[76] To judge from the newspaper reports, neither Mr. Francis nor any of his fellow magistrates were so callous as to ignore a battered woman's attempted suicide, as happened elsewhere.[77] Still, the "poor man's friend"[78] in Southwest London could approach marital issues with a stunning lack of tact.

Such insensitivity flowed partly from inexperience, since the South-Western Court was known as "a sort of nursery" for new magistrates. Judicial tyros and veterans alike, however, found it taxing to tell a stream of applicants that what they sought could not be obtained in a police court: recovering custody of a child; making a lazy husband work; getting even with a name-calling neighbor; stopping juvenile street games with a "football summons."[79] By far the most misunderstood aspect of a magistrate's power was his supposed ability to issue "protection orders." One can only speculate about the roots of this misunderstanding. Perhaps the language of the 1857 Divorce Act first led women to view the police court as a refuge for domestic oppression. Section 21 of that Act designated a police court as the only place where deserted wives could obtain "an order to protect any money or property she may acquire by her own lawful industry, and property which she may become possessed of after such desertion."[80] Parliament did not intend this safeguard to shield the average wage-earner's wife, nor would a poor woman often have had enough personal wealth to tempt her departed spouse. Yet just as a few working-class persons did manage to gain divorces against daunting odds, so a sufficient number of working-class wives may have secured property protection orders to launch what one magistrate described in 1949 as an undying "popular superstition."[81]

Whatever its beginnings, this "superstition" persisted among poor women in Southwest London. Police court reports in the *Star* saw nothing noteworthy about the daily requests for "a protection," unless they sparked quotable exchanges between applicants and magistrates. One such exchange involved the peevish Mr. Garratt:

Long cherished delusions as to "protection" were ruthlessly shattered by Mr. Garrett [sic] this morning. It must not be supposed that his worship made any pronouncement concerning matters financial and political. No, the "protection" of which he spake was of the kind that magistrates are so often importuned by distressed females to grant. "I want a protection order against my husband," said a sad-faced woman. "You want a summons," suggested Mr. Garrett [sic]. "No," replied the applicant, "I want a protection order." "I don't know what you mean by a protection order. I can only give you a summons for assault," Mr. Garrett [sic] said. Again the woman repeated her request for a "protection." Then, becoming impatient, his worship said, somewhat testily, "Can't you understand? There's no such thing as a protection order. People talk about a protection order, but it means nothing." But the woman was too slow of comprehension to understand, and as she mournfully turned away, after declining the offer of a summons, she was heard to murmur, "I only wanted protection."[82]

Both judge and reporter here believed that a dull mind was responsible for this wife's confusion. It is just as plausible, though, that her confusion stemmed from despair. For if some wives in Southwest London conceived of police court protection as "a piece of paper, in hue, official blue, typifying the arm of the law, and rendering the person of the possessor . . . immune from assault,"[83] then the sudden withdrawal of this imagined last line of defense might have shaken even the most quick-witted woman.

By no means all those seeking to transform their married lives labored under legal delusions. On the contrary, fragmentary evidence suggests that common men and women sometimes made a point of familiarizing themselves with summary procedure, a fact which suggests that some working-class individuals saw the police court as an agency whose coercive power could be harnessed to their own ends. Mary Knott, the wife of a Clapham painter, had suffered twelve years of carefully calculated abuse before she turned to Mr. Gibson for help in 1898. At first Mary's husband used to throw hot potatoes at her. Later George's attacks grew more menacing, although rarely did they go so far as to constitute "aggravated assaults" in the narrow sense of that phrase. This was no coincidence. For early on in the marriage George "developed a habit of attending the police court and listening to all the matrimonial summonses." He had taken special note of the "persistent cruelty" clause of the 1895

Summary Jurisdiction Act. George soon realized that since his wife was formally the tenant of the house they rented, she would be loathe to leave it in order to satisfy the law. Secure in his legal immunity, George took to punching Mary in the face nearly every night after the pubs closed. Finally the stoic woman could bear no more. Late one evening Mary sought refuge in rooms she had sublet to her lodgers, and the next day she approached Mr. Gibson for advice. Clever as well as sympathetic, the magistrate urged her to thwart George by returning to her lodgers' rooms for several days—thereby demonstrating that she had technically left her home without actually abandoning the premises. Mary followed this advice, with the result that Mr. Gibson felt justified in granting her a separation order and generous terms for maintenance.[84] The defendant's manipulation of law had forced Gibson to bend that same law in defense of the victim. Magistrates in other police courts faced similar predicaments, and sometimes took similar liberties.[85]

Working-class wives could also be well versed in matrimonial law. According to Alfred Plowden, a longtime magistrate at Marylebone Police Court and an occasional visitor to the South-Western bench, the Archbishop of Canterbury had erred in declaring that adultery was rare among the poor. True, applications for separation orders seldom alleged adultery, but only because, "People do not usually ask for what they cannot get." Plowden added that, "Wives who make these applications in a Police Court as a rule are surprisingly well informed of the legal grounds on which alone they are entitled to succeed."[86]

Magistrates regularly assigned to the South-Western bench would have agreed with this assessment, save for the mythology surrounding "protection orders." Late in the summer of 1891 a woman came to court with the complaint that her husband had been "carrying on" so for the past few days that she was afraid to go home. All she wanted was to collect her clothing and leave, nothing more. Mr. Denman initially refused to help; he would not interfere with a "domestic dispute." Taking careful aim, she shot back: "The law is all for the men, and none for the women. I wish I was Mrs. Jackson." This timely allusion to a celebrated case of wife-abduction (and court-ordered release) in Lancashire[87] impressed Denman, who, breaking into a smile, now appeared willing to hear more. The woman seized her chance, conveniently recalling that her husband had threatened her with a gun. Mr. Denman thereupon ordered a constable to guarantee her safety while she retrieved her clothing.[88] The 1880's saw flamboyant Georgina Weldon win fame for her "plantiff in person" suits against doctors who had tried to immure her in a lunatic asylum.[89] Anonymous by comparison, more than a few poor women who sought matrimonial relief in Southwest London were likewise equipped to act as their own counsel.

Some of the same commentators who found poor wives "surprisingly" well informed about their rights under summary jurisdiction also marveled that they were willing to accept such terrible treatment from their husbands. The wife with two black eyes who pleaded for legal help yet refused to give evidence against her mate was a stock figure in police court lore. She was, alternately, a paragon of female forgiveness or an obstructor of justice who would "lie unblushingly to the magistrate in order to save [her] husband from prison."[90] Data presented to the Royal Commission on Divorce confirm that "aggravated assault" was rarely the ground upon which working-class wives sought judicial separations. Although magistrates assigned to the South-Western Police Court were silent on this point, stipendiaries elsewhere were not. In Wolverhampton and its hinterland, a West Midlands district of about 350,000 where coal mining and iron manufacture dominated the economy, less than 1 percent of all separation orders granted between 1906 and 1909 cited aggravated assault as the cause for action. During the same period the stipendiary magistrate of Grimsby, a northeastern fishing port of 70,000, granted just 8.5 percent of his separation orders on account of aggravated assault. Finally, at London's Tower Bridge Police Court, a mere 4 percent of the orders were so based. At each of these widely dispersed courts a husband's "desertion" was what drove roughly half of all applicants to seek permission (and means) to set up new households, while "persistent cruelty" and "failure to maintain" also bulked large as causes.[91]

Judicial disagreement over what constituted an "aggravated" assault may explain in part why poor women complained so infrequently about gross physical abuse. More often, probably, a wife refused to summons her mate for aggravated assault because his conviction meant that she and her children would be left with a drastically reduced income during his jail term.[92] The much-discussed forbearance of working-class wives stemmed also from a conception of marriage that bore only a vague resemblance to the "companionate" ideal then in favor among the comfortable classes. That is, while working-class conjugal relationships generally did respect the norm of monogamy, they often lacked the associated element of emotional intimacy. Poor women were more likely to regard their marriages as economic support systems than as partnerships based on love. As Ellen Ross has remarked about life in the East London slums, "If marriage did not enjoin trust, sharing, and partnership, then it was far less surprising that conflict would frequently erupt here."[93] The social meaning of violence within marriage varied according to social and economic circumstances; an act that might outrage bourgeois sensibilities could stir far less indignation among the poor. Thus, while passing sentence on a Battersea carpenter who had pummeled his wife's head with clenched fists, Magistrate Plowden in 1889 issued the dictum that "men of the prisoner's class must understand that they cannot be allowed to assault women with impunity." Meanwhile, the carpenter's wife was tearfully urging his release.[94] Within many working-class communities there endured an expectation of friction between husbands and wives, friction produced as often by the assertion of matriarchal claims as by patriarchal aggression. From time to time magistrates in Southwest London felt obliged to remind wives that there were limits to their right of remonstration against husbands, and to exhort husbands to deal resolutely with "nagging" wives.[95] For women who suffered male violence without enjoying substantial autonomy within their own sphere, a police court summons might appear capable of restoring domestic equilibrium. So apparently reasoned the unmarried mother of eight who complained to Mr. Fordham in 1913 that the man she lived with "knocks me about just as if I was his wife." The remedy

"IT'S ALL A MISTAKE, YOUR WUSHIP, ALL A MISTAKE; HE
DIDN'T DO NUFFING, HE WOULDN'T 'URT A FLY!"

"I'LL DO FOR YOU WEN I COME OUT."

George Sims (*How the Poor Live*, 1883) thought he understood why the working-class wife so often refused to press charges against her abusive mate: "The woman knows . . . that the three months' sentence means comfort and luxury to the man—misery and starvation to [her] and her little ones."

seemed obvious to her: "If you would please grant me a summons. He'd be a better man then, I know."[96]

Reminded each day in their courtrooms that violence was sadly commonplace in working-class marriage, a few magistrates grew to believe that only a vast liberalization of divorce law would bring peace to humble homes. After twenty years in London police courts, Alfred Plowden had concluded that without divorce as a practical option for the poor, marriage remained a "dangerous mad gamble." During testimony to the Royal Commission on Divorce, Plowden confessed that when marital violence was at issue, breaking up a family gave him no pause:

Rightly or wrongly, I can assure the Commission I never sleep so soundly after a day's work as when I feel I have separated some woman from a brute of a husband on grounds which are unanswerable. . . . I feel I have done a charitable work more than a legal one, and I should rejoice more if, instead of being able to give that qualified partial relief, . . . I would give what is at that moment her heart's desire, . . . a divorce.[97]

Cecil Chapman likewise believed that the vaunted sanctity of marriage should not condemn common folk to lives of physical and mental anguish. Chapman saw judicial separation as a valuable but ultimately crude tool with which to relieve "obvious misery." For although a separation order might cost a poor wife just two shillings and save her from decades of further abuse, it might also buy "a life of celibacy or immorality" since, with remarriage impossible for her, the separated mother would feel strong economic pressure to form an irregular union. Chapman therefore wished to expand the grounds for judicial separation and, after the lapse of several years, to permit spouses to convert their separation orders into divorces.[98]

The pronouncements of Chapman and Plowden were, however, exceptional in two respects. First, even if they did privately agree that universal access to divorce made sense, the great majority of police court magistrates in late-Victorian and Edwardian England kept discretely silent on this issue. Second and more important, where Chapman and Plowden saw judicial separation as a useful if imperfect method for offering relief to misused spouses, most of their judicial peers viewed the cure as worse than the illness. What troubled magistrates above all was that working-class husbands and wives often did not use separation and maintenance orders as the law intended. Poor women, they complained, put the separation process in motion not because they wanted new lives apart from their husbands but rather because they hoped to jolt them out of bad habits.[99] Jealousy, more often than fear or want, allegedly lay at the root of applications made in "the heat of the moment."[100] Whether or not this was true is difficult to tell from the case summaries featured in local newspapers. Plainly, though, among the matrimonial oddities with which magistrates in Southwest London had to cope on a regular basis was the wife who had obtained several separation orders yet kept returning to her mate. Less commonly, a wife might urge the magistrate to order her husband's return despite the existence of a valid separation agreement.[101] Such apparent fickleness convinced several magistrates that poor women did not appreciate the gravity of a judicial separation, and thus should be dissuaded from seeking one. From the perspective of a working-class wife, on the other hand, the wish to modify or even ignore a legal separation order might have been a rational first step toward patching up a marriage worth saving. Still more likely, she might have learned the hard lesson that winning the right to weekly maintenance payments was one thing, and actually receiving the stipulated sum was quite another.

Indeed, the difficulty of enforcing maintenance orders, which accompanied separation orders in over 95 percent of such police court cases,[102] persuaded many magistrates that their energies would best be devoted to keeping couples together. For some husbands who defaulted on their scheduled maintenance payments, the prospect of prison held no terror. When "smartly dressed" Adeline Robinson, a lady's maid, came before the South-Western Police Court in 1900 seeking payment of maintenance arrears, few observers would have predicted success. Samuel, her husband, a "dirty and insolently indolent" man, had already proclaimed his aversion to work, and the way he slouched against the side of the dock while leering at his wife seemed to say that the threatened two months behind bars was a matter of indifference to him.[103] The Criminal Justice Administration Act of 1914[104] enabled police courts to appoint collecting officers (often the court clerk), with the result that working-class wives no longer had the onus of confronting delinquent husbands. The violation of maintenance orders nevertheless continued to plague England's summary justice system through the mid-1930's. Husbands were often willing to pay something toward the support of their separated wives, but because these payments tended to be irregular, large arrears could accumulate. Since police courts had no authority to excuse a portion of such debts, even well-intentioned men might end up in prison.[105] Thus, beyond the moral argument that judicial separation encouraged "libertinage" on the part of the husband and drove the wife to seek financial security with "a husband who is no husband,"[106] there were practical reasons why magistrates often tried to coax working-class petitioners into giving their marriages one more chance.

The work of marital mediation began to weigh heavily on magistrates in the 1880's. What made this work feasible in the first place was the help of voluntary agents known as "police court missionaries." By the time that Lord Gorell's commission launched its painstaking study of proposals to democratize divorce in 1909, police court missionaries had become the principal social investigators for magistrates throughout England. Significantly, missionaries constituted the largest single category of witnesses to testify before the Royal Commission on Divorce.[107] The missionaries' combined testimony was equivocal on the key question of working-class preferences: whereas the "Majority Report" cited their evidence as proof that a pent-up demand for divorce existed among the poor, the "Minority Report" brandished the same evidence to show that it did not.[108] On the matter of salvaging marriages, however, little doubt seemed to surround the missionaries' record. Working hand-in-hand with police court magistrates, these men and women had reportedly been so successful at reconciling poor spouses that a "very large proportion" of the separation orders granted each year eventually became moot. So at least argued the Archbishop of Canterbury on the eve of the Royal Commission's appointment.[109] The Archbishop, an implacable foe of divorce law liberalization, naturally had every reason to contend that existing legal resources were adequate to deal with the marital difficulties of the masses. Yet in less exaggerated form many Edwardian contemporaries shared this confidence in the conciliatory power of the missionaries. Robert Holmes, a missionary in Sheffield, kept a rough tally of the "matrimonial cases" he encountered during twelve years of service. Of the 1,600 men and women who approached him with separation orders in mind, about half left the interview resolved to remake their marriages, Holmes claimed. Some missionaries elsewhere reportedly enjoyed even greater success at persuading working-class spouses to put God's wishes ahead of their own.[110]

Originally dispatched to police courts as church-sponsored temperance workers in the late 1870's, these missionaries unexpectedly evolved into *de facto* probation officers for some magistrates. Salvation had been the chief concern of the earliest police court missionaries. In 1876, the Church of England Temperance Society appointed a special agent whose job it was to visit certain London police courts and from them scoop up drunkards for "restoration and reclamation." Nearly from the start of this venture CETS officials were ready to give their corps of male (and, after 1885, female) missionaries a long leash, since drink-induced sin assumed so many forms.[111] But the rapid expansion of such rescue work hinged upon the conjunction of two specific developments. First, the theological bent of the CETS disposed it to encourage direct intervention in private lives. Canon Henry Ellis, longtime Chairman of the Society, espoused a pragmatic evangelicalism which held that it was pointless to preach the gospel to people while the "stumbling-block" of alcohol hardened their hearts. Although faith remained paramount in the quest for God's grace, good works, including those that tended to coerce the sinner, might at times be essential supplements. Second, the 1870's and 1880's found English judges under mounting pressure to adopt more uniform sentencing standards in criminal cases. As judges felt increasingly compelled to justify acts of mercy that produced "disparate sentencing," therefore, they grew correspondingly more eager to find plausible justifications for exercising leniency.[112] The social inquiries made by police court missionaries furnished magistrates with these justifications, while the work itself honored the CETS's commitment to assisted salvation. How effectively the police court mission served to impose an "ideology of moral individualism"[113] on working-class culture remains a largely unanswerable question, not least because it would be difficult to recognize the signs of successful indoctrination. That late-Victorian legal reforms opened up new room for missionary activism is incontestable, however. In permitting magistrates to discharge persons convicted of minor offenses provided they behaved themselves, for example, the 1879 Summary Jurisdiction Act prompted police courts to seek help with supervising these offenders.[114] Furthermore, as we have seen, the Matrimonial Causes Act of 1878 empowered magistrates to issue separation and maintenance orders. It appeared that no one was better positioned than the missionary to act as a voluntary probation officer, or to intercede in those cases of marital strife that would soon deluge the courts.

The Church of England Temperance Society was not the only sponsor of court-centered voluntarism, nor was its missionary organization monolithic. Throughout England, representatives of the Salvation Army also made occasional courtroom appearances to support misused females or "respectable" men whose wives had succumbed to drink.[115] In Birmingham during the 1890's, a local women's association saw to it that "lady visitors" were present to assist young females brought before the magistrates. Cambridge women organized a similar service in 1912. By 1916 the CETS was just one of five societies supplying missionaries to police courts in Liverpool.[116] The CETS itself abandoned centralized administrative control in 1892, thereby permitting each diocese to run its own reclamation program. Thereafter, even in the Society's London stronghold, doubts lingered about the relative value of police court "rescue" work versus such "preventive" efforts as children's temperance education in the Band of Hope movement.[117] Outside London, police court missions often faced stiff competition for philanthropic support. In Edwardian Oxfordshire, the Additional Curates Society might raise twice the annual income of the local Police Court and

Prison Gate Mission. The Norwich Mission in the same period suffered from economic rivalry with the Discharged Prisoners' Aid Society, when their kindred efforts could easily have been coordinated.[118] And most significantly, the advent of a state-controlled probation system in 1907 marked the start of a process by which "scientific" training for missionaries gained prestige at the expense of the old CETS ideal of spiritual inspiration. Although professionalism and a sense of religious calling coexisted in the person of the "missionary probation officer" throughout most of the interwar years, the role of social diagnostician grew steadily more important.[119]

If missionaries were neither a well organized nor a uniformly influential force across the land, it nevertheless remains true that they were believed to play leading roles in most of the marital dramas brought to court. In the reminiscences of magistrates and police court clerks, missionaries emerge as virtual saints: firm but fair in remonstrating with drunkards; sage in recommending how poor-box charity should be distributed; tactful in dealing with warring spouses; "accomplished . . . in handling any symptoms of hysteria"; capable of "draw[ing] money from a skinflint, and goodness from a wastrel."[120] Well after credentialed probation officers had superseded the missionary "old-timers," some magistrates continued to prize "personal spirit" above scholastic attainment in their assistants.[121] The missionaries who told their own stories were eager to stress themes of triumph over adversity. Thomas Holmes, a largely self-taught Staffordshire iron worker who rose through police court work to become Secretary of the Howard Association in 1905, was surely the best known specimen. His vignettes depict a sensitive warrior who could be sickened to tears by the sordidness of police court routine yet spend days orchestrating a happy homecoming for a wife-beater released from jail. Although Holmes's tales of decency amidst degeneration would strike a modern reader as annoyingly self-righteous, they earned praise from his contemporaries.[122]

At London's South-Western Police Court, the partnership between missionaries and magistrates appears to have been tenuous until mid-1917. There is little evidence to suggest that, prior to

Ralph Bankes's joining the South-Western bench, local missionaries acted as "the friend of all alike, and the friend simply; never the prosecutor."[123] The first reference to a missionary at the court on Lavender Hill dates from early 1897, when the *Star* noted that a young servant seen wading into (and out of) Eagle House Pond, Clapham, had been charged with attempted suicide. The court missionary, a Mr. McGowan, believed that Louisa Parsons should be institutionalized, and his insistence on this point set off a shouting match with the young woman's outraged mother. Magistrate Francis settled the dispute by discharging Louisa.[124] McGowan gave way to a Miss Reade as the court's lone missionary seven years later, but it was not until 1914 that a magistrate averse to granting separation orders began to employ her as his "semi-official peacemaker" in domestic disputes. Up to this time Miss Reade had been used sparingly, most often to counsel women charged with public drunkenness or vagrancy.[125] In the absence of any press commentary on her background, we may surmise that Miss Reade was a Church of England Temperance Society agent as well as a probation officer who, unlike the Chelsea doctor's wife with a "superior education" then performing the same duties at Thames Police Court, had working-class roots.[126] At some point during the early war years a second missionary–probation officer, Mr. Wrigley, joined the court. When appeals to a feuding couple's "better nature" failed, Wrigley tried "din[ning] straightforward common-sense into minds temporarily inflamed," by stressing the economic costs of separation.[127]

Under Magistrate Bankes's scrutiny, these two missionaries compiled a stunning record in the mediation of marital complaints. The Home Office was gratified to report that in 1923, 46.3 percent of the 3,448 London-wide "separation cases" referred to probation officers had ended in reconciliation.[128] But this record paled beside that of the South-Western Police Court. During the two years 1918 and 1919, 747 applications "arising out of marital differences" came before Mr. Bankes, and in 655 of these cases "no subsequent proceedings" took place. Strictly speaking the two sets of statistics were not comparable, since requests other than for judicial separation (e.g., applications to amend maintenance awards) were included in

Bankes's figures. Neither calculation, moreover, differentiated between reconciliations achieved before and those achieved after court-ordered separations. Nor was there any way to tell from such totals how many wives agreed to make peace with their husbands out of rekindled affection, and how many agreed to try again out of economic necessity. Yet, riddled with ambiguity as these statistics were, a reconciliation rate of 87.7 percent, accomplished amidst the social and economic dislocation of world war, still seemed nearly miraculous.[129]

On closer examination this achievement appears less impressive, for Magistrate Bankes's commitment to middle-class moral standards sometimes blinded him to the plight of women trapped in desperate circumstances.[130] The South-Western Police Court's strategy for preserving working-class marriage may actually have prolonged as much misery as it relieved. If, as Jan Lambertz has speculated, the reconciliation work of the police courts helped to divert public attention from the problem of violence within the home,[131] then the experiment at Lavender Hill was a prime example of misdirected energy. What admirers of this matrimonial work also failed to appreciate was that its author exercised limited influence over his own court. Ralph Bankes died in October 1921, a little more than four years after he took over as the senior stipendiary. Frequent periods of illness during 1920 and 1921 had not only kept Bankes off the bench but also brought replacement magistrates to court who gave short shrift to the goal of reconciliation. The "patriarchal" Mr. d'Eyncourt cared less about regulating marriage than articulating the duties of wives.[132] Mr. Disney struck reporters as resentful of "advice and guidance, be they [ever] so tactfully tendered."[133] Whereas Mr. Boyd was too "curt" and "easily irritated" to play a leading part in marital fence-mending, Mr. Symmons was perhaps too phlegmatic, a magistrate so inert that his monocle seemed permanently suspended over his right eye.[134] These and other substitutes obviously brought their own prejudices to bear on disputes between wives and husbands. Although London's South-Western Police Court was acquiring a national reputation for its matrimonial peacekeeping during the immediate postwar years, it was probably fame built as much on wishful thinking as on solid success. After all, many of those who governed during the early 1920's still shuddered at the thought of divorce becoming universally available—a thought that seemed particularly troubling given the wartime toll of broken marriages. Thus the stage was nearly set for England's most ambitious experiment in matrimonial regulation.

Claud Mullins and Coercive Conciliation

By the mid-1920's legal reforms had equalized the grounds for divorce as well as enlarged the matrimonial jurisdiction of police courts. Of these two developments only the story of divorce law reform is well known. World War One dramatically altered English divorce patterns: roughly four times as many persons petitioned for divorce in 1919 as had in 1913.[135] Although the relative importance of factors responsible for such a striking change is difficult to judge, certainly the expansion of legal aid in 1914 along with generally rising real wages meant that divorce was growing more affordable during the war years. Additionally, since impulsive wartime marriages were often followed by lonely periods of separation, the more visible infidelity of wives also fueled this trend.[136] Feminists in the immediate postwar years therefore took up the challenge of securing equal grounds for divorce. Largely as a result of pressure from the National Union of Societies for Equal Citizenship, then England's leading feminist interest group, the 1923 Matrimonial Causes Act did indeed create a new legal standard, making a husband's adultery equivalent to a wife's.[137] Thoroughgoing champions of divorce law reform remained impatient, however. These activists argued that until the grounds for divorce were expanded, the dissolution of marriage would continue to be a process that encouraged deceit among petitioners and sent shudders of disgust through the judges who drew Divorce Court duty.[138] In a telling turn of phrase one reformer complained as late as 1935 that "matrimonial surgery" was all but impossible to perform in this court, since it offered a judge no room to operate.[139] By contrast, mechanisms for conciliation were plentiful in English police courts.

Magistrates and their missionary–probation officers showed a growing preference for reconciling rather than separating couples during the 1920's partly because the law itself was making it easier for poor spouses to leave one another. In this sense the work of marital "adjustment"[140] may be viewed as a preemptive strike directed against working-class wives and husbands who plainly *were* exercising their legal prerogatives with increasing frequency.[141] At the level of case law, judicial decisions such as *Thomas v. Thomas* (1923) had gradually clarified the concept of "desertion" to the advantage of wronged women. That is, by defining desertion as withdrawal from "a state of things," these decisions allowed a wife who had been driven from home by her husband's behavior to refuse to return when he asked for another chance.[142] At the level of parliamentary statute, the 1925 Summary Jurisdiction (Separation and Maintenance) Act empowered police court magistrates to grant separation orders under new circumstances: when a spouse had been found guilty of persistent cruelty to the children; when a husband insisted on intercourse while knowingly suffering from venereal disease; or when he had forced his wife into prostitution. Although the 1925 Act was introduced as a government measure, the ground for it had been cleared by a persistent private Member, Sir Robert Newman.[143] Nor should Baldwin's Conservatives be credited here with anticipating a shift in public opinion. Rather, the government was promoting what it saw as a cheap alternative to the foreign, and thus suspect idea of "domestic courts."

The notion of a special court of summary jurisdiction where the "adjustment" of most family problems might take place generated both enthusiasm and alarm within the English legal community. Since domestic courts were clearly American inventions, having emerged as the adult extension of juvenile courts, they troubled those who already resented "the increasing Americanization of Great Britain." Such contamination was especially foul when it assumed the form of "a multitude of pettifogging Statutes, each destroying piecemeal some little vestige of a period when a man could call his soul his own." The author of this rant was E. S. P. Haynes, among the most outspoken advocates of English divorce law reform.

Curiously, in the same tract Haynes lauded the work of American domestic courts, arguing that as specialist tribunals they were better equipped to deal with family conflict than English police courts.[144] Haynes's self-contradiction reflected a deep ambivalence among those concerned with legal administration. On the one hand, most scholars and high-ranking jurists agreed with the Royal Commission on Divorce that it was inappropriate for the nation's common criminal courts to entertain civil applications—"applications which, if granted, may produce the practical although not the legal dissolution of the marriage tie."[145] On the other hand, to abolish the matrimonial jurisdiction of police courts without simultaneously democratizing divorce procedure was to slam law's door on the poor.

Given such ambivalence about the American domestic court, its first English champions not surprisingly occupied the outskirts of legal power. In 1914, Cecil Leeson, a Birmingham probation officer, praised the judicial experiments then being conducted in New York, Illinois, and Massachusetts. What Leeson admired most about the legal pioneers in these states was their willingness to tackle head-on the problem of the deadbeat husband. For although America's first domestic courts theoretically aimed to reconcile estranged mates, most of their effort was devoted to extracting money from men who had abandoned their wives and children.[146] Leeson's enthusiasm proved less than infectious. Five years passed before the Home Office learned that a social work center in East London had recently opened a "Domestic Troubles Court" at which its volunteer barrister sought to settle quarrels between poor spouses.[147] Another seven years elapsed before an aged General Booth decided that his Salvation Army needed a "Reconciliation Bureau" to complement its "Anti-Suicide Bureau."[148] By the late 1920's news of the successful "social diagnosis" provided in American domestic courts, where judges worked as "human adjuster[s] of human difficulties," had convinced a handful of Labour MPs to take legislative action.[149] What resulted was the 1928 Courts of Domestic Relations Bill. At least one newspaper found it amusing that the force behind this proposal was a bachelor, Harry Snell, the Member for Woolwich, but Snell himself saw nothing humorous about the police court "stigma" that allegedly poisoned all reconciliation work. If only family matters could be aired behind closed doors, he believed, then surely men and women "would learn to go to the judge for . . . help with the same ready confidence that they now go to a doctor when they are physically ill."[150]

Although Snell's bill died upon introduction, his faith in the transforming potential of the domestic court echoed a growing body of opinion that viewed summary jurisdiction as an appropriate realm for weighing "social evidence." It appeared that the police court could be modified to carry out the highest mandate of American social science: to promote happiness through the realignment of expectations with reality.[151] Thus, for example, a new breed of magistrate, presiding over a clinic-like court, might save marriages by helping to restore sexual balance to troubled relationships.[152] Many of the older, CETS missionaries were receptive to the idea of a domestic court held *in camera*. Their generally younger and better educated peers, members of the National Association of Probation Officers, likewise welcomed the prospect of greater involvement in reconciliation work, also known as finding "sparks beneath the ashes."[153] By 1934 a new champion of the domestic court model had stepped forward in Parliament. This time, however, the champion was an earl rather than a socialist MP, and his plan called for a drastic revision of English legal practice.

Lord Listowel's Summary Jurisdiction (Domestic Procedure) Bill, introduced in late March and debated on May 15, aimed not only to shield a poor couple's strife from the "vulgar curiosity of gaping onlookers," but also to turn a trial into a friendly chat. Henceforth, according to this plan, stipendiary magistrates would hear domestic disputes in private sessions flanked by two lay justices (one of whom had to be a woman), since "common sense is more urgently needed than legal knowledge where a marriage is going wrong."[154] This was novel enough. But by seeking to make conciliation *obligatory* "before the fatal legal process [of separation] begins," and by abolishing oaths and direct cross-examination, Listowel's scheme challenged some of the most hallowed elements of trial procedure. Equally unorthodox was its proposed "conciliation summons." This was to be a non-compulsory request from either spouse that husband and wife vent their grievances before sympathetic magistrates "whenever . . . married life seems on the verge of disaster." Taken together these reforms would change the "whole atmosphere" of the new domestic court "from one of litigation to one of investigation and reconciliation."[155]

Press reactions to Listowel's plan were overwhelmingly positive.[156] The twenty-seven-year-old earl nonetheless hit a stone wall in the form of a hostile House of Lords and a skeptical Civil Service. His bill, their lordships complained, shook the foundations of English justice and snubbed generations of experience.[157] The Home Office worried that the proposal would damage the prestige of the police courts by conferring on them "patriarchal" functions, while a ranking member of the Lord Chancellor's Office dismissed it as "ridiculous."[158] No one in the Government wished publicly to denounce the Bill's American antecedents, so to placate Listowel the Lord Chancellor promised to conduct a full-scale review of the "social character" of police court justice. His promise proved good, for six months later the Home Office launched an in-house study of this sensitive matter.[159]

Significantly, the driving force behind Listowel's plan emanated from the magistracy itself. After the death in 1932 of Sir William Clarke Hall, doyen of English juvenile court judges,[160] Claud Mullins emerged as the nation's most visible magistrate. Unlike Clarke Hall, however, Mullins's reputation has nearly disappeared with time.[161] Yet during the 1930's and 40's his judicial activism went far toward defining the limits of summary justice.

By the time that Claud Mullins took his place on the South-Western Police Court bench in November 1934, he was already a lightning rod for controversy. Mullins's path to the magistracy had been unusual, and his famous—or infamous—judicial independence was the natural extension of a life lived on the edge of middle-class security. One of four sheltered children, Mullins grew up in Northwest London, where his father, a talented sculptor, earned just enough to maintain the trappings of household respectability. Due not only to the family's modest means but also to his distaste for the second-rate education he had endured, young Mullins left school at the age of sixteen. Thanks to an uncle's generosity he spent the next two years studying German on the Continent. But at eighteen the need to make his own way drove Mullins into a mind-numbing junior clerkship with the London County Council, a job he kept while later reading for the Bar at night. The same self-discipline that enabled him to win a Gray's Inn fellowship without university training continued in evidence during his years as an apprentice barrister, when Mullins's legal education had to compete with his part-time job as a writer for various London newspapers. Throughout the 1920's Mullins was a well-regarded if financially unsuccessful advocate. Thus as a "keen" but professionally frustrated man of forty-three, he leapt at the chance to become a metropolitan magistrate in 1931. Claud Mullins would later recall that he did not set out to be a reformer when first assigned to the North London Police Court. He nonetheless approached the job of stipendiary magistrate holding two iron-clad convictions: that the "gloomy security" of socialism in any form was toxic; and that virtually all marriages were worth saving, a faith inspired by the "model" relationship of his own father and mother.[162]

Within a year of his appointment to the metropolitan bench Mullins had earned the Chief Magistrate's ire for out-of-court activism. Sir Chartres Biron, already well known for banning (and thus publicizing) Radclyffe Hall's lesbian novel, *The Well of Loneliness*, declared it unseemly that London's youngest magistrate should spend so much time discussing the application of psychiatry to criminal justice with "dangerous" innovators such as Sir William Clarke Hall and Dr. J. R. Rees, head of the Tavistock Clinic. Far from humoring Biron, however, Mullins concluded their tense interview with a barb about the superiority of golf as judicial recreation. Biron's successor as Chief Magistrate, Sir Rollo Graham Campbell, inherited a still less tractable judge. By 1934 Mullins was writing widely about the police court as a place where working-class couples should be able to obtain the latest birth control information, and from which they might be referred to sex experts for the cure of physical difficulties.[163] But Mullins's overriding concern was the way that matrimonial matters continued to be "jumbled up" with criminal cases in English police courts. If only magistrates could find a way to "burrow more deeply" into the domestic difficulties brought before them, "the real causes of . . . estrangements would be revealed and . . . then more hopeful efforts could be made to reconcile" unhappy mates.[164] Pursuing this project, Mullins tried in turn to interest the National Council of Women, the Salvation Army, and the Mothers' Union in a campaign for legislative reform of police court procedure. After three successive rebuffs he pounced on an offer of parliamentary backing from the young Earl of Listowel, with the controversial result we have seen. When Mullins was transferred to the South-Western Police Court in late 1934, then, he was eager to conduct his own domestic court despite legislative foot-dragging and the fond wish of some judicial colleagues that he be "muzzled."[165]

Claud Mullins was lucky to draw Southwest London as his new post because here both the senior magistrate and his two missionaries already viewed their court as a "sphere of social welfare work." The genial William Brodrick, with whom Mullins was now paired, had a popular following at Lavender Hill so strong that complainants "flocked in shoals" to the court when he was sitting.[166] The new magistrate struck local newspaper reporters as less likely to win such affection. Mullins's deep bass voice, curt delivery, and "impatience with trifles" hinted at a man of "individuality," perhaps even ambition. Together, these attributes made his first day in court a noteworthy one:

Not a murmur, not a whisper, not the suggestion of a laugh fell from the crowd at the back of the court during the morning. The mere presence of Mr. Mullins subdued them, not only into silence but into motionlessness. One little untoward incident there was. A man in the throng . . . kept his hat on his head. Had another magistrate been sitting the man would have been openly rebuked, perhaps ordered to leave the court. But the influence of the new stipendiary was such as to create the impression that even the lawful exercise of subordinate authority would be undesirable. Therefore, an official tip-toed towards the back of the court, and gently tapped the side of his head, gazing steadily the while at the man who was wearing the cap. The hint had the desired effect. Off came the cap, and the man was frowned on by all who stood near him.

Mullins might "prove to be the Napoleon of police court magistrates," mused the *Star*.[167]

He certainly wasted no time overhauling the machinery of domestic justice. For several years Mr. Brodrick had seen to it that all women applying for a matrimonial summons either whispered their complaints in his ear or else saw the female missionary before stating their cases in open court. When poor applicants appeared to need a solicitor, the court provided one at no cost. Finally, to enlarge its social services, six local clergymen scattered throughout the district had been enlisted as "referees" before whom husbands and wives might lay out their differences. Short of resorting to secret hearings, which Brodrick feared would anger the press and alienate working-class clients, the South-Western Court had "exhausted all methods of conciliation."[168] Mullins disagreed, though for once he resisted saying so in public. He decided instead to "improve" on the law by taking huge liberties with accepted police court procedure. Accordingly, within a month of his arrival at Lavender Hill Mullins began holding "domestic afternoons" in a small side room. Because the door to this room was closed but not locked, such sessions were not technically private, while the size of the new chamber excluded "idle spectators" without requiring Mullins to declare a prohibition of any sort.[169]

The new magistrate regarded "strict law" as the enemy of matrimonial salvation. At first Mullins sought to soothe fears that conciliation as practiced in his district was a coercive process. Clergymen who served as "referees" in Southwest London, he assured the Home Office, might well argue against reconciliation depending on the intimate details of a case. For example, when Rev. F. H. Grimwade of Battersea learned that lurking behind "Mrs. O's" request for child support lay the fact of intercourse between her husband and her mother, the referee was quick to recommend separation.[170] But in his everyday work Mullins himself found it very hard to concede that any marriage had failed for good. In "forced" unions—those compelled by unwanted pregnancy—"careful treatment" could often keep "rash" parents together.[171] Working-class mates for whom sex had become a source of resentment allegedly benefited from visiting one of the medical psychologists on Mullins's lengthening list of volunteers.[172] Most poor husbands were purportedly "glad" to talk through their troubles with a missionary, especially when the magistrate issued him a confidential invitation to do so. Even after a couple had been judicially separated, legerdemain might turn a maintenance arrears case into a reunion. That is, by ordering the delinquent husband to jail for just one day, Mullins could wipe out the man's legal debt. Then, by prohibiting the jailer from enforcing this order, Mullins could create such gratitude in the husband that he would warmly agree to support his wife, and perhaps even ask her to take him back. The police court magistrate, it seemed, might be in a better position to determine a couple's best interest than the couple itself. "Life is long," Mullins observed. Hence, "Those who have to decide marriage cases should always have an eye to the distant future, although the law and the evidence concerns the past and present only."[173]

If not quite Napoleonic, Mullins's domestic campaign was coercive by most contemporary standards save his own. Hopkin Morris, a four-year veteran of the South-Western Court, found it "odiously impertinent" that Mullins and his staff devoted such energy to investigating private lives.[174] Although the Home Office's Departmental Committee was less disturbed, its report, released in the winter of 1936, had Mullins in mind when it cautioned that more harm than good might be done by "ill-judged efforts" to keep incompatible mates together.[175] But counsels of moderation made no impression on the most headstrong of metropolitan magistrates. With requests for separation orders in police courts still far outnumbering petitions for divorce in the High Court, Mullins saw judicial restraint as a luxury the nation could not afford.

Predictably, Mullins grew belligerent when his methods met resistance. The Home Office observers who visited his self-styled "matrimonial court" were welcome.[176] The same was not true for interfering reporters. When Mullins learned that a brewer's assistant

had been sacked on account of publicity given to his wife's application for maintenance arrears, the *South Western Star* received a sharp
rebuke. More often his wrath fell on the large London dailies whose
agents made regular forays into the court on Lavender Hill. Reporters who paid Charles Calvert a pound for a picture of his wife and
details concerning her charge that he was a "sexual maniac" drove
Mullins to fury. Similarly, one pandering daily chose to publicize a
charge of persistent cruelty under the heading "SPANKED WIFE."
This notice, in turn, prompted a hire-purchase firm to repossess its
furniture, thereby worsening the odds against a couple that had been
induced to give their relationship one more go.[177] Such reportage was
morally wrong if technically legal, in Mullins's mind, because the
public's right to know about the inhumanity still possible in English
homes did not equal society's need to resuscitate marriage among its
laboring majority.

That Mullins remained free to practice his legal brinksmanship
was above all testimony to a widely shared fear for the future of the
working-class family. Although the mid-1930's saw no dramatic rise
in requests for separation and maintenance orders, urban élites in
this period did link soaring rates of juvenile crime and an increasing
incidence of "high grade mental defect" to "family disorganization"
among the poor.[178] The Home Office, to be sure, had traditionally
allowed police court magistrates much latitude, believing that executive government ought not to obstruct the exercise of independent
judicial discretion.[179] But the extent to which Mullins's maverick
methods went unchecked suggests that something more than a reverence for constitutional ideals was at issue. When, "boiling with
rage," he used a case of gross child neglect to condemn religious opponents of birth control, the Home Office finally sent him a mild
warning.[180] Yet in a far more crucial vote of confidence, that which
saw the metropolitan bench try to gag its most voluble member,
highly placed civil servants backed Mullins.[181] His vice, after all, was
also his saving virtue. At times he may have been "more provocative
than wise," but on balance his cry that England was becoming a "di-
vorce-minded nation" gave focus to a prevailing social concern.[182] In
Liverpool, Bradford, and several other cities, as well as throughout

ANGERED by the story of a beautiful young wife and her artist husband, who lived together before they were married and separated less than a year afterwards, Magistrate Claud Mullins declared in the South-Western Matrimonial Court yesterday:—

"These parties have nothing but false ideas about the morals of marriage. They tried a novel experiment and called it marriage, but it was not."

He threatened to make an order for a penny a week for the bride, dark-haired Mrs. Florence Knight, twenty-five-year-old secretary, of Parkhill, Clapham, S.W., but he finally adjourned the case for three weeks, making an interim order for £1 a week.

Mrs. Knight applied for a separation from her husband because, she said, he had failed to maintain her.

Lived in Luxury Flat

She said they were married in November, 1936, but that Knight, who earned £6 a week as a commercial artist, had failed to maintain her.

They had lived in a luxury flat when she was earning £3 a week.

Recently her husband had asked for his freedom, and she was asked to sign an agreement to take the furniture and a cash payment of £30 in full liquidation of his liability towards her. She would not sign the agreement.

"The trouble is," she told Mr. Mullins, "that we lived together for two months before our marriage, unknown to our parents.

"We spent week-ends together in Jersey and Birmingham. It had been a secret until my husband told my father about it, and said I was not a fit person to return to."

Mr. Claud Mullins, the magistrate: Has there ever been any genuine love?

Mrs. Knight (bursting into tears): Yes. There has on my part. There is now. I want him back.

Husband Joseph Victor Knight, of Motley-street, Battersea, said: "I did have a bit of feeling for my wife, although she said she only married me to make use of me. But if I went back to her there would be no happiness between us."

"BEAUTIFUL BRIDE THREATENED WITH 1d. A WEEK ORDER," read the *Daily Mirror*'s headline for this case heard before Claud Mullins on July 6, 1937. Mullins loathed the way that reporters sensationalized his marriage-mending efforts. Courtesy: British Library.

London, news of "Mullins' way" with domestic disharmony offered urban élites hope. Perhaps America's apparent stampede toward divorce could be prevented from occurring in England through refinement of police court conciliation work?[183] Either his admirers did not know, or else they did not care, that Mullins's campaign against Americanized marriage hinged in part on the deployment of therapeutic strategies first made popular across the Atlantic.

What mattered most to civil servants and concerned amateurs

alike was that Mullins's strategy for preserving working-class marriage seemed to be succeeding. His conciliation schemes, moreover,
were only the most visible variations on a theme now commonly
heard. During the first seven months of 1935, the South-Western
Police Court, through its probation officers and clergymen "referees," had managed to persuade 60 percent of the applicants for separation orders that they should cease legal action.[184] In several parts of
the country it was even more difficult to obtain a judicial separation.
The Home Office learned from a questionnaire returned by sixty-
five clerks throughout England and Wales that only 28.6 percent of
the 6,222 "matrimonial disputes" brought to summary courts between April 1st and July 1st, 1935, reached the hearing stage. Just
14.7 percent of all disputes ended in separation or maintenance orders. These figures exploded the charge—voiced so often during testimony before the Royal Commission on Divorce—that magistrates
dispensed such orders indiscriminately. More important, these figures hinted strongly that "some denial of justice" was taking place,
most probably at the hands of zealous probation officers whose reverence for the "sanctity of the marriage tie" had impelled them to
press for out-of-court settlements.[185]

How much greater would the demand for judicial separations
have been if poor wives and husbands had not faced the prospect of
one or more meetings with proselytizing court agents? We cannot
answer this question, though we should note the revealing fact that
very few contemporaries bothered to ask it. For the comfortable
classes it was enough to know that matrimonial conciliation was being practiced in many ways and in many places. At the Jewish
Court of Bethdin in East London, "wise men" were striving to heal
family wounds among their co-religionists. Behind the dockyards of
Southeast London, missionary Grace Harrison saw to it that distraught wives took tea with her overlooking the soothing expanse of
Blackheath.[186] On the Sussex coast at Eastbourne, Mrs. Kimpton, the
local probation officer, regularly invited husbands and wives to
separate meetings in her home followed by two-hour joint interviews. In Bury, on the outskirts of Manchester, Mr. and Mrs. Som-
erville were so well known as probation experts in matrimonial fric-

tion that solicitors urged poor women to see one of them before stepping foot in court.[187] Given the range of conciliation schemes in effect, therefore, the overriding concern of legal reformers was not with guaranteeing due process to spouses at odds but rather with regularizing the domestic work of police courts. If legislation could create a universal "atmosphere of understanding" in which to "adjust" marriages, then one root cause of family disintegration might be removed.[188] By early 1937 the government was ready to accept this argument and to tolerate a new "Summary Procedure" bill.

The Act that resulted[189] gave Claud Mullins much of what he had been demanding. This was hardly surprising, since the Home Office had worked closely with Mullins in drafting the legislation that a private Member, Maurice Petherick, brought before the House of Commons.[190] Classified as merely another small step in the "great movement towards what one might call the humanising of the administration of justice," and justified as a product of magisterial experience, the Act in fact constituted a fundamental redefinition of summary justice. To preserve the working-class family home "at a time when it is in real danger of breaking up," the Act altered domestic proceedings in three essential ways. Henceforth, most disputes between husbands and wives would be aired at special court sittings which "busybody neighbors" could not attend; newspaper reports were limited to a bare recital of case particulars; and magistrates were empowered to conduct cross-examination in cases where a defendant appeared unequal to this task.[191] More broadly, the Act gave explicit legal standing to probation officers as mediators in domestic conflict, and implicit recognition of their superiors, the police court magistrates, as the law's best defense against working-class family breakdown.

The same parliamentary session saw passage of another milestone in English domestic law. Judged by its impact on divorce rates, the 1937 Matrimonial Causes Act deserves the historical attention it has received. By expanding the grounds for divorce to cover cruelty, incurable insanity, and most important, desertion, A. P. Herbert's legislative coup doubled the number of divorce petitions in one year. To contemporaries it appeared that the old objection to divorce law reform—that "hard cases make bad laws"—had been turned on its head.[192] Yet thoughtful contemporaries also understood that in terms of its ability to improve English family life, the Divorce Court remained vastly inferior to the lowly police court. Writing in the same year that Herbert's Act took effect, Margaret Cole wondered how much had really changed:

Divorce is still prohibitive in cost for the very poor; but in compensation, as it were, the State, in the person of the magistrate, does provide a means of helping married couples who differ to reconcile themselves. Their superiors either do not reconcile themselves, and part; or they have recourse to expensive psychologists, or to their friends, which latter is a great waste of everybody's time and nervous energy.[193]

Cole might have given more thought to the double-edged quality of such legal "compensation." Instead, she was echoing Claud Mullins's point that given the noble but inevitably superficial nature of "Poor Persons'" representation in the Divorce Court, many of its future clients would receive no "social investigation" into their cases.[194]

Mullins helped draft the Matrimonial Causes Act of 1937, and was solely responsible for insuring that it gave police court magistrates the important power to grant separation orders for adultery. But one feature of the Act troubled Mullins deeply, and his worry was soon justified. Section 6 specified that women who had obtained separation orders in police courts could later present these orders to the Divorce Court, without proving afresh the facts on which these orders had been granted.[195] The consequences of this legal change soon became apparent in Mullins's own court. On October 13, 1937, Kathleen Stevens, age and occupation unstated, appeared at Lavender Hill to obtain a judicial separation, contending that her husband refused to maintain her. The facts of the case gave Mullins pause. Three years earlier Mrs. Stevens and her husband Arthur, a chauffeur, had agreed to live apart. Arthur remained near his employer in the West End, while Kathleen settled down with her mother in Streatham and found a job paying £2 17s. per week. When Arthur testified that he wished his wife would return to him, Mullins sensed a ruse. So he asked Kathleen directly whether the real purpose of her application was not to lay the groundwork for a divorce, and she "candidly" replied "yes." Mullins thereupon dismissed her application. For him, the case revealed an "alarming" new opportunity for wives to subvert the intent of the law.[196] What rarely occurred to Mullins, the celebrated marriage-mender, was that even the most enlightened forms of conciliation were useless when one spouse had determined to end a relationship. Worse, it can be argued, he was temperamentally incapable of appreciating that the poor might prefer their own marital mistakes to the intrusive counsel of strangers, however well trained.

The Stevens case merits mention for another reason. The Matrimonial Causes Act did not come into force until January 1, 1938. Yet anticipating its impact, Kathleen had calculated precisely how she might win a divorce on her own. Since she had almost certainly not consulted a solicitor (who otherwise would have accompanied her into court), it follows that Kathleen was either legally astute or else had sought advice from a "Poor Man's Lawyer."[197] If the latter were true, one must wonder to what extent the volunteer barristers and solicitors who provided the only free counsel then available were helping working-class wives and husbands to circumvent a judicial system designed to uphold conventional marriage. If, on the other hand, Kathleen never saw a "Poor Man's Lawyer," then she must have been very unlike the instinctively conservative and fatalistic working-class wives sometimes portrayed in historical studies.[198] It may well have been true, of course, that Mrs. Stevens sought legal aid precisely because she already saw law as a resource to further her own interests. Like those late-Victorian women who were "surprisingly well informed" about summary procedure, Kathleen probably viewed the police court in frankly instrumental terms.

Mrs. Stevens was the first, but not the last wife to try to build a case for divorce under Mullins's nose.[199] We cannot know how many women pursued similar strategies at the thousand-odd police courts then operating in England and Wales, though it would be safe to assume that the average magistrate, particularly the average lay magistrate, was less eagle-eyed than Claud Mullins. Indeed, his domestic regime represented the conciliatory thrust of summary justice in its most aggressive form. As contemporaries realized, how well schemes for "adjusting" marriage might work hinged on the nature of relationships among a court's magistrates, probation officers, and voluntary assistants.[200] On the eve of the Second World War, London's South-Western Police Court had built a well-oiled engine for regulating disputes between husbands and wives. Elsewhere, this engine sputtered, or did not run at all.

The emotional strains, forced separations, and housing shortages brought on by world war only increased middle-class demands for systematic conciliation work. The "Denning Committee" on Procedure in Matrimonial Causes, which reported in 1947, was so alarmed about the soaring resort to divorce that it recommended establishing a state-sponsored "Marriage Welfare Service" whose first ambassadors would be probation officers.[201] For a time Mullins thought that concern over the child casualties of "broken homes" was about to bring even divorce petitions within his therapeutic grasp.[202] He found further cause for optimism when, in the autumn of 1948, a Home Office panel urged that experimental work in the field of marriage guidance be encouraged with government grants. Mullins had been a founding member of the Marriage Guidance Council in 1938, and he believed as fervently as any of the clergymen who dominated this group that premarital counseling was a vital weapon in the battle against divorce.[203] But hopes that the central government might soon assume responsibility for all marriage preservation work went unfulfilled. The legal machinery for conciliation in divorce proceedings varied widely throughout postwar Europe, from explicit prohibition of court-sponsored mediation in Norway to obligatory counseling conducted by the Orthodox Church in Greece. In England, argued the former head of an Army Legal Advice Bureau, "Service divorce cases" presented an emotional minefield so perilous that *any* form of mandatory reconciliation would deepen marital discord. Ultimately, what the Royal Commission on Marriage decided in 1955 would remain a fixed assumption of English social policy: that although the state has every interest in reducing conflict between husbands and wives, such "intimate and personal problems" demand the expertise of voluntary as well as statutory bodies.[204]

One practical outcome of this logic is that police courts have retained their curious identity as criminal tribunals with a concurrent domestic mission. Much to the dismay of modern legal critics, institutions that "still carry the stigma of criminality, public degradation and punitiveness" continue to be the courts of first resort for many poor spouses at odds.[205] For Claud Mullins, who retired as a magistrate in 1947 but lived until 1968, the ongoing power of police courts to "adjust" relations between spouses was a source of solace. He clung to the conviction that many marriages needed to be saved from themselves. His guiding faith reeked of class bias and offered an ideal pretext for wielding a benevolent tyranny over the poor.

Had English police courts generally followed Mullins's lead, then a strong argument could be made for the existence of a pervasive marital "policing" strategy. For as recent critics have emphasized, a wholesale resort to conciliation in matrimonial cases would give startling power to the conciliators themselves, power that is all the more worrisome because it conflates dispute resolution and therapy, and thus masks a shift from one form of social discipline to another.[206] But in fact the English police court in the second half of the twentieth century is a legal hybrid. With respect to its matrimonial work, summary jurisdiction remains tangled in a web of conflicting intentions, only some of which can be called coercive. Working-class spouses meanwhile still approach the police court for help with marital problems. They do so, however, as did many of their late nineteenth- and early twentieth-century predecessors, on their own terms.

FIVE

Families on Trial?

The Work of the Juvenile Court

HOWEVER DETERMINED some English police courts may have been to shape the marital relations of the poor, still higher hopes attended the creation of a juvenile court system. Established in 1908,[1] courts for boys and girls under sixteen embodied what optimists have variously labeled the "enlightened," "humanitarian," or "liberal and generous"[2] trend in modern English penal policy. But on the wider stage of social criticism, juvenile courts and the machinery of surveillance they came to operate have been roundly denounced. This critique insists that far from epitomizing a current of compassion in modern criminal law, tribunals built with tender youth in mind have since their inception been patrolling the family with a suffocating vigor that masquerades as kindness. The French juvenile court, Jacques Donzelot declares, is "an arrangement that recalls the oldest patriarchal rules, the only difference being that the father has been replaced by the judge and the kinsfolk by social mentors and technicians."[3] Surveying the American experience, Christopher Lasch is equally emphatic. The spread of juvenile courts throughout America during the first third of the twentieth century, Lasch contends, "best exemplifies the connections between therapeutic conceptions of society, the rise of social pathology as a profession, and the appropriation of familial functions by agencies of socialized reproduction."[4] Critics of English juvenile justice have been less unremittingly bleak in characterizing the work of the children's court. Nonetheless, by emphasizing the court's creation of a "special domain" in criminological practice, such studies echo Foucault's maxim that the goal of modern penal policy has been "not to punish less, but to punish better; . . . to insert the power to punish more deeply into the social body."[5]

Given these interpretive extremes of relentless manipulation on the one hand and simpleminded meliorism on the other, it is understandable that scholars might wish to recast the history of the juvenile court in less tendentious terms. Thus, both Radzinowicz and Hood's monumental fifth volume of the *History of the Criminal Law*[6] and Victor Bailey's judicious *Delinquency and Citizenship*[7] mark a reassertion of the view that legal reform can best be understood as the story of administrative experts responding practically to problems as they arose. Although painstakingly researched, these books leave us with a curiously incomplete picture of penal policy in general and of juvenile justice in particular because they fail to study the cultural matrix within which legal change was embedded and from which it derived its meaning.[8]

Most noticeable is their silence about the relationship between cures for juvenile delinquency and representations of working-class family life. As we have seen, a not-so-small army of English philanthropists, health and education officials, physiologists, psychologists, and psychiatrists made the "adjustment" of domestic relations their overriding concern. We have also seen, however, that their quest for order in the home proved frustrating because the disciplinary strategies they employed were themselves matters of competition and dispute.[9] Between 1908 and the outbreak of World War Two, English juvenile courts emerged as the single most celebrated weapon in the arsenal of domestic regulation. Yet we will find that even this vaunted disciplinary system—a perfect example, it would seem, of the Foucauldian power / knowledge technology at work[10]—could not begin to realize the ambitions of its designers. The therapeutic metaphors that framed most discussions of juvenile justice in the early twentieth century rarely reflected judicial practice. For such language conveniently ignored the fact that retribution, not therapy, remained the dominant goal of many children's courts.

The Birth of the English Juvenile Court

Whereas the idea that young offenders should receive correction and guidance in a court of their own is partly English, the model for such a scheme is American. But tracing the institution's genealogy matters less than understanding the shift in cultural assumptions about criminality that made these courts attractive in the first place. The view of human nature generally accepted as animating mid-Victorian jurisprudence is that of Bentham's rational individual pursuing the path of greatest pleasure. Save for lunatics and infants, each individual was deemed completely free to choose his or her own destiny. Criminals, too, supposedly made a rational calculation that crime might pay. It followed from this utilitarian premise that criminals must be shown that they had miscalculated, that in a civilized social order the road to lawlessness was paved with pain. Hence the proper response to the rational criminal so conceived was a penal policy of deterrence and retribution, "the former to deny the utility of crime, the latter to reconstruct the social order after its breach."[11]

At the center of this vision was the ideal of the responsible individual. It is necessary to appreciate, however, that the exultation of individual responsibility hid an altogether different cultural preoccupation. As Martin Wiener has shown, people were not necessarily thought to be fully responsible agents. On the contrary, the purpose of law was "as much instrumental as declarative," since the best way to make men (and women) self-governing was to treat them as if they were.[12] Thus, laws intelligently drafted could and would build character by encouraging the growth of sound habits—habit, according to one interpretation, being nothing more than "congealed will."[13] What made character building such a vital enterprise, in turn, was the specter of rampaging instinct that haunted polite society during the first three-quarters of the nineteenth century. One may debate whether a preoccupation with instinct entered English social thought through Malthusian images,[14] but little doubt can exist that a fear of destructive passion pervaded mid-Victorian society. From alarms over urban murder in the 1840's to hysteria over infanticide and garrotting in the 1860's, the champions of law reform had more on their minds than a straightforward calculus of pleasure and pain. There were also "folk devils" to exorcise. That is, widespread cultural anxieties occasionally fixed on certain persons or groups, attributing to them stereotypical vices and demanding legislative protection against them. Criminal youth sometimes bore the brunt of these moral panics.[15]

The first important reforms of the law concerning young offenders took root in a soil rich with worry about the reproduction of savagery. Most accounts of the creation of reformatories and industrial schools between 1854 and 1861 stress the extent to which these new penal institutions marked a "progressive" step: they recognized the "blindingly obvious" distinction between juvenile and adult lawlessness.[16] Although the champions of reformatory methods were far from unanimous in viewing young offenders as more sinned against than sinning, the thrust of historical analysis has been to see in Mary Carpenter's famous dictum of 1852 that a child should be treated "as a child" the seed of an idea that reached fruition in the Children Act of 1908.[17] According to this unproblematic reading of legal history, the kind of procedural barbarity that traumatized little Oliver Twist as he sat in Magistrate Fang's police court was a perversion of justice so gross that humane men and women felt compelled to take remedial action.[18]

But the mid-Victorian rhetoric of reform had another face. Many of those who urged Parliament to save young offenders from mixing with adult criminals believed that the working-class home was becoming a caldron of cruelty. Some acknowledged experts on crime stressed the malice of step-parents, whose abuse forced the child on to the streets, "an alien from his natural home, to starve or to steal."[19] Others argued that alcohol induced violence, for the habitually drunken father soon became a monster.[20] The "improper conduct of parents" had long been identified as a principal cause of juvenile crime in England.[21] What lent special urgency to this problem at mid-century, however, was a growing recognition among the urban élites that city life had produced a physical separation of the classes and, consequently, a weakening of what Matthew Davenport

Hill termed the "natural police" of custom "operating upon the conduct of each individual" in small towns and villages. Hill, the Recorder of Birmingham for twenty-six years and one of the reformatory movement's leading lights, observed that so long as "rich and poor lived in proximity, . . . the superior classes exercised [a] species of silent but very efficient control over their neighbours." But now (in 1852), cities permitted the poor to live "in absolute obscurity with little or no control from outside."[22] The logic for criminologists, as it had been for the advocates of district visiting, seemed self-evident. Since the urban working-class home had been allowed to turn increasingly violent, and since children were "copyists" whose habits formed through imitating those around them,[23] the next generation of city-bred poor would grow up still more brutal. Somehow this cycle of savagery had to be broken.

Two legal strategies, complementary in their aims, offered hope that working-class children might yet escape a brutalized future. The first strategy called for building a variety of institutions in which both young offenders and non-offenders who seemed on the brink of moral ruin could find the family-like supervision and correction that they lacked in their own homes. Reformatories and industrial schools sought to bring about a transformation of character such as rarely occurred in traditional prisons. The second strategy, focused on amending the criminal law, sought to give magistrates greater flexibility in dealing with juvenile crime. Like reformatory institutions, the broadening of summary jurisdiction to deal with childish error aimed at keeping young offenders out of jail, where the "unnatural" habits learned in "unnatural" homes would only harden. Both strategies were pursued with vigor. Together, after a half-century's work, they had achieved far less than their architects would have wished.[24]

What went wrong in the experiment with reformatories and industrial schools? The answer is important because it reveals how ambivalent the legal establishment remained about the nature of working-class family life. Reformatories, created in 1854, received most of the public attention, although industrial schools, introduced through legislation in 1857 and 1861, soon outnumbered them.[25]

The law allowed reformatories to accept only convicted delinquents under sixteen who had served at least two weeks (after 1866, ten days) in prison. Industrial schools, by contrast, supposedly provided for younger children deemed to be potential offenders, some of whom were "entirely free from criminal taint." After 1870, however, the similarities between these two penal institutions struck contemporaries as more important than their differences. A Home Office expert identified the "leading common characteristic" of reformatories and industrial schools in 1880: "Both ... are places of training, under voluntary management, but largely subsidized by Government and subject to Government rules and Government inspection, in which the inmates are legally detained by order of a Court of Justice, against the will both of themselves and their parents."[26]

What this description fails to note is that both kinds of institutions embraced a schizophrenic view of working-class parenthood. On the one hand, most reformers believed that constant parental supervision was necessary to prevent the mistakes of youthful inexperience. Where parents failed to maintain close supervision, allowing their children to stray from the path of self-control and delayed gratification, the state had a duty to act *in loco parentis*.[27] Such parents were feckless, incompetent, or perhaps just "demoralized" by their own life struggles. On the other hand, a large proportion—perhaps a majority—of those who backed reformatories and industrial schools remained convinced that poor parents were shrewd manipulators of the legal system who would stop at nothing to dump their young. To deter these supposedly crafty fathers and mothers, the reformatory system tried not only to force parents to pay part of their children's keep but also to expose parental deceit whenever possible.

Particularly among chroniclers of police court drama there seemed to be agreement that working-class parents favored the ruse of declaring their children to be "beyond control" and thus candidates for industrial school care.[28] One police court missionary railed against the "wholesale and easy way in which parents get rid of their children at the expense of the State," assuring his readers that even "stalwart fathers" hauled their eight-year-old boys into court and charged them with being uncontrollable.[29] It may be true that the lack of uniformity with which policemen collected contributions from parents encouraged some fathers and mothers to pester magistrates for an industrial school order.[30] But impressionistic evidence drawn from newspaper accounts in several parts of England paints a different picture, of parents who were desperate for help. In early 1875, for example, a laborer named James Hebdon seemed at wit's end as he entered a Northeastern police court. Lifting his "little lad" of ten on to the clerk's table, Hebdon asked the Stockton magistrates for advice in dealing with a boy who would not go to school and was constantly running away, creeping aboard boats and trains and sleeping wherever night found him. The father noted that ever since his son's twin brother died, three years before, the boy had "been in the habit of wandering about." An attending policeman corroborated this story, adding that the boy had been shockingly ill-treated by his stepmother. Here was precisely the sort of family breakdown with which industrial schools had been designed to deal. Yet even though Hebdon expressed well-grounded fear for his son's future, the court was unmoved: it "could not relieve [Hebdon] of his responsibility."[31]

In the same year another Northeastern police court did accept a father's "beyond control" story, but only in the face of evidence that he had exercised force to halt his son's wandering ways. The father, a metalworker, had chained up ten-year-old James with "thick links of iron, about ten feet long," for nearly thirty hours. Two decades before anti-cruelty societies arrived in this corner of the country, the Hartlepool bench dismissed charges of child abuse against the father, reasoning that he was only trying to "correct" a boy who had become unmanageable. James was committed to an industrial school for six years.[32]

Esther Wilsdon, the aunt of a wild boy, received less latitude from Oxfordshire magistrates in 1885. Esther had generously agreed to care for him so long as his mother remained a domestic servant. But when the child began stealing from relatives and disrupting lessons at school, Esther realized that she could not cope with him. Magistrates at the Bullingdon Petty Sessions, however, refused to consider an industrial school for the lad unless his aunt pledged to pay a small weekly contribution. Poor herself and already responsible for an invalid husband, Esther could ill afford even a shilling per week.[33] Similarly, despite being saddled with what a London newspaper called "*un enfant terrible*," Susannah Hardy also hit a stone wall. Her nine-year-old boy would not go to school, come home at night, or heed the message of a "good thrashing." Although an attending policeman swore that the child was "most audacious," Justice Denham of the South-Western Police Court ordered him sent to the workhouse for a week rather than to an industrial school. Denham, like his fellow magistrate, Justice DeRutzen, believed that "[s]uch establishments . . . were choked and crowded with children sent there . . . [by] parents who wished to relieve themselves of their maintenance."[34]

Thus industrial schools, a key weapon in the fight to civilize unruly children, failed to achieve their goal in large part due to judicial sabotage. Another strategy for halting the reproduction of savagery, the broadening of summary jurisdiction, likewise faltered at the level of application. The notion that juvenile justice might be better served if magistrates had greater flexibility in matching punishment with offense predates the Victorian period.[35] But a series of legal modifications, beginning with the Summary Jurisdiction Act of 1847 and culminating in the amending Act of 1899,[36] substantially changed judicial procedure for dealing with child crime. By the turn of the century all offenses, except murder, committed by those under the age of seventeen could be brought before summary courts, where two magistrates dispensed instant justice. Theoretically, the right to be tried before a jury remained intact, since parents of children under twelve, and youths between the ages of twelve and sixteen speaking for themselves, could refuse summary disposition of their cases. That youths and parents very rarely demanded a trial by jury does not necessarily mean that the English working classes placed great faith in the fairness of summary proceedings. On the contrary, magistrates who prescribed whipping as a remedy for youthful misbehavior could enrage a whole community. When the birch rod was being wielded at Bow Street Police Court in the 1860's, "the screams of the boys disturbed the neighbourhood, attracting an unruly crowd around the Court, and caused so much angry excitement that it became necessary to discontinue the practice."[37] But skeptical though the poor may sometimes have been about the merits of summary justice for their offspring, by the end of the nineteenth century most English penal reformers applauded this trend toward judicial informality as a tactic for fighting juvenile crime.

In one sense the application of "short, sharp shocks" rather than long months behind prison bars was working too well. For the gradual enlargement of summary jurisdiction over youthful misdeeds had the effect of substantially increasing the number of boys and girls brought into magistrates' courts. As John Gillis has shown, the prosecution rate for males under the age of nineteen in Oxford City rose sharply after 1890. Most pronounced was the growing rate of prosecution for non-indictable crimes—that is, for offenses such as gambling, loitering, trespassing, and setting off fireworks.[38] Gillis demonstrates that the law enforcement authorities in Oxford, under pressure from philanthropists, teachers, and clergymen, "were engaged in a process of redefining as 'delinquent' those patterns of behavior which had traditionally been tolerated by the community." What was happening in turn-of-the-century Oxford was occurring throughout England and indeed throughout the industrialized West: a stage of life called "adolescence" was replacing a sociological category called "class" as the presumed cause of delinquency.[39] And in England at least, the self-appointed guardians of public morality were now demanding that the new discretionary power of magistrates be applied to subduing assertive behavior in teenagers.

Scholars may argue about exactly when the "idea" of adolescence coalesced into a "social fact,"[40] or about the extent to which this socially constructed category served hegemonical ends and provoked proletarian resistance.[41] But to the comfortable classes of late-Victorian England, juvenile delinquency seemed far from an academic issue. Although their courts of summary jurisdiction were bringing unprecedented numbers of young offenders to justice, the supply of child crime appeared inexhaustible. Their reformatory and industrial school system had grown alarmingly expensive and grotesquely un-"home-like."[42] Their bold experiment with compulsory elementary education had, over the course of a generation, succeeded in stimulating common intellects but not, it appeared, common morality.[43] City streets seemed to be more perilous than at anytime within recent memory. The *Echo* sounded an alarmist note when it exclaimed in 1898:

No one can have read the London, Liverpool, Birmingham, Manchester, and Leeds papers and not know that the young street ruffian and prowler, with his heavy belt, treacherous knife and dangerous pistol, is amongst us. . . . The question for every man who cares for streets that are safe after dark, decent when dark, not disgraced by filthy shouts and brutal deeds, is what is to be done with this new development of the city boy and slum denizen?[44]

If respectable citizens differed as to what generated "hooliganism," most agreed at century's end that the specter of instinctualism had returned in the body of the young street tough. This "worshipper of muscle" had allegedly learned his trade through gang warfare, so the graduation to bashing solitary gentlemen over the head with damp sandbags was easy.[45]

Whereas the "hooligan" panic soon ebbed, the cultural concern from which it emerged did not. Young ruffians, as the *Echo*'s comment implied, were only the most dangerous specimens of a much larger and rapidly growing breed, the city child who had been physically and morally stunted by its slum environment. For London, interestingly enough, children aged fifteen and under constituted a smaller segment of the metropolitan population in 1901—around one-third—than they had a generation earlier.[46] Nevertheless, well before the disturbing proportion of unfit volunteers for the Boer War ignited worry about the "degeneration of the race" and "national efficiency," penal reformers had been warning of a new generation of urban youth whose inferior height, weight, and intelligence were excluding them from a favored place in the labor market.[47] In what contemporaries widely regarded as the most thorough study of juvenile delinquency published during the late-Victorian era, the prison chaplain W. D. Morrison dressed his grim vision of the future in Lamarckian garb: "The doctrine of heredity teaches us to believe [that] this mental inertia, this defect of will and character, is transmissible . . . from the parents to the child." If, as the Rev. Morrison deduced from his study of six hundred juveniles in reformatories, nearly half of the parents of young offenders had shown an incapacity to control their offspring, then this weakness should be reproduced in a like percentage of children as an incapacity to control themselves.[48] Lacking self-possession, these victims of heredity seemed condemned to lives of poverty and vice.

Whether criminologists emphasized the eugenic basis of debility or chose to view juvenile misdeeds through the psychological lens of adolescence, the implications for penal policy were identical. Young offenders who showed signs of physical or moral weakness could not be effectively helped if their home lives were ignored. Adolescents who broke the law may have been expressing merely the rebelliousness characteristic of that life stage, but they nevertheless needed guidance from those who understood the domestic context of their rebellion. In either vision it was essential to attempt what C. S. Loch called the "concurrent treatment of child and family."[49] The juvenile court, first deployed in America, had precisely this ambition.

English penal reformers greeted the American model so enthusiastically in large part because they were already familiar with the notion of a separate judicial system for children. Twice during the Victorian years legal activists sketched the shape of a juvenile court. The first of these plans soon lapsed into legislative obscurity. The second, although more accurately described as a dream than as a plan, would become a permanent goal of England's chief child-protection pressure group.

In 1840, Sir John Eardley Wilmot, a magistrate and Conservative MP for Warwickshire North, brought before the House of Commons a bill to establish "an intermediate tribunal" in which "trivial" first offenses by children under the age of thirteen might be heard.

The bill dealt with other subjects dear to Wilmot's heart, such as doing away with petty sessions held in pubs. But its primary goal was to keep children out of jails. Wilmot hoped "to invest magistrates, not with an arbitrary power to inflict punishment, but to give them an authority similar to that [of a] . . . father over his son—a moral authority, which would enable them to bring juvenile offenders under a course of moral training and discipline which should have the effect of reclaiming them to the paths of honesty and industry."[50] The laudable ends of this scheme seemed to outweigh its novel means, for the Commons passed Wilmot's bill by a wide margin. The Lords, however, reasoned differently. Any modification of the criminal law that meant restricting a prisoner's right to trial by jury was suspect. Wilmot's bill therefore died in the Upper House.

One generation later, Benjamin Waugh, then a Congregational minister and member of the first London School Board, offered a more compelling vision. Waugh's work with poor families near his East Greenwich chapel had convinced him that finding alternatives to prison for young offenders was a Christian duty as well as a penal necessity.[51] In 1873, *The Gaol Cradle—Who Rocks It?* crystalized Waugh's thinking. Evangelical in temper if not in theology, Waugh evoked the spirit of Wilburforce when he prophesied that "the time will come when Englishmen will be ashamed that they ever dealt with the naughtiness of a child by police-courts and prisons, as they are now ashamed that they had ever traded in slaves."[52] Righteous indignation meshed with pragmatism in Waugh's plea for change. Imprisonment brought dishonor, he observed. Thus, "if the deprivation of a decent reputation tends to exclude the deprived from the labor market," children who had been jailed stood little or no chance of becoming honest, productive adults. Criminal court proceedings, moreover, were stacked against the child offender, whose fear virtually guaranteed that it could not account for its actions. It would be far more just and also more efficient to create a "new and distinct tribunal" composed of "ordinary citizens . . . whose functions should be magisterial, whose qualifications should be [the] ability to read the living literature of English children, whose Act of Parliament should be their own moral instincts, and, above all, who had committed and had not forgotten the appetitive and pugnacious follies common to youth." Waugh believed that a model for this wise tribunal was already at hand: the London School Board. With a minimum of effort, he argued, school boards might gather the "exact, vast, and varied facts" on child-life, as well as details on the background of each delinquent. Meeting with the young offender in private, these bodies could quickly reach "the bottom of the matter"—where, Waugh sensed, parental neglect would usually be found.[53]

In the short term, Waugh's castigation of bad parents may have seemed to suggest an expanded use of reformatories and industrial schools.[54] But later, after he assumed leadership of the NSPCC, Waugh made plain his commitment to keeping families united by means of treating both young offenders and their parents in the same place. Abandoning his earlier faith in school boards as the proper forum for such matters, the truculent Waugh and his rapidly expanding Society began agitating for a court "without technical limitation" wherein "[t]he delinquencies of children should be regarded ... as the delinquencies of their parents."[55] By the mid-1890's, NSPCC propaganda was promoting the ideal of a juvenile court in every population center, and branding judges who still sent young offenders to jail as "their country's enemies."[56]

Prior to 1900, the NSPCC and its philanthropic ally, the Howard Association, were England's chief advocates of new judicial techniques to treat child crime.[57] But it took the example of America's first juvenile courts to transform this pressure into something irresistible. If experience had been the critical issue, then the juvenile court that opened in Adelaide, South Australia, in April of 1890 should have been the center of interest. With the exception of a few brief notices in English newspapers,[58] however, the Australian scheme remained far less visible than its slightly more recent counterparts in Chicago, New York, and Denver. Since New York was twenty-four and Chicago twelve times the size of Adelaide at the turn of the century, legal innovations in these American cities were bound to generate greater interest among English penal reformers. But relative city size was less important than the self-promotion char-

This photograph shows two boys, aged eleven and thirteen, who in 1899 were convicted of willfully damaging a door by throwing mortar at it. For their "grave" offense these boys were sentenced to five days' hard labor. Note the special prison clothes for children. From Home Office, *Third Report on the Work of the Children's Branch* (1925).

acteristic of early American juvenile courts. Chicago, where the first such tribunal opened its doors in 1899, was the preserve of Richard Tuthill and Timothy Hurley, the new court's first Judge and Chief Probation Officer, respectively. Both men possessed in full measure the blinkered self-righteousness that became a hallmark of American Progressivism.[59] Yet more visible was Judge Ben Lindsey of Denver's juvenile court, established in 1900. "A one-man traveling road show," Lindsey seized every opportunity to advertise his success—success based on conducting his juvenile court in the manner of a "wise parent." Any judge whose methods had allegedly coaxed more than 150 boys to turn themselves in for probationary treatment was worth close study.[60]

Between 1900 and 1905, a few English reformers made pilgrimages to American juvenile courts, while many more found inspiration in the secondhand reports that circulated at home.[61] Glowing accounts of Ben Lindsey's work in Denver spurred a Birmingham businessman, J. Courtenay Lord, to press for the holding of children's cases in a room uncontaminated by adult offenders. A member of Birmingham's Watch Committee, Lord convinced his fellow city fathers that they should worry about what young ears heard in a common police court (this despite the fact that he himself was nearly deaf). Thus, on April 13, 1905, Birmingham judges began to sort out juvenile offenses in weekly, private court sessions whose illegality went unchallenged, one admirer has explained, due to the public's "natural reverence . . . [for] the authority of the magistrates and the police."[62] However questionable the presumed deference of Birmingham's working classes to legal authority may seem, little doubt can exist that the judicial experiment launched there reinforced the now considerable pressure for legal reform. The weight of opinion among teachers, managers of children's homes, and foes of "blind alley" labor for boys was being added to that of the Howard Association and the NSPCC.[63] Henrietta Barnett, the assertive queen of East London philanthropy, could now describe the demand for children's courts as "a sort of microbe [that] seems to start simultaneously the same movement in the minds of various people, often without previous communication or contact." Thoughts of reforming England's juvenile justice system were not merely "in the air."[64] They were also on official record. For in July of 1904, the Report of the Inter-Departmental Committee on Physical Deterioration had recommended that, "In all cases touching the young where the assistance of a magistrate is invoked he should, where possible, be a specially selected person sitting for the purpose."[65]

Edwardian fears about "national efficiency" had converged with long-contemplated penal reform to create a cause ripe for parliamentary action.

When, in the summer of 1905, a bill to authorize the holding of juvenile courts failed in the Commons only because its backers could not "move" a lone opponent's "bowels of compassion,"[66] Home Office experts grew concerned. The measure that Sir Howard Vincent and four fellow MPs brought before Parliament was permissive. But if, as some Home Office personnel thought likely, a successful bill in the future should *require* the creation of separate juvenile courts throughout the land, such action would involve "absolutely prohibitive expense."[67]

The next two years saw an easing of Home Office anxiety. By May, 1907, there appeared to be much merit in the Australian state of Victoria's new law giving juvenile courts exclusive jurisdiction in nearly all children's cases.[68] What happened to bring about this change of heart was surely linked to the Liberal Government that assumed power in late 1905 and, more directly, to the appointment of a reform-minded Herbert Samuel as Home Office Under-Secretary at the same time.[69] Surely, too, the fact that children's courts of one kind or another had been established at Bradford, Dublin, and Cork, as well as at Birmingham, was dragging the issue of comprehensive legislation onto center stage. When it finally arrived, the 1908 Children Act disappointed few who held advanced legal views. Dazzled by new American methods for enforcing "parental responsibility," English penal reformers hailed the nationwide establishment of juvenile courts as the dawn of the modern age.[70]

William Clarke Hall and the Ideal of Fatherly Justice

Even the most ardent supporters of England's first juvenile court legislation knew that their victory was incomplete. After all, part 5 of the Children Act fell far short of creating a "system" of courts for children. The law of 1908 merely ordered that a court of summary jurisdiction, when hearing charges against boys and girls under the age of sixteen, must meet either in a different room or building, or on a different day or at a different time, from the ordinary court session. Children's court hearings were to be closed in the sense that only "persons directly concerned in the case" might attend—a restriction that did not, significantly, bar representatives of the press. If located, the parent or guardian of a child under fourteen charged with any offense, or brought in on an industrial school application, was obliged to attend throughout the court proceedings.[71] Beyond these stipulations, uncertainty reigned.

In London, where the Home Secretary, Herbert Gladstone, hoped to build juvenile court models for the rest of Britain, resistance of several kinds forced compromise from the start. Gladstone wished to establish four juvenile tribunals in London, and to appoint a "special" police court magistrate so that the existing twenty-five-member bench would not be overburdened. Treasury officials, however, refused to fund such a plan.[72] The idea of designating specialist judges sparked still more controversy. Penal reformers such as the NSPCC's Robert Parr insisted that a children's magistrate was essential not only to preside over juvenile court sessions but also to supervise probation officers and visit detention centers. Yet several London magistrates shared Cecil Chapman's worry that a specialist judge would tend "to get one-sided, perhaps faddist; his bias or fads [would] quickly get known to the people, and there will be much more chance of their being able to . . . 'pull his leg.'"[73] In terms of facilities, champions of "modern" penal methods such as the State Children's Association dreamed of separate juvenile courtrooms with entrances reserved for impressionable youth. But the facts of urban economics dealt hard with dreams. Adding a separate children's entrance to the new police court building planned in West London, for example, meant that property values along Devonshire Street would likely plunge by one-third, obliging the Metropolitan Police to compensate homeowners. Thus, by late 1909 the Home Secretary had accepted a more modest scheme of six juvenile courts for London, none blessed with showcase facilities or magistrates wise in the ways of childhood.[74]

Although England could not pack its juvenile courts with judges resembling the magnetic Ben Lindsey of Denver, enthusiasts clung to the hope that, with experience, many magistrates might learn the American lesson that even young "prodigies of crime" could be reclaimed as productive citizens. To accomplish this goal, the officers of English juvenile courts would have to focus on the needs of the individual child rather than on his or her misdeeds. Such individual attention, in turn, demanded detailed knowledge of the child's home life and a readiness to provide "help and instruction for ignorant and careless parents."[75] Fortunately, a tool ready to accomplish both tasks was at hand. This tool was England's new probation system, and penal reformers understood that probation officers would have to act as the eyes and ears of all juvenile courts.

As previously discussed, a state-sanctioned probation system did not exist in Britain prior to 1907, although "police court missionaries" had been at work in some large towns for nearly a generation.[76] The usefulness of these denominationally tied workers must have helped to reassure magistrates that probation was not entirely an American craze.[77] In any event, what English advocates of juvenile courts wanted during the Edwardian years was less a new breed of probation officer than more men and women who possessed the best qualities of the old police court missionary. As two leaders in the boy's club movement explained:

[Z]eal and devotion were key qualities in a good probation officer: but zeal and devotion can do little without the magic touch which will make the boy [offender] realize at once that he is understood, that his character is laid before a just and stern, but kind judge—a man who stands so much above any friend he has ever known that he is uplifted, and his nature expands to feelings of reverence and admiration.[78]

If this was aiming high, the founders of Birmingham's juvenile court wished to accept nothing less in the three, full-time children's officers they hired during 1906, one of whom was an Oxford graduate.[79] When English juvenile courts began operating on a national basis in 1909, it remained to be seen whether Birmingham's aggressive use of the probation system would win acceptance elsewhere. The early signs did not look encouraging. In 1910, the first year for which national statistics were published, 10.6 percent of the

TABLE I

Persons Tried for Criminal Offenses in Juvenile Courts, 1910–1925

	Persons Tried in Juvenile Courts		
Year	Total Number Tried	Number Placed on Probation	Percentage on Probation
1910	33,598	3,568	10.62
1911	32,977	3,454	10.47
1912	38,351	4,537	11.83
1913	37,520	4,465	11.90
1914	36,929	4,496	12.17
1915	43,981	5,719	13.00
1916	47,342	6,781	14.32
1917	51,323	6,548	12.76
1918	49,915	5,868	11.76
1919	40,473	4,188	10.35
1920	36,064	4,691	13.01
1921	30,253	4,147	13.71
1922	31,056	4,715	15.18
1923	28,769	5,448	18.94
1924	29,624	5,812	19.62

SOURCE: William Clarke Hall, *Children's Courts* (1926), Appendix J.

33,598 boys and girls tried for criminal offenses in English juvenile courts were placed on probation. As expected, males under sixteen committed the large majority (88.3 percent) of these offenses. Those who believed in the character-mending power of the new penalty did not expect, however, that the percentage of delinquent children placed on probation would remain below 15 percent until 1922 (Table 1).[80]

The problem was not just that probation officers saw too few children. Rather, as the Home Office learned during its first careful study of probation, one court's friend of the family might be another court's spy. A Home Office report of 1910 noted approvingly that legally appointed probation officers enjoyed a "much stronger hold over the offender" than the old-style police court missionaries.[81] But at what cost? The report confessed that one major reason for an uneven application of probationary powers was the concern of some magistrates that a probation officer's home visit might seem an "intrusion," causing the offender "to be marked by the neighbours, and to become a subject of gossip, leading to keen resentment, and even to the possibility of violence." If "greatly exaggerated," in the words of the report, such a concern could not be dismissed. J. M. Yates, a Stipendiary Magistrate at the Manchester Petty Sessions, assured his examiners that "it would be a very awkward time" for the probation officer who called at a collier's home. Yates went on to speculate that perhaps because of the concentration of Sunday schools in Lancashire, working-class families there could accept the Sunday school teacher, the clergyman, or the police court missionary as having a "right" to make home visits, but not a formal agent of the courts.[82] Nor was such feeling unknown in London. Explained a metropolitan magistrate, "nothing is so jealously guarded as even the one room of a person in a lodging-house." Since probation officers were also policemen in some places, and more, because preliminary inquiries into the domestic life of an accused person might occasionally be used against that person at his or her subsequent trial, the grounds for suspicion were quite rational.[83] Besides, judges—especially juvenile court judges—could be misled by their most important advisers. As one critic complained:

Magistrates do not sufficiently appreciate that official evidence has frequently been obtained recently and at second hand. I have heard [a probation] officer relate the story of the family to the magistrate as though he had known the parents for years when he was merely retailing the statement of the mother whom he had met for the first time outside the court. There is hardly a sitting of any [juvenile] court which does not receive with profound attention an equally irresponsible statement.[84]

The early champions of English juvenile courts, then, had to contend both with ignorance about new legal procedure and with considerable hostility. Some frustrated reformers chided magistrates for placing considerations of economy ahead of child welfare, and others demanded new legislation so that parents might be better "advised, admonished, and assisted" in dealing with their wayward offspring.[85] Meanwhile, the American model of juvenile justice continued to excite envy. Cecil Leeson, Secretary of the Howard Association, praised the vision of a Massachusetts authority in which not just the child offender but indeed all the "inmates of the home circle" would become objects of the probation officer's scrutiny. To-ward this end, unannounced home visits on Saturday afternoons and Sundays were essential if an officer hoped to sway the child's fa-ther.[86]

Of course, such probationary surveillance would never be com-mon in England until enlightened magistrates took control of chil-dren's courts. The conduct of individual juvenile court magistrates therefore became a subject of great interest between the outbreak of war in 1914 and passage of the next major installment of child wel-fare law in 1933. Much of this interest focused on William Clarke Hall. If England has ever had a children's magistrate who ap-proached the celebrity of America's Ben Lindsey or France's Louis Albanel and Henri Rollet, it was Clarke Hall. Whether, like them, he should be held accountable for trying to destroy due process in the administration of juvenile justice—and, simultaneously, to strip parents of their disciplinary prerogative—is a question worth asking. The answer is revealing. As the following analysis of Clarke Hall's regime in East London will suggest, interwar England's most thor-oughly modern juvenile court judge ill fits the profile of the thera-peutic expert drawn by Donzelot and Lasch.[87]

William Clarke Hall had established his own expertise in child law long before he was appointed a metropolitan magistrate. The son of a humorless Church of Ireland curate and the eldest of six children, William was born in Durham in 1866. Following eight years of public school education he won a scholarship to Christ Church College, Oxford, where he read history and developed a taste for Christian Socialist politics and the art of Edward Burne-Jones.[88] Why Clarke Hall chose a career in the law and what he learned about his profession during a three-year stay in Ireland can-not be determined from the biographical threads that survive. A panegyric published shortly before Clarke Hall's death alleges that, "The turning point in his life appears to have come one day at Ox-ford when, happening to see upon a table a copy of the 'Child's Guardian,' published by the National Society [NSPCC], his imagi-native mind was filled with a burning sense of indignation at the wrongs of children and a great desire was engendered to put these right."[89] Whatever the truth of this tale, it is clear that in 1893 Clarke Hall began to volunteer as a speaker for the Society, and that by the following year he had become one of its chosen counsel.

The young barrister's association with the NSPCC and its combative Secretary, Benjamin Waugh, proved critically important. As the author of *The Gaol Cradle*, Waugh was a prophet to heed; as chief of the nation's child-protection police, he was someone to fight beside; and as the father of Clarke Hall's future wife, he was an elder to be cultivated.[90] Two books emerged from Clarke Hall's early work for the NSPCC. *The Law Relating to Children* (1894) offered a detailed commentary on existing legislation, whereas *The Queen's Reign for Children* (1897) was a more popular piece whose "account of the horrors practiced upon children within the memory of living men" could, according to *The Star*, "curdle the blood and hold one spellbound."[91] Despite such billing, *The Queen's Reign* aimed not so much to sensationalize the hazards of English childhood as to press for greater state involvement in this theater of concern—involvement that might range from defraying the NSPCC's prosecution costs to creating a Home Office "Children's Department" for the supervision of all children at risk.[92] Clarke Hall's grasp of existing statutory flaws and his flair for sketching a more hopeful legal future, both evident in *The Queen's Reign*, would later animate his famous books on the state and the child (1918), children's courts (1926), and adoption (1928).

Acting as the NSPCC's head prosecutor while maintaining his own criminal law practice apparently did not exhaust his professional ambition, since in late 1909 he agreed to stand as a Liberal MP for Hythe. Although Clarke Hall lost decisively to his Tory opponent in the first general election of 1910, he used the campaign to declare his impatience with those who sought to rule England "by the orders of an irresponsible oligarchy."[93] Nor did he show much tolerance for those who wished to proceed cautiously with the nation's new juvenile courts. In early 1909, Clarke Hall explained to Robert Parr that the "ideal" children's tribunal should function as a father treating a naughty child.[94] For its time such legal thinking hardly qualified as orthodox. When the Liberal Home Secretary,

Reginald McKenna, tapped Clarke Hall to fill a vacancy at the Thames Police Court in 1913, therefore, London's fraternity of magistrates found a brash partisan of the new penality thrust upon them. And when, one year later, he moved to Old Street Police Court, the East End received a judge who for the next eighteen years would make news as "a lover of children, a counsellor of parents, with a will of iron and a heart of gold."[95]

William Clarke Hall's demeanor, both outside his Old Street bastion and within it, gained wide notice in part because the English legal community could not agree about what a juvenile court judge should do. Since children's courts aimed to rehabilitate the individual delinquent rather than to inflict a just measure of pain, the discretionary power of their judges should ideally have been broad. "[T]ranslated into practice," as David Rothman writes of the American experience, "this grant of authority meant that juvenile courts would be as different from each other as judges were different from each other."[96] What such institutional heterogeneity made possible was, in effect, a cult of judicial personality. Compared to Ben Lindsey's following, the Clarke Hall cult seems fairly bland. After all, the "kid's judge" of Colorado was an idol of Progressive America, a "benevolent judicial despot"[97] who convinced many of his contemporaries that the secret to saving young offenders was empathy. As far as Lincoln Steffens could tell:

The Judge didn't turn away hate, quiet fear, and dry tears by any 'methods.' When a child is brought weeping or scowling before him, Ben Lindsey is dragged off that bench by his heartstrings, and when he sits on a stool beside the boy in trouble, or goes for a walk with him, or takes him home to dinner . . . , this is no act thought out by a wise man. This is nothing but a good man putting into his work what he wants to get out of it—'faith, hope, and love.'[98]

That Lindsey did in fact have a method (he called it "the artistry of human approach"), and that his method might sometimes involve the denigration of a child's parents mattered little to his admirers. On the contrary, Ben Lindsey's "little revolution in Denver" struck many English reformers as a wondrous thing.[99]

Like Lindsey, William Clarke Hall believed that "knowledge of a child's mind is very much more important than a knowledge of Blackstone."[100] No one ever went so far as to ascribe Clarke Hall's hold over his young probationers to hypnotism, but both judges reveled in the scent of salvation that surrounded their work.[101] Also like his American counterpart, the Old Street Judge maintained an "invincible optimism" about his mission, and took "infinite pains" to see that it was done right. Visitors to Clarke Hall's courtroom often confessed that "it was a lesson to see him, with his arm around the shoulder of a waif, . . . talk to the boy not as a magistrate, but as if the lad had been his own child."[102]

Despite such similarities, though, these two men cut quite different public figures. Ben Lindsey made a fetish out of his iconoclasm, going so far as to invent a name ("the beast") for the rottenness he saw pervading American society.[103] Although this muckraking judge rubbed elbows with some of his era's most eminent reformers, he remained outside the walls of privilege. By contrast, from the start of his career Clarke Hall was part of a "progressive alliance" of English voluntary organizations whose aim was to pressure both Parliament and the Home Office into reforming the criminal law. We may debate the assertion that this alliance was determined above all to push the state into previously unregulated realms of civil society,[104] but there can be no doubt that the leaders of these pressure groups were near the center of policy-making power. And Clarke Hall stood nearer than most. At various points during his tenure in East London juvenile courts he served as Chairman of both the National Association of Probation Officers and the Magistrates' Association, participated actively in the Penal Reform League and the London Police Court Mission, and was a member of the influential Home Office Advisory Committee on Probation. Some of his crusty colleagues on the metropolitan court bench dismissed Clarke Hall as "an enthusiast" whose kindly imagination had allowed his courtroom to become a "happy hunting ground for all the cranks, male and female," in London—worst among them "psycho-analysts, psychiatrists, [and] Christian scientists."[105] No doubt Home Office civil servants, particularly Sidney Harris of the Children's Branch, sometimes wished that he took himself and his legal crusade a bit less seriously. Then again, the bureaucrats who had to brace themselves against Clarke Hall's reforming ardor also recognized his gifts, and wondered about who would be "fit to receive the succession" when he retired or died.[106] The knighthood that he received in 1932 confirmed what had always been clear: Clarke Hall agitated from within the walls.

Beyond his reputed grasp of the child mind, William Clarke Hall's fame rested on his fierce commitment to probation as a reformatory tool. Some of his judicial peers viewed this commitment as an expression of dangerous "sentimentality." When in 1913 the new judge granted probation to a man with twenty-five prior convictions, the public took notice, particularly because "C.H." blamed this life of crime on a one-month prison term for stealing apples that the man had received as a teenager. Even at the end of his judicial career he remained convinced that many adults with multiple convictions should be "given a trial" on probation.[107] But Clarke Hall was keener yet on granting young offenders a second chance, and his enthusiasm for this course of action was rooted as much in a sober assessment of the penal alternatives as in misplaced compassion. Reformatories and industrial schools, for example, would have looked especially uninviting to a young magistrate joining the bench on the eve of the Great War. A government analysis of these institutions published in 1913 attributed most of their flaws to a combination of underfunding by the voluntary groups that ran them and the government's lack of authority to enforce needed improvements.[108]

Underneath this rather bland definition of the problem, however, lay a crisis of confidence regarding institutional treatment. The Chief Inspector of Reformatories and Industrial Schools admitted that the trades taught to boys rarely resulted in steady, skilled employment, though he hastened to blame meddlesome parents for this fact. Parents were also at fault for "interfering" with daughters placed as domestic servants, alleged the longtime manager of an industrial school for girls. Other managers found a convenient scapegoat in the new probation system itself, arguing that boys and girls unwisely given probation for second and third offenses became so "habituated to an undisciplined life" that subsequent attempts by industrial schools to reshape their characters were often futile.[109] But Clarke Hall and like-minded activists saw these complaints as incidental to the core problem. The Victorian goal of correcting more perfectly by classifying offenders more precisely had failed to appreciate that institutions of any kind threatened to crush "the sheer exuberance of spirits" in children.[110] East London's juvenile judge made it a rule never to commit a child to any place that he himself had not visited; and after committal he did his best to stay in touch with "his" boys and girls. Clarke Hall's preference for probation over institutionalization was nonetheless plain. "Regulation *within*, rather than removal *from* the community" is a fair assessment of his goal, although to impute a "crude psychology of 'personal influence'" to Clarke Hall's work is to forget that in exalting probation he was attacking a penal psychology that seemed to him cruder still.[111]

Probation appeared all the more attractive in light of the social disruption brought on by total war. Well before August 1914, as we have seen, concerns about the working-class family as an incubator of savagery had given way to worry about the frailty of poor parents as they struggled with the pressures of modern urban life. But with Britain's awakening to the horrors of trench warfare, the alleged "disorganization" of working-class home life gained new prominence. It happened that Dr. William Healy, Director of the Juvenile Psychopathic Institute of Chicago, chose a London publisher for his massive study of *The Individual Delinquent*. Thus in 1915, just as the public began to wonder what a war of attrition might mean, it learned from Healy "that the child who is not controlled under the united efforts of both father and mother is at great disadvantage, and readily acquires anti-social tendencies."[112] By late winter 1916, the chief constables of Britain's seventeen largest towns could confirm what the newspapers already suspected: that a rampage of juvenile theft, gambling, and "malicious damage" had begun.[113] If Healy was right—and few doubted that he was—then this epidemic of lawlessness among the young could be ascribed in large part to further weakening of parental control in working-class homes, particularly where fathers were at the front and mothers labored long hours in munitions factories. Cecil Leeson offered some interesting contradictions in his study of the domestic crisis. While admitting that "exercise of discipline generally falls upon the mother," Leeson still insisted that "a large number" of delinquent lads somehow lacked a focus of authority with their fathers abroad. As for mothers who decided to share their homes for reasons of economy, the presence of boarders reduced the chance that children would be left alone and therefore get into trouble. Yet a disruption of the "home atmosphere" for any reason, Leeson maintained, could "scarcely fail to interfere with the children's upbringing" and thus promote crime.[114] Although the Juvenile Organisations Committee's report on child crime, released in 1918, cast doubt on many of Leeson's allegations, this came as cold comfort to a penal community that by and large believed the Secretary of the Howard Association.[115]

Presiding over London's East End, Clarke Hall never doubted that the reports of a juvenile crime wave were true, although he preferred to explain delinquency as an outgrowth of wartime restlessness. Greater police vigilance in his court's jurisdiction would, he believed, quadruple the number of charges brought against boys and girls.[116] What could be done? For "C.H.," the answer lay in supplementing London's small cadre of probation officers with volunteers who showed keen sympathy with the young. Beginning in 1915 with the appointment of a young woman whose experience was confined to work at a labor exchange, the Old Street Judge sought to provide every wayward child in his court an "education by friendship."[117] It became Miss Bishop's job to match each delinquent with a "volunteer helper" who, in turn, would submit periodic reports on the child's progress. When Clarke Hall realized that Miss Bishop's limited education hampered her ability to evaluate the helpers' reports, he found a new "protege," to use the Judge's own word. This was Miss Evelyn Sander, the twenty-one-year-old daughter of refugees from Bruges, a woman whose Cambridge education and volunteer experience with the Charity Organisation Society spoke well of her "fitness for social work." Armed with assistants such as Miss Sander, a network of "helpers," and, after mid-1921, a "Special Children's Probation Officer," the Judge directed a sizable corps of childsavers.[118] An observer who was allowed to shadow Clarke Hall in 1927 learned that this probationary force had won an impressive reputation:

The 'probation ladies' are doing the pioneering in the slums, and the magistrate at Old Street, Mr. Clarke-Hall, gives special time to visiting his probation officers in their little offices—those 'outposts' of the Law in a wilderness. The 'probation lady' gets a reputation for infallibility. After Tommy has visited her, then comes Sis to see the lady; then Mum, to ask advice about Jim, who is so trying lately. Sometimes Dad comes, too. One day this magistrate was visiting a certain 'outpost' when in strode 'Mum,' bringing with her a rather sheepish Dad. He had given her two fine black eyes, and she hoped that the omnipotent 'probation lady' would talk him into a better frame of mind. To his immense surprise he got a severe dressing-down from the 'Beak' himself, and has, I believe, treated Mum better every since.[119]

Here, it may seem, is clear proof of how probation served to browbeat parents as well as children into submission before the agents of state power. And Clarke Hall would appear to be the legitimizing force behind this harassment, a charismatic bully intent on showing working-class family members that their conduct was being watched and weighed. The parents of delinquent children, urged an American study widely read in England, should also be placed on probation: "A nurse or civil service employee is a probationer when he is permitted to carry a limited responsibility and to practice the arts of his profession under supervision, but he is not ready yet for a final appointment. Parents [of young offenders] are in this class."[120] Even if this manipulative language accurately represented judicial aims in some American courts, however, it did not convey what actually occurred on Clarke Hall's watch.

For the judge's disciplinary reach was never as long as his contemporaries assumed. The first two probation officers sent to Old Street, Miss Croker-King and Miss Cheshire, worked diligently to subvert his volunteer scheme. To Clarke Hall and his allies at the Home Office, Miss Croker-King seemed an Irish Protestant snob "who has a habit of trailing her coat and is apt to say much more than she really means." In the fullness of hindsight one can appreciate the resentment that these two women must have felt toward the Judge's experiment, not least because his *ad hoc* "helpers" diluted the professional status that the women had struggled for years to win.[121] Very much against their will, Croker-King and Cheshire were reassigned to different juvenile courts in 1921. But although Clarke Hall's probationary machine ran more smoothly after their banishment, its power as a tool of family surveillance probably diminished. The administrative demands on urban probation officers throughout the interwar years were increasing to the point where home-visitation—that most potent opportunity "to be a friend to the family"—was declining as formal interviews at probation offices grew more common. The "home and domestic side of the work" was imperceptibly losing ground, and as it did so any hegemonic ambitions that Clarke Hall may have cherished were growing more illusory.[122]

The fact is, however, that the nation's most famous juvenile court judge did *not* cherish such ambitions. As Victor Bailey has pointed out, the ideal "draft bill" which appeared as an appendix to *Children's Courts* shows that Clarke Hall was uncomfortable with the idea, popular in America, that such tribunals should exercise a purely "chancery" (non-criminal) jurisdiction.[123] Historians and sociologists have often observed that those portions of the 1908 Children Act dealing with juvenile delinquency established a curious mix of criminal and exclusively welfare-oriented procedures. Clarke Hall thought that notions of punishment figured far too prominently in this Edwardian legislation. He went so far as to admit that "the American [juvenile] Courts are surely right in laying supreme emphasis upon the question, not 'What has the child's past conduct deserved in the way of punishment?' but 'What past conditions have led up to this conduct?'"[124] Yet ready as the Judge was to befriend rather than to threaten his young clients, and eager as he seemed to "assist" parents who had thus far "failed" their offspring, he never lost sight of the juvenile court's deterrent role. The 1927 Departmental Committee on Young Offenders noted that "there is also the duty of restraining those who commit offences from [joining] the ranks of hardened criminals at a later stage and becoming a serious menace and public burden."[125] Clarke Hall understood and accepted this duty.

Indeed, what made him Britain's most "progressive"—or, alternatively, "dangerous"[126]—magistrate was his willingness to test new techniques that held out the promise of improved deterrence. The Judge's much-publicized opposition to judicial whipping, for example, was based on concerns about the efficacy, not the humanity, of corporal punishment. Between 1920 and 1926 no child received the birch rod in Clarke Hall's courtroom, and yet the incidence of larceny committed by East End juveniles declined during these years. His explanation was, as he put it, "psychological." The sort of lad who appeared in a children's court charged with theft had little to be proud of except "his own pluck and enterprise" and the admiration of his "small circle" of friends; so the "the last thing in the world he would wish them to think" is that he had been "cowed." The only proof of undiminished "pluck" would be another theft. Hence any judicial action that forced the lad to save face was worse than useless.[127] Similarly, while sitting on the Islington bench, Clarke Hall saw a parade of boy thieves whose most notable courtroom characteristic was their complete *lack* of anxiety. Such youth were beyond intimidation. Whipping them, in fact, seemed more likely to activate "sadistic impulses" than to curb a tendency to steal.[128]

Clarke Hall's receptivity to the emerging mental sciences was also rooted in a desire to save young offenders from "the ranks of the hopelessly irreclaimable,"[129] rather than in a fondness for covert manipulation. Cyril Burt remembered him as the first London magistrate to ask for full psychological reports on the juvenile cases that came before him. By 1931 Clarke Hall's court sessions regularly involved volunteer psychiatrists from the Tavistock Clinic or the London Child Guidance Clinic.[130] Such open-mindedness demanded thick skin. For throughout the 1920's and particularly in the immediate postwar period, even urbane civil servants such as Sir Edward Troup might warn judges that, "Only mischief can come of listening to foolish persons who have dabbled a little in the obscene publications of Freud and his school."[131] Clarke Hall favored no one psychotherapeutic approach. Instead, he considered whatever advice was available from the People's League of Health, the National Council for Mental Hygiene, or any of the specialized London clinics. That at least some of this expert counsel seemed to pay dividends—as, for example, in coping with young "exhibitionists"—confirmed the wisdom of following a judicial course that is best termed pragmatic.[132]

There *is* an unrecognized aspect of Clarke Hall's juvenile court work, but it has nothing to do with a scheme to smother the working-class home with therapeutic expertise. It is, rather, that he allowed his courtrooms to become such public places. "The great essential in the regulation of children's courts," Clarke Hall proclaimed, "is to secure the utmost possible simplicity in the proceedings." If a judge quietly told a child, "in the simplest possible way," what the charge against him was, the child would almost always admit his guilt.[133] While laboring to maintain this strategic calm in his East London courtrooms, however, "C.H." welcomed a steady stream of observers whose presence surely disrupted the ritual. Along with interested psychologists, psychiatrists, and students studying mental health at the London School of Economics, the years 1928 and 1929 saw representatives of assorted women's groups, several foreign judges, and one of Mahatma Gandhi's aides apply for entrance. During the last three years of the Judge's life this list of visitors could only have grown. An American observer in early 1932 found his courtroom "very over-crowded," and added, "one had a feeling that the child was facing [a] considerable . . . ordeal."[134] In a sense, then, Clarke Hall's work became a hostage of its own fame.

The Dematerialization of the Offense

If England's best known juvenile judge failed to wield the sort of coercive kindness that some historians might expect, it remains to be seen whether English children's courts in general contributed to the enfeeblement of working-class family life. Analyzing penal strategies in mid-twentieth-century France, Jacques Donzelot maintains that the juvenile court's intrusive power derives from its skill at cloaking punishment in "assistancial" forms. "There is a dematerialization of the offense," Donzelot explains, "which places the minor in a mechanism of interminable investigation, of perpetual judgment." As the young offender's conduct becomes ever more closely watched, so inevitably does the conduct of its home.[135] Paradoxically perhaps, the shape of English juvenile court politics grows clearer if viewed in these reductionist terms. For they suggest that in England, as in France (and America), a generation of mind-numbing debate over the minutiae of courtroom procedure reflected a determination to produce what one judge called "exactly the right kind of atmosphere."[136] This meant—to "progressive" reformers, at any rate—creating an arena wherein parents as well as their children would be specially receptive to the help offered them.

Not surprisingly, England's penal reformers enjoyed only modest success in creating an "atmosphere" by statute. What *is* surprising, however, is the extent to which they underestimated the obstructive force of legal custom. The rancor generated by the 1920 Metropolitan Juvenile Courts Bill was a preview of controversy to come. Starting in mid-1918, a Home Office subcommittee began reviewing the nation's juvenile court system. The evidence gleaned from children's magistrates, probation officers, and social workers pointed to some glaring problems. Above all, too few judges approached their work with "a sympathetic understanding of child life," and too many juvenile courtrooms still terrorized sensitive children or, just as bad, gave young offenders "a contemptuous . . . familiarity with the 'majesty of the law.'"[137] So long as magistrates kept "groping in a twilight of uncertainty" for a "remedy . . . to suit the constitution of [each] patient," the goal of individual case treatment would remain unreachable; and until children's cases could be heard in places other than the morally tainted police court building, preferably in the "calm surroundings of a dull committee room," neither the young offenders nor their parents would be adequately impressionable.[138] To legislate new juvenile court rules for the whole war-weary nation seemed unwise, but a modification of procedure for London might be possible. Together, therefore, the Lord Chancellor, Birkenhead, and the Home Secretary, Edward Shortt, proposed to solve two problems at once. The same bill would require not only that all London juvenile hearings convene outside police court premises but also that each children's bench include a woman lay magistrate. The addition of maternal instinct to a neutral courtroom could only enhance the quality of juvenile justice, or so they assumed.[139]

Such logic struck others as mad. Save for Clarke Hall, the London police court magistrates were vehemently opposed to any measure that challenged their authority. The magistrates might agree to sit beside female "assessors" in the hearing of children's cases, but nothing more. The press added fuel to this fire by hinting that a sex war was imminent, a conflict pitting the "clamourous feminist section" of London society against the "women-haters" who dominated the legal establishment.[140] The battle lines were not in fact so simply drawn. All ten of London's female probation officers, for example, believed that to elevate untrained women to the level of seasoned magistrates would be a "retrograde step," because such action would "make a distinction between men and women which is not desired by women." Nor did these probation officers (or most of the magistrates) like the idea of creating one, central juvenile court for all of London.[141] To counter opposition from "legal big-wigs" outside Parliament and from wary Lords within, the Government was forced to orchestrate a "full dress" deputation of leading women's groups and penal reform organizations.[142] What finally emerged from this political maelstrom was an arrangement that gave childsavers cause for guarded optimism. In London, henceforth, juvenile courts were to be ruled by a stipendiary magistrate, assisted by two lay justices, one of whom had to be a woman. The courtrooms themselves were to be located in premises completely separate from those used for adult offenders. How many children's courts London should have, and where they should be located, were matters left for the Home Secretary to settle.[143]

This was a small victory for promoters of the juvenile court ideal, but during the rest of the interwar period they would be more often vexed than encouraged. Within London, the popular press remained skeptical about efforts to decriminalize justice for young offenders. The *South Western Star* sprinkled sarcasm in its report on the founding of a neighborhood juvenile court in January 1930:

The new court for children opened at Battersea yesterday. It is not a police-court. . . . As far as possible [children] will be kept from knowing that there are such things as policemen and Repressive Institutions. Kindness and leading are the keynotes of the new system. Children will perhaps commit misdemeanours. Possibly, if sufficiently unregenerate and if they have the right (which means wrong) kind of ancestry, they may steep themselves in crime. But they will never know it. They will never have to face

THE TERRORS OF THE LAW

For them the law will shed its terrors and will disguise itself. Even the policemen will be disguised. A constable's helmet will not be allowed to show itself within the precincts or anywhere near the court. There will be a magistrate, but he will adopt the demeanour of a friendly relative.[144]

Outside London, Birmingham, and Liverpool, especially in rural districts, children's courts often mocked the spirit of "assistancial" justice. Despite a steady stream of Home Office circulars to clerks of summary courts, the "progressive" examples of William Clarke Hall and Geraldine Cadbury bred as much suspicion as admiration. It was not until the spring of 1925 that the Home Office obtained any comprehensive data on juvenile courts throughout England, and what it learned then boded ill for those who expected these institutions to serve as "crime hospitals."[145]

Almost everywhere, it appeared, parents really did accompany their children to court. But all too often confronting them were judges deemed "temperamentally unsuited" to the subtle work of family adjustment. As late as 1930 in the closely watched London juvenile court complex, Sidney Harris was appalled at the number of "white beards" whose job obliged them to empathize with the very young.[146] By 1936 the Home Office had decided that the time for diplomacy was long past. In yet another circular to clerks of summary courts it noted the "obvious advantage attaching to quickness of hearing and sight in a justice," and urged that magistrates who dealt with children should be of "parental age," rather than of the "grandfatherly period." In early 1937 the Home Secretary estimated that nearly a quarter of male juvenile court judges were seventy or older. That some magistrates needed an ear trumpet to follow the evidence was lamentable above all because signs of infirmity played havoc with the job of "capturing" parental confidence.[147]

The chasm between penal theory and judicial practice yawned just as wide in terms of courtroom routine. Reformers in the mid-twenties pleaded for simplified examination procedures, arguing that if the questions put to a child remained "as intelligible as one of Euclid's theorems," the court's ambition to befriend—and thus to influence—him would be forever frustrated.[148] Yet as late as 1942 an authority on the subject was still condemning "ridiculous" formalism.[149] It was not until 1933 that newspapers were expressly forbidden to reveal the names of, or otherwise to identify, boys and girls who appeared in juvenile courts. Earlier, voluntary restraint by the press had proven to be a thin shield against poisonous publicity; and afterwards some newspapers continued to violate both the letter and the spirit of the law, particularly where a juvenile case involved charges of serious violence.[150] Some magistrates and most penal reformers basked in the knowledge that juvenile courts functioned *in loco parentis*. But since the fathers of children brought before juvenile courts typically appeared in only a small fraction of the cases, one may wonder how broadly influential these tribunals were as dispensers of "scientific and friendly advice" to the working poor.[151]

Precisely because the reality of juvenile court procedure fell so far short of the ideal, pressure for new, national legislation mounted during the late twenties and early thirties.[152] Both "Whiggish" accounts of progress in penal administration and inverted-Whig diatribes against the rise of the carceral society tend to view the 1933 Children and Young Persons Act as a legal landmark, the former because it shored up existing law and the latter because it marked a further dematerialization of the offense. Consider the semantic changes that the new statute demanded. Henceforth in juvenile cases the word "conviction" was to be replaced with the phrase "findings

The interior of the new Liverpool Juvenile Court (from Home Office, *Third Report on . . . the Children's Branch*, 1925). Such purpose-built chambers for "treating" the young offender and his family were still rare on the eve of World War Two.

of guilt," and the word "sentence" with the phrase "order upon such finding." That these euphemisms formed part of a larger penal strategy to "encircle"[153] the family with the social expertise of the court might seem a plausible reading of the evidence. Similarly, other provisions of the Act may appear to support the charge that the architects of modern juvenile justice have aimed to administer and control all children, not just young offenders. Section 35 (2) ordered that in every case where a child was found to be "in need of care and protection," the local authority *must* investigate and report to the court on the child's home environment, school record, health, and character. The formula "in need of care and protection," moreover, now covered everyone under age seventeen who had no parent or guardian, had an "unfit" parent or guardian, or had grown "out of control," not to mention all those children found wandering, begging, or loitering. Claud Mullins proclaimed these redefinitions "a step toward the psycho-analytical conception of the needs of both individuals and the community."[154] At least since the depths of the Depression, therefore, England's juvenile justice system might appear to have filled the "cavity"[155] once occupied by punishment with an all-permeating program of family regulation dressed as friendship.

Despite its sweeping terms of reference, however, even this new weapon in the childsavers' armory proved a disappointment. Any suggestion that the 1933 Act marked the end of retributive justice for children ignores the "savage patricians of the House of Lords" who stood firm against the idea that all whipping of children should cease.[156] But their Lordships were far from the only force ranged against modernization of England's juvenile justice system. Passage of the Children and Young Persons Act coincided with a sharp rise in juvenile crime rates throughout the nation. Thus, the mid- and late-thirties found many magistrates and senior police officials declaring that a wave of lawlessness had been generated by the Act's "sentimental" provisions. According to the Stipendiary Magistrate of Salford, public safety would benefit from abolishing the "nice consulting-room idea" that had recently gained standing in children's courts. Or as other critics put it, "the Clarke Hall movement" had gone too far toward creating an atmosphere of "cheerful informality" in these tribunals.[157] A court whose "slovenly, informal methods" hid behind a veil of "semi-secrecy" seemed un-English. Similarly, a law whose broad construction of "moral danger" and "destitution" had more than doubled the number of children sent to approved schools (as reformatories and industrial schools were now known) seemed dangerous.[158] Although the immediate prewar years saw Parliament nearly abolish corporal punishment for young offenders, the demand for it continued to be strong in many localities. A worried James Crichton-Browne saw the recrudescence of schemes for judicial whipping as evidence of a cultural turn toward sadism. As he noted ominously in 1937, "The Hitler Government has issued an injunction to all schoolmasters in Germany to resort to a free use of the cane, and the London County Council has been occupying itself in the selection of different grades of that instrument of torture . . . for use on children of different ages in its schools."[159] If anything, resort to the birch grew more common during the tense early years of the Second World War.[160]

Those who favored judicial whipping and attacked the 1933 Act for its corrosive sentimentalism have been labeled "reactionaries."[161]

Certainly these individuals were backward-looking in their fixation with deterrence and narrow-minded in their reluctance to connect rising juvenile crime rates with harsh economic conditions. But was their case so implausible? Explanations for an alleged "tidal wave of iniquity amongst the young" ranged from the increasing number of automobiles left unattended to the corrupting influence of the cinema, from a decline in religious teaching to a wrecking of home life through resort to judicial separation.[162] Whereas in Birmingham there appeared to exist a close relationship between residence in the new public housing estates and rising rates of juvenile crime, in London's East End no such correlation held.[163] E. M. Rich, the London County Council's Education Officer, seized national attention with a report asserting that among the deleterious forces of modern life was the experience of the "present generation of fathers" during World War One: wartime scarcity had placed a premium on "scrounging" skills, and out of want had emerged a "new morality" that "persists in all classes."[164] The eminent criminologist Hermann Mannheim argued that national statistics could not accurately gauge the volume of juvenile crime; they might, in fact, reflect merely a greater willingness to prosecute delinquent behavior. The period's most thorough study of juvenile crime found nothing to prove that "specific new and adverse influences" had been brought to bear on English children.[165] Thus, the "reactionaries" may have misjudged cause and effect when they linked a presumed outburst of lawlessness to juvenile court procedure, but if so their misjudgment was one among many.

As for their charge that juvenile court procedure was "loose" and "irregular," the reactionaries had a point.[166] For example, confusion over the intent of section 35 (2) in the 1933 Act meant, practically, that a juvenile court's probation officers and the local school authorities sometimes viewed each other as rivals for control of a child's future. Since this future might include committal to an approved school until the age of nineteen, the human stakes were high.[167] Equal ambiguity surrounded the vital question of how a court was to know when a parent had failed to exercise "proper" care. Deciding "where the balance lies between parental autocracy and filial autonomy" was a delicate task that understandably concerned the Home Office.[168] But most unpredictable was the extent to which juvenile court magistrates might permit the parents of a child on trial to cross-examine its accusers. Despite the court's stated aim—repeated, mantra-like, throughout the interwar years—of treating all family members as friends, many judges appear to have held the "wit" of working-class parents in low esteem. Magistrates who followed John Watson's lead, allowing parents to ask only "relevant questions" on behalf of their young, were unlikely to have earned much gratitude.[169] In some cases, one may speculate, this short leash actually tugged against a just result.

For a generation after their birth, English juvenile courts remained "inefficient" in two senses.[170] First, they appeared unable to reduce delinquency during crisis periods. However distorted the national statistics on child crime may have been, they offered small consolation to a public hungry for good news. Juvenile courts had not been in operation long enough, their defenders argued, to cope with the plague of youthful lawlessness that struck England in the midst of World War One. But inexperience could not be pled when these instruments of progressive penality failed to staunch the flow of child crime during the thirties. By the middle of World War Two, the continuing upward spiral of juvenile crime statistics drove some critics to propose that children's courts be scrapped altogether, while even professionals within the juvenile justice system were resigned to spending the next half-generation struggling to counteract the "evil consequences" of mass evacuation, blackouts, and the "bizarre troglodyte" behavior spawned in air raid shelters.[171]

More fundamentally, juvenile courts remained inefficient in their role as agencies of family regulation. In *some* localities, at *certain* times, the dedication of juvenile court officers was everything that Clarke Hall could have wished. The experience of Mrs. Eda Collier spoke well of the care with which several institutions coordinated their work during the early months of the Second World War. In February 1940, a distraught Mrs. Collier brought her fourteen-year-old daughter to Buckinghamshire's High Wycombe Juvenile Court, declaring Suzanne to be "out of control." Prone to serious "fits" for which extended hospitalization had been necessary, Suzanne was an unruly child who alternately stole from her mother and ran away from home. Following a thorough psychological examination, the Court decided to place Suzanne with a capable foster mother who lived in the nearby village of Weston Turville. Unfortunately, as a probation officer explained to the Court, Suzanne's "passion to be in [the] limelight" together with her "very advanced ideas" and "sexual problems" made her a poor candidate for permanent foster placement. The only alternative, it seemed, was for the local education authority to take Suzanne into its care until she reached the age of nineteen. Mrs. Collier consented to this plan and to the weekly contribution of seven shillings, six pence (about 7 percent of her total weekly income) set by the Court. Yet a happy ending for all was not soon to be. Over the next six months Suzanne suffered a series of small "fits" at the school where she had been placed, followed soon thereafter by an escape back to High Wycombe, and thence, in the company of an older man, to London, Portsmouth, and Amersham. When the Court register ceases to mention Suzanne, she had been found and, accompanied by her mother and a female probation officer, taken to the St. Christopher Home for Girls, in Liverpool.[172] Whatever psychic scars she may have borne, Suzanne received the most attentive treatment then available to young persons in her straits.

But the majority of girls and boys who appeared before English juvenile courts received much less personalized attention. Because court registers rarely offer the sort of detail recorded in the Collier case, we must usually infer judicial logic from cryptic notations. If, for instance, both fifteen-year-old Roland Vaughan, who was found to have stolen a dynamo worth twelve shillings, and sixteen-year-old Arthur Taylor, who had indecently assaulted a much younger boy, received exactly the same sanction ("bound over £5 for 12 months"), it is safe to assume that as late as the mid-1930's Coventry's juvenile court still paid little heed to the notion of treating each child as a patient in need of individual care.[173] The medical model of treatment seems to have made an equally small dent in the thinking of Cambridge magistrates. The early summer of 1938 saw Leonard

John Veal, a lad of fifteen, embark on a kinky crime spree. To start, he "did steal and take and carry away one pair of lady's artificial silk knickers of the value of 1/3." Not satisfied, that same day Leonard purloined a lady's cotton vest and her brassiere. These souvenirs contented him at first, but a month later he was caught in the act of liberating a third lady's knickers and bra—from a clothesline, one presumes. If ever teenage larceny begged for psychosexual assessment, Leonard Veal's did. Significantly, the Cambridge Juvenile Court merely fined him for theft. The magistrates made no effort at all to dematerialize Veal's offense. And they missed a golden opportunity to use the lad's strange behavior as a pretext for treating his whole family.[174]

Today, as during the interwar years, English juvenile courts remain less imposing instruments of family regulation than their purportedly "scientific" forms of surveillance and examination might suggest. For a regulatory system to work effectively there must first exist a clear conception of desired ends. In the case of juvenile justice, the agents of regulation—magistrates and probation officers— are far from united in their views of how best to cope with young delinquents, particularly those who have committed serious offenses.[175] This divergence in opinion follows naturally from a yet more basic confusion. That is, precisely how should a child behave? By late 1994, the citizens of Elland, a struggling textile mill town in West Yorkshire, were desperate to halt the larcenous onslaught of a fourteen-year-old boy. Arrested eighty-eight times and convicted of 130 offenses over a period of six years, he was deemed almost single-handedly responsible for causing insurance premiums to soar and driving some firms out of town. Local shopkeepers entertained thoughts of hanging the boy or perhaps locking him in stocks on the central square. Any sympathy with the view that his age should shield him from the terror of the law had long since evaporated.[176] Indeed, with persons under eighteen now responsible for a fifth of all crime and nearly 40 percent of burglaries in England, both Tory and Labour leaders have advocated stripping some of the confidentiality from juvenile court proceedings. "Shaming," it seems, is the juvenile peacekeeping tactic *du jour*.[177]

Even louder was the outcry over the killing of Jamie Bulger in 1993. Late that year a Preston jury convicted Robert Thompson and Jon Venables, both then eleven, of murdering a toddler whom they lured from his mother's side. Nine months earlier these boys had snatched little Jamie from a busy shopping center in Liverpool, frog-marched him through the city, and then beaten him to death with stones and an iron bar on a railway line, leaving his body to be dismembered by a train. Sentencing them to indefinite detention, Justice Morland called the boys "both cunning and very wicked," a characterization that struck some sections of the public as generous. By lodging an appeal against Morland's sentence with the European Court of Human Rights in Strasbourg, counsel for the defense have done much to keep the Bulger case at the forefront of demands for greater personal accountability from young offenders.[178] The ideological uncertainty that pervades England's juvenile justice system has rarely been more apparent.

SIX

Artificial Families

The Politics of Adoption

J UST AS THE judicial treatment of young offenders remained a controversial matter throughout the period of this study, so the problem of regulating English adoption practice proved vexing for politicians and philanthropists alike. Writing in 1887, two American historians gazed enviously across the Atlantic: "In a stable society, like that of England, where distinctions of rank and social position are settled by birth rather than by achievement, the questions connected with the family do not present such complications as in our own American life."[1] Ironically, it was in fact England's social stability that helped to make the issue of adoption so complex. For although legal adoption—the process by which parental rights and responsibilities become fully transferable—was not possible in England until 1926, children had been adopted *de facto* since time out of mind. Thus for generations there endured a glaring contradiction between common law and popular practice. During the first quarter of the twentieth century, however, a confluence of demographic and psychological forces brought about an end to this anomaly. Along the way thorny questions involving the rights of illegitimate children, the status of unmarried mothers, and the privacy of domestic life were thrust before the public.

Adoption can serve several ends. Viewing the phenomenon in broad, cross-cultural terms, Jack Goody suggests three functions: to provide homes for orphans, bastards, and foundlings; to give childless couples "social progeny"; and to create heirs for property.[2] Whereas in the late twentieth-century West adoption as a cure for childlessness tends to dominate discussion of the subject, this is a relatively recent preoccupation. In pre-industrial societies, by contrast, concern over preventing extinction of family lines was far more likely to be the impetus for action.[3] Yet as legal scholars are quick to point out, England's common law tradition early on developed an aversion to the idea that parenthood might be transferable, an idea originally rooted in the requirements of Roman ancestor worship.[4] Precisely why such a dislike of Roman practice should have evolved in England has not been satisfactorily analyzed. To contend, for example, that "[t]he English had an inordinately high regard for blood lineage" is to beg the question. Glanville's oft-quoted dictum that "Only God can make a heres [an heir], not man" epitomizes early modern English fears for the safety of inheritance rights without explaining these fears. That the "individualistic character" of common law rendered it hostile to the Roman concept of *patria potestas* (absolute paternal authority) is an equally vague formulation.[5] If, as previously suggested, English society dating back to medieval times was obsessed with the acquisition and preservation of property, it follows that legal adoption, insofar as it complicated the transmission of property, might have appeared to threaten the economic order.

Whatever the logic of English common law, there is no doubt that functional alternatives to adoption were readily available in medieval and early modern times. Where childlessness posed an economic threat, farmers sometimes sold or leased land to younger persons in exchange for support during old age. Known technically as a "use," this contractual arrangement has occasionally been labeled an "adoption," though it more closely resembled modern social security schemes.[6] By the sixteenth century another custom was increasingly coming to offer some of the benefits of adoption: the custom of sending children to other families as servants or apprentices. In creating a labor market of young people who might be hired as needed, Tudor-Stuart England was practicing what amounted to after-the-fact family planning. That is, whereas in many preindustrial societies it was "essential to produce, or even to over-produce, children in order to provide the right labor force in terms of age and sex, and to adopt children if nature did not give the right number, in England it was possible to use the much more flexible mechanism of hiring children for a year at a time as servants, or taking an apprentice for a longer period."[7] If this widespread hiring of the young as servants constituted a "quasi-adoptive device," it was not a device designed primarily to safeguard the "best interests" of the child.[8]

We should not of course assume that economic calculation governed all decisions to send children away from, or take them into, early modern households. Parents may sometimes have agreed to "put out" their illiterate sons and daughters with other families in the hope of exposing them to a higher standard of education.[9] Puritan parents, Edmund Morgan has suggested, sometimes placed their offspring in other homes because they were afraid of "spoiling" them with too much affection.[10] It seems that for at least one Puritan family in Stuart London, compassion was the animating force behind a *de facto* adoption. When Nehemiah and Grace Wallington learned that a relative's boy had lost his father during the Irish rebellion of 1641, they wasted no time offering to care for him. Thus for eight years young Charles was treated as a member of the Wallington family.[11] In an age when perhaps a sixth of all children under the age of eighteen had lost at least one parent,[12] Charles's experience must have been relatively common.

The Dark Side of "Adoption"

As we approach England's industrial heyday, however, the term "adoption" increasingly becomes associated with the criminal treatment of illegitimate children. This dark side of the subject would haunt Victorian social reformers, color the early infant welfare movement, and ultimately complicate the campaign for legalized adoption. Although the story of efforts to protect illegitimate children in England is convoluted,[13] one straightforward fact did much to shape it. This was that a combination of legal and moral prejudice had created a hostile climate for the unmarried mother who wished to keep her young child. Aware that the social odds were stacked against such women, the reading public of mid-Victorian England could not ignore those doctors, journalists, and charity workers who began warning about a wholesale "slaughter of the innocents."[14] The preoccupation of polite society with savage instincts, particularly those attributed to the poor,[15] only heightened fears that the disposal of illegitimate offspring had become a thriving trade by the 1860's.

A few charities dedicated to protecting such children did exist. By far the best known of these was London's venerable Foundling Hospital, whose doors had opened in 1741 "to prevent the frequent murders of poor miserable children at their birth." After its unrestricted admissions policy proved ruinously expensive, however, the Foundling Hospital grew increasingly selective, eventually establishing a kind of philanthropic inquisition before which unwed mothers were obliged to confess their carnal sins.[16] Yet by the mid-Victorian era even this degree of coercion seemed inadequate. As the voice for London's "magdalen" charities declared, "We should be sorry to see Foundling Hospitals multiplied, thus affording an *unnatural* means of escape from the terrible retribution of maternity, to those whom nature has branded with this just mark of shame."[17] Numerous "homes," "refuges," and "penitentiaries," for unmarried mothers operated in Victorian cities, although they concentrated on helping the "respectable" girl who had "fallen" but once. In London, where such work had become a charitable speciality, the length of time during which mothers might find shelter varied from several weeks at the Temporary Home for Friendless Women to a minimum of a year at St. Mary Magdalene's Home. Some charities imposed no age limit on the women they stooped to save, whereas others, such as St. Cyprian's Beth Esda in Dorset Square, would admit only girls under eighteen.[18] These institutions shared a confidence that by extending "sisterly" concern to the "fallen," helping them find work as domestic servants, and arranging to place their children with foster parents, an antidote was at hand for the kind of maternal desperation that expressed itself as suicide or infanticide.[19] Unfortunately, few mid-Victorian rescue societies paid close attention to the fate of the children for whom they had found homes.

It was the often fatal fostering of illegitimate children that caused some social reformers to cringe at the word "adoption." By the mid-1860's public health activists, physicians and lay sanitarians alike, were acutely conscious that England's legal system made unmarried motherhood a hazardous condition. The New Poor Law Act of 1834 was bad enough. Under its terms a single woman with a child could receive food and shelter at public expense only if they entered the workhouse together. In keeping with Utilitarian precepts, the New Poor Law aimed to render the condition of the unwed mother "less eligible" than that of her married counterpart, and so provide a powerful deterrent to sexual nonconformity. In one important respect, however, the 1834 Act actually improved the lot of the single mother. Because it authorized Poor Law Guardians to help her track down the child's putative father and, if possible, to extract child support from him, the Act gave her administrative support that she had previously lacked. But sustained protest against the involvement of Poor Law authorities in affiliation and maintenance actions—chiefly on the grounds that such involvement encouraged "concubinage" and menaced innocent men—produced the "Little Poor Law" of 1844.[20] Simply put, the latter retained the hated workhouse deterrent but prohibited Poor Law authorities from helping women in paternity suits. Now obliged to launch her own maintenance action in a police court, and entitled to a paltry maximum award of two shillings and sixpence if she proved her case, the unwed mother without supportive kin faced a bleak future.[21] As an anonymous reformer mused in 1864, England already had a Divorce Court for the rich when what it really needed was an "Affiliation Court" for poor women.[22] It is true that illegitimacy ratios declined during the latter half of the nineteenth century. But to deduce from such statistical aggregates that the "deserted mother . . . was not a serious problem in Victorian England," as Gertrude Himmelfarb has done, would be foolish.[23]

The comfortable classes knew better. They were understandably worried about the placement of illegitimate children with strangers. Public health crusaders had long warned that the absence of any stillbirth registration procedure offered an ideal cover for abortion and infanticide. "How many children who have survived their birth a few hours, a few days, weeks perhaps, are cast into that ever-yawning and indiscriminate grave . . . of the still-born!," exclaimed *The Lancet* in 1859.[24] After the infamous Torquay murder trial of Charlotte Winsor seven years later, polite society began to speculate about an equally clandestine yet perhaps more widespread crime. For if the cold-blooded Mrs. Winsor had managed to run a brisk business killing bastards in rural Devonshire, how much busier were entrepreneurs in England's great cities, where "a system with regular practitioners and fixed fees" surely flourished?[25] Large urban centers, after all, provided not only the anonymity useful for criminal deeds but also large concentrations of "seduced and abandoned" servant girls who accounted for so many illegitimate births. If early twenti-eth-century census figures are any indication of demographic trends a generation before, it may well have been the case that domestic servants in fact produced proportionally *fewer* illegitimate children than several other female occupational groups, most notably char-women, agricultural laborers, and laundresses.[26] And we may question the degree to which a servant's drive to "emancipate herself from her position" through marriage made her easy prey for preda-tory men.[27] But with nearly a million female servants employed in English households during the 1860's,[28] there were bound to be thousands of children born out of wedlock each year to women whose livelihood demanded that evidence of their indiscretions be erased as quickly as possible.

Short of outright murder, the quickest way for a friendless female to get rid of her child was by paying to have it "adopted." This meant, in practice, finding foster parents to take the child in ex-change for weekly payments or else a lump sum at the time of trans-fer. What public health activists in the late 1860's discovered was that a flourishing trade along these lines was already being con-ducted through the newspapers. J. B. Curgenven, a general surgeon and Honorary Secretary of London's reform-minded Harveian Soci-ety, and Ernest Hart, an ophthalmic surgeon, Dean of the St. Mary's Hospital Medical School, and from 1866 to 1898 editor of the *Brit-ish Medical Journal*, formed the nucleus of a determined effort to eradicate what they called the "baby farming" business.[29] The scope of baby farming could be inferred, they thought, from the advertisements for "villanously cheap" adoption placed in publications catering to the masses. At least a few reputable London papers also carried such advertisements. It was, for example, a simple matter to insert these notices in the *Daily Telegraph*: "Send a boy of fourteen with three and sixpence and an offer to manage the birth of a baby in concealment, or to dispose of one by adoption, and your money will be taken without a word of inquiry, and your little advertisement will appear in due course, to tempt women eager to have done with their children. . . ."[30] Under Ernest Hart's direction, the *British Medical Journal* set out to show how prevalent baby farming had grown. Within a week of offering a £5 premium for full care of a child, the *Journal*'s undercover agent received 333 replies. The visits he subsequently paid to respondents' homes proved "beyond doubt" that many of these women "carried on the business [of adoption] with a deliberate knowledge that the children would die very quickly." No more than a third of those answering the *Journal*'s decoy advertisements genuinely wanted a child in their lives. Here was a social "gangrene," as *The Times* put it, that had to be cut out.[31]

Despite a well-publicized estimate that about 30,000 illegitimate children fell into the hands of paid "nurses" each year,[32] it took a more disturbing exposé to convince Parliament that baby farming was an ill in need of legislative cure. This time the Metropolitan Police became involved. Since no fewer than sixteen infant bodies had been recovered from the streets of Brixton during the spring of 1870, police were keenly interested when yet another tiny corpse, this one wrapped in a piece of paper bearing the name "Mrs. Waters," was found among some lumber in the same South London neighborhood. Soon thereafter *Lloyd's Weekly* carried an advertisement that stank of foul play:

ADOPTION: A GOOD home, with a mother's love and care, is offered to any respectable person wishing her Child to be entirely adopted. Premium £5, which sum includes everything. Apply, by letter only, to Mrs. Oliver. Post office, Goar-place, Brixton.[33]

The *Illustrated Police News* (Oct. 15, 1870) was keen to document the "baby farm-ing" crimes of Margaret Waters. Courtesy: British Library.

Sergeant Relf, the policeman selected to play the part of a reluctant father, met "Mrs. Oliver" at Camberwell Railway Station and fol-lowed her home. Once Relf traced the illegitimate child of a seven-teen-year-old girl to this same house he was ready to act. Accompa-nied by the baby's grandfather, he gained entry to 4 Frederick Ter-race, and discovered there not one but eleven infants, all grossly ne-glected.

Evidence gathered about "one of the most horrible . . . stories ever brought to light in a Court of Justice" soon showed that "Mrs. Oliver" was actually Margaret Waters, aged 35. For several years Waters and her husband had prospered in Newfoundland. But upon his death in 1864, the widow returned to London with £300 and a plan to start her own collar-sewing business. When this scheme soured she turned to renting out rooms in her home, and it was as a landlady that she discovered how eager some women were to part with their babies. So Waters and her sister, Sarah Ellis, 29, took to feeding their young charges a formula consisting of common lime and water, sometimes spiked with tincture of opium. Receipts found in the house proved that during May and June of 1870 alone, the sisters had pawned over a hundred items of children's clothing.

Thus, once five of the infants died from the combined effects of starvation and narcotic poisoning, the charges against Waters and Ellis grew to include murder, manslaughter, conspiracy, and obtaining money under false pretenses. Sarah Ellis was lucky to escape with a conviction on the last charge alone. Margaret Waters went to the gallows on October 1, 1870.[34]

Chilling though the "Brixton Horrors" were, Waters's hanging struck some contemporaries as a pointless gesture. By demonstrating the risks that baby farming entailed, they argued, the state was merely encouraging mercenary nurses to demand higher fees, thereby increasing the chances that unwed mothers would perform their own killings.[35] More fundamental was the objection that English law, not Mrs. Waters, had created a social system in which "the whole onus and disgrace" of illegitimacy fell on women. Very much as foes of the Contagious Diseases Acts kept insisting, what made sexual vice rampant was the "safe indulgence of man's vicious propensities."[36] But just as public health reformers wielded the threat of epidemic syphilis and gonorrhea to win support for the mandatory inspection of suspected prostitutes, so they also exploited the Waters trial to publicize formation of an Infant Life Protection Society and, ultimately, to push Parliament toward launching a full-scale study of the traffic in young children.[37] The all-male ILPS was well positioned to argue for the regulation of baby farming. Supported by a parade of policemen, coroners, and medical officers of health as witnesses, and a Select Committee membership generally sympathetic to regulation, J. B. Curgenven, Ernest Hart, and their fellow sanitarians managed to represent adoption as a commonly fatal act. In doing so they were not only validating contemporary fears about a subculture of urban savagery but also arguing for the indispensability of professional medicine.

Testimony presented to the 1871 Select Committee on Infant Life Protection failed in fact to answer several key questions about the nature and extent of baby farming. It was curious, for example, that whereas London, Edinburgh, and Glasgow had apparently become booming centers of this trade, the conurbations of Lancashire and Yorkshire seemed untouched: Manchester's Coroner had encountered just one case of fraudulent adoption in twenty-two years. Perhaps the unmarried mothers employed in Northern factories did not need baby farmers because they could leave their infants with child-minders during working hours? If Salford's Medical Officer of Health was right that between 80 and 90 percent of these daycare babies died during infancy, then did Northern mothers prefer what was in effect a cheaper form of child disposal?[38] Nor was it clear how much "adoption" took place at the point of birth, in suspect lying-in establishments. The Metropolitan Police already knew of at least one thriving center for criminal abortion in a Soho midwife's home.[39] The unmasking of another abortionist, Mrs. Hall, showed that in South London the midwife and the baby-farmer could form a lucrative if unholy alliance. It was Hall's Camberwell lying-in home that had supplied several drugged infants to the nearby Brixton baby farm of Waters and Ellis—and to households located as far away as Gloucestershire.[40] Finally, the Select Committee was unsure how to classify the business of professional adoption. Were baby farms commercial ventures analogous to lodging houses, which already required periodic inspection in several municipalities? And what of the "farmers"? Since persons who cared for certified imbeciles and lunatics had to be licensed, why should those who fostered helpless infants for profit be exempt from licensing?[41]

Despite these uncertainties the 1871 Select Committee proposed taking a cautious first step toward monitoring the traffic in illegitimate children. Its report pleased neither the friends nor the foes of regulation. Mid-Victorian feminists railed against the "increasing officialism, police interference, and espionage" that they felt sure would accompany any regulatory scheme. The male backers of protective legislation, Lydia Becker pointed out, had once again confused cause with effect: bastards would not *need* to be "farmed" out if English law properly punished seduction.[42] Ernest Hart would later blame Northern feminists for the "emasculation" of England's first statute to deal with professional adoption.[43] This statute, the 1872 Infant Life Protection Act, instituted compulsory registration of persons who accepted "for hire or reward" more than a single child under one year of age. Taken together with the 1872 Bastardy

Laws Amendment Act and the 1874 Registration Act,[44] also products of pressure from the medical establishment, it constituted a modest victory for those who held that the sanctity of English home life should not be respected at the cost of forsaking illegitimate children.

The alarm over baby farming that arose in the late 1860's endured for a generation. Although the doctor-dominated Infant Life Protection Society soon faded from the political scene, there emerged new and more powerful defenders of "nurse children," principally the NSPCC and the London County Council. With support from the medical press, these groups insisted that by limiting registration to homes where more than one child had been taken for reward, the 1872 Infant Life Protection Act was ignoring a potentially vast reservoir of crime. For if, as the LCC's well-named Samuel Babey believed, 95 percent of the children given up for "adoption" were illegitimate,[45] then there could be hundreds of homes where unscrupulous people "put away" such children one at a time. The 1872 Act's restrictive application to infants under the age of one likewise left a great many children at risk. Moreover, with the significant exception of London, where the LCC's Public Control Department monitored newspaper advertisements and kept close watch over its registered homes,[46] most local authorities did little to enforce the law. Trying to shock Parliament into closing these legal loopholes, the NSPCC's Benjamin Waugh announced in 1896 that, "I could baby-farm [to death] a million children a year in this country and never be convicted, and make a good fortune."[47]

Waugh was exaggerating and he knew it. Never a patient man, the NSPCC's leader had grown frustrated with the time and expense needed to prosecute baby farmers. It had cost the Society over £80 to win a manslaughter conviction against Alice Reeves, in whose Lambeth home twelve starving infants were found during the winter of 1891. Married to a lawyer and feeling so secure that she conducted business while living next door to a policeman, the notorious Mrs. Reeves was allegedly but one of "hundreds of traders in baby slaughter" whose far-flung advertisements hinted at a "prodigious business."[48] So single-minded did the NSPCC and the London

County Council become in their drive for stringent control of this business that they dismissed concerns about popular resentment of inspection. Some people objected at first to his home visits, Samuel Babey confessed, but "when they get used to it [inspection] they do not mind." As far as Benjamin Waugh could see, the only individuals apt to fear strict supervision of professional adoption were those who *should* feel a "very proper dread" of the law.[49]

The Home Office, on the other hand, worried about "subjecting the houses of the poor to no small intrusion" in order to prevent "occasional crime."[50] It was justifiably concerned. Edwin Baxter, Coroner for the Eastern Division of London, declared that very little criminal fostering went on among the destitute folk of his district: "When a daughter of a working man gets into trouble," Baxter noted, "as a rule . . . she marries at the eleventh hour, whereas, amongst those in a more affluent position there is an endeavour to screen the shame and get rid of the child; and so baby farming starts."[51] If a last-minute marriage did not take place, an East End child was more likely to be absorbed into the woman's natal family than sent out to a paid nurse. And where commercial baby nursing did occur in the East End, as Ellen Ross has shown, its practitioners tended to be widows or older women with grown children, recruited through word of mouth rather than newspaper advertisements.[52] The denizens of inner-city slums were often passionate about preserving family honor despite—or perhaps because of—their poverty. Hence the presumption of misconduct personified by the visit of an infant life protection inspector aroused more than "sentimental objections" among the masses. Only where the registration of a home served to blunt the "malicious insinuation of neighbours" might poor people welcome such scrutiny.[53]

Nor were proletarian mores the only source of opposition to tighter control of baby farming. Charities committed to helping unwed mothers applauded the idea of saving bastard children from that "cult of Moloch" whose rituals included "murder, deception, and sordid greed."[54] But applause turned to protest as soon as reformers mentioned the possibility of inspecting one-child homes. Robert Peel Wethered, representing eighteen constituent members of the London Diocesan Council for Rescue and Preventive Work, assured a Lords Select Committee in 1896 that the small-scale fostering associated with such charity would vanish if kindly nurse mothers became the objects of registration and inspection.[55] Most late-Victorian and Edwardian philanthropy aimed at "friendless girls" continued to place moral rehabilitation ahead of concern for the happiness of mother and child. This held true for charities of all sizes. Florence Smith, 22, found the rules at tiny St. Faith's Shelter in Coventry so confining that she fled to a circus troupe in 1897. The regimen was likewise austere in the large Salvation Army homes, 90 percent of whose unwed mothers had supposedly been "saved from falling over the precipice" into the social "abyss."[56] Judgmental as such charity may seem in retrospect, its adherents nonetheless managed until 1908 to exempt from inspection all homes where a single child had been "adopted" in exchange for weekly payments. Nor until 1908 did Parliament see fit to repeal the "£20 rule." Written into the Infant Life Protection Act of 1897 largely at the behest of philanthropists, this escape clause allowed local authorities to ignore placements of children under two years old so long as any accompanying fee exceeded £20. Only the well paid, it seemed, could be trusted with the offspring of others.[57]

Baby farming continued to trouble England even after passage of the 1908 Children Act. Robert Parr, Waugh's successor as NSPCC Secretary, kept reminding the public that baby farming was an iceberg phenomenon. To detach its submerged criminal element would require acceptance of radical legal reform—such as William Clarke Hall's plan to make every illegitimate child a ward of its local police court.[58] Until such reform became law, charity workers, Poor Law authorities, and health visitors would need to comb their areas for those who had already devised new ways to circumvent registration and inspection procedures.[59] This abiding concern with the deceit that sometimes masqueraded as "adoption" survived the First World War and would leave its mark on interwar social policy.

Fostering and Kindred Care

Illegitimate infants were not of course the only young to be separated from their parents. Often, for example, the children of middle-class families stationed abroad on Imperial business were left with foster parents in England. Rudyard Kipling was one such child, and if Kipling's account of the "House of Desolation" where he spent nearly six miserable years is at all representative, then this custom may have traumatized many otherwise well-off boys and girls.[60] But better known was the use to which both private charities and Poor Law authorities put fostering as a way to simulate "the divine institution of the family" for abandoned children.[61] To Poor Law children, fostering meant "boarding-out" in humble homes. Although boarding-out had taken root in Scotland as early as 1843,[62] it was not until 1870 that England's Poor Law Board authorized Guardians to place selected children with foster parents. This liberalization of policy stemmed largely from the pressure of middle-class women concerned about the plight of girls in workhouses and the "barracks schools" associated with them. One can identify less high-minded concerns here as well, the most evident of which was worry about the future supply of reliable servants. Writing from her Wiltshire home in 1861, Hannah Archer, the wife of a Guardian, warned that a "race" of shameless workhouse girls was unleashing a "torrent of sin" that threatened not only to pollute other child minds but also to render all paupers unfit for domestic service. By boarding-out the younger workhouse girls with "trustworthy cottagers" and allowing ladies to supervise them, Archer believed, Guardians might salvage some productive citizens. More immediately influential were the women who met G. J. Goschen, President of the Poor Law Board, in early 1870. This deputation was the idea of Miss Preusser, a German-born activist whose attempts to transplant children from London's East End to cottages near her Lake District home had run afoul of Poor Law regulations.[63] Miss Preusser's group argued successfully that Guardians should have the option of sending orphaned and deserted young to foster homes, even when these homes lay outside local Union boundaries.[64]

The public response to boarding-out was at first mixed. Those who, like Henry Fawcett, saw the Poor Law as England's chief weapon against working-class sloth predicted that the new system would teach parents how they could "best secure physical comfort for their children by deserting them."[65] Nor were those asked to supervise boarded-out boys and girls uniformly impressed. After a careful assessment of the new system at Swansea, for instance, Inspector Andrew Doyle wondered how well pauper children would learn "lessons of industry, frugality, and self-reliance" when consigned to homes with drunken lodgers, rag piles for beds, and privies under the stairs.[66] Still other critics insisted that small-scale rural settlements, each with a resident house-mother, offered the best alternative to workhouse life for pauper young.[67] Balanced against these objections were the hopes of many solid citizens that foster care might offer the kind of "natural training" in "human conduct" that would enable girls to remain chaste and equip boys to resist the lure of crime. "The low villains who insult women, garotte and plunder," after all, "were once neglected little boys"; they had gone bad "because none deemed it worth their while to provide them when young with shelter under a good woman's care."[68]

Although initially skeptical, Poor Law officials resorted to boarding-out with increasing frequency. As a leading London philanthropist explained in 1883, "notwithstanding much prejudice and obstruction," the new system was gaining ground not only because it cost less to board-out a child than to maintain it in a workhouse or Poor Law school, but also because kindly folk were awakening to the fact that by opening their homes they could revive boys and girls so emotionally stunted that some "actually *did not know how to kiss!*"[69] Two administrative reforms helped to popularize boarding-out. The Poor Law Acts of 1889 and 1899 effectively permitted Guardians to "adopt" certain boys and girls.[70] By the start of the twentieth century Guardians could assume legal custody over workhouse children under the age of eighteen whose parents had died, deserted the home, gone to prison for offenses against their young, been judged morally or mentally unfit, or become permanently disabled while in receipt of Poor Law aid. Where Guardians chose to exercise these prerogatives a child's parent retained the right of appeal to a police court. But judging from the fact that in 1908 alone Guardians adopted 12,417 such children, these appeals must have been either few in number or else singularly ineffective.[71]

A Poor Law adoption did not necessarily end in foster care. And we should understand that Poor Law foster care—that is, boarding-out arrangements—affected just 3.7 percent of all English and Welsh children receiving public relief of some kind in the early twentieth century.[72] It remains true nonetheless that Guardians began wielding their new power as a way to reconfigure working-class families. In Edwardian Essex, Poor Law authorities at Braintree used adoption to "break the family tradition" of "vicious habits" that poisoned some rural homes.[73] At about the same time Guardians elsewhere started trying to protect abused children through adoption. Such solicitude could prove to be as much a curse as a blessing, Margaret Nevinson found:

We once had a case [*circa* 1902] on the Hampstead Board of a husband and father so cruel and brutal . . . that the Guardians adopted the children, and sent them away to school, though the wife, a decent woman and devoted mother, came regularly to beg that some of them, at least, should be left to her, loyally promising her husband should reform. But she was left in her loneliness till the war broke out. Her husband then departed and slaughtered Germans with great vigour, covering himself with glory; the children returned to their mother, now independent with a separate allowance, and the little home was carried on in peace and quiet under matriarchy.[74]

Prewar evidence drawn from the minute books of Poor Law Unions in the North of England suggests that Guardians there most often resorted to adoption where gross "neglect by parents" was at issue: less than 10 percent of the children adopted in Carlisle were either orphans or illegitimate.[75] Curiously, in at least two Northern Unions children who had already been adopted by the Guardians were sometimes then re-adopted by local citizens. Darlington's Boarding-Out Committee felt no qualms about allowing respectable folk to tour the workhouse so that they might hand-pick promising youngsters.[76] In County Durham's Chester-le-Street Union, the Workhouse Visiting Committee permitted one girl, Sarah Thompson, to be re-adopted *twice* within a span of fourteen months. Although the minutes are mute as to why young Sarah returned to the workhouse after both placements, it may have been the case that she, like Poor Law children in several other localities, had been exploited as a short-term servant.[77]

The volunteer committees that oversaw such strange placements naturally tended to be middle-class in composition, with "ladies" shouldering much of the visiting work. Ideally at least, "the relationship between the foster-parents and the committee lady . . . becomes one of real friendship, both being deeply interested in the welfare of a little child. If misfortune falls upon the family, the lady is at hand to assist; but if wrong-doing takes place, undesirable lodgers be admitted, . . . it is the duty of the lady to inform the committee, so that they may remove the child to a more desirable home."[78] By 1909, however, it was clear to the Royal Commission on the Poor Laws that children boarded-out within a Union's boundaries usually received less attentive supervision than those placed with foster parents living "without" the Union. The reason seemed obvious: whereas within Union boundaries boarding-out committees remained optional and unregulated, outside the Union these bodies were compulsory and, after 1884, the objects of Local Government Board scrutiny. Miss M. H. Mason, who became the LGB's first inspector of foster children in 1885, was nothing if not earnest about her job. For "[i]f the boarding-out system spreads widely," she believed, "only strict rules can save it from degenerating into baby-farming." Thus Mason gave short shrift to lady visitors whose investigative protocol differed from her own. All too often, she assured a parliamentary committee in 1896, these volunteers failed to check for signs of mistreatment "hidden under tidy clothes," yet tended to be unrealistically demanding about the housekeeping habits of foster mothers.[79]

Very rarely do records allow us to glimpse the Poor Law's boarding-out work through a child's eyes. Still, it is probable that the disorientation which Catherine B. experienced on leaving her Essex workhouse home would have been common. Born in 1890, Catherine could recall her earliest memory more than seventy years later—eating "skilly" (a mush made of corn and hot water) at a large workhouse table. She was lame ("my toes were where my heels were"), and perhaps because of that she became a special favorite of the workhouse matron. But one day when she was four Catherine found herself in a dogcart heading to a strange place:

> Oh, I was frightened. I hadn't been told a thing, you see. And when I got in [to her new home, in nearby Great Bentley] . . . there was a chair, a little chair in front of the fire and this lady asked me to sit on it. She said, 'sit down,' and I did and she gave me some biscuits, but I remember I couldn't eat them . . . 'cos I was too upset, couldn't think where I was. And after they [the workhouse Master and Matron] said they were going, I got up to go, thinking I was going back, but I didn't. I had to stop. So I cried, I said, 'I don't want to stop here. I want to go back to my other home!' I remember as if it was yesterday. And I was a . . . frail little thing, white face, and they cropped my hair like a boy.

Catherine remained in Great Bentley until she was old enough to earn her own keep as a domestic servant.[80] For her, and perhaps for many other wards of the workhouse, resettlement in a new home, whether through boarding-out or adoption, did not necessarily lead to a happier life.

Catherine B. might just as easily have spent her first years in one of the many charitable institutions dedicated to saving children classified variously as "friendless," "homeless," or "outcast." For running parallel with the Poor Law's foster care system was a dense if uncoordinated complex of private agencies specializing in virtually the same work. By the end of the nineteenth century there were several hundred of these bodies operating throughout England and Wales, although three of them—the Barnardo group, the Children's Home and Orphanage, and the Church of England Waifs and Strays Society—together accounted for as much as half the voluntary effort in this field. Dr. Barnardo's Homes, expanding rapidly from their base in London's East End, was the oldest (1866) and largest of the triumvirate. Thomas John Barnardo, an Irish Protestant zealot whose philanthropic style is best described as martial, proclaimed "the ever-open door" for young outcasts.[81] Barnardo's policy of ad-

"The Bull's Eye" (from Doré and Jerrold, *London: A Pilgrimage*, 1872) refers to the lantern favored by police and waif-hunting philanthropists alike. The Church of England Waifs and Strays Society explained that the prime time for such hunts was 1 A.M.—when homeless children who had been turned out of lodging-house kitchens were just settling into their outdoor digs.

mitting ragged boys and girls to his homes before investigating their personal circumstances followed naturally from his belief that successful reclamation work often came down to a race against time. "If the children of the slums can be removed from their surroundings early enough, and can be kept sufficiently long under training," he averred, "heredity counts for little, environment counts for everything."[82]

A sense of urgency therefore pervaded Barnardo's work and sometimes drove him to take rash action. Early enemies had lobbed into the Barnardo camp several incendiary charges, the best documented of which centered on his resort to posed photographs of "street arabs."[83] Partly no doubt as a fund-raising ploy but partly also because he deemed divine command superior to human law, Barnardo later confessed to kidnapping in 1885. This confession was shrewdly timed. W. T. Stead, Editor of the *Pall Mall Gazette* and crusader against child prostitution, was then England's most famous prisoner, having been convicted of buying thirteen-year-old Eliza Armstrong as part of a campaign to expose the white slave trade. Not to be outdone, Barnardo revealed that by kidnapping no fewer than forty-seven homeless children he had elevated "philanthropic abduction" to a "fine art."[84] Although no legal challenges followed this announcement, the combative "Doctor" ran out of luck four years later. In 1889, the parents of three children admitted to his homes demanded their return. Subsequent litigation showed that Barnardo had acted irresponsibly, hustling two of these children out of the country in such a way that they could not be traced.[85] Some of Barnardo's well-placed supporters tried to shield him from future legal liability by urging Parliament to limit the rights of parents who had permitted charities to "adopt" their young. The resulting 1891 Custody of Children Act did at least allow courts to prevent the return of children to parents judged unfit. But this was too little too late. Not until the mid-1890's could the Barnardo group once more devote its full attention to the fostering and vocational training of slum children, 4,357 of whom were boarded-out by 1906.[86]

Despite Barnardo's "buccaneering"[87] example, it is important to realize that by no means all the children in his organization's care had been wrested from bad parents. Sometimes the press of circumstance left no obvious alternative to parting with one's young. The experience of Kathleen Dayus is telling in this regard. However difficult her Edwardian childhood in a Birmingham slum may have been, motherhood for Dayus brought only more pain. After marrying at the age of eighteen in 1921, she went on to bear five children. Life proved hard but endurable until 1927 when, in quick succession, her father died, her eldest son was crushed by a van, she lost her job, and her husband became an invalid. When her husband, too, died in 1931, Kathleen felt "shattered." Left with a harpy of a mother and four children, she was reduced to seeking public assistance:

I was given food and coal vouchers eventually, but not before I had pawned everything except the clothes we stood up in. Still, what was given was not enough for us and I had to moonlight as an enameller in order to survive. Even then I couldn't cope. Life was unbearable with Mum, and I was at my wit's end. Finally, I had to let my children go into a Dr. Barnardo's home. I was heartbroken, but what could I do? We were starving and helpless; there was only Mum and me and so I decided to let them go where they would at least be clothed and fed. The home turned out to be better than I expected. It was in Moseley [a southern suburb of Birmingham] which was still quite rural then, and the matron was a kindly soul. I still wept bitterly when I had to leave them there, but they were laughing and chatting with the other kids soon enough, and I knew I'd done the right thing.[88]

The Barnardo group, like the New York Children's Aid Society in an earlier era, may therefore have been less significant as a family-policing agency than as "part of a normative and reasonable family strategy for coping with . . . the vicissitudes of proletarianization."[89]

   Dr. Stephenson's Children's Home and the Church of England Waifs and Strays Society also emerged as leading providers of foster care. As was true of Barnardo's work, the line between fostering and adoption could easily become blurred in these organizations. Thomas Bowman Stephenson, a Methodist minister, had launched his rescue mission on the mean streets of South London in 1869. Although best known during the late-Victorian period as an orphanage, Stephenson's society actually admitted few total orphans. His charges tended rather to be the offspring of widows, deserted wives, and prostitutes—precisely the sort of children who needed saving from the "workhouse system."[90] During their first quarter-century the Stephenson institutions helped about half their children to find unskilled employment abroad, principally in Canada, where economic opportunity and a better moral climate appeared to exist.[91] Most of those who remained in England managed to find jobs in domestic service and agriculture. But roughly 2 percent of the Stephenson children are listed in annual reports as "adopted." We are assured that "homes of comfort and happiness" had been located for these fortunate few, although published material sheds no real light on the nature of such adoptions.[92]

The experience of the Church of England Waifs and Strays Society is more revealing. The CEWSS owed its founding in 1881 to Edward de Montjoie Rudolf, a young civil servant. Like the charities of Barnardo and Stephenson, the "Waifs and Strays" (as it was popularly known) began work in London, sometimes "hunted" its outcast "quarry" at night inside dustbins and under tarpaulins, and later turned to emigration as one outlet for the children under its care.[93] But whereas the older charities tended to ignore sectarian distinctions, Rudolf from the first ran his agency for the benefit of Anglican young. Moreover, unlike the Barnardo group, which continued to be the fiefdom of its founder until his death in 1905, the CEWSS adhered closely to a constitution, thereby earning full support—financial as well as spiritual—from the Established Church.[94]

Boarding-out children in foster homes soon became a key feature of the Waifs and Strays' mission. By 1896 the Society had 2,300 boys and girls on its books, 700 of them in foster homes; and the proportion of CEWSS children boarded-out would remain in the range of 20 percent to 30 percent for several more years.[95] The large majority (69 percent) of children under CEWSS care received no financial support from their relatives. Contributions from Poor Law Unions, other charities, and individuals who sponsored particular boys and girls helped to offset the considerable cost of fostering. But such assistance never fully covered the boarding-out bill, with the result that CEWSS administrators were always eager to economize.[96] One way to cut costs was to engineer the adoption of the Society's children. This is not to imply that the Waifs and Strays pounced on every adoption offer it received. Where Nonconformists made the offer, Anglican administrators might return a child to its parent rather than place it with those outside the faith.[97] Nor would CEWSS officials automatically tear a child away from its foster parents, particularly if they made an attractive counteroffer:

Alice, a child of 3, was boarded out with Mrs. Worley, of Hillingdon [West London]. Her mother dead; father unknown. An offer is made by a lady to adopt her. The foster-parent is in great trouble on hearing this; and one morning presented herself at headquarters with the child, and with tears in her eyes, pleaded that she might keep her. She was quite willing to forego the payment made to her by the Society [five shillings per week] if she could only keep the little one as her own. The child had become most dear to her; she had twined herself around her foster-mother's heart. The request was granted; for who could have refused it?[98]

But if a child had been admitted to CEWSS care as a "free case," or if its source of outside support had dried up, the prospect of adoption must have been very attractive. Thus, because the mother of John S., an illegitimate child, had disappeared along with her weekly contribution of four shillings, the Society was delighted to adopt him off its account book. Despite having spent three years as a "happy well cared for and loved" foster child, John S. was taken from the only home he knew and given to prospective adopters "on approval."[99]

Quite apart from the baby farming trade there existed a market for adoption in late-Victorian England, and CEWSS officials were more than willing to supply it. Early in 1887 the Society learned that an orphanage in Leominster called the "Christian Million Mission" had long sought to match homeless children with childless couples.[100] Four years later an unidentified philanthropist announced that he or she had spent the past two decades arranging adoptions for orphan girls. *Our Waifs and Strays* piously reminded its readers that the CEWSS, too, had become "a middleman or distributor of a most happy and beneficial kind, . . . penetrated with the idea that, wherever there is an orphan or a waif wanting a parent, there is also somewhere a parental heart seeking a child, for the mutual advantage and blessing of both."[101] By the turn of the century England's largest merchandising newspaper, *The Bazaar, Exchange and Mart*, was regularly carrying adoption advertisements. The wording of these notices hinted at the broad range of motivations behind them, from the Staffordshire "lady of position" who wanted a "baby girl, 3 years, orphan, bright, good looking, healthy," to the Surrey woman who frankly sought "an orphan girl as one of the family, for general domestic work." Some advertisers were prepared to pay for the right sort of child, while others wished to be compensated for their kindness. Mrs. Merton from the Isle of Wight, for example, was forty, "without family," and lived in "a pretty seaside home." She wanted a young child of either sex but expected a "premium in accordance with refined upbringings."[102]

CEWSS officers did not need to scour *The Bazaar, Exchange and Mart*.[103] An analysis of nineteen cases involving children born between 1877 and 1909 shows that adoption most commonly took place when the Society's foster parents volunteered to give up their weekly boarding-out fees in return for the right to keep a child.[104] Often the Society's only detailed information about would-be adopters came from "ladies" and "gentlemen" who had agreed to sponsor individual children. The case of Edith B., an illegitimate girl born in the Marylebone Union workhouse, suggests how influential these sponsors could be. Since Edith's mother, a servant, had been "a respectable girl before & since her fall," Headquarters decided to accept her baby and thereby save the twenty-one-year-old mother from further exposure to the "demoralizing influence of a workhouse." The baby was boarded-out with Mrs. Smith of Pelham Street, Mile End, and a Mrs. Billing offered to underwrite this placement. The latter agreed not only to remain responsible for Edith's maintenance but also to collect one shilling per week from her mother. Mrs. Billing subsequently had to persuade a dubious E. de M. Rudolf that this unusual arrangement with an East End foster mother was worth continuing:

I placed [Edith] where she is when we were living very near at Spitalfields. She was a most delicate child & many nurses wd not have undertaken the care of her. Mrs. Smith was a kind & motherly lady on whom I could depend to be kind to the child. She has given her a Mother's love & care & the child is better & stronger now than I ever supposed she could be. I quite agree that Pelham Street is not an ideal boarding out spot—not what wd be called a desirable place—but I think this is more than compensated for by the real love the child has enjoyed & under which she has thrived. I feel I would not remove her merely for the sake of a better neighbourhood.

Thanks to Mrs. Billing's intervention Edith remained in her East End foster home. Six years later the nurturing Mrs. Smith chose to adopt her foster child.[105]

A child's sponsor might also spare CEWSS administrators some of the adoption-related headaches that so pained Dr. Barnardo. Soon after Alice N. was admitted to a receiving home near Brighton in 1902, a Mrs. Desborough agreed to shoulder the expense of maintaining this seven-year-old girl. By late 1906 the Society was poised to send Alice to Canada as she had shown herself to be intelligent and trustworthy. But because Mrs. Desborough had had the good sense to keep the girl's relatives apprised of her progress, this sponsor was able to warn Headquarters that an elder sister and an uncle objected to emigrating Alice. Soon thereafter Mrs. Desborough managed to convince the girl's relatives that adoption would now be the best course of action and later to warn the prospective adopter that she was taking a risk. "'[A]doption' has no legal sanction," Mrs. Desborough explained, "and it would not be possible to retain a child in opposition to the claim of a natural guardian, should one appear at any time in the future."[106]

Not every CEWSS child received such close attention from a sponsor, and in some cases no amount of supervision could have anticipated the perils that attended adoption in this era. Lilian W., an illegitimate girl of fourteen, appears to have had no sponsor. Thus, when a Mrs. Edwards of Glamorganshire wrote to the Society asking to adopt a female, there was no one who could vouch for the

Boarded-out children with their CEWSS foster mother, circa 1900. Foster parents sometimes "adopted" such children even though there was no legal mechanism for doing so. Courtesy: Children's Society Archives.

Welshwoman. Mrs. Edwards, it turned out, reneged on the adoption after two years because Lilian was once "a bit rude."[107]

The adoption of Hubert B., an eight-year-old orphan boy, failed despite careful precautions. Thanks to the interest that the Reverend Badcock of Leeds took in Hubert, the boy was "boarded out free" with Mr. and Mrs. Roberts, genteel friends of the clergyman. Seven months after this *de facto* adoption, all seemed well. As the Rev. Badcock reported to Headquarters:

The . . . boy was baptised by me on July 25 . . . last year [1886]. I have frequent opportunities of seeing the boy in his home & certainly I could desire no more happy position for any boy. Both his 'parents' are devoted to him, but at the same time they treat him very wisely & judiciously. [Hubert] is developing into a fine manly boy both physically and mentally.

That Mr. and Mrs. Roberts would soon move to New Jersey gave the Rev. Badcock no pause. Three years later, however, trouble arose in the person of Hubert's married sister, who now wanted custody of him. The Rev. Badcock was bewildered. Surely the Society had impressed the conditions of this adoption upon Hubert's relatives, and by accepting these conditions they had just as surely "yielded up all claims to the child"? Informed that Hubert's relatives could not legally be deprived of his custody, the Reverend urged CEWSS officials to appeal instead to the sister's "sense of gratitude":

Probably the sister does not realize that the boy is brought up as the only child of a gentleman & lady who are in a good position in America & who *are* giving him a future which is far more promising than any that his relatives can offer him. Then too, the sister cannot realize that after 4 years of love and affection from the adopted parents the boy wd. not at 13 years of age take kindly to a home or friends who had taken him from parents he had learned to love and respect.

But once young Hubert learned of his sister's bid for custody he could not "settle down at all," so obsessed did he become with seeing his siblings again. By mid-August 1890, Mr. and Mrs. Roberts had sadly accepted that they must give up their son.[108]

The Waifs and Strays worked hard to discourage relatives from disrupting an adoption. To protect adopting parents as well as its own financial interests the Society began in the late 1890's to use a typed and formidably legalistic "Adoption Agreement" in these cases. All known relatives were asked to sign the document, which enjoined kinfolk from interfering "in any way with any arrangement that may be made in regard to [an adopted child's] future." In the event that relatives later tried to remove a child from its adoptive home, they would be liable, under this Agreement, to reimburse the CEWSS for its "expenses"—at a rate of between £10 and £13 per year of care.[109]

How often such coercion served its intended purpose is impossi-

ble to know, since the CEWSS did not routinely continue to supervise an adoption, as modern social work "aftercare" is designed to
do. Clearly some of the middle-class men and women who ran the
Society's receiving centers believed that poor people could be intimidated. As one Lady Superintendent observed about the Adoption Agreement that she hoped Kathleen H.'s servant mother would
sign in 1915: "*I* know it is just paper, but she would not."[110] Still,
there was no real security for the kind of *ad hoc* adoption work carried on at the CEWSS and similar children's charities. The cata-
clysm of world war would soon transform such insecurity into a
demand for legal protection.

The Campaign for Legal Adoption

By the outbreak of war in 1914 both charitable institutions and
Poor Law authorities had been arranging adoptions of English children for a generation, despite the legally suspect nature of this work.
Adoptions of a less formal sort must have been even more common
during these years. Both in mid-Victorian Lancashire and in East
London at the turn of the century, 29 percent of all children could
expect to lose one parent, and 8 percent both, before they reached
the age of fifteen.[111] Desertion and judicial separation would have
created additional one-parent households. Under these demographic
conditions what seems remarkable is that *more* children did not end
up in public or private institutions. A large—but unknowable—
proportion of orphans and children from troubled homes must have
been taken in by other families. Unlike nineteenth-century France,
where the adoption of orphan young was often arranged through a
council of relatives,[112] kinfolk in English working-class districts
tended to open their doors spontaneously. Anecdotal evidence suggests that adoption was also undertaken as a neighborly act. A London police court magistrate was "greatly moved" to learn that during the hard winter of 1886–87 four Greenwich children with disabled parents had joined a poor family in the next street.[113] Another
patrician student of plebeian culture, Lady Bell, found adoption to
be the highest expression of "hospitality" among the ironworkers of

Edwardian Middlesborough.[114] Even in Campbell Road, notorious as North London's worst street between the wars, one mother's inability to cope with a sick baby led to its becoming permanently part of a neighbor's brood.[115]

These "articulated notions of community obligation" accounted for many, but not all, working-class adoptions. Some stemmed from the same sense of maternal deprivation that features so prominently in late twentieth-century discussions of the subject. Childlessness was a source of regret but not "passionate sorrow" for the Northern wives whom Elizabeth Roberts interviewed principally because they had played active and satisfying roles in the rearing of nieces and nephews. But what of poor women without surrogate young? Having suffered seven miscarriages in her thirteen years of marriage, the childless wife of one manual worker explained that she had "consoled myself by adopting an orphan boy, who is the sunshine of my life."[116] Thus we should treat with caution literary representations of adoption as an unnatural act. "To adopt a child, because children of your own had been denied you," reasoned Nancy in George Eliot's *Silas Marner* (1861), "was to try and choose your lot in spite of Providence." If fatalism remained a defining feature of working-class culture, it did not deter the poor from opening their homes to children who needed them.[117]

All the same, compared to other Anglophone nations England was very slow to grant *de facto* adoptions full legal security.[118] As early as 1852 one Englishwoman marveled "how easily and frankly children are adopted in the United States, how pleasantly the scheme goes on, and how little of the wormwood of domestic jealousies . . . seems to interfere with it." She concluded that three factors might account for this happy circumstance: America's comparative "abundance of food and . . . unoccupied room"; a high demand for labor; and the absence of primogeniture in U.S. legal codes.[119] It is true that within a decade of the American Revolution nearly all the States had abolished primogeniture. But the first genuinely "modern" adoption law did not appear until 1851, when a milestone Massachusetts statute overruled centuries of English precedent by legalizing the irrevocable transfer of parental power to third persons. The Massachusetts statute provided a legal mechanism for severing the ties created by birth and replacing them with binding artificial ties. Just as significantly, this law made plain that the core considerations in any adoption process should be the welfare of the child and the parental qualifications of the adopters.[120] Partly the product of growing concern with a child's "best interests" in custody disputes, the Massachusetts statute soon became a national model for most of the other States. By 1900, Michael Grossberg observes, judicial adoption was widely accepted in America and the formation of artificial families had become "routine."[121] Indeed, the routine was such that by 1915 the *New York Times Magazine* could complain that adoption had evolved into an "exact science," with U.S. children subjected to a battery of medical and mental tests, as well as vetted for "anatomical stigmata," before "any play of the affections" might be considered.[122] Adoption in Progressive era America was actually far less systematic than this lament implies. The General Secretary of the Boston Children's Friend Society warned in 1915, for example, that "numerous" babies offered through local newspapers had come from mothers with mental defects, venereal diseases, or non-white lovers.[123] Even so, American adoption was becoming an increasingly well-regulated practice.

In early twentieth-century England, by contrast, a child was judged suitable for adoption not on the basis of diagnostic tests but rather on the grounds that he or she had no known kin left alive. Middle-class people who hoped to cure their childlessness faced a frustrating dilemma. Because they lived in an age which had reached "the calmly deliberate conclusion that . . . children are its most important concern," the childless found themselves "very much out in the cold." But entering the "privileged area" of parenthood "by the side-door of adoption" was no easy matter. Since exceedingly few children of their own "caste" were available to adopt, these middle-class people perforce turned to workhouses and orphanages for promising candidates. Yet in taking a child from either source, the genteel adopter "lays himself open to blackmail once he has become attached to it," for a "deserting parent" or a "depraved" relative might well lurk in the child's background.[124] We cannot know how

often blackmail of the sort attempted in *Pygmalion* (1913)[125] actually
occurred, although, as we have seen, kinfolk could and sometimes
did demand an adopted child's return. That poor relatives might
have sought custody of an older child for reasons other than extor-
tion rarely occurred to midle-class critics. Since teenagers were expected in many poor communities to contribute either wages or
substantial daily labor to their households, retrieving an able-bodied
child from foster care may have been perfectly consistent with
working-class custom.[126]

The twin demographic catastrophes of war and pandemic disease
nevertheless magnified middle-class concerns on this point. Nearly
three-quarters of a million British soldiers died during the Great
War, and in England and Wales combat deaths accounted for just
under 7 percent of all males between the ages of fifteen and forty-
nine. An estimated 150,000 more citizens perished during the lethal
influenza outbreak of 1918–1919, many of them young adults.[127]
An alarming number of "war orphans" therefore lost at least one
parent during a brief, five-year period. Swelling these ranks were the
"war babies," the illegitimate issue of wartime liaisons whose numbers temporarily reversed a long-term decline in bastardy rates:
whereas in 1913, 4.29 percent of all live births had been illegitimate, by 1918 the figure stood at 6.26 percent. Not all contemporaries believed that "dead heroes" had fathered these babies, or that
the "girls" who conceived them should be praised. Yet never in living memory had there been so many children who needed new
homes, or so many grieving parents ready to provide them.[128]

As *The Times*'s "personal" columns began to suggest, especially after the start of the Somme offensive in July 1916, more well-off
adults were now prepared to overlook eugenic fears about the underclass and bring up the children of others as their own. Often,
however, these advertisements demanded "absolute surrender."[129] If
The Spectator was right that an "epidemic of adoption" had broken
out, it was spreading among those who "lived in constant dread"
that their new sons and daughters might be "snatched away."[130]
Catherine Hartley, the author of two well-received books on
woman's nature, typified the sort of middle-class parent for whom

adoption entailed terrifying uncertainty. Late in 1917 she implored the Home Secretary to provide legal relief:

I myself have an adopted son now at a public school, & dearer to me than anyone in the world. [H]e was deserted by his mother under peculiarly painful circumstances in early childhood, but for the last few years I have had terrible trouble, anxiety, & expense as the mother though she had signed a deed giving him up to me, said she wished to have him back. I need not trouble you with further details, which I mention only to show you how earnestly I care. I ask you, in the name of these little ones, to do something to help & protect them.[131]

The legal limbo in which parents like Mrs. Hartley lived drove another advocate of reform to declare, "The law has gone so far in the direction of restricting the exercise of parental rights that it might [as] well go a little further" and recognize the validity of these new family arrangements. For without law's blessing, well-to-do adopters would be forced to dodge a child's birth parents by ever more devious means.[132]

Such anxiety fueled the founding of at least two child placement services toward the end of the war. What distinguished these new bodies from hundreds of other child welfare groups then operating in England was their exclusive focus on adoption. The National Adoption Society, better known as the "Baker Street Society" due to the site of its headquarters in West London, grew out of prewar charity work in Cambridgeshire.[133] More immediately influential was the National Children Adoption Association (NCAA), likewise formed in 1917 and based in West London. Miss Clara Andrew, a philanthropic whirlwind from Exeter, made certain that both the Home Office and the Local Government Board knew of her group's mission. While tending to the needs of tubercular patients, Belgian war refugees, and munitions workers, Andrew had learned to value adoption as a way to stimulate a sense of moral purpose within receiving families. Early in 1918, therefore, she wrote to the Local Government Board seeking official status as an "adoption officer." "I believe," Andrew explained, "that it [her work] would be greatly expedited if would-be parents had some one person to whom they could apply when willing to care for a child with 'full surrender.'"[134] The NCAA could already count on socially prominent women to supervise its activities in several Southern towns, and soon it planned to open a hostel for children awaiting adoption. Andrew failed to add that her NCAA "Associates," most of them privileged, single women, were keen on shoring up social barriers that had begun to crumble during the war. As she assured a Plymouth newspaper, "We have homes suited for all classes, and always endeavour to . . . plac[e] the children in the class of homes from which they have come."[135]

Local Government Board officials remained aloof. Since adoption did not form part of their Maternity and Child Welfare scheme and, in any case, possessed no legal sanction, they refused to accommodate Andrew.[136] By 1920 English civil servants had grown wary of proposals to legalize adoption, not least because the advocates of reform held such varied and often conflicting agendas. Some demanded legalization on the grounds that baby farming still flourished "under the cloak" of adoption.[137] The Baker Street Society saw adoption as a patriotic act, the legalization of which would help comfort more "mourning mothers, wives and sisters . . . whose nearest and dearest have died gallantly."[138] Whereas Clara Andrew's NCAA claimed to be agitating on behalf of "thousands of unwanted babies crying in the wilderness for . . . motherly care," the National Council for the Unmarried Mother and Her Child (NCUMHC), organized in 1918, declared that legalizing adoption would do little good so long as England's harsh bastardy and affiliation codes remained in place.[139] Home Secretary Edward Shortt eventually decided that an official investigation must sort out this welter of rhetoric. Thus, under the chairmanship of Sir Alfred Hopkinson, a respected barrister and advocate of legalization,[140] a Home Office Departmental Committee began to gather evidence in late summer 1920.

Hopkinson's Committee cast a wider net and issued a more forceful report than expected. The Home Office had carefully removed from the Committee's purview questions dealing with reform of the bastardy laws, convinced that "well meaning people intent on . . . children's welfare cannot safely be trusted" with this matter. Yet in an "Interim Report," the Committee nevertheless urged Parliament to follow the lead of "almost all civilised countries" and recognize legitimation by subsequent marriage.[141] The rest of the Committee's recommendations, published in May 1921, reflected the influence of adoption laws in America, Western Australia, and New Zealand.[142] Hopkinson and his colleagues moreover accepted English philanthropists at their word that the "lack of security" plaguing *ad hoc* adoptions had deterred "many suitable people" from taking children into their homes. The need for legal machinery to regulate adoption was therefore "urgent." County courts, rather than police courts with their supposed criminal taint, should supervise the adoption process. Husbands and wives should be entitled to adopt a child jointly, if both spouses were over twenty-five years of age, whereas single persons of either sex should have the same privilege if over thirty. Finally, Hopkinson's Committee joined the NSPCC and other foes of baby farming in urging Parliament to amend the 1908 Children Act. Henceforth all private homes and institutions assuming "the entire custody and control" of any child under fourteen, whether for payment or not, should be open to inspection.[143]

Much to the annoyance of legal reformers, precedent-shy civil servants declined to accept all of these recommendations, and in fact refused (on the grounds of economy) to publish the Committee's evidence. Representatives from the Home Office, Board of Education, Ministry of Health, and Ministry of Pensions conceded that legislation to address the legitimation issue was overdue. But because Hopkinson and his colleagues had failed to produce statistics on the extent of long-term fostering, civil servants preferred to assume that "there is no real necessity for any measure legalising adoption."[144] This stance seemed all the more ostrich-like in view of the publicity then starting to dramatize tales of misguided placement. A *Daily Mail* piece on the "New Mayflower Pilgrimage" lamented that fifteen babies had recently been shipped to rich couples in New York City while good families were waiting in England. Indeed, a body known as the British-American Adoption Society now existed to help Miss Andrew's NCAA find "little orphan babies" elegant homes on the far side of the Atlantic.[145] One could also point to

troubling cases closer at hand. *The Spectator* described how a childless couple had lavished "all the luxuries that wealth can command"
on their adopted daughter, only to return her to the workhouse
many years later when they happened to conceive a boy of their
own.[146] England's "mania" for adoption had driven a well-educated
young woman from the Southwest to take possession of four poor
children, give them posh names, and, when she could no longer pay
her bills, abandon them in various seaside towns.[147]

With three private members' adoption bills brought before Parliament in 1923 alone, it was growing clear even to denizens of the
Home Office that legislative action could not be put off much
longer. Meanwhile, scandals continued to surface. The NSPCC had
prosecuted fourteen adoptive parents during recent months, including a diabolical couple from Wigan whose little girl, "outraged con-
tinuously from the age of four," had contracted acute gonorrhea.[148]
Private agencies also appeared less than reliable now. Clara Andrew's NCAA made much of its selectivity, pointing out that all its
boys and girls had been carefully screened for medical problems, and
that "the majority" of its adopting parents came from the professional middle class, had been married ten or more years, and were
childless. But as *John Bull* revealed in damning detail, NCAA verifi-
cation of an adopter's credentials sometimes involved no more than
a few words exchanged in a railway station waiting room when the
baby was handed over. Vetting procedures were equally lax at the
National Adoption (Baker Street) Society.[149] These two organizations saw themselves as philanthropic rivals and consequently refused to share information about prospective clients. Faced with an
increasingly chaotic situation, therefore, the Home Office agreed to
mount yet another investigation, this time under the chairmanship
of Justice Tomlin.[150]

The Tomlin Committee, like its predecessor, sifted through a
great deal of often conflicting testimony before deciding that there
was indeed a case for legalized adoption. Its three-part report all but
guaranteed that the government would soon support legislative action of some kind. This was true in large measure because Tomlin
and his colleagues took a more conservative line than had the Hop-

kinson committee three years before. The "demand" for legalized adoption remained uncertain. If anything, Tomlin and company observed, "the people wishing to get rid of children are far more numerous than those wishing to receive them, and partly on this account the activities in recent years of societies arranging systematically for the adoption of children would appear to have given to adoption a prominence which is somewhat artificial and may not be in all respects wholesome."[151] Even so, because the adoptive relationship deserved community acknowledgment, legalization made sense. This relationship should not, however, stay shrouded in secrecy. Both the NCAA and its rival, the Baker Street Society, numbered among those charities that sought "to fix a gulf between the child's past and future," partly to guard against meddlesome birth parents and partly also to hide from the child its illegitimate origins.[152] Adoption should become a judicial matter, the Tomlin Committee wrote, with all parties represented in proceedings at either the Chancery Division of the High Court or, for those of modest means, at magistrates' courts, whose juvenile tribunals could add adoption to their family preservation work. Lastly, in keeping with its cautionary approach to legal reform, the Committee argued that an adopted child should be allowed to inherit only from its birth parents. In this and other respects Tomlin's recommendations stopped well short of creating a new nuclear family.[153]

The measure that eventually became law in the summer of 1926 was a private member's bill. But unlike the other nine adoption bills introduced since 1922, James Galbraith's (Conservative, East Surrey) measure earned a warm welcome from civil servants, closely based as it was on the Tomlin Committee's recommendations. A year earlier the House of Commons had heard Sir Geoffrey Butler describe adoption as "a sacramental ministry of reconstruction," England's most poignant effort, as yet "unrecognised and unofficial," to heal the wounds of war.[154] Now, in early 1926, Galbraith's bill satisfied both hardheaded champions of child life and those who preferred to view adoption as a patriotic exercise. Parliamentary backers of the NCUMHC were pleased that the Bill enabled an unmarried mother to legitimate her own child by adopting it.[155] MPs representing working-class districts, such as Clement Attlee (Labour, Limehouse), demanded a scheme that would bring adoption "within the reach of people who are not only on the poverty line but under it." With the great majority of such cases destined to be heard *in camera* at police courts—the courts now designed "for helping people in their troubles"—Attlee could rest easy.[156] Some Members wanted more teeth in the bill. Miss Ellen Wilkinson (Labour, Middlesborough East) wondered what would deter an "empty-headed" single woman from adopting "some fluffy-haired, blue-eyed little thing," only to return it to a workhouse once the child had ceased to be "a pet to play with."[157] But such doubts were rare. Thus, amidst confident predictions that it would bring happiness into lives young and old, England's first adoption law reached the statute book.[158]

Regulating the Artificial Family

Despite the fanfare accompanying its passage, the 1926 Act marked a victory for conservative social policy. The Act erected no barrier to marriage between adoptive parent and adopted child, for example, suggesting that its architects were less eager to forge new family ties than to provide homeless children with a more satisfactory environment than they could likely find in an orphanage or workhouse.[159] One can of course view the legislation of 1926 as a service to childless couples as much as to homeless children. In nine years the NCAA and the Baker Street Society together had brokered over 3,500 *de facto* adoptions.[160] As we have seen, the adopting parents in these cases, many of them middle-class, often worried about the permanence of their new domestic arrangements. For such parents the Adoption Act offered a measure of security. But as William Clarke Hall observed, "comparatively few people have chosen to take upon themselves the responsibility of maintaining in their own homes orphan and destitute children." Encouraging more "kind-hearted people" to nurture disadvantaged boys and girls was therefore the Act's fundamental aim.[161]

One incentive to undertake legal adoption lay in the promise of confidentiality. Henceforth the Registrar-General was to keep a special record of all those adopted through court action. Only by means of the Adopted Children Register could an original birth certificate be traced, and only a court order—very rarely granted—could open this Register to inspection. Such safeguards would enable the adopted child to produce evidence of its date of birth "without disclosing any circumstances, such as illegitimacy, connected with it." The Register also served a broader purpose: to give adopted children a "fresh start" by removing any possible link between their privileged present and their dubious past. Adoptive parents, too, might gain from a "fresh start" by pretending that a child was biologically their own.[162]

Because the 1926 Act could not guarantee strict secrecy, however, England's large adoption agencies soon began agitating for its amendment. In doing so they clashed head-on with Home Office mandarins. According to the latter, "a novel principle of law ha[d] been brought into operation with ... marked success." During its first year the Act had generated 3,173 adoption orders, 88 percent of them issued at low cost in juvenile courts. About two-thirds of those adopted were illegitimate, whereas the overwhelming majority (85 percent) of new parents were married couples adopting jointly. Initially at least, the median age of children being adopted appears to have been around six years. The Act had specified that as soon as possible after receiving a written adoption application, courts must appoint a guardian *ad litem* who would become responsible for the conduct of all subsequent legal proceedings on the child's behalf. Civil servants were gratified to learn that responsible public authorities, most often school boards, had volunteered to work in this capacity along with probation officers, clergymen, and NSPCC leaders.[163]

But some adoption agencies saw matters differently. Clara Andrew's National Children's Adoption Association complained that "many hundreds" of potential parents had lost their enthusiasm for legal adoption, having been "humiliated" at juvenile courts. Andrew pointed out that although case particulars were aired *in camera*, "there is nothing private at all about the preliminaries." Too often the NCAA's prospective adopters were pillars of their communities, and so found themselves obliged to reveal "the secret" of a child's birth before a magistrate who happened also to be a social acquaintance. There was, moreover, a danger that court proceedings might disturb young minds. Hence a prominent Exeter tradesman and his wife had applied through their solicitor to legalize the adoption of their ten-year-old son. But when told that they must bring the boy to court, where his "whole history" would be reviewed, this couple decided to forgo the ordeal. Their son did not know that he was illegitimate, and his parents vowed that he would remain innocent of his origins until he left for preparatory school.[164]

The National Adoption (Baker Street) Society felt no less strongly about keeping family secrets. In common with Andrew's agency, the NAS's adopting parents were typically "gentlefolk," "of the educated class," or "in good position," whereas the children they aimed to raise as their own generally had more "humble" backgrounds. Interestingly, well-off adopters and their philanthropic allies imputed to poor birth mothers not only a penchant for blackmail but also a "natural" maternal power which, if brought to bear again on an adopted child, might unravel the affective bonds holding together an artificial family. The NAS added, rather as an afterthought, that greater secrecy in adoption cases was also necessary to protect the birth mother. Some of these women, still single, lived with unsuspecting parents; some had married men who knew nothing about their wives' former "disgrace"; and yet others had borne adulterous children during their husbands' absence. All would suffer should court action betray their deeds.[165]

Adoptions stemming from a wife's infidelity, although few in number, posed the greatest challenge to courts intent on honoring both the ideal of family unity and the new requirements of civil procedure. A case from Southend-on-Sea well illustrated the problem. In 1914, soon after a young couple married in this Essex town, the husband went abroad on military service for a year. During his absence the wife was unfaithful once, had a baby girl as a result of this lone indiscretion, and immediately gave it to her mother's sister-in-law, who generously raised the child as her own. Because the girl's biological father had been killed in France, no threat to her extended family's peace could come from that quarter. In fact, for many years the only cause for concern was the girl's appearance: she was such an "exact copy" of her biological mother that neither the latter's husband nor her three legitimate children had ever been allowed to see her. Then, as the girl neared her sixteenth birthday, a crisis arose. At this age registration under the National Health and Unemployment Insurance Acts became mandatory, but registration required one to produce a birth certificate. Since the girl's birth certificate listed her as a child of her biological mother's marriage, the impending registration process would expose a skeleton long buried. To prevent this from happening the girl's *de facto* mother applied for an adoption order. The biological mother gladly gave her written consent, surreptitiously. Since "the presumption of law" deemed the girl to be legitimate, however, the unsuspecting husband was required to give his consent as well. H. R. Fanner, Clerk to the County Court at Southend-on-Sea, agonized over a case that "bristle[d] with difficulties." Should the justices "screen from an innocent husband the guilt and deceit of a wife" in the interests of preserving domestic harmony? Alas, there is no accessible record of how the justices answered this question.[166]

Civil servants understood that the Act of 1926 was imperfect. It plainly *had* strained the resources of some juvenile courts, especially in London. William Clarke Hall, for one, found it impossible to deal with more than a quarter of the adoption applications he was receiving each week in 1927.[167] Doubts about legal principle also troubled the Home Office for several years after the Act's passage. Could a birth mother nullify an adoption on the grounds that her child was being raised in a faith different from her own?[168] What, precisely, were the rights and responsibilities of separated spouses with regard to adopted children?[169] But far more worrisome to the Home Office was the discovery that many adoption societies had decided to ignore the Act altogether. By 1936, private agencies of one sort or another were arranging about half the adoption cases brought before the High Court. In urban juvenile courts, which presided over most of the legal adoptions, private agencies introduced between 12 percent and 25 percent of such cases.[170] Yet a growing number of studies suggested that extra-legal adoptions—those consummated without court sanction—were at least as common, and often unwisely arranged.

The NSPCC and its allies diligently compiled these studies during the early thirties. Baby farming in the mid-Victorian sense of murder-by-neglect disguised as "adoption" was now thankfully rare; after the 1933 Children and Young Persons Act banned the use of anonymous advertisements it was difficult for shady operators to stay in business.[171] But as child-protection experts found, "entirely unsuitable" people still managed to adopt. Children had been entrusted to drunkards, to the mentally incompetent, and to those who wanted a "domestic drudge," their only qualification being a character reference from a local clergyman.[172] In March of 1933, a joint letter from William Elliott, Director of the NSPCC, J. C. Pringle, Secretary of the Charity Organisation Society, and Cecil Chapman, a veteran police court magistrate, urged the Home Office to conduct a full-scale investigation of adoption societies. Chapman was a devout member of the National Children Adoption Association, and the NCAA, as Home Office personnel knew full well, was "prepared to drive a coach and four through the [Adoption] Act" when it chose to do so—generally in pursuit of secrecy.[173] Then too, the NCAA enjoyed the backing of several distinguished patrons, most notably its President, Princess Alice, the Countess of Athlone. Prudence therefore dictated that civil servants treat the organization more gently than perhaps it deserved.

Philanthropic pressure nonetheless led to the appointment in January 1936 of the so-called Horsbrugh Committee. A careful study of adoption societies, its report went far toward regularizing the legal work begun in 1926. Although the Committee unearthed no nefarious "traffic" in adopted children, it learned that a disturbingly large number of babies travelled straight from their mother's arms in nursing homes to new parents. Sometimes well-meaning doctors and midwives arranged these adoptions free of charge as a favor to unwed mothers. But in other cases nursing home matrons or their intermediaries received from the mother up to £150 in brokerage fees.[174] Such sums were one reflection of a rising demand for

TABLE 2

Adoptions Registered in the Years 1927–1936

Year	Entries in the Adopted Children Register	Number of Adoption Orders Covered by Entries			
		Total	High Court	County Courts	Juvenile Courts
1927	2,967	2,943	133	184	2,626
1928	3,303	3,278	124	236	2,918
1929	3,307	3,294	72	224	2,998
1930	4,517	4,511	74	317	4,120
1931	4,127	4,119	68	274	3,777
1932	4,467	4,465	38	264	4,163
1933	4,528	4,524	61	262	4,201
1934	4,758	4,756	45	290	4,421
1935	4,852	4,844	64	342	4,438
1936	5,185	5,180	62	372	4,746

SOURCE: Home Office, Fifth Report on the Work of the Children's Branch (1938), pp. 112–13.

NOTE: The slight discrepancy between the number of entries in the Adopted Children Register and the number of adoption orders was due to the fact that a few orders in the High Court and the county courts applied to more than one child.

healthy children. Court-sanctioned adoption had grown more popular over the past decade, as Home Office statistics clearly showed (Table 2). How many extra-legal adoptions had been consummated during the same period could not be determined. Clearly, though, both individual brokers and most adoption societies were accustomed to placing children in new homes without judicial blessing.

None of England's adoption societies possessed a staff of trained social workers, few used case committees to screen applicants' homes, only some required a Wasserman test of birth mothers, and probationary periods for new placements ranged from three months to none at all.[175] Most agencies had regularly sent English children to adopters living abroad, particularly in the United States and Holland. These foreign cases involved unacceptable risk for the obvious reason that prior examination of an adopter's home was impossible. Although the Horsbrugh Committee carefully avoided criticizing foreign placements on nationalistic grounds, it took note of newspaper stories about the "astonishing" hemorrhage of "Anglo-Saxon" young. Revelations concerning "the world's wickedest trade" may have hastened the Committee's deliberations and certainly received center stage when its Report appeared.[176] But of greater consequence was the strong stand that Florence Horsbrugh (Conservative, Dundee) and her colleagues took against total secrecy in the adoption process. All birth mothers had to sign a consent form on which appeared the name(s) of the adopter(s). Yet in direct violation of the law, some societies made a "regular practice" of asking birth mothers to sign blank consent forms so as to preserve the anonymity of adopting parents. This tactic was intolerable. It suggested that the societies "regard themselves as owing no duty to the mother in the choice of adopters, but only to the child and those who wish to adopt it." Henceforth "constant vigilance" on the part of the courts must insure that biological parents fully understood the consequences of giving up a child.[177]

The Horsbrugh Committee's report, published in July of 1937, left important problems unresolved. Most evident was its failure to urge the banning of all private, "third-party" adoptions: its recommendations applied only to adoption societies.[178] But given the ideological climate within which the Committee worked, its Report was bold. For on the eve of the Second World War a number of influential English citizens still believed that whereas adoptions should be finalized in court, the preliminary steps in a process so closely associated with private "family feeling" ought to be left to voluntary effort.[179]

Florence Horsbrugh's Adoption of Children (Regulation) Bill became law in mid-1939, although its provisions did not take effect until June 1, 1943. By this time England's local authorities were of course already mired in emergency work. Churchill's War Cabinet nevertheless decided to add to these burdens by making the Act operational. The rising tide of illegitimacy suggested that adoptions were increasing in tandem, and government officials saw evidence of "growing public anxiety" over abuse of the adoption process.[180] A more general concern with the care of deprived children expressed itself in the appointment and recommendations of the famous Curtis Committee, whose 1946 Report characterized adoption as "the most completely satisfactory method of providing a substitute home." That same year saw over 21,000 adoption orders granted in

England and Wales. This was seven times the volume of orders approved back in 1927, when legal adoption first became possible, and would remain the peak year for this judicial category until 1966. Obviously, much had changed during the two decades since the Tomlin Committee insisted that the number of people wishing "to get rid of children by way of adoption" exceeded the number eager to adopt.[181]

In the immediate postwar period, adoption emerged as a "fashionable" way to fill "the child-hungry homes of people of high quality but low fertility."[182] Although most students of modern English social policy would resent the élitist tone of this formula, preferring instead to emphasize children's needs as the sanctifying force behind adoption,[183] the politics of the artificial family defy neat dichotomy. Since the Second World War courts have imposed substantial order on what was once, for parent and child alike, a notoriously chaotic process. But many of the emotional risks that accompany an adoption must remain beyond judicial control.

Conclusion

Family Values and Moral Panic

It is no mere accident that the best-loved English song is about home;
it is not by chance that the best-known English proverb concerns the
Englishman's home. That lovely little word evokes in all of us an
intensity of feeling that steals resolve, for in the love of home is found
one of the sources of England's strength.
—Advertisement issued by the Co-operative Wholesale Society, Apr. 1942[1]

NEITHER THE onset of World War Two nor the subsequent
building of a modern welfare state in Britain silenced debate
about how best to defend home and family. Indeed, the bombing of
British cities and the later provision of a "mixed economy of social
care"[2] intensified public scrutiny of the private sphere. An account
of family politics in the years after 1940 lies beyond the scope of
this book. It is nonetheless worth emphasizing that there are powerful continuities between recent themes in family policy and the pre-
occupations of prewar activists.

Most fundamental among these continuities may be the problem
of apportioning responsibility for family assistance. By no means
everyone will accept that the state is "too blunt and impersonal an
instrument to provide security for the British family without rein-
forcements from volunteers."[3] Yet several of the nation's current
family-centered disputes are framed in exactly these terms. Today,
for example, the main obstacle to adoption is a dearth of British babies. Partly because single mothers are now more apt to keep their
infants than in decades past, and partly also because childless couples
are increasingly keen on adopting newborns, demand far exceeds
supply. Given such circumstances the conduct of local authorities'
child welfare officers has come under fire. Their rigid protocols, it is

alleged, keep the childless in agonizing suspense, especially where trans-racial or foreign adoptions are involved.[4] Just as private adoption agencies did during the interwar years, many critics today hold that the transfer of parental responsibility is too delicate an operation for bureaucratized servants of the state.

Disenchantment with state action likewise suffuses debate over juvenile delinquency. Behind the game of law-and-order one-upmanship that has characterized recent Tory and Labour pronouncements on child crime, one finds a common concern with "character." Sometimes expressed as a need to stimulate "emotional intelligence,"[5] this critique harkens back to the moral physiology of Charlotte Mason. No less reminiscent of prewar thinking is the current enthusiasm for "saving saveable marriages." As his contribution to National Marriage Week in February of 1997, the Tory Lord Chancellor, Lord Mackey of Clashfern, explained that although the state cannot hope to legislate harmony between husbands and wives, it can—and must—enlist the aid of voluntary organizations to "support" marriage.[6] Claud Mullins would approve.

What Mullins would not admire is the alarmist tone of today's talk about the private sphere. The nuclear family now is falling apart, or so we hear at every turn. Historians should be in a position to dampen, if not defuse, this moral panic over the alleged erosion of "traditional family values" because the history of private life during the past two centuries makes it clear that "family" has *never* been able to meet the expectations placed upon it. But in many rich nations, and certainly in Britain and America, evidence from the long term has been buried beneath short-term fears that a "permissive society" is fostering self-indulgence at the expense of self-discipline. In our rush to catalog the symptoms of moral decay we accentuate the negative. For when we talk about the family in terms of tradition we necessarily conjure up a static image. And if family life in the past is conceived as a frozen social form, then almost any change in that form is apt to be seen as "decline," "loss," or "corruption."[7]

There are, of course, sane reasons to worry about the future of the family. Even a capsule account of certain demographic trends is sobering. For the first sixty years of this century, except during and immediately after the two world wars, illegitimate births accounted for roughly 5 percent of all live births in Britain. Between 1960 and 1980, this figure rose to more than 12 percent. By 1992, illegitimate births—now officially redesignated "births outside marriage"—had climbed to nearly one in three. Among those who wed, many apparently do not view marriage as a commitment for life: whereas in 1961, 25,000 divorces were granted in England and Wales, by 1981 this number had leapt to 146,000, and by 1990 higher still to 153,000. The multiplication of single-parent families has been one much-lamented result of these soaring divorce and illegitimacy figures. Between 1971 and 1991, single-parent families with dependent children as a proportion of all families with dependent young more than doubled, a trend that rapidly accelerated during the late 1980's and early 1990's as "lone mothers" came to head just over 17 percent of such households.[8] Although family desertion and fatherlessness in Britain have not approached the spectacular levels of black American households, more than 60 percent of which had a single mother at their head in 1994, Charles Murray's warning seems increasingly germane on both sides of the Atlantic. Murray, among America's most influential critics of social welfare administration, contends that the breakdown of the traditional, two-parent nuclear family must lead to poverty, crime, and a hopeless, isolated underclass. "Sometimes," as Murray puts it, "the sky really is falling."[9]

Yet before accepting his fix for the family, which is the abolition of all welfare benefits, the other side of the ledger must be examined. Despite its flaws, the married couple household remains the norm. The great majority of children—about 70 percent in America and 80 percent in Britain—still live in families with two parents. According to the 1996-97 *British Social Attitudes* survey, parent-child relations seem to be in better shape than the doomsayers would have us believe. In an age of unprecedented mobility, two British adults in three still live within an hour's journey of their mothers. Half of the adults questioned apparently see their mothers at least once per week; just 19 percent of parents report seeing their adult children less than once per month. Only 9 percent of the British population with a living father "never" visit him. A mere 3 percent with a living mother "never" visit her. A third of the respondents provided their parents with regular care or help because of illness, disability, or some other problem during the past five years. Almost three-quarters disagree with the proposition that children should no longer expect help from their parents once they leave home. "For the bulk of people," concludes this survey, "their family continues to be a central and enduring part of their lives—as secure as can reasonably be expected against the supposed threats from social, cultural and even occupational pressures."[10]

The key qualifier here is *reasonably*. Unfortunately, politicians, journalists, and think-tank pundits have done much to whip sensible public concern about the family into a froth of free-floating anxiety. The private predicaments of the famous tend to be viewed as proof of a more general pathology at work. Madonna, arguably the most successful exhibitionist alive, has been depicted as a victim of prying eyes: "[W]hen I'm in the confines of my own home, my sanctuary, I can't help but feel violated by the invasion of my privacy."[11] It appears that even the Material Girl has a castle to defend. And in Britain today a real castle such as Balmoral cannot fully shield the private life of royalty from photographers' lenses. Walter Bagehot, who in 1867 cautioned that, "We must not let in daylight upon magic," would be shocked to find how overexposed the queen's family has become.[12] In the wake of Princess Diana's traumatic death, it remains uncertain whether the press will allow her young sons time and space to grieve.

Precisely because the ideal of domestic privacy remains sacred in Anglo-American culture, the language of family disintegration commands special notice. Our thinking about the family, as Stephanie Coontz has shown, is caught in a "nostalgia trap"; we persist in eulogizing the way we never were.[13] There are no doubt several reasons why the myth of a golden age of family autonomy should appeal to late-twentieth-century imaginations, but one bulks large. Above all, it is *easy* to pine for a lost world of domestic bliss. It is far more taxing to confront the possibility that our present family "cri-

sis" is not so much about the need for thicker doors and higher walls
as about constructing a different sort of community—one in which
the private and public spheres are treated as symbiotic rather than
antagonistic. We need not accept the thesis that the nuclear family is
"anti-social"[14] in order to recognize that such plagues as drug addic-
tion, teen pregnancy, and gang violence cannot be cured through
the isolated exertions of individual homes, however re-moralized.

Although it is convenient to locate social salvation in a bygone
era of inviolate family values, this era defies discovery. *Friends of the
Family* has insisted that at no time between the Victorian high noon
and the outbreak of World War Two was the English home seen as
sufficient unto itself. Any suggestion that the English family's
apotheosis has been more recent falls just as flat. For example, the
Second World War may have brought out the best in Britain's civilian population; the fierce self-possession of ordinary people was no
figment of state propaganda. Yet home life on the home front constituted a source of grave concern throughout the war. Richard
Titmuss believed that among the most compelling reasons for resistance to urban evacuation plans during the dangerous months of
1940 and 1941 was "the solidarity of family life among the mass of
the people." The precautionary exodus staged during the late summer of 1939, according to Titmuss, had given some families a taste
of what it meant to be divided and to live in "unfamiliar and often
unsympathetic surroundings."[15] This first experience with separation
had apparently soured citizens on the idea of evacuation. But the
evacuations of 1939 had also cast a "merciless searchlight" on "family life as actually lived by a section of Britain's people in the denser
portions of industrial cities."[16] The resulting illumination of the
"problem" family intensified demands for greater state and voluntary aid to households variously labeled as "unsatisfactory," "in
trouble," or "derelict." In view of such evidence, Mass Observation's
wartime finding that English housewives were militant about family
privacy must have offered cold comfort.[17]

If the war years fail to qualify as a family Eden, the succeeding era
looks no more promising. Neither the austere late 1940's, with
their prolonged rationing and peaking rate of divorce, nor the more

affluent 1950's, when new welfare services were rendering less vital
the help traditionally derived from extended kin networks,[18] can
pass as a golden age. In Britain, as in America, the advent of a high-
spending consumer society brought unprecedented material prosperity to certain sectors of the population but something less than tranquillity where family was concerned. Over the course of the fifties,
expenditure on household appliances rose dramatically. The number
of families owning a vacuum cleaner doubled, ownership of refrig-
erators tripled, while homes with a washing machine increased ten-
fold. Perhaps these conveniences, along with more furniture, car-
pets, and water heaters, *did*, for the first time, make the working-
class home a place that was truly "warm, comfortable, and able to
provide its own fireside entertainment."[19] But balanced against these
consumer gains was the belief, common among social critics of the
time, that an era of economic hardship had given way to an age of
self-absorption. Whereas by the mid-1950's divorce rates had declined markedly from 1947, the leveling off of the birth rate suggested that deliberate family-limitation practices were being adopted
among nearly all classes. The specter of widespread resort to birth
control outside marriage sent moralists into an apocalyptic tailspin.
As one historian of religion prophesied, "when the 'unfettered de-
lights' of free love have become exhausted, only the ruins of broken
homes and spoilt lives [will] remain on a scene of utter desolation."[20]
Nor did the future of Britain's youth seem assured. Those young
folk devils of the 1960's, the Mods and Rockers, had a "deviant"
forebear in the Teddy Boy.[21] New youth cultures were already playing havoc with the ideal of home as the forge of character.

Thus, at the center of our fantasies about a family golden age lies
an explanatory black hole.[22] That no real enlightenment can escape
from it hardly matters to most politicians, however, since discussion
about "restoring" family values connotes bold action without the
encumbrance of policy particulars. Useful because it is so vague, the
rhetoric of family values transcends party affiliation.

In Britain, the so-called "New Right," which usually refers to
Margaret Thatcher's brand of free market conservatism, is often
seen as synonymous with the "pro-family" lobby. This is in fact a

conflation of sometimes compatible yet distinct political forces. Well before Mrs. Thatcher came to power in May of 1979, there existed in Britain several pressure groups concerned with sexual politics in general, and with what they regarded as specific forms of moral backsliding, spawn of permissiveness, in particular. Although it did not wield the born-again clout of Jerry Falwell's "Moral Majority" in the U.S., Mary Whitehouse's campaign against sexually explicit television in Britain, launched in 1964, sank deep organizational roots during the 1970's. Responsible Society (later renamed Family and Youth Concern) set about scrutinizing British sex education as early as 1971. The Society for the Protection of Unborn Children, founded in 1967, and LIFE, established three years later, cast their anti-abortion case in "pro-life" terms, but neither body cared much about the "enterprise culture" so dear to Thatcherite hearts.[23]

Still, a professed admiration for family values—often "Victorian"—superficially linked these pressure groups to Tory government during the 1980's. Mrs. Thatcher's political agenda hinged on the revival of "standards." If privatizing industry, curbing trade union power, and restoring British prestige on the world stage were to succeed, then the importance of discipline, best learned in a good home, had to be grasped. As the Prime Minister exhorted a woman's journal in 1981: "The people who give everything to their children because they don't like to exercise family discipline don't get it right. And it's the same in politics. You've got to do the things you believe to be right and explain them. Some of them will hurt. But you just can't retreat."[24] In Thatcherite terms, a prosperous Britain demands that families function as the incubators of responsibility, since only a responsible citizenry will be able to carry on the work of reviving entrepreneurial capitalism. The New Right is adamant on this point: to continue treating families as clients of a welfare bureaucracy is to produce more "scroungers." Indeed, it was by riding a wave of panic over welfare fraud that Mrs. Thatcher's party sought to gain the moral high ground during the general election of 1979.[25]

Contrary to at least one prediction,[26] Margaret Thatcher's resignation in late 1990 has not yet led to an eclipse of "family values" rhetoric. If anything, that incantatory phrase grew more familiar once the Labour party under Tony Blair decided to enter the civic morality sweepstakes. Blair's timing was impeccable. For in the autumn of 1993, the Tory government of John Major had proclaimed a "back to basics" plan to energize Britain. Its legislative core was a crackdown on crime, including the abridgment of a suspect's right to remain silent under police questioning, along with fervent calls for a renewed commitment to the two-parent family. Where U.S. Republicans had failed to translate their family values theme into reelection for George Bush in 1992, British Conservatives would wage a similar but more appealing campaign. After all, as the *Sunday Times* had proclaimed earlier that year, "the family" was "back in fashion."[27] But scandal in the private life of a Tory cabinet member soon scuttled these plans. As it became known in the waning days of 1993 that Tim Yeo, Mr. Major's Environment Minister and a married man, had fathered a child out of wedlock, the din of criticism grew deafening.[28] When Blair became Labour's leader six months later, therefore, he was quick to capitalize on what seemed to be Tory hypocrisy. Praising the family as Britain's "essential, stable social unit," Mr. Blair has subsequently tried to trump the Tories on such emotive issues as trimming welfare benefits for single mothers. "Suddenly," in the words of one editorialist, "we've got values coming out of our ears."[29]

Back in the early eighties, two American sociologists counseled retreat to a "middle ground" in formulating family policy. The delicate balancing of children's and parents' rights, they observed, could not occur in a political climate of mutual recrimination.[30] A half-generation later, in both Britain and America, grave disagreements persist about how much and in what form the state should help families at risk. Indeed, the very meaning of "risk" is contested. But more disheartening yet is the way that a *fin-de-siècle* hysteria over private life and public virtue has poisoned debate. Those weary of the politics of panic may find some solace in recalling that social disintegration, like beauty, remains very much in the eye of the beholder.

Reference Matter

Notes

Complete authors' names, dates, and publication data are given in the Bibliography, pages 389-442. The following abbreviations are used in the Notes:

B.M.J.	*British Medical Journal*
HO	Home Office Papers
MEPO	Metropolitan Police Papers
MH	Ministry of Health Papers
P.P.	Parliamentary Papers
P.R.O.	Public Record Office
R.C.	Royal Commission
S.C.	Select Committee
SWS	*Southwestern Star*

Introduction

1. B. Anderson, pp. 5-7.

2. Ariès, "Introduction," p. 5. Ariès bases his assertion on the fact that private diaries were widely kept in England earlier than anywhere else.

3. Beales, pp. 344-45.

4. Douglas, pp. 289-90.

5. Rybczynski, pp. 20-22.

6. *Oxford English Dictionary*, 2nd ed., s.v. "comfortable" and "homely."

7. Duby, pp. vii-viii. Another Frenchman, the Saint-Simonian theorist Émile Barrault, once praised the Ottoman harem as a "domestic temple" where Islamic men "shook off at the door the dust of the world." Barrault, pp. 342-43. For a more gender-conscious discussion of public and private spheres in "traditional" Mediterranean society, see Pitkin.

8. Moore, pp. 59-62. Among some small and very isolated groups, such as the Baktaman of the New Guinea highlands and the Mehinaku of central Brazil, it is arguable that privacy as understood in the industrial West did not exist when anthropologists began studying them. On the former, see Barth; on the latter, Gregor. And more broadly, see Krygier.

9. Emerson, pp. 104–8, 149, 159. Emerson's direct exposure to English culture consisted of five weeks in 1833, on his return to America from a tour of Italy, and seven months in 1847–48, when he lectured throughout Lancashire and Yorkshire. See Von Frank, pp. 84–85, 219–37.

10. Census of Great Britain, 1851. Report of the Registrar-General, P.P., 1852–53, LXXXV: xxxvi. In support of his contention that domestic possessiveness was "stronger in England than . . . on the Continent," the Registrar-General quoted at length from *The King of Saxony's Journey Through England and Scotland in the Year 1844*. Dr. C. G. Carus, a naturalist, had written this book for a German audience in 1845. Translated into English the following year, its "Continental" view of English character chimed with the cultural self-perception of many mid-Victorian gentlemen. Carus took special note of middle-class English homes, "which stand in close connection with that long-cherished principle of separation and retirement, lying at the very foundation of national character."

11. F. M. L. Thompson, *Rise*, pp. 168–71.

12. See Grumbler; and *The Times*, Oct. 24, 1857.

13. *The Times*, Jan. 4, 1873; ibid., Jan. 27, 1875.

14. Dickens, *Dombey*, chap. 9.

15. 2 Samuel 4:5.

16. Coke, *Third Part of the Institutes*, chap. 73, p. 162; "Semayne's Case," in idem, *Reports*, part 5, p. 339.

17. Lambard, book 2, chap. 7, p. 257: ". . . and our law calleth a mans house, his castle, meaning that he may defend himselfe therein"; Stanford, p. 14b: "*ma measo e a moy: coe mo castel, hors de quel, le ley ne moy arta a fuer.*" Translated from its law French, this phrase reads, "My house is to me as my castle, from which the law does not compel me to flee."

18. Mulcaster, chap. 40, p. 225.

19. William Harrison, p. 222.

20. Orlin, pp. 1–3.

21. On the rise and tenacity of that specialized branch of mortgage law known as the "equity of redemption," see Sugarman and Warrington.

22. Kelley, pp. 170–71.

23. Macfarlane, *Origins*, pp. 80, 163, and passim. Macfarlane credits F. W. Maitland, the great constitutional historian, with anticipating part of this revisionist argument.

24. The least defensible aspect of Macfarlane's model may be his assumption that English family structure changed very little between the thirteenth and the eighteenth centuries. For a critique of this assumption, see Razi.

25. Punctuation varies considerably among modern accounts of Pitt's speech. In some versions a concluding phrase appears: "—all his [the King of England's] force dare not cross the threshold of the ruined tenement!" For accounts that append this last phrase, see B. Stevenson, p. 936; and J. Bartlett, p. 426.

26. Brougham, 1: 18–19, 41–42.

27. *Anecdotes*, 1: 250–51.

28. Brewer, *Sinews*, pp. 67–68; Thane, "Government and Society," pp. 4–5.

29. Brewer, *Sinews*, p. 68.

30. Gerald Newman, pp. 169–71; [Nash] *Essay*, pp. iv–v.

31. Colley, "Britishness," pp. 321–22; and idem, *Britons*, pp. 322, 364–71.

32. Cannon, p. 30.

33. E. P. Thompson, p. 79. Thompson's depiction of this moral consensus is a bit slippery, shifting as it does between a "constitutionalism" that emphasized the right to be left alone, and a rather different demand for political "fair play." See ibid., pp. 81, 689–90.

34. Baugh, p. 386.

35. Rogers, pp. 107–8.

36. [Butler] *Essay*, pp. 50–55, 61; *Discourse*, pp. 45–46, 59–60; *Rights*, pp. 19–21.

37. Dugan, pp. 58–59.

38. Hunt, "Unstable," pp. 13–14. Hunt argues elsewhere that the Revolution constructed new narratives of family relations to replace those associated with the old patriarchal-absolutist model. See idem, *Family Romance*.

39. Wollstonecraft, p. 457. Five years before Wollstonecraft offered this account, an ardent admirer of the French queen, Edmund Burke, had used very similar language to describe the October outrage: "A band of cruel ruffians and assassins, reeking with ... blood, rushed into the chamber of the queen, and pierced with an hundred strokes of bayonets and poniards the bed, from whence this persecuted woman had but just time to fly almost naked. ..." Indeed, Burke summed up the threat of revolution in terms of defilement: "All the decent drapery of life is to be rudely torn off." Burke, *Reflections*, pp. 164, 171.

40. Lefebvre, pp. 113–16; Scott and Rothaus, 1: 68–71; Schama, *Citizens*, pp. 389–93, 399–415.

41. During the post-revolutionary generation in England, a hybridized metaphor blending "castle" with "cottage" occasionally appears. This amalgam of images would have reasserted the old claim of household sovereignty while promoting the ruling-class ideal of a deferential and apolitical proletariat. See, for example, *My Cottage*, pp. 3, 6–7. On the linkage of rural and domestic "idylls," see Davidoff, L'Esperance, and Newby.

42. M. Turner, pp. 143–44.

43. *The Times*, Dec. 11, 1871; Gammond, p. 273; Sadie, 2: 741–43; Brown and Stratton, pp. 48–49; Gillett, pp. 5–7. For an extended discussion of the place of "Home, Sweet Home" in late-Victorian culture, see Paula Gillett's forthcoming book on women musicians in England, 1870-1920.

44. G. Harrison, pp. 106–7; Overmyer, pp. 209–10.

45. *Home, Sweet Home* (Dublin [1823?]), p. 4; *Home! Sweet Home!* (Glasgow [1823?]), n.p.; "*Home, Sweet Home*" (London, 1874), pp. 7, 9; Ensor, *England*, p. 169; R. Roberts, p. 53; Bunner, pp. 210–16.

46. Undocumented attribution to Payne, in M. Turner, p. 144.

47. Paulding, pp. 29–30.

48. "Home's Home," n.p. Letters from the *Gentleman's Magazine* of this period discuss "an old *breaking up* song" that public schoolboys sang at the approach of their summer holiday. Its chorus would have been uncomfortably familiar to John Howard Payne: "Home, the seat of joy and pleasure, / Home, sweet home, inspires our lay! / Welcome, freedom! Welcome, leisure! / Every care be far away." See *Gentleman's Magazine*, 66, pt. 1 (Mar. 1796): 208–9; and ibid. (Apr. 1796): 287.

49. S. Johnson, *The Rambler*, 2, no. 68 (London, 1763): 73–74.

50. Cotton, 18: 19.

51. Erasmus's project had begun as a commentary on 818 Greek and Latin proverbs published in 1500 under the title *Collectanea Adagiorum Veterum*. The enlarged and renamed version of 1508, *Adagiorum Veterum*, contained 3,260 entries. On the history of the *Adagia*, see M. Phillips. For a thumbnail biography of Richard Taverner, see Taverner, pp. v–xv. I thank Prof. Mary O'Neil for pointing me to Erasmus.

52. "*Patriae fumus* . . . ," in Erasmus, 31: 161. Lucian's essay, as rendered by an early eighteenth-century translator, concludes with this rhetorical flourish: "And even the Islander himself will make haste into his own Country, and tho' he might live happily abroad, wou'd refuse offer'd Immortality else-where for a Grave in his paternal Soil: He will even prefer the Smoke of his own Country to the Fires of another." See *Works of Lucian*, 2: 67.

53. Taverner, p. 7.

54. John Clarke, *Paroemiologia*, p. 101.

55. Seed, passim. On French possession ceremonies, see Wintroub. For the cartographic strategies of the Dutch, see Schmidt.

56. Beaumont, pp. 60–61.

57. Shaw, *Getting Married*, p. 132.

58. Temple, p. 156.

59. Schama, *Embarrassment*, pp. 380–83.

60. Mook, pp. 32, 43; Praz, pp. 50, 53, 58–60; Rybczynski, pp. 106–8.

61. MacDonald, pp. 75–81. Among the general studies that have reinforced MacDonald's case, see especially Wrightson, pp. 112–13; and Houlbrooke, pp. 136–37. The orthodoxy thus overturned rested on the work of Ariès, *Centuries*, pp. 38–40; Shorter, pp. 170, 172; and L. Stone, *Family*, pp. 64–73, 161–78, 470–80, 679. For an incisive discussion of this "sentiments" school, see M. Anderson, *Approaches*, chap. 3.

62. On patriarchalism and the Reformation, cf. Roper with Ozment. On patriarchalism in political theory, cf. Schochet with Elshtain, chap. 3.

63. Habermas holds that eighteenth-century European society witnessed the emergence of a "political sphere," distinct from the state, in such settings as the salon and the theater. The "private sphere," by contrast, included not only family life (the *Intimsphäre*) but also the realm of commodity exchange. See Habermas, pp. 14–31. For the classic account of the "cult of true womanhood," see Welter.

64. Clark, "Contested," pp. 269–70. Paula Backscheider makes a similar point about "sphere"-induced myopia. Backscheider, pp. 2–11.

65. Welter, pp. 151–52.

66. See, for example, Cott, chap. 2; Epstein, p. 81; Smith-Rosenberg, pp. 85–86; and, most recently, Skocpol, p. 322. Among American feminist historians at work during the 1970's and 80's, Mary Ryan offered the most balanced analysis of the "doctrine of the spheres." Ryan, chap. 5.

67. Davidoff and Hall, p. 33.

68. C. Hall, pp. 23–24, 29–30; Davidoff and Hall, pp. 90–91, 359–61; Davidoff, "Family," pp. 75–76.

69. Vickery; Wahrman.

70. Thane, "Late Victorian Women"; Colley, *Britons*, pp. 249–50, 262–63, 273–74.

71. Although the literature on these diverse subjects is large, several works merit mention. For a brief but suggestive discussion of "psychological interiority," see Maus. On confession, see Bossy. Lying in the face of religious and political intolerance is treated by Zagorin. On the changing nature of hospitality, see Heal. The architectural implications of a growing demand for privacy among the landed élite receive attention in Girouard.

72. See the pioneering essay on pre-industrial domesticity by Shammas. The rigors of housework are examined in Davidson; and B. Hill. For a searching account of domesticity within the context of working-class radicalism, see Clark, *Struggle*.

73. Mayhew, "Home," pp. 258–64; idem, *London Labour*, 3: 214–19; Himmelfarb, *Idea*, pp. 332–34.

74. Walton and Wilcox, p. 116. On incest, see Wohl, "Sex ."

75. For more on child prostitution, see Gorham, "'Maiden Tribute'"; and Walkowitz, *City*, pp. 81–83, 94–120.

76. Disraeli, 2: 494. The idea that the British monarchy was a royal *family* originated not during Victoria's reign but during that of George III. See Marilyn Morris.

77. The queen to her eldest daughter, June 15, 1859, in Fulford, p. 115; ibid., May 4, 1859, p. 191; ibid., Nov. 17, 1858, p. 143; ibid., July 11, 1860, p. 265. See also J. H. Miller.

78. [Linton] "Domestic Life," pp. 405–6, 415; "Home Life," p. 180; "Home Happiness," p. 115.

79. On a kindred issue, the relationship between humanitarianism and capitalism, note the debate among Thomas Haskell, David Brion Davis, and John Ashworth in the pages of the *American Historical Review*. See especially, 90 (Apr. 1985): 339–61; 90 (June 1985): 547–66; and 92 (Oct. 1987): 797–812, 813–28.

80. Prochaska, "Philanthropy," p. 358; Conybeare, p. 6; José Harris, "Society," p. 68.

81. Arblaster, pp. 43–45, 70–71. See also Benn and Gaus.

82. Burke, *Thoughts*, 5: 166–67.

83. Auden, "Dedication," ["To Stephen Spender"] in *The Orators*, n.p.; W. Taylor, p. 574.

84. B. Mitchell, pp. 9, 25; M. Anderson, "Social Implications," pp. 1, 5, 24, 57–58.

85. Perkin, p. 123; Boyer, p. 46.

86. F. M. L. Thompson, *Rise*, pp. 118–19.

87. M. Anderson, *Family Structure*, passim. Less convincing is Anderson's rational choice model of kinship assistance, a model that views such help as the calculated product of individual self-interest. For a critique of Anderson's instrumentalism, see Dupree, pp. 20–28.

88. M. Anderson, "Social Implications," p. 65; Davidoff, "Separation." Anna Davin provides useful particulars on fluctuating household compositions. See her *Growing Up Poor*, pp. 42–43, and passim.

89. Census of 1871, as quoted in José Harris, *Private Lives*, p. 63.

90. Crowther, pp. 132–33.

91. See, among other proponents of this view, Mintz.

92. Lasch, passim.

93. Donzelot, pp. 89, xxv, 6. Donzelot's study was originally published in 1977 as *La Police des Familles*.

94. Mount, pp. 1, 150, 161–63, 175; Ranelagh, pp. 243–44.

95. Himmelfarb, *De-Moralization*, pp. 78, 165, 250, 256–57; idem, "The Victorians Get a Bad Rap," *New York Times*, Jan. 9, 1995.

96. Speaker of the U.S. House of Representatives Newt Gingrich anchors his argument that "the time [has] come to reestablish shame as a means of enforcing proper behavior" in Himmelfarb's account of the Victorian eagerness to "stigmatize and censure" antisocial acts. Gingrich, p. 77; Himmelfarb, *De-Moralization*, p. 142.

97. Gillis, *World*, p. xv.

Chapter 1

1. Ruskin, p. 85; Patmore, *Angel*. The sanctification of English domestic life reached its literary climax in the late-Victorian era. Among many other tributes to the home, see J. B. Brown; Greenhough; J. R. Miller; and W. Mitchell.

2. Bentham, 1: 350.

3. S.C. on the Health of Towns, P.P., 1840, XI, QQ. 732–34; Report of the Commissioners for Inquiry into the State of Large Towns and Populous Districts, P.P., 1844, XVII, QQ. 951–53.

4. Symons, pp. 8–9.

5. Saville, pp. 9–10.

6. Summers, "Home," p. 33.

7. J. Simon, pp. 131–32; Prochaska, *Women*, pp. 98–100; Summers, "Home," p. 36.

8. Prochaska, *Women*, pp. 103–4; D. Lewis, pp. 40–41. The GSPDV collapsed in the late 1830's and was reorganized as the Metropolitan Visiting and Relief Association in 1843.

9. Rack, pp. 367–68; A. Kidd, pp. 47–48; Heeney, p. 27.

10. *The Devotional Remains of Mrs. Cryer* (1854), as quoted in Prochaska, *Voluntary Impulse*, pp. 46–47. Cf. the visiting commitment of Adelaide Newton, in Claudia, pp. 272–73.

11. Dickens, *Bleak House*, chap. 8.

12. Lascelles, 2: 337; Hilton, pp. 66–67.

13. R. Morris, pp. 106–7.

14. Clough, as quoted in Simey, p. 65.

15. Walkowitz, *City*, pp. 16–17, 46–48, 52–54; Wechsler, pp. 175–76; Posnock, pp. 100, 141. The systematic nature of much district visiting further distinguished it from the capriciousness of the *flâneur*. As Jeanne Peterson aptly remarks, district visitors became England's first "social surveyors." Peterson, *Family*, p. 134. But for a credible "challenge to the utter impossibility of female spectatorship," see Deborah Nord's *Walking the Victorian Streets*.

16. Jalland, p. 257; Walvin, *Victorian Values*, p. 96.

17. Davidoff and Hall, p. 436; Koven, "Borderlands," pp. 94–95.

18. [Rathbone] *Social Duties*, p. 14.

19. Chalmers, 2: 36–37. For more on Chalmers's philanthropic activity, see Stewart Brown, especially chap. 3.

20. The "charm" that Chalmers's deacons supposedly carried into working-class homes depended upon a temporary inversion of social roles: "The readiest way of finding access to a man's heart, is to go into his house, and there to perform the deed of kindness. . . . By putting ourselves under the roof of a poor neighbour, we in a manner put ourselves under his protection—we render him for the time our superior—we throw our reception on his generosity, and we may be assured that it is a confidence which will almost never fail us." Chalmers, 1: 29–30.

21. *District Visitors' Record*, 1 (Jan. 1836): 1–2.

22. Poovey, *Making*, p. 35; Shuttleworth, pp. 66–67. On the dubious application of "social control" theory to history, see especially Gareth Stedman Jones, "Class Expression"; and F. M. L. Thompson, "Social Control." A social control interpretation of district visiting is most plausibly applied to rural culture. See, for example, Gerard.

23. *District Visitors' Record*, 2 (Jan. 1837): 16–17; *Friendly Visitor*, Nov. 1856, pp. 207–9.

24. *Home Visitor*, n.s., 4 (1877): 281; Weylland, *Man*, pp. 102–6.

25. *District Visitor's Manual*, pp. 248–56; *District Visitors' Record*, 2 (Oct. 1837): 107–8. On popular prejudice against English Gypsies, see Behlmer, "Gypsy Problem."

26. *Cottager's Monthly Visitor*, June 1856, pp. 207–9; ibid., Nov. 1856, pp. 383–88; *London City Mission Magazine*, 4 (July 1839): 124. For a thoughtful discussion of the evangelical war on brutal amusements, see B. Harrison, "Religion."

27. *Hints*, p. 6; *District Visitors' Record*, 3 (Jan. 1838): 22.

28. *District Visitor's Manual*, pp. 267–68; Kemble, pp. 10–11.

29. *London City Mission Magazine*, 34 (Apr. 1, 1869): 61–62; *Advance! The*

Monthly Magazine of the West London Mission, Aug. 1894, pp. 118-19; ibid., Jan. 1897, pp. 2-3; ibid., June 1897, p. 81.

30. J. L. Davies, p. 123; *District Visitors' Record*, 1 (Apr. 1836): 47-48.

31. *District Visitor's Manual*, pp. 23-24, 28; Weylland, *Man*, p. 8.

32. E. H. Mitchell, pp. 6-17; *Hints*, pp. 3-5; Surridge, pp. 7-9; J. L. Davies, p. 123; Clergyman's Daughter, p. 194.

33. See, for example, *London City Mission Magazine*, 2 (Mar. 1837): 56-57.

34. *District Visitor's Manual*, p. 31; Lees, pp. 68-69; Goffman, *Presentation*, Chapter 6.

35. E. Chase, pp. 9-10; E. Ross, *Love*, pp. 18-19.

36. Shairp, p. 19; *District Visitors, Deaconnesses*, p. 7.

37. Blunt, pp. 325-26.

38. *Mother's Companion*, 4 (1890): 183; ibid., 5 (1891): 11-12; *Friendly Visitor*, Mar. 1856, p. 43; *Woman's Secret*, pp. 1-2.

39. For an extended discussion of wife-beating and the judicial responses to it, see Chapter 4.

40. *Home Visitor*, 1 (July 1864): 192; *Friendly Visitor*, June 1862, pp. 107-8; Bell, pp. 78-79.

41. *Home Visitor*, 1 (Aug. 1864): 222-24; *Cottager's Monthly Visitor*, July 1852, p. 233; ibid., May 1850, p. 172-73.

42. *Friendly Visitor*, Mar. 1856, p. 44; *District Visitors' Record*, 1 (Apr. 1836): 36-37.

43. *Mother's Companion*, 2 (1888): 103. On the "medicalization" of motherhood in England, see J. Lewis, *Politics*; Dwork; and E. Ross, *Love*, chap. 7.

44. Bradford District Archives: Bradford Town Mission, *First Annual Report* (1851), pp. 7-8; *Twenty-Third Annual Report* (1873). p. 7. On the paternalism that gave rise to such industrial monuments as Saltaire, see Joyce, chap. 4; and D. Roberts, chap. 7.

45. Bradford Town Mission, Managing Comm. Mins. for 1850-59: May 1, 1850.

46. Bradford Town Mission, *First Annual Report*, pp. 10, 12; Best, pp. 196-201.

47. Bradford Town Mission, *First Annual Report*, p. 11. According to the Bye Laws of 1850, full-fledged missionaries were to earn at least £52 annually. One, Mr. Ilingworth, received £60, a wage equivalent to that paid by the London City Mission. A General Agent, paid £100 per year, supervised the missionaries. See Bradford Town Mission, Managing Comm. Mins. for 1850-59: Feb. 12, 1850.

48. Bradford Town Mission, *Second Annual Report* (1852), pp. 9-10.

49. Bradford Town Mission, *Twenty-Third Annual Report*, p. 9; *Seventy-Second Annual Report* (1922), pp. 5-6; Managing Comm. Mins. for 1865-72: May 18, 1870. The Mission remains active today, although its doors shut between 1977 and 1990.

50. Bradford Town Mission, *First Annual Report*, p. 24; *Sixtieth Annual Report* (1910), p. 14; *Thirty-Second Annual Report* (1882), pp. 3-4; *Thirty-Ninth Annual Report* (1889), p. 9; Lady, pp. 27-29.

51. Bradford Town Mission, *Sixth Annual Report* (1856), p. 6.

52. Bradford Town Mission, *Forty-Sixth Annual Report* (1896), pp. 6–7; *Bradford Weekly Telegraph*, Mar. 19, 1904.

53. Garland, *Punishment*, pp. 50–51.

54. *District Visitors, Deaconesses*, pp. 2–3; Sewell, pp. 3–4. "Socialistic" visitors really *did* come to the door of Grace Foakes's tenement flat in Edwardian East London. One Saturday evening when their parents were out, Grace and her four siblings found a "smart lady and gentleman" on the landing. Announcing that they had come to take one child for a holiday, these strangers settled for the bold Grace. The ten-year-old girl soon arrived at a large house in the Northwest suburbs, where she took her first real bath and slept beneath an eiderdown duvet. "I thought I was in heaven," Grace later recalled. But heaven was not what the posh strangers had in mind. For only when she was shushed after singing "Gentle Jesus meek and mild" in a nearby hall next morning, did Grace learn that she had been transported to a Communist youth club rather than a Sunday school. Foakes, p. 81.

55. Barnett, as quoted in Meacham, *Toynbee Hall*, p. 38. For more on Henrietta Barnett's philanthropic service, see Koven, "Henrietta."

56. H. Barnett, *Making*, pp. 108–9; *Mother's Companion*, 1 (1887): 134.

57. Reynolds, *Poor Man's*, pp. 280–81; Orwell, pp. 16–17.

58. Prochaska, "Body," p. 337. My discussion of the Ranyard nurses owes much to Dr. Prochaska's essay.

59. Engels, pp. 33–34. Although parts of St. Giles were razed to make way for New Oxford Street, this demolition, Parliament learned in 1851, had exacerbated overcrowding along some hellish lanes. See Wohl, *Eternal Slum*, p. 34.

60. R[anyard], *Missing Link*, pp. 7, 274, 14–22.

61. *Missing Link Magazine*, 1 (Jan. 2, 1865): 2; E. Platt, pp. 47–48; R[anyard], *Missing Link*, pp. 247, 274–75; Abel-Smith, pp. 4–5, 19–20. Cf. Anne Summers's assessment of nursing sisterhoods. See Summers, "Costs." Mary Poovey has argued that the "feminized epistemology of sympathy" so prominent in Mrs. Ranyard's work challenged the growing authority of abstraction in Victorian society. Poovey, *Making*, pp. 43–54. Then again, the same claim could be made for most female-dominated visiting schemes.

62. D. Lewis, p. 221; R[anyard], *Missing Link*, p. 271; Mort, pp. 58–59. Mrs. Ranyard's use of working-class women "to enter with keen sympathy into the details of [degraded persons'] daily troubles" soon spawned imitation. See Hamilton, pp. 984–85.

63. *The Times*, Aug. 28, 1862; letter from Hill to Baumgartner, Dec. 5, 1859, in Maurice, p. 171.

64. *Missing Link Magazine*, 3 (May 1, 1867): 137–40; R[anyard], *True Institution*, pp. 4–5; *The Book and Its Missions, Past and Present*, 7 (Sept. 1, 1862): 231–32; Ducrocq, n. 10, p. 269; Mrs. Ranyard, as quoted in Pope, p. 141.

65. Anne Summers has argued persuasively that the quality of medical care provided by pre-professional home nurses was often no worse—and sometimes better—than the nursing offered in early-Victorian hospitals. See Summers, "Mysterious."

66. Most urban district nurses lived together in residential institutions often far removed from their assigned neighborhoods. Mrs. Ranyard and her successors, however, believed that "institution life does not tend to develop individuality," a characteristic prized in Bible-nurses. Moreover, "To live amongst [the poor], constantly coming into personal contact with their lives, gives the nurse a great hold over her patients, and her influence in matters of simple cleanliness and hygiene has a far more lasting effect than the fleeting visits of a stranger from strange parts can possibly have." *Nursing Times*, 2 (June 9, 1906): 469.

67. R[anyard], *Nurses*, p. 48; J. Woodward, p. 69.

68. E. Ross, *Love*, p. 173.

69. Cf. the hostile assessment of Dr. Lewis Hawkes, a general practitioner in Edwardian Finsbury. Report of the Inter-Departmental Committee on Physical Deterioration, P.P., 1904, XXXII, QQ. 12,944–45, 12,986, 13,213.

70. Baines, p. 676; Rathbone, "Social Disintegration," pp. 28–31, 35; idem, *Sketch*, pp. 15–22.

71. Stocks, *Hundred Years*, pp. 28, 30; Baly, pp. 6–8; Dingwall et al., pp. 176–80.

72. *Report of the Sub-Committee of Reference and Enquiry*, pp. 13–14.

73. Holcombe, *Victorian Ladies*, pp. 89–90; Stocks, *Hundred Years*, pp. 41–42.

74. Lees, as quoted in Stocks, *Hundred Years*, p. 50.

75. *Public Health*, 5 (Aug. 11, 1876): 121.

76. *Lancet*, Dec. 20, 1879, p. 919; *Medical Officer*, May 15, 1909, p. 913.

77. Nightingale, pp. 199–200; *Hospital*, Dec. 29, 1888, p. 201; facsimile of a letter from Nightingale to the Duke of Westminster, Dec. 16, 1896, Durham County R.O., D/Lo/F 1124: Queen's Jubilee Institute for Nurses, misc. papers; Greta Allen, pp. 78–79. The QVJI preferred gentlewomen as nurse trainees. In the Institute's early years, an applicant had to specify the occupation of her father and, if married, of her husband as well. See *Regulations*.

78. E. Ross, *Love*, p. 173. On the much-discussed uniforms for Queen's Nurses, see Baly, pp. 35–36.

79. *Banner of Faith*, 5 (1886): 115; *Nursing Times*, 2 (Aug. 25, 1906): 720.

80. *Hospital*, Nov. 16, 1889, p. 101. Ranyard nurses in London averaged twenty-one visits per patient during 1894, down from a startling average of fifty visits per patient in 1868. See Prochaska, "Body," p. 343.

81. *Hospital* ("Nursing Supplement"), Sept. 16, 1893, p. ccxlvi; ibid., May 6, 1893, p. lv.

82. Ibid., Aug. 5, 1893, p. clxxxiv; *Nursing Times*, 1 (Oct. 14, 1905): 467; "Poor at Home," pp. 622–23. On the function of "gossip" in English working-class neighborhoods, see Tebbutt.

83. McKibbin, *Ideologies*, pp. 170, 181, 195–96; Loane, *Common Growth*, p. 53. Loane did not see the very poorest folk since, as she explained, a district nurse could only function "where there is *some* kind of a home." Idem, *Queen's Poor*, pp. 27–28.

84. *Queen's Nurses Magazine*, 1 (Dec. 1904): 77–79; *Nursing Times*, 2 (Mar. 10, 1906): 198–99.

85. Loane, *Outlines*, pp. 141–42.

86. *Queen's Nurses Magazine*, 7 (Oct. 1910): 127; Loane, *From Their Point*, p. 140.

87. Idem, *Englishman's Castle*, p. 1.

88. Idem, *Next Street*, pp. 19–20, 144–45.

89. Idem, "Husband," p. 223; idem, *From Their Point*, pp. 62–64.

90. Idem, *Neighbours*, p. 152.

91. Idem, *Common Growth*, p. 198.

92. Idem, *Next Street*, pp. 154–55.

93. Tebbutt, pp. 34–35.

94. *Queen's Nurses Magazine*, 7 (Apr. 1910): 9–10; *Hospital* ("Nursing Supplement"), Aug. 5, 1893, p. clxxxiv; Cambridgeshire County R.O., R70 / 18 (pt): "A Morning with a Queen's Nurse" (London [1924?]), pp. 1–2.

95. *Kelly's Directory*, pp. 159, 221; Cambridgeshire County R.O.: Trumpington and Grantchester District Nursing Association, Executive Comm. Mins.: Dec. 14, 1905; July 9, 1906; July 20, 1908; May 4, 1911.

96. *Kelly's Directory*, pp. 207–9; Cambridgeshire County R.O.: Soham Nursing Association, Mins., Oct. 2, 1911, and Feb. 26, 1912. The Queen's Institute was never comfortable assigning midwifery work to its nurses on account of the lower status associated with childbirth duties. See E. Fox, pp. 239–46.

97. *National Health*, 3 (May 1912): 265–66.

98. *Medical Officer*, Nov. 2, 1912, pp. 206–7; ibid., July 26, 1913, pp. 37–38; ibid., Dec. 6, 1913, pp. 282.

99. C. Booth, *Life and Labour*. Final Volume: *Notes on Social Influences*, p. 157; Macadam, *New Philanthropy*, p. 120; *Survey of the Social Services*, pp. 204, 219–20; Blythe, p. 197. When the National Health Service Act took effect in mid-1948, a district nursing service was within the reach of 98 percent of the English population. Merry and Irven, p. 10.

100. *English Woman's Journal*, 3 (June 1, 1859): 217–18. As Celia Davies has argued, the LSA in some areas "deliberately blurred" the dichotomy between public and private spheres by creating a semi-professional space for its members. See C. Davies, p. 44.

101. *English Woman's Journal*, 3 (Aug. 1, 1859): 387; *B.M.J.*, Oct. 23, 1858, p. 892; Davin, "Imperialism," pp. 9–10; *Lancet*, Apr. 19, 1862, p. 415.

102. Shonfield, pp. 19–20; *Truth*, June 27, 1878, pp. 806–7.

103. *English Woman's Journal*, 6 (Dec. 1, 1860): 237.

104. Dowling, pp. i–ii, 139, 148–49; McCleary, *Early History*, pp. 84–85.

105. *Thirty-Eighth Report of the Manchester Board of Health*, as quoted in Dowling, p. 49.

106. F. B. Smith, p. 114.

107. *How to Manage*, pp. 5, 13.

108. *Wasps*, p. 11.

109. *Whose Fault*, pp. 3–4. The governing classes of mid-Victorian England were obsessed with fresh air in large part because they associated stale atmosphere with disease-bearing "miasma." One speaker at the Social Science Association in 1862 went so far as to assert that, "Inadequate dwelling-house ventilation was . . . the monster of civilization." Mr. Prideaux, as quoted in Wohl, *Endangered Lives*, pp. 285–86.

110. *Inspector*, pp. 31–32.

111. Begg, pp. 10–11; *Sanitary Duties*, pp. 7–8.

112. *Twenty-Fourth Annual Report of the L.S.A.* (1882), pp. 5–6, 17–18; *Remarks*, pp. 17–18. A few of the LSA's tracts were in fact directed at middle-class homes. See, for example, *Why Do Not Women Swim?* [1865?]; and *The Evils of Perambulators* [1863?].

113. *Twenty-Third Annual Report of the L.S.A.* (1881), p. 21; *Twenty-Fourth Annual Report of the L.S.A.*, p. 16; *Hospital*, Sept. 22, 1888, p. 404; *Public Health*, 1 (Oct. 1888): 170; *Sanitary Record*, Mar. 19, 1897, p. 236. Carbolic (phenylic) acid was widely available in the form of soap, powder, and a 1:20 lotion.

114. Scannell, pp. 8, 13, 45, 47–49.

115. *Public Health*, 4 (May 26, 1876): 402; *Sanitary Record*, Nov. 19, 1897, p. 566; ibid., Oct. 15, 1880, pp. 144–45.

116. Buckinghamshire County R.O., AR 48/86: Reprint of a letter from Nightingale to Frederick William Verney, Oct. 17, 1891, in "Village Lecturing and Visiting."

117. S. and B. Webb, *State and the Doctor*, pp. 177–79; Dwork, pp. 126, 156–61; Wohl, *Endangered Lives*, p. 38. The Relieving Officer was the "portal" through which all applications for Poor Law relief had to pass. There were, the Webbs estimated, between 1,700 and 1,800 of these officials in England and Wales as of 1909. See their edited volume, *Break-Up of the Poor Law*, pp. 50–51, 56; and Riverside Visitor, pp. 345–52.

118. G. Newman, pp. 263–64; Kanthack, p. 3.

119. E. Ross, *Love*, p. 209.

120. R. Roberts, p. 78.

121. Darlington Branch Library, Local Studies Department, Da/PH/4/3: *Report of the Medical Officer of Health on Health Visitors*, County Borough of Darlington (June 12, 1915), pp. 3–4.

122. *Sanitary Record*, Jan. 16, 1902, pp. 59–60; Keeling, pp. 70–71.

123. *National Health*, 3 (Aug. 1911): 120. Section 11 of the 1855 Nuisances' Removal Act gave local authorities or "any of their officers" the power of entry into private homes between 9 A.M. and 6 P.M., provided they had reasonable grounds for believing that a "nuisance" existed on the premises. See E. Smith, p. 149.

124. One could argue that avoidance of the health visitor constituted passive resistance. As a former Chief Woman Inspector of the Leeds Public Health Department observed in 1915, "No sooner does an inspector turn into certain streets than she will see children fly off to their homes, and when she arrives at the doors in due course they will be found locked and no response will be

made to her knocking." But this sanitarian added, significantly, that explanations of a health visitor's intent "given through the keyhole" often opened the door. Maynard, p. 54.

125. *Medical Officer*, Apr. 3, 1909, p. 792; ibid., Jan. 20, 1912, p. 31; ibid., Oct. 25, 1913, p. 207. For more on Bostock Hill's place in the health visiting campaign, see C. Davies, pp. 45–46.

126. *Medical Officer*, June 17, 1911, p. 314; Eve, pp. 4–5. The champions of health visiting complained that nursing journals were partly to blame for whipping up public concern over "interference with the sacredness of family life." See *Medical Officer*, July 1, 1916, p. 250.

127. G. Allen, pp. 9–10; Hubert Smith, p. 9.

128. Mount, p. 174.

129. Prochaska, "Mother's Country," p. 379.

130. E. Twining, pp. iii–iv; Bayly, *Ragged Homes*, p. 110.

131. Weylland, *These Fifty Years*, pp. 137–38. For a discussion of the symbolic significance of needlework, see Rozsika Parker.

132. Bayly, *Ragged Homes*, p. 116. Mrs. Bayly provided clothing patterns at no cost. Other mothers' meeting organizers cut out patterns for mothers who wished such help. See *Missing Link Magazine*, 18 (Dec. 1, 1882): 353–54. One working-class woman summed up the issue of cloth quality: "We never find no rubbish on the mothers' meeting table." See Mother, *Bright Glimpses*, p. 13.

133. Bayly, *Ragged Homes*, pp. 118–19, 197–98.

134. *Missing Link Magazine*, 1 (Mar. 1, 1865): 75–76.

135. Bradford Town Mission, *Nineteenth Annual Report* (1869), p. 8.

136. Lloyd, p. 230.

137. Meacham, *Life Apart*, p. 91; *Advance!*, Aug. 1890, p. 169. See also *Advance!*, Aug. 1894, pp. 115–16.

138. Flora Thompson, p. 246.

139. Dowling, pp. 189–90.

140. *English Woman's Journal*, 3 (June 1, 1859): 226; Report of the Inter-Departmental Committee on Physical Deterioration, P.P., 1904, XXXII, QQ. 7,221, 7,223, 7,225, 7,320–25.

141. H. Barnett, *Canon Barnett*, 1: 100–101; National Health Society, *Eighth Annual Report* (1881), pp. 8–9; Louisa Twining, *Recollections of Life*, p. 208; E. Ross, *Love*, pp. 36–37; Stackpoole, p. 1; Homersham, p. 30.

142. Mother, *Bright Glimpses*, pp. 2–3; [Stanley] *Work*, p. 9.

143. *London City Mission Magazine*, 33 (Aug. 1, 1868): 161; Mother, *Bright Glimpses*, p. 3; J. E. Hopkins, *Home Thoughts*, pp. 1–5.

144. *Advance!*, Apr. 1899, p. 55; H. Bosanquet, p. 37.

145. Parson, *My District Visitors*, p. 58; M. L. Davies, p. 40.

146. S. and B. Webb, *Consumers' Co-operative Movement*, p. 168. See also C. Webb, pp. 26, 52.

147. V. Crawford, pp. 62–63.

148. Bedwell, p. 181; *Ranyard Magazine*, Jan. 1929, pp. 3–4. On the absorption of twentieth-century mothers' meetings into more modern forms of voluntary effort, see Prochaska, "Mother's Country," pp. 394–99.

149. M. M. Gordon, pp. 4, 8, 47–50; Yonge.

150. J. Cox, pp. 71–72; *Happy Mothers' Meeting*, p. 7.

151. C. Booth, *Life and Labour*, 3rd series, vii: 18–19, 277. Lord Shaftesbury, the embodiment of evangelical philanthropy, offered a more glowing assessment. The mothers' meeting, Shaftesbury held, was "one of the most remarkable inventions of modern times." Weylland, *Fifty Years*, pp. 137–38.

152. *Fathers' Meeting*, pp. 3–6, 15–17, 30–31; Bradford Town Mission, *Twentieth Annual Report* (1870), p. 8; J. E. Hopkins, *English Woman's Work*, p. 27.

153. Hubbard, pp. 278–79; O. Parker, p. 7; *Mothers in Council*, 3 (1893): 129–30.

154. Coombs, p. 82; *Church Times*, June 6, 1913; Peterson, *Family*, pp. 149–50. It was in the summer of 1876, while living at the Rectory in the Hampshire village of Old Alresford, that Mrs. Sumner first distributed advice cards to local mothers. This event is generally regarded as marking the inception of the Mothers' Union. Not until the autumn of 1885 at the Portsmouth Church Congress, however, did her society become established on a national footing. See H. Porter, pp. 21–24.

155. O. Parker, pp. 1–2; *Mothers in Council*, 2 (1892): 60; Coombs, p. 188.

156. *Mothers' Union Journal*, Apr. 1888, p. 14; Mothers' Union, Oxford Diocese, *First Report* (1891), p. 8; *Mothers in Council*, 6 (1896): 250.

157. *Mothers in Council*, 8 (1898): 31–32. "Associates" of the Mothers' Union were expected to recruit working-class "Members," conduct mothers' meetings, and occasionally visit poor women at home. Ladies who wished to support such work without getting personally involved in it had the option of becoming "Subscribing Members" for an annual contribution of one shilling. See *Mothers' Union Journal*, Jan. 1888, p. 2. Whereas "Associates" in England had to be Anglicans, this requirement did not apply to Associates in Scotland or the colonies. See *Mothers in Council*, 7 (1897): 196.

158. Couchman, p. 16.

159. *Mothers' Union Annual Conference* (1893), p. 6.

160. For the child-rescue work of the CEWSS, see Chapter 6. On the GFS as a bastion of conservative social thought, see B. Harrison, "For Church."

161. Shrewsbury, pp. 957–58; Tuckwell, *State*, pp. 70–71; B. Harrison, "For Church," pp. 123–24, 127–28.

162. *Mothers' Union Journal*, Jan. 1903, p. 15; *Mothers in Council*, 10 (1900): 35; Bailward, pp. 2, 5–8, 21–22.

163. Phillip, pp. 5–6.

164. Sumner, *To Mothers*, pp. 11, 14–15; *Mothers in Council*, 12 (1902): 28; Sumner, *Mothers' Union*, pp. 5–6.

165. Dauncey, pp. 604–5.

166. Sumner, *Nursery Training*, pp. 14–15; *Mothers in Council*, 1 (1891): 57; ibid., 5 (1895): 17.

167. Dyhouse, *Girls*, p. 12.

168. *Mothers in Council*, 5 (1895): 84–86; *The Queen: The Lady's Newspaper*

and Court Chronicle, Oct. 27, 1894; Crackanthorpe, pp. 23, 25–26; Sumner, *Home Life*, pp. 13–14; Bailward, p. 17. On mother-daughter conflict in the prosperous families of this era, see Susan Pedersen, "Ambition"; and Oppenheim, "Mother's Role."

169. *Mothers in Council*, 12 (1902): 227–33.

170. Sumner, *Home Life*, p. 26.

171. *Mothers' Union Journal*, July 1894, pp. 38–39; ibid., July 1898, p. 58; ibid., July 1896, p. 59.

172. *Mothers in Council*, 16 (1906): 51.

173. *Mothers' Union Journal*, Oct. 1908, p. 94; ibid., July 1912, p. 71.

174. *Church Times*, June 3, 1938; *Mothers' Union, Chester Diocese*, pp. 7–8; Jo Harris, *Mother, Child*, pp. 5–6, 9–10. The marshaling of Mothers' Union resources against divorce law reform is an important—and neglected—research subject.

175. Macadam, *New Philanthropy*, pp. 145–46. The Mothers' Union was far larger than its socialist counterpart, the Women's Co-operative Guild. See, for example, Tibbits, p. 147.

176. B. Harrison, "For Church," p. 133; Heeney, pp. 16–17.

177. José Harris, *Private Lives*, pp. 17–23.

178. Donzelot, p. 36.

179. Mill, *Subjection*, p. 36.

Chapter 2

1. The phrase belongs to W. L. Burn, but reflects a standard periodization in which the mid-Victorian "consensus" is seen as dissolving into a period of heightened uncertainty, at least for England's middle and upper classes. Among many other examples of this scholarly convention, see G. M. Young, pp. 114–17; Ensor, *England*, pp. xix–xxiii; and R. K. Webb, pp. 285–415.

2. Collini, "Idea," pp. 30–31, 48. In a preliminary discussion of this subject, Collini referred to the idea of character as the "Trojan horse" of Victorian political theory, suggesting that it unintentionally prepared the way for certain collectivist proposals. See idem, *Liberalism*, pp. 28–29.

3. Smiles, pp. 42–43.

4. Masterman, pp. 49–50.

5. C. Pearson, p. 270.

6. Ibid.

7. The evolution of social casework in Britain has been the subject of several studies, most notably C. Morris; Young and Ashton; and Woodroofe. All three studies emphasize the operational differences between "modern" social casework methods and older, less self-consciously "scientific" forms of charity, a distinction that tends to trivialize the latter and eulogize the former. More reliable, but also narrower in focus, is Jane Lewis's *The Voluntary Sector*.

8. Hardy, "Public Health," p. 131; Brand, pp. 109–10. Medical officers attached to Poor Law institutions constituted a separate health corps. See Hodgkinson. The most famous—and controversial—champion of public health

as an arena to be policed was Bentham's bulldog, Edwin Chadwick. On his administrative style, see Brundage.

9. Rumsey, pp. 48–49, 280–81; Bynum, pp. 56–57. Unlike medical officers of health, nineteenth-century inspectors of nuisances were not obliged to show proof of professional competence. Toward century's end, however, increasing numbers of them voluntarily earned certification from the Sanitary Institute. For more on the partnership between these two groups, see Wohl, "Unfit."

10. *How to Make Home*, pp. 2–3, 6, 30–38; Stewart and Jenkins, p. 91; *Public Health*, 6 (June 8, 1877): 425–26; *Sanitary Record*, Nov. 9, 1877, pp. 296–301.

11. "Dwellings," p. 153; Sykes, pp. 27–28; *Medical Officer*, July 19, 1913, pp. 31–32.

12. See, for example, *Sanitary Record*, June 14, 1878, p. 380; ibid., June 16, 1884, p. 578; ibid., June 4, 1897, p. 545; *Public Health*, 3 (Nov. 1890): 209.

13. *Lancet*, Dec. 16, 1876, p. 867; *Public Health*, 5 (Dec. 22, 1876): 472. Medical officers of health fanned the flames of professional rivalry by alleging that private practitioners were slow to report outbreaks of infectious disease for fear of embarrassing their patients. See *Public Health*, 4 (Apr. 28, 1876): 300–301, 314.

14. Dudfield, *Metropolitan*, p. 31.

15. Hardy, *Epidemic Streets*, pp. 112–13. Smallpox, according to one calculation, was directly responsible for between 8 and 20 percent of all deaths in parts of eighteenth-century Europe. See Mercer, p. 307.

16. F. B. Smith, pp. 156–57. The World Health Organization has recommended that the last two remaining stocks of smallpox virus, located in Russia and the U.S., be destroyed by June 30, 1999.

17. Frazer, pp. 6–7, 88; Gay, 2: 22–23.

18. R. Lambert, *Sir John Simon*, pp. 249–50.

19. *Public Health*, 3 (July 8, 1875): 409–10; Beck, pp. 316–17; A. Chase, pp. 66, 72.

20. Gibbs, "The Compulsory Vaccination Act Briefly Considered . . . ," P.P., 1856, LII: 11, 26; Wilkinson, p. 36; Tebb, *Premature Burial*. For a careful analysis of Wilkinson's "rearguard action" against medical orthodoxy, see Barrow.

21. Bridges, p. 129; Parliamentary Debates, 3rd ser., 280 (June 19, 1883): 1026; Beck, p. 316; E. P. Thompson, p. 12. Among the studies of antivaccination sentiment in Victorian England, three are noteworthy for their balanced treatments. See MacLeod, "Law"; F. B. Smith, pp. 161–70; and Dorothy and Roy Porter, "Politics."

22. P. A. Taylor, p. 785; Parliamentary Debates, 3rd ser., 280 (June 19, 1883): 1006. See also Tebb, *Brief Story*; and *Compulsory Vaccination*.

23. *Opinions of Statesmen*, pp. 6–7.

24. Wilkinson, p. 29.

25. F. B. Smith, pp. 158–59; Burnett, p. 54. For popular attitudes toward the inoculation of children in eighteenth-century England and America, see Pollock, pp. 231–34.

26. J. Simon, pp. 282–86; R. J. Lambert, "A Victorian."

27. *Encyclopedia Britannica*, 9th ed., s.v. "vaccination"; *Lancet*, Nov. 11, 1854, p. 404; Rosen, p. 654.

28. The question of syphilis transmission through vaccination was bitterly debated in the medical press. Among many clinical reports, see especially *B.M.J.*, Apr. 12, 1862, p. 387; ibid., Jan. 21, 1871, pp. 66, 69–70; ibid., Apr. 29, 1871, pp. 448–49; ibid., July 1, 1871, p. 15; *Medical Times and Gazette*, Feb. 1, 1873, pp. 114–15. Antivaccinationists insisted that rising rates of syphilitic mortality were "largely due" to compulsory vaccination. See, for example, [Longman] *Fifteen Years*, p. 11.

29. Rumsey, p. 378; Copland, 9: 1423.

30. Hardy, *Epidemic Streets*, p. 121.

31. W. White, pp. 540–41.

32. MacLeod, "Frustration"; idem, "Law," pp. 114–15, 122–28, 189–207; F. B. Smith, pp. 167–70.

33. MacLeod, "Medico-Legal," pp. 44, 46–47; *Cases of Disease*, pp. 6, 8, 14–16.

34. S.C. on the Operation of the Vaccination Act (1867), P.P., 1871, XIII, QQ. 78, 3,318–19.

35. Ibid., QQ. 26, 29, 57, 2,369–70, 2,373, 2,447–50.

36. Ibid., QQ. 4,174–76.

37. *The Times*, Mar. 21, 1872; *Croydon Advertiser*, June 15, 1872.

38. *B.M.J.*, Aug. 26, 1871, pp. 239, 251–52; ibid., Sept. 2, 1871, p. 269; ibid., Dec. 2, 1871, p. 649.

39. Bynum, p. 86; Report of the Medical Officer of the Local Government Board for 1874, P.P., 1875, XL, Appendix 5, pp. 51–54. Public health activists could not agree on an explanation for the terrible smallpox mortality of 1870–72. Some sanitarians attributed its toll to "imperfect" vaccinations provided in earlier years, many harped on the outbreak's "exceptional potency of infection," while others argued that only revaccinated individuals were truly safe. Richard Thorne Thorne, President of the Epidemiological Society, advanced all three explanations. See Thorne, pp. 6–11.

40. Wohl, *Endangered Lives*, p. 321; C. Bosanquet, p. 57; *Lancet*, Aug. 7, 1869, p. 208. The Ladies' Sanitary Association did, however, support noncompulsory vaccination of young children. See *Too Late*.

41. *The Times*, Jan. 26, 1872; *The Anti-Vaccinator and Public Health Journal*, May 1, 1872, p. 22; *B.M.J.*, Oct. 14, 1871, p. 444.

42. *Birmingham Daily Post*, Aug. 2, 1879; *Vaccination Inquirer*, Sept. 1879, p. 80.

43. *Public Health*, 6 (July 6, 1877): 3; Report of the Medical Officer of the Local Government Board for 1883, P.P., 1884–85, XXXIII: i–ii. The antivaccinationists argued that all government smallpox statistics were suspect since medically trained coroners often refused to hold inquests on children alleged to have died from the effects of vaccination. Although Victorian anti-vaccinationists were themselves notoriously quick to distort health statistics, their suspicion of smallpox mortality figures was probably justified. See S.C. on the Op-

eration of the Vaccination Act (1867), QQ. 2,385-90, 2,401-4, 2,407, 2,410, 2,413-18, 2,430; Tebb, "What Is the Truth," pp. 187-90; and Eyler, pp. 347-48.

44. *Public Health*, 5 (Nov. 10, 1876): 381; *B.M.J.*, June 1, 1878, p. 778; ibid., Apr. 3, 1875, p. 452.

45. *Sanitary Record*, Mar. 6, 1875, p. 163; ibid., Aug. 26, 1876, pp. 135-36; *B.M.J.*, Apr. 17, 1875, pp. 513-14; *Public Health*, 4 (Mar. 31, 1876): 210; ibid., 4 (June 30, 1876): 530; ibid., 4 (Sept. 15, 1876): 224; ibid., 5 (Oct. 13, 1876): 301; ibid., 5 (Dec. 22, 1876): 481; Dupree, pp. 323-24.

46. *Leicester Daily Post*, June 15, 1887; *B.M.J.*, Apr. 15, 1871, p. 406; *Public Health*, 5 (Oct. 6, 1876): 282; *Medical Press and Circular*, Dec. 24, 1884, p. 558; *Vaccination Inquirer*, Sept. 1879, p. 79; *The Anti-Vaccinator and Public Health Journal*, July 1, 1872, p. 91.

47. Judith Walkowitz has suggested that East London mobs were primed to riot against doctors during the "Ripper" scare of late 1888 in part because they already harbored deep antivaccinationist feeling. Walkowitz, *City*, p. 214.

48. *Oxford Times*, June 26, 1880.

49. E. Chase, pp. 182-84; S.C. on the Operation of the Vaccination Act (1867), p. iv.

50. M. Elliott, pp. 95-96; *Sanitary Record*, Mar. 16, 1885, pp. 405-6; Picton, p. 126; *Lancet*, May 29, 1886, p. 1036.

51. *Vaccination Inquirer*, Apr. 1883, p. 9; Dudgeon, p. 520. For a detailed account of Dr. Johnston's sanitary crusade, see Fraser.

52. *The Times*, Mar. 24, 1885; *Leicester Daily Post*, Mar. 24, 1885; Biggs, *Leicester*, p. 79.

53. [Potts] *Vaccination*, p. 3; *Report of the Sixth Annual Meeting of the London Society for the Abolition of Compulsory Vaccination* (1886), pp. 10, 13.

54. Shonfield, pp. 186-87.

55. *Encyclopedia Britannica*, 9th ed., s.v. "vaccination"; Picton, pp. 114-15; *Hospital*, Feb. 7, 1891, p. 290.

56. Hardy, *Epidemic Streets*, p. 148.

57. [Longman] *Fifteen Years*, p. 21; Final Report of the Royal Commission [on] . . . Vaccination, P.P., 1896, XLVII: 1, 134-35, 137.

58. Malcolm Morris, pp. 971-72.

59. *Public Health*, 11 (1898-99): 461; ibid., 12 (1899-1900): 267; Report of the Departmental Committee on Vaccination Expenses, P.P., 1905, LXXIII (Lords): 8, 14-15.

60. P.R.O., MH55/404, H.O. circular dated May 18, 1906.

61. Elmy, "Woman and the Law" [1907], p. 397; P.R.O., MH53/53, memo by Reece, Dec. 8, 1921.

62. *Daily Telegraph*, Dec. 30, 1925; P.R.O., MH55/404, Joyson-Hicks to Day, May 10, 1926.

63. *Lancet*, Sept. 4, 1926, pp. 504-5; ibid., Sept. 15, 1928, pp. 547-48; Report of the Committee on Vaccination [Ministry of Health], P.P., 1928, XII: 65-66, 83-86, 199-201; Further Report of the Committee on Vaccination [Ministry of Health], P.P., 1930-31, XVII: 3-4.

64. *Medical Officer*, Jan. 21, 1911, p. 36; ibid., Mar. 25, 1911, pp. 148–49; P.R.O., MH55/408, Loat [Sect., National Anti-Vaccination League] to Minister of Health, Apr. 29, 1924; *Brief Summary*.

65. On smallpox vaccination in nineteenth- and early twentieth-century India, see Arnold, "Colonial Prison," pp. 181–82; and idem, *Colonizing the Body*, pp. 136–44. Still more intrusive was the public health response of the Bombay Government to an outbreak of bubonic plague in 1897. See Nanda, pp. 102–7.

66. Adamson, pp. 349–60; Armytage, pp. 142–45; James Murphy, pp. 54–63. As of 1869, denominational elementary instruction was providing 1.7 million places for England's 2.5 million school-age children. Musgrave, p. 40.

67. Davison, p. 130; Pomeroy, p. 6.

68. "Lex," pp. 397–98.

69. G. Sutherland, *Policy-Making*, pp. 115, 118.

70. Chalmers, 1: 68–69.

71. On poor parents as consumers of education, see Laqueur; and P. Gardner. For an opposing view that stresses the "haphazard" transmission of literacy, see D. Levine, "Education."

72. B. Simon, pp. 115–16; Rubinstein, *School Attendance*, pp. 5–7. For evidence that rote learning was less unpopular than many historians have assumed, see J. Rose; and Burnett, pp. 151–52.

73. G. M. Young, p. 116.

74. Springhall, p. 50; Ellis, pp. 314–15, 317–19. By legislation passed in 1899 the school-leaving age rose to twelve. Not until 1918 did full-time education up to the age of fourteen become the norm in England and Wales, and not until 1972 did the school-leaving age reach its present level of sixteen years.

75. *School Attendance Officers' Gazette*, Feb. 1901, pp. 180–81; Report of the Inter-Departmental Committee on Partial Exemption from School Attendance, P.P., 1909, XVII: 1–3, 11–12.

76. Hurt, pp. 155–56; R.C. on the Working of the Elementary Education Acts in England and Wales, Second Report, P.P., 1887, XXIX, Q. 32,134. One section of the "residuum" did, however, feel the pinch of compulsion early on: parents who received payment of school fees as part of their outdoor relief. After 1873, if these pauper parents did not regularly send their children to school they could lose such Poor Law assistance.

77. Rubinstein, "Socialization," pp. 235–36; Hurt, p. 158; R.C. on the Working of the Elementary Education Acts, Second Report, Q. 34,614; B. Simon, p. 127.

78. Dyhouse, *Girls*, pp. 101–4; Turnbull, p. 84; Davin, *Growing Up Poor*, pp. 102–11.

79. E. Ross, *Love*, pp. 24–25; Seccombe, p. 109.

80. C. Morley, pp. 218–19.

81. Gautrey, p. 35; J. Lewis, "Parents, Children," pp. 301–2.

82. Gautrey, p. 35; Sims, *How*, p. 27; J. Reeves, pp. 13, 29, 34–35.

83. Sims, *How*, p. 19; Philpott, p. 91; Runciman, pp. 21–32.

84. Pringle, p. 255.

85. Sims, *How*, p. 21.

86. Return from London School Board, showing . . . the Number of Cases of Wife Desertion . . . during the Twelve Months Ended the 30th day of June 1875, P.P., 1875, LVIII.

87. Rubinstein, "Socialization," pp. 232–33; R.C. on the Housing of the Working Classes, P.P., 1884-85, XXX, QQ. 17,674-75, 17,731-36.

88. O'Day and Englander, pp. 43–44.

89. Jephson, pp. 129–30; C. Morley, pp. 210–11.

90. Pomeroy, p. 24; Loane, *Neighbours*, p. 182.

91. R.C. on the Working of the Elementary Education Acts, Second Report, QQ. 14,750, 40,908, 40,943; P.R.O., HO45/9496/6739, Williams to Croad, Nov. 13, 1883.

92. J. Reeves, pp. 15–16; R.C. on the Working of the Elementary Education Acts, Second Report, QQ. 31,384-85; *South Western Star*, Sept. 10, 1892.

93. Rubinstein, "Socialization," p. 248; idem, *School Attendance*, p. 99.

94. This issue is discussed at length in Chapter 4.

95. Plowden, pp. 221–23.

96. Magistrate, p. 53; *South Western Star*, Feb. 2, 1889; ibid., Mar. 1, 1890; ibid., Oct. 7, 1893.

97. Late-Victorian education authorities in such large towns as Manchester, Salford, Liverpool, and Hull assured the Cross Commission that local magistrates were sympathetic to the cause of compulsory school attendance. R.C. on the Working of the Elementary Education Acts, Second Report, QQ. 32,145, 34,198, 35,869, 40,210.

98. P. Horn, pp. 134–35, 138–39; Flora Thompson, p. 44.

99. Blatchford, pp. 170–77. See also Robert Holmes's description of the midnight "roust-out" of a Sheffield father wanted for his "foolish contempt of the law" on school attendance. R. Holmes, *My Police Court*, pp. 21–22.

100. Lady, pp. 18–19.

101. *School Attendance Officers' Gazette*, Nov. 1900, pp. 130–31; ibid., May 1900, pp. 21–22; ibid., Apr. 1901, p. 23. As of May 1900, the School Attendance Officers' National Association claimed 777 members, leaving roughly 4,000 school visitors unaffiliated with this guild. Some "punishment men" remained obsessed with attendance percentages long thereafter. See, for example, I. Briggs, pp. 110–11.

102. R.C. on the Working of the Elementary Education Acts, Second Report, QQ. 27,092-93, 27,213-14, 35,982.

103. This preoccupation is thoroughly analyzed in Searle.

104. *Sanitary Record*, Mar. 27, 1902, p. 271; Board of Education, Report . . . upon the School Attendance of Children Below the Age of Five, P.P., 1908, CIXX (Lords): 31–32.

105. *Medical Officer*, June 12, 1909, p. 1002; ibid., Aug. 19, 1911, p. 90; ibid., June 29, 1912, p. 310; ibid., July 27, 1912, pp. 39–40; ibid., May 24, 1913, p. 250.

106. Report of the Departmental Committee on Reformatory and Indus-

trial Schools, P.P., 1913, XXXIX, Q. 6,300; Report of the Inter-Departmental Committee on Partial Exemption from School Attendance, P.P., 1909, XVII, QQ. 4,524–25; *Probation*, July 1935, p. 10.

107. Marsden, pp. 212–13.

108. Coventry City R.O., SEC/MB/37/1: Coventry School Attendance Sub-Committee Min. Bk., Jan. 29, 1908; July 15, 1908; Sept. 29, 1909; Sept. 7, 1910; and Mar. 29, 1911.

109. Bingham, p. 57.

110. Sheffield City Archives, CA 400: School Attendance Sub-Committee Min. Bk. no. 1, Aug. 17, 1903. See also CA 397: School Board, Bye Laws Comm. Min. Bk. no. 1, Dec. 14, 1888; Jan. 11, 1889; and Dec. 13, 1889. Sheffield and Liverpool were the first English towns to build industrial schools for habitual truants. For a glimpse into the disciplinary regime at Hollow Meadows, see Sheffield City Archives, CA 35/69 and CA 35/81: Log Bks., Truants' Industrial School, 1884–89 and 1895–1901.

111. Sheffield City Archives, CA 397–99: School Board, Bye Laws Comm. Min. Bks. 1–3, passim; CA 400: School Attendance Sub-Comm. Min. Bks. 1–3, passim.

112. Sheffield City Archives, CA 400: School Attendance Sub-Comm. Min. Bk. no. 1, June 7, 1905; Aug. 23, 1905; and Dec. 6, 1905.

113. *School Attendance Officers' Gazette*, July 1902, pp. 130–31. For more on educational politics in late-Victorian Leicester, see Gill.

114. Loane, *Neighbours*, p. 182; Garland, *Punishment*, pp. 159–264.

115. London SPCC, *First Annual Report* (1885), p. 9.

116. NSPCC, *Fiftieth Annual Report* (1934), pp. 38–39, 47. The category "centres of work" is misleading, conflating as it does both "district committees" and "branches." A "branch" of the NSPCC was a regional outpost of the child protection bureaucracy typically composed of middle-class volunteers who carried out their own fund-raising campaigns and met regularly with the inspector(s) assigned to them. A "district committee," on the other hand, was a smaller and more loosely knit band of volunteers—again, overwhelmingly middle-class—who did not have ready access to a cruelty man. See *Child's Guardian*, Nov. 1906, p. 125. For a revealing study of the politics of NSPCC branch formation, see Ferguson, "Cleveland," pp. 149–53.

117. *Child's Guardian*, June 1908, p. 71.

118. The first substantial studies of late-Victorian and Edwardian child protection were Housden; and Allen and Morton. A comprehensive analysis was attempted by Behlmer, *Child Abuse*. The NSPCC's changing role as a voluntary body has received attention from Sherrington. Harry Ferguson has done important work on the social construction of child abuse in England. See Ferguson, "Cleveland"; and idem, "Rethinking."

119. Pollock, pp. 91–95.

120. Mill, *Principles*, pp. 957–58; idem, *On Liberty*, p. 107.

121. M. Anderson, *Family Structure*, pp. 104–5; Conley, pp. 105–6.

122. Although a "Society for the Protection of Women and Children from

Aggravated Assaults" had operated in London since 1857, this body never won wide public support, perhaps because its dual focus proved too diffuse. See *The Times*, Jan. 11, 1884; and May, "Violence," pp. 145–46.

123. L. Gordon, pp. 9, 20, 30–31. The so-called "padroni system," which involved the display of Italian begging children in city streets, captured attention in the late 1870's. But this was a fleeting concern and hardly typified later anticruelty campaigns in England. See Ribton-Turner, pp. 303–4.

124. Pleck, p. 84; E. Townsend, pp. 12–13.

125. NSPCC, *Fiftieth Annual Report*, pp. 38–39. In 1934, after a half-century of work, the NSPCC was taking a mere 1.1 percent of its cases to court.

126. NSPCC Archives, London: copy of a letter from Ranfurly to Rosa Waugh, June 6, 1910; NSPCC, *Nineteenth Annual Report* (1903), pp. 4–5; NSPCC, *Fifteenth Annual Report* (1899), p. 57. Although the NSPCC was far less inclined to prosecute offenders than its New York counterpart, the London public may have been more censorious of parental misbehavior. The childhood experience of Buster Keaton certainly suggests as much. Born in 1895, Keaton joined his parents' rough-and-tumble vaudeville show just before has fourth birthday. For more than a decade thereafter "The Three Keatons" delighted audiences throughout the American Northeast with a comedy routine that featured young Buster, "The Human Mop," being swept across floors and hurled into scenery. When the trio took their act to London in 1911, however, the Palace Theatre lapsed into a "blood-chilling silence" once the mock combat began. "You actually scared the audience," a fellow American explained to Mr. Keaton. "They think you are hurting Buster." Keaton, pp. 11–14, 21–22, 60–62.

127. See, for example, J. Lewis, "Anxieties," p. 38.

128. NSPCC, *Fifth Annual Report* (1889), pp. 67–69.

129. Mager, p. 13.

130. NSPCC, *Fiftieth Annual Report*, pp. 42–43. The category "moral corruption" would have included persons investigated for incest and indecent exposure, although the most numerous "offenders" under this heading tended to be mothers who worked either full- or part-time as prostitutes. While NSPCC case statistics do not permit us to distinguish sexual from non-sexual violence against the young, there is little in the Society's voluminous records to support suffragist Frances Swiney's claim that 37 percent of all assaults against British children were incestuous. Swiney, *The Sons of Belial*, as uncritically cited in S. Kent, p. 143. What NSPCC Director Robert Parr *did* assert was that 37.8 percent of the comparatively small number of criminal sexual assault cases (186) investigated during 1909–1910 involved incest. R. Parr, *Assaults*, pp. 4–5.

131. *Child's Guardian*, June 1902, p. 68; Hendrick, *Child Welfare*, pp. 57–58; *Hospital*, Apr. 24, 1897, p. 57.

132. Loane, *Neighbours*, pp. 159–60.

133. NSPCC, *Eighteenth Annual Report* (1902), pp. 6–7. For a thoughtful discussion of Victorian attitudes toward animals, see J. Turner.

134. Saleeby, p. 32; B. Kidd, pp. 316–17; Pick, pp. 109–39.

135. *Child's Guardian*, Feb. 1889, p. 17; NSPCC, *First Annual Report*, p. 9; "Happiness," p. 332. For an account of the NSPCC's shifting stance on poverty and drink as contributing factors to cruelty, see Behlmer, *Child Abuse*, pp. 177–81.

136. Parton, pp. 20, 34–35; Thane, "Childhood," p. 18.

137. Manning and Waugh, p. 699. Unlike the three French child protection laws passed in 1889, 1898, and 1912, the English statutes did not substantially enhance the power of "philanthropic notables, magistrates, and children's doctors" to "penetrate into families from the angle of violations committed *by* children." Donzelot, pp. 83–84.

138. *Child's Guardian*, Aug. 1894, p. 107; ibid., Dec. 1890, p. 146; ibid., Mar. 1898, p. 34; ibid., Jan. 1894, p. 6; ibid., Feb. 1905, p. 20.

139. Cecil, p. 1011.

140. *Child's Guardian*, Sept. 1903, p. 97; ibid., Oct. 1906, p. 113; ibid., Mar. 1892, p. 29; ibid., Apr. 1891, pp. 25–26; ibid., Nov. 1895, p. 145.

141. Storch, "Policeman," p. 487.

142. *Child's Guardian*, Apr. 1907, p. 38; *School Child*, 1 (May 1911): 5.

143. *Advance!*, June 1890, p. 136; S.C. on Infant Life Protection/Safety of Nurse Children, P.P., 1896, X (Lords), Q. 2,672; *Annual Report of the Manchester and Salford Sanitary Association . . . for 1902*, p. 5; *Lancet*, May 15, 1897, p. 1356.

144. NSPCC, *Thirteenth Annual Report* (1897), pp. 46–47; NSPCC, *Twenty-Sixth Annual Report* (1910), p. 61. Information about mistreated children obtained from voluntary workers must have been added to the "general public" category. Local case statistics reveal a strikingly similar pattern. Both in York between 1898 and 1903, and in Stockton-on-Tees during 1898–99, the "general public" provided 55 and 54 percent of the new referrals, respectively. See Behlmer, *Child Abuse*, p. 171; and Ferguson, "Rethinking," p. 136.

145. A. Morrison, p. 69; Loane, *From Their Point*, p. 63; idem, *Next Street*, p. 208; NSPCC, *Twenty-Fifth Annual Report* (1909), p. 16.

146. L. Gordon, pp. 6, 55–56.

147. Ferguson, "Rethinking," 136.

148. Case cited in Hammerton, *Cruelty*, p. 41. Hammerton reads "cruelty man" as a reference to the local police court, but this interpretation seems unlikely.

149. Dayus, pp. 6–7. Cf. Jasper, p. 47. For more on the assertive nature of working-class matriarchy, see E. Ross, "'Fierce Questions.'"

150. Loane, as quoted in José Harris, *Private Lives*, p. 79.

151. *Hospital*, Apr. 24, 1897, p. 57; C. Booth, *Life and Labour*, 2nd Series, 5: 332; R. Roberts, p. 29.

152. *Essays on Duty*, pp. 2–3; Sims, *Black Stain*, passim; E. Bayly, pp. 3–5.

153. An Oxford couple, as quoted in Gillis, "Evolution," p. 118; Loane, *Englishman's Castle*, pp. 217–18.

154. Loane, *Common Growth*, p. 249.

155. [NSPCC] *Inspector's Directory*, pp. 25, 39, 12; B. Harrison, "Animals," p. 809; *Our Waifs and Strays*, Aug. 1892, p. 12. For an autobiographical account, see [Payne] *Cruelty Man*.

156. P.R.O., MEPO2/1426, Cooper to Fordham, Dec. 20, 1910.

157. Mrs. Benjamin, as quoted in E. Ross, "Hungry Children," pp. 168, 191 (n. 27).

158. Reynolds, Woolley, and Woolley, pp. 25–26; Ferguson, "Rethinking," p. 133.

159. Paterson, p. 23; Gillis, "Evolution," p. 117. The distinction being drawn here does not assume the existence of a "labor aristocracy" but rather a cultural gulf between what the mid-Victorian metal worker Thomas Wright called the "artisans" and the "rough." For more on Wright's nomenclature, see Reid.

160. R. Roberts, pp. 28–29; NSPCC Archives: York Branch Case Records, Plaint #993. Well into the 1950's Liverpool slum dwellers viewed cruelty to children as a cultural anathema. See Kerr, p. 116. Cf. F. M. L. Thompson's assertion that "the postman was the only representative of authority encountered in ordinary daily experience who was generally regarded as benign and helpful." See idem, *Rise*, pp. 358–59.

161. Thane, "Women and the Poor Law," pp. 39–40.

162. Dyhouse, *Feminism*, p. 134; Bell, pp. 51, 104, 207. So ubiquitous were Lady Bell and her assistants in the homes of Middlesborough ironworkers that at least one wife asked a visitor to decide whether "it was right" to leave an abusive husband (237). A similar point may be made about the "drearily decent" homes of North Lambeth that Maud Reeves investigated on behalf of the Fabian Women's Group. Her illustrative family budgets could not have been derived except through close questioning of working-class wives. See M. Reeves, passim.

163. "Laborers' Homes," pp. 268–69.

164. Pedder, pp. 853, 846–47.

165. Haw, pp. 5–6.

166. Preston-Thomas, pp. 363–64. Edwardian England's most systematic attack on this regulatory impulse came from the Liberty and Property Defence League. See Soldon.

167. T. Holmes, "Youthful Offenders," pp. 845–46.

168. Muirhead, p. 114; Pelham, p. 22.

169. A. Page, pp. 589–90; Pepler, *Justice*, pp. 21–23; Shand, p. 39; Bray, pp. 308–9.

170. McCleary, "State as Over-Parent," pp. 47–48.

171. Pennybacker, chap. 3.

172. Du Maurier; *Spectator*, 102 (Feb. 6, 1909): 208–9; R. Roberts, p. 180. Du Maurier's foreign enemy, as in most Edwardian invasion tales, was German. It is worth noting that early twentieth-century Germany had its own chroniclers of family disintegration. See, for example, Müller-Lyer, pp. 251–52.

173. Pelling, pp. 1–3, 17–18; Barker, p. 64; Yeo, p. 70. Barker and Yeo

treat Stephen Reynolds and Bob and Tom Woolley's 1911 study, *Seems So!*, as unimpeachable evidence of working-class outrage over legislation that interfered with their home lives. For a different reading of this text, see Thane, "Working Class," pp. 894–95.

174. Berdoe, p. 562; F. B. Smith, pp. 67–68; E. Ross, *Love*, pp. 132–33.

175. R.C. on the Poor Laws and Relief of Distress, P.P., 1909, XLI [Appendix no. CLVII]: 791; J. Lewis, "Working-Class Wife," pp. 102–3. It was Eleanor Rathbone who mounted the first sustained critique of the male-breadwinner norm in her 1924 study, *The Disinherited Family*.

176. Hobsbawm, pp. 200–208; G. S. Jones, *Languages*, pp. 217–20.

177. Crossick, pp. 146–47.

178. M. Reeves, p. 3.

179. Flint, p. 17; E. Roberts, *Woman's Place*, pp. 137–38, 195–96; Burnett, p. 218; D. Vincent, pp. 241–42. "There were housewives," Robert Roberts recalled about his corner of the Salford slums, "who finally lost real interest in anything save dirt removing. Almost every working hour of the week they devoted to cleaning and re-cleaning the same objects so that their family, drilled into a slavish tidiness, could sit in state, newspaper covers removed, for a few hours each Sunday evening. On Monday purification began all over again. Two of these compulsives left us for the 'lunatic asylum,' one of them, I remember vividly, passing with a man in uniform through a group of us watching children to a van, still washing her hands like a poor Lady Macbeth." R. Roberts, p. 37.

180. Loane, *Next Street*, pp. 45–46; José Harris, *Private Lives*, pp. 93–94.

181. Light, pp. 8, 12, 106–7, 217–18; J. White, *Worst Street*, pp. 134, 197–98; Gittins, pp. 57–58, 175–78.

182. On the resuscitation of "Mothering Sunday," see C. Penswick Smith, *Short History*; and idem, *Revival*. The tradition of "Children's Sunday" was an Edwardian invention and dealt more narrowly with public support for anti-cruelty work. See *Manchester Guardian*, Oct. 2, 1911; and Morton, pp. 15–16.

183. Daunton, pp. 277–80; West, as quoted in José Harris, *Private Lives*, p. 81.

184. Rowan, p. 230; E. Ross, *Love*, p. 202.

185. Dyhouse, "Working-Class," pp. 261–62; J. Lewis, *Politics*, p. 76; Report of the Inter-Departmental Committee on Physical Deterioration, P.P., 1904, XXXII, QQ. 13,017–18.

186. Horsley, p. 194; *B.M.J.*, Nov. 19, 1910, p. 1657; John Harris, "Unfit," pp. 579–80; Pick, pp. 157–59, 162–63, 184–85.

187. Dwork, pp. 226–30. For a useful comparative analysis of maternalist politics, see Koven and Michel, "Womanly."

188. Fremantle, p. 115.

189. See, especially, B. Gilbert, pp. 102–3, 113–14, 156–57; and Pipkin, pp. 70–73. More recently, Susan Pedersen has discussed school meals in the context of precedents for the "disaggregation of family income" in modern British social policy. See Pedersen, *Family*, pp. 52–55.

190. For contemporary support of school feeding, see Gorst, chap. 5; and

S. and B. Webb, *Prevention*, pp. 66–68. The opposing case was argued in Lightbody; "Underfed Children"; and O'Brien.

191. A. Martin, *Married Working Woman*, pp. 29–31.

192. NSPCC, *Twenty-Fourth Annual Report* (1908), pp. 26–27. As of mid-1913, the average attendance rate of English parents (often the mother alone) at school medical inspections was 40.2 percent. See *Medical Officer*, July 12, 1913, p. 20.

193. A. Martin, "The Mother," pp. 1241–42; Mackenzie and Matthew, pp. 12–16; J. Stewart, pp. 93–95; Steedman, *Childhood*, p. 57.

194. *Medical Officer*, Mar. 20, 1909, p. 742; ibid., Nov. 25, 1911, p. 257; ibid., May 25, 1912, pp. 233–34.

195. Report on the Working of the Education (Provision of Meals) Act, P.P., 1910, XXIII: 5–6; Pepler, *Justice*, pp. 15–19; A. Martin, "The Mother," p. 1240.

196. Pepler, *Care Committee*, pp. 58–65; Frere, pp. 24–32; Iselin; B. Rowntree and Lasker, pp. 20–21. For a detailed analysis of "blind alley" labor for juveniles, see Hendrick, *Images*; and for the relationship between child labor and school medical care, see idem, "Child Labour."

197. Stocks, *My Commonplace*, pp. 57–58; *The School Child and Juvenile Worker*, 3 (Jan. 1913): 6; ibid., 1 (Jan. 1911): 7–8.

198. Macadam, *New Philanthropy*, p. 170; M. Longman, pp. 733–35. Coventry was one of the few provincial cities to build a care committee structure closely modeled on London's. For its experience in the prewar period, see Coventry City R.O., SEC/MB/19/4: Children's Care Sub-Comm. Min. Bk.

199. Saleeby, pp. 94–95; Haynes, *Decline*, pp. 69–70, 212–13.

200. Chesterton, *Autobiography*, pp. 190–91, 197; idem, *Eugenics*, p. 166; Belloc, pp. 16–17, 138–39, 144; Barker, pp. 86–91.

201. *National Health*, 12 (Mar. 1920): 208–9; *Maternity and Child Welfare*, Dec. 1919, pp. 414–17; *Medical Officer*, Nov. 29, 1919, p. 205.

202. This diagram appeared first in Margaret G. Bondfield's *The National Care of Maternity* (1914), a publication of the Women's Cooperative Guild. One year later it reappeared, slightly altered, as "Appendix A" in Douglas Pepler's *Justice and the Child*. More recently it has seen rhetorical service in both David Garland's *Punishment and Welfare* (1985), p. 251; and Seth Koven and Sonya Michel's "Womanly Duties" (1990), p. 1104.

203. N. Rose, pp. 146–50.

204. R. Roberts, pp. 13, 185; P. Fox, pp. 32–34.

205. Meacham, *Life Apart*, p. 207; Hoggart, p. 21.

Chapter 3

1. Gorer, pp. 72, 74.

2. Spock, pp. 2–4; Zuckerman, pp. 179, 183–88.

3. Lasch, pp. 171–72. For a perceptive reading of *Baby and Child Care* as "a document in cultural disintegration," see Graebner.

4. Childrearing prescriptions during the 1920's and 30's are analyzed in Urwin and Sharland.

5. Cole, p. 185.

6. Guthrie, pp. 4, 23.

7. Oppenheim, *"Shattered Nerves,"* pp. 10, 51–52.

8. Haley, pp. 23, 35.

9. Oppenheim, *"Shattered Nerves,"* pp. 8–9. Calling tetanus a "neurosis" was not as farfetched as we today might assume, since some of its symptoms closely resemble the paralysis of classic "hysteria." I thank Lisa Nakamura for drawing my attention to this point.

10. For a lucid discussion of the relationship between experimental physiology and psychological understanding in Victorian England, see R. M. Young.

11. Crichton-Browne, *Story*, pp. 2–5. On the appeal of Victorian phrenology, see Cooter.

12. Spencer, *Principles*, 1: 573–74; R. M. Young, pp. 201–2.

13. W. Carpenter, *Principles*, pp. 12–14.

14. G. Harris, pp. 5–6; Ribot, pp. 113–14; Prince, pp. 259–60; Sully, *Human Mind*, 1: 33.

15. Gotch, 2: 453–55; Sully, *Human Mind*, 1: 48; idem, *Outlines of Psychology*, pp. 12–14.

16. Clouston, *Hygiene*, p. v.

17. Maudsley, *Physiology and Pathology*, pp. 26–27; idem, "Sex," p. 467.

18. Oppenheim, *"Shattered Nerves,"* pp. 54, 66–68, 70–71. In 1878, Crichton-Browne, together with another alienist, joined Hughlings-Jackson and Ferrier in founding the neurological journal *Brain*.

19. Hearnshaw, *Short History*, pp. 132–33.

20. Sully, *My Life*, pp. 182, 189–91; idem, "Physiological Psychology," pp. 20–21, 26–27.

21. Sully, *Outlines*, pp. 516–20; *Brain*, 8 (1885): 94–95.

22. Bain, *Education*, p. 12.

23. For an illuminating study of this ideal, see Haley.

24. Flora Thompson, p. 19.

25. Warner, "Recurrent Headaches," pp. 889–90; idem, "Spontaneous Postures." Like several late-Victorian nerve-doctors, Warner, then Assistant Physician to the East London Hospital for Children, was confident that certain muscular irregularities could be linked to lesions in particular parts of the brain. Uncontrollable spasms of the face or body, for example, signaled a "choreic brain."

26. Mercier, pp. 67–68; Preyer, *Mind of the Child*, pp. 344–46; Sully, *Outlines*, pp. 216, 288–89; W. Carpenter, *Principles*, pp. 133–35.

27. Riley, pp. 52–53.

28. *The Times*, Apr. 16, 1853.

29. Collini, "Idea," p. 35; Haley, pp. 43–45; Bain, *On the Study*, pp. 199–200.

30. Sully, *Outlines*, pp. 664–66; Schofield, *Enquiry*, pp. 13–14; idem, *Springs*, p. 36.

31. T. Hughes, p. 20; Greg, pp. 32–33. Greg's equation of "the high pressure and rapid pace" of urban life with heart failure was derived from health statistics first published in the *British Medical Journal*.

32. Gowers, pp. 1059–63; Richardson, pp. 82–86.

33. Spencer, *Education*, pp. 275–76; Allbutt, pp. 61, 71; Dennis, p. 232; A. B. Robertson, p. 316. For the "rising crescendo of complaints" about scholastic overpressure in Victorian America, see Duffy.

34. Teale, p. 11; R. A. Armstrong, pp. 6–7, 13–15. Among several historical accounts of the educational politics behind charges of "overpressure," see especially Sutherland, *Policy-Making*, pp. 245–57; and Hurt, pp. 106–8.

35. *B.M.J.*, Feb. 9, 1884, pp. 279–80; ibid., Mar. 1, 1884, p. 445; *Lancet*, Mar. 1, 1884, p. 410; ibid., Mar. 8, 1884, p. 445; ibid., June 21, 1884, pp. 1132–33.

36. Report of Dr. Crichton-Browne [to the Education Department] upon the Alleged Over-pressure of Work in Public Elementary Schools, P.P., 1884, LXI: 56, 22, 6.

37. Buxton, pp. 806–7, 814–15; Return of Cases Which Have Been Reported to the [Education] Department, in which Overpressure Has Been Alleged as the Cause of Illness, P.P., 1884–85, LXI; *The Times*, Jan. 10, 1885.

38. Warner, *The Children*, pp. 2, 11–15.

39. Idem, *Nervous System*, p. 14; Wooldridge, p. 34.

40. Galton, *Memories*, pp. 244–49; Supplement to the Seventy-Fifth Report of the Registrar-General, P.P., 1914–16, VIII: xciii–xcv; *Hospital*, Mar. 2, 1889, p. 349; *Child's Guardian*, Jan. 1893, p. 6; Kern, pp. 454–57; O. Anderson, pp. 256, 353.

41. Chrisman, pp. 7–8; Zelizer, pp. 22–55; Steedman, *Childhood*, p. 63; idem, "'Mother,'" pp. 151–52.

42. Spencer, *Education*, pp. 236–38, 240–41, 262–64; Preyer, *Mental Development*, pp. xv–xvi, 75–76.

43. Schofield, *Unconscious Mind*, pp. 408–9; Stoner, p. 1; Guthrie, p. 89.

44. Among many examples of this normative literature, see especially Henry; and Mosher.

45. Taine; Darwin; Preyer, *Mind*.

46. Riley, pp. 44, 48–49; Sully, "Babies and Science," pp. 539–40, 543, 545.

47. Sully, "Baby Linguistics," pp. 110–11; Robinson, pp. 836–39. See also Buckman, "Babies and Monkeys," which dwells on the prognathism of infants.

48. Galton, *Hereditary Genius*, p. 12, and passim; Sully, "Genius," pp. 603–4.

49. Sikorskii, pp. 245–46.

50. Clouston, *Neuroses*, pp. 134–35; Sully, "Studies . . . V," pp. 362–63.

51. Oppenheim, *"Shattered Nerves,"* pp. 156, 166, 168; Tuke, p. 50; Sully, *Studies of Childhood*, pp. 298, 305–6; idem, "Studies . . . X," p. 656; idem, "Studies . . . III," pp. 733–34, 742; idem, "Studies . . . I," pp. 324–25.

52. Keir, pp. 6–9; Hearnshaw, *Short History*, p. 134.

53. Sully, "Studies . . . XIII," pp. 176, 180; idem, "New Study," pp. 728–29.

54. Ibid., 731–33. An English doctor put the case against mothers even

more dismissively: "[T]he average mother, in spite of many unquestioned merits, is about as competent to take an unprejudiced view of the facts bearing on the natural history of her infant as a West African negro would do to carry out an investigation of the anatomy and physiology of a fetish." Robinson, p. 832.

55. See, for example, Baldwin, pp. 213–14.

56. In the "Authorities" section of its long article on "Psychology," the eleventh edition of the *Encyclopedia Britannica* lists Sully's *The Human Mind* (1892) first among the most important "systematic" surveys in the field, ahead of William James's *Principles of Psychology* (1890).

57. Monroe, pp. 2–3; Wooldridge, pp. 36–37.

58. Reeder, pp. 86–87; Dyhouse, *Girls*, p. 129.

59. Hearnshaw, *Short History*, chap. 15; Riley, pp. 59, 55–57; R. Jones, pp. 431–32.

60. José Harris, *Private Lives*, p. 82.

61. *Parents' Review. A Monthly Magazine of Home-Training and Culture*, 1 (1890): 1–2.

62. "Cry of the Parents," pp. 55–56.

63. Whitbread, p. 19; Curtis and Boultwood, pp. 115–16.

64. See, for example, *Short Account*.

65. *Parents' Review*, 5 (1894): 923, 927.

66. Froebel, pp. 64–66; Steedman, "'Mother,'" pp. 153–54.

67. Woodham-Smith, pp. 36–37; Whitbread, p. 47; *Then and Now*, p. 20; Ballard, pp. 181–82; R. Hill and F. Hill, n. 2, pp. 356–57.

68. Simpson, pp. 16, 24, 33, 37–39, 44, 52–54.

69. Shirreff, *Kinder-garten in Relation*, pp. 1–2; idem, *Kindergarten at Home*, pp. 3, 41–43, 153.

70. Herford, 1: 5; Froebel Society, *Twenty-Fifth Annual Report* (1900), pp. 19–22.

71. *Mothers in Council*, 1 (1891): 147; E. Abbott, pp. 13–16; Rooper, pp. 335–37; *Parents' Review*, 1 (1890): 26–30.

72. *Parents' Review*, 5 (1894): 928.

73. Obituary in *The Times*, Jan. 17, 1923; Cholmondeley, *Story*, pp. 5–6, 14–15; *In Memoriam*, pp. 56–58, 118–21.

74. C. Mason, *Home Education*, pp. 1–2. For an analysis of related anti-suffrage arguments, see B. Harrison, *Separate Spheres*.

75. C. Mason, *Home Education*, pp. 1–2, 6, 14, 19, 27–30.

76. Ibid., pp. v, 16–17, 65–66, 71–72, 80. *Home Education* went through six editions between 1886 and 1906, selling over 10,000 copies.

77. Carolyn Steedman's fine biography clarifies this connection. See her *Childhood*.

78. McMillan, *Education*, pp. 50–51.

79. Idem, *Nursery School*, pp. 21–22, 24–26, 172–74.

80. *Parents' Review*, 1 (1890): 70–71.

81. I. Taylor, pp. 20–21, 30, 32–39; *Mothers' Companion*, 3 (1889): 133–34; National Home Reading Union, *Eighth Annual Report* (1897), p. 11; G.

Radford, pp. 8–13. Inspired by New York State's Chautauqua Assembly, the NHRU was founded in 1889 and sought to promote the reading of wholesome books in local "circles."

82. *Parents' Review*, 8 (1897): 51–56.

83. Ibid., 1 (1890): 320.

84. Ibid., 9 (1898): 509; ibid., 8 (1897): 409; ibid., 4 (1893): 16–22, 920–21; Cholmondeley, *Story*, pp. 52–54.

85. *Mothers' Companion*, 8 (1894): 78–79; *The Times*, Jan. 17, 1923.

86. Gorham, "Ideology," p. 47.

87. Poovey, *Uneven Developments*, pp. 127–29; *In Memoriam*, pp. 22–23.

88. *Parents Review*, 2 (1891): 311–13; ibid., 3 (1892): 284; ibid., 13 (1902): 733–34.

89. Loane, *Neighbours*, pp. 23–24.

90. R. Jones, pp. 428–29.

91. Foster, as quoted in Schofield, *Enquiry*, p. 14. For Foster's place in nineteenth-century British science, see Geison.

92. *Parents' Review*, 2 (1891): 568; C. Mason, *Parents*, p. 18.

93. Schofield, *Springs*, pp. 1–3, 6; *Parents' Review*, 12 (1901): 849–52.

94. *Parents' Review*, 17 (1906): 324–25; ibid., 12 (1901): 702–3. In a variation on this theme, one contributor to the *Parents' Review* declared that mild hysteria was preventable "by teaching self-control and strengthening the will-power." Ibid., pp. 847–52.

95. Ibid., 1 (1890): 3, 437–38; ibid., 8 (1897): 138–41, 262; ibid., 10 (1899): 411–12.

96. Ibid., 1 (1890): 323–24; ibid., 16 (1905): 424–25.

97. *Times Educational Supplement*, Feb. 6, 1912, p. 17; ibid., Apr. 19, 1917, p. 137. The book-based knowledge of which Mason wrote also served, she argued, to mute class conflict. For such knowledge was not so much the mastery of information as "a generous view of men and their motives."

98. Boyd, pp. 140–41; Culverwell, pp. 55–61; Cecil Grant, pp. 28–29, 92–93. As enthusiastic as some English converts to the Montessori method were, they paled beside American advocates. See, for example, D. Fisher, pp. viii–ix, 7–11; and Tozier.

99. *Journal of Education*, 45 (June 1913): 385–86; Collins, p. 393.

100. Selleck, pp. 28–29; Mannin, pp. 209–10.

101. *Parents' Review*, 23 (1912): 578; ibid., 24 (1913): 408–9; *Times Educational Supplement*, Nov. 2, 1915, pp. 127–28.

102. Cecil Grant, pp. v–vii; Crichton-Browne, *Doctor's Second Thoughts*, pp. 103–4. Crichton-Browne's interwar praise for Montessori principles followed from the assumption that children educated under her system matured into "healthy well-balanced men and women" who would "mate wisely." For a crypto-fascist extension of this logic, see "The Montessori Child—Super Citizen," *Montessori Notes*, 1 (Mar. 1934): 15; and "Montessori and the New Social Order," ibid., 1 (Apr. 1934): 40, 42.

103. *Times Educational Supplement*, Dec. 7, 1915, pp. 139–40.

104. *Parents' Review*, 26 (1915): 7–8, 11–13; ibid., 30 (1919): 20; Andrews, pp. 100–102, 108.

105. *Parents' Review*, 30 (1919): 371; Seaborne, p. 219; P.R.O., HO45/14111/169846, St. Mary's Industrial School, correspondence, 1930.

106. *In Memoriam*, pp. 101, 16–17.

107. Donzelot, pp. 189–90, 209. For a thoughtful study of French concerns with *dénatalité*, as well as a comparison of pronatalist policy in the two countries, see Pedersen, *Family*, especially pp. 59–77, 130–32, 233–36, and 358–73. Useful for linking depopulation fears with social welfare reform in an earlier period is Fuchs, "France." The most thorough analysis of English depopulation politics is Soloway.

108. As late as 1944, one of Mason's faithful was touting PNEU principles as the key to "win[ning] the peace." See Cholmondeley, *Parents*.

109. Urwin and Sharland, pp. 175, 184. For popular accounts of changing childrearing advice, see Hardyment; and Beekman.

110. D. Armstrong, pp. 7–9, 21, 26.

111. Oppenheim, "*Shattered Nerves*," pp. 92–93, 97, 99, 109.

112. Keegan, pp. 270–71, 327–28.

113. Macpherson et al., 2: 1, 8–9; M. Stone, 2: 250–51.

114. For Mott's somatic case, see *Lancet*, Feb. 12, 1916, pp. 331–38; ibid., Feb. 26, 1916, pp. 441–49; ibid., Mar. 11, 1916, pp. 545–53; and Mott, "Punctiform Haemorrhages." For the "wind of the bullet" theory, see *Lancet*, Mar. 27, 1915, p. 663; ibid., Aug. 14, 1915, pp. 348–49; and ibid., Oct. 2, 1915, p. 766. The opposing case was best summarized by Hugh Crichton-Miller in idem, ed., *Functional Nerve Disease*, pp. 4–5.

115. Ibid., pp. vi–vii; Hadfield, "Treatment," pp. 63–65.

116. Nicoll and Young, pp. 130–31; McDougall, p. 184; Hadfield, *Psychology*, pp. 2–3; Alcock, pp. 68–69.

117. Graves and Hodge, pp. 102–4.

118. Tansley, pp. 180–81, 222, 242; Hadfield, *Psychology*, pp. 17–19; Flugel, pp. 157–58; *The Times*, Dec. 31, 1925; ibid., Jan. 5, 1926; ibid., Jan. 15, 1926; ibid., Jan. 20, 1926.

119. C. Fox, pp. 231–37; Tansley, pp. 13–15.

120. Ackerknecht, p. 86; Beekman, pp. 113–17; Hardyment, pp. 176–81.

121. John B. Watson, *Behaviorism*, p. 11; idem, *Psychological Care*, pp. 5–7, 81–82.

122. Crichton-Miller, *New Psychology*, pp. 12, 245–46, 208.

123. Ibid., pp. 24, 33.

124. Scharlieb, *Psychology*, pp. 58–59; Isaacs, *Nursery Years*. Isaacs, trained in psychology and logic, as well as in psychoanalysis, cautioned parents about correcting the naughty child. "[W]henever the child behaves in a way that does not please us, we are ready to act. We do so, out of our own good or bad humour at the moment, out of a habit of acting so, out of our 'principles'; but rarely out of a full knowledge of what in the child's mind has led him to do the thing we don't like. Yet without that knowledge, we cannot be sure that we are dealing with him in the way most likely to help him." Ibid., p. 2.

125. Tavistock Square Clinic for Functional Nervous Disorders [hereafter TSCFND], *Report for . . . 1920–1927*, p. 6; Irvine, pp. 17–25; *Hugh Crichton-Miller*, pp. 40–41; Crichton-Miller, *Functional Nerve Disease*, p. 4.

126. Trist and Murray, pp. 1–3; Dicks, p. 2.

127. Ramon, pp. 60–61, 64; Dicks, pp. 26–27, 2.

128. Ibid., pp. 16–17; *Hugh Crichton-Miller*, p. 43.

129. TSCFND, *Report for . . . 1920–1927*, p. 6.

130. Hugh Crichton-Miller, p. 42; Dicks, pp. 17, 28, 44; TSCFND, *Report for . . . 1920–1927*, p. 35; idem, *Report for . . . 1929 to . . . 1930*, p. 6; idem, *Report for . . . 1930 to . . . 1931*, p. 7; idem, *Report for . . . 1935*, p. 11. In 1931, the Tavistock Clinic changed its name to the Institute of Medical Psychology.

131. TSCFND, *Report for . . . 1920–1927*, pp. 9–10, 14.

132. D. Armstrong, p. 25.

133. TSCFND, *Report for . . . 1927 to . . . 1929*, p. 12; Dicks, p. 31.

134. TSCFND, *Report for . . . 1927 to . . . 1929*, pp. 12, 7.

135. Crichton-Miller, "Foreword," in *Advances in Understanding*, pp. 5, 7.

136. Rees, p. 197. Rees, too, had trained in general medicine rather than in psychiatry, although he did attend seminars and ward rounds at the Bethlem Royal Hospital, then London's main teaching hospital for psychiatrists.

137. Hugh Crichton-Miller, pp. 44–45; *Probation*, Jan. 1932, p. 160; *Montessori Notes*, 1 (Mar. 1934): 9, 11.

138. Thom, p. 205.

139. Dicks, pp. 39, 45; TSCFND, *Report for 1st Apr. to 31st Dec. 1931*, p. 7.

140. LeMesurier, *Handbook*, pp. 208–10.

141. Institute of Child Psychology, *Annual Report 1937*, p. 4; *Probation*, July 1929, p. 12. See also Burns.

142. N. Rose, pp. 173–74; Donzelot, p. 150.

143. MacCalman, pp. 257–59; Leeson, *Probation System*, pp. 24–25; M. Horn, "Moral Message," p. 26; Healy, *Honesty*, pp. 2, 170; idem, "Psychology," pp. 44–45.

144. This reorientation is well analyzed in M. Horn, *Before It's Too Late*, chap. 2.

145. Hamilton-Pearson, "Some Aspects," p. 116; Howard Association, *Gift*, p. 1. For more on the police court missionaries, see Chapter 4.

146. Mental Deficiency Act of 1927 (17 & 18 Geo. 5, c. 33), section 1 (2); *Education and Care*, pp. 18–19. For an illustration of charity along these lines persisting into the 1920's, see Bucks. County R.O.: Bucks. Voluntary Association for the Care of the Mentally Defective, Min. Bk. no. 3 (Oct. 19, 1920–Feb. 20, 1923).

147. Feversham Committee, *Voluntary*, p. 55; National Council for Mental Hygiene, *Seventh Report* (1930), pp. 1, 3; Greta Jones, *Social Hygiene*, p. 137.

148. N. Rose, chap. 7; D. Armstrong, pp. 26–29.

149. Burt, "Symposium," p. 27; idem, *Young Delinquent*, pp. 594–95; Hearnshaw, *Cyril*, pp. 97–98.

150. Gath et al., p. 6.

151. B. Smart, pp. 73-77.

152. Renton, pp. 309-11; Feldman, pp. 359-66; Thom, p. 207. The Commonwealth Fund assumed financial sponsorship of the East London Clinic in 1929.

153. Child Guidance Council [hereafter CGC], *Report for 1935*, p. 4; Harvey and Abrams, pp. 1-18; CGC, Report for 1931, p. 9; Beveridge, *London School*, p. 86.

154. CGC, Report for 1931, p. 5; CGC, *Report for 1937*, pp. 7-9; CGC, *Report for 1938*, pp. 11, 15; Feversham Committee, *Voluntary*, p. 77.

155. Gesell, pp. 194-95; M. Horn, "Moral Message," p. 26; idem, *Before It's Too Late*, pp. 138-39, 176.

156. *Report of the Proceedings of the Conference on Mental Health* (1930), p. 6; London Child Guidance Clinic, *Report for... 1929 to ... 1931*, pp. 7-8, 11-12, 20-24; Moodie, *Address*, n.p.

157. Deborah Thom makes a similar point. See her "Wishes, Anxieties," pp. 200-201, 208-9.

158. *Magistrate*, Apr.–May 1930, p. 391; Hardcastle, pp. 536-37.

159. Establishment, p. 4; *London Child Guidance Clinic, Report for... 1929 to ... 1931*, pp. 8-9, 20; *B.M.J.*, June 3, 1939, p. 1131. Apart from cases where, for example, the provision of eyeglasses brought immediate classroom improvement, the criteria for judging treatment successful (i.e., achieving full or partial "adjustment") were seldom examined. A widely cited American study admitted that it had "dodge[d]" this issue "by saying that a successfully adjusted case is one that the clinic staff says is successfully adjusted!" See Witmer, p. 432.

160. *Report, Inter-Clinic Conference*, p. 7.

161. W. P. Brown, pp. 125-26.

162. Moodie, *Doctor*, pp. 16-18; idem, *Child Guidance by Team Work*, pp. 1, 4, 6; idem, *Enuresis*, pp. 1-2. Psychiatric jargon was all the more suspect due to its loose use among "ignorant amateurs [and] ... pure charlatans." Home Office, *Fifth Report... Children's Branch*, pp. 17-18.

163. CGC, *Report for 1936*, pp. 7-8.

164. Ertz, p. 201; *Establishment*, p. 3; *Young Offenders and the Courts*, p. 3.

165. P.R.O., HO45/18118/697558, extract from Report of Chief Constable of Exeter, Dec. 1935; Craig, pp. 300, 303-5.

166. *Medical Officer*, May 19, 1934, p. 197; Cadbury, p. 133.

167. *Lancet*, Feb. 10, 1940, p. 287; Mullins, *Crime*, p. 11; Hendrick, *Child Welfare*, p. 173. On the rapid expansion of postwar child psychiatric services, see Gath et al., pp. 1-2.

168. Riley, pp. 97-101.

169. Rees, p. 28; Burbury et al., pp. 5-6.

170. Kimmins, pp. 37-38; *The Times*, Dec. 13, 1934. It was A. S. Neill who put the case most starkly. "There is never a problem child," Neill insisted, "there is only a problem parent." Thus, a "great many" cases of maladjusted children were traceable to "illmatched" parents. Neill, pp. 9, 21, 23.

171. Mullins, *Marriage*, pp. 72-75; *Advances in Understanding*, pp. 8-9.

172. J. Lewis, "Public Institution," pp. 234–38; Mace, "Family Life," p. 180.

173. Keeling, pp. 62–63; Sanctuary, p. 13; Mace, *Marriage Counselling*, p. 8; *The Times*, Nov. 21, 1938.

174. Wallis and Booker, pp. 3–4; J. Lewis, "Public Institution," pp. 243–44; Sanctuary, p. 14; Mace, *Does Sex*, p. 128; *B.M.J.*, May 17, 1947, p. 697.

175. Mace, *Marriage Counselling*, pp. 24, 50–51.

Chapter 4

1. Wiener, "March," pp. 87–88. See also idem, *Reconstructing the Criminal*, pp. 7–10; Gatrell, "Crime"; and McGowen. The continuing influence of local values on criminal justice administration receives attention from Conley.

2. Davis, "Poor Man's," pp. 309, 313.

3. John Gillis is surely right to characterize marriage as a "social drama in which not just the couple but several parties play crucial roles." Gillis has tried with considerable success to balance the standard conception of marriage "in legal, institutional terms" with a fresh focus on the dynamic (and inherently political) interactions among the couple and their family, friends, and neighbors. See Gillis, *For Better*, pp. 5–6, 8. Yet certain "legal" and "institutional" dimensions of English marriage are equally well suited to analysis as social drama.

4. Giles, *Magistrates' Courts*, p. 8.

5. For the summary powers of early modern magistrates, see Landau; and for magistrates' roles in misdemeanor prosecutions, see Shoemaker.

6. By 1860, 73 percent of all larcenies (without violence) were being tried summarily; by 1900, this figure would rise to 88 percent. See Gatrell, "Decline," pp. 274, 301–2.

7. Giles, *Magistrates' Courts*, p. 8; Solicitor, p. 7. Over grave felonies such as murder, consummated rape, and arson, the police court never gained jurisdiction. The job of the magistrate in such cases was to determine whether enough evidence of guilt existed to send the accused on to Quarter Sessions or Assizes for trial by jury. As regards training, the 1949 Justices of the Peace Act established "schemes for instructing" magistrates but provided nothing like systematic legal education. As late as 1967 it was merely a "status symbol" for lay magistrates to tour corrective institutions in rural Suffolk. See the interview with Mrs. Annersley, in Blythe, pp. 268–69.

8. Tobias, pp. 137–38; Manchester, pp. 77–78. Not all large towns chose to appoint stipendiaries, nor were stipendiaries appointed only in the largest urban centers. As of 1935, Sheffield, Newcastle, Bristol, and Nottingham relied upon lay magistrates, for example, whereas Grimsby and Pontypridd employed stipendiaries. See Mullins, "Justices," pp. 224–25; and Ensor, *Courts*, p. 18.

9. *Daily News*, Feb. 11, 1873.

10. *Saturday Review*, 35 (Feb. 15, 1873): 213–14; *Punch*, 64 (Mar. 15, 1873): 105. The Chief Metropolitan Magistrate, traditionally attached to Bow

Street Police Court, received a higher salary. Theoretically, the Chief Magistrate served as a conduit through whom information passed between the metropolitan bench and the Home Office. *Magistrate*, p. 8.

11. Police court melodrama was among the most popular elements of Victorian sensationalism. On the latter subject, see Boyle; W. Hughes; and Walkowitz, *City*, pp. 85–102. "I have seen nothing in the theatres so dramatic," remarked the editor Robert Blatchford about his first visit to a police court in Manchester: "I shall go again." Blatchford, pp. 156.

12. T. Holmes, *Pictures*, pp. 32, 35. Similarly, see Potter, p. 24; and *Sanitary Record*, Oct. 26, 1877, p. 270.

13. [F. Longman] *Fifteen Years*, pp. 2–3; *Lancet*, Feb. 11, 1905, p. 378; Bygott, 2: 513–17; Nevinson, p. 93.

14. *Report of the Committee on the Metropolitan Police Courts and Juvenile Courts*, p. 4; *Church of England Temperance Chronicle*, Oct. 18, 1884, p. 291.

15. Dark, pp. 15–16.

16. *South Western Star*, Mar. 8, 1907.

17. Ibid., May 5, 1911.

18. Plowden, p. 175; Galsworthy, *Silver Box* [first performed in 1906], act 3.

19. *The Times*, Aug. 24, 1844.

20. P. Fitzgerald, 1: 214–15.

21. *Morning Advertiser*, Feb. 12, 1873; Biron, pp. 265–66. Unlike the general public, members of the press could be present during the "applications" phase of police court business. Magistrates were therefore under constant scrutiny.

22. M. Williams, *Later Leaves*, pp. 395–97; *Law Times*, 164 (Oct. 1, 1927): 225; Cairns, *Loom*, pp. 272–74.

23. Foucault, pp. 296–98. Cf. Walkowitz, Jehlen, and Chevigny, pp. 28–29.

24. Davis, "Prosecutions," pp. 413–14; idem, "Poor Man's," pp. 330–31; Ignatieff, pp. 90–91.

25. Although the derivation of this slang term for a magistrate remains uncertain, "beak" was in common use by the middle of the nineteenth century. *Oxford English Dictionary*, 2nd ed., s.v. "beak"; Milton, pp. 8–9.

26. *The Times*, Nov. 17, 1860; Pinero, *Magistrate* [first performed in 1885], act 1.

27. Waddy, pp. 162–63; M. Williams, *Later Leaves*, pp. 242–43; idem, *Round London*, pp. 46–47.

28. Chapman, *From the Bench*, pp. 30–31.

29. P.R.O., MEPO 2/1426, Cooper to Fordham, Dec. 20, 1910; Davis, "Poor Man's," pp. 328–29.

30. Plowden, p. 217; Waddy, pp. 56–58.

31. Storch, "Police Control," pp. 53–56; *South Western Star*, Apr. 18, 1891.

32. *Manchester Guardian*, Oct. 24, 1891.

33. Timewell, pp. 4–8.

34. Gamon, *London Police*, pp. vii–viii.

35. Davis, "Poor Man's," pp. 333–34.

36. Gamon, *London Police*, p. viii.

37. Criminal Statistics, England and Wales, 1934, P.P., 1935–36, XXV: xv. Even contemporaries who should have known better sometimes misunderstood both the variety and the volume of police court business. In 1931, a High Court judge was startled to learn that a serious larceny case had been tried summarily in "a place where small motoring offences and such things were dealt with." *The Times*, Oct. 22, 1931.

38. Mullins, "Justices," pp. 223–24.

39. Rowntree and Carrier, pp. 189–90.

40. The total number of judicial separations sought each year is best approximated by combining the applications for maintenance orders and the applications for separation orders without maintenance. Working-class wives, who typically accounted for 94–97 percent of the applicants, rarely asked for maintenance orders that did not include some provision for non-cohabitation. In several years the official statistics do not differentiate between separation orders and maintenance orders.

41. 20 & 21 Vict., c. 85.

42. These equivalencies are rough. Charles Tibbits reckoned that the average undefended divorce case in 1907 cost £50, and the average defended case about £121. Tibbits, p. 58. A. L. Bowley gave twenty-six shillings as the average weekly wage for a fully employed British male in 1911. Bowley, p. 74. Had Bowley excluded Scottish and Irish males from his figures, the resulting average weekly wage would have been somewhat higher. Similar caveats must surround his estimate that the average weekly wage for British women in 1911 (including domestic servants and shop assistants) was just under fourteen shillings.

43. Rowntree and Carrier, p. 222. See also Savage, "Operations," pp. 106–7; idem, "Marital Conflict," pp. 5–6; and Hammerton, *Cruelty*, pp. 104–5. "Poor Man's Lawyers," barristers and solicitors at first associated with certain East London settlement houses, began their volunteer legal advice work in the mid-1890's. See *Law Journal*, 28 (Dec. 30, 1893): 898; *Annual Report of Mansfield House* (1896), pp. 38–39; and Meacham, *Toynbee Hall*, pp. 79–80.

44. [Gladstone] "Bill," p. 286; L. Stone, *Road*, pp. 385–86.

45. Gillis, *For Better*, pp. 237–42.

46. See Behlmer, "Deadly Motherhood"; and Higgenbotham, "Sin."

47. Shanley, p. 161. For a discussion of how newspapers helped propagate a "middle-class myth of rape," see Clark, *Women's Silence*, pp. 16–18. On domestic violence generally during the Victorian period, see Tomes.

48. Justice Archibald to the Home Secretary, *Reports . . . on the State of the Law Relating to Brutal Assaults*, P.P., 1875, LXI: 9.

49. E. Cox, pp. 87–88; Pulling, pp. 345–46; Hammerton, *Cruelty*, pp. 34–35.

50. Cobbe, *Life*, 2: 534–37; idem, "Wife-Torture," pp. 80, 82. Miss Cobbe was not the first to propose judicial separation as a shield for abused wives.

Forty years earlier Richard Mence had argued for allowing magistrates to grant "provisional separations" in such cases. Mence, pp. 59–61.

51. 41 Vict., c. 19. See Parliamentary Debates, 3rd ser., 239 (Mar. 29, 1878): 191–92; Manchester, p. 123.

52. M. Crawford, pp. 298–99. On the nineteenth-century feminist analysis of wife-beating, see Doggett, pp. 26–33.

53. *Women's Suffrage Journal*, 11 (July 1880): 123.

54. *Manchester Guardian*, Oct. 5, 1881. Cf. a strikingly similar judicial response to a wife-beating "charivari" in late-Victorian Yorkshire: Hammerton, *Cruelty*, p. 15.

55. Bauer and Ritt, p. 199. More broadly, Iris Minor has argued that the *ad hoc* nature of matrimonial law reform in the late-Victorian and Edwardian years probably increased the vulnerability of working-class wives. Minor, pp. 103–24.

56. 49 & 50 Vict., c. 52.

57. 58 & 59 Vict., c. 39.

58. Parliamentary Debates, 4th ser., 34 (May 22, 1895): 62.

59. Tibbits, p. 66; M'Ilquham, p. 440.

60. 2 Ed. 7, c. 28. On the social dangers of section 5, see T. Holmes, "New Licensing Bill."

61. Lushington and Lushington, pp. vi–vii.

62. Elmy, *Woman* [1896], p. 15. See also British Library, Elmy Papers: Add. MS. 47451, Elmy to M'Ilquham, Aug. 15, 1897. On Elmy's place in the late-Victorian feminist "network," see P. Levine, pp. 69–70.

63. C.H.D., p. 71.

64. Although Jacques Donzelot cites mainly French evidence, his frame of reference is far wider, suggesting indeed that all "advanced liberal" societies have suffered from the invasive regulation of domestic life. See Donzelot, p. 228. As the evidence analyzed here will show, however, the "policing" of working-class marriage in the world's most "advanced liberal" society was far from uniform and often ineffective.

65. Corder, p. 10.

66. *Post Office London Directory for 1899*, 2: 2519.

67. Besant, *South London*, pp. 319–20.

68. P.R.O., HO45/10566/173881, Troop's minute of Oct. 22, 1909; Besant, *London South of the Thames*, pp. 163–65, 246; Ezard, p. 12.

69. S. Myers, p. 112.

70. *New Survey*, 6: 439–42, 447–50; ibid., 1: 357; W. Kent, pp. 36, 696.

71. Although the *South Western Star* began publication in 1877, the British Library holds no issue before 1889.

72. Since surviving police court records are rare, and when extant amount to terse entries on printed ledgers, the historian is left with local newspaper reports. Although the *Star*'s police court reportage clearly did emphasize the sensational or humorous elements in domestic disputes, there is no evidence that these accounts consistently suppressed relevant information.

73. T. Holmes, *Pictures*, pp. 53–54.

74. *South Western Star* [hereafter *SWS*], June 28, 1901. For a similar case of husband-beating, see ibid., Jan. 5, 1889.

75. Ibid., Sept. 11, 1908.

76. Ibid., Mar. 25, 1904.

77. See Fishman, p. 203. Cf. R. Roberts, p. 29.

78. *Justice of the Peace and Local Government Review Annual, 1928*, p. 12.

79. *SWS*, Mar. 25, 1904; ibid., May 6, 1893; ibid., July 25, 1913; Waddy, pp. 136–37.

80. 20 & 21 Vict., c. 85, s. 21. This provision fell into disuse after the 1870 Married Women's Property Act became law. Mullins, *Wife*, p. 23. See also Holcombe, "Victorian Wives."

81. Giles, *Magistrates' Courts*, p. 192.

82. *SWS*, July 31, 1903.

83. Ibid., May 22, 1903.

84. Ibid., Apr. 1, 1898.

85. Cecil Chapman, another metropolitan magistrate, devised a way to outwit husbands who nominally "maintained" their wives while bringing other women home to bed. Chapman advised victims of this cynical strategy to leave their domiciles and summons their husbands for "persistent cruelty." At the subsequent trial Chapman would rule that such gross humiliation of a wife did in fact constitute "persistent cruelty," even though prevailing legal standards were much less elastic. Chapman, *Poor Man's*, pp. 62–63; MacQueen, pp. 224–25. For an excellent analysis of "cruelty" in Divorce Court decisions, see Hammerton, "Victorian Marriage."

86. *The Times*, July 19, 1909. Adultery did not become a ground for judicial separation in courts of summary jurisdiction until 1937.

87. Mrs. Jackson's predicament drew wide press coverage. See *The Times*, Mar. 10, 11, 12, 13, 17, and 20, 1891; and Linton, "Judicial Shock." For a discussion of the legal significance of *R. v. Jackson*, see Doggett, pp. 1–4, 142–48.

88. *SWS*, Sept. 8, 1891. As another London magistrate described this legal savvy, "[working-class] wives, under various pretexts, invite the Courts to cooperate with them in bringing the husband to a proper frame of mind." Cairns, *Drab Street*, p. 124.

89. On Weldon as a "lunacy lawyer in petticoats," see Walkowitz, *City*, pp. 183–87.

90. Greenwood, pp. 16–17; Plowden, pp. 249–51; T. Holmes, *Pictures*, p. 75. Cf. Magistrate, p. 37; and Sims, *How the Poor*, pp. 53–54.

91. R.C. on Divorce and Matrimonial Causes, P.P., 1912–13, LXVIII (Lords), QQ. 6,953, 7,573, 2,182.

92. A. Martin, "Mother," p. 1075.

93. Gillis, *For Better*, p. 259; J. Lewis, *Women*, p. 10; E. Ross, "'Fierce Questions,'" p. 593.

94. *SWS*, Mar. 9, 1889. To point out that working-class wives expected a greater degree of violence from husbands than would be tolerated today is not to suggest that these women were strangers to deep emotional pain.

95. *SWS*, May 15, 1914; ibid., June 18, 1915.

96. E. Ross, "'Fierce Questions,'" p. 592; *SWS*, Oct. 17, 1913.

97. R.C. on Divorce, P.P., 1912–13, LXIX (Lords), QQ. 18,999, 19,021. At the same time that he was taking this liberal line on divorce, Plowden was regretting that he could not punish women's suffrage activists more severely for staging a bell-ringing protest. M. Nevinson, p. 198. Viewed theoretically, Plowden's schizophrenia over women's rights becomes intelligible in terms suggested by Gayatri Spivak: his "liberalism" was confined to an arena wherein bourgeoise men could save poor women from poor men. See Spivak, pp. 92–93.

98. Chapman, *Marriage*, pp. 75, 141–42.

99. The Chairman of the Durham County Police Court, for example, was irate when a miner's wife announced that she wanted to withdraw her charge of aggravated assault: "You make use of this court just to threaten your husband. That's the case with you women. You get into a tantrum with your husbands, and then you come here. Well, it's your own look out." *Newcastle Weekly Chronicle*, Mar. 22, 1890.

100. R.C. on Divorce, P.P., 1912–13, LXIX (Lords), Q. 12,950.

101. See, for example, *SWS*, Oct. 31, 1913; and ibid., June 6, 1913.

102. National statistics for the years 1907–9. R.C. on Divorce, P.P., 1912–13, LXIX (Lords), Q. 23,435.

103. *SWS*, Apr. 6, 1900.

104. 4 & 5 Geo. 5, c. 58, s. 4.

105. Report of the Departmental Committee on Imprisonment By Courts of Summary Jurisdiction in Default of Payment of Fines and Other Sums of Money, P.P., 1933–34, II: 12–13, 42–43, 47; Ayers and Lambertz, p. 210. On the "silting up" of local prisons with maintenance defaulters, see McGregor, Blom-Cooper, and Gibson, pp. 22–23.

106. Haynes, "Divorce Law" [1909], p. 727.

107. R.C. on Divorce, P.P., 1912–13, LXVII (Lords): 3.

108. "Marriage, Divorce," pp. 18–19. The question of working-class demand for divorce was addressed most directly in the testimony of two very different women's organizations. Among the 25,897 members of the socialist Women's Co-operative Guild, most of whom were wives of "respectable artisans," there existed an "overwhelming" desire for drastic reform of the divorce laws. In stark contrast, the conservative Mothers' Union submitted to the Commission an anti-divorce law reform petition from 21,389 working-class (and mostly Anglican) wives. R.C. on Divorce, P.P., 1912–13, LXVII (Lords): 47–48; and ibid., LXX (Lords), QQ. 36,964–65; 36,976–78. Cf. Reynolds, "Divorce," p. 488.

109. Parliamentary Debates, 5th ser. (Lords), 2 (July 14, 1909): 488–91.

110. R.C. on Divorce, P.P., 1912–13, LIX (Lords), QQ. 17,972–74; ibid., LXVII (Lords): 178–79.

111. Potter, pp. 7–10, 57.

112. McWilliams, "Mission," pp. 131–33, 140–42.

113. P. Young, p. 57.

114. LeMesurier, *Handbook*, pp. 22–23. Similarly, the 1887 Probation of

First Offenders Act intensified pressure on the magistrates to use missionary supervision of offenders released on recognizance.

115. On strategies for reforming female alcoholics, see Zedner, pp. 219–63.

116. Burdett-Coutts, p. 389; Hutchinson, pp. 25–28; D'Aeth, p. 135.

117. Potter, p. 6; Lambeth Palace Library, MS. 2031: mins. of the CETS Council, Apr. 29, 1895. By 1910 there were sixteen male and seven female CETS missionaries assigned to the London police courts. Report of the Departmental Committee on the Probation of Offenders Act, 1907, P.P., 1910, XLV, QQ. 221–23, 282.

118. Women's Home Mission Association, *Report for 1910*, p. 7; Oxford Police Court and Prison Gate Mission, *Fourth Annual Report* (1910), p. 22; Hawkins, p. 253. Cf. Lambeth Palace Library, #H5013 T3: Dioceses of Canterbury and Rochester, *Annual Report of the . . . Police Court Mission for the Year 1932*, p. 21.

119. Lloyd, p. 198. For an institutional study of the probation service, see Bochel.

120. Plowden, pp. 235–37; Biron, p. 249; Cancellor, pp. 89–90; Waddy, pp. 78–79; Lieck, *Bow Street*, pp. 86–87; C. Morley, pp. 242–44.

121. Pettifer, *Court Resumes*, pp. 55–58.

122. G. Rose, *Struggle*, pp. 68–70; T. Holmes, *Pictures*, pp. 11–15, 42, 76–84; idem, *Known*, pp. 101–7. Equally self-righteous accounts of police court service appear in R. Holmes, *Them*; idem, *My Police Court*; and Orchard.

123. Gamon, *London Police*, p. 161.

124. *SWS*, Mar. 5, 1897.

125. Ibid., May 1, 1914; ibid., Oct. 8, 1909.

126. P.R.O., HO45/22774/272425, H.O. notes for Feb. 1, 1918.

127. Cancellor, p. 123; *Answers: A Weekly Journal of Instruction*, Dec. 14, 1918, p. 52.

128. Home Office, *Second Report of the Work of the Children's Branch* (1924), p. 18.

129. Waddy, p. 79; R.C. on Divorce, P.P., 1912–13, LXVII (Lords): 178–79; Cancellor, pp. 95–99. Cf. *Journal of the Divorce Law Reform Union*, Apr. 1924, p. 11.

130. See especially the cases of Mmes. Smith, Clark, and Maile: *SWS*, Oct. 3, 1917; ibid., Oct. 17, 1917; ibid., July 15, 1921; ibid., Feb. 11, 1921. Bankes's insensitivity to the lot of working-class wives may also have stemmed from overconfidence in the transfiguring influence of female probation officers, whom he once described as "walking in the footsteps of Christ." Quoted in R. Walton, p. 125.

131. Lambertz, p. 31.

132. *SWS*, June 15, 1917.

133. Ibid., Mar. 1, 1918.

134. Ibid., Feb. 1, 1918; ibid., Oct. 21, 1921.

135. Civil Judicial Statistics for 1913, P.P., 1914–16, XIX (Lords): 23; Civil Judicial Statistics for 1919, P.P., 1921, XLI: 19.

136. Gibson, p. 92; Winter, pp. 263–64; R. Phillips, pp. 519–22; L. Stone, *Road*, p. 394. As Stone points out, although a larger proportion of English husbands may have committed wartime adultery overseas, their deeds were more easily concealed.

137. Stetson, pp. 106–12.

138. MacKinnon, pp. 112–13; A. Holmes, pp. 223–29.

139. Thomas Bucknill, in *The Times*, Mar. 2, 1935.

140. *Law Journal*, 65 (May 12, 1928): 391.

141. Much of the evidence for this assertion must be inferential. Occasionally, however, the strategy was explicit. As G. E. Franey, a probation officer attached to the Greenwich Police Court, explained to a Home Office committee in 1934, "At the end of 1919 the late Mr. W. H. Disney sent for me to say, that in view of the largely increased applications for Separations, one of the after-results of the Great War, it was his wish, before any application for process was made, I should interview the parties, talk over the difficulties, and try and effect a reconciliation." Home Office Library: testimony before the Summary Courts (Social Services) Committee, 1934–35, I, written evidence, B2.

142. *Justice of the Peace*, 88 (Jan. 26, 1924): 68–69; Lieck and Morrison, pp. 23–25, 29–33.

143. Reiss, pp. 86–87; Parliamentary Debates, 5th ser. (Lords), 61 (May 26, 1925): 525–27; Mullins, *Wife*, pp. 26–27.

144. Haynes, *Lycurgus*, pp. 92, 47–50. Since on a *per capita* basis the U.S. was producing roughly twenty times as many divorces as England and Wales during the mid-1920's, the proposed "Americanization" of legal procedure in this area made many middle-class people in the old country understandably nervous.

145. R.C. on Divorce, P.P., 1912–13, LXVII (Lords): 68–69; McGregor, *Social History*, pp. 50–51.

146. Leeson, *Probation*, pp. 36–37; Spadoni, p. 15; Gemmill, pp. 115–16; Pleck, pp. 136–37.

147. P.R.O., HO45/15719/520977, Miss Bolton [Administrator of the Given-Wilson Institute, Plaistow] to the Home Secretary, Apr. 15, 1919.

148. *Reconciled*, pp. 5–6, 9.

149. Mowrer and Mowrer, p. 10; Haynes, *Lycurgus*, pp. 61–68.

150. *Evening News*, May 11, 1928; ibid., May 14, 1928; *Law Journal*, 65 (May 12, 1928): 391.

151. Lasch, pp. 42–43.

152. *Preparation*, pp. 87, 93–94; *Advances*, pp. 8–9.

153. Lambeth Palace Library, MS. 2060: mins. of the CETS Police Court Missionaries' Guild, Oct. 17, 1929; *Probation*, Jan. 1935, pp. 349–50; Ellison, pp. 100–111.

154. *Evening News*, Apr. 21, 1934.

155. Parliamentary Debates, 5th ser. (Lords), 92 (May 15, 1934): 365; *Evening News*, Apr. 21, 1934; "Police Courts," p. 567.

156. See, for example, *The Times*, May 15, 1934; and "Marriage in the Police Court," p. 587.

157. Parliamentary Debates, 5th ser. (Lords), 92 (May 15, 1934): 366–72, 378, 380–85.

158. P.R.O., HO45/15719/520977, memo by Maxwell, ca. May 2, 1934; ibid., Schuster to Dawson, Apr. 19, 1934.

159. *The Times*, July 26, 1934. Lord Merrivale's Matrimonial Causes (Amended Procedure) Bill, introduced on Oct. 30, 1934, was designed primarily to remind the government that pressure for regularizing police court matrimonial work had not diminished. Parliamentary Debates, 5th ser. (Lords), 94 (Oct. 30, 1934): 1–2; ibid., 94 (Nov. 7, 1934): 173–76, 186.

160. For an analysis of Clarke Hall on the juvenile court bench, see Chapter 5.

161. Modern historical scholarship has completely overlooked Mullins as a legal reformer and judicial innovator. He now receives only casual mention, as, for example, in J. Lewis, *Women*, p. 47; and V. Bailey, *Delinquency*, p. 157.

162. Mullins, *One Man's*, pp. 13, 52–53, 100, 103; idem, *Fifteen Years'*, pp. 13–20.

163. Mullins, *One Man's*, pp. 104–8; idem, *Marriage*, pp. 77–78; *Magistrate*, July–Aug. 1933, pp. 707–8; Mullins, "Christianity," pp. 152–53. See also Barry, Mullins, and White. As if Mullins's open advocacy of birth control were not controversial enough, he also wrote at least one article on the psychic prowess of Fräulein Oesterreicher, a German "intuitive graphologist." See Mullins, "Graphologin."

164. Mullins, *Marriage*, p. 196; idem, *One Man's*, p. 110.

165. Ibid., pp. 110–12; P.R.O., HO45/15719/520977, Powell to Robinson, May 1, 1934.

166. *SWS*, Nov. 2, 1934; ibid., June 16, 1933; ibid., June 23, 1933. By early 1939, Mullins had persuaded the Home Office to assign his court two additional missionaries. *SWS*, Mar. 10, 1939.

167. Ibid., Nov. 9, 1934.

168. Home Office Library: testimony before the Summary Courts (Social Services) Committee, 1934–35, I, E.V. 9, p. 2.

169. Mullins, *Wife*, pp. 50–53; idem, *One Man's*, p. 113; *SWS*, Nov. 23, 1934.

170. Home Office Library: testimony before the Summary Courts (Social Services) Committee, 1934–35, I, E.V. 10, n.p.

171. Mullins, *Wife*, pp. 16–17.

172. *SWS*, May 17, 1935. Mullins compiled his panel of medical psychologists with help from the British Social Hygiene Council. On the BSHC's work with the "physiology of marriage," see Collier, p. 9.

173. Mullins, *Wife*, pp. 41–42, 116–19, 15–16.

174. *SWS*, July 24, 1936.

175. Report of the Departmental Committee on the Social Services in Courts of Summary Jurisdiction, P.P., 1935–36, VIII: 11.

176. *SWS*, Feb. 22, 1935; ibid., Jan. 3, 1936.

177. *SWS*, Feb. 7, 1936; ibid., Nov. 13, 1936; Mullins, *Fifteen Years'*, pp. 148–49. See also *Daily Mirror*, July 7, 1937.

178. Report of the Departmental Committee on Sterilisation, P.P., 1933–34, XV: 21; Mowrer, passim. Mullins himself was convinced that juvenile crime usually stemmed from what Cyril Burt called "defective family relationships." In addition to Burt's *The Young Offender* (1925), two studies by American criminologists, Sheldon and Eleanor Glueck's *One Thousand Juvenile Delinquents* (1934), and Albert Morris's *Criminology* (1935), did much to shape Mullins's views on the causal connection between divorce and delinquency. See Mullins, *Wife*, pp. 23–24.

179. Maxwell, *Treatment*, pp. 11–12.

180. *The Times*, July 19, 1939; P.R.O., HO45/21034/590660, Maxwell to Mullins, Aug. 4, 1939.

181. P.R.O., HO45/21034/590660, memo of Mar. 10, 1936; Mullins, *One Man's*, p. 126. Nor would Neville Chamberlain's Tory Government listen to the Labour MP who wished to brand Mullins a judicial misfit for declaring that two untrustworthy witnesses should be placed in a "concentration camp" and forced to study history for five years. Parliamentary Debates, 5th ser., 341 (Nov. 17, 1938): 1050–51; *SWS*, Nov. 4, 1938.

182. *SWS*, July 16, 1937.

183. *Liverpool Post*, Oct. 5, 1937; *Yorkshire Observer*, Oct. 5, 1937.

184. *SWS*, Aug. 9, 1935.

185. Report of the Departmental Committee on the Social Services in Courts of Summary Jurisdiction, P.P., 1935–36, VIII: 12; *Probation*, Oct. 1936, p. 83.

186. Geeson, pp. 44–46.

187. Home Office Library: testimony before the Summary Courts (Social Services) Committee, 1934–35, I, E.V. 23(a), p. 12; ibid., E.V. 36, p. 2.

188. Latey and Rees, p. 416.

189. The Summary Procedures (Domestic Proceedings) Act, 1937: 1 Edw. 8 and 1 Geo. 6, c. 58. This legislation took effect on Oct. 1, 1937.

190. P.R.O., HO45/17152/695967, Harris to Mullins, Jan. 14, 1937; ibid., Mullins to Harris, Jan. 17, 1937.

191. Parliamentary Debates, 5th ser., 319 (Feb. 5, 1937): 1977–78, 1948, 1953.

192. R. Phillips, pp. 529–30; L. Stone, *Road*, p. 401; Stetson, pp. 115–17; F. Acland, p. 226.

193. Cole, p. 187.

194. *The Times*, Apr. 23, 1934; ibid., July 8, 1937; ibid., Sept. 9, 1937. Mullins and Herbert, one-time allies in the cause of divorce law reform, came to rhetorical blows over the former's public criticism of the "Marriage Bill." See Herbert, *Ayes*, pp. 57–63; and *The Times*, Sept. 8, 1937.

195. [Mullins] "Divorce *via* Magistrates' Courts," pp. 230–31.

196. *SWS*, Oct. 15, 1937.

197. By the late 1930's, the practice of lawyers giving free legal advice to working-class people had spread far beyond the East End university settlements where it had begun. In London, a voluntary body called the Bentham Committee gave some organizational coherence to work that had long lacked any uni-

formity. Beyond offering counsel, a "Poor Man's Lawyer" generally would do no more than draft letters for his clients. To gain representation in court, a laborer had to apply to one of the ninety "Poor Persons' Committees" operating in England and Wales under the auspices of various professional legal societies. "Poor Persons' " representation was limited to actions taken in the High Court of Justice, mostly undefended divorce cases. On the eve of World War Two there existed no scheme for cheap legal representation in police courts. Law Society, *Annual Report, 1937*, pp. 132, 142, 152; Jackson, pp. 252–53, 256–57; Egerton, p. 22.

198. R. Roberts, pp. 41–44, 77–78; Meacham, *Life Apart*, pp. 62–66, 199; G. S. Jones, "Working-Class Culture," pp. 226–27, 234. The "language of fatalism," as Ellen Ross has remarked about London slum mothers, may have been "the safest posture for the[se] women to adopt with middle-class professionals." E. Ross, *Love*, pp. 98, 167.

199. See, for example, the case of Ethel Flintham: *SWS*, Jan. 14, 1938.

200. Jackson, p. 152.

201. Final Report of the Committee on Procedure in Matrimonial Causes, P.P., 1946–47, XIII: 5–6, 13–14; Dawtry, p. 184.

202. Mullins, "Conciliation," p. 376; idem, "Divorce." Cf. *Magistrate*, July–Aug. 1938, p. 81; and *Justice of the Peace*, 105 (July 12, 1941): 386.

203. Report of the Departmental Committee on Grants for the Development of Marriage Guidance, P.P., 1948–49, XVII: 14–15; *The Times*, Nov. 21, 1938; Sanctuary, pp. 13–14.

204. Cohn, "Reconciliation," p. 409; R.C. on Marriage and Divorce, P.P., 1955–56, XXIII: 97.

205. C. Smart, pp. 71–72, 75–76; McGregor, *Social History*, pp. 50–52. See also Bottomley, "What Is Happening "; and Eekelaar, pp. 199–201.

206. Szwed, pp. 276–77; Bottomley, "Resolving," pp. 296–97, 300.

Chapter 5

1. By part 5, section 3, of the 1908 Children Act (8 Edw. 7, c. 67).

2. Pinchbeck and Hewitt, 2: 493; Heywood, p. 108; Carlebach, pp. 82–83.

3. Donzelot, p. 104.

4. Lasch, p. 15. On the similarities between Lasch and Donzelot with respect to the meaning of juvenile courts, see J. Scott, pp. 510–11.

5. Garland, *Punishment*, pp. 222–23; Foucault, p. 82.

6. Radzinowicz and Hood.

7. Bailey, *Delinquency*.

8. See Martin Wiener's perceptive review of Radzinowicz and Hood, "The March."

9. Ignatieff, p. 95.

10. Foucault, passim.

11. Garland, *Punishment*, p. 17.

12. Wiener, *Reconstructing the Criminal*, pp. 54–55. My discussion in this paragraph owes much to Wiener's analysis.

13. Ibid., p. 43.

14. Wiener offers few clues about why Malthusian images so effectively infiltrated "early Victorian social description, both fictional and factual." *Reconstructing the Criminal*, p. 29. Perhaps the psychic ground had been cleared by earlier, primarily evangelical, remonstrations over the power of human depravity?

15. On infanticide, see Chapter 6. On garrotting, see Davis, "London Garrotting." Stanley Cohen offers a sociological model of this process in his *Folk Devils and Moral Panics*, especially chap. 1.

16. Springhall, p. 164.

17. S.C. on Criminal and Destitute Juveniles, P.P., 1852, VII, Q. 818; May, "Innocence," p. 7. For similar assessments, see Boss, pp. 25, 28; G. Rose, *Schools*, pp. 3–7; and Manton, pp. 249–50. This meliorist line of interpretation is attacked in Humphries, pp. 238–39.

18. Dickens, *Oliver Twist*, chap. 11.

19. [S. Turner] "Juvenile Delinquency," p. 406; S.C. on Criminal and Destitute Children, P.P., 1852–53, XXIII, Q. 1,516.

20. Worsley, p. 140; S.C. on Criminal and Destitute Juveniles, P.P., 1852, VII, QQ. 1,557, 2,091.

21. See, for example, *Report of the Committee for Investigating the Causes of the Alarming Increase of Juvenile Delinquency in the Metropolis* (1816), quoted in Carr-Saunders, Mannheim, and Rhodes, p. 2.

22. S.C. on Criminal and Destitute Juveniles, P.P., 1852, VII, Q. 386. Cf. the urban crisis of the 1880's: G. S. Jones, *Outcast London*.

23. May, "Innocence," pp. 21–22.

24. The point here is *not* to suggest that overall levels of criminal activity failed to decline in England during the second half of the nineteenth century. Crimes involving major theft and serious violence did in fact grow less common during the late-Victorian period. See Gatrell, "Decline." Nor is there much doubt that reformatories and industrial schools served to keep children out of jail. Actually, the number of youths under seventeen committed to prison (as their only form of punishment) fell from 10 percent of all persons so treated in 1857 to 4 percent by 1877. By 1900, the flow of young people to jail had become "a mere trickle." Radzinowicz and Hood, pp. 624, 627. The point is, rather, that reformatories and industrial schools achieved disappointingly mixed results.

25. Reformatories expanded rapidly to a maximum of fifty-four institutions in 1878, thereafter steadily declining in number to thirty-nine in 1900. Their peak inmate population was about 4,000. Industrial schools gained favor more slowly. As of 1859, just eighteen had received government certification, but by 1900 there were 109 industrial schools in England and Wales housing about 28,000 boys and girls. Carlebach, pp. 66–67; Radzinowicz and Hood, pp. 180–81; Forty-Fourth Report of the Inspector of Reformatory and Industrial Schools, Part II, P.P., 1902, XLVII: 9–10.

26. P.R.O., HO45/9594/93897H, "Reformatories and Industrial Schools, and Juvenile Offenders," memo by Lushington, Oct. 5, 1880.

27. M. Carpenter, *Reformatory Schools*, pp. 348–49; idem, *Juvenile Delinquents*, pp. 119, 132–33, 156–57.

28. The Industrial Schools Act of 1861 (24 & 25 Vict., c. 113) allowed parents to charge their children under age fourteen with being "beyond control." If the charge proved true, and so long as parents pledged to pay the full costs, their children could be committed to a state-certified industrial school for a period of between two and five years. In practice, magistrates almost never held parents fully responsible for industrial school expenses.

29. T. Holmes, "Youthful Offenders," pp. 846–47. See also Greenwood, *Prisoner*, pp. 92–95; and Waddy, p. 115.

30. Most often, it appears, maintenance orders on parents were made *after* the committal of the child. Thus it often became the policeman's task to collect payments. P.R.O, HO45/10992/127059, "Inquiry re the Management of the Police Agencies for the Collection of Contributions from Parents of Children in Certified Schools," memo by Lushington, May 20, 1914.

31. *Northern Echo*, Jan. 22, 1875.

32. Ibid., Apr. 28, 1875.

33. *Oxford Times*, Sept. 26, 1885.

34. *South Western Star*, Sept. 15, 1894; ibid., Oct. 6, 1894. Cf. Davis, "Prosecutions," p. 416.

35. See, for example, S.C. on the Police of the Metropolis, P.P., 1834, XVI, QQ. 1,875–76, 2,713–14.

36. 10 & 11 Vict., c. 82 (1847); and 62 & 63 Vict., c. 22 (1899). One early twentieth-century study traced "the idea in germ" of juvenile courts to the Act of 1847 insofar as it introduced "a much-needed distinction between younger and elder delinquents." Courtney, p. 629.

37. Sir Thomas Henry to T. Baring, as quoted in Radzinowicz and Hood, p. 715.

38. Gillis, "Evolution," pp. 98–99.

39. Idem, *Youth*, p. 177; idem, "Evolution," p. 97.

40. Hendrick, *Images*, pp. 83–118.

41. See P. Cohen, "Policing," 121–22; and Humphries, passim.

42. "Cry of the Children," p. 41.

43. *Juvenile Offenders* [1898], pp. 5–6.

44. *Echo*, Feb. 7, 1898.

45. Drew, pp. 93–99; E. Morley; *Manchester Guardian*, Oct. 4, 1901; Rook, 2: 229–32. For an extended study of this moral panic, see G. Pearson. On strategies for countering the threat of masculinity run amok, see Koven, "Rough Lads." Joan Neuberger has contributed a useful analysis set in the context of tsarist Russian society. See her *Hooliganism*.

46. E. Ross, *Love*, p. 13. By today's standards, however, turn-of-the-century London was aswarm with children. As of 1991, persons aged fifteen and under comprised just 19.5 percent of the metropolitan population. *Key Statistics*, p. 51.

47. For the rise of intelligence testing in England, see G. Sutherland, *Ability*.

48. W. D. Morrison, pp. 99–101, 111.

49. Loch, "State," pp. 44–45.

50. Parliamentary Debates, 3rd ser., 52 (Feb. 26, 1840): 651–57.

51. On Waugh's early career, see R. Waugh. For Waugh's later involvement in the child protection campaign, see Behlmer, *Child Abuse*, passim.

52. B. Waugh, *Gaol Cradle*, p. 4.

53. Ibid., pp. 28–29, 79, 88–89, 101.

54. Wiener, *Reconstructing the Criminal*, p. 287.

55. NSPCC, *Seventh Annual Report* (1891), pp. 52–53; [Stead] "Two Champions," p. 701.

56. *Leeds Mercury*, Apr. 24, 1890; *Child's Guardian*, Jan. 1893, p. 8.

57. In terms of publicizing how various American states used probation officers to supervise young offenders, the Howard Association was more important than the NSPCC. See, for example, the Association's pamphlet, *Juvenile Offenders* [1881], pp. 1–2; and its *Annual Report* (1896), pp. 6–7.

58. Florence Davenport-Hill's letter to *The Times* (Oct. 27, 1903) offered English readers the most detailed account of Adelaide's juvenile court.

59. S. Fox, pp. 1229–30. On the publicity-seeking style of Chicago's philanthropic community, see Mennel, *Thorns*, pp. 128–30; and A. Platt, pp. 140–46.

60. Rothman, *Conscience*, p. 215; Lindsey, "Reformation," pp. 5, 10–11.

61. E. P. Hughes, p. 8; L. Bartlett, pp. 392–93.

62. Whitney, pp. 71–72, 76–77. For an account of Birmingham's new juvenile court during its first year, see *Seeking and Saving*, 16 (Oct. 1906): 185–88.

63. *The Times*, Nov. 3, 1904; *Hospital*, Nov. 12, 1904, p. 130.

64. H. Barnett, "Special Police Courts," p. 735. At least one influential segment of governing opinion was skeptical about children's tribunals, however—the London police court magistrates. See *The Times*, Oct. 17, 1904.

65. Report of the Inter-Departmental Committee on Physical Deterioration, P.P., 1904, XXXII: 63.

66. H. Vincent, p. 760; Jeyes, p. 248.

67. P.R.O., HO45/10311/123946, memo, n.d.

68. P.R.O., HO45/10535/152076, memo, May 7, 1907.

69. On Samuel's tenure as Home Office Under-Secretary during the legislatively crucial years of 1905–1908, see Wasserstein, chap. 4.

70. H. Vincent, p. 760; NSPCC, *Twenty-Second Annual Report* (1906), p. 23; *Legislation in Regard*, pp. 28–30; *Our Waifs and Strays*, Mar. 1908, pp. 297–98.

71. The 1908 Act defined "child" as someone under fourteen and "young person" as someone who was at least fourteen but less than sixteen years old. Parents or guardians who did not live "within a reasonable distance" of the juvenile court were exempt from attendance.

72. P.R.O., HO45/10566/173881, draft letter to the Treasury, Dec. 29, 1908; ibid., Treasury to Gladstone, Mar. 29, 1909.

73. P.R.O., HO45/10566/173881, Parr to Gladstone, Oct. 13, 1909; ibid., typescript report by A. L. Dixon, May 11, 1909.

74. P.R.O., HO45/10566/173881, Metropolitan Police to Under Sect. of State, Apr. 2, 1909; ibid., H.O. to Chief Magistrate, Bow Street, Nov. 18, 1909. London's original juvenile courts were established at Bow Street, Clerkenwell, Greenwich, Old Street, Tower Bridge, and Westminster.

75. An unnamed "American expert," as quoted in H. Barnett, "Special Police Courts" p. 745.

76. See Chapter 4.

77. Cf. Bochel, pp. 6-14; and S. W. Harris, p. 7.

78. Russell and Rigby, pp. 148-49.

79. Cadbury, pp. 74-75.

80. Home Office, [First] *Report on the Work of the Children's Branch* (1923), p. 110; W. C. Hall, *Children's Courts*, p. 281.

81. Report of the Departmental Committee on the Probation of Offenders Act, 1907, P.P., 1910, XLV: 3.

82. Ibid., pp. 4, 6-7; and QQ. 1,830, 1,837, 1,840, 1,846, 1,879, 1,882.

83. Ibid., Q. 2,612.

84. Pepler, *Justice*, p. 53. See also Chapman, *Poor Man's*, pp. 262-63.

85. J. Myers, p. 126; Devon, p. 125.

86. Leeson, *Probation*, p. 117; Flexner and Baldwin, p. 136.

87. Donzelot, p. 100; Lasch, pp. 15-16. For the broader scholarly context, see Mennel, "Attitudes," p. 211; and Haskell, pp. xii-xiii.

88. William Clarke Hall Papers: Arthur R. L. Gardner, "William Clarke Hall. A Record" [typescript mss.], pp. 2-6, 13, 23-37.

89. *Probation*, Jan. 1932, p. 145.

90. Clarke Hall Papers: Gardner, "William Clarke Hall," pp. 47-48; and Edna Clarke Hall, "A Biographical Sketch of the Life of William Clarke Hall" [typescript mss.], pp. 37-39. William met Edna Waugh, thirteen years his junior, at her father's home in 1893. They married in 1899.

91. As quoted in Gardner, "William Clarke Hall," pp. 61-62.

92. W. C. Hall, *Queen's Reign*, pp. 136-38, 179-81.

93. *Hythe and Sandgate Advertiser*, Dec. 25, 1909.

94. NSPCC Archives: #FX111-64, "Memorandum on the Principles and Procedure for Children's Courts," Clarke Hall to Parr [Jan. 1909].

95. *The Times*, Oct. 29, 1932; *Probation*, Jan. 1932, p. 146. Cf. Horace Smith, pp. 4-5.

96. Rothman, p. 238.

97. Schlossman, pp. 55-56.

98. Steffens, pp. 114-15.

99. "Judge Lindsey"; St. John, p. 322.

100. "Can A Child," p. 846.

101. Larsen, pp. 50-51.

102. L. Page, *Justice*, pp. 32-33. At Clarke Hall's urging the East London juvenile court eventually moved to purpose-built quarters in Toynbee Hall. By 1931 he was also serving as President of the Islington Juvenile Court. *Toynbee Hall*, p. 6.

103. See Lindsey and O'Higgins.

104. As John Clarke contends in "Managing the Delinquent," pp. 249-51.

105. Biron, p. 259.

106. P.R.O., HO45/10970/404139, Schuster to Troup, June 23, 1920.

107. Biron, p. 259; *Probation*, Jan. 1932, p. 146; Clarke Hall Papers: Illinois Commission on Prisons, Probation and Parole [typescript interview with Clarke Hall et al.], July 31, 1931, p. 5.

108. Report of the Departmental Committee on Reformatory and Industrial Schools, P.P., 1913, XXXIX: 7.

109. Ibid., QQ. 820-21, 6,755; and 64.

110. W. C. Hall, *Children's Courts*, p. 175.

111. *The Times*, Oct. 31, 1932; Clarke, "Managing the Delinquent," p. 251. For an example of Clarke Hall's contact with his industrial school charges, see Clarke Hall Papers: "Miscellaneous," letter from Joseph Cordes, July 17, 1928.

112. Healy, *Individual Delinquent*, p. 291.

113. P.R.O., HO45/11008/272403, draft circular, May 11, 1916.

114. Leeson, *Child*, pp. 22-27.

115. P.R.O., HO45/1096213/101986, Juvenile Organisations Committee, *Report on Juvenile Delinquency* (1918).

116. David Smith, p. 121.

117. Flexner and Baldwin, p. 122.

118. P.R.O., HO45/11912/397140, memo on Clarke Hall's volunteer scheme, July 30, 1919; HO45/11924/413703, Clarke Hall to Harris, July 16, 1921; ibid., Sept. 10, 1921.

119. Woollcombe, p. 1143.

120. Van Waters, pp. 4-5. See also Beard, pp. 51-52.

121. *Probation*, Jan. 1934, p. 284; P.R.O., HO45/11912/397140, memo on Clarke Hall's volunteer scheme, July 30, 1919. Note Miss Cheshire's moving letter to Houston, HO45/11924/413703, June 26, 1921.

122. *Probation*, Dec. 1929, pp. 23-24. This conclusion is consistent with the fact that slowly, throughout the interwar years, England's probation officers were becoming better educated, better paid, and more fully conscious of themselves as "professionals." For more on these changes, see McWilliams, "Mission Transformed."

123. Bailey, *Delinquency*, pp. 26-27.

124. W. C. Hall, *Children's Courts*, pp. 58-59.

125. Report of the Departmental Committee on the Treatment of Young Offenders, P.P., 1927, XII: 16.

126. Sir Chartres Biron, as quoted in Mullins, *Fifteen Years'*, p. 163.

127. W. C. Hall, *Children's Courts*, pp. 75-81. See also his letter to *The Times*, Apr. 3, 1919; *Magistrate*, June 1929, p. 318; and Clynes, 2: 162-63.

128. Moodie, *Stealing*, p. 4; Glover, p. 11.

129. L. Page, *Justice*, pp. 32-33.

130. Clarke Hall Papers: Edna Clarke Hall, "Biographical Sketch," pp. 66-67; W. C. Hall, "Extent and Practice," p. 293.

131. P.R.O., HO45/17943/451656, typescript copy of Troup's speech to the Magistrates' Association, 1923.

132. W. C. Hall, *Children's Courts*, pp. 96–99; idem, "Extent and Practice," pp. 293–94; *Report of the Proceedings of the Conference on Mental Health*, p. 77.

133. W. C. Hall, *Children's Courts*, pp. 59, 61–62.

134. Clarke Hall Papers: "Miscellaneous," typescript summary of Clarke Hall's schedule for 1928 and 1929; G. Abbott, 2: 485–86.

135. Donzelot, pp. 108–10.

136. B. Henriques, *Indiscretions*, p. 17.

137. P.R.O., HO45/11152/240518, mins., July 30, 1919; ibid., Juvenile Organisations Committee, *Report of the Sub-Committee on Juvenile Courts* (n.d.).

138. P.R.O., HO45/16515/375684, draft report (1920), pp. 25–26; *Times Educational Supplement*, Oct. 2, 1919.

139. P.R.O., HO45/10970/404139, Schuster to Troup, Feb. 16, 1920. The Sex Disqualification (Removal) Act of 1919 enabled women to serve as justices of the peace.

140. *Daily Telegraph*, May 25, 1920; *West London Press*, June 26, 1920; *South East Herald*, Nov. 19, 1920; *Daily Herald*, June 29, 1920.

141. *The Times*, May 21, 1920.

142. *Daily Herald*, June 29, 1920; P.R.O., HO45/10970/107489, Schuster to Troup, June 25, 1920; ibid., summary of the deputation (n.d.).

143. Juvenile Courts (Metropolis) Act of 1920, 10 & 11 Geo. 5, c. 68.

144. *SWS*, Jan. 3, 1930.

145. Home Office, *Third Report on the Work of the Children's Branch* (1925), pp. 6–10; Rankin, passim.

146. P.R.O., HO45/11152/240518, Hawkins to Shortt, May 22, 1921; HO45/13777/498902, Harris to Schuster, Jan. 13, 1930.

147. P.R.O., HO45/21107/694989, "Election of New Juvenile Court Panels 1936," and Simon to Lord Liverpool, Jan. 30, 1937; L. Page, *Justice*, p. 182; J. A. F. Watson, *Child and the Magistrate*, p. 197.

148. I. Briggs, p. 108; Courtney, pp. 630–31; W. C. Hall, *Children's Courts*, p. 59.

149. J. A. F. Watson, *Child and the Magistrate*, pp. 72–73.

150. For examples of imperfect press self-censorship, see P.R.O., HO45/13655/180010. A well-documented example of strictly illegal newspaper coverage is the case of William Abbott, age sixteen. See Greater London R.O.: Ch/D/6/7 (1939).

151. Cairns, *Loom*, pp. 182, 185; Home Office, *Fourth Report on the Work of the Children's Branch* (1928), pp. 11–12; B. Henriques, "Child in Trouble," p. 881; P.R.O., HO45/15746/568968, minutes, Feb. 21, 1934. Since juvenile sessions most often met in the late morning or early afternoon, fully employed fathers could not easily accompany their children to court.

152. For an analysis of this pressure, see Bailey, *Delinquency*, pp. 110–13.

153. Donzelot, p. 108.

154. Mullins, *Crime*, p. 165.

155. Donzelot, p. 109.

156. Clynes, 2: 163.

157. "Sentimental Justice"; *Manchester Guardian*, Oct. 27, 1936. Cf. Walling, p. 501.

158. *Newcastle Chronicle*, Oct. 14, 1936; ibid., Oct. 15, 1936.

159. Crichton-Browne, *From the Doctor's*, p. 101.

160. *Justice of the Peace and Local Government Review*, Nov. 25, 1939, p. 745; *Daily Mirror*, Oct. 23, 1940; *Nottingham Evening Post*, Jan. 16, 1941; *Liverpool Daily Post*, May 1, 1941.

161. Bailey, *Delinquency*, pp. 117–18.

162. Home Office, *Fifth Report on the Work of the Children's Branch* (1938), pp. 9–10.

163. *Magistrate*, Nov. 1936, pp. 1089–90; Greater London R.O.: Ch/D/4/ 7, "Juvenile Delinquency on Council's Housing Estates," June 15, 1937.

164. Greater London R.O.: CH/D/4/6, "Report of the Education Officer on Juvenile Delinquency," Feb. 1937, pp. 11–12; *Liverpool Daily Post*, Feb. 26, 1937; *Schoolmaster and Woman Teacher's Chronicle*, Mar. 4, 1937, p. 411.

165. Mannheim, *Social Aspects*, pp. 79–80; Carr-Saunders et al., p. 156. See also Giles, *Juvenile Courts*, pp. 9–11.

166. *Newcastle Chronicle*, Oct. 14, 1936; *Suffolk Chronicle and Mercury*, Sept. 10, 1937. "Reactionaries" were not of course alone in lamenting the lack of uniformity in juvenile court procedure. See, for example, Hermann Mannheim's wartime essay, "The Juvenile Court."

167. P.R.O., HO45/18118/697558, "Juvenile Delinquency" (1938), pp. 15, 19; Greater London R.O.: CH/D/6/9, Griggs to Robertson, Jan. 21, 1939; ibid., CH/D/4/11, "Committal of Children Under the Age of Ten Years to Approved Schools" (n.d.).

168. Home Office, *Fifth Report on the Work of the Children's Branch*, pp. 37–38.

169. L. Page, *Justice*, pp. 189–90; J. A. F. Watson, *Child and the Magistrate*, pp. 44–45. See also Parliamentary Debates, 5th ser., 261 (Feb. 12, 1932): 1172–73.

170. *Probation*, Mar. 1941, pp. 183–84.

171. Pettifer, *Court Resumes*, pp. 27–28; J. A. F. Watson, "Child and the Aftermath," p. 256; Bathhurst, p. 292; Godwin, pp. 253–54.

172. Buckinghamshire County R.O.: PS/WB/MJ/1, min. book, High Wycombe Borough Juvenile Court (Jan. 3, 1939–Mar. 7, 1945).

173. Coventry City R.O.: MG/REG/4/1, juvenile court register, entries for Nov. 3, 1933, and Mar. 2, 1934.

174. Cambridgeshire County R.O.: Petty Sessional Division of Cambridge, juvenile court register (Mar. 24, 1934–Dec. 30, 1944). The female head of a rural Suffolk magistrates' court, interviewed in 1967, asserted that the theft of women's underwear was "a fairly recent thing." "Perhaps women didn't have dainty underwear years ago," Mrs. Annersley suggested, "or perhaps it is because all the underwear ads are so extremely erotic now. Pantie-stealers and in-

decent exposure people are the same type of man, lonely, nervous, fantasist. Of course, they are always put on probation. We never treat them unkindly." As quoted in Blythe, p. 271.

175. R. Harris, pp. 165–68.

176. *The Times*, Nov. 23, 1994.

177. *Sunday Times*, Sept. 1, 1996.

178. *The Economist*, Feb. 27, 1993, p. 62; *The Times*, Nov. 25, 1993; *Daily Express*, May 24, 1994.

Chapter 6

1. Thwing and Thwing, p. 164.

2. Goody, p. 57.

3. This was true for certain non-Western societies as well. See, for example, Hayami and Uchida.

4. McCauliff, pp. 656–57.

5. Huard, p. 745; Presser, pp. 447–48. For an analysis of prejudice against adoption in early modern France, see Gager.

6. Hanawalt, pp. 252–53.

7. Macfarlane, *Marriage*, p. 83. The classic study of service as a defining feature of early modern English society is Peter Laslett's *The World We Have Lost*, especially chap. 3.

8. Grossberg, pp. 268–69; Kirk and McDaniel, p. 76.

9. Demos, p. 72.

10. Morgan, p. 77. Alan Macfarlane speculates that parental motivations for sending children away when they reached puberty may also have included a desire to minimize "incestuous temptations." Macfarlane, *Family Life*, p. 205.

11. Seaver, pp. 78–84. Fear that Charles might fall under Catholic influence if allowed to remain with his mother in Ireland probably also moved the Wallingtons to open their home.

12. Laslett, *Family Life*, pp. 162, 170–73.

13. Older accounts include McCleary, *Early History*; Hopkirk; and Housden. More recent analyses appear in Behlmer, *Child Abuse*; L. Rose, *Massacre*; and Higgenbotham, "Unmarried Mother."

14. "Infanticide," p. 161.

15. See Chapter 5.

16. McClure, pp. 32–35, 49; Weisbrod, pp. 208–9; Barret-Ducrocq, pp. 160–62.

17. *The Magdalen's Friend, and Female Homes' Intelligencer*, 2 (1862): 39.

18. S.C. on Protection of Infant Life, P.P., 1871, VII, QQ. 4,631–39; Barret-Ducrocq, pp. 150–51. For an analysis of mid-Victorian "magdalene" institutions and the controversy surrounding them, see Mahood, chaps. 5 and 6.

19. *The Magdalen's Friend*, 1 (1860): 13–16; ibid., 5 (1864): 64.

20. S.C. on Protection of Infant Life, P.P., 1871, Q. 3,848; U. Henriques, p. 119.

21. Acton, pp. 498–99.

22. J.B., p. 59.

23. Himmelfarb, *De-Moralization*, pp. 41–42.

24. *Lancet*, Oct. 22, 1859, p. 415. See also G. Graves, p. 11; Wynter, p. 609; and Havard, p. 74.

25. *Life and Trial; The Times*, Aug. 2, 1865.

26. See statistical tables from the 1911 Census, P.P., 1913, XXXVIII [Lords]: xxx. At the same time, mid-Victorian social critics were well aware that illegitimacy levels could be considerably higher in country districts than in large cities. Whether expressed as a rate or as a ratio, for example, "bastardy" in rural Cumberland far surpassed that in teeming East London. See Mayhew, *London Labour*, 4: 467; and Laslett et al., *Bastardy*, pp. 62–64.

27. J.B., pp. 22, 24. Cf. "Seduction," p. 481.

28. Best, pp. 122–23.

29. For more on Curgenven, Hart, and the politics of baby farming see Behlmer, *Child Abuse*, pp. 22–38; and idem, "Ernest Hart."

30. Greenwood, *Seven Curses*, pp. 24–25; *Pall Mall Gazette*, Jan. 31, 1868; L. Rose, *Massacre*, p. 165.

31. *B.M.J.*, Jan. 15, 1898, pp. 178–79; ibid., May 27, 1871, p. 563; S.C. on Protection of Infant Life, P.P., 1871, QQ. 18–26, 30, 44; *The Times*, Dec. 14, 1867.

32. Curgenven, *On Baby-Farming*, pp. 6, 9. According to official figures, 44,691 English children were born out of wedlock during the year 1869. See Thirty-Second Annual Report of the Registrar General, P.P., 1871, XV: 28.

33. *Lloyd's Weekly Newspaper*, June 5, 1870.

34. *The Times*, June 16, 1870; June 21, 1870; July 2, 1870; July 4, 1870; July 7, 1870; July 28, 1870; Sept. 24, 1870; *Illustrated Police News*, Oct. 15, 1870.

35. *Daily Telegraph*, Oct. 12, 1870; Dickson, pp. 325–26.

36. *Morning Advertiser*, Oct. 10, 1870. On the ideological content of the Contagious Diseases Acts and the opposition to them, see Walkowitz, *Prostitution*; and McHugh.

37. Curgenven, *Infant Life Protection*, p. 1. For a provocative attempt to "deconstruct" the baby farming scandal of 1870–71, see Arnot.

38. S.C. on Protection of Infant Life, P.P., 1871, QQ. 597–98, 1,118–22. Although "day nursing" was a common practice in the factory towns of Lancashire, well-run crèches were rare there before the First World War. See Hewitt, pp. 129–34; and Wohl, *Endangered Lives*, p. 31.

39. P.R.O., MEPO 3/92. Since Mrs. Martin of 33 Dean Street charged between £20 and £50 for the delivery and subsequent disposal of a baby, the average London servant could not have afforded her services without help from an accomplice.

40. S.C. on Protection of Infant Life, P.P., 1871, Q. 1,325.

41. Ibid., QQ. 230–31, 235, 259–61, 1,275–82.

42. *Infant Mortality*, pp. 7, 30–31. Lydia Becker and her Manchester branch of the National Society for Women's Suffrage led the feminist charge against regulation.

43. *B.M.J.*, Feb. 22, 1896, p. 489.

44. The Bastardy Laws Amendment Act of 1872 made life a little less harsh for unmarried mothers in three ways: first, Poor Law Guardians were once again empowered to assist mothers in recovering child support from putative fathers; second, a father's liability to support his illegitimate child would now continue until it turned sixteen; and third, a woman's maximum weekly support rose from two-and-a-half to five shillings. The Registration Act of 1874 established a fine of up to forty shillings for failure to report live births within forty-two days, and deaths within eight days. It said nothing about stillbirths, however, which would continue to go unregistered until 1915.

45. S.C. on the Infant Life Protection Bill and Safety of Nurse Children Bill, P.P., 1896, X, Q. 693.

46. Ibid., QQ. 10,27–28, 1,032–33; *B.M.J.*, Feb. 29, 1896, p. 543.

47. S.C. on I.L.P./S.N.C., P.P., 1896, Q. 1,595.

48. NSPCC, *Seventh Annual Report* (1891), p. 50; *Child's Guardian*, Apr. 1891, p. 31; B. Waugh, "Baby Farming," p. 704.

49. S.C. on the Infant Life Protection Bill, P.P., 1890, XIII, Q. 376; B. Waugh, "Baby Farming," p. 713.

50. S.C. on I.L.P./S.N.C., P.P., 1896, Q. 24.

51. Ibid., QQ. 1,423–26.

52. E. Ross, *Love*, pp. 135–36; S.C. on I.L.P./S.N.C., 1896, Q. 1,046.

53. R. Roberts, pp. 22–26, 30; S.C. on I.L.P./S.N.C., 1896, QQ. 199–201, 1035–37.

54. C.R., pp. 239–40.

55. S.C. on I.L.P./S.N.C., P.P., 1896, QQ. 2,859–63. See also F. H. Low, pp. 281–82; *Report of the . . . Third International Congress*, pp. 165, 169; and *Hospital*, Dec. 13, 1902, p. 173.

56. Coventry City R.O.: St. Faith's Shelter, case histories, vol. 1, no. 12; *Social Work*, p. 66.

57. Hendrick, *Child Welfare*, p. 48.

58. Parr, *Baby Farmer*, pp. 27–29, 52–53.

59. *B.M.J.*, July 16, 1910, p. 165.

60. Kipling, pp. 6–19.

61. *The Times*, Nov. 7, 1874.

62. W. Anderson, p. 98.

63. L. Twining, *Recollections of Workhouse Visiting*, pp. 196–99; Davenport-Hill, pp. 183–84.

64. The boarding-out of pauper children *within* Union boundaries was already taking place at Bath. See C. W. Grant, pp. 2–3, 33–34.

65. Fawcett, pp. 81–84.

66. Fourth Annual Report of the Local Government Board, P.P., 1875, XXXI, Appendix 15, pp. 171–79. The Local Government Board replaced the Poor Law Board in 1871.

67. Offen. Cf. Joanna Hill.

68. *The Times*, Nov. 7, 1874; ibid., Mar. 29, 1872; ibid., Sept. 3, 1872; Surr, p. 656.

69. Peek, pp. 58, 43–44.

70. Even before 1889, Guardians in some Poor Law Unions had encouraged foster parents to "adopt" boarded-out children in the sense of offering them permanent homes to which they could return at any age. See Report from the Select Committee of the House of Lords on Poor Law Relief, P.P., 1888, XV, QQ. 3,939–42.

71. Report of the Departmental Committee on the Treatment of Young Offenders, P.P., 1927, XII: 116.

72. R.C. on the Poor Laws and Relief of Distress, P.P., 1909, XVIII, Appendix, p. 2. As of Jan. 1, 1907, 234,004 persons under sixteen years of age were receiving Poor Law relief in England and Wales. Boys and girls boarded-out numbered 8,659.

73. Cuttle, p. 116.

74. Loane, *Next Street*, pp. 216–17; M. Nevinson, pp. 255–56.

75. See Cumbria County R.O.: Carlisle Poor Law Union, Register of Children Under Control, 1912–1955, #SPU/Ca/5/11.

76. Darlington Branch Library, Local Studies Dept.: Darlington Poor Law Union, Mins. of the Boarding Out Committee (July 8, 1889–Nov. 25, 1897), #U/Da 720, entry for Jan. 14, 1892.

77. Durham County R.O.: Chester-le-Street Poor Law Union, Mins. of the Workhouse Visiting Committee, 1913–1915, #U/CS 27, entries for Jan. 23, 1913; July 24, 1913; and Mar. 5, 1914. Joseph Brown, President of the Association of Poor Law Unions, testified that workhouse adoption was in "too many instances" a kind of forced labor, with strangers taking away children between the ages of nine and thirteen to use as "little house slaves and nurses" before and after school. R.C. on the Poor Laws and Relief of Distress, P.P., 1909, XL, QQ. 24,790–92.

78. H. Barnett, *Matters*, pp. 170–71.

79. R.C. on the Poor Laws and Relief of Distress, P.P., 1909, LXVIII [Lords]: 183–85; *Hospital*, Aug. 31, 1889, pp. 340–41; Report of the Departmental Committee [on] . . . the Maintenance and Education of Children Under the Charge of . . . Boards of Guardians, P.P., 1896, XLIII, Q. 14,326. The much-publicized death of Dennis O'Neill at the hands of his Shropshire foster parents in 1945 would recall Miss Mason's plea for vigilance. See R. A. Parker, "Gestation," pp. 203–4.

80. Family Life and Work Experience Archive, Sociology Dept., University of Essex: interview #19, "Catherine B."

81. *Night and Day*, Feb./Mar. 1882, pp. 32–34. Middle-class moralists often denounced "street arabism," pointing out that children swarming in city thoroughfares produced social disorder and bred contempt for authority. See Samuels.

82. Barnardo, as quoted in Heywood, pp. 53–54.

83. Seth Koven offers a shrewd reading of the "artistic fictions" flap of 1874. See Koven, "Dr. Barnardo's."

84. *Night and Day*, Nov. 1885, pp. 149–52. See also T. Barnardo, *Worse than Orphans*. The "Maiden Tribute of Modern Babylon" scandal has received

careful attention from M. Pearson; Gorham, "'Maiden Tribute'"; and Walkowitz, *City*, passim.

85. Wagner, pp. 218–25. The *habeas corpus* actions taken against Barnardo in the case of Harry Gossage were perhaps the most celebrated of the Doctor's legal woes. For full—and to date unexploited—particulars on this boy's family background, see Warwick County R.O.: Leamington Charity Organisation Society, Case Record Book, CR51/1878, record #890.

86. On efforts to shield the philanthropic "adoption" of children, see Parliamentary Debates, 3rd ser. (Lords), 338 (July 16, 1889): 502–14. For the growth of Barnardo's boarding-out work, see S. Barnardo and J. Marchant, pp. 190, 194, 201–2.

87. José Harris, *Private Lives*, p. 75.

88. Dayus, pp. 192–93.

89. Bellingham, pp. 128–29, 151–52.

90. Gillis, *For Better*, p. 246; Children's Home and Orphanage, *Annual Report for 1895–96*, p. 8.

91. For the treatment of English children sent to Canada, see Joy Parr.

92. Children's Home and Orphanage, *Annual Report for 1879–80*, p. 7; ibid., *Annual Report for 1886–87*, p. 6; ibid., *Annual Report for 1895–96*, p. 13. By Dec. 1920, what was then known as the National Children's Home and Orphanage had arranged for the care and education of 15,048 children. Of this number just 262 (1.74 percent) "had been found in every way available for adoption." P.R.O., HO45/11540/354040, Litten to Sharpe, Dec. 21, 1920.

93. *Our Waifs and Strays*, Aug. 1886, p. 2; Ward, pp. 304–5.

94. Stroud, pp. 29–30, 54; Wrong, pp. 36–37. At various times Barnardo seems to have viewed the CEWSS as a philanthropic upstart whose financial support had been gained through "crooked methods," chief among them denigrating the Doctor's work. *Our Waifs and Strays*, June 1895, pp. 94–95.

95. S.C. on Infant Life Protection/Safety of Nurse Children, P.P., 1896, X, QQ. 860, 865; Stroud, p. 67.

96. Report of the Departmental Committee [on] . . . the Maintenance and Education of Children Under the Charge of . . . Boards of Guardians, P.P., 1896, XLIII, QQ. 12,956, 12,960.

97. Children's Society Archives, London: Executive Comm. Min. Book #7: mins. for Aug. 19, 1901.

98. *Our Waifs and Strays*, Aug. 1891, p. 1.

99. Ward, pp. 295–96.

100. *The Christian Million*, Jan. 20, 1887; ibid., Feb. 17, 1887.

101. *Our Waifs and Strays*, Aug. 1891, p. 13; ibid., Feb. 1887, p. 8.

102. *The Bazaar, Exchange and Mart*, May 25, 1898; ibid., May 13, 1898; ibid., June 17, 1898. *The Exchange and Mart* first appeared in 1868 as a weekly newspaper "established to provide a medium between the seller and buyer, and at a very cheap rate to enable anyone who wishes to dispose of any article, either by exchange or by sale, to do so to the very best advantage": May 13, 1868.

103. But on at least one occasion the mother of a child boarded-out by the

Waifs and Strays Society used *The Bazaar, Exchange and Mart* to find adoptive parents. This mother, a widow "unable owing to a reverse of fortune to bring up the Child in a way befitting [her] station," soon located a Mr. A. B. Watson, owner of an engineering firm in Hull. See Children's Society Archives: "Correspondence Between Bruce Millar & Company, Solicitors, and A. B. Watson re Adoption of a Little Girl," 1898–99, accession #89.53.

104. E. de M. Rudolf assured a Local Government Board committee that, "I have known instances repeatedly where foster-parents have come forward and offered to adopt children who have been placed with them, and have volunteered to forgo all payments as long as the children are allowed to remain entirely as their own." Report of the Departmental Committee [on] . . . the Maintenance and Education of Children Under the Charge of . . . Boards of Guardians, P.P., 1896, XLIII, QQ. 12,870, 12,891.

105. "Edith B.," born in Aug. 1885. Children's Society Archives: case file #715. For similar examples of local ladies smoothing the path for adopting parents, see case files #243 and #318.

106. "Alice N.," born in Aug. 1894. Children's Society Archives: case file #8,762.

107. "Lilian W.," born in Apr. 1896. Children's Society Archives: case file #15,499.

108. "Hubert B.," born in 1878. Children's Society Archives: case file #674.

109. See the draft Agreement in case file #8,762.

110. "Kathleen H.," born in Apr. 1896. Children's Society Archives: case file #15,438.

111. M. Anderson, *Family Structure*, pp. 148–49; Young and Willmott, pp. 21–22.

112. Fuchs, *Abandoned Children*, pp. 30–31.

113. M. Williams, *Later Leaves*, pp. 257–59.

114. Bell, pp. 116, 192–93.

115. J. White, *Worst Street*, pp. 137–38.

116. E. Ross, *Love*, p. 134; E. Roberts, *Woman's Place*, p. 103; *Maternity*, pp. 160–61. District nurse Margaret Loane complained that "children are far too lightly handed over to childless [working-class] persons offering to adopt them." Loane, *Englishman's Castle*, p. 105.

117. G. Eliot, pp. 238–39. The adoption of Tattycoram likewise appears ill conceived in Dickens's *Little Dorrit* (1857). See also the adoption of a foundling by the crusty wife of a Shadwell chimney sweep in "Mrs. Simon's Baby," chap. 4 of Henry W. Nevinson's *Neighbours of Ours* (1895).

118. There was in fact one predominantly Anglophone nation still more wary of legalized adoption: the Republic of Ireland did not grant legal recognition until 1952, and even then clamped religious restrictions on the adoption process.

119. [Lundie] *America*, pp. 93–96.

120. McCauliff, pp. 666–67; Zainaldin, pp. 1042–43; Presser, p. 465.

121. Grossberg, p. 278.

122. *New York Times Magazine*, Oct. 31, 1915, p. 9. Wealthy childless couples in the U.S. did on occasion insist that children's charities administer the Simon-Binet intelligence test to prospective adoptees, along with the more routine tuberculosis test, but well into the twentieth century American social workers remained skeptical of adoption, particularly for illegitimate children. See Carp.

123. C. Howard, pp. 285–86.

124. Macnair, pp. 704–8.

125. Shaw, *Pygmalion*. In act 2, Mr. Doolittle attempts to blackmail Professor Higgins over the "adoption" of Eliza.

126. E. Ross, *Love*, pp. 152–54.

127. J. Stevenson, pp. 94, 210.

128. Eighty-Second Annual Report of the Registrar General, P.P., 1920, XI: xxxiv–xxxv; L. Fisher, "Unmarried Mother and Her Child," pp. 485–86; *The Times*, Apr. 19, 1915; Skrine. The newly patriotic Women's Social and Political Union was the first major feminist group to advocate adoption as a remedy for the "war babies" problem. See *The Times*, May 6, 1915.

129. See, for example, *The Times*'s front pages for August through November 1916. Since the minimum charge for a small "personal" advertisement was then five shillings, those seeking to adopt children most likely enjoyed a degree of financial comfort.

130. "Epidemic of Adoption," p. 79; British Agencies for Adoption and Fostering, London: typescript "History of the [Lancashire and Cheshire Child] Adoption Council" [1977].

131. P.R.O., HO45/11540/354040, Hartley to the Home Secretary, Dec. 6, 1917. Hartley also advocated "free divorce," and argued that where divorced parents could not amicably share childcare duties, the state might award custody of their children to childless couples. See Hartley, p. 358.

132. Croom-Johnson, pp. 53–54.

133. Kornitzer, pp. 8–9, 60–61; McWhinnie, p. 7.

134. P.R.O., MH57/53, Andrew to Stutchbury, Jan. 15, 1918.

135. *Western Morning News*, July 3, 1918; Benet, p. 72.

136. P.R.O., MH57/53, Stutchbury to Willis, Feb. 19, 1919; HO45/11540/354040, "Notes on Progress of N.C.A.A.," Oct. 25, 1920.

137. See the Earl of Winterton's question, Parliamentary Debates, 5th ser. (Lords), 119 (Aug. 14, 1919): 1963–64; and Grey, p. 1.

138. *National Adoption Society*, pp. 1–2.

139. *The Times*, Mar. 2, 1920; ibid., Aug. 19, 1918; *The Unmarried Mother*, pp. 15–16; Barnes, p. 557.

140. Hopkinson, pp. 3–4.

141. P.R.O., HO45/11540/354040, H.O. minutes for May 4, 1920; and "Interim Report," Oct. 30, 1920. Legitimation *per subsequens matrimonium* had long been legal in Scotland and intermittently the focus of reform efforts in England. The Legitimation League, a coterie of libertines active in the mid-1890's, advocated a "crusade against custom" through free love and the creation of "a machinery for acknowledging offspring born out of wedlock." The

League collapsed after its secretary was brought to trial for selling a "scandalous libel," namely Havelock Ellis's *Sexual Inversion.* See *Natural Rights,* pp. 9–10, 13–14, 18; *Legitimation League,* pp. 2–3; and Weeks, pp. 180–81.

More influential was the work of Lettice Fisher's National Council for the Unmarried Mother and Her Child, which made "humanizing public attitudes to illegitimacy" a high priority. See Graham-Dixon, p. 2; Lens; and NCUMHC, *2nd Report* (1920), p. 3. Not until 1926 did English law recognize legitimation *per subsequens matrimonium.* Yet even then the concession was grudging because it specified that legitimation could occur only if the parents had been free to wed at the time of their child's birth. The Legitimacy Act of 1959 finally removed this remnant of punitive morality.

142. Report of the [Hopkinson] Committee on Child Adoption, P.P., 1921, IX: 3–4; P.R.O., HO45/11540/354040, Julia Lathorp [Chief, U.S. Dept. of Labor, Children's Bureau] to Sharpe, Oct. 20, 1920; D. Stanley Smith, pp. 165–66.

143. Report of the [Hopkinson] Committee, pp. 4–8, 10–11; "Legalizing of Adoptions."

144. P.R.O., HO45/11540/354040, Hurst to Bridgeman, Nov. 13, 1923; ibid. "Conference on Child Adoption," Nov. 28, 1921.

145. *Daily Mail,* May 14, 1921; P.R.O., HO45/11540/354040, Wethered and Maddison to the Home Secretary, May 18, 1921; Macnaghten to Porter, June 30, 1921; *Seeking and Saving,* 21 (Apr. 1921): 82–83.

146. "Child Adoption" [*Spectator*].

147. *Child's Guardian,* Mar. 1921, p. 17; ibid., June 1922, p. 41. See also *Child Adoption* [NSPCC].

148. *Child's Guardian,* Mar. 1923, p. 18; P.R.O., HO45/11540/354040, Parr to Harris, May 31, 1923.

149. P.R.O., HO45/11540/354040, "Summary of Evidence by Miss Clara Andrew," Oct. 5, 1920; *John Bull,* Nov. 18, 1922, p. 8; P.R.O., MH57/53, Andrew to Puxley, Mar. 21, 1923.

150. Home Office, *Second Report on the Work of the Children's Branch* (1924), p. 47.

151. Child Adoption [Tomlin] Committee, First Report, P.P., 1924–25, IX: 3–4.

152. Ibid., p. 9.

153. Ibid.; McCauliff, p. 674.

154. Parliamentary Debates, 5th ser., 182 (Apr. 3, 1925): 1708–9.

155. *The Woman's Leader,* Mar. 19, 1926, p. 65; NCUMHC, *Annual Report, 1926,* p. 12.

156. Parliamentary Debates, 5th ser., 192 (Feb. 26, 1926): 932, 936, 948–49. Galbraith's Bill was amended in committee to give county courts jurisdiction in adoption cases.

157. Ibid., col. 950.

158. The Adoption of Children Act (16 & 17 Geo. 5, c. 29) took effect on Jan. 1, 1927. Legal adoption came to Northern Ireland in 1929, and to Scotland in 1930.

159. Not until 1949 did legislation finally prohibit marriages between adopted children and their adopting parents. This legislation (12, 13 & 14 Geo. 6, c. 98) also allowed adopted children for the first time to inherit from intestate adopting parents.

160. Parliamentary Debates, 5th ser., 192 (Feb. 26, 1926): 918; P.R.O., HO45/12695/496773, "Notes on the Present Difficulties . . . of the Adoption of Children Act," Apr. 27, 1927.

161. W. C. Hall, *Law of Adoption*, pp. 5–6.

162. Home Office, *Fourth Report on the Work of the Children's Branch* (1928), p. 80; Haimes and Timms, pp. 12–13. The story of how adopted people in England gained the right to view their own birth records is summarized in Triseliotis.

163. *Fourth Report . . . of the Children's Branch*, pp. 81–84; W. C. Hall, *Law of Adoption*, p. 41.

164. P.R.O., HO45/12695/496773, [NCAA] "Notes on Adoption Act," Feb. 23, 1927. The National Children's Home and Orphanage may have been the only English charity to recommend telling children at an early age that they had been adopted. See P.R.O., HO45/11540/354040, Litten to Sharpe, Dec. 21, 1920.

165. P.R.O., HO45/12695/496773, [N.A.S.] "Notes on the Present Difficulties . . . ," Apr. 27, 1927; *Magistrate*, Feb. 1929, pp. 276–77.

166. P.R.O., HO45/20466/563548, Fanner to Harris, Apr. 13, 1931. The process of adoption through county courts more often involved a minimum of legal fuss. Wishing to adopt a baby boy as a companion for their young daughter, James Drawbell and his wife in 1933 appeared before a judge who asked one rhetorical question: "You have [a] little girl of your own?" Drawbell, pp. 136–37.

167. P.R.O., HO45/12695/496773, Clarke Hall to Harris, Jan. 31, 1927; W. C. Hall, *Law of Adoption*, pp. 6–7.

168. *Daily Telegraph*, Dec. 3, 1930.

169. Lieck and Morrison, pp. 55–57; "Adoption of Children Act."

170. Report of the Departmental [Horsbrugh] Committee on Adoption Societies and Agencies, P.P., 1936–37, IX: 6.

171. L. Rose, *Massacre*, p. 185.

172. NSPCC, *Annual Report for 1930-31* (1931), pp. 13–14; P.R.O., HO45/20467/563548, "Adoption Cases, NSPCC Private," Mar. 1933.

173. P.R.O., HO45/20467/563548, Elliot, Pringle, and Chapman to Gilmour, Mar. 4, 1933; Chapman, *Poor Man's*, pp. 275–76; P.R.O., HO45/17061/669162, H.O. notes, Aug. 1, 1935.

174. Report of the Departmental [Horsbrugh] Committee on Adoption Societies, pp. 35–39.

175. Ibid., pp. 11, 14–17; Kaye, p. 43.

176. Report of the Departmental [Horsbrugh] Committee on Adoption Societies, pp. 28–32; *Day Nursery Journal*, Aug. 1933, p. 14; *Tit-Bits*, July 13, 1935, pp. 3–4; ibid., July 17, 1937, p. 3; *John Bull*, Mar. 13, 1937, p. 7; *Yorkshire Observer*, July 7, 1937; *Manchester Guardian*, July 7, 1937. An "urgent

American desire" for eugenic improvement allegedly lay behind the demand for babies "bearing the clear characteristics of the English race." Holland also figured prominently as a destination for English children because Dutch citizens at that time were without legal protection for their adoptions. Hence by taking foreign children into their homes, Dutch adopters could avoid almost any possibility of interference from birth parents.

177. Report of the Departmental [Horsbrugh] Committee on Adoption Societies, pp. 19–22.

178. L. Fisher, "Adoption," pp. 261–62; Kornitzer, pp. 10–11.

179. Report of the Departmental [Horsbrugh] Committee on Adoption Societies, pp. 43–44.

180. P.R.O., HO45/19299/823375, "Extracts from . . . a Meeting of the Lord President's Committee," Jan. 25, 1943.

181. Report of the Care of Children [Curtis] Committee, P.P., 1945–46, X: 148; Report of the Departmental [Hurst] Committee on the Adoption of Children, P.P., 1953–54, VIII: 4; Report of the Departmental [Houghton] Committee on the Adoption of Children, P.P., 1971–72, XXXVIII: 122.

182. Kornitzer, pp. 7–8.

183. T. Hall, pp. xiv–xv.

Conclusion

1. As quoted in *Enquiry into People's Homes*, p. 53.

2. Judge and Knapp, pp. 133. For the case that "welfare and "state" need not be linked, see Finlayson, *Citizen*, pp. 1–18.

3. Prochaska, *Voluntary Impulse*, p. 87.

4. *The Observer*, Dec. 29, 1996; *The Times*, Feb. 18, 1997.

5. On "a different way of being smart," see Goleman, passim.

6. "How Can Government Best Support Marriage?" Reuter Textline, U.K. Government Press Releases, Feb. 11, 1997.

7. Gillis, *World*, p. 4.

8. Office of Population and Censuses, *Social Trends*, 12 (1982): 36–39; ibid., 23 (1993): 30–33; ibid., 24 (1994): 38–40.

9. Murray, as quoted in *The Economist*, Sept. 9, 1995, p. 19.

10. *British Social Attitudes*, pp. 54–71; P. Johnson, pp. 12–13.

11. *USA Today*, Oct. 25, 1996.

12. *Sunday Telegraph*, Aug. 18, 1996; Bagehot, p. 100.

13. Coontz, passim.

14. For an elaboration of this thesis, see Barrett and McIntosh.

15. Titmuss, pp. 175–77, 180–82, 345–46. For more on the uneasy billetings of 1939, see R. Inglis, chap. 2.

16. *The Times*, Mar. 29, 1943; Mary Hamilton, p. 15.

17. Tomlinson, pp. 7–8; *Enquiry into People's Homes*, pp. 6–7, 171–72. Although the label "social problem group" originated in the 1929 Wood Report on mental deficiency, it owed much to Charles Booth's earlier notion of a "submerged tenth." Between 1929 and 1943 several eugenic tracts kept alive

discussion of malfunctioning families, but it was the publication in the latter year of *Our Towns*, a study sponsored by the National Federation of Women's Institutes, that captured public attention. A raft of similar works appeared over the next nine years.

18. Marwick, pp. 64–65; Chris Harris, pp. 49–50.

19. Mark Adams, "The Home-Centered Society" [a radio talk given in Nov. 1959], as quoted in R. Fletcher, p. 184.

20. James, p. 164. Cf. self-indulgence and teen pregnancy in America during the 1950's: Coontz, pp. 38–40.

21. Rock and Cohen; S. Cohen, pp. 9–26; *The Guardian*, Nov. 4, 1996.

22. G. Pearson, pp. 7–8.

23. Durham, chap. 1; P. Abbott and C. Wallace, chap. 3.

24. Mrs. Thatcher interviewed in *Woman's Own* [Oct. 17, 1981], as quoted in T. Fitzgerald, p. 51.

25. J. Lewis, "Anxieties," p. 32; A. Clarke.

26. Durham, p. 4.

27. *Sunday Times*, Feb. 28, 1993.

28. *The Guardian*, Jan. 6, 1994.

29. *Sunday Times*, Nov. 13, 1994; *Daily Mail*, Oct. 14, 1996; *Daily Telegraph*, Oct. 16, 1996; *The Observer*, Apr. 2, 1995.

30. Berger and Berger, passim.

Bibliography

Archival Sources

Bradford District Archives
Bradford Town Mission, Committee Minute Books, 1850–1881: 32D80/72–75.

British Agencies for Adoption and Fostering, London
Typescript "History of the [Lancashire and Cheshire Child] Adoption Council" (n.d.).

British Library, London
Wolstenholme Elmy Papers: Additional Manuscripts 47449; 47450; 47451.

Buckinghamshire County Record Office, Aylesbury
Bucks. Country Probation and After Care Committee, Minute Books, 1927–1941: AR 16/79.
High Wycombe Borough Juvenile Court, Minute Book, 1939–1945: PS/WB/MJ/1.

Cambridgeshire County Record Office, Cambridge
Cambridge Petty Sessional Division, Juvenile Court Register, 1934–1944.
Cambridge School Board, School Attendance Committee Minute Book, 1882–1889.
Linton Petty Sessional Division, Probation Minute Book, 1927–1954.
Soham Nursing Association, Minutes, 1910–1921.
Trumpington and Grantchester District Nursing Association, Executive Committee Minutes, 1904–1915.

Children's Society, London
Case File Summaries.
C.E.W.S.S., Executive Committee Minute Books, 1894–1906.

Correspondence between Bruce Millar . . . and A. B. Watson, 1898–1899: #89.53.

Coventry City Record Office

Children's Care Sub-Committee, Minute Book: SEC/MB/19/4.
Juvenile Court Registers, 1933–1940: MG/REG/3/28-35; MG/REG/4/1-2.
Juvenile Employment Bureau Sub-Committee, Minute Book, 1911–1927: SEC/MB/47/1.
Poor Law Union, Boarding-Out Committee, Minute Book, 1891–1936: CU/MB/3/1.
St. Faith's Shelter, Case Histories, vols. 1 and 2 (1897–1903).
School Attendance Sub-Committee, Minute Book, 1904–1922: SEC/MB/37/1-2.

Cumbria County Record Office, Carlisle

Carlisle Poor Law Union, Register of Children Under Control, 1912–1955: SPU/Ca/5/11.
Cockermouth Poor Law Union, Boarding-Out Committee Minute Books, 1910–1930: SPUCo/2/16-18.
Whitehaven Petty Sessions, Juvenile Court Registers, 1909–1914 and 1933–1948: CPQ/Wh/16-17, and 44.

Darlington Branch Library

Darlington Poor Law Union, Boarding-Out Committee, Minute Book, 1889–1897: U/Da 720.
Darlington Town Council meeting, news cuttings: DA/DM/10/21.

Durham County Record Office, Durham

Chester-le-Street Poor Law Union, Workhouse Visiting Committee, Minute Books, 1913–1926: U/CS 27-29.
Durham County Juvenile Court Register, 1933–1939: PS/DU 41.
Queen's Jubilee Institute for Nurses, misc. papers: D/Lo/F 1124.

Family Life and Works Experience Archive, Colchester

(Sociology Department, University of Essex)
Interview No. 19, "Catherine B.," born 1890.

Gray's Inn Library, London

William Clarke Hall Papers: Gardner, Arthur R. L. "William Clarke Hall. A Record," unpublished typescript biography, no date. Hall, Edna Clarke. "A Biographical Sketch of the Life of William Clarke Hall," unpublished typescript biography, no date. "Miscellaneous" papers on the Shoreditch Juvenile Court. Typescript interview with William Clarke Hall conducted by the Illinois Commission on Prisons, Probation and Parole, July 31, 1931.

Greater London Record Office

Old Street Children's Court, Registers, 1911-1929.
Toynbee Hall Juvenile Court, Register, 1929-1940.

Hertfordshire County Record Office, Hertford

Dacorum Petty Sessional Division, Probation Officer's Registers of Offenders, 1908-1935: PS 6/10/6-7.
Hertfordshire Probation Committee, Minute Book, 1923-1938.

Home Office Library, London

Summary Courts (Social Services) Committee, Minutes of Evidence, 1934-1935.

Lambeth Palace Library, London

Benson Papers, 1883-1896: vol. 78, ff. 35-42.
Church of England Temperance Society, Council Meetings, Minutes, 1894-1908: MS. 2031.
C.E.T.S., Police Court Missionaries' Guild, Minutes, 1923-1938: MS. 2060.

London School of Economics

Charles Booth Manuscripts: Group B, School Board Visitors' Notebooks, vols. 39 and 45.

NSPCC Archives, London

Hall, William Clarke, "Memorandum on . . . Children's Courts" (Jan. 1909): FXIII-64.
Record Book of Inspectors, 1889-1910.
York Branch, case records, 1898-1903.

Northumberland County Record Office, Newcastle

Bedlington, Blyth and Whitley Bay Moral Welfare Association, Minute Book, 1936-1943: EP 112/63.
Northumberland and Tyneside Council of Social Services, case papers, 1920-1978: NRO 2281/4a.

Public Record Office, London

Home Office Records, HO45 and HO136.
Metropolitan Police Records, MEPO2 and MEPO3.
Ministry of Health Records, MH55 and MH57.
Poor Law Correspondence, MH15.

Sheffield City Archives

Sheffield School Attendance Sub-Committee, Minute Books, 1903-1915: CA 400-402.

Sheffield School Board, Bye Laws Committee, Minute Books, 1888–1903: CA 397–99.
Sheffield School Board, Minute Books, 1877–1881: 379.4274 SF.
Truants' Industrial School, Hollow Meadows, Log Books, 1884–1889 and 1895–1901: CA 35/69 and CA 35/81.

Warwick County Record Office, Warwick
Leamington Charity Organisation Society, Case Record Book, 1879–1893: CR 51/1877.

Parliamentary Papers (individual reports only)

Report from the Select Committee on the Police of the Metropolis: 1834, vol. 16.
Report from the Select Committee on the Health of Towns: 1840, vol. 11.
Report [on] . . . Large Towns and Populous Districts: 1844, vol. 17.
Report from the Select Committee on Criminal and Destitute Juveniles: 1852, vol. 7.
Report from the Select Committee on Criminal and Destitute Children: 1852–1853, vol. 23.
Gibbs, John. Letter to the Board of Health [on] . . . Compulsory Vaccination: 1856, vol. 52.
Report from the Select Committee on Protection of Infant Life: 1871, vol. 7.
Select Committee on the Operation of the Vaccination Act (1867): 1871, vol. 13.
Return from London School Board [on] . . . Wife Desertion: 1875, vol. 58.
Reports . . . on the State of the Law Relating to Brutal Assaults: 1875, vol. 61.
Copy of Report of Dr. Crichton-Browne [on] . . . Over-pressure . . . in Public Elementary Schools: 1884, vol. 61.
Royal Commission on the Housing of the Working Classes: 1884–85, vol. 30.
Return of Cases . . . in Which Overpressure Has Been Alleged as the Cause of Illness: 1884–85, vol. 61.
Royal Commission on the . . . Elementary Education Acts in England and Wales: 1886, vol. 25; 1887, vols. 29 and 30; 1888, vols. 35 and 37.
Report . . . of the House of Lords on Poor Law Relief: 1888, vol. 15.
Report from the Select Committee on the Infant Life Protection Bill: 1890, vol. 13.
Report of the Departmental Committee [on] . . . School Attendance and Child Labour: 1893–94, vol. 68.
Return Showing . . . the Number of Separation Orders Granted Under the Matrimonial Causes Act, 1878: 1895, vol. 81.
Report from the [Lords] Select Committee . . . on the Infant Life Protection Bill and Safety of Nurse Children Bill: 1896, vol. 10.
Report of the Departmental Committee [on] . . . the Maintenance and Education of Children Under the Charge of Managers of District Schools and Boards of Guardians: 1896, vol. 43.

Final Report of the Royal Commission [on] . . . Vaccination: 1896, vol. 47.

Report of the Inter-Departmental Committee on Physical Deterioration: 1904, vol. 32.

Report of the Departmental Committee on Vaccination Expenses: 1905, vol. 73 (Lords).

Board of Education, Report of the Consultative Committee upon the School Attendance of Children Below the Age of Five: 1908, vol. 119 (Lords).

Report . . . on Debtors (Imprisonment): 1909, vol. 7.

Report of the Inter-Departmental Committee on Partial Exemption from School Attendance: 1909, vol. 17.

Royal Commission on the Poor Laws and Relief of Distress: 1909, vols. 18, 40, and 68 (Lords).

Board of Education, Report on the Working of the Education (Provision of Meals) Act: 1910, vol. 23.

Report of the Departmental Committee on the Probation of Offenders Act, 1907: 1910, vol. 45.

Report of the Royal Commission on Divorce and Matrimonial Causes: 1912–13, vols. 67–70 (Lords).

Report of the Departmental Committee on Reformatory and Industrial Schools: 1913, vol. 39.

Report of the [Hopkinson] Committee on Child Adoption: 1921, vol. 9.

Report of the Departmental Committee on the Training, Appointment and Payment of Probation Officers: 1922, vol. 10.

Child Adoption [Tomlin] Committee: First and Second Reports, 1924–25, vol. 9; Final Report, 1926, vol. 8.

Report of the Departmental Committee on Sexual Offences Against Young Persons: 1924–25, vol. 15.

Report of the Departmental Committee on the Treatment of Young Offenders: 1927, vol. 12.

Report of the Departmental Committee on Vaccination: 1928, vol. 12.

Report of the Poor Persons (Divorce Jurisdiction) Committee: 1929–30, vol. 17.

Further Report of the Committee on Vaccination: 1930–31, vol. 17.

Report of the Departmental Committee on Imprisonment by Courts of Summary Jurisdiction in Default of Payment of Fines: 1933–34, vol. 11.

Report of the Departmental Committee on Sterilisation: 1933–34, vol. 15.

Report of the Departmental Committee on the Social Services in Courts of Summary Jurisdiction: 1935–36, vol. 8.

Report of the Departmental [Horsbrugh] Committee on Adoption Societies and Agencies: 1936–37, vol. 9.

Report of the Departmental Committee on Corporal Punishment: 1937–38, vol. 9.

Report of the Tribunal Appointed Under the Tribunals of Inquiry (Evidence) Act, 1921: 1942–43, vol. 4.

Report of the Care of Children [Curtis] Committee: 1945–46, vol. 10.

Committee on Procedure in Matrimonial Causes: First and Second Interim
    Reports, 1945–46, vol. 13; Final Report, 1946–47, vol. 13.
Report of the Departmental Committee on Grants for . . . Marriage Guidance:
    1948–49, vol. 17.
Report of the Departmental Committee on the Adoption of Children: 1953–
    54, vol. 8.
Royal Commission on Marriage and Divorce: 1955–56, vol. 23.
Report of the Departmental Committee on Matrimonial Proceedings in Magis-
    trates' Courts: 1958–59, vol. 16.
Report of the [Ingleby] Committee on Children and Young Persons: 1959–60,
    vol. 9.
Report of the Departmental [Houghton] Committee on the Adoption of Chil-
    dren: 1971–72, vol. 38.

Newspapers and Periodicals (substantially consulted)

Advance! The Monthly Magazine of the West London Mission
The Anti-Vaccinator and Public Health Journal
The Book and Its Missions, Past and Present
Brain: A Journal of Neurology
British Medical Journal
Charity Organisation Review
Child Life
Child Study
Child's Guardian
Church of England Temperance Chronicle
City Mission Magazine
Contemporary Review
The Cottager's Monthly Visitor
District Visitor's Record
The Englishwoman
Fortnightly Review
The Friendly Visitor
The Home Visitor
The Hospital
Justice of the Peace and Local Government Review
The Lancet
The Magdalen's Friend, and Female Homes' Intelligencer
The Magistrate
The Medical Officer
Mind: A Quarterly Review of Philosophy
The Missing Link Magazine
The Mothers' Companion
Mothers in Council
Mothers' Union Journal
New Era

Nineteenth Century
Nursing Times
Our Waifs and Strays
The Parents' Review: A Monthly Magazine of Home-Training and Culture
Probation
Public Health: A Journal of Sanitary Science and Progress
Public Health: The Journal of the Society of Medical Officers of Health
Punch
Quarterly Review
Queen's Nurses Magazine
The Sanitary Record
The School Attendance Officers' Gazette
The School Child
Seeking and Saving
Solicitors' Journal
South Western Star
The Spectator
The Times
The Vaccination Inquirer and Health Review
Westminster Review

Other Works

Abbott, Edwin A. *Hints on Home Teaching*. London, 1883.

Abbott, Grace. *The Child and the State*. 2 vols. Chicago, 1938.

Abbott, Pamela, and Claire Wallace. *The Family and the New Right*. London, 1992.

Abel-Smith, Brian. *A History of the Nursing Profession*. London, 1960.

Ackerknecht, Erwin H. *A Short History of Psychiatry*. Trans. Sulammith Wolff. New York, 1959.

Acland, E. A. *Marriage as the Foundation of the Home*. Oxford, 1902.

Acland, F. D. "The Marriage Bill." *The Fortnightly*, n.s. 141 (Feb. 1937): 224-29.

Acton, William. "Observations on Illegitimacy in the London Parishes of St. Marylebone, St. Pancras, and St. George's, Southwark, During the Year 1857." *Statistical Journal* (Dec. 1859): 491-505.

Adamson, John W. *English Education 1789-1902*. Cambridge, 1964.

Adkins, Frank J. "Holidays for Children." *Westminster Review*, 170 (Nov. 1908): 574-81.

"The Adoption of Children Act in Working." *Solicitors' Journal*, 75 (Feb. 14, 1931): 107-8.

Advances in Understanding the Child. London, 1935.

Alcock, J. A. M. "Psycho-Analysis." *Education for the New Era*, 1 (July 1920): 68-70.

Allbutt, T. Clifford. "On Brain Forcing." *Brain*, 1 (Apr. 1878): 60-78.

Allen, Anne, and Arthur Morton. *This Is Your Child*. London, 1961.

Allen, Greta. *Practical Hints to Health Visitors*. London, 1908.

Amussen, Susan. *An Ordered Society: Gender and Class in Early Modern England*. Oxford, 1988.

Anderson, Benedict. *Imagined Communities: Reflections on the Origin and Spread of Nationalism*. Revised ed. London, 1991.

Anderson, Michael. *Approaches to the History of the Western Family, 1500–1914*. London, 1980.

———. *Family Structure in Nineteenth Century Lancashire*. Cambridge, 1974.

———. "The Social Implications of Demographic Change." In F. M. L. Thompson, ed., *The Cambridge Social History of Britain 1750–1950*, vol. 2. Cambridge, 1990.

Anderson, Olive. *Suicide in Victorian and Edwardian England*. Oxford, 1987.

Anderson, William. *Children Rescued from Pauperism: or, the Boarding-Out System in Scotland*. Edinburgh, 1871.

Andrews, O. M. "Teach Yourself: An Account of Miss Mason's Methods." In Ernest Young, ed., *The New Era in Education*. London, 1922.

Anecdotes of the Life of the Right Hon. William Pitt, Earl of Chatham. 2 vols. London, 1792.

Arblaster, Anthony. *The Rise and Decline of Western Liberalism*. Oxford, 1984.

Ariès, Philippe. *Centuries of Childhood: A Social History of Family Life*. Trans. Robert Baldick. New York, 1962.

———. "Introduction." In Roger Chartier, ed., *A History of Private Life*, vol. 3. Trans. Arthur Goldhammer. Cambridge, MA, 1989.

Armstrong, David. *Political Anatomy of the Body: Medical Knowledge in Britain in the Twentieth Century*. Cambridge, 1983.

Armstrong, R. A. *The Overstrain in Education*. London, 1883.

Armytage, W. H. G. *Four Hundred Years of English Education*. Cambridge, 1970.

Arnold, David. "The Colonial Prison: Power, Knowledge and Penology in Nineteenth-Century India." In idem and David Hardiman, eds., *Subaltern Studies VIII*. Delhi, 1994.

———. *Colonizing the Body: State Medicine and Epidemic Disease in Nineteenth-Century India*. Berkeley, CA, 1993.

Arnot, Margaret L. "Infant Death, Child Care and the State: The Baby-Farming Scandal and the First Infant Life Protection Legislation of 1872." *Continuity and Change*, 9 (Aug. 1994): 271–311.

Auden, W. H. *The Orators: An English Study*. New York, 1967 [1932].

Ayers, Pat, and Jan Lambertz. "Marriage Relations, Money, and Domestic Violence in Working-Class Liverpool, 1919–39." In Jane Lewis, ed., *Labour and Love: Women's Experience of Home and Family, 1850–1940*. Oxford, 1986

Backscheider, Paula R. "Introduction." In idem and Timothy Dykstal, eds., *The Intersections of the Public and Private Spheres in Early Modern England*. London, 1996.

Bagehot, Walter. *The English Constitution*. London, 1973 [1867].

Bagot, J. H. *Juvenile Delinquency*. London, 1941.

Bailey, Victor. *Delinquency and Citizenship: Reclaiming the Young Offender, 1914-1948*. Oxford, 1987.

Bailey, Victor, and Sheila Blackburn. "The Punishment of Incest Act 1908: A Case Study of Law Creation." *Criminal Law Review* (Nov. 1979): 708-17.

Bailward, Margaret E. *Mothers and Their Responsibilities*. London, 1904.

Bain, Alexander. *Education as a Science*. New York, 1896 [1879].

———. *On the Study of Character*. London, 1861.

Baines, Thomas. *History of the Commerce and Town of Liverpool*. London, 1852.

Baldwin, J. Mark. "A New Method of Child Study." *Science*, 21 (Apr. 21, 1893): 213-14.

Ballard, Philip Boswood. *Things I Cannot Forget*. London, 1937.

Baly, Monica E. *A History of the Queen's Nursing Institute*. London, 1987.

Barker, Rodney. *Political Ideas in Modern Britain*. London, 1978.

Barnardo, Syrie, and James Marchant. *Memoires of the Late Dr. Barnardo*. London, 1907.

Barnardo, Thomas J. *Worse than Orphans: How I Stole Two Girls and Fought for a Boy*. London, 1885.

Barnes, Annie E. "The Unmarried Mother and Her Child." *Contemporary Review*, 112 (Nov. 1917): 556-59.

Barnett, Henrietta. *Canon Barnett: His Life, Work, and Friends*. 2 vols. London, 1921.

———. *The Making of the Home*. London [1885].

———. *Matters That Matter*. London, 1930.

———. "Special Police Courts for Children." *Cornhill Magazine*, 3rd series, 18 (1905): 735-45.

Barnett, Mary G. *Young Delinquents*. London, 1913.

Barrault, Émile. *Occident et Orient*. Paris, 1835.

Barret-Ducrocq, Françoise. *Love in the Time of Victoria*. Trans. John Howe. London, 1991.

Barrett, Michèle, and Mary McIntosh. *The Anti-social Family*. London, 1982.

Barrett, Rosa M. "Hooligans at Home and Abroad." *Good Words* (June 1901): 388-95.

Barrister-at-Law. "Police Courts and Husbands and Wives." *The Spectator*, 152 (Apr. 13, 1934): 567.

Barrow, Logie. "An Imponderable Liberator: J. J. Garth Wilkinson." In Roger Cooter, ed., *Studies in the History of Alternative Medicine*. New York, 1988.

Barry, F. R., Claud Mullins, and Douglas White. *Right Marriage*. London, 1934.

Barth, Fredrik. *Ritual and Knowledge Among the Baktaman of New Guinea*. New Haven, CT, 1975.

Bartlett, John. *Familiar Quotations*. 14th ed. Boston, 1968.

Bartlett, Lucy C. "Probation and Children's Courts in Italy." *Hibbert Journal* (1908-9): 391-403.

Bathurst, M. E. "Juvenile Delinquency in Britain During the War." *Journal of Criminal Law and Criminology*, 34 (Jan.-Feb. 1944): 291-302.

Bauer, Carol, and Lawrence Ritt. "Wife-Abuse, Late-Victorian English Feminists, and the Legacy of Frances Power Cobbe." *International Journal of Women's Studies*, 6 (May/June 1983): 195-207.

Baugh, Daniel. *British Naval Administration in the Age of Walpole.* Princeton, NJ, 1965.

Bayly, Elisabeth Boyd. *England's Answer to the Children's Cry.* London, 1908.

[Bayly, Mary.] *Lancashire Homes, and What Ails Them.* 2nd ed. London, 1863.

———. *Ragged Homes, and How to Mend Them.* London, 1860.

Beales, H. L. "The Victorian Family." In *Ideas and Beliefs of the Victorians.* London, 1949.

Beard, Belle B. *Juvenile Probation.* New York, 1934.

Beaumont, Joseph. "House and Home" [ca. 1640]. In H. J. C. Grierson and G. Bullough, eds., *The Oxford Book of Seventeenth Century Verse.* Oxford, 1934.

Beck, Ann. "Issues in the Anti-Vaccination Movement in England." *Medical History*, 4 (Oct. 1960): 310-21.

Bedwell, C. E. A. "The Fatherless and Widows." *Contemporary Review*, 108 (Aug. 1915): 179-82.

Beekman, Daniel. *The Mechanical Baby: A Popular History of the Theory and Practice of Child Rearing.* Westport, CT, 1977.

Begg, James. *Happy Homes for Working Men, and How to Get Them.* London, 1866.

Behlmer, George K. *Child Abuse and Moral Reform in England, 1870-1908.* Stanford, CA, 1982.

———. "Deadly Motherhood: Infanticide and Medical Opinion in Mid-Victorian England." *Journal of the History of Medicine and Allied Sciences*, 34 (Oct. 1979): 403-27.

———. "Ernest Hart and the Social Thrust of Victorian Medicine." *British Medical Journal* (Oct. 3, 1990): 711-13.

———. "The Gypsy Problem in Victorian England." *Victorian Studies*, 28 (Winter 1985): 231-53.

Bell, Lady. *At the Works: A Study of a Manufacturing Town.* London, 1907.

Bellingham, Bruce. "Waifs and Strays: Child Abandonment, Foster Care, and Families in Mid-Nineteenth-Century New York." In Peter Mandler, ed., *The Uses of Charity: The Poor on Relief in the Nineteenth-Century Metropolis.* Philadelphia, 1990.

Belloc, Hilaire. *The Servile State.* London, 1912.

Benet, Mary K. *The Politics of Adoption.* New York, 1976.

Benn, Stanley I., and Gerald F. Gans. "The Liberal Conception of the Public and Private." In idem, eds., *Public and Private in Social Life.* London, 1983.

Bentham, Jeremy. "Principles of the Civil Code" [ca. 1802]. In John Bowring, ed., *The Works of Jeremy Bentham.* 11 vols. Edinburgh, 1859.

Berdoe, Edward. "Slum-Mothers and Death Clubs: A Vindication." *Nineteenth Century*, 29 (Apr. 1891): 560-63.

Berger, Brigitte, and Peter L. Berger. *The War over the Family.* Garden City, NY, 1983.

Besant, Walter. *London South of the Thames.* London, 1912.

————. *South London*. London, 1899.

Best, Geoffrey. *Mid-Victorian Britain 1851–1875*. Frogmore, St. Albans, Herts., 1973.

Beveridge, William. *The London School of Economics and Its Problems 1919–1937*. London, 1960.

————. *Voluntary Action: A Report on Methods of Social Advance*. London, 1948.

Biggs. J. T. *Leicester: Sanitation Versus Vaccination*. London, 1912.

————. *Smallpox at Middlesborough: A Reply to Dr. Dingle's Report*. 2nd ed. London [1902].

Bingham, J. H. *The Period of the Sheffield School Board 1870–1903*. Sheffield, 1949.

Biron, Chartres. *Without Prejudice: Impressions of Life and Law*. London, 1936.

Blatchford, Robert. *Dismal England*. New York, 1984 [1899].

Blunt, John Henry. *Directorium Pastorale*. London, 1864.

Blythe, Ronald. *Akenfield: Portrait of an English Village*. London, 1969.

Bochel, Dorothy. *Probation and After-Care: Its Development in England and Wales*. Edinburgh, 1976.

Bondfield, Margaret. *The National Care of Maternity*. London, 1914.

Booth, Charles. *Life and Labour of the People in London*. 17 vols. London, 1892–1903.

Booth, William. *In Darkest England and the Way Out*. London, 1890.

Bosanquet, Charles. *A Handy-Book for Visitors of the Poor in London*. London, 1874.

Bosanquet, Helen. *Rich and Poor*. London, 1896.

Boss, Peter. *Social Policy and the Young Delinquent*. London, 1967.

Bossy, John. "The Social History of Confession in the Age of the Reformation." *Transactions of the Royal Historical Society*, 5th series, 25 (1975): 21–38.

Bottomley, Anne. "Resolving Family Disputes: A Critical View." In Michael D. A. Freeman, ed., *The State, the Law, and the Family: Critical Perspectives*. London, 1984.

————. "What Is Happening to Family Law? A Feminist Critique of Conciliation." In Julia Brophy and Carol Smart, eds., *Women-In-Law*. London, 1985.

Bowley, Arthur L. *Wages and Income in the United Kingdom Since 1860*. Cambridge, 1937.

Boyd, William. *From Locke to Montessori*. New York, 1914.

Boyer, Paul. "The Witching Hour." *New Republic*, 188 (Jan. 17, 1983): 44–46.

Boyle, Thomas. *Black Swine in the Sewers of Hampstead*. New York, 1989.

Brand, Jeanne L. *Doctors and the State: The British Medical Profession and Governmental Action in Public Health, 1870–1912*. Baltimore, 1965.

Bray, Reginald A. *The Town Child*. London, 1907.

Brewer, John. *The Sinews of Power: War, Money and the English State, 1688–1787*. New York, 1989.

Bridges. J. H. "The Moral and Social Aspects of Health." *Eclectic Magazine*, n.s. 27 (Feb. 1878): 129–41.

Brief Summary of Past Work [National Anti-Vaccination League]. London, 1926.

Briggs, Asa, and Anne Macartney. *Toynbee Hall: The First Hundred Years.* London, 1984.

Briggs, Isaac G. *Reformatory Reform.* London, 1924.

British Social Attitudes: The 13th Report. Aldershot, Hants., 1996.

Brougham, Henry. *Historical Sketches of Statesmen Who Flourished in the Time of George III.* 3 vols. London, 1839–43.

Brown, James Baldwin. *The Home: In Its Relation to Man and to Society.* London, 1883.

Brown, James D., and Stephen S. Stratton, eds., *British Musical Biography.* Birmingham, 1897.

Brown, Stephen. *Reform and the Rise of Family Law.* Birmingham, 1990.

Brown, Stuart J. *Thomas Chalmers and the Godly Commonwealth in Scotland.* Oxford, 1982.

Brown, W. Paterson. "The Family Neurosis." In R. G. Gordon, ed., *A Survey of Child Psychiatry.* London, 1939.

Brundage, Anthony. *England's "Prussian Minister": Edwin Chadwick and the Politics of Government Growth, 1832–1854.* University Park, PA, 1988.

Buckman, S. S. "Babies and Monkeys." *Nineteenth Century,* 36 (Nov. 1894): 727–43.

Bunner, H. C. "'Home, Sweet Home,' with Variations"[1881]. In William Harmon, ed., *The Oxford Book of American Light Verse.* New York, 1979.

Burbury, W. Mary, Edna M. Balint, and Bridget J. Yapp. *An Introduction to Child Guidance.* London, 1945.

Burke, Edmund. *Reflections on the Revolution in France.* Harmondsworth, Middlesex, 1976 [1790].

———. *Thoughts and Details on Scarcity* [1795]. In *The Writings and Speeches of the Right Honorable Edmund Burke.* 12 vols. Boston, 1901.

Burn, W. L. *The Age of Equipoise.* New York, 1965.

Burnett, John, ed. *Destiny Obscure: Autobiographies of Childhood, Education and Family from the 1820s to the 1920s.* London, 1982.

Burns, C. L. C. "Why Children Steal." *The Spectator,* 159 (Dec. 24, 1937): 1140–41.

Burt, Cyril. "Symposium on Psychologists and Psychiatrists in the Child Guidance Service, VII." *British Journal of Educational Psychology,* 23 (Feb. 1953): 8–28.

———. *The Young Delinquent.* New York, 1925.

[Butler, Charles.] *An Essay on the Legality of Impressing Seamen.* London, 1777.

Buxton, Sydney. "Over-Pressure." *Nineteenth Century,* 16 (Nov. 1884): 806–25.

Bygott, A. H. "The Minor Courts in Their Relation to Public Health." In *Report of the Proceedings of the National Conference on Destitution.* 2 vols. London, 1911–12.

Bynum, W. F. *Science and the Practice of Medicine in the Nineteenth Century.* Cambridge, 1994.

Cadbury, Geraldine S. *Young Offenders: Yesterday and Today*. London, 1938.
Cairns, J. A. R. *Drab Street Glory*. London, 1934.
———. *The Loom of the Law*. London, 1922.
"Can a Child Trust the Law?" *The Outlook*, 110 (Aug. 11, 1915): 845-47.
Cancellor, H. L. *The Life of a London Beak*. London, 1930.
Cannon, John. *Parliamentary Reform 1640-1832*. Cambridge, 1973.
Carlebach, Julius. *Caring for Children in Trouble*. London, 1970.
Carp, E. Wayne. "Professional Social Workers, Adoption, and the Problem of Illegitimacy, 1915-1945." *Journal of Policy History*, 6, no. 3 (1994): 161-84.
Carpenter, Mary. *Juvenile Delinquents, Their Condition and Treatment*. London, 1853.
———. *Reformatory Schools for the Children of the Perishing and Dangerous Classes, and for Juvenile Offenders*. London, 1851.
Carpenter, William B. *Principles of Mental Physiology*. New York, 1889 [1874].
———. "Small-Pox and Vaccination in 1871-1881." *Nineteenth Century*, 11 (Apr. 1882): 526-46.
Carr-Saunders, A. M., Hermann Mannheim, and E. C. Rhodes. *Young Offenders: An Enquiry into Juvenile Delinquency*. Cambridge, 1944.
Cases of Disease, Suffering and Death Reported by the Injured Families [tract no. 5]. In *Vaccination Tracts*. London, 1879.
Cecil, Hugh. "The Rights of Parents." *The Spectator*, 109 (Dec. 14, 1912): 1011.
Chalmers, Thomas. *The Christian and Civic Economy of Large Towns*. 3 vols. Glasgow, 1821-26.
Chapman, Cecil. *From the Bench*. London, 1932.
———. *Marriage and Divorce*. London, 1911.
———. *The Poor Man's Court of Justice: Twenty-Five Years as a Metropolitan Magistrate*. London, 1925.
Chase, Allan. *Magic Shots*. New York, 1982.
Chase, Ellen. *Tenant Friends in Old Deptford*. London, 1929.
C.H.D. "An East End Police Court." *Toynbee Record*, 11 (Feb. 1899): 70-71.
Chesterton, G. K. *The Autobiography of G. K. Chesterton*. New York, 1936.
———. *Eugenics and Other Evils*. London, 1922.
Child Adoption [NSPCC Occasional Papers, X]. London, 1921.
"Child Adoption." *The Spectator*, 129 (Aug. 12, 1922): 200-201.
Child Guidance Council. *Note on Present Activities*. London, 1940.
———. *Reports*. London, 1931-1940.
Children's Home and Orphanage. *Annual Reports*. London, 1879-1896.
Cholmondeley, Essex. *Parents Are Peacemakers: Six Talks*. London [1944].
———. *The Story of Charlotte Mason*. London, 1960.
Chrisman, Oscar. *Paidology: The Science of the Child*. Boston, 1920.
Clark, Anna. "Contested Space: The Public and Private Spheres in Nineteenth-Century Britain." *Journal of British Studies*, 35 (Apr. 1996): 269-76.
———. *The Struggle for the Breeches: Gender and the Making of the British Working Class*. Berkeley, CA, 1995.

————. *Women's Silence, Men's Violence: Sexual Assault in England 1770–1845*. London, 1987.

Clarke, Alan. "Prejudice, Ignorance and Panic! Popular Politics in a Land Fit for Scroungers." In Martin Loney, David Boswell, and John Clarke, eds., *Social Policy and Social Welfare*. Milton Keynes, 1983.

Clarke, John. "Managing the Delinquent: The Children's Branch of the Home Office, 1913–30." In Mary Langan and Bill Schwarz, eds., *Crises in the British State 1880–1930*. London, 1985.

Clarke, John. *Paroemiologia Anglo-Latina in Usum Scholarum Concinnata*. London, 1639.

Claudia [Mary P. Hack]. *Consecrated Women*. London, 1880.

Clergyman's Daughter, A [Maria L. Charlesworth]. *The Female Visitor to the Poor*. London, 1846.

Clouston, T. S. *The Hygiene of the Mind*. London, 1906.

————. *The Neuroses of Development*. Edinburgh, 1891.

Clynes, J. R. *Memoirs*. 2 vols. London, 1937.

Cobbe, Frances Power. *Life of Frances Power Cobbe*. 2 vols. Boston, 1894.

————. "Wife Torture in England." *Contemporary Review*, 32 (Apr. 1878): 55–87.

Cohen, Phil. "Policing the Working-Class City." In Bob Fine et al., eds., *Capitalism and the Rule of Law*. London, 1979.

Cohen, Stanley. *Folk Devils and Moral Panics: The Creation of the Mods and Rockers*. New York, 1980.

Cohn, E. J. "Reconciliation and Divorce." *The Fortnightly*, n.s. 160 (Dec. 1946): 403–9.

Coke, Edward. "Semayne's Case." In idem, *The Reports of Sir Edward Coke*. 2nd ed. London, 1680.

————. *Third Part of the Institutes of the Laws of England*. 3rd ed. London, 1660.

Colcord, Joanna C. *Broken Homes: A Study of Family Desertion and Its Social Treatment*. New York, 1919.

Cole, Margaret. *Marriage Past and Present*. London, 1938.

Colley, Linda. "Britishness and Otherness: An Argument." *Journal of British Studies*, 31 (Oct. 1992): 309–29.

————. *Britons: Forging the Nation 1707–1837*. New Haven, CT, 1992.

Collier, Howard E. *Happy Marriage in Modern Life*. Birmingham, 1937.

Collini, Stefan. "The Idea of 'Character' in Victorian Political Thought." *Transactions of the Royal Historical Society*, 5th series, 35 (1985): 29–50.

————. *Liberalism and Sociology: L. T. Hobhouse and Political Argument in England 1880–1914*. Cambridge, 1979.

Collins, William J. "The Place of Volition in Education." *International Journal of Ethics*, 23 (July 1913): 379–96.

Compulsory Vaccination a Desecration of Law, a Breaker of Homes. . . [tract no. 11]. In *Vaccination Tracts*. London, 1879.

Conley, Carolyn A. *The Unwritten Law: Criminal Justice in Victorian Kent*. New York, 1991.

Conybeare, William J. *Charity of Poor to Poor*. London, 1908.

Coombs, Joyce. *George and Mary Sumner: Their Life and Times*. London, 1965.

Coontz, Stephanie. *The Way We Never Were: American Families and the Nostalgia Trap*. New York, 1992.

Cooter, Roger. *The Cultural Meaning of Popular Science: Phrenology and the Organization of Consent in Nineteenth-Century Britain*. Cambridge, 1984.

Copland, James. *A Dictionary of Practical Medicine*. 9 vols. New York, 1845–1859.

Corder, R. E. [James Dunn]. *Tales Told to the Magistrate*. London, 1925.

Cott, Nancy F. *The Bonds of Womanhood: "Women's Sphere" in New England, 1780–1835*. New Haven, CT, 1977.

Cotton, Nathaniel. "The Fireside" [1751]. In Alexander Chalmers, ed., *The Works of the English Poets, from Chaucer to Cowper*. 21 vols. London, 1810.

Couchman, Mary. *More Homely Words for Mothers*. London, 1899.

Courtney, Janet E. "Children's Courts." *Fortnightly Review*, 127 (May 1927): 629–36.

Cox, E. W. *The Principles of Punishment, as Applied . . . by Judges and Magistrates*. London, 1877.

Cox, Jeffrey. *The English Churches in a Secular Society: Lambeth, 1870–1930*. New York, 1982.

C.R. "Moloch in England." *Westminster Review*, 139 (Mar. 1893): 239–46.

Crackanthorpe, B. A. "The Revolt of the Daughters." *Nineteenth Century*, 35 (Jan. 1894): 23–31.

Craig, R. N. "Report on the Work of the Exeter Child Guidance Clinic." In Leon Radzinowicz and J. W. C. Turner, eds., *Mental Abnormality and Crime*. London, 1944.

Crawford, Mabel S. "Maltreatment of Wives." *Westminster Review*, 139 (Mar. 1893): 292–303.

Crawford, Virginia M. *Ideals of Charity*. Edinburgh, 1908.

Crichton-Browne, James. *The Doctor's Second Thoughts*. London, 1931.

———. *From the Doctor's Notebooks*. London, 1937.

———. *The Story of the Brain*. Edinburgh, 1924.

Crichton-Miller, Hugh. *The New Psychology and the Parent*. London [1922].

———, ed. *Functional Nerve Disease: An Epitome of War Experience for the Practitioner*. London, 1920.

Croom-Johnson, Norman. "The Adoption of Children." *The Englishwoman*, 116 (Aug. 1918): 49–54.

Crossick, Geoffrey. *An Artisan Elite in Victorian Society: Kentish London 1840–1880*. Totowa, NJ, 1978.

Crowther, M. A. "Family Responsibility and State Responsibility in Britain Before the Welfare State." *Historical Journal*, 25, no. 1 (1982): 131–45.

"The Cry of the Children." *Quarterly Review*, 205 (July 1906): 29–53.

"The Cry of the Parents." *Macmillan's Magazine*, 62 (May 1890): 55–58.

Culverwell, E. P. *The Montessori Principles and Practice*. 2nd ed. London, 1914.

Cunnington, C. Willett. *Nursery Notes for Mothers*. London, 1913.

Curgenven, J. B. *On Baby-Farming and the Registration of Nurses*. London, 1869.

————. *Infant Life Protection Society Prospectus*. London [1870].

Curtis, S. J., and M. E. A. Boultwood. *An Introductory History of English Education Since 1800*. 4th ed. London, 1970.

Cuttle, George. *The Legacy of the Rural Guardians: A Study of Conditions in Mid-Essex*. Cambridge, 1934.

D'Aeth, Frederic G., ed. *Liverpool Social Workers' Handbook*. 2nd ed. Liverpool, 1916.

Dark, Sidney. *Inasmuch . . . Christianity in the Police Courts*. London, 1939.

Darwin, Charles. "A Biographical Sketch of an Infant." *Mind*, 2 (July 1877): 285-94.

Dauncey, Enid C. "Ignorant Mothers." *Contemporary Review*, 97 (May 1910): 603-7.

Daunton, M. J. *House and Home in the Victorian City*. London, 1983.

Davenport-Hill, Florence. *Children of the State*. 2nd ed. London, 1889.

Davidoff, Leonore. "The Family in Britain." In F. M. L. Thompson, ed., *The Cambridge Social History of Britain 1750-1950*, vol. 2. Cambridge, 1990.

————. "The Separation of Home and Work? Landladies and Lodgers in Nineteenth- and Twentieth-Century England." In Sandra Burman, ed., *Fit Work for Women*. New York, 1979.

Davidoff, Leonore, and Catherine Hall. *Family Fortunes: Men and Women of the English Middle Class, 1790-1850*. London, 1987.

Davidoff, Leonore, Jeanne L'Esperance, and Howard Newby. "Landscape with Figures: Home and Community in English Society." In Davidoff, ed., *Worlds Between: Historical Perspectives on Gender and Class*. Cambridge, 1995.

Davidson, Caroline. *A Woman's Work Is Never Done: A History of Housework in the British Isles 1650-1950*. London, 1983.

Davies, Celia. "The Health Visitor as Mother's Friend: A Woman's Place in Public Health, 1900-14." *Social History of Medicine*, 1 (Apr. 1988): 39-59.

Davies, J. L. "District Visiting." In F. D. Maurice, ed., *Lectures to Ladies on Practical Subjects*. Cambridge, 1855.

Davies, Margaret Llewelyn, ed. *Life as We Have Known It*. London, 1931.

Davin, Anna. *Growing Up Poor: Home, School and Street in London 1870-1914*. London, 1996.

————. "Imperialism and Motherhood." *History Workshop*, 5 (Spring 1978): 9-65.

Davis, Jennifer. "The London Garrotting Panic of 1862: A Moral Panic and the Creation of a Criminal Class in Mid-Victorian England." In V. A. C. Gatrell, Bruce Lenman, and Geoffrey Parker, eds., *Crime and the Law: The Social History of Crime in Western Europe Since 1500*. London, 1980.

————. "A Poor Man's System of Justice: The London Police Courts in the Second Half of the Nineteenth Century." *Historical Journal*, 27 (June 1984): 309-35.

————. "Prosecutions and Their Context: The Use of the Criminal Law in Later Nineteenth-Century London." In Douglas Hay and Francis Snyder, eds., *Policing and Prosecution in Britain 1750-1850*. Oxford, 1989.

Davison, Ronald C. "The Revolt Against Officialdom." *Westminster Review*, 177 (Feb. 1912): 126–32.

Dawtry, Frank. "Whither Probation?" *British Journal of Delinquency*, 8 (Jan. 1958): 180–87.

Dayus, Kathleen. *Her People*. London, 1982.

Demos, John. *A Little Commonwealth: Family Life in Plymouth Colony*. New York, 1970.

Dennis, Wayne. "Historical Beginnings of Child Psychology." *Psychological Bulletin*, 46 (May 1949): 224–35.

Devon, James. *The Criminal and the Community*. London, 1912.

Dickens, Charles. *The Adventures of Oliver Twist*. New York, 1980 [1838].

———. *American Notes*. London, 1985 [1842].

———. *Bleak House*. New York, 1924 [1852–53].

———. *Dombey and Son*. New York, 1885 [1846–48].

———. *Little Dorrit*. London, 1857 [1856–57].

Dicks, H. V. *Fifty Years of the Tavistock Clinic*. London, 1970.

Dickson, Thompson. "On Baby Farming." *Medical Press and Circular*, n.s. 10 (Oct. 1870): 323–27.

Dingwall, Robert, Anne Marie Rafferty, and Charles Webster. *An Introduction to the Social History of Nursing*. London, 1988.

A Discourse on the Impressing of Mariners. London [1768].

Disraeli, Benjamin. *Selected Speeches of the late . . . Earl of Beaconsfield*. 2 vols. London, 1882.

District Visitors, Deaconesses, and a Proposed Adaptation . . . of the Third Order. London, 1890.

The District Visitor's Manual. 2nd ed. London, 1840.

Doggett, Maeve E. *Marriage, Wife-Beating and the Law in Victorian England*. London, 1992.

Donzelot, Jacques. *The Policing of Families*. Trans. Robert Hurley. New York, 1979.

Doré, Gustave, and Blanchard Jerrold. *London: A Pilgrimage*. London, 1872.

Douglas, Mary. "The Idea of a Home: A Kind of Space." *Social Research*, 58 (Spring 1991): 287–307.

Dowling, W. C. "The Ladies' Sanitary Association and the Origins of the Health Visiting Service." M.A. thesis, University of London, 1963.

Drawbell, James W. *Experiment in Adoption*. London, 1935.

Drew, Andrew A. W. "Hooliganism and Juvenile Crime." *Nineteenth Century*, 48 (July 1900): 89–99.

Duby, Georges. "Foreword." In Paul Veyne, ed., *A History of Private Life*, vol. 1. Trans. Arthur Goldhammer. Cambridge, MA, 1987.

Ducrocq, Françoise. "The London Biblewomen and Nurses Mission, 1857–1880: Class Relations / Women's Relations." In Barbara J. Harris and Jo Ann K. McNamara, eds., *Women and the Structure of Society*. Durham, NC, 1984.

Dudfield, Thomas O. *Metropolitan Sanitary Administration*. London, 1889.

———. *Woman's Place in Sanitary Administration*. London, 1904.

Dudgeon, Henry D. "Compulsory Vaccination." *Westminster Review*, n.s. 65 (Apr. 1884): 496–528.

Duffy, John. "Mental Strain and 'Overpressure' in the Schools: A Nineteenth-Century Viewpoint." *Journal of the History of Medicine and Allied Sciences*, 23 (Jan. 1968): 63–79.

Dugan, James. *The Great Mutiny*. London, 1966.

Du Maurier, Guy. *An Englishman's Home*. New York, 1909.

Dupree, Marguerite W. *Family Structure in the Staffordshire Potteries 1840–1880*. Oxford, 1995.

Durham, Martin. *Sex and Politics: The Family and Morality in the Thatcher Years*. London, 1991.

"The Dwellings of the Poor." *Quarterly Review*, 157 (Jan. 1884): 144–68.

Dwork, Deborah. *War Is Good for Babies and Other Young Children: A History of the Infant and Child Welfare Movement in England 1898–1918*. London, 1987.

Dyhouse, Carol. *Feminism and the Family in England 1880–1939*. Oxford, 1989.

———. *Girls Growing Up in Late Victorian and Edwardian England*. London, 1981.

———. "Working-Class Mothers and Infant Mortality in England, 1895–1914." *Journal of Social History*, 12 (Winter 1978): 248–67.

Education and Care of Idiots, Imbeciles, and Harmless Lunatics. London, 1877.

Eekelaar, John. *Family Law and Social Policy*. London, 1978.

Egerton, Robert. *Legal Aid*. London, 1945.

Eliot, George. *Silas Marner*. New York, 1906 [1861].

Elkin, Winifred A. *English Juvenile Courts*. London, 1938.

Elliott, Malcom. *Victorian Leicester*. London, 1979.

Elliott, W. H. H. "Children's Care Committees." In J. H. Whitehouse, ed., *Problems of Boy Life*. London, 1912.

Ellis, A. C. O. "Influences on School Attendance in Victorian England." *British Journal of Educational Studies*, 21 (Oct. 1973): 313–26.

Ellison, Mary. *Sparks Beneath the Ashes: Experiences of a London Probation Officer*. London, 1934.

Elmy, Elizabeth C. W. *Woman and the Law*. Congleton, Cheshire [1896].

———. "Woman and the Law." *Westminster Review*, 168 (Oct. 1907): 394–97.

Elshtain, Jean B. *Public Man, Private Woman: Women in Social and Political Thought*. Princeton, NJ, 1981.

Emerson, Ralph Waldo. *English Traits*. Boston, 1884 [1856].

Engels, Friedrich. *The Condition of the Working Class in England*. Trans. and ed. W. O. Henderson and W. H. Chaloner. Stanford, CA, 1968 [1845].

An Enquiry into People's Homes: A Report Prepared by Mass-Observation for the Advertising Service Guild. London, 1943.

Ensor, R. C. K. *Courts and Judges in France, Germany, and England*. London, 1933.

———. *England 1870–1914*. Oxford, 1975 [1936].

Epstein, Barbara L. *The Politics of Domesticity: Women, Evangelicalism, and Temperance in Nineteenth-Century America.* Middletown, CT, 1981.

Erasmus, Desiderius. *Collected Works of Erasmus*, vol. 31: *Adages.* Trans. Margaret M. Phillips. Toronto, 1982.

Ertz, Susan. "Child Guidance: A New Social Service." *The Spectator*, 154 (Feb. 8, 1935): 201–2.

Essays on Duty and Discipline: A Series of Papers on the Training of Children in Relation to Social and National Welfare. London, 1910.

The Establishment of a Child Guidance Clinic. London [1938].

Eve, Enid, ed. *Manual for Health Visitors and Infant Welfare Workers.* London, 1921.

The Evils of Perambulators: A Word to Mothers. 2nd ed. London [1861].

Eyler, John M. "Mortality Statistics and Victorian Health Policy: Program and Criticism." *Bulletin of the History of Medicine*, 50 (Fall 1976): 335–55.

Ezard, Edward. *Battersea Boy.* London, 1979.

The Fathers' Meeting: Half-An-Hour's Reading for Working Men. London [1873?].

Fawcett, Henry. *Pauperism: Its Causes and Remedies.* London, 1871.

Feldman, David. *Englishmen and Jews: Social Relations and Political Culture 1840–1914.* New Haven, CT, 1994.

Ferguson, Harry. "Cleveland in History. The Abused Child and Child Protection, 1880–1914." In Roger Cooter, ed., *In the Name of the Child: Health and Welfare, 1880–1940.* London, 1992.

———. "Rethinking Child Protection Practices: A Case for History." In *Taking Child Abuse Seriously.* London, 1990.

Feversham Committee. *The Voluntary Mental Health Services.* London, 1939.

Finlayson, Geoffrey. *Citizen, State, and Social Welfare in Britain 1830–1990.* Oxford, 1994.

———. "A Moving Frontier: Voluntarism and the State in British Social Welfare 1911–1949." *Twentieth Century British History*, 1, no. 2 (1990): 183–206.

Fisher, Dorothy C. *A Montessori Mother.* New York, 1912.

Fisher, Lettice. "The Adoption of Children." *Fortnightly*, n.s. 158 (Oct. 1945): 260–64.

———. "The Unmarried Mother and Her Child." *Contemporary Review*, 156 (Oct. 1939): 485–89.

Fishman, W. J. *East End 1888.* Philadelphia, 1988.

Fitzgerald, Percy. *Chronicles of Bow Street Police-Office.* 2 vols. London, 1888.

Fitzgerald, Tony. "The New Right and the Family." In Martin Loney, David Boswell, and John Clarke, eds., *Social Policy and Social Welfare.* Milton Keynes, 1983.

Fletcher, Ian C. "'A Star Chamber of the Twentieth Century': Suffragettes, Liberals, and the 1908 'Rush the Commons' Case." *Journal of British Studies*, 35 (Oct. 1996): 504–30.

Fletcher, Ronald. *Britain in the Sixties: The Family and Marriage.* Harmondsworth, Middlesex, 1962.

Flexner, Bernard, and Roger N. Baldwin. *Juvenile Courts and Probation*. London, 1915.

Flint, Elizabeth. *Hot Bread and Chips*. London, 1963.

Flugel, J. C. *The Psycho-Analytic Study of the Family*. London, 1948 [1921].

Foakes, Grace. *My Part of the River*. London, 1974.

Foucault, Michel. *Discipline and Punish: The Birth of the Prison*. Trans. Alan Sheridan. New York, 1979.

Fox, Charles. *Educational Psychology: Its Problems and Methods*. New York, 1925.

Fox, Enid. "An Honourable Calling or a Despised Occupation: Licensed Midwifery and Its Relationship to District Nursing in England and Wales Before 1948." *Social History of Medicine*, 6 (Aug. 1993): 237–59.

Fox, Pamela. *Class Fictions: Shame and Resistance in the British Working-Class Novel, 1890–1945*. Durham, NC, 1994.

Fox, Sanford J. "Juvenile Justice Reform: An Historical Perspective." *Stanford Law Review*, 22 (1969–70): 1187–1239.

Fraser, Stuart M. "Leicester and Smallpox: The Leicester Method." *Medical History*, 24 (July 1980): 315–32.

Frazer, W. M. *A History of English Public Health 1834–1939*. London, 1950.

Frere, Margaret. *Children's Care Committees*. London, 1909.

Froebel, Friedrich. *The Education of Man*. Trans. W. N. Hailmann. New York, 1910 [1826].

Froebel Society of Great Britain and Ireland. *Twenty-Fifth Annual Report*. London, 1900.

Frost, Ginger. *Promises Broken: Courtships, Class, and Gender in Victorian England*. Charlottesville, VA, 1995.

Fuchs, Rachel. *Abandoned Children: Foundlings and Child Welfare in Nineteenth-Century France*. Albany, NY, 1984.

———. "France in a Comparative Perspective." In Elinor A. Accampo et al., eds., *Gender and the Politics of Social Reform in France, 1870–1914*. Baltimore, 1995.

Fulford, Roger, ed. *Dearest Child: Letters Between Queen Victoria and the Princess Royal*. New York, 1965.

Gager, Kristin E. *Blood Ties and Fictive Ties: Adoption and Family Life in Early Modern France*. Princeton, NJ, 1996.

Galsworthy, John. *The Silver Box*. New York, 1909.

Galton, Francis. *Hereditary Genius: An Inquiry into Its Laws and Consequences*. London, 1925 [1869].

———. *Memories of My Life*. 3rd ed. London, 1909.

Gammond, Peter, ed. *The Oxford Companion to Popular Music*. Oxford, 1991.

Gamon, Hugh R. P. *The London Police Court To-Day and To-Morrow*. London, 1907.

Gardiner, Phil. *The Lost Elementary Schools of Victorian England*. London, 1984.

Garland, David. "Foucault's *Discipline and Punish*: An Exposition and Critique." *American Bar Foundation Research Journal*, no. 4 (Fall 1986): 847–80.

————. *Punishment and Welfare: A History of Penal Strategies.* Aldershot, Hants., 1985.

Gath, Dennis et al. *Child Guidance and Delinquency in a London Borough.* Oxford, 1977.

Gatrell, V. A. C. "Crime, Authority and the Policeman-State." In F. M. L. Thompson, ed., *The Cambridge Social History of Britain 1750–1950,* vol. 3. Cambridge, 1990.

————. "The Decline of Theft and Violence in Victorian and Edwardian England." In idem, Bruce Lenmen, and Geoffrey Parker, eds., *Crime and the Law: The Social History of Crime in Western Europe Since 1500.* London, 1980.

Gautrey, Thomas. *"Lux Mihi Laus": School Board Memories.* London, 1937.

Gay, Peter. *The Enlightenment: An Interpretation.* 2 vols. New York, 1969.

Geeson, Cecil. *Just Justice? Husbands and Wives in the Police Courts.* London, 1936.

Geison, Gerald L. *Michael Foster and the Cambridge School of Physiology.* Princeton, NJ, 1978.

Gemmill, William. "Chicago Court of Domestic Relations." *Annals of the American Academy of Political and Social Science,* 52 (Mar. 1914): 115–23.

Gerard, Jessica. "Lady Bountiful: Women of the Landed Classes and Rural Philanthropy." *Victorian Studies,* 30 (Winter 1987): 183–209.

Gesell, Arnold. *The Guidance of Mental Growth in Infant and Child.* New York, 1930.

Gibson, Colin. "The Effect of Legal Aid on Divorce in England and Wales." *Family Law,* 1 (May/June 1971): 90–96.

Gilbert, Bentley, B. *The Evolution of National Insurance in Great Britain.* London, 1966.

Giles, F. T. *The Juvenile Courts: Their Work and Problems.* London, 1946.

————. *The Magistrates' Courts.* Harmondsworth, Middlesex, 1949.

Gill, Angela. "The Leicester School Board 1871–1903." In Brian Simon, ed., *Education in Leicester 1540–1940.* Leicester, 1968.

Gillett, Paula. "From Hayden to *Home, Sweet Home*: Music in Late-Victorian Philanthropy." Unpublished paper (1994).

Gillis, John R. "The Evolution of Juvenile Delinquency in England 1890–1914." *Past and Present,* 67 (May 1975): 96–126.

————. *For Better, for Worse: British Marriages, 1600 to the Present.* New York, 1985.

————. *A World of Their Own Making: Myth, Ritual, and the Quest for Family Values.* New York, 1996.

Gingrich, Newt. *To Renew America.* New York, 1995.

Girouard, Mark. *Life in the English Country House.* New Haven, CT, 1978.

Gittins, Diana. *Fair Sex: Family Size and Structure, 1900–39.* London, 1982.

[Gladstone, W. E.] "The Bill for Divorce." *Quarterly Review,* 102 (July 1857): 251–88.

Glover, Edward. *The Psycho-Pathology of Flogging.* 2nd ed. London, 1937.

Godwin, George. "War and Juvenile Delinquency." *Contemporary Review,* 160 (Oct. 1941): 251–55.

Goffman, Erving. *The Presentation of the Self in Everyday Life*. Garden City, NY, 1959.

——. *Relations in Public: Microstudies of the Public Order*. New York, 1971.

Goleman, Daniel. *Emotional Intelligence*. New York, 1995.

Goody, Jack. "Adoption in Cross-Cultural Perspective." *Comparative Studies in Society and History*, 11 (1969): 55–78.

Gordon, Linda. *Heroes of Their Own Lives: The Politics and History of Family Violence, Boston 1880–1960*. New York, 1988.

Gordon, M. M. *Rights and Wrongs: or, Begin at Home*. London, 1869.

Gorer, Geoffrey. *The American People: A Study in National Character*. New York, 1948.

Gorham, Deborah. "The Ideology of Femininity and Reading for Girls, 1850–1914." In Felicity Hunt, ed., *Lessons for Life: The Schooling of Girls and Women, 1850–1950*. Oxford, 1987.

——. "The 'Maiden Tribute of Modern Babylon' Re-Examined: Child Prostitution and the Idea of Childhood in Late-Victorian England." *Victorian Studies*, 21 (Spring 1978): 353–79.

Gorst, John. *The Children of the Nation*. 2nd ed. London, 1907.

Gotch, Francis. "Nerve." In E. A. Schäfer, ed., *Text-Book of Physiology*. 2 vols. Edinburgh, 1900.

Gowers, William R. *A Manual of Diseases of the Nervous System*. Philadelphia, 1888.

Graebner, William. "The Unstable World of Benjamin Spock: Social Engineering in a Democratic Culture, 1917–1950." *Journal of American History*, 67 (Dec. 1980): 612–29.

Graham-Dixon, Sue. *Never Darken My Door: Working for Single Parents and Their Children 1918–1978*. London, 1981.

Grant, C. W. *The Advantages of the Boarding Out System*. London [1869].

Grant, Cecil. *English Education and Dr. Montessori*. London, 1913.

Graves, George. "Observations on Some of the Causes of Infanticide." *Transactions of the Manchester Statistical Society* (1862–63): 1–24.

Graves, Robert, and Alan Hodge. *The Long Week-End: A Social History of Great Britain 1918–1939*. New York, 1963.

"The Great Underpaid." *Punch*, 64 (Mar. 15, 1873): 105.

Greenhough, J. G. *Our Dear Home Life*. London, 1896.

Greenwood, James. *The Prisoner in the Dock: My Four Years' Daily Experiences in the London Police Courts*. London, 1902.

——. *The Seven Curses of London*. Boston, 1869.

Greg, W. R. *Enigmas of Life*. Boston, 1873.

Gregor, Thomas. *Mehinaku: The Drama of Daily Life in a Brazilian Indian Village*. Chicago, 1977.

Grey, Mrs. Edwin. *The Case for Legalising Adoption*. London [1920].

Grossberg, Michael. *Governing the Hearth: Law and the Family in Nineteenth-Century America*. Chapel Hill, NC, 1985.

Grumbler, A. "The 'Englishman's-House-His-Castle' Theory; Or a Glance at the Police of the Streets." *Fraser's Magazine*, 56 (Dec. 1857): 719–24.

Guthrie, Leonard G. *Functional Nervous Disorders in Childhood.* London, 1909.

H., F. *Hints to District Visitors.* London, 1858.

Habermas, Jürgen. *The Structural Transformation of the Public Sphere: An Inquiry into a Category of Bourgeois Society.* Trans. Thomas Burger. Cambridge, MA, 1989.

Hadfield, J. A. *Psychology and Morals: An Analysis of Character.* London, 1955 [1923].

———. "Treatment by Suggestion and Persuasion." In Hugh Crichton-Miller, ed., *Functional Nerve Disease.* London, 1920.

Haimes, Erica, and Noel Timms. *Adoption, Identity and Social Policy: The Search for Distant Relatives.* Aldershot, Hants., 1985.

Haley, Bruce. *The Healthy Body and Victorian Culture.* Cambridge, MA, 1978.

Hall, Catherine. "The Early Formation of Victorian Domestic Ideology." In Sandra Burman, ed., *Fit Work for Women.* New York, 1979.

Hall, Tony. "Foreword." In Philip Bean, ed., *Adoption: Essays in Social Policy, Law, and Sociology.* London, 1984.

Hall, William Clarke. *Children's Courts.* London, 1926.

———. "The Extent and Practice of Probation in England." In Sheldon Glueck, ed., *Probation and Criminal Justice.* New York, 1933.

———. *The Law of Adoption and Guardianship of Infants.* London, 1928.

———. *The Law Relating to Children.* London, 1894.

———. *The Queen's Reign for Children.* London, 1897.

———. *The State and the Child.* London, 1917.

Hamilton, Mary Agnes. "Britain Fights for Family Life." *Annals of the American Academy of Political and Social Science,* 229 (Sept. 1943): 11–19.

Hamilton, Maud C. "Misson Women." *Nineteenth Century,* 16 (Dec. 1884): 984–90.

Hamilton-Pearson, E. A. "Particular Problems: Lying, Stealing, etc." In *Some Causes of Difficult Behaviour in Children.* London, 1936.

———. "Some Aspects of Child Delinquency." *New Era,* 3 (Oct. 1922): 116–21.

Hammerton, A. James. *Cruelty and Companionship: Conflict in Nineteenth-Century Married Life.* London, 1992.

———. "Victorian Marriage and the Law of Matrimonial Cruelty." *Victorian Studies,* 33 (Winter 1990): 269–92.

Hanawalt, Barbara A. *The Ties That Bound: Peasant Families in Medieval England.* New York, 1986.

"The Happiness of Children." *The Spectator,* 68 (Mar. 5, 1892): 331–32.

A Happy Mothers' Meeting. London [1911?].

Hardcastle, Dorothy H. "A Follow-Up Study of One Hundred Cases Made for the Department of Psychological Medicine, Guy's Hospital." *Journal of Mental Science,* 80 (July 1934): 536–49.

Hardy, Anne. *The Epidemic Streets: Infectious Disease and the Rise of Preventive Medicine, 1856–1900.* Oxford, 1993.

———. "Public Health and the Expert: The London Medical Officers of

Health, 1856–1900." In Roy MacLeod, ed., *Government and Expertise: Specialists, Administrators and Professionals, 1860–1919*. Cambridge, 1988.

Hardyment, Christina. *Dream Babies: Three Centuries of Good Advice on Child Care*. New York, 1983.

Harris, Chris. "The Family in Post-war Britain." In James Obelkevich and Peter Catterall, eds., *Understanding Post-war British Society*. London, 1994.

Harris, George. "The Psychology of Memory." *Proceedings of the Psychological Society of Great Britain, 1875–1879*. London, 1880.

Harris, Jo. *Probation: A Sheaf of Memories*. Lowestoft, Suffolk, 1937.

Harris, Mrs. Jo. *Mother, Child, and Home*. Lowestoft, Suffolk, 1914.

Harris, John. "Unfit for Parenthood." *Westminster Review*, 177 (May, 1912): 579–81.

Harris, José. *Private Lives, Public Spirit: A Social History of Britain 1870–1914*. Oxford, 1993.

———. "Society and the State in Twentieth-Century Britain." In F. M. L. Thompson, ed., *The Cambridge Social History of Britain 1750–1950*, vol. 3. Cambridge, 1990.

Harris, Robert J. "A Changing Service: The Case for Separating 'Care' and 'Control' in Probation Practice." *British Journal of Social Work*, 10 (Summer 1980): 163–84.

Harris, Sidney W. *Probation and Other Social Work of the Courts*. Rochester, Kent, 1937.

Harrison, Brian. "Animals and the State in Nineteenth-Century England." *English Historical Review*, 88 (Oct. 1973): 786–820.

———. "For Church, Queen, and Family: The Girls' Friendly Society 1874–1920." *Past and Present*, 61 (Nov. 1973): 107–38.

———. "Religion and Recreation in Nineteenth-Century England." In idem, *Peaceable Kingdom: Stability and Change in Modern Britain*. Oxford, 1982.

———. *Separate Spheres: The Opposition to Women's Suffrage in Britain*. London, 1978.

Harrison, Gabriel. *John Howard Payne*. Philadelphia, 1885.

Harrison, William. *The Description of England*. Ithaca, NY, 1968 [1587].

Hartley, Catherine Gasquoine. *The Truth About Woman*. London, 1913.

Harvey, A. M., and S. L. Abrams. *"For the Welfare of Mankind": The Commonwealth Fund and American Medicine*. Baltimore, 1986.

Haskell, Thomas L., ed. *The Authority of Experts*. Bloomington, IN, 1984.

Havard, J. D. J. *The Detection of Secret Homicide*. London, 1960.

Haw, George. *The Englishman's Castle: The Problem of the People's Homes*. London [1906].

Hawkins, C. B. *Norwich: A Social Study*. London, 1910.

Hayami, Akira, and Nobuko Uchida. "Size of Household in a Japanese County Throughout the Tokugawa Era." In Peter Laslett and Richard Wall, eds., *Household and Family in Past Time*. Cambridge, 1974.

Haynes, E. S. P. *The Decline of Liberty in England*. London, 1916.

———. "Divorce Law Reform." *English Review*, 3 (Nov. 1909): 724–29.

———. *Lycurgus, or the Future of Law*. London, 1925.

Heal, Felicity. *Hospitality in Early Modern England*. Oxford, 1990.

Healy, William. *Honesty: A Study of the Causes and Treatment of Dishonesty Among Children*. Indianapolis, IN, 1915.

———. *The Individual Delinquent*. London, 1915.

———. "The Psychology of the Situation: A Fundamental for Understanding and Treatment of Delinquency and Crime." In Jane Addams et al., eds., *The Child, the Clinic and the Court*. New York, 1925.

Hearnshaw, L. S. *Cyril Burt: Psychologist*. Ithaca, NY, 1979.

———. *A Short History of British Psychology 1840-1940*. New York, 1964.

Heeney, Brian. *The Women's Movement in the Church of England 1850-1930*. Oxford, 1988.

Hendrick, Harry. "Child Labour, Medical Capital, and the School Medical Service, c. 1890-1918." In Roger Cooter, ed., *In the Name of the Child: Health and Welfare, 1880-1940*. London, 1992.

———. *Child Welfare: England 1872-1989*. London, 1994.

———. *Images of Youth: Age, Class, and the Male Youth Problem 1880-1920*. Oxford, 1990.

Henriques, Basil. "The Child in Trouble." *The Listener* (May 23, 1934): 881-82.

———. *The Indiscretions of a Magistrate*. London, 1950.

Henriques, U. R. Q. "Bastardy and the New Poor Law." *Past and Present*, 37 (July 1967): 103-29.

Henry, S. M. I. *Confidential Talks on Home and Child Life*. Edinburgh, 1898.

Herbert, A. P. *The Ayes Have It*. London, 1937.

———. "Morals and Divorce." *The Spectator*, 155 (Aug. 2, 1935): 181-82.

Herford, William H. *The Student's Froebel*. 2 vols. London, 1893.

Hewitt, Margaret. *Wives and Mothers in Victorian Industry*. London, 1958.

Heywood, Jean S. *Children in Care*. London, 1959.

Higgenbotham, Ann R. "'Sin of the Age': Infanticide and Illegitimacy in Victorian London." *Victorian Studies*, 32 (Spring 1989): 319-37.

———. "The Unmarried Mother and Her Child in Victorian London." Ph.D. dissertation, Indiana University, 1985.

Hill, Bridget. *Women, Work, and Sexual Politics in Eighteenth-Century England*. Oxford, 1989.

Hill, Joanna M. "The Pseudo and the Real 'Cottage Homes' for Pauper Children." *Westminster Review*, 146 (Dec. 1896): 660-75.

Hill, Rosamond Davenport, and Florence Davenport Hill. *The Recorder of Birmingham: A Memoir of Matthew Davenport Hill*. London, 1878.

Hilton, Boyd. *The Age of Atonement*. Oxford, 1991.

Himmelfarb, Gertrude. *The De-Moralization of Society: From Victorian Virtues to Modern Values*. New York, 1995.

———. *The Idea of Poverty: England in the Early Industrial Age*. New York, 1984.

Hints to District Visitors. London, 1858.

Hobsbawm, E. J. *Worlds of Labour*. London, 1984.

Hodgkinson, Ruth G. "Poor Law Medical Officers in England 1834-1871."

Journal of the History of Medicine and Allied Sciences, 11 (July 1956): 299–338.

Hoggart, Richard. *The Uses of Literacy*. Harmondsworth, Middlesex, 1960.

Holcombe, Lee. *Victorian Ladies at Work: Middle-Class Working Women in England and Wales 1850-1914*. Hamden, CT, 1973.

———. "Victorian Wives and Property: Reform of the Married Women's Property Law, 1857-1882." In Martha Vicinus, ed., *A Widening Sphere: Changing Roles of Victorian Women*. Bloomington, IN, 1977.

Holmes, Ann Sumner. "Hard Cases and Bad Laws: Divorce Reform in England, 1909-1937." Ph.D. dissertation, Vanderbilt University, 1986.

Holmes, Robert. *My Police Court Friends with the Colours*. Edinburgh, 1915.

———. *Them That Fall*. Edinburgh, 1923.

Holmes, Thomas. *Known to the Police*. London [1915].

———. "The New Licensing Bill." *Contemporary Review*, 81 (Apr. 1902): 508-15.

———. *Pictures and Problems from London Police Courts*. London [1911].

———. "Youthful Offenders and Parental Responsibility." *Contemporary Review*, 77 (June 1900): 845-54.

"Home Happiness." *The Queen* (Aug. 15, 1874): 115-16.

"Home Life—English Dwellings." *Westminster Review*, o.s. 103 (Jan. 1875): 173-92.

Home Office. *Reports on the Work of the Children's Branch* [1st-6th Reports]. London, 1923-1951.

Home, Sweet Home. Dublin [1820?].

Home! Sweet Home! Glasgow [1820?].

"Home, Sweet Home." London, 1874.

Home, Sweet Home. London [1890].

Homersham, E. Margery. "The Spread of Sanitary Knowledge by District Nurses." *Nurses' Journal*, 1 (May 1891): 30-33.

Home's Home. London [1792?].

Hopkins, Eric. *Childhood Transformed: Working-Class Children in Nineteenth-Century England*. Manchester, 1994.

Hopkins, Jane Ellice. *An English Woman's Work Among Workingmen*. New Britain, CT, 1875.

———. *Home Thoughts for Mothers and Mothers' Meetings*. 2nd ed. London, 1869.

Hopkinson, Alfred. "Adoption." *Journal of Comparative Legislation and International Law*, 3rd series, 2 (1920): 3-9.

Hopkirk, Mary. *Nobody Wanted Sam: The Story of the Unwelcomed Child, 1530-1948*. London, 1949.

Horn, Margo. *Before It's Too Late: The Child Guidance Movement in the United States, 1922-1945*. Philadelphia, 1989.

———. "The Moral Message of Child Guidance 1925-1945." *Journal of Social History*, 18 (Fall 1984): 25-36.

Horn, Pamela. *Education in Rural England 1800-1914*. Dublin, 1978.

Horsley, J. W. *How Criminals Are Made and Prevented*. London, 1913.

Houlbrooke, Ralph A. *The English Family 1450–1700*. London, 1984.
Housden, Leslie G. *The Prevention of Cruelty to Children*. London, 1955.
How to Make Home Unhealthy. London, 1850.
How to Manage a Baby. London [1861].
Howard Association. *Annual Reports*. London, 1874–1899.
———. *The Gift of Guidance*. London, 1901.
Howard, Carrington. "Adoption by Advertisement." *The Survey*, 35 (Dec. 11, 1915): 285–86.
Huard, Leo Albert. "The Law of Adoption: Ancient and Modern." *Vanderbilt Law Review*, 9 (1955–56): 743–63.
Hubbard, Miss. "The Organization of Women Workers." In Angela Burdett-Coutts, ed., *Woman's Mission*. London, 1893.
Hugh Crichton-Miller 1877–1959: A Personal Memoir by His Friends and Family. Dorchester, Dorset, 1961.
Hughes, E. P. *The Probation System of America*. London, 1903.
Hughes, Thomas. *Tom Brown's School Days*. New York, 1968 [1857].
Hughes, Winifred. *The Maniac in the Cellar*. Princeton, NJ, 1980.
Hughlings-Jackson, J. "Evolution and Dissolution of the Nervous System." *Popular Science Monthly*, 25 (June 1884): 171–80.
Humphries, Stephen. *Hooligans or Rebels? An Oral History of Working-Class Childhood and Youth 1889–1939*. Oxford, 1981.
Hunt, Lynn. *The Family Romance of the French Revolution*. Berkeley, CA, 1992.
———. "The Unstable Boundaries of the French Revolution." In Michelle Perrot, ed., *A History of Private Life*, vol. 4. Cambridge, MA, 1990.
Hurt, J. S. *Elementary Schooling and the Working Classes 1860–1918*. London, 1979.
Hutchinson, Evaline. "Women in the Police Courts." *The Englishwoman*, 20 (Oct. 1913): 25–29.
Ignatieff, Michael. "State, Civil Society and Total Institutions: A Critique of Recent Social Histories of Punishment." In Stanley Cohen and Andrew Scull, eds., *Social Control and the State*. New York, 1983.
In Memoriam: Charlotte M. Mason. London, 1923.
Infant Mortality: Its Causes and Remedies. Manchester, 1871.
"Infanticide." *Saturday Review*, 20 (Aug. 5, 1865): 161–62.
Inglis, Ruth. *The Children's War: Evacuation 1939–1945*. London, 1989.
The Inspector: or, How to Get Rid of Bad Smells Without, and of Bad Tempers Within. London [1867].
Institute of Child Psychology. *Annual Reports* for 1933, 1934, and 1937. London, 1934, 1935, and 1938.
Irvine, E. F. *A Pioneer of the New Psychology: Hugh Crichton-Miller, 1877–1959*. Chatham, Kent, 1963.
Isaacs, Susan. "Cambridge Evacuation Survey." *Fortnightly*, o.s. 153 (June 1940): 619–30.
———. *The Nursery Years: The Mind of the Child from Birth to Six Years*. New York, 1970 [1929].

Iselin, Henry. "The Story of a Children's Care Committee." *Economic Review*,
    22 (Jan. 1912): 42–64.
Jackson, R. M. *The Machinery of Justice in England*. Cambridge, 1940.
Jalland, Pat. *Women, Marriage and Politics 1860–1914*. Oxford, 1986.
James, E. O. *Marriage and Society*. London, 1952.
Jasper, A. S. *A Hoxton Childhood*. London, 1969.
J.B. *Thoughts and Suggestions Having Reference to Infanticide*. London, 1864.
Jephson, Arthur W. *My Work in London*. London, 1910.
Jeyes, S. H. *The Life of Sir Howard Vincent*. London, 1912.
Johnson, Paul. "Introduction." In idem, ed., *Twentieth-Century Britain: Eco-
    nomic, Social and Cultural Change*. London, 1994.
Johnson, Samuel. *The Rambler*, vol. 2. 6th ed. London, 1763.
Jones, Gareth Stedman. "Class Expression Versus Social Control? A Critique
    of Recent Trends in the Social History of 'Leisure.'" In idem, *Languages of
    Class: Studies in English Working Class History 1832–1982*. Cambridge,
    1983.
———. *Outcast London: A Study in the Relationship Between Classes in Victo-
    rian Society*. Oxford, 1971.
———. "Working-Class Culture and Working-Class Politics in London,
    1870–1900." In idem, *Languages of Class*. Cambridge, 1983.
Jones, Greta. *Social Hygiene in Twentieth Century Britain*. London, 1986.
Jones, Robert. "Mental Hygiene in Childhood." *Westminster Review*, 167 (Apr.
    1907): 423–35.
Joyce, Patrick. *Work, Society and Politics: The Culture of the Factory in Later Vic-
    torian England*. Brighton, 1980.
Judge, Ken, and Martin Knapp. "Efficiency in the Production of Welfare: The
    Public and the Private Sectors Compared." In Rudolf Klein and Michael
    O'Higgins, eds., *The Future of Welfare*. Oxford, 1985.
"Judge Lindsey No 'Snitcher.'" *The Outlook*, 110 (June 23, 1915): 399–400.
Justice of the Peace and Local Government Review Annual, 1928. London, 1928.
Juvenile Offenders. London [Howard Association], 1881.
Juvenile Offenders. London [Howard Association], 1898.
Kanthack, Emilia. *The Preservation of Infant Life: A Guide for Health Visitors*.
    London, 1907.
Kaye, Michael. *Child Welfare Outside the School*. Edinburgh, 1936.
Keaton, Buster. *My Wonderful World of Slapstick*. Garden City, NY, 1960.
Keegan, John. *The Face of Battle*. New York, 1977.
Keeling, Dorothy C. *The Crowded Stairs: Recollections of Social Work in Liver-
    pool*. London, 1961.
Keir, Gertrude. "A History of Child Guidance." *British Journal of Educational
    Psychology*, 22 (Feb. 1952): 5–29.
Kelley, Donald R. *The Human Measure: Social Thought in the Western Legal Tra-
    dition*. Cambridge, MA, 1990.
Kemble, Charles. *Suggestive Hints on Parochial Machinery*. 3rd ed. London,
    1865.

Kent, Susan Kingsley. *Sex and Suffrage in Britain, 1860-1914*. Princeton, NJ, 1987.

Kent, William. *An Encyclopedia of London*. New York, 1937.

Kern, Stephen. "Explosive Intimacy: Psychodynamics of the Victorian Family." *History of Childhood Quarterly*, 1 (Winter 1974): 437-61.

Kerr, Madeline. *The People of Ship Street*. London, 1958.

Key Statistics for Local Authorities, Great Britain. London, 1994.

Kidd, Alan J. "Charity Organization and the Unemployed in Manchester. 1870-1914." *Social History*, 9 (Jan. 1984): 45-66.

Kidd, Benjamin. *Social Evolution*. New York, 1902 [1894].

Kimmins, C. W. *The Child in the Changing Home*. London, 1926.

Kipling, Rudyard. *Something of Myself*. Garden City, NY, 1937.

Kirk, H. David, and Susan A. McDaniel. "Adoption Policy in Great Britain and North America." *Journal of Social Policy*, 13 (Jan. 1984): 75-84.

Kornitzer, Margaret. *Child Adoption in the Modern World*. London, 1952.

Koven, Seth. "Borderlands: Women, Voluntary Action, and Child Welfare in Britain, 1840 to 1914." In idem and Sonya Michel, eds., *Mothers of a New World*. New York, 1993.

———. "Dr. Barnardo's 'Artistic Fictions': Photography, Sexuality and the Ragged Child in Victorian London." *Radical History Review*, 69 (Fall 1997): 7-45.

———. "From Rough Lads to Hooligans: Boy Life, National Culture and Social Reform." In Andrew Parker et al., eds., *Nationalisms & Sexualities*. London, 1992.

———. "Henrietta Barnett 1851-1936. The (Auto) Biography of a Late Victorian Marriage." In Peter Mandler and Susan Pedersen, eds., *After the Victorians: Private Conscience and Public Duty in Modern Britain*. London, 1994.

Koven, Seth, and Sonya Michel. "Womanly Duties: Maternalist Politics and the Origins of Welfare States in France, Germany, Great Britain, and the United States, 1880-1920." *American Historical Review*, 95 (Oct. 1990): 1076-1108.

Krygier, Martin. "Publicness, Privateness and 'Primitive Law.'" In S. I. Benn and G. F. Gaus, eds., *Public and Private in Social Life*. London, 1983.

"Labourers' Homes." *Quarterly Review*, 107 (Apr. 1860): 267-97.

Lady, A. *Afternoons in the Manchester Slums*. Manchester, 1887.

Lambard, William. *Eirenarcha: or of the Office of the Justices of Peace*. London, 1588 [1581].

Lambert, R. J. *Sir John Simon . . . and English Social Administration*. London, 1963.

———. "A Victorian National Health Service: State Vaccination 1855-71." *Historical Journal*, 5 (1962): 1-18.

Lambertz, Jan. "Feminists and the Politics of Wife-Beating." In Harold L. Smith, ed., *British Feminism in the Twentieth Century*. Aldershot, Hants., 1990.

Landau, Norma. *The Justices of the Peace, 1679–1760*. Berkeley, CA, 1984.

Laqueur, Thomas. "Working-Class Demand and the Growth of Elementary Education, 1750–1850." In Lawrence Stone, ed., *Schooling and Society: Studies in the History of Education*. Baltimore, 1976.

Larsen, Charles. *The Good Fight: The Life and Times of Ben B. Lindsey*. Chicago, 1972.

Lascelles, E. C. P. "Charity." In G. M. Young, ed., *Early Victorian England*. 2 vols. London, 1951.

Lasch, Christopher. *Haven in a Heartless World: The Family Besieged*. New York, 1979.

Laslett, Peter. *Family Life and Illicit Love in Earlier Generations*. Cambridge, 1977.

———. *The World We Have Lost: England Before the Industrial Age*. 2nd. ed. New York, 1971.

Laslett, Peter, Karla Oosterveen, and Richard M. Smith, eds., *Bastardy and Its Comparative History*. London, 1980.

Latey, William, and D. Perronet Rees. *Latey's Law and Practice in Divorce & Matrimonial Causes*. 12th ed. London, 1940.

The Law Society. *Annual Report, 1937*. London, 1937.

Lees, Lynn Hollen. "The Survival of the Unfit: Welfare Policies and Family Maintenance in Nineteenth-Century London." In Peter Mandler, ed., *The Uses of Charity: The Poor on Relief in the Nineteenth-Century Metropolis*. Philadelphia, 1990.

Leeson, Cecil. *The Child and the War*. London, 1916.

———. *The Probation System*. London, 1914.

Lefebvre, Georges. *The Coming of the French Revolution*. Trans. R. R. Palmer. Princeton, NJ, 1967 [1939].

"The Legalizing of Adoptions." *Child Welfare Worker*, 2 (Nov. 1920): 203–4.

Legislation in Regard to Children. London, 1906.

The Legitimation League: Its Objects and Principles. London [1897].

Le Mesurier, Lilian. *A Handbook of Probation and Social Work of the Courts*. London, 1935.

Lens. "The Unmarried Mother." *New Statesman*, 14 (Mar. 6, 1920): 639–40.

Levine, David. "Education and Family Life in Early Industrial England." *Journal of Family History*, 4 (Winter 1979): 368–80.

———. "'For Their Own Reasons': Individual Marriage Decisions and Family Life." *Journal of Family History*, 7 (Fall 1982): 255–64.

Levine, Philippa. *Feminist Lives in Victorian England*. Oxford, 1990.

Lewis, Donald M. *Lighten Their Darkness: The Evangelical Mission to Working-Class London, 1828–1860*. Westport, CT, 1986.

Lewis, Jane. "Anxieties About the Family and the Relationships Between Children and the State in Twentieth Century England." In Martin Richards and Paul Light, eds., *Children of Social Worlds*. Cambridge, 1986.

———. "Parents, Children, School Fees and the London School Board 1870–1890." *History of Education*, 11 (Dec. 1982): 291–312.

———. *The Politics of Motherhood: Child and Maternal Welfare in England, 1900–1939.* London, 1980.

———. "Public Institution and Private Relationship: Marriage and Marriage Guidance, 1920–1968." *Twentieth Century British History,* 1 (1990): 233–63.

———. *The Voluntary Sector, the State and Social Work in Britain.* Aldershot, Hants., 1995.

———. *Women in England 1870–1950: Social Divisions and Social Change.* Brighton, 1984.

———. "The Working-Class Wife and Mother and State Intervention, 1870–1918." In idem, ed., *Labour and Love: Women's Experience of Home and Family 1850–1940.* Oxford, 1986.

"Lex v. the Poor." *The Eye-Witness,* 3 (Sept. 12, 1912): 397–98.

Lieck, Albert. *Bow Street World.* London, 1938.

———. *The Justice at Work.* London, 1922.

Lieck, Albert, and A. C. L. Morrison. *Matrimonial and Family Jurisdiction of Justices.* 2nd ed. London, 1932.

The Life and Trial of the Child Murderess, Charlotte Winsor. London, n.d.

Light, Alison. *Forever England: Femininity, Literature and Conservatism Between the Wars.* London, 1991.

Lightbody, W. M. "The State and Parental Responsibility." *Westminster Review,* 163 (Mar. 1905): 288–93.

Lindsey, Benjamin B. "The Reformation of Juvenile Delinquents Through the Juvenile Court." 1903.

Lindsey, Benjamin B., and Harvey J. O'Higgins. *The Beast.* New York, 1910.

[Linton, Eliza Lynn.] "Domestic Life." *Temple Bar,* 4 (Feb. 1862): 402–15.

———. "The Judicial Shock to Marriage." *Nineteenth Century,* 29 (May 1891): 691–700.

Lloyd, Katharine. "Social Work in the Diocese." In W. S. F. Pickering, ed., *A Social History of the Diocese of Newcastle.* Stocksfield, Northumberland, 1981.

Loane, Margaret. *The Common Growth.* London, 1911.

———. *An Englishman's Castle.* London, 1909.

———. *From Their Point of View.* London, 1908.

———. "Husband and Wife Among the Poor." *Contemporary Review,* 87 (Feb. 1905): 222–30.

———. *Neighbours and Friends.* London, 1910.

———. *The Next Street but One.* London, 1907.

———. *Outlines of Routine in District Nursing.* London, 1905.

———. *The Queen's Poor: Life as They Find It in Town and Country.* London, 1905.

———. *Simple Sanitation.* London [1905].

Loch, C. S. *Charity and Social Life.* London, 1910.

———. "The State and Parental Control." In Sir William Chance, ed., *Report of the Proceedings of the Third International Congress for the Welfare and Protection of Children.* London, 1902.

London Child Guidance Clinic. *Report for the Period July 29th, 1929 to Dec. 31st, 1931*. London, 1932.

[Longman, F.] *Fifteen Years Fight Against Compulsory Vaccination*. 4th ed. London [1900].

Longman, Mary. "Children's Care Committees." *Contemporary Review*, 98 (Dec. 1910): 733–42.

Low, Florence B. "Will the Family Disappear?" *Contemporary Review*, 162 (Sept. 1942): 164–69.

Low, Frances H. "A Remedy for Baby-Farming." *Fortnightly Review*, 69 (Feb. 1898): 280–86.

[Lundie, Mary Grey.] *America as I Found It*. New York, 1852.

Lushington, Sydney G., and Guy Lushington. *The Summary Jurisdiction (Married Women) Act, 1895*. 2nd ed. London, 1904.

Macadam, Elizabeth. *The New Philanthropy: A Study of the Relations Between the Statutory and Voluntary Social Services*. London, 1934.

MacCalman, D. R. "The General Management of Maladjustment in Children." In R. G. Gordon, ed., *A Survey of Child Psychiatry*. London, 1939.

McCauliff, C. M. A. "The First English Adoption Law and Its American Precursors." *Seton Hall Law Review*, 16 (1986): 656–77.

McCleary, G. F. *The Early History of the Infant Welfare Movement*. London, 1933.

———. "The Importance of Children." *Fortnightly Review*, 148 (Oct. 1937): 451–57.

———. "The State as Over-Parent." *Albany Review* (Oct. 1907): 46–59.

McClure, Ruth K. *Coram's Children: The London Foundling Hospital in the Eighteenth Century*. New Haven, CT, 1981.

MacDonald, Michael. *Mystical Bedlam: Madness, Anxiety, and Healing in Seventeenth-Century England*. Cambridge, 1981.

McDougall, William. "Summary." In Hugh Crichton-Miller, ed., *Functional Nerve Disease*. London, 1920.

Mace, David R. *Does Sex Morality Matter?* London, 1943.

———. "Family Life in Britain Since the First World War." *Annals of the American Academy of Political and Social Science*, 272 (Nov. 1950): 179–84.

———. *Marriage Counselling*. London, 1948.

Macfarlane, Alan. *The Family Life of Ralph Josselin*. New York, 1977.

———. *Marriage and Love in England: Modes of Reproduction 1300–1840*. Oxford, 1986.

———. *The Origins of English Individualism: The Family, Property and Social Transition*. Oxford, 1992 [1978].

McGowen, Randall. "A Powerful Sympathy: Terror, the Prison, and Humanitarian Reform in Early Nineteenth-Century Britain." *Journal of British Studies*, 25 (July 1986): 312–34.

McGregor, O. R. *Divorce in England*. London, 1957.

———. *Social History and Law Reform*. London, 1981.

McGregor, O. R., Louis Blom-Cooper, and Colin Gibson. *Separated Spouses*. London, 1970.

McHugh, Paul. *Prostitution and Victorian Social Reform.* New York, 1980.

M'Ilquham, Harriett. "Marriage: A Just and Honourable Partnership." *Westminster Review,* 157 (Apr. 1902): 433–42.

Mackenzie, W. Leslie, and Edwin Matthew. *The Medical Inspection of School Children.* Edinburgh, 1904.

McKibbin, Ross. *The Ideologies of Class: Social Relations in Britain 1880–1950.* Oxford, 1990.

MacKinnon, Frank Douglas. *On Circuit 1924–1937.* Cambridge, 1940.

MacLeod, Roy M. "The Frustration of State Medicine 1880–1899." *Medical History,* 11 (Jan. 1967): 15–40.

———. "Law, Medicine and Public Opinion: The Resistance to Compulsory Health Legislation 1870–1907." *Public Law* (Summer 1967): 107–28 (Autumn 1967): 189–211.

———. "Medico-Legal Issues in Victorian Medical Care." *Medical History,* 10 (Jan. 1966): 44–49.

McMillan, Margaret. *Education Through the Imagination.* New York, 1924 [1904].

———. *The Nursery School.* London, 1919.

Macnair, J. H. "The Case for Adoption." *Contemporary Review,* 105 (May 1914): 704–11.

Macpherson, W. G., et al., eds., *History of the Great War: Medical Services: Diseases of the War.* 2 vols. London, 1923.

MacQueen, John Fraser. *The Rights and Liabilities of Husband and Wife.* 4th ed. London, 1905.

McWhinnie, Alexina M. *Adopted Children: How They Grow Up.* London, 1967.

McWilliams, William. "The Mission to the English Police Courts." *Howard Journal,* 22 (1983): 129–47.

———. "The Mission Transformed: Professionalisation of Probation Between the Wars." *Howard Journal,* 24 (Nov. 1985): 257–74.

Mager, Alfred. *Children's Rights: A Social and Philanthropic Question.* Bolton, Lancs., 1886.

Magistrate, A. *Metropolitan Police Court Jottings.* London, 1882.

Mahood, Linda. *The Magdalenes: Prostitution in the Nineteenth Century.* London, 1990.

Manchester, A. H. *A Modern Legal History of England and Wales 1750–1950.* London, 1980.

Mannheim, Hermann. "The Juvenile Court: Its Procedure." In Margery Fry et al., eds., *Lawless Youth.* London, 1947.

———. *Social Aspects of Crime in England Between the Wars.* London, 1940.

Mannin, Ethel. *Common-Sense and the Child: A Plea for Freedom.* Philadelphia, 1932.

Manning, Henry Edward, and Benjamin Waugh. "The Child of the English Savage." *Contemporary Review,* 49 (May 1886): 687–700.

Manton, Jo. *Mary Carpenter and the Children of the Streets.* London, 1976.

"Marriage, Divorce and the Divorce Commission." *Edinburgh Review,* 217 (Jan. 1913): 1–20.

"Marriage in the Police Court." *New Statesman and Nation*, n.s. 7 (Apr. 21, 1934): 587.

Marsden, W. E. "Social Environment, School Attendance and Educational Achievement in a Merseyside Town 1870-1900." In Phillip McCann, ed., *Popular Education and Socialization in the Nineteenth Century*. London, 1977.

Martin, Anna. *The Married Working Woman*. New York, 1980 [1911].

———. "The Mother and Social Reform." *Nineteenth Century and After*, 73 (May 1913): 1060-79; (June 1913): 1235-55.

Marwick, Arthur. *British Society Since 1945*. Harmondsworth, Middlesex, 1982.

Mason, Charlotte M. *Home Education: A Course of Lectures to Ladies Delivered in Bradford, in the Winter of 1885-1886*. London, 1886.

———. *Parents and Children: A Sequel to "Home Education."* London, 1897.

Mason, Michael. *The Making of Victorian Sexuality*. Oxford, 1994.

Masterman, C. F. G. "Realities at Home." In *The Heart of the Empire*. London, 1901.

Maternity: Letters from Working-Women. New York, 1980 [1915].

Maudsley, Henry. *The Physiology and Pathology of the Mind*. New York, 1867.

———. "Sex in Mind and in Education." *Fortnightly Review*, n.s. 15 (1874): 466-83.

Maurice, C. E., ed. *Life of Octavia Hill as Told in Her Letters*. London, 1914.

Maus, Katharine Eisaman. "Proof and Consequences: Inwardness and Its Exposure in the English Renaissance." *Representations*, 34 (Spring 1991): 29-52.

Maxwell, Alexander. *Treatment of Crime*. London, 1938.

May, Margaret. "Innocence and Experience: The Evolution of the Concept of Juvenile Delinquency in the Mid-Nineteenth Century." *Victorian Studies*, 17 (Sept. 1973): 7-29.

———. "Violence in the Family: An Historical Perspective." In J. P. Martin, ed., *Violence and the Family*. Chichester, Sussex, 1978.

Mayhew, Henry. "Home Is Home, Be It Ever So Homely." In Viscount Ingestre, ed., *Meliora: or, Better Times to Come*. 1st series, 2nd ed. London, 1852.

———. *London Labour and the London Poor*. Facsimile ed., 4 vols. New York, 1968 [1861-62].

Maynard, Edith L. *Women in the Public Health Service*. London, 1915.

Meacham, Standish. *A Life Apart: The English Working Class 1890-1914*. Cambridge, MA, 1977.

———. *Toynbee Hall and Social Reform 1880-1914*. New Haven, CT, 1987.

Mence, Richard. *The Mutual Rights of Husband and Wife*. London, 1838.

Mennel, Robert M. "Attitudes and Policies Toward Juvenile Delinquency in the United States: A Historiographical Review." In Michael Tonry and Norval Morris, eds., *Crime and Justice*, vol. 4. Chicago, 1983.

———. *Thorns and Thistles: Juvenile Delinquents in the United States 1825-1940*. Hanover, NH, 1973.

Mercer, A. J. "Smallpox and Epidemiological-Demographic Change in Europe: The Role of Vaccination." *Population Studies*, 39 (July 1985): 287-307.

Mercier, Charles. "The Nervous System in Childhood." *Brain*, 15 (1892): 65-75.

Merry, Eleanor J., and Iris D. Irven. *District Nursing: A Handbook for District Nurses*. London, 1960.

Middleton, Nigel. *When Family Failed: The Treatment of Children in the Care of the Community During the First Half of the Twentieth Century*. London, 1971.

Mill, John Stuart. *On Liberty*. Arlington Heights, IL, 1947 [1859].

———. *Principles of Political Economy*. 2 vols. New York, 1899 [1848].

———. *The Subjection of Women*. Arlington Heights, IL, 1980 [1869].

Miller, J. R. *Home-Making, or the Ideal Family Life*. London, 1895.

Miller, John Hawkins. "'Temple and Sewer': Childbirth, Prudery, and Victoria Regina." In Anthony Wohl, ed., *The Victorian Family: Structure and Stresses*. New York, 1978.

Milton, Frank. *In Some Authority: The English Magistracy*. London, 1959.

Minor, Iris. "Working-Class Women and Matrimonial Law Reform, 1890–1914." In David E. Martin and David Rubinstein, eds., *Ideology and the Labour Movement*. London, 1979.

Mintz, Steven. *A Prison of Expectations: The Family in Victorian Culture*. New York, 1983.

Mitchell, B. R. *British Historical Statistics*. Cambridge, 1988.

Mitchell, Elizabeth Harcourt. *Lay Help in District Visiting*. London, 1899.

Mitchell, William. *House and Home: or, The Value and Virtue of Domestic Life*. London [1896].

Monroe, Will S. *Status of Child Study in Europe*. Worcester, MA, 1899.

Montessori, Maria. *The Montessori Method*. Trans. Anne George. New York, 1912.

Moodie, William. *An Address to the Presidents and Justices of the Metropolitan Juvenile Courts*. London, 1930.

———. *Child Guidance by Team Work*. London, 1931.

———. *The Doctor and the Difficult Child*. New York, 1940.

———. *Enuresis: Drawing-Room Talks, No. 5*. London, 1938.

———. *Stealing: Drawing-Room Talks, No. 6*. London, 1938.

Mook, Bertha. *The Dutch Family in the 17th and 18th Centuries*. Ottawa, 1977.

Moore, Barrington, Jr. *Privacy: Studies in Social and Cultural History*. Armonk, NY, 1984.

Morgan, Edmund S. *The Puritan Family*. New York, 1966.

Morley, Charles. *Studies in Board Schools*. London, 1897.

Morley, Ernest. "Hooliganism & Working Boys' Clubs." *Westminster Review*, 155 (May 1901): 560–67.

Morris, Cherry, ed. *Social Case-Work in Great Britain*. 2nd ed. New York, 1955.

Morris, Malcolm. "The Superfluous Vaccination Commission." *Nineteenth Century*, 40 (Dec. 1896): 958–73.

Morris, Marilyn. "The Royal Family and Family Values in Late Eighteenth-Century England." *Journal of Family History*, 21 (Oct. 1996): 519–32.

Morris, R. J. "Voluntary Societies and British Urban Elites, 1780–1850: An Analysis." *Historical Journal*, 26 (Mar. 1983): 95–118.

Morrison, Arthur. *A Child of the Jago*. London, 1969 [1896].

Morrison, William Douglas. *Juvenile Offenders*. London, 1896.

Mort, Frank. *Dangerous Sexualities: Medico-Moral Politics in England Since 1830*. London, 1987.

Morton, Arthur. *The Directorate of Sir Robert Parr*. London, n.d.

Mosher, Martha B. *Child Culture in the Home*. London, 1898.

Mother, A. *Bright Glimpses for Mothers' Meetings*. London, 1868.

The Mothers' Union, Chester Diocese: Diamond Jubilee 1898–1958. Chester, 1958.

Mothers' Union, Oxford Diocese. 1st–20th *Reports*. Oxford, 1892–1912.

Mott, F. W. "Punctiform Haemorrhages of the Brain in Gas Poisoning." *Proceedings of the Royal Society of Medicine*, 10, pt. 3 (1916–17): 73–90.

Mount, Ferdinand. *The Subversive Family: An Alternative History of Love and Marriage*. New York, 1992.

Mowrer, Ernest R. *Family Disorganization: An Introduction to a Sociological Analysis*. Chicago, 1927.

Mowrer, Ernest, and Harriet Mowrer. *Domestic Discord: Its Analysis and Treatment*. Chicago, 1928.

Mulcaster, Richard. *Positions . . . Necessaire for the Training Up of Children*. London, 1581.

Müller-Lyer, F. *The Family*. Trans. F. W. Stella Browne. London, 1931 [1912].

Mullins, Claud. "Christianity and the Family." *The Spectator*, 152 (Feb. 2, 1934): 152–53.

———. "Conciliation in Divorce Cases." *Quarterly Review*, 285 (July 1947): 376–83.

———. *Crime and Psychology*. London, 1943.

———. "Divorce in the Post-War World." *Quarterly Review*, 279 (Oct. 1942): 155–67.

[———.] "Divorce *via* Magistrates' Courts." *Law Journal*, 84 (Oct. 9, 1937): 230–31.

———. *Fifteen Years' Hard Labour*. London, 1948.

———. "The Graphologin: A Unique Experience." *Cornhill Magazine*, n.s. 72 (Apr. 1932): 398–406.

———. "Justices of the Peace: Abolition or Reform?" *Quarterly Review*, 265 (Oct. 1935): 223–37.

———. *Marriage, Children and God*. London, 1933.

———. *One Man's Furrow*. London, 1963.

———. *Wife v. Husband in the Courts*. London, 1935.

Murphy, James. *The Education Act 1870*. Newton Abbot, Devon, 1972.

Musgrave, P. W. *Society and Education in England Since 1800*. London, 1968.

My Cottage Is My Castle; or, the Free-born Englishman. London, 1817.

My Own Dearest Home ["To be sung to the Marseillaise"]. In *Poetical Broadsides*. London [ca. 1850?].

Myers, J. M. "The Boy Criminal." In J. H. Whitehouse, ed., *Problems of Boy Life*. London, 1912.

Myers, Sam Price. *London South of the River*. London, 1949.

Nanda, B. R. *Gokhale: The Indian Moderates and the British Raj*. Delhi, 1979.

[Nash, Thomas.] *An Essay on the Pernicious Practice of Impressing Seamen into the King's Service*. London, 1760.

The National Adoption Society. London [1920].

National Conference on the Prevention of Destitution. *Report of the Proceedings*. 2 vols. London, 1911–12.

National Children's Home [Children's Home and Orphanage]. *Annual Reports* for 1879–80, 1886–87, and 1895–96. London, 1880, 1887, and 1896.

National Council for the Unmarried Mother and Her Child. 2nd–23rd [annual] *Reports*. London, 1919–1942.

National Council for Mental Hygiene. 6th and 7th [annual] *Reports*. London, 1929 and 1930.

National Health Society. *Annual Reports* for 1879–1899. London, 1880–1900.

National Home Reading Union. 1st and 8th *Annual Reports*. London, 1890 and 1897.

National League for Physical Education and Improvement. 1st–6th *Annual Reports*. London, 1906–1911.

National Society for the Prevention of Cruelty to Children. 1st–50th *Annual Reports*. London, 1884–1934.

———. *Inspector's Directory*. London, 1901.

The Natural Rights of Children: Verbatim Report of the Inaugural Proceedings of the Legitimation League. London, 1893.

Neill, A. S. *The Problem Parent*. London, 1932.

Neuberger, Joan. *Hooliganism: Crime, Culture, and Power in St. Petersburg, 1900–1914*. Berkeley, CA, 1993.

Nevinson, Henry W. *Neighbours of Ours: Slum Stories of London*. New York, 1895.

Nevinson, Margaret Wynne. *Life's Fitful Fever*. London, 1926.

The New Survey of London Life & Labour. 9 vols. London, 1930–1935.

Newman, George. *Infant Mortality: A Social Problem*. London, 1906.

Newman, Gerald. *The Rise of English Nationalism: A Cultural History 1740–1830*. New York, 1987.

Nicoll, Maurice, and James Young. "Psycho-Analysis." In Hugh Crichton-Miller, ed., *Functional Nerve Disease*. London, 1920.

Nightingale, Florence. "Sick-Nursing and Health-Nursing." In Angela Burdett-Coutts, ed., *Woman's Mission*. London, 1893.

Nord, Deborah Epstein. *Walking the Victorian Streets: Women, Representation, and the City*. Ithaca, N.Y., 1995.

O'Brien, M. D. "The Child and the Home." *Westminster Review*, 165 (June 1906): 668–75.

O'Day, Rosemary, and David Englander. *Mr. Charles Booth's Inquiry: Life and Labour of the People in London Reconsidered*. London, 1993.

Offen, C. R. "The Pseudo and the Real 'Cottage Homes' for Pauper Children: A Reply." *Westminster Review*, 147 (May 1897): 570–81.

Opinions of Statesmen, Politicians, Publicists, Statisticians and Sanitarians [tract no. 3]. In *Vaccination Tracts*. London, 1879.

Oppenheim, Janet. "A Mother's Role, a Daughter's Duty: Lady Blanche Balfour, Eleanor Sidgwick, and Feminist Perspectives." *Journal of British Studies*, 34 (Apr. 1995): 196–232.

———. *The Other World: Spiritualism and Psychical Research in England, 1850–1914*. Cambridge, 1985.

———. *"Shattered Nerves": Doctors, Patients, and Depression in Victorian England*. New York, 1991.

Orchard, H. Courtenay. *The Police Court Missionary's Story*. Walsall, Staffordshire, 1931.

Orlin, Lena Cowen. *Private Matters and Public Culture in Post-Reformation England*. Ithaca, NY, 1994.

Orwell, George. *Down and Out in Paris and London*. New York, 1961 [1933].

Our Towns: A Close-Up. London, 1943.

Overmyer, Grace. *America's First Hamlet*. New York, 1957.

Oxford Police Court and Prison Gate Mission. 2nd–4th and 6th–9th *Annual Reports*. Oxford, 1908–1910 and 1912–1915.

Ozment, Steven. *When Fathers Ruled: Family Life in Reformation Europe*. Cambridge, MA, 1983.

Page, Arthur. "What Is Social Reform?" *Blackwood's Magazine*, 192 (Nov. 1912): 589–602.

Page, Leo. "The Child and the Law." *Contemporary Review*, 149 (June 1936): 696–703.

———. *Justice of the Peace*. London, 1936.

Pardailhé-Galabrun, Annik. *The Birth of Intimacy: Privacy and Domestic Life in Early Modern Paris*. Trans. Jocelyn Phelps. Cambridge, 1991.

Parker, Olive. *For the Family's Sake: A History of the Mothers' Union 1876–1976*. Folkestone, Kent, 1975.

Parker, R. A. "The Gestation of Reform: The Children Act of 1948." In Philip Bean and Stewart MacPherson, eds., *Approaches to Welfare*. London, 1983.

Parker, Rozsika. *The Subversive Stitch: Embroidery and the Making of the Feminine*. New York, 1989.

Parr, Joy. *Labouring Children: British Immigrant Apprentices to Canada, 1869–1924*. London, 1980.

Parr, Robert J. *Assaults on, and Corruption of Children*. London, 1910.

———. *The Baby Farmer: An Exposition and Appeal*. London, 1909.

———. *N.S.P.C.C. Inspectors and the Work of Care Committees*. London, 1917.

Parson, A. *My District Visitors*. London, 1891.

Parton, Nigel. *The Politics of Child Abuse*. London, 1985.

Paterson, Alexander. *Across the Bridges, or Life by the South London River-Side*. London, 1911.

Patmore, Coventry. *The Angel in the House*. Boston, 1856.

———. "The Social Position of Women." *North British Review*, 14 (Feb. 1851): 515–40.

Paulding, J. K. "The Backwoodsman." Philadelphia, 1818.

[Payne, W.] *The Cruelty Man: Actual Experiences of an Inspector of the N.S.P.C.C. Graphically Told by Himself*. London, 1912.

Pearson, Charles H. *National Life and Character: A Forecast.* London, 1894.

Pearson, Geoffrey. *Hooligan: A History of Respectable Fears.* London, 1983.

Pearson, Michael. *The Age of Consent: Victorian Prostitution and Its Enemies.* Newton Abbot, Devon, 1972.

Pedder, D. C. "Without House or Home." *Contemporary Review,* 81 (June 1902): 845–53.

Pedersen, Susan. "Ambition, Collaboration, and Social Reform: The Choices of Eleanor Rathbone and Elizabeth Macadam." Unpublished paper (1994).

———. *Family, Dependence, and the Origins of the Welfare State: Britain and France, 1914–1945.* Cambridge, 1993.

———. "Gender, Welfare, and Citizenship in Britain During the Great War." *American Historical Review,* 95 (Oct. 1990): 983–1006.

Peek, Francis. *Social Wreckage; A Review of the Laws of England as They Affect the Poor.* 3rd ed. London, 1888.

Pelham, H. S. *The Training of a Working Boy.* London, 1914.

Pelling, Henry. *Popular Politics and Society in Late-Victorian Britain.* London, 1968.

Pennybacker, Susan D. *A Vision for London 1889–1914: Labour, Everyday Life and the LCC Experiment.* London, 1995.

Pepler, Douglas. *The Care Committee.* London, 1912.

———. *Justice and the Child.* London, 1915.

Perkin, Joan. *Women and Marriage in Nineteenth-Century England.* London, 1989.

Peterson, M. Jeanne. *Family, Love, and Work in the Lives of Victorian Gentlewomen.* Bloomington, IN, 1989.

———. "The Victorian Governess: Status Incongruence in Family and Society." In Martha Vicinus, ed., *Suffer and Be Still: Women in the Victorian Age.* Bloomington, IN, 1974.

Pettifer, Ernest W. *The Court Resumes.* Bradford, 1946.

Phillip, Mrs. Arthur. "A 'Spoilt Child': The Nation's Wasted Wealth." In *Essays on Duty and Discipline.* London, 1910.

Phillips, Margaret Mann. *The "Adages" of Erasmus; A Study with Translations.* Cambridge, 1964.

Phillips, Roderick. *Putting Asunder: A History of Divorce in Western Society.* Cambridge, 1988.

Philpott, Hugh B. *London at School: The Story of the School Board, 1870–1904.* London, 1904.

Pick, Daniel. *Faces of Degeneration: A European Disorder, c. 1848–c. 1918.* Cambridge, 1989.

Picton, J. Allanson. "Compulsory Vaccination." *Contemporary Review,* 55 (Jan. 1889): 114–32.

Pinchbeck, Ivy, and Margaret Hewitt. *Children in English Society.* 2 vols. London, 1969, 1973.

Pinero, Arthur W. *The Magistrate.* London, 1909 [1885].

Pipkin, Charles W. *Social Politics and Modern Democracies.* London, 1931.

Pitkin, Hanna F. *Fortune Is a Woman: Gender and Politics in the Thought of Nic-colò Machiavelli.* Berkeley, CA, 1984.

Platt, Anthony M. *The Child Savers: The Invention of Delinquency.* 2nd ed. Chicago, 1977.

Platt, Elspeth. *The Story of the Ranyard Mission 1857-1937.* London, 1937.

Pleck, Elizabeth. *Domestic Tyranny: The Making of Social Policy Against Family Violence from Colonial Times to the Present.* New York, 1987.

Plowden, Alfred C. *Grain or Chaff? The Autobiography of a Police Court Magistrate.* London, 1903.

"Police Courts and Husbands and Wives." *The Spectator,* 152 (Apr. 13, 1934): 567.

Pollock, Linda A. *Forgotten Children: Parent-Child Relations from 1500 to 1900.* Cambridge, 1983.

Pomeroy, Ernest. *The Education Tyranny.* London, 1910.

"The Poor at Home." *Westminster Review,* 131 (June 1889): 619-25.

Poovey, Mary. *Making a Social Body: British Cultural Formation 1830-1864.* Chicago, 1995.

———. *Uneven Developments: The Ideological Work of Gender in Mid-Victorian England.* Chicago, 1988.

Pope, Norris. *Dickens and Charity.* New York, 1978.

Porter, Dorothy, and Roy Porter. "The Politics of Prevention: Anti-Vaccinationism and Public Health in Nineteenth-Century England." *Medical History,* 32 (1988): 231-52.

Porter, Mrs. Horace. *Mary Sumner: Her Life and Work.* 2nd ed. Winchester, 1928.

Posnock, Ross. *The Trial of Curiosity: Henry James, William James, and the Challenge of Modernity.* New York, 1991.

Potter, J. Hasloch. *Inasmuch: The Story of the Police Court Mission 1876-1926.* London, 1927.

[Potts, John F.] *Vaccination: A Moral Evil; A Physical Curse; and a Psychological Wrong.* London[?] [1885?].

Praz, Mario. *An Illustrated History of Furnishing from the Renaissance to the 20th Century.* Trans. William Weaver. New York, 1964.

Preparation for Marriage: A Handbook Prepared by a Special Committee on Behalf of the British Social Hygiene Council. London, 1932.

Presser, Stephen B. "The Historical Background of the American Law of Adoption." *Journal of Family Law,* 11, no. 3 (1972): 443-516.

Preston-Thomas, Herbert. *The Work and Play of a Government Inspector.* Edinburgh, 1909.

Preyer, William T. *Mental Development in the Child.* Trans. H. W. Brown. New York, 1897.

———. *The Mind of the Child, Part I: The Senses and the Will.* Trans. H. W. Brown. New York, 1905 [1882].

Prince, Morton. "Hughlings-Jackson on the Connection Between Mind and Brain." *Brain,* 14 (1891): 250-69.

Pringle, J. C. "The Sociology of Compulsory School Attendance." *Charity Organisation Review* (May 1910): 255-65.

The Probation Service: Its Objects and Its Organisation. London, 1938.

Prochaska, Frank K. "Body and Soul: Bible Nurses and the Poor in Victorian London." *Historical Research*, 60 (1987): 336-48.

———. "A Mother's Country: Mothers' Meetings and Family Welfare in Britain, 1850-1950." *History*, 74 (Oct. 1989): 379-99.

———. "Philanthropy." In F. M. L. Thompson, ed., *The Cambridge Social History of Britain 1750-1950*, vol. 3. Cambridge, 1990.

———. *The Voluntary Impulse: Philanthropy in Modern Britain.* London, 1988.

———. *Women and Philanthropy in Nineteenth-Century England.* Oxford, 1980.

"Publicity in the Divorce Court." *The Spectator*, 102 (Feb. 13, 1909): 253-54.

Pulling, Serjeant. "What Legislation Is Necessary for the Repression of Crimes of Violence?" *Transactions of the National Association for the Promotion of Social Science* (1876): 345-49.

Rack, H. D. "Domestic Visitation: A Chapter in Early Nineteenth Century Evangelism." *Journal of Ecclesiastical History*, 24 (Oct. 1973): 357-76.

Radford, George. *The Faculty of Reading: The Coming of Age of the National Home Reading Union.* Cambridge, 1910.

Radzinowicz, Leon, and Roger Hood. *A History of English Criminal Law and Its Administration from 1750*, vol. 5. London, 1986.

Ramon, Shulamit. *Psychiatry in Britain: Meaning and Policy.* London, 1985.

Ranelagh, John. *Thatcher's People.* London, 1991.

Rankin, Charles. *Crime Hospitals.* London [1923].

R., L. N. [Ellen Ranyard]. *The Missing Link; or Bible-Women in the Homes of the London Poor.* London, 1860.

———. *Nurses for the Needy or Bible-Women Nurses in the Homes of the London Poor.* London, 1875.

———. *The True Institution of Sisterhood; or, A Message and Its Messengers.* London [1862].

Rathbone, Eleanor F. *The Disinherited Family.* London, 1924.

———. *William Rathbone: A Memoir.* London, 1905.

Rathbone, William. *Sketch of the History & Progress of District Nursing.* London, 1890.

———. "Social Disintegration." *Macmillan's Magazine*, 16 (May–Oct. 1867): 28-35.

[———.] *Social Duties....* London, 1867.

Razi, Zvi. "The Myth of the Immutable English Family." *Past and Present*, 140 (Aug. 1993): 3-44.

Reconciled, Being the First Annual Account of the Work of the Reconciliation Bureau of the Salvation Army. London [1928].

Reeder, D. A. "Predicaments of City Children: Late Victorian and Edwardian Perspectives on Education and Urban Society." In idem, ed., *Urban Education in the Nineteenth Century.* London, 1977.

Rees, J. R. *The Health of the Mind*. New York, 1951.

Reeves, John. *Recollections of a School Attendance Officer*. London [1915?].

Reeves, Maud Pember. *Round About a Pound a Week*. New York, 1980 [1913].

Regulations as to the Training and Engagement of District Nurses for the Sick Poor. London [1888?].

Reid, Alastair. "Intelligent Artisans and Aristocrats of Labour: The Essays of Thomas Wright." In Jay Winter, ed., *The Working Class in Modern British History*. Cambridge, 1983.

Reiss, Erna. *Rights and Duties of Englishwomen*. Manchester, 1934.

Remarks on Woman's Work in Sanitary Reform. 3rd ed. London [1867?].

Renton, George. "The East London Child Guidance Clinic." *Journal of Child Psychology and Psychiatry*, 19 (Oct. 1978): 309–12.

Report, Inter-Clinic Conference 1935. London, 1935.

Report of the Committee on the Metropolitan Police Courts and Juvenile Courts. London, 1929.

Report of the Proceedings of the Conference on Mental Health. London, 1930.

Report of the Proceedings of the Third International Congress for the Welfare and Protection of Children. Sir William Chance, ed. London, 1902.

Report of the Sixth Annual Meeting of the London Society for the Abolition of Compulsory Vaccination. London, 1886.

Report of the Sub-Committee of Reference and Enquiry [to the National Association for Providing Trained Nurses for the Sick Poor]. London, 1875.

Reynolds, Stephen. "Divorce for the Poor." *Fortnightly Review*, n.s. 88 (Sept. 1910): 487–96.

———. *A Poor Man's Home*. London, 1909.

Reynolds, Stephen, Bob Woolley, and Tom Woolley. *Seems So! A Working-Class View of Politics*. London, 1911.

Ribot, Théodule. *The Psychology of Attention*. 3rd ed. Chicago, 1896.

Ribton-Turner, C. J. *A History of Vagrants and Beggars and Begging*. London, 1887.

Richardson, Benjamin Ward. *Diseases of Modern Life*. New York, 1882.

The Rights of the Sailors Vindicated. London, 1772.

Riley, Denise. *War in the Nursery: Theories of the Child and Mother*. London, 1983.

Riverside Visitor, The [Thomas Wright]. *The Pinch of Poverty: Suffering and Heroism of the London Poor*. London, 1892.

Roberts, David. *Paternalism in Early Victorian England*. New Brunswick, NJ, 1979.

Roberts, Elizabeth. *A Woman's Place: An Oral History of Working-Class Women 1890–1940*. Oxford, 1984.

———. *Women's Work 1840–1940*. Cambridge, 1995.

Roberts, Katherine. *Five Months in a London Hospital*. Letchworth, Herts., 1911.

Roberts, Robert. *The Classic Slum: Salford Life in the First Quarter of the Century*. Harmondsworth, Middlesex, 1987.

Robertson, A. B. "Children, Teachers, and Society: The Over-Pressure Controversy, 1880–1886." *British Journal of Educational Studies*, 20 (Oct. 1972): 315–23.

Robinson, Louis. "Darwinism in the Nursery." *Nineteenth Century*, 30 (Nov. 1891): 831–42.

Rock, Paul, and Stanley Cohen. "The Teddy Boy." In Vernon Bogdanor and Robert Skidelsky, eds., *The Age of Affluence: 1951–1964*. London, 1970.

Rogers, Nicholas. "Vagrancy, Impressment and the Regulation of Labour in Eighteenth-Century Britain." *Slavery and Abolition*, 15 (Aug. 1994): 102–13.

Rook, Clarence. "Hooligan London." In George R. Sims, ed., *Living London*. 3 vols. London, 1902–3.

Rooper, T. G. *School and Home Life*. London [1896].

Roper, Lyndal. *The Holy Household: Women and Morals in Reformation Augsburg*. Oxford, 1991.

Rose, Gordon. *Schools for Young Offenders*. London, 1967.

———. *The Struggle for Penal Reform: The Howard League and Its Predecessors*. London, 1961.

Rose, Jonathan. "Willingly to School: The Working-Class Response to Elementary Education in Britain, 1875–1918." *Journal of British Studies*, 32 (Apr. 1993): 114–38.

Rose, Lionel. *The Erosion of Childhood: Child Oppression in Britain 1860–1918*. London, 1991.

———. *The Massacre of the Innocents: Infanticide in Britain 1800–1939*. London, 1986.

Rose, Nikolas. *The Psychological Complex: Psychology, Politics and Society in England, 1869–1939*. London, 1985.

Rosen, George. "Disease, Debility, and Death." In H. J. Dyos and Michael Wolff, eds., *The Victorian City: Images and Realities*, vol. 2. London, 1973.

Ross, Dale. "Leicester and the Anti-Vaccination Movement 1853–1889." *Transactions of the Leicestershire Archaeological and Historical Society*, 43 (1967–68): 35–44.

Ross, Ellen. "'Fierce Questions and Taunts': Married Life in Working-Class London, 1870–1914." *Feminist Studies*, 8 (Fall 1982): 575–602.

———. "Good and Bad Mothers: Lady Philanthropists and London Housewives Before World War I." In Dorothy O. Helly and Susan M. Reverby, eds., *Gendered Domains: Rethinking Public and Private in Women's History*. Ithaca, NY, 1992.

———. "Hungry Children: Housewives and London Charity, 1870–1918." In Peter Mandler, ed., *The Uses of Charity: The Poor on Relief in the Nineteenth-Century Metropolis*. Philadelphia, 1990.

———. *Love and Toil: Motherhood in Outcast London 1870–1918*. New York, 1993.

Rothman, David J. *Conscience and Convenience: The Asylum and Its Alternatives in Progressive America*. Boston, 1980.

Rowan, Caroline. "Child Welfare and the Working-Class Family." In Mary Langan and Bill Schwarz, eds., *Crises in the British State, 1880–1930*. London, 1985.

Rowntree, B. Seebohm, and Bruno Lasker. *Unemployment: A Social Study.* London, 1911.

Rowntree, Griselda, and Norman H. Carrier. "The Resort to Divorce in England and Wales, 1858-1957." *Population Studies,* 11 (Mar. 1958): 188-233.

"The Royal Commission on Divorce." *The Spectator,* 109 (Nov. 16, 1912): 797-98.

Rubinstein, David. *Before the Suffragettes: Women's Emancipation in the 1890s.* Brighton, 1986.

————. *School Attendance in London, 1870-1904: A Social History.* New York, 1969.

————. "Socialization and the London School Board 1870-1904: Aims, Methods and Public Opinion." In Phillip McCann, ed., *Popular Education and Socialization in the Nineteenth Century.* London, 1977.

Rumsey, Henry W. *Essays on State Medicine.* London, 1856.

Runciman, James. *School Board Idylls.* London, 1885.

Ruskin, John. *Sesame and Lilies.* New York [1865?].

Russell, Charles E. B. *Social Problems of the North.* London, 1913.

Russell, Charles E. B., and L. M. Rigby. *The Making of the Criminal.* London, 1906.

Ryan, Mary P. *Cradle of the Middle Class: The Family in Oneida County, New York, 1790-1865.* Cambridge, 1981.

Rybczynski, Witold. *Home: A Short History of an Idea.* New York, 1987.

Ryerson, Ellen. *The Best-Laid Plans: America's Juvenile Court Experiment.* New York, 1978.

Sadie, Stanley, ed. *The New Grove Dictionary of Music and Musicians.* 20 vols. Washington, D. C., 1980.

St. John, Arthur. "Have Reformatory Methods Failed?" *Westminster Review,* 170 (Sept. 1908): 317-24.

Saleeby, C. W. *Individualism and Collectivism.* London, 1906.

Samuels, Emma. "The Adoption of Street Arabs by the State." *Fortnightly Review,* o.s. 69 (Jan. 1898): 111-18.

Sanctuary, Gerald. *Marriage Under Stress.* London, 1968.

The Sanitary Duties of Private Individuals. London [1872?].

Savage, Gail. "Marital Conflict Among the Respectable: Middle-Class Divorce in Victorian England." Unpublished paper (1989).

————. "The Operations of the 1857 Divorce Act, 1860-1910: A Research Note." *Journal of Social History,* 16 (Summer 1983): 103-10.

Saville, John. "The Origins of the Welfare State." In Martin Loney, David Boswell, and John Clarke, eds., *Social Policy and Social Welfare.* Milton Keynes, 1983.

Scannell, Dorothy. *Mother Knew Best: An East End Childhood.* London, 1975.

Schäfer, E. A. *Text-Book of Physiology.* 2 vols. Edinburgh, 1900.

Schama, Simon. *Citizens: A Chronicle of the French Revolution.* New York, 1989.

————. *The Embarrassment of Riches: An Interpretation of Dutch Culture in the Golden Age.* New York, 1987.

Scharlieb, Mary. *The Psychology of Childhood*. London, 1927.

Schlossman, Steven L. *Love and the American Delinquent: The Theory and Practice of "Progressive" Juvenile Justice, 1825–1920*. Chicago, 1977.

Schmidt, Benjamin. "Mapping an Empire: Cartographic and Colonial Rivalry in Seventeenth-Century Dutch and English North America." *William and Mary Quarterly*, 54 (July 1997): 549–78.

Schochet, Gordon, J. *Patriarchalism in Political Thought*. New York, 1975.

Schofield, Alfred T. *An Enquiry into the Formation of Habit in Man*. London [1896].

———. *The Springs of Character*. London, 1900.

———. *The Unconscious Mind*. London, 1898.

Scott, Joan. "Review Essay: The History of the Family as an Affective Unit." *Social History*, 4 (Oct. 1979): 509–16.

Scott, Samuel F., and Barry Rothaus. *Historical Dictionary of the French Revolution, 1789–1799*. 2 vols. Westport, CT, 1985.

Seaborne, Malcolm. "William Brockington, Director of Education for Leicestershire 1903–1940." In Brian Simon, ed., *Education in Leicestershire 1540–1940*. Leicester, 1968.

Searl, G. R. *The Quest for National Efficiency*. Berkeley, CA, 1971.

Seaver, Paul. *Wallington's World: A Puritan Artisan in Seventeenth-Century London*. Stanford, CA, 1985.

Seccombe, Wally. *Weathering the Storm: Working-Class Families from the Industrial Revolution to the Fertility Decline*. London, 1993.

"Seduction and Infanticide." *Saturday Review*, 22 (Oct. 20, and Nov. 3, 1866): 481–82 and 545–46.

Seed, Patricia. *Ceremonies of Possession in Europe's Conquest of the New World, 1492–1640*. Cambridge, 1995.

Selleck, R. J. W. *English Primary Education and the Progressives, 1914–1939*. London, 1972.

"Sentimental Justice." *The Spectator*, 155 (Sept. 27, 1935): 457–58.

Sewell, Margaret A. *District Visiting*. London, 1893.

Shairp, Leslie V. *Hints for Visitors*. Leeds, 1910.

Shammas, Carole. "The Domestic Environment in Early Modern England and America." *Journal of Social History*, 14 (Fall 1980): 3–24.

Shand, Alexander F. *The Foundations of Character*. London, 1914.

Shanley, Mary Lyndon. *Feminism, Marriage, and the Law in Victorian England, 1850–1895*. Princeton, NJ, 1989.

Shaw, George Bernard. *Getting Married*. In idem, *The Doctor's Dilemma*. New York, 1913 [1908].

———. *Pygmalion*. London, 1913.

Sherrington, Christine. "The NSPCC in Transition, 1884–1983: A Study in Organizational Survival." Ph.D. thesis, University of London, 1985.

Shirreff, Emily A. *The Kinder-garten in Relation to Family Life*. London, 1878.

———. *The Kindergarten at Home*. London, 1884.

Shoemaker, Robert B. *Prosecution and Punishment: Petty Crime and the Law in London and Rural Middlesex, c. 1660–1725*. Cambridge, 1991.

Shonfield, Zuzanna. *The Precariously Privileged: A Professional Family in Victorian London.* Oxford, 1987.

A Short Account of the System Pursued in the Pestalozzian Academy, South Lambeth. London, 1826.

Shorter, Edward. *The Making of the Modern Family.* New York, 1975.

Shrewsbury, Theresa. "Prevention." *Nineteenth Century,* 18 (Dec. 1885): 957–64.

Shuttleworth, James P. K. *The Moral and Physical Condition of the Working Classes Employed in the Cotton Manufacture in Manchester.* 2nd ed. London, 1832.

Sikorskii, I. A. "Le Développement Psychique de l'Enfant." *Revue Philosophique,* 19 (Mar.–May 1885): 241–64; 403–25; and 533–54.

Simey, Margaret B. *Charitable Effort in Liverpool in the Nineteenth Century.* Liverpool, 1951.

Simon, Brian. *Education and the Labour Movement 1870–1920.* London, 1965.

Simon, John. *English Sanitary Institutions.* 2nd ed. London, 1897.

Simpson, Lucie. *The Privilege of Motherhood.* London, 1905.

Sims, George R. *The Black Stain.* London, 1907.

———. *How the Poor Live.* London, 1883.

———. *Living London.* 3 vols. London, 1902–3.

Skocpol, Theda. *Protecting Soldiers and Mothers: The Political Origins of Social Policy in the United States.* Cambridge, MA, 1992.

Skrine, Mary J. H. "The Little Black Lamb." *The Spectator,* 119 (Aug. 11, 1917): 137.

Smart, Barry. "On Discipline and Social Regulation: A Review of Foucault's Genealogical Analysis." In David Garland and Peter Young, eds., *The Power to Punish.* London, 1983.

Smart, Carol. *The Ties That Bind: Law, Marriage and the Reproduction of Patriarchal Relations.* London, 1984.

Smiles, Samuel. *Character.* New York, 1872.

Smith, Adolphe, and John Thompson. *Street Life in London.* New York, 1969 [1877–78].

Smith, C. Penswick. *The Revival of Mothering Sunday.* London, 1921.

———. *A Short History of Mothering Sunday.* Nottingham, 1915.

Smith, D. Stanley. "Adoption of Children in New Zealand." *Journal of Comparative Legislation and International Law,* 3rd series, 3 (1921): 165–77.

Smith, David. "Juvenile Delinquency in Britain in the First World War." *Criminal Justice History,* 11 (1990): 119–45.

Smith, Edward. *Manual for Medical Officers of Health.* 2nd ed. London, 1874.

Smith, F. B. *The People's Health 1830–1910.* New York, 1979.

Smith, Horace. "A Magistrate's View of Slack Discipline." In *Essays on Duty and Discipline.* London, 1910.

Smith, Hubert L. *The Borderland Between Public and Voluntary Action in the Social Services.* London, 1937.

Smith-Rosenberg, Carroll. *Disorderly Conduct: Visions of Gender in Victorian America.* New York, 1985.

Snell, Harry. *Men, Movements, and Myself.* London, 1936.

Social Work in Principle and Practice: A Study in Applied Optimism. London [1921].

Soldon, Norbert. "*Laissez-Faire* as Dogma: The Liberty and Property Defence League, 1882–1914." In Kenneth D. Brown, ed., *Essays in Anti-Labour History.* London, 1974.

Solicitor. *English Justice.* London, 1932.

Soloway, Richard A. *Demography and Degeneration: Eugenics and the Declining Birthrate in Twentieth-Century Britain.* Chapel Hill, NC, 1990.

Spadoni, Adriana. "In the Domestic Relations Court." *Collier's,* 47 (Aug. 26, 1911): 15, 27.

Spencer, Herbert. *Education, Intellectual, Moral, and Physical.* New York, 1929 [1860].

———. *The Principles of Psychology.* 3 vols. New York, 1896 [1855].

Spivak, Gayatri Chakravorty. "Can the Subaltern Speak?" In Patrick Williams and Laura Chrisman, eds., *Colonial Discourse and Post-Colonial Theory.* New York, 1994.

Spock, Benjamin. *The Common Sense Book of Baby and Child Care.* New York, 1945.

Springhall, John. *Coming of Age: Adolescence in Britain 1860–1960.* Dublin, 1986.

Stacpoole, Florence. *Homely Hints for District Visitors.* London [1897?].

Stanford, William. *Les Plees del Coron: Diuisees in Plusiours Titles.* London, 1567 [1557].

[Stanley, Maude Aletha.] *Work About the Five Dials.* London, 1878.

"The State and the Mother." *Quarterly Review,* 228 (Oct. 1917): 465–86.

[Stead, W. T.] "Two Champions of the Children." *Review of Reviews,* American ed., 4 (Jan. 1892): 689–701.

Steedman, Carolyn. *Childhood, Culture and Class in Britain: Margaret McMillan, 1860–1931.* London, 1990.

———. "'The Mother Made Conscious': The Historical Development of a Primary School Pedagogy." *History Workshop,* 20 (Autumn 1985): 149–63.

Steffens, Lincoln. *Upbuilders.* New York, 1909.

Stetson, Dorothy. *A Woman's Issue: The Politics of Family Law Reform in England.* Westport CT, 1982.

Stevenson, Burton, ed. *The Home Book of Quotations.* 10th ed. New York, 1967.

Stevenson, John. *British Society 1914–45.* Harmondsworth, Middlesex, 1984.

Stewart, Alexander P., and Edward Jenkins. *The Medical and Legal Aspects of Sanitary Reform.* New York, 1969 [1867].

Stocks, Mary. *A Hundred Years of District Nursing.* London, 1960.

———. *My Commonplace Book.* London, 1970.

Stone, Lawrence. *The Family, Sex, and Marriage in England 1500–1800.* New York, 1977.

———. *Road to Divorce.* Oxford, 1990.

Stone, Martin. "Shellshock and the Psychologists." In W. F. Bynum, Roy Porter, and Michael Shepherd, eds., *The Anatomy of Madness: Essays in the History of Psychiatry*, vol. 2. London, 1985.

Stoner, Winifred Sackville. *Natural Education*. Indianapolis, IN, 1914.

Storch, Robert D. "Police Control of Street Prostitution in Victorian London: A Study in the Contexts of Police Action." In David H. Bayley, ed., *Police and Society*. Beverly Hills, CA, 1977.

———. "The Policeman as Domestic Missionary: Urban Discipline and Popular Culture in Northern England, 1850-1880." *Journal of Social History*, 9 (June 1976): 481-509.

Stroud, John. *Thirteen Penny Stamps: The Story of the Church of England Children's Society (Waifs and Strays) from 1881 to the 1970s*. London, 1971.

Sugarman, David, and Ronnie Warrington. "Land Law, Citizenship, and the Invention of 'Englishness': The Strange World of the Equity of Redemption." In John Brewer and Susan Staves, eds. *Early Modern Conceptions of Property*. London, 1996.

Sully, James. "Babies and Science." *Cornhill Magazine*, 43 (May 1881): 539-54.

———. "Baby Linguistics." *English Illustrated Magazine* (Oct. 1884): 110-18.

———. "Genius and Precocity." *Popular Science Monthly*, 29 (Aug. 1886): 469-82; and (Sept. 1886): 594-604.

———. *The Human Mind: A Text-book of Psychology*. 2 vols. New York, 1892.

———. *My Life and Friends: A Psychologist's Memories*. London, 1918.

———. "The New Study of Children." *Fortnightly Review*, 64 (Nov. 1895): 723-37.

———. *Outlines of Psychology, with Special Reference to the Theory of Education*. New York, 1891 [1884].

———. "Physiological Psychology in Germany." *Mind*, 1 (Jan. 1876): 20-43.

———. *Studies of Childhood*. London, 1895.

———. "Studies of Childhood, I." *Popular Science Monthly*, 45 (July 1894): 323-30.

———. "Studies of Childhood, III." *Popular Science Monthly*, 45 (Oct. 1894): 733-42.

———. "Studies of Childhood, V." *Popular Science Monthly*, 46 (Jan. 1895): 348-63.

———. "Studies of Childhood, X." *Popular Science Monthly*, 47 (Sept. 1895): 648-64.

———. "Studies of Childhood, XIII." *Popular Science Monthly*, 48 (Dec. 1895): 166-80.

Summers, Anne. "The Costs and Benefits of Caring: Nursing Charities, c. 1830-c. 1860." In Jonathan Barry and Colin Jones, eds., *Medicine and Charity Before the Welfare State*. London, 1991.

———. "A Home from Home—Women's Philanthropic Work in the Nineteenth Century." In Sandra Burman, ed., *Fit Work for Women*. New York, 1979.

———. "The Mysterious Demise of Sarah Gamp: The Domiciliary Nurse and Her Detractors, c. 1830-1860." *Victorian Studies*, 32 (Spring 1989): 365-86.

Sumner, Mary. *Home Life: Addresses to Members of Mothers' Union*. London, 1895.

———. *The Mothers' Union: Its Aims and Objects*. Winchester [1890].

———. *Nursery Training: A Book for Nurses*. 3rd ed. London [1892].

———. "The Responsibilities of Mothers." In Angela Burdett-Coutts, ed., *Woman's Mission*. London, 1893.

———. *To Mothers of the Higher Classes*. London, 1888.

Surr, Elizabeth. "The Child-Criminal." *Nineteenth Century*, 9 (Apr. 1881): 649–63.

Surridge, H. A. D. *A Manual of Hints to Visiting Friends of the Poor*. London, 1871.

A Survey of the Social Services in the Oxford District, II: Local Administration in a Changing Area. London, 1940.

Sutherland, Gillian. *Ability, Merit and Measurement: Mental Testing and English Education 1880–1940*. Oxford, 1984.

———. *Policy-Making in Elementary Education 1870–1895*. London, 1973.

Sykes, John F. J. "Hygiene and Sanitation in the Home and at School." In *Report of the Proceedings of the Third International Congress for the Welfare and Protection of Children*. London, 1902.

Symons, Jelinger C. *Tactics for the Times: as Regards the Condition and Treatment of the Dangerous Classes*. London, 1849.

Szwed, Elizabeth. "The Family Court." In Michael D. A. Freeman, ed., *The State, the Law, and the Family: Critical Perspectives*. London, 1984.

Taine, Hippolyte. "Note sur l'Acquisition du Langage." *Revue Philosophique*, 1 (Jan. 1876): 5–23.

Tansley, A. G. *The New Psychology and Its Relation to Life*. London, 1921.

Taverner, Richard. *Proverbs or Adages by Desiderius Erasmus Gathered Out of the Chiliades and Englished*. Gainsville, FLA, 1956 [1569].

Tavistock Square Clinic for Functional Nervous Disorders. *Annual Reports*, 1920–1935. London, 1928–1936.

Taylor, Isaac. *Home Education*. London, 1838.

Taylor, P. A. "Anti-Vaccination." *Nineteenth Century*, 11 (May 1882): 782–802.

Taylor, Whately Cooke. "What Influence Has the Employment of Mothers in Manufactures on Infant Mortality?" *Transactions of the National Association for the Promotion of Social Science* (1874): 569–84.

Teale, T. Pridgin. *Hurry, Worry, and Money: The Bane of Modern Education*. Leeds, 1883.

Tebb, William. *Brief Story of Fourteen Years' Struggle for Parental Emancipation from the Vaccination Tyranny*. London, 1894.

———. *Premature Burial and How It May Be Prevented*. London, 1896.

———. "What Is the Truth About Vaccination?" *Westminster Review*, 131 (Feb. 1889): 187–200.

Tebbutt, Melanie. *Women's Talk? A Social History of "Gossip" in Working-Class Neighbourhoods, 1880–1960*. Aldershot, Hants., 1995.

Temple, William. *Observations upon the United Provinces of the Netherlands.* 5th ed. London, 1690.

Thane, Pat. "Childhood in History." In Michael King, ed., *Childhood, Welfare and Justice.* London, 1981.

———. "Government and Society in England and Wales, 1750-1914." In F. M. L. Thompson, ed., *The Cambridge Social History of Britain 1750-1950,* vol. 3. Cambridge, 1990.

———. "Late Victorian Women." In T. R. Gourvish and Alan O'Day, eds., *Later Victorian Britain, 1867-1900.* London, 1988.

———. "Women and the Poor Law in Victorian and Edwardian England." *History Workshop,* 6 (Autumn 1978): 29-51.

———. "The Working Class and State 'Welfare' in Britain, 1880-1914." *Historical Journal,* 27 (Dec. 1984): 877-900.

Then and Now: The Froebel Society's Jubilee Pamphlet. London, 1925.

Thom, Deborah. "Wishes, Anxieties, Play and Gestures: Child Guidance in Inter-War England." In Roger Cooter, ed., *In the Name of the Child.* London, 1992.

Thompson, E. P. *The Making of the English Working Class.* New York, 1963.

Thompson, F. M. L. *The Rise of Respectable Society: A Social History of Victorian Britain 1830-1900.* Cambridge, MA, 1988.

———. "Social Control in Victorian Britain." *Economic History Review,* 34 (May 1981): 189-208.

Thompson, Flora. *Lark Rise to Candleford.* Harmondsworth, Middlesex, 1977.

Thorne, Richard Thorne. *On the Progress of Preventive Medicine During the Victorian Era.* London, 1888.

Thwing, Charles F., and Carrie F. B. Thwing. *The Family: An Historical and Social Study.* Boston, 1887.

Tibbits, Charles. *Marriage Making and Marriage Breaking.* London, 1911.

Timewell, James. *The Police and the Public: The Southwark Police Case and Its Moral.* 2nd ed. London, 1898.

Titmuss, Richard M. *Problems of Social Policy.* London, 1950.

Tobias, J. J. *Crime and Police in England 1700-1900.* Dublin, 1979.

Tomes, Nancy. "A 'Torrent of Abuse': Crimes of Violence Between Working-Class Men and Women in London, 1840-1875." *Journal of Social History,* 11 (Spring 1978): 328-45.

Tomlinson, Charles G. *Families in Trouble: An Enquiry into Problem Families in Luton.* Luton, 1946.

Too Late: A Tract for Mothers on Vaccination. London [1872?].

Townsend, Edward W. *A Daughter of the Tenements.* New York, 1895.

Toynbee Hall: 1884-5–1934-5. London, 1935.

Tozier, Josephine. "An Educational Wonder-Worker: The Methods of Maria Montessori." *McClure's Magazine,* 37 (May 1911): 3-19.

Triseliotis, John. "Obtaining Birth Certificates." In Philip Bean, ed., *Adoption: Essays in Social Policy, Law, and Sociology.* London, 1984.

Trist, Eric, and Hugh Murray. *The Social Engagement of Social Science: A Tavistock Anthology.* Philadelphia, 1990.

Trumbach, Randolph. *The Rise of the Egalitarian Family: Aristocratic Kinship and Domestic Relations in Eighteenth-Century England*. New York, 1978.

Tuckwell, Gertrude. *The State and Its Children*. London, 1894.

Tuke, J. Batty. *The Insanity of the Over-Exertion of the Brain*. Edinburgh, 1894.

Turnbull, Annmarie. "Learning Her Womanly Work: The Elementary School Curriculum, 1870-1914." In Felicity Hunt, ed., *Lessons for Life: The Schooling of Girls and Women, 1850-1950*. Oxford, 1987.

Turner, James. *Reckoning with the Beast: Animals, Pain, and Humanity in the Victorian Mind*. Baltimore, 1980.

Turner, Michael R., ed. *The Parlour Song Book*. New York, 1972.

[Turner, Sidney.] "Juvenile Delinquency." *Edinburgh Review*, 94 (Oct. 1851): 403-29.

Twenty-Third and *Twenty-Fourth Annual Report of the Ladies' Sanitary Association*. London, 1881-82.

Twining, Elizabeth. *Readings for Mothers' Meetings*. London, 1861.

Twining, Louisa. *Recollections of Life and Work*. London, 1893.

———. *Recollections of Workhouse Visiting and Management*. London, 1880.

"Underfed Children." *The Spectator*, 94 (Apr. 1, 1905): 467-68.

The Unmarried Mother and Her Child in England and Wales. London, 1924.

Urwin, Cathy, and Elaine Sharland. "From Bodies to Minds in Childcare Literature: Advice to Parents in Inter-War Britain." In Roger Cooter, ed., *In the Name of the Child*. London, 1992.

Valenze, Deborah. *The First Industrial Woman*. New York, 1995.

Van Waters, Miriam. *Parents on Probation*. New York, 1927.

Vickery, Amanda. "Golden Age to Separate Spheres? A Review of the Categories and Chronology of English Women's History." *Historical Journal*, 36 (June 1993): 383-414.

Vincent, David. "Love and Death and the Nineteenth-Century Working Class." *Social History*, 5 (May 1980): 223-47.

Vincent, Howard. "Children's Courts." *The Graphic* (June 24, 1905): 760.

The Voluntary Mental Health Services: The Report of the Feversham Committee. London, 1939.

Von Frank, Albert J. *An Emerson Chronology*. New York, 1994.

Waddy, Henry Turner. *The Police Court and Its Work*. London, 1925.

Wagner, Gillian. *Barnardo*. London, 1979.

Wahrman, Dror. "'Middle-Class' Domesticity Goes Public: Gender, Class, and Politics from Queen Caroline to Queen Victoria." *Journal of British Studies*, 32 (Oct. 1993): 396-432.

Walkowitz, Judith. *City of Dreadful Delight: Narratives of Sexual Danger in Late-Victorian London*. Chicago, 1992.

———. *Prostitution and Victorian Society: Women, Class, and the State*. Cambridge, 1980.

Walkowitz, Judith, Myra Jehlen, and Bell Chevigny. "Patrolling the Borders: Feminist Historiography and the New Historicism." *Radical History Review*, 43 (Winter 1989): 23-43.

Walling, R. A. J. "Are Children's Courts Sentimental?" *The Spectator*, 155 (Oct. 4, 1935): 501–2.

Wallis, J. H., and H. S. Booker. *Marriage Counselling*. London, 1958.

Walton, John K., and Alastair Wilcox, eds. *Low Life and Moral Improvement in Mid-Victorian England: Liverpool Through the Journalism of Hugh Shimmin*. Leicester, 1991.

Walton, Ronald G. *Women in Social Work*. London, 1975.

Walvin, James. *A Child's World: A Social History of English Childhood 1800–1914*. Harmondsworth, Middlesex, 1982.

———. *Victorian Values*. London, 1987.

Ward, Harriet. "The Charitable Relationship: Parents, Children and the Waifs and Stray Society." Ph.D. thesis, University of Bristol, 1990.

Warner, Francis. *The Children: How to Study Them*. London, 1887.

———. *The Nervous System of the Child*. New York, 1900.

———. "Recurrent Headaches in Children, and Associated Pathological Conditions." *British Medical Journal* (Dec. 6, 1879): 889–90.

———. "Spontaneous Postures of the Hand Considered as Indications of the Condition of the Brain." *Brain*, 6 (1883): 342–60.

Wasps Have Stings; or, Beware of Tight-Lacing. London [1863].

Wasserstein, Bernard. *Herbert Samuel: A Political Life*. Oxford, 1992.

Watson, John A. F. "The Child and the Aftermath of War." *Fortnightly*, o.s. 167 (Apr. 1947): 254–60.

———. *The Child and the Magistrate*. London, 1942.

Watson, John B. *Behaviorism*. New York, 1925.

———. *Psychological Care of Infant and Child*. New York, 1928.

Waugh, Benjamin. "Baby Farming." *Contemporary Review*, 57 (May 1890): 700–714.

[———.] *The Gaol Cradle, Who Rocks It?* 3rd ed. London, 1876.

Waugh, Rosa. *The Life of Benjamin Waugh*. London, 1913.

Webb, Catherine. *The Woman with the Basket: The History of the Women's Co-operative Guild 1883–1927*. Manchester, 1927.

Webb, Robert K. *Modern England*. 2nd ed. New York, 1980.

Webb, Sidney, and Beatrice Webb. *The Consumers' Co-operative Movement*. London, 1921.

———. *The Prevention of Destitution*. London, 1911.

———. *The State and the Doctor*. London, 1910.

———, eds. *The Break-Up of the Poor Law*. London, 1909.

Wechsler, Judith. *A Human Comedy: Physiognomy and Caricature in 19th Century Paris*. Chicago, 1982.

Weeks, Jeffrey. *Sex, Politics & Society: The Regulation of Sexuality Since 1800*. 2nd ed. London, 1989.

Weisbrod, Bernd. "How to Become a Good Foundling in Early Victorian London." *Social History*, 10 (May 1985): 193–209.

Welter, Barbara. "The Cult of True Womanhood: 1820–1860." *American Quarterly*, 18 (Summer 1966): 151–74.

Weylland, John M. *The Man with the Book; or, The Bible Among the People.* Boston [1871].

———. *These Fifty Years: Being the Jubilee Volume of the London City Mission.* London [1884].

Whitbread, Nanette. *The Evolution of the Nursery-Infant School.* London, 1972.

White, Jerry. *Rothschild Buildings: Life in an East End Tenement Block 1887–1920.* London, 1980.

———. *The Worst Street in North London: Campbell Bunk, Islington, between the Wars.* London, 1986.

White, William. *The Story of a Great Delusion.* London, 1885.

Whitney, Janet. *Geraldine S. Cadbury 1865–1941.* London, 1948.

Whose Fault Is It?, or How to Make a Happy Home. 3rd ed. London [1872].

Why Do Not Women Swim? A Voice From Many Waters. London, n.d.

Wiener, Martin. "The March of Penal Progress?" *Journal of British Studies,* 26 (Jan. 1987): 83–96.

———. *Reconstructing the Criminal: Culture, Law, and Policy in England, 1830–1914.* Cambridge, 1990.

Wilkinson, James John Garth. *On Human Science.* London, 1876.

Williams, Montague. *Later Leaves.* London, 1891.

———. *Round London.* London, 1892.

Winter, J. M. *The Great War and the British People.* London, 1986.

Wintroub, Michael. "To Triumph in Paradise: The New World and the New Learning in the Royal Entry Festival of Henri II (Rouen 1550)." Ph.D. dissertation, U.C.L.A., 1995.

Witmer, Helen L. "Parental Behavior as an Index to the Probable Outcome of Treatment in a Child Guidance Clinic." *American Journal of Orthopsychiatry,* 3 (Oct. 1933): 431–44.

Wohl, Anthony S. *Endangered Lives: Public Health in Victorian Britain.* Cambridge, MA, 1983.

———. *The Eternal Slum: Housing and Social Policy in Victorian London.* Montreal, 1977.

———. "Sex and the Single Room: Incest Among the Victorian Working Classes." In idem, ed., *The Victorian Family: Structures and Stresses.* New York, 1978.

———. "Unfit for Human Habitation." In H. J. Dyos and Michael Wolff, eds., *The Victorian City,* vol. 2. London, 1973.

Wollstonecraft, Mary. *An Historical and Moral View of the Origin and Progress of the French Revolution.* 2nd ed. Delmar, NY, 1975 [1795].

A Woman's Secret; or, How to Make Home Happy. London, 1860.

Women's Home Mission Association, Oxford Diocesan Branch. *Report for 1910.* Oxford, 1911.

Woodham-Smith, P. "History of the Froebel Movement in England." In Evelyn Lawrence, ed., *Froebel and English Education.* New York, 1969.

Woodroofe, Kathleen. *From Charity to Social Work in England and the United States.* Toronto, 1962.

Woodward, John. "Medicine and the City: The Nineteenth-Century Experience." In idem and Robert Woods, eds., *Urban Disease and Mortality in Nineteenth-Century England*. London, 1984.

Wooldridge, Adrian. *Measuring the Mind: Education and Psychology in England, c. 1860–c. 1990*. Cambridge, 1994.

Woollcombe, Joan. "The 'Children's Court.'" *The Spectator*, 139 (Dec. 31, 1927): 1142–43.

The Works of Lucian: Translated from the Greek by Several Eminent Hands. 4 vols. London, 1710–11.

Worsley, Henry. *Juvenile Depravity*. London, 1849.

Wrightson, Keith. *English Society 1580–1680*. London, 1982.

Wrong, R. M. "Some Voluntary Organizations for the Welfare of Children." In A. F. C. Bourdillon, ed., *Voluntary Social Services*. London, 1945.

Wynter, Andrew. "The Massacre of the Innocents." *Fortnightly Review*, 4 (Apr. 15, 1866): 607–12.

Yeo, Stephen. "Working-Class Association, Private Capital, Welfare and the State in the Late-Nineteenth and Twentieth Centuries." In Noel Parry et al., eds., *Social Work, Welfare and the State*. Beverly Hills, CA, 1980.

Yonge, Charlotte M. *Burnt Out: A Story for Mothers' Meetings*. 3rd ed. London, 1882.

Young, A. F., and E. T. Ashton. *British Social Work in the Nineteenth Century*. London, 1956.

Young, G. M. *Victorian England: Portrait of an Age*. 2nd ed. London, 1953.

Young, Michael, and Peter Willmott. *Family and Kinship in East London*. Harmondsworth, Middlesex, 1957.

Young, Peter. "A Sociological Analysis of the Early History of Probation." *British Journal of Law and Society*, 3 (Summer 1976): 44–58.

Young, Robert M. *Mind, Brain and Adaptation in the Nineteenth Century: Cerebral Localization and Its Biological Context from Gall to Ferrier*. Oxford, 1970.

Young Offenders and the Courts. London [1938].

Zagorin, Perez. *Ways of Lying: Dissimulation, Persecution, and Conformity in Early Modern Europe*. Cambridge, MA, 1990.

Zainaldin, Jamil S. "The Emergence of a Modern American Family Law: Child Custody, Adoption, and the Courts, 1796–1851." *Northwestern University Law Review*, 73 (Feb. 1979): 1038–89.

Zaretsky, Eli. *Capitalism, the Family, & Personal Life*. New York, 1976.

Zedner, Lucia. *Women, Crime, and Custody in Victorian England*. Oxford, 1991.

Zelizer, Viviana A. *Pricing the Priceless Child: The Changing Social Value of Children*. New York, 1985.

Zuckerman, Michael. "Dr. Spock: The Confidence Man." In Charles E. Rosenberg, ed., *The Family in History*. Philadelphia, 1975.

Index

In this index an "f" after a number indicates a separate reference on the next page, and an "ff" indicates a separate reference on the next two pages. *Passim* is used for a cluster of references in close but not consecutive sequence.

Library of Congress Cataloging-in-Publication Data

Behlmer, George K.
    Friends of the family : the English home and its guardians,
    1850–1940 / George K. Behlmer.
          p.   cm.
    Includes bibliographical references and index.
    ISBN 0-8047-3313-9 (cloth : alk. paper).
    1. Family—England—History—19th century.   2. Family—
    England—History—20th century.   3. England—Social
    conditions—19th century.   4. England—Social conditions—
    20th century.   I. Title.
    HQ615.B45   1998
    306.85'0942—dc21

                                                    98-11235
                                                    CIP

This book is printed on acid-free, recycled paper.

Original printing 1998
Last figure below indicates year of this printing:
07   06   05   04   03   02   01   00   99   98